ENVIRONMENTAL DESIGN RESEARCH

THE BODY, THE CITY, AND THE BUILDINGS IN BETWEEN

Third Revised Edition

EDITED BY

Galen Cranz and

Eleftherios Pavlides

Bassim Hamadeh, CEO and Publisher
Christopher Foster, General Vice President
Michael Simpson, Vice President of Acquisitions
Jessica Knott, Managing Editor
Kevin Fahey, Cognella Marketing Manager
Jess Busch, Senior Graphic Designer
Stephanie Sandler, Licensing Associate

Copyright © 2013 by Cognella, Inc. All rights reserved. No part of this publication may be reprinted, reproduced, transmitted, or utilized in any form or by any electronic, mechanical, or other means, now known or hereafter invented, including photocopying, microfilming, and recording, or in any information retrieval system without the written permission of Cognella, Inc.

First published in the United States of America in 2013 by Cognella, Inc.

Trademark Notice: Product or corporate names may be trademarks or registered trademarks, and are used only for identification and explanation without intent to infringe.

16 15 14 13 12   1 2 3 4 5

Printed in the United States of America

ISBN: 978-1-62131-879-8

www.cognella.com 800.200.3908

Dedication

To our current students, our future colleagues, who will join us to design, in a full-bodied way, the places where we live and work.

We hope this collection stimulates and inspires students in architecture everywhere to design with heightened awareness of the social significance of architecture.

We thank the authors and publishers whose work has helped us present the field, make our points, and introduce us to new perspectives.

CONTENTS

	Editor's Introduction	xi
	Galen Cranz and Eleftherios Pavlides	

1969
1	**Proxemics in a Cross-Cultural Context: Germans, English, and French**	1
	Edward T. Hall	

1973
2	**"Natural Surveillance" and "Image and Milieu"**	13
	Oscar Newman	

1974
3	**The Search for Environmental Theory**	43
	W. H. Ittelson, H. M. Prohansky, L. G. Rivlin, G. H. Winkel	
4	**Understanding Behavior in Conflict**	59
	Kenneth W. Thomas and Ralph H. Kilmann	

1976
5	**The Anthropology of Space: An Organizing Model**	67
	Edward T. Hall	
6	**Signs of Life: Symbols in the American City**	81
	Robert Venturi and John Rauch	

1977
7	**Environmental Messages**	97
	Franklin Becker	

8   Does Post-Modernism Communicate?   109
Linda Groat and David Canter

1980

9   The Social Life of Small Urban Spaces   119
William H. Whyte

10 What Would a Non-Sexist City Look Like?   135
Dolores Hayden

1981

11 Perception and Awareness: What Is This Setting?   147
Fritz Steele

1984

12 The Homeless in Urban Parks:
Is Exclusion the Solution?   157
Louise Mozingo

1985

13 Models of Design in Studio Teaching   159
Stefani Ledewitz

1987

14 Territoriality   173
Barbara B. Brown

15 Observation: The World Under a Glass   209
Robert B. Bechtel and John Zeisel

16 Ethnicity and Urban Recreation: Whites, Blacks,
and Hispanics in Chicago's Public Parks   237
Ray Hutchison

1988

17 Inside Spatial Relations   253
Ellen J. Pader

18 Vernacular Architecture as an Expression of Its
Social Context in Eressos, Greece 269
Eleftherios Pavlides and Jana E. Hesser

19 Fengshui: Its Application in
Contemporary Architecture 283
Teh Tien Yong

1989

20 Overview of Collective and Shared Housing 297
Karen A. Franck

21 Women and Downtown Open Spaces 313
Louise Mozingo

22 Designing to Orient the User 325
Gerald Weisman

1991

23 A New Look at the Person in
Person–Environment Relations:
Theoretical Assumptions About the Body 329
Galen Cranz

24 Missing Dimension in Environmental Research:
Detailed Visual Documentation 337
Eleftherios Pavlides

1992

25 The Park and the People 345
Roy Rosenzweig and Elizabeth Blackmar

1993

26 The Enacted Environment of East Los Angeles 355
James T. Rojas

1995
27 Architect à la Mode 367
Deborah Singmaster

1996
28 The Psychology of Sustainability: What Planners Can Learn from Attitude Research 369
Alice Jones

2000
29 The Hidden Program of the High School (or Six Metaphors in Search of a Box) 385
Herb Childress

2001
30 Environmental Logic and Minority Communities 401
David R. Diaz

31 Reinterpreting Sustainable Architecture: The Place of Technology 417
Simon Guy and Graham Farmer

2002
32 Post-Occupancy Evaluation: Issues and Implementation 433
Craig Zimring

2003
33 Environmental Correlates to Behavioral Health Outcomes in Alzheimer's Special Care Units 451
John Zeisel, Nina M. Silverstein, Joan Hyde, Sue Levkoff, M. Powell Lawton, and William Holmes

2004
34 A New Way of Thinking About Taste 475
Galen Cranz

35 Defining the Sustainable Park:
A Fifth Model for Urban Parks 485

Galen Cranz and Michael Boland

2005

36 Cohousing: An Old Idea—
A Contemporary Approach 511

Charles Durrett

2006

37 Interview with Jaime Lerner 521

2009

38 Three Theoretical Assumptions Needed
to Create Useful Applied Social Science
Research for Architecture 525

Eleftherios Pavlides and Galen Cranz

2010

39 Levels of Analysis in Environmental Design 535

Galen Cranz

40 How Post-Occupancy Evaluation Research
Effected Design and Policy at the San Francisco
Public Library 543

Galen Cranz

41 Healthy Cities: Key Principles for
Professional Practices 551

Roderick J. Lawrence

42 Landscape Design: Patient-Specific
Healing Gardens 563

Clare Cooper Marcus

Editor's Introduction

Galen Cranz and Eleftherios Pavlides

This reader supports courses that focus on the significance of the physical environment in human life. Theoretical knowledge in this field is important to all of us as citizens and to future design professionals in particular. Through this reader, we want to help architecture students identify various ways to take a social perspective on architecture. Accordingly, the reader (and the course) has multiple objectives:

TRANSDISCIPLINARY

Our perspective is transdisciplinary. We have incorporated environmental psychology, sociology, anthropology, architecture, landscape architecture, and urban design to develop our understanding of the profound relationship between humans and their environments.

This introduction to the field of human-environment studies offers a working knowledge of the basic concepts in person-environment relations: density, privacy, personalization, personal space, proxemics, territoriality, defensible space, appropriation, class, gender, stage in life cycle, and sustainability. We have added sustainability to the basic concepts because of its fundamental importance to the future of our life on Earth, and because we need to remind ourselves that it is ultimately a social problem having to do with human attitudes and behavior.

CROSS-CULTURAL AND AMERICAN SUBCULTURES

In order to demonstrate that the relationships between social-cultural life and physical form are different in different contexts, we include case studies from other cultures (Greece, China, Brazil, Mongolia) and American subcultures. We teach content from the point of view of three different American subcultures in order to bring home the point that American life expresses multiple experiences, not a singular one. We have chosen to compare and contrast Anglo-American, Chinese-American, and Hispanic-American experiences, so some of the readings reflect that choice. For example, we have selected articles that show variation in regard to how key concepts (like privacy, territoriality, recreational behavior) are expressed within American culture.

METHOD AND DATA COLLECTION TECHNIQUES

Third, such a course raises awareness of the social side of architecture, but it also builds on awareness to engage students in questions about how we learn more about people's involvement with buildings and places, that is, how do we do research? How do we use other people's published research, and how do we do our own original research? We want students to learn to use the methodological skills needed to contribute to architectural programming and evaluation research. Hence, the reader includes articles about methodological issues and data collection techniques that support students' hands-on field research projects. We emphasize observation and interviewing, especially photo elicitation and semantic ethnography, both important to us as ways to learn the insider's "emic" point of view.

CRITICAL THINKING

Fourth, we want to model how to think critically about the values embedded in design and the humanistic consequences for people, their behavior, and feelings.

THEORY, METHOD, APPLICATION, AT ALL SCALES

We define environment broadly to include all scales from the object and the body to the room, building, yard, and garden on up to the park, the neighborhood, and city. Accordingly, the readings cover all scales. Furthermore, the readings include theory, method, and applications to different scales.

In order to be parsimonious, each reading has to do double—or triple—duty. It might be about ethnic differences but also about parks. It might be about popular VS architectural views of architecture but also about a data collection technique. It might be about sustainability but also how to measure sustainable behavior. Communication theory might also offer information about housing. Our annotations at the beginning of each article indicate different ways that we think the article can be used pedagogically.

CHRONOLOGICAL ORGANIZATION

Because the articles can be used in different ways by different teachers, we did not organize the readings by topic. The idea is that the readings can be assigned in different sequences in different years by different professors since we each have related but different needs in our courses. We chose to list them by year, rather than author, in order to show development of the field since its inception in the 1960s. The editors of this anthology will be happy to share their syllabi illustrating two different ways of organizing the articles in this volume for teaching undergraduate and graduate classes. Email <galen@berkeley.edu> to receive Galen Cranz's syllabus for "Social and Cultural Processes in Architecture and Urban Design" that she teaches at the College of Environmental Design at the University of California, Berkeley. Email <epavlides@rwu.edu> to receive Eleftherios Pavlides's syllabus for "Environmental Design Research" that he teaches at the school of the School of Architecture, Art, and Historic Preservation, Roger Williams University.

ENVIRONMENTAL DESIGN RESEARCH

THE BODY, THE CITY, AND THE BUILDINGS IN BETWEEN

1 Proxemics in a Cross-Cultural Context: Germans, English, and French

Edward T. Hall

This is a classic study of how the tacit meaning of space is experienced in different cultures. It examines how the untold rules that implicitly regulate how we occupy space in relation to each other and in everyday work environments in relation to environmental features differs for the Germans, English, and the French. Written forty years ago before globalization of the business environment, it is still surprisingly relevant today.

The Germans, the English, the Americans, and the French share significant portions of each other's cultures, but at many points their cultures clash. Consequently, the misunderstandings that arise are all the more serious because sophisticated Americans and Europeans take pride in correctly interpreting each other's behavior. Cultural differences which are out of awareness are, as a consequence, usually chalked up to ineptness, boorishness, or lack of interest on the part of the other person.

THE GERMANS

Whenever people from different countries come into repeated contact they begin to generalize about each other's behavior. The Germans and the German Swiss are no exception. Most of the intellectual and professional people I have talked to from these two countries eventually get around to commenting on American use of time and space. Both the Germans and the German Swiss have made consistent observations about how Americans structure time very tightly and are sticklers for schedules. They also note that Americans don't leave any free time for themselves (a point which has been made by Sebastian de Grazia in *Of Time, Work, and Leisure*).

Since neither the Germans nor the Swiss (particularly the German Swiss) could be regarded as completely casual about time, I have made it a point to question them further about their view of the American approach to time. They will say that Europeans will schedule fewer events in the same time than Americans do and they usually add that Europeans feel less "pressed" for time than Americans. Certainly, Europeans allow more time for virtually everything involving important human relationships. Many of my European subjects observed that in Europe human relationships

Edward T. Hall, "Proxemics in a Cross-Cultural Context: Germans, English, and French in The Hidden Dimension," from *The Hidden Dimension*, pp. 131–148. Published by Anchor Books, 1969. Copyright by CPP, Inc. Permission to reprint granted by the rights holder.

are important whereas in the United States the schedule is important. Several of my subjects then took the next logical step and connected the handling of time with attitudes toward space, which Americans treat with incredible casualness. According to European standards, Americans use space in a wasteful way and seldom plan adequately for public needs. In fact, it would seem that Americans feel that people have no needs associated with space at all. By overemphasizing the schedule, Americans tend to underemphasize individual space needs. I should mention at this point that all Europeans are not this perceptive. Many of them go no further than to say that in the United States they themselves feel pressured by time and they often complain that our cities lack variety. Nevertheless, given these observations made by Europeans one would expect that the Germans would be more upset by violations of spatial mores than the Americans.

Germans and Intrusions

I shall never forget my first experience with German proxemic patterns, which occurred when I was an undergraduate. My manners, my status, and my ego were attacked and crushed by a German in an instance where thirty years' residence in this country and an excellent command of English had not attenuated German definitions of what constitutes an intrusion. In order to understand the various issues that were at stake, it is necessary to refer back to two basic American patterns that are taken for granted in this country and which Americans therefore tend to treat as universal.

First, in the United States there is a commonly accepted, invisible boundary around any two or three people in conversation which separates them from others. Distance alone serves to isolate any such group and to endow it with a protective wall of privacy. Normally, voices are kept low to avoid intruding on others and if voices are heard, people will act as though they had not heard. In this way, privacy is granted whether it is actually present or not. The second pattern is somewhat more subtle and has to do with the exact point at which a person is experienced as actually having crossed a boundary and entered a room. Talking through a screen door while standing outside a house is not considered by most Americans as being inside the house or room in any sense of the word. If one is standing on the threshold holding the door open and talking to someone inside, it is still defined informally and experienced as being *outside*. If one is in an office building and just "pokes his head in the door" of an office he's still outside the office. Just holding on to the door-jamb when one's body is inside the room still means a person has one foot "on base" as it were so that he is not quite inside the other fellow's territory. None of these American spatial definitions is valid in northern Germany. In every instance where the American would consider himself *outside* he has already entered the German's territory and by definition would become involved with him. The following experience brought the conflict between these two patterns into focus.

It was a warm spring day of the type one finds only in the high, clean, clear air of Colorado, the kind of day that makes you glad you are alive. I was standing on the doorstep of a converted carriage house talking to a young woman who lived in an apartment upstairs. The first floor had been made into an artist's studio. The arrangement, however, was peculiar because the same entrance served both tenants. The occupants of the apartment used a small entryway and walked along one wall of the studio to reach the stairs to the apartment. You might say that they had an "easement" through the artist's territory. As I stood talking on the doorstep, I glanced to the left and noticed that some fifty to sixty feet away, inside the studio, the Prussian artist and two of his friends were also in conversation. He was facing so that if he glanced to one side he could just see me. I had noted his presence, but not wanting to appear presumptuous or to interrupt his conversation, I unconsciously applied the American rule and assumed that the two activities—my quiet conversation and his conversation—were not involved with each other. As I was soon to learn, this was a mistake, because in less time than it takes to tell, the artist had detached himself from his friends, crossed the intervening space, pushed my friend aside, and with eyes flashing, started shouting at me. By what right had I entered his studio without greeting him? Who had given me permission?

I felt bullied and humiliated, and even after almost thirty years, I can still feel my anger. Later study has given me greater understanding of the German pattern and I have learned that in the German's eyes I really had been intolerably rude. I was already "inside" the building and I intruded when I could *see* inside. For the German, there is no such thing as being inside the room without being inside the zone of intrusion, particularly if one looks at the other party, no matter how far away.

Recently, I obtained an independent check on how Germans feel about visual intrusion while investigating what people look at when they are in intimate, personal, social, and public situations. In the course of my research, I instructed subjects to photograph separately both a man and a woman in each of the above contexts. One of my assistants, who also happened to be German, photographed his subjects out of focus at public distance because, as he said, "You are not really supposed to look at other people at public distances *because it's intruding.*" This may explain the informal custom behind the German laws against photographing strangers in public without their permission.

The "Private Sphere"

Germans sense their own space as an extension of the ego. One sees a clue to this feeling in the term "Lebensraum," which is impossible to translate because it summarizes so much. Hitler used it as an effective psychological lever to move the Germans to conquest.

In contrast to the Arab, as we shall see later, the German's ego is extraordinarily exposed, and he will go to almost any length to preserve his "private sphere." This was observed during World War II when American soldiers were offered opportunities to observe German prisoners under a variety of circumstances. In one instance in the Midwest, German P.W.s were housed four to a small hut. As soon as materials were available, each prisoner built a partition so that he could have *his own space.* In a less favorable setting in Germany when the *Wehrmacht* was collapsing, it was necessary to use open stockades because German prisoners were arriving faster than they could be accommodated. In this situation each soldier who could find the materials built his own tiny dwelling unit, sometimes no larger than a foxhole. It puzzled the Americans that the Germans did not pool their efforts and their scarce materials to create a larger, more efficient space, particularly in view of the very cold spring nights. Since that time I have observed frequent instances of the use of architectural extensions of this need to screen the ego. German houses with balconies are arranged so that there is visual privacy. Yards tend to be well fenced; but fenced or not, they are sacred.

The American view that space should be shared is particularly troublesome to the Germans. I cannot document the account of the early days of World War II occupation when Berlin was in ruins but the following situation was reported by an observer and it has the nightmarish quality that is often associated with inadvertent cross-cultural blunders. In Berlin at that time the housing shortage was indescribably acute. To provide relief, occupation authorities in the American zone ordered those Berliners who still had kitchens and baths intact to share them with their neighbors.

The order finally had to be rescinded when the already overstressed Germans started killing each other over the shared facilities.

Public and private buildings in Germany often have double doors for soundproofing, as do many hotel rooms. In addition, the door is taken very seriously by Germans. Those Germans who come to America feel that our doors are flimsy and light. The meanings of the open door and the closed door are quite different in the two countries. In offices, Americans keep doors open; Germans keep doors closed. In Germany, the closed door does not mean that the man behind it wants to be alone or undisturbed, or that he is doing something he doesn't want someone else to see. It's simply that Germans think that open doors are sloppy and disorderly. To close the door preserves the integrity of the room and provides a protective boundary between people. Otherwise, they get too involved with each other. One of my German subjects commented, "If our family hadn't had doors, we would have had to change our way of life. Without doors we would have had many, many more fights. … When you can't talk, you retreat behind a door. … If there hadn't been doors, I would always have been within reach of my mother."

Whenever a German warms up to the subject of American enclosed space, he can be counted on to comment on the noise that is transmitted through walls and doors. To many Germans, our doors epitomize American life. They are thin and cheap; they seldom fit; and they lack the substantial quality of German doors. When they close they don't sound and feel solid. The click of the lock is indistinct, it rattles and indeed it may even be absent.

The open-door policy of American business and the closed-door patterns of German business culture cause clashes in the branches and subsidiaries of American firms in Germany. The point seems to be quite simple, yet failure to grasp it has caused considerable friction and misunderstanding between American and German managers overseas. I was once called in to advise a firm that has operations all over the world. One of the first questions asked was, "How do you get the Germans to keep their doors open?" In this company the open doors were making the Germans feel exposed and gave the whole operation an unusually relaxed and unbusinesslike air. Closed doors, on the other hand, gave the Americans the feeling that there was a conspiratorial air about the place and that they were being left out. The point is that whether the door is open or shut, it is not going to mean the same thing in the two countries.

Order in Space

The orderliness and hierarchical quality of German culture are communicated in their handling of space. Germans want to know where they stand and object strenuously to people crashing queues or people who "get out of line" or who do not obey signs such as "Keep out," "Authorized personnel only," and the like. Some of the German attitudes toward us are traceable to our informal attitudes toward boundaries and to authority in general.

However, German anxiety due to American violations of order is nothing compared to that engendered in Germans by the Poles, who see no harm in a little disorder. To them lines and queues stand for regimentation and blind authority. I once saw a Pole crash a cafeteria line just "to stir up those sheep."

Germans get very technical about intrusion distance, as I mentioned earlier. When I once asked my students to describe the distance at which a third party would intrude on two people who were talking, there were no answers from the Americans. Each student knew that he could tell when he was being intruded on but he couldn't define intrusion or tell how he knew when it had occurred.

However, a German and an Italian who had worked in Germany were both members of my class and they answered without any hesitation. Both stated that a third party would intrude on two people if he came within seven feet!

Many Americans feel that Germans are overly rigid in their behavior, unbending and formal. Some of this impression is created by differences in the handling of chairs while seated. The American doesn't seem to mind if people hitch their chairs up to adjust the distance to the situation—those that do mind would not think of saying anything, for to comment on the manners of others would be impolite. In Germany, however, it is a violation of the mores to change the position of your chair. An added deterrent for those who don't know better is the weight of most German furniture. Even the great architect Mies van der Rohe, who often rebelled against German tradition in his buildings, made his handsome chairs so heavy that anyone but a strong man would have difficulty in adjusting his seating position. To a German, light furniture is anathema, not only because it seems flimsy but because people move it and thereby destroy the order of things, including intrusions on the "private sphere." In one instance reported to me, a German newspaper editor who had moved to the United States had his visitor's chair bolted to the floor "at the proper distance" because he couldn't tolerate the American habit of adjusting the chair to the situation.

THE ENGLISH

It has been said that the English and the Americans are two great people separated by one language. The differences for which language gets blamed may not be due so much to words as to communications on other levels beginning with English intonation (which sounds affected to many Americans) and continuing to ego-linked ways of handling time, space, and materials. If there ever were two cultures in which differences of the proxemic details are marked it is in the educated (public school) English and the middle-class Americans. One of the basic reasons for this wide disparity is that in the United States we use space as a way of classifying people and activities, whereas in England it is the social system that determines who you are. In the United States, your address is an important cue to status (this applies not only to one's home but to the business address as well). The Joneses from Brooklyn and Miami are not as "in" as the Joneses from Newport and Palm Beach. Greenwich and Cape Cod are worlds apart from Newark and Miami. Businesses located on Madison and Park avenues have more tone than those on Seventh and Eighth avenues. A corner office is more prestigious than one next to the elevator or at the end of a long hall. The Englishman, however, is born and brought up in a social system. He is still Lord no matter where you find him, even if it is behind the counter in a fishmonger's stall. In addition to class distinctions, there are differences between the English and ourselves in how space is allotted.

The middle-class American growing up in the United States feels he has a right to have his own room, or at least part of a room. My American subjects, when asked to draw an ideal room or office, invariably drew it for themselves and no one else. When asked to draw their present room or office, they drew only their own part of a shared room and then drew a line down the middle. Both male and female subjects identified the kitchen and the master bedroom as belonging to the mother or the wife, whereas Father's territory was a study or a den, if one was available; otherwise, it was "the shop," "the basement," or sometimes only a workbench or the garage. American women who want to be alone can go to the bedroom and close the door. The closed door is the sign meaning "do not disturb" or "I'm angry." An American is available if his door is open at home or at his office. He is expected not to shut himself off but to maintain himself in a state of constant readiness to answer the demands of others. Closed doors are for conferences, private conversations, and business, work that requires concentration, study, resting, sleeping, dressing, and sex.

The middle- and upper-class Englishman, on the other hand, is brought up in a nursery shared with brothers and sisters. The oldest occupies a room by himself which he vacates when he leaves for boarding school, possibly even at the age of nine or ten. The difference between a room of one's own and early conditioning to shared space, while seeming inconsequential, has an important effect on the Englishman's attitude toward his own space. He may never have a permanent "room of his own" and seldom expects one or feels he is entitled to one. Even members of Parliament have no offices and often conduct their business on the terrace overlooking the Thames. As a consequence, the English are puzzled by the American need for a secure place in which to work, an office. Americans working in England may become annoyed if they are not provided with what they consider appropriate enclosed work space. In regard to the need for walls as a screen for the ego, this places the Americans somewhere between the Germans and the English.

The contrasting English and American patterns have some remarkable implications, particularly if we assume that man, like other animals, has a built-in need to shut himself off from others from time to time. An English student in one of my seminars typified what happens when hidden patterns clash. He was quite obviously experiencing strain in his relationships with Americans. Nothing seemed to go right and it was quite clear from his remarks that we did not know how to behave. An analysis of his complaints showed that a major source of irritation was that no American seemed to be able to pick up the subtle clues that there were times when he didn't want his thoughts intruded on. As he stated it, "I'm walking around the apartment and it seems that whenever I want to be alone my roommate starts talking to me. Pretty soon he's asking 'What's the matter?' and wants to know if I'm angry. By then I am angry and say something."

It took some time but finally we were able to identify most of the contrasting features of the American and British problems that were in conflict in this case. When the American wants to be alone he goes into a room and shuts the door—he depends on architectural features for screening. For an American to refuse to talk to someone else present in the same room, to give them the "silent treatment," is the ultimate form of rejection and a sure sign of great displeasure. The English, on the other hand, lacking rooms of their own since childhood, never developed the practice of using space as a refuge from others. They have in effect internalized a set of barriers, which they erect and which others are supposed to recognize. Therefore, the more the Englishman shuts himself off when he is with an American the more likely the American is to break in to assure himself that all is well. Tension lasts until the two get to know each other. The important point is that the spatial and architectural needs of each are not the same at all.

Using the Telephone

English internalized privacy mechanisms and the American privacy screen result in very different customs regarding the telephone. There is no wall or door against the telephone. Since it is impossible to tell from the ring who is on the other end of the line, or how urgent his business is, people feel compelled to answer the phone. As one would anticipate, the English, when they feel the need to be with their thoughts, treat the phone as an intrusion by someone who doesn't know any better. Since it is impossible to tell how preoccupied the other party will be they hesitate to use the phone; instead, they write notes. To phone is to be "pushy" and rude. A letter or telegram may be slower, but it is much less disrupting. Phones are for actual business and emergencies.

I used this system myself for several years when I lived in Santa Fe, New Mexico, during the Depression. I dispensed with a phone because it cost money. Besides, I cherished the quiet of my tiny mountainside retreat and didn't want to be disturbed. This idiosyncrasy on my part produced a shocked reaction in others. People really didn't know what to do with me. You could see the consternation on their faces when, in answer to the question, "How do I get in touch with you?" I would reply, "Write me a post card. I come to the post office every day."

Having provided most of our middle-class citizens with private rooms and escape from the city to the suburbs, we have then proceeded to penetrate their most private spaces in their home with a most public device, the telephone. Anyone can reach us at any time. We are, in fact, so available that elaborate devices have to be devised so that busy people can function. The greatest skill and tact must be exercised in the message-screening process so that others will not be offended. So far our technology has not kept up with the needs of people to be alone with either their families or their thoughts. The problem stems from the fact that it is impossible to tell from the phone's ring who is calling and how urgent his business is. Some people have unlisted phones but then that makes it hard on friends who come to town who want to get in touch with them. The government solution is to have special phones for important people (traditionally red). The red line bypasses secretaries, coffee breaks, busy signals, and teenagers, and is connected to White House, State Department, and Pentagon switchboards.

Neighbors

Americans living in England are remarkably consistent in their reactions to the English. Most of them are hurt and puzzled because they were brought up on American neighboring patterns and don't interpret the English ones correctly. In England propinquity means nothing. The fact that you live next door to a family does not entitle you to visit, borrow from, or socialize with them, or your children to play with theirs. Accurate figures on the number of Americans who adjust well to the English are difficult to obtain. The basic attitude of the English toward the Americans is tinged by our ex-colonial status. This attitude is much more in awareness and therefore more likely to be expressed than the unspoken right of the Englishman to maintain his privacy against the world. To the best of my knowledge, those who have tried to relate to the English purely on the basis of propinquity seldom if ever succeed. They may get to know and even like their neighbors, but it won't be because they live next door, because English relationships are patterned not according to space but according to social status.

Whose Room Is the Bedroom?

In upper middle-class English homes, it is the man, not the woman, who has the privacy of the bedroom, presumably as protection from children who haven't yet internalized the English patterns of privacy. The man, not the woman, has a dressing room; the man also has a study which affords privacy. The Englishman is fastidious about his clothes and expects to spend a great deal of time and attention in their purchase. In contrast, English women approach the buying of clothes in a manner reminiscent of the American male.

Talking Loud and Soft

Proper spacing between people is maintained in many ways. Loudness of the voice is one of the mechanisms which also varies from culture to culture. In England and in Europe generally, Americans are continually accused of loud talking, which is a function of two forms of vocal control: (a) loudness, and (b) modulation for direction. Americans increase the volume as a function of distance, using several levels (whisper, normal voice, loud shout, etc.). In many situations, the more gregarious Americans do not care if they can be overheard. In fact, it is part of their openness showing that we have nothing to hide. The English do care, for to get along without private offices and not intrude they have developed skills in beaming the voice toward the person they are talking to, carefully adjusting it so that it just barely overrides the background noise and distance. For the English to be overheard is to intrude on others, a failure in manners and a sign of socially inferior behavior. However, because of the way they modulate their voices the English in an American setting may sound and look conspiratorial to Americans, which can result in their being branded as troublemakers.

Eye Behavior

A study of eye behavior reveals some interesting contrasts between the two cultures. Englishmen in this country have trouble not only when they want to be alone and shut themselves off but also when they want to interact. They never know for sure whether an American is listening. We, on the other hand, are equally unsure as to whether the English have understood us. Many of these ambiguities in communication center on differences in the use of the eyes. The Englishman is taught to pay strict attention, to listen carefully, which he must do if he is polite and there are not protective walls to screen out sound. He doesn't bob his head or grunt to let you know he understands. He blinks his eyes to let you know that he has heard you. Americans, on the other hand, are taught not to stare. We look the other person straight in the eye without wavering only when we want to be particularly certain that we are getting through to him.

The gaze of the American directed toward his conversational partner often wanders from one eye to the other and even leaves the face for long periods. Proper English listening behavior includes immobilization of the eyes at social distance, so that whichever eye one looks at gives the appearance of looking straight at you. In order to accomplish this feat, the Englishman must be eight or more feet away. He is too close when the 12-degree horizontal span of the macula won't permit a steady gaze. At less than eight feet, one *must* look at either one eye or the other.

THE FRENCH

The French who live south and east of Paris belong generally to that complex of cultures which border the Mediterranean. Members of this group pack together more closely than do northern Europeans, English, and Americans. Mediterranean use of space can be seen in the crowded trains, buses, automobiles, sidewalk cafés, and in the homes of the people. The exceptions are, of course, in the châteaus and villas of the rich. Crowded living normally means high sensory involvement. Evidence of French emphasis on the senses appears not only in the way the French eat, entertain, talk, write, and crowd together in cafés, but can even be seen in the way they make their maps. These maps are extraordinarily well thought out and so designed that the traveler can find the most detailed information. One can tell from using these maps that the French employ all their senses.

These maps make it possible for you to get around and they also tell you where you can enjoy a view; where you'll find picturesque drives, and, in some instances, places to rest, refresh yourself, take a walk, and even eat a pleasant meal. They inform the traveler which senses he can expect to use and at what points in his journey.

Home and Family

One possible reason why the French love the outdoors is the rather crowded conditions under which many of them live. The French entertain at restaurants and cafés. The home is for the family and the outdoors for recreation and socializing. Yet all the homes I have visited, as well as everything I have been able to learn about French homes, indicate that they are often quite crowded. The working class and the petite bourgeoisie are particularly crowded, which means that the French are sensually much involved with each other. The layout of their offices, homes, towns, cities, and countryside is such as to keep them involved.

In interpersonal encounters this involvement runs high; when a Frenchman talks to you, he really looks at you and there is no mistaking this fact. On the streets of Paris he looks at the woman he sees very directly. American women returning to their own country after living in France often go through a period of sensory deprivation. Several have told me that because they have grown accustomed to being looked at, the American habit of *not* looking makes them feel as if they didn't exist.

Not only are the French sensually involved with each other, they have become accustomed to what are to us greatly stepped-up sensory inputs. The French automobile is designed in response to French needs. Its small size used to be attributed to a lower standard of living and higher costs of materials; and while there can be no doubt but that cost is a factor, it would be naïve to assume that it was the major factor. The automobile is just as much an expression of the culture as is the language and, therefore, has its characteristic niche in the cultural biotope. Changes in the car will reflect and be reflected in changes elsewhere. If the French drove American cars, they would be forced to give up many ways of dealing with space which they hold quite dear. The traffic along the Champs-Elysées and around the Arc de Triomphe is a cross between the New Jersey Turnpike on a sunny Sunday afternoon and the Indianapolis Speedway. With American-size autos, it would be mass suicide. Even the occasional "compact" American cars in the stream of Parisian traffic look like sharks among minnows. In the United States, the same cars look normal because everything else is in scale. In the foreign setting where they stand out, Detroit iron can be seen for what it is. The American behemoths give bulk to the ego and prevent overlapping of personal spheres inside the car so that each passenger is only marginally involved with the others. I do not mean by this that all Americans are alike and have been forced into the Detroit mold. But since Detroit won't produce what is wanted, many Americans prefer the smaller, more maneuverable European cars which fit their personalities and needs more closely. Nevertheless, if one simply looks at the styles of the French cars, one sees greater emphasis on individuality than in the United States. Compare the Peugeot, the Citroen, the Renault and the Dauphine and the little 2 C.V. shoebox. It would take years and years of style changes to produce such differences in the United States.

French Use of Open Spaces

Because total space needs must be maintained in balance, the urban French have learned to make the most of the parks and the outdoors. To them, the city is something from which to derive satisfaction and so are the people in it. Reasonably clean air, sidewalks up to seventy feet wide, automobiles that will not dwarf humans as they pass on the boulevards make it possible to have outdoor cafés and open areas where people congregate and enjoy each other. Since the French savor and participate in the city itself—its varied sights, sounds, and smells; its wide sidewalks and avenues and parks—the need for insulating space in the automobile may be somewhat less than it is in the United States where humans are dwarfed by skyscrapers and the products of Detroit, visually assaulted by filth and rubbish, and poisoned by smog and carbon dioxide.

The Star and the Grid

There are two major European systems for patterning space. One of these, "the radiating star" which occurs in France and Spain, is sociopetal. The other, the "grid," originated in Asia Minor, adopted by the Romans and carried to England at the time of Caesar, is sociofugal. The French-Spanish system connects all points and functions. In the French subway system, different lines repeatedly come together at places of interest like the Place de la Concorde, the Opéra, and the Madeleine. The grid system separates activities by stringing them out. Both systems have advantages, but a person familiar with one has difficulty using the other.

For example, a mistake in direction in the radiating center-point system becomes more serious the farther one travels. Any error, therefore, is roughly equivalent to taking off in the wrong direction. In the grid system, baseline errors are of the 90-degree or the 180-degree variety and are usually obvious enough to make themselves felt even by those with a poor sense of direction. If you are traveling in the right direction, even though you are one or two blocks off your course, the error is easily rectified at any time. Nevertheless, there are certain inherent advantages in the center-point system. Once one learns to use it, it is easier, for example, to locate objects or events in space by naming a point on a line. Thus it is possible, even in strange territory, to tell someone to meet you at the 50 KM mark on National Route 20 south of Paris; that is all the information he needs. In contrast, the grid system of coordinates involves at least two lines and a point to locate something in space (often many more lines and points, depending on how many turns one has to make). In the star system, it is also possible to integrate a number of different activities in centers in less space than with the grid system. Thus, residential, shopping, marketing, commercial, and recreation areas can both meet and be reached from central points.

It is incredible how many facets of French life the radiating star pattern touches. It is almost as though the whole culture were set up on a model in which power, influence, and control flowed in and out from a series of interlocking centers. There are sixteen major highways running into Paris, twelve into Caen (near Omaha Beach), twelve into Amiens, eleven for Le Mans, and ten for Rennes. Even the figures don't begin to convey the picture of what this arrangement really means, for France is a series of radiating networks that build up into larger and larger centers. Each small center has its own channel, as it were, to the next higher level. As a general rule, the roads between centers do not go through other towns, because each town is connected to others by its own roads. This is in contrast to the American pattern of stringing small towns out like beads on a necklace along the routes that connect principal centers.

In *The Silent Language* I have described how the man in charge of a French office can often be found in the middle—with his minions placed like satellites on strings radiating outward from him. I once had occasion to deal with such a "central figure" when the French member of a team of scientists under my direction wanted a raise because his desk was in the middle! Even De Gaulle bases his international policy on France's central location. There are those, of course, who will say that the fact that the French school system also follows a highly centralized pattern couldn't possibly have any relationship to the layout of offices, subway systems, road networks, and, in fact, the entire nation, but I could not agree with them. Long experience with different patterns of culture has taught me that the basic threads tend to be woven throughout the entire fabric of a society.

The reason for the review of the three European cultures to which the middle class of the United States is most closely linked (historically and culturally) is as much as anything else a means of providing contrast to highlight some of our own implicit patterns. In this review it was shown that different use of the senses leads to very different needs regarding space no matter on what level one cares to consider it. Everything from an office to a town or city will reflect the sense modalities of its builders and occupants. In considering solutions to problems such as urban renewal and city sinks it is essential to know how the populations involved perceive space and how they use their senses. The next chapter deals with people whose spatial worlds are quite different from our own, and from whom we can learn more about ourselves.

2 "Natural Surveillance" and "Image and Milieu"

Oscar Newman

This book examines how architectural form can be shown, when controlling for all other co-producer variables, to affect crime rates. It examines how architectural form and features impact crime rates both by making surveillance possible as well as influencing the sense of ownership and territoriality. This is one of the most influential studies to come out of the environment behavior field because of its impact on policy, leading to massive rethinking of design guidelines for public housing.

SURVEILLANCE AND TERRITORIALITY

Improvements in surveillance capacity—the ability to observe the public areas of one's residential environment and to feel continually that one is under observation by other residents while on the grounds of projects and within the public areas of building interiors—can have a pronounced effect in securing the environment for peaceful activities. An additional benefit, of possibly greater import, is that surveillance has a demonstrable effect in reducing irrational fears and anxieties in inhabitants. This may have some self-fulfilling attributes in that residents, feeling that an area is secure, will make more frequent use of it and so further improve its security by providing the safety which comes with intensive use.

However, experience has shown that the ability to observe criminal activity will not, in and of itself, impel the observer to respond with assistance to the person or property being victimized. The decision to act will also depend on the presence of the following conditions:

- The extent to which the observer has a developed sense of his personal and proprietary rights and is accustomed to defending them.
- The extent to which the activity observed is understood to be occurring in an area within the sphere of influence of the observer.
- Identification of the observed behavior as being abnormal to the area in which it occurs and therefore warranting response.

Oscar Newman, "Natural Surveillance & Image and Milieu," from *Defensible Space; Crime Prevention Through Urban Design*, pp. 78–117. Copyright © 1973 by Oscar Newman. Permission to reprint granted by the author.

- The observer's identification with either the victim or the property being vandalized or stolen.
- The extent to which the observer feels he can effectively alter (by personal or collective response) the course of events being observed.

Physical means for furthering the development of proprietary feelings and extending the zone of identification were discussed under mechanisms for the definition of zones of territorial influence.

The Kitty Genovese incident, perhaps one of the most widely known examples in which the many observers of a crime were incapable of mounting an effective response, has been the subject of many studies, some involving in-depth interviews with witnesses. The common excuses given for inaction were that the victim was unknown to the observers, and that the incident occurred on a public street. These two factors, it seems, precluded intervention. This and other similar incidents happening in urban areas point out a serious breakdown in traditional social values and responsibilities.

The provision of surveillance should not be interpreted as a universal panacea for a complex problem. It is necessary to reinforce the point that the effectiveness of increased surveillance depends on whether the area under surveillance is identified by the observer as falling under his sphere of influence. Improved surveillance operates most effectively when linked with the territorial subdivision of residential areas, allowing the resident to observe those public areas which he considers to be part of his realm of ownership and hence responsibility. A further operating factor has also been introduced which will be more fully discussed later—the recognition of or identification (on the part of the observer) with the victim. This implies an ability to distinguish strangers and has been found to be closely related to the number of families sharing a particular defined area at each level of a development's subdivision. The unilateral success of surveillance capacities as a mechanism of crime control is, therefore, by no means implied.

The following set of mechanisms are directed to the design of the grounds and internal semipublic areas of housing developments to facilitate natural visual and auditory monitoring of activities taking place within them.

Most crime in housing occurs in the visually deprived semipublic interiors of buildings: the lobbies, halls, elevators, and fire stairs. However, it is possible, through the relative juxtaposition of apartment windows with stairs and corridors, as well as with the outside, to ensure that all public and semiprivate spaces and paths come under continual and natural observation by the project's residents.

It is our hypothesis that the provision of such surveillance opportunities is a significant crime deterrent that markedly lessens the anxiety of inhabitants, and serves to create an overall image of a safe environment. Most important, this image is also perceived by the potential criminal, who is deterred from initial consideration of this area as an easy hit.

The glazing, lighting, and positioning of nonprivate areas and access paths, in buildings and out, to facilitate their surveillance by residents and formal authorities. (Access paths refer to vertical paths as well as horizontal ones and include stairs, elevators, corridors, and lobbies, along with the more obvious outside paths.)

EXTERNAL AREAS

Following the directives of early planning manuals, many housing projects have been intentionally designed to look inward on themselves, with the result that residents cannot view bordering streets. In medium-density, row-type housing projects, only the ends of buildings meet adjacent streets; their entrances and windows face the interior of the project. As a result, these bordering streets have been deprived of continual surveillance by residents and have proven unsafe to walk along—for both project residents and the members of the surrounding community. Residents often find that the nighttime journey from the bus stop to the project interior assumes harrowing proportions. Many project residents choose to remain at home rather than use these streets in the evening, further adding to the lack of path surveillance and to feelings of insecurity.

Formal motor patrol of the interior areas of these projects is made impossible. This difficulty has been somewhat overcome in New York City projects through the use of motor scooters by housing police. Nevertheless, the opportunity for the informal supervision provided by passing cars and pedestrians is lost. Similarly, it is impossible for city police to include the internal grounds of such projects in their normal routes.

The traditional row-house street is considered by both residents and police to be superior in design to the superblock configuration most often employed in medium and high-density residential developments. The front entrances of the row-house units are easily surveyed by patrolling automobiles. Well-lit front-door paths, with individual lights over the entrances, allow cruising

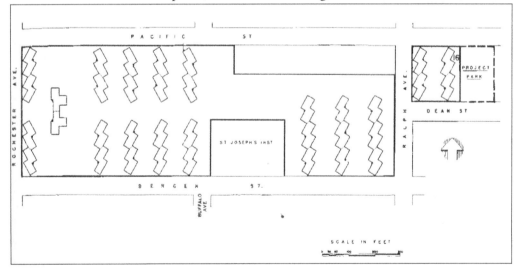

Site Plan of Kingsborough Houses, Brooklyn, New York. Because the project buildings are oriented inward, the streets surrounding the project are considered unsafe. The activity along Pacific and Bergen streets cannot be observed by residents from their apartment windows.

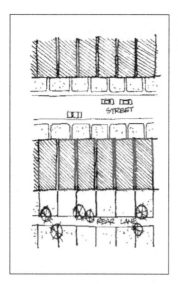

Plan of a portion of a row-house street.

Aerial view of Baruch Houses, New York. (Courtesy of New York City Housing Authority)

police to spot at a glance any peculiar activity taking place on a row-house street. The positioning of front entrances along the street provides them with continuous natural supervision by passersby; the residents within their houses, in turn, provide these passersby with protective surveillance. The New York City Housing Authority Police consider projects with buildings having entrances facing the street superior to those with entrances facing the interior project grounds.

The random positioning of high-rise towers on housing sites has produced systems of access paths which are filled with sharp turns and blind corners. Circuitous paths of movement through the interior of large projects are a recurring complaint of residents, especially in projects where the main building entries face interior project grounds rather than public streets. Woodhill Estates in Cleveland, Baruch Houses in New York, and Columbus Homes in Newark are examples. Winding access paths provide many opportunities for muggers to conceal themselves while awaiting the arrival of a victim. The circuitous access route to building entries is made even more dangerous by the common practice of positioning shrubs exactly at the turn in a path. Compositionally satisfying as this practice might be, such visual barriers provide natural hiding places and vantage points for potential criminals.

Regardless of how well-lit these areas are, residents express strong fears about turns in the path system connecting the street to the building lobby. This problem does not of course arise in the traditional row-house pattern where buildings are set back only a few yards from the street. Nor does it occur in projects such as Breukelen and Brownsville (discussed in chapters 2 and 3) where the entry is only slightly set back from the street. In these projects, residents are able to scan the terrain they are about to use; they move in a straight line from the relative safety of the public street to what they can observe to be the relative safety of the well-lit lobby area in front of their building.

The design of such projects as Columbus Homes in Newark, Pruitt-Igoe in St. Louis, and Baruch in New York requires residents to leave the comparative safety of the neighborhood street and enter the project grounds without knowing what lies ahead. Access to the building entry requires entering the project interior, circumnavigating a few corners, and finally approaching a point from which they are able to observe the lobby of their own apartment building.

To test the soundness of our theories on building location and its effect on crimes, existing New York City housing projects were divided into three categories:

- Those with buildings facing and within fifty feet of the street.
- Those with buildings facing and within fifty feet of the street and with good lobby visibility (large window area)—a subcategory of (1).
- Those with less than 30 percent of the buildings facing and within fifty feet of the street.

The total number of felonies, misdemeanors, and offenses was calculated for all projects, as well as for those in the three categories, and a rate per thousand population was determined.

The lowest crime rates were recorded for the second category (optimum surveillance possible). The highest rates occurred in the third category, where most buildings had poor surveillance potential. Evidently, the orientation of a building to the street and the open design of its lobby have a direct effect on the attractiveness it possesses to criminal elements. A project with buildings facing and close to a street, with lobbies visible to passersby, is decidedly less likely to experience as much crime as one where these factors do not interplay. (See table 9.)

As a further test of the effect of visibility on crime rate, the same projects were divided into two groups according to type of lobby entry. Those projects with buildings having little or no definition were labeled "poor" and those with significant or precise entry definition were, labeled "good." (See figure 61 design criteria.)

In addition, the same projects were also divided into two groups, "good" and "bad" according to quality of lobby visibility, from the outside primary door. Those projects that fell into "good" design categories, for both entrance definition and visibility, were labeled Category I; those that qualified as "good" on only one design criterion formed Category II; and finally, those projects in which buildings were rated "poor" on both criteria were listed under Category III. Felonies, misdemeanors, and offenses occurring in both lobbies and elevators were totaled for all projects concerned.

The results, shown in table 10, underline the importance of the effect of design on discouraging crime.

Surveillance (Building in Relation to Street)

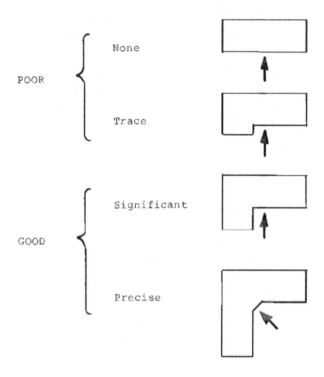

Extent of definition of lobby entry as formed by shape of building.

TABLE 9
Surveillance (Building in Relation to Street)

FMOs* in Lobby	All Projects	(a) Projects where All Buildings Are Facing and within 50 feet of Street	(b) Projects where All Buildings Are Facing and within 50 feet of Street and Having Good Lobby Visibility	(c) Projects Where Less Than 30% of the Buildings are Facing and within 50 feet of Street
Rate per 1000 Population	7.5 (140 projects)	5.3 (22 projects)	4.4 (12 projects)	9.7 (21 projects)

*Felonies, misdemeanors, and offenses.

TABLE 10
Effect of Lobby Visibility and Entry Design on Crime Rate

		Crime Rate (FMOs) per 1,000 Population	
		Lobby	Elevator
Category I	good visibility/good entry definition	7.3	3.8
Category II	(a) or (b) poor visibility/good entry definition good visibility/poor entry definition	7.8	4.5
Category III	poor visibility/poor entry definition	8.6	4.6

Category I projects, in which buildings were rated "good" on both counts, had a comparatively lower crime average. Category II had slightly higher crime rates. The highest rates were recorded for Category III, where both design factors were considered "poor."

When separate scores were calculated for both parts of Category II (see table 11), it was discovered that for both the elevator and lobby, crime rates were higher in buildings with poor visibility, clearly indicating that of the two design factors, visibility seems to be the determining one for crime rate and *not* entry definition.

TABLE 11
Breakdown of Category II

		Crime Rate (FMOs) per 1,000 Population	
		Lobby	Elevator
Category II	(a) poor visibility/good entry definition	8.9	4.9
	(b) good visibility/good entry definition	7.2	4.1

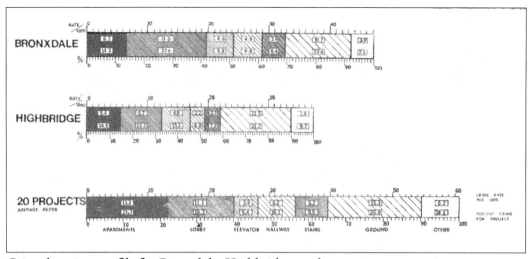

Crime location profile for Bronxdale, Highbridge, and twenty average projects.

A final indication of the relationship between visibility and crime was discovered when robberies occurring in elevators were examined (elevator robberies were the most numerous of the major crimes in 1969). The annual rate per thousand population for elevators judged not visible from outside the main entrance was 65 percent higher than for elevators that were visible (3.8 compared to 2.3).

INTERNAL AREAS

The internal areas of high-rise buildings contain many zones devoid of any opportunity for surveillance. Lobbies, elevators, hallways, and fire stairs are, by definition, public rather than private spaces and are intended for use by all building residents. Yet, these zones differ from other public areas, like city streets, in that they exist without benefit of continual observation by either patrolling officers, residents, or passersby. It would have been preferable to design all these internal public areas so that activities within them could be readily observed from outside the building.

Lobby

Lobby design is easily provided with surveillance from outside a building, and it is possible and preferable to design the lobby so that internal activity—getting mail, waiting for the elevator, using the pram room, or, as the case may be, purse snatching or drug dealing—is observable from the streets and exterior grounds of the project. As an example of how poorly lobbies can be designed, the entrance of the Bronxdale Houses project in The Bronx, New York, requires one to make a double turn before reaching the elevator waiting area. Residents of Bronxdale are required to enter the building "blind" with no foreknowledge of what awaits them; once inside they are completely isolated from visual or auditory observation by persons within the apartment units or outside on the project grounds.

By contrast, the design of the lobby of Highbridge Gardens is clearly preferable. In these buildings, elevators are located directly opposite the entry doors which were designed as a part of a large window wall. Similarly, at Edenwaid Houses in The Bronx, the lobby is glazed, well-lit, and open to visual observation from as far away as fifty yards. Figure 65 compares crime location in Bronxdale

Transitional path at Breukelen Houses. View of the transitional path lead-in from the common play area of the buffer zone to one of the entries and stair-wells within the L-shaped building. This area is considered to be sufficiently defined as semiprivate (serving only the nine families in the building) so that a baby can be left in a pram alone beside the entry. Note however, that the kitchen windows of the apartment units on both sides of the entry and at each level are immediately adjacent to the entry and stairwell and look out upon this area. (Photo by author)

Transitional Buffer and Parking Area at Breukelen. The transitional zones formed by the L-shaped buildings at Breukelen at times include parking. This combination of parking, seating, and play space adjacent to the multiple-entry buffer serves to create a well-peopled and well-watched-over semiprivate outside zone serving the apartment building. In this L-shaped building, five entries share a common buffer area and parking lot. Each entry, in turn, has its own transition zone leading from the common buffer area. (Photo by author)

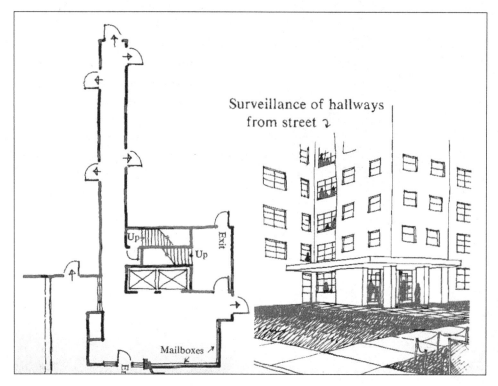

Tilden Houses, Brooklyn, New York. The positioning of windows at the end of the corridor on each floor and at the stairwell landings allows a patrolling officer on the street to observe activity in these public interior spaces.

and Highbridge with an average of twenty projects. Where allover crime rates are three-fourths the average at Bronxdale and two-thirds at Highbridge, lobby crime at Bronxdale is 52 percent higher than the average, while at Highbridge, it is 33 percent below the average.

Fire Stairs

Another area of high-rise buildings devoid of both visual and auditory surveillance opportunities is the fire stair system. Because of changes in fire code regulations, fire stairs in elevator buildings must be enclosed in fireproof wells. These regulations have resulted in the widespread adoption of the scissors-stair design. This solution has precipitated a wide range of allied problems.

Due to fire code requirements, the stairs are virtually sealed off from heavily traversed areas of the buildings they serve. The stairwells are commonly constructed of concrete, with access provided through heavy, fireproof steel doors in which the only opening is a one-foot-square area of wired glass. This arrangement effectively precludes the possibility of visual or auditory monitoring of activity in the stairwells. Consequently, most residents rarely make use of the stairwell for entry and exit, thereby increasing its isolation.

A disproportionate amount of crime has been found to occur on these stairs. It is common practice for criminals to accost their victim in a more heavily used public area of the building—the lobby, elevator, or corridors—and then move him or her, by threat or force, to the sealed fire stairs. Not surprisingly, fire stairs are the area in which a high percentage of the rapes occur, and in which narcotics addicts congregate.

Ground Floor Plan of Breukelen Houses. The design of the apartment units facilitates surveillance. Kitchen windows face out on front entries, allowing parents to observe the movements of children and passersby.

In older buildings and projects, fire stairs were constructed with glass areas larger than contemporary fire codes permit. For example, at Breukelen Houses the landing areas and a good portion of the stairs are surveyable both from the interior corridors and from the grounds and street. Large windows at the stair landings flood the internal stair with daylight. Users of these well-trafficked stairwells feel that they are under observation by other residents and that in an emergency they can call out to people in the street below.

Effective formal police surveillance is a difficult task in high-rise buildings with scissors stairs. Housing police patrol the interior of a building of double-loaded corridor design by taking the elevator to the top floor and descending one fire stair after another, observing activity in the corridors at each floor level as they go down. In addition to being burdensome and boring this method is not particularly effective; it is difficult to see more than a few yards ahead, and it is impossible for a man to cover more than one stair at a time. Conversely, evading a patrolman is very easily done. A criminal can hear a patrolman coming three floors away, by the sound of his footsteps and the opening of doors at each level. Eluding pursuit by police is further facilitated by the double, scissors-stair configuration which produces an exit door on each side of the building. Police officers may be going down one of the staircases while the intruder slips down and out of the other.

Members of the staff of the Project for Security Design accompanied officers of the New York City Housing Authority Police in their nightly and daily patrols and witnessed the comparative ease of formal patrol of buildings which have features such as (1) windows in the fire-stair walls, (2) lobbies and mailbox areas that are well lit and easily viewed from the street; and (3) elevator waiting areas at each floor which can be seen from the street below. These areas can be surveyed from the ground at a glance. Trouble spots in buildings can be pinpointed easily from the street. Someone moving down a set of stairs can be observed in progress. Dark landings resulting from smashed or unscrewed light bulbs provide a warning that some activity may be taking place there.

Tilden Houses illustrates the increased surveillance opportunities made possible by simple modification of what is otherwise a standard floor plan: windows were inserted at the end of the corridor on each floor and at each landing of the fire stair. As a result, the patrolling officer on the street can observe much of the activity in the public interior space of the building.

Roof landings (the last landing of the fire stair before exit onto the roof) have presented a similar surveillance problem, because they are used by addicts as a gathering place. At Brownsville Houses, two kinds of roof landings are employed: one set of landings is dark, and one has windows and is well lit. Drug addicts are seldom found in the second, but the first is the location of numerous arrests on narcotics charges.

THE JUXTAPOSITION OF ACTIVITY AREAS IN APARTMENT INTERIORS WITH EXTERIOR NONPRIVATE AREAS TO FACILITATE VISUAL SURVEILLANCE FROM WITHIN

Design that facilitates the surveillance of outside areas from within the apartment can be accomplished in many ways. This involves designing apartments so that people *within* them will naturally view the communally used paths, entries, play, and seating areas of a project during their normal household activities.

Breukelen Houses, discussed in the previous chapter, has employed this technique. The result is very little crime, or fear of crime, on its grounds. The architects of Breukelen located kitchen windows in each apartment so that they face the building entries, and then incorporated play areas and parking lots adjacent to these entries. As adult occupants spend a good portion of their time in the kitchen-dining area, they easily and naturally observe their children at play outside, while at the same time monitoring the comings and goings of residents and strangers.

Surveillance of the public areas of building interiors from the apartments can be provided for equally well. Apartment buildings of "single-loaded corridor" design provide ready opportunity for natural surveillance of their corridors from within the apartment. "Double-loaded corridors" are, by contrast, devoid of surveillance opportunity except where tenants choose to use the peepholes in their doors. As was described earlier, a double-loaded corridor denotes a building designed with apartment units positioned on either side of a central corridor; a "single-loaded" corridor designates a building design in which apartment units are located exclusively on one side of the corridor and face an exterior wall which is glazed or, in mild climates, left open to the weather. The open corridor allows designers to locate windows in the apartment wall facing the corridor to achieve cross-ventilation of the apartment unit. The provision of windows allows as well for excellent surveillance opportunities. Cross-ventilation of units in a double-loaded corridor design is, of course, impossible. The setting of windows in the corridor wall is further precluded by fire regulations and the lack of privacy that would result from the close proximity of windows in the facing apartment.

An example of single-loaded corridor design in a public housing project is Stapleton Houses in Staten Island, New York. Here, the corridor approaching an apartment unit can be monitored by residents through both their kitchen-dining room and their living room windows. These corridors also receive marginal monitoring from the bedroom windows of opposite buildings. The open-corridor window wall also facilities effective police surveillance from the ground level. It is easy to understand, therefore, why the corridors of single-loaded buildings have almost no crime problems, whereas double-loaded corridors are responsible for some 20 percent of all crimes committed in the interiors of buildings.

Typical of the single-loaded corridor building design is a floor plan in which the elevators and fire stairs are located centrally. The open corridor runs from one end of the building to the other, through the central area which is usually enclosed. At least one apartment is located in this enclosed central space, opposite the elevators. These centrally-located apartments have no windows onto the corridors and no visual link to the other apartment entrances because of the two doors closing off the central interior space. Despite the fact that the apartments with windows provide an easy access for criminals, they are the least burglarized. Rather, the central apartments opposite the elevator, with no windows on the corridor, are the most consistently burglarized. In one such middle-income single-loaded corridor building in Manhattan, Columbus Towers, there has been a recent rash of burglaries—averaging four per month. All the apartments burglarized were those located within this central elevator area of the corridor, that is, those immediately opposite the elevators.

At Stapleton Houses, continual surveillance of the gallery corridors is provided through apartment windows: threats such as loitering strangers are detected quickly and reported to the Housing Authority police. By contrast, the entry lobbies of Stapleton Houses are not related to apartment units and suffer from poor visibility. These are the most littered areas of the buildings, suffer the most vandalism, and are where most of the crime occurs.

Housing Authority management is concerned that the pattern of corridor use at Stapleton Houses constitutes a breach of the rules of occupancy. The Authority quite painstakingly informs tenants that there is to be no loitering or other activity in the public areas of the building. Management is further troubled by tenants bickering over their conflicting claims to territory and

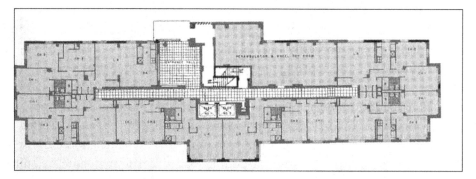

Ground-floor plan at Edenwald Houses.

Entry to building at Highbridge Houses, New York. The large window wall at the building entry provides an excellent surveillance opportunity. Residents can see the lobby interior and elevator waiting area from the path outside the building. (Photo by author)

boundaries in the outside gallery. Settling those arguments is apparently very time consuming. As a result, management continues to issue directives to prevent this occupation of the public corridor, emphasizing the fire hazard and nuisance of it all.

For all its nuisance value, however, territorial bickering has an important function in framing tenants' attitudes toward this space and its violation by intruders. Arguments over the minutiae of territorial boundaries are insignificant when weighted against the benefits accrued: tenants have assumed responsibility for the corridor's maintenance and policing and thereby insure its freedom from crime and vandalism.

Admittedly, the single-loaded corridor is more costly than the typical double-loaded layout, and this is a strong inhibiting factor to its general adoption in low-income housing. However, as we shall see in Chapter 6, in the discussion of Riverbend Houses, the problem is not without solution.

THE REDUCTION IN AMBIGUITY OF PUBLIC AND PRIVATE AREAS AND PATHS IN PROJECTS SO AS TO PROVIDE FOCUS AND MEANING TO SURVEILLANCE

The interior layout and organization of many housing projects is often very difficult to comprehend, particularly when long blocks of buildings are grouped together: interior corridors flow into

Fire exits at Highbridge Houses. The secondary exit at Highbridge is located at the opposite side of the building and is often jammed to stay open. Although at times this makes access to the building easier, it also creates an opportunity for vandals and criminals to enter and leave unobserved. Children rarely realize the potential danger of playing in such an unsupervised and unsafe area. (Photo by author)

one another through fire doors; fire stairs are positioned in leftover corners; exits and entrances to long, slab buildings are numerous and difficult to locate. Descending a scissors-type fire stair, positioned identically to its twin, is as likely to deposit one at the rear of the building as at the front. City and Housing Authority police, responding to calls in housing projects with which they are unfamiliar, find it difficult to distinguish one building from another, let alone find their way through the building to the right apartment. The locational simplicity provided by the address system in the grid layout of streets is, by comparison, a much desired attribute.

CIRCULATION CONFUSION: FIRE STAIRS

As was discussed previously, many large high-rise buildings are required by law to have fire stairs no further than a hundred feet from any apartment. This regulation is commonly satisfied by the provision of a scissors stairs in a central location behind the elevator. Separate exits at the ground floor are also required, and it is quite common to have the second exit at the rear of the building, opposite the lobby entry. This practice results in an ambiguity of building layout, with tenants using front and rear entries interchangeably. Criminals evade pursuit simply by alternating fire stairs as they flee the building. There is only a 50 percent chance that a single pursuing officer will exit at the same side of the building as the criminal he is chasing.

A similar scissors-stair arrangement, with separate exits at the ground floor, is provided at Edenwald Houses. It was through an accident of design, however, that the architect was able to exit both the first and second fire stairs adjacent to the main entry. This modification enabled him to achieve three things.

- Any person attempting to evade pursuit by using either fire stair would, regardless of which route he chose, exit at approximately the same point in front of the main building entrance.
- Residents and visitors alike, regardless of which entry they choose, must use the same circulation paths and pass within view of the sitting area adjacent to the front door, thus becoming subject to the surveillance provided by this facility.
- Much of the reason for using the fire stair as a more convenient route disappears when access doors to the fire stair and the main lobby are positioned adjacently.

As a result of this design, the fire exit remains predominantly unused as a secondary means of circulation at the ground level. Edenwald is consequently one of the few projects under the aegis of the New York City Housing Authority in which the security hardware on the emergency exit doors has not been destroyed.

Interviews with Edenwald residents indicate that the securing of the stairwell entrance at the ground level has greatly increased the security of the stairwell at upper levels of the building. The stairs, avoided as unsafe in other projects, are readily used for secondary vertical circulation and for visiting between floors.

Where the fire exit of a building is positioned on the side of the building opposite the main entrance, as in Highbridge, the opportunity it affords to leave a building and move directly toward one's destination becomes a convenience too useful to be resisted. Tenants have often resorted to jamming the latches on these doors to provide easy access for themselves. However, this practice has had a detrimental side effect: the superintendents have fixed the doors to remain open rather than be continually repairing the latches. The permanently open fire door now provides an easy entrance point for criminals. The stairwell eventually comes to be recognized as a danger zone and falls into disuse by all, save intruders.

Buildings that are longer than the standard 100 to 150 feet (or come under other fire codes), such as those at Columbus Homes in Newark and Pruitt-Igoe in St. Louis, have additional sets of stairs which exit to the ground and are connected at every floor through the common double-loaded corridor. Ambiguity of building plan is even more rampant in such designs. The labyrinthine access routes and corridors make recognition of neighbors difficult to impossible; there are simply too many people coming and going. Consequently, residents express fear in using the interior corridors. The many access doors to fire stairs provide almost endless opportunities for intruders to make their way through the building and to surprise tenants at any point along the way. There is no way to tell where someone will appear or where he will exit.

LEGIBILITY OF THE PROJECT AS A WHOLE

Perhaps even more critical than functional ambiguities of building design are those ambiguities which are a consequence of the superblock concept common to large-scale government-supported low- and middle-income housing design.

Elevator waiting area in the high-rise buildings of Schuylkyll Falls Housing Project, Philadelphia. (Photo by author)

The problems of orientation in large high-rise projects may be as much the result of uniformity in their design as of their internal labyrinthine arrangements. All buildings are designed and positioned alike so that it is difficult to discern any differences. There is also no orderly, or ritualized, means of progression from street to home. The project looks the same from all angles; all facets of buildings echo the same form. Nothing that tenants do to their apartments or windows can modify the appearance of their buildings so as to impart identity and individuality. Project residents almost universally refer to buildings by the number given them by the Housing Authority on the original site plan. Few know the numbers of buildings beyond their own or even of those immediately adjacent to theirs. When tenants have to describe a building or location to an outsider or to a policeman who does not know the building number system, they are forced to revert to primitive terms—"down that way," "at the other side of the project." Use of city street names or street addresses as a means of locating buildings in a superblock is usually impossible.

In conclusion we find that there are many aspects and facets to surveillance which contribute to the improvement of security. Stated simply, if there is any modicum of morality and accompanying social pressures in a community, opening up all activity in public spaces to natural supervision proves a very powerful deterrent to criminal acts. An existing proof of this principle may be found in New Orleans, by a comparison of Fisher Homes and Guste Homes with St. Bernard Homes and Desire Houses. Fisher Homes and Guste Homes were built in 1965 and 1963, respectively, and

Elevator and Mailbox Area at Pruitt-Igoe, St. Louis. Typically vandalized breezeway entry to the high-rise at Pruitt-Igoe. (Photo by author)

follow the open court and corridor design. St. Bernard Homes and Desire Houses were built in 1942 and 1956, respectively, and follow the old double-loaded corridor designs. In New Orleans, after years of building public housing with interior stairs and corridors, the Housing Authority began to build two- and three-story walk-ups with single-loaded corridors around open courts, accessible by open stairwells. The net result: the virtual elimination of all robberies in the public areas of the project, and the elimination of much of the burglarizing of apartments.

The subdivision of housing projects into small, recognizable and comprehensible-at-a-glance enclaves is a further contributant to improving the visual surveillance mechanism. Simultaneously, this subdivision serves to provide identity and territorial definition; gives focus, involvement, and commitment to the act of surveillance. In some housing developments, where the surveillance of the activity of one's neighbors, outside their apartments, was possible, residents were found to be very familiar indeed with everyone's comings and goings—and, occasionally, somewhat critical. The overall effect, however, was to cement collective identity and responsibility—through these social pressures. For those, however, who intentionally choose the anonymity and unsupervised life of large apartment towers to pursue a life style distant from the social norms, the supervised environment is one to be shunned. For these, however, a secure environment may be quite a secondary concern. There is a probable correlation between those who seek anonymity and dissociation from physical neighbor and the young. Equally, family life and middle age probably correlates highly with expectations of neighbor obedience to a moral code—of whatever definition—as it also does with expectations of a secure existence.

With a little bit of searching everyone in this day and age should be able to find a living environment where one's neighbors share one's moral values, however antagonistic they may be to middle-class norms, but still share a common desire for ensuring a safe residential environment.

The introduction of a large grouping of new buildings of distinctive height and texture into an existing urban fabric singles out these buildings for particular attention. If this distinctive image is also negative, the project will be stigmatized and its residents castigated and victimized.

Government-sponsored housing developments in America, for a variety of reasons seldom articulated, are designed so that they stand out and are recognized as distinctively different residential complexes. It is our contention that this differentiation serves in a negative way to single out the project and its inhabitants as "easy hits." The idiosyncratic image of publicly-assisted housing,

View of the High-Rise at Schuylkyll Falls Housing Project. Philadelphia. Note the pervading graffiti, smashed windows, and other vandalism. (Photo by author)

coupled with other design features and the social characteristics of the resident population, makes such housing a peculiarly vulnerable target of criminal activity.

The following is a discussion of those many formal ingredients which are felt to negatively differentiate a housing project from a surrounding residential area. Ironically, many of these physical features may have been intentionally provided by the architects as what they felt were positive contributions to the living environment of intended residents.

THE DISTINCTIVENESS RESULTING FROM INTERRUPTIONS OF THE URBAN CIRCULATION PATTERN

One ingredient, mentioned in Chapter 2, that contributes to the stigma and isolation of a project is the practice of closing off city streets for the purpose of gaining open space for the interior project grounds. The rectangular grid which is the texture of most American cities has been criticized by planners as an incredibly naive and simplistic approach to urban form and development. Nevertheless, this street pattern, with its constant flow of vehicular and pedestrian traffic, does provide an element of safety for every dwelling unit.

The design of a huge project which closes off internal streets and provides vehicular access only at the periphery, originally heralded as an important new design tool for the redevelopment of cities, has served to single out these areas and make them vulnerable. This, coupled with the obvious disadvantages that come from closing streets which were considered safe areas, serves to further handicap low-income housing design.

THE DISTINCTIVENESS OF BUILDING HEIGHT, PROJECT SIZE, MATERIALS, AND AMENITIES

Publicly supported housing is usually designed to replace high-density slums. Although it is densely designed (to reduce land cost per unit), it is seldom that a housing project is able to achieve the density of the slum it is replacing, since most slum-dwelling units have double or even triple family occupancy. Most architects, faced with the problem of designing a high-density project, opt for high-rise elevator buildings, in order to free ground areas sufficiently large for green and recreation facilities.

High-rise projects stand out very clearly and identifiably from their surrounding community, whether an old tenement area or new, middle-income residential complex.

There are, however, many instances of upper-middle-income, high-rise housing that are in sharp contrast with adjacent, older low-density developments, but which present a more positive image than their surroundings. Therefore, it is important to understand and articulate what it is, exactly, in the form of housing project buildings that makes these differences evident.

High-density, upper-middle-income, high-rise buildings are seldom grouped in projects of more than two or three buildings. In contrast, many public housing estates are designed to include from ten to thirty towers, and because of this scale of development, become predominant visual elements in the urban fabric. An effort is usually made in upper-middle-income housing to treat the facades with high-quality materials—an expensive brick, precast concrete, or stone facing—a luxury not usually possible in public housing. Similarly, a percentage of the units in upper-middle-income housing are provided with outdoor balconies, a feature normally economically prohibitive in public housing.

One should not conclude that public housing is built cheaply, even though for certain reasons—and many have been suggested—frills are strictly forbidden. In fact, the cost per square foot of public housing at times equals the cost per square foot of luxury high-rise housing. Public housing, built by a housing authority, is usually built extremely carefully, with good attention to detail and meticulously supervised construction. The exception to this rule is the current "Turnkey" practice. The turnkey program is a relatively new device whereby housing is built by private developers expressly to be sold to housing authorities for use as public housing.

One of the reasons for intentionally maintaining the visual stigma of public housing was suggested by Adam Walinsky in his article, "Keeping the Poor in Their Place."[1] He reasons that in this country, unlike our Western European counterparts, the middle and working-class population do not look favorably on those members of our society who require government assistance to pay their rent. While we have come a long way from our laissez-faire attitudes of the 1920s in developing a more enlightened approach toward less able members of our society, we are still apparently incapable of providing housing for them which looks better than the worst we provide for ourselves.

THE DISTINCTIVENESS OF INTERIOR FINISHES AND FURNISHINGS

It has long been the policy of housing authorities to design and equip buildings with furnishings which are vandal-proof and wear-resistant. Glazed tiles of the kind employed in hospitals and prisons are standard in the corridors of public housing projects. They are convenient to wash down, graffiti erases from them, and they wear appreciably longer than plaster walls. Corridor lights are now being enclosed in unbreakable plastic, and it is hoped these new fixtures will survive forever. Exterior lighting, with its own unbreakable housing, is usually of the mercury-vapor type, which casts a strong, purplish light.

This attitude toward interior finishes and furnishings creates an institutional atmosphere, not unlike that achieved in our worst hospitals and prisons. Even though the materials are in fact stronger and more resistant to wear, tenants seem to go out of their way to test their resistance capacities. Instead of being provided with an environment in which they can take pride and might desire to keep up, they are provided with one that begs them to test their ability in tearing it down. In the long run, even the institutional wall tiles and vandal-resistant radiators at Pruitt-Igoe met their match.

DESIGN AND LIFE STYLE SYMBOLIZATION

Our interviews with tenants have led us to the unmistakable conclusion that living units are assessed by tenants not only on the basis of size and available amenities but on the basis of the life style they symbolize and purport to offer. Building prototypes, from row housing to high-rise, symbolize various forms of class status. The small, two-story row-house unit totaling 1,200 square feet, with a couple hundred feet taken away by an interior staircase, is universally held by tenants to be more desirable than the 1,000 square foot apartment in an elevator building, equipped with more modern conveniences. As with most of American society, low-income groups aspire to the lifestyle symbolized by this housing prototype and by the suburban bungalow. They view the row house as more closely resembling the individual family house than the apartment within a communal building. A piece of ground adjacent to a unit, provided for the exclusive use of a family, is cherished and defended, regardless of how small.

By gentlemen's agreement, public housing must never approach the luxurious in appearance, even though it may cost more per square foot. It must retain an institutional image. Unfortunately, this practice not only "puts the poor in their place" but brings their vulnerability to the attention of others. Parallel to this, and much more devastating, is the effect of the institutional image as perceived by the project residents themselves. Unable to camouflage their identities and adopt the attitudes of private apartment dwellers, they sometimes overreact and treat their dwellings as prisoners treat the penal institutions in which they are housed. They show no concern for assisting in the care, upkeep, and maintenance of the buildings, no inclination toward the decoration of their apartment units with paint or curtains. Lee Rainwater, in his discussion of Pruitt-Igoe, observes that finally, the consequences for conceptions of the moral order of one's world, of one's self, and of others, are very great. Although lower class people may not adhere in action to many middle class values about neatness, cleanliness, order and proper decorum, it is apparent that they are often aware of their deviance, wishing that their world could be a nicer place, physically and socially. The presence of non-human threats conveys in devastating terms a sense that they live in an immoral and uncontrolled world. The physical evidence of trash, poor plumbing and the stink that goes with it, rats and other vermin, deepens their feeling of being moral outcasts. Their physical world is telling them that they are inferior and bad just as effectively perhaps as do their human interactions.[2]

We are not advocating aesthetic treatment of halls and apartments for the sake of beautification alone, although even the President's Commission on Law Enforcement and Criminal Justice recognized the debilitating effect on the spirit of a deteriorated living environment.[3] In our discussion, aesthetic considerations assume importance for the ways in which they can contribute to

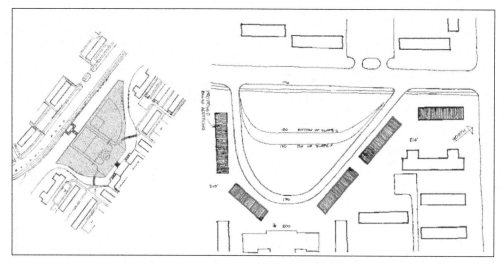

Site Plan of Woodhill Estates, Cleveland. The existing recreation area is located in an isolated area of high ground and lacks any visual association or relationship to project buildings or surrounding public streets. The plan for modification of the grounds shows the positioning of additional dwellings to improve safety, and earth-moving to bring the play area in closer association with the street.

the definition and subdivision of the environment as well, as to the psychological state of the inhabitants. Halls and lobbies with uniform fixtures and materials are at times more the result of an aesthetic ideal of uniformity than a commitment to lowering costs. Uniformity and durability represent an attempt to achieve the maximum of neatness, order, and maintenance ease for the project as a whole. This universal denominator eliminates the environmental highs and lows that characterize the private housing market where individuals are responsible for property upkeep. Everyone is aware of how the individual efforts of homeowners—curtains on windows, treatment and disposal of garbage—can grace or disgrace a street. Their most important attribute may be their individual differences: a public display of individualism indicates as much in its precious concern as occasional examples of indifferent neglect. A resident who has resigned himself to not caring about the condition of his immediate surroundings—who has come to accept his ineffectualness in modifying his condition—is not about to intercede, even in his own behalf, when he becomes the victim of a criminal.

URBAN LOCALE

If particular urban areas, streets, or paths are recognized as being safe, adjoining areas benefit from this safety in a real sense and also by association.

It is possible to increase the safety of residential areas by positioning their public zones and entries so that they face on areas which, for a variety of reasons, are considered safe. Certain sections and arteries of a city have come to be recognized as being safe—by the nature of the activities located there; by the quality of formal patrolling; by the number of users and extent of their felt responsibility; and by the responsibility assumed by employees of bordering institutions and establishments. The areas most usually identified as safe are heavily trafficked public streets and arteries combining both intense vehicular and pedestrian movement; commercial retailing areas during shopping hours, institutional areas, and government offices.

These areas have a reputation of safety which is occasionally reflected in low precinct crime rates. There are contradictory statistics available, however. A commercial street which may have been identified by surrounding inhabitants and users as safe will, occasionally, be found to have a higher crime rate than adjoining areas which were rated unsafe. This may be explained by a difference in the type of crime occurring and by the lower chance of its occurrence per area user. Where a purse snatching which occurs on an identified safe street will usually be of the grab and run sort, in an area identified as less safe, it may further involve an assault on the victim. One concludes that both victim and criminal assume that aggravated assault would not be tolerated by witnesses (shopkeepers and/or other shoppers) on a well-trafficked commercial street, or that escape time is critical to a criminal in what is considered a more formally patrolled area. Some commercial street corners, identified as safe, have records, showing up to three times more crimes than any other place in the immediately surrounding residential area. However, the number of pedestrians passing any point on the commercial street is over twenty times the average of surrounding streets and areas. The rate of occurrence may be higher, but the chance of occurrence per user may be lower. However, this explanation is, for the moment, hypothetical. It may also be that where shoppers have come to understand that there is potential risk in using a shopping street, they will not tolerate this same condition on their own streets.

JUXTAPOSITION OF RESIDENTIAL AREAS WITH OTHER "SAFE" FUNCTIONAL FACILITIES: COMMERCIAL, INSTITUTIONAL, INDUSTRIAL, AND ENTERTAINMENT

Some institutional and commercial areas have come to be recognized as safe areas during their periods of intensive use; others have a decidedly opposite image. The reason identified for their being safe involves the presence of many people engaged in like activities; thus providing a number of possible witnesses who might choose to come to the aid of a victim. Most importantly, the presence of many people is seen as a possible force in deterring criminals. Many of those interviewed identified staff in charge of commercial and institutional facilities, storekeepers, librarians, or security guards as highly concerned about the safety of adjoining areas. Shoppers feel that neighborhood employees have a more significant stake in ensuring safety than do uninvolved passersby or fellow shoppers. The juxtaposition of the entries to residential units with safe institutional areas was considered of positive benefit by many of those interviewed, although apprehension was expressed about the days and hours when these facilities are closed and radiate no security whatsoever. The juxtaposition preferred was one which created a transitional buffer between apartment building entry and the street and establishments.

The provision of parks and playgrounds within and around housing projects has been a program considered highly desirable by communities, planners, and housing authority officials alike. It therefore comes as a particular disappointment to learn of instances where their provision has been a cause of crime and vandalism.

At Edenwald, the park on the west corner of the project was beneficently designed and positioned to serve both the project residents and the surrounding community. In addition, it is located near a commercial strip which contains a bar and liquor store. Housing Authority police and residents claim the park attracts all the bums and addicts from the neighborhood. Because the relationship between park and adjacent project buildings is not clearly identified, the park has become a no-man's-land—an open congregation area controlled by no particular group. The

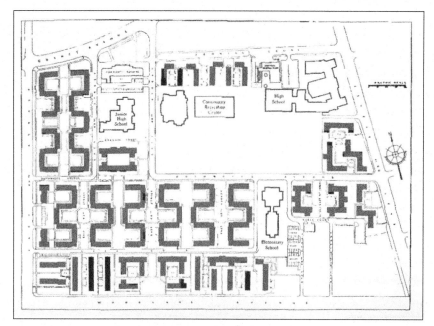

Site Plan of Outhwaite Houses, Cleveland. The Outhwaite Houses project borders on three different schools. The buildings and grounds of the project which suffer most from vandalism and loitering are those located directly across the street from the schools.

buildings at Edenwald which suffer the most crime and vandalism are those immediately adjacent to this park. Residents and management feel that the park would have been much safer if its relationship to the project had been more clearly defined. The park, they say, should have been designed so that only one side remained accessible from the street, while the other three sides were enclosed by housing units and their entry areas. The adoption of this design would have facilitated natural surveillance of park activities by adjacent residents.

A similar problem exists at the Woodhill Homes project in Cleveland. The recreation area at Woodhill is isolated from all other activity areas by a rise of ground which segregates it from project buildings and public streets. Use of the recreation facilities by teenagers has been found to degenerate quickly into fighting over claims to territory. In an effort to prevent such encounters, the project manager has removed the basketball hoops and the baseball field backstop. As a result, the grounds have fallen into disuse, even though they are the only recreation facilities available for blocks around. The disposition of new housing units adjacent to these grounds and the addition of a service road could provide surveillance of the area. Such subdivision would serve to define the grounds as a territorial extension of adjacent housing, while hopefully not restricting its use to residents only. If the recreation area could be further landscaped so that part of it were lowered to the level of the street below, this portion would receive additional surveillance from the street and from facing buildings.

It should be mentioned, however, that there are examples where the proximity of certain types of institutions act to impair the safety of a neighborhood. A recurring problem of juxtaposition results from the close proximity of housing projects with high schools and junior colleges. The Outhwaite project in Cleveland is a particularly notorious case-in-point since one area of the project actually borders on three different schools. The buildings suffering most frequent burglaries are those juxtaposed with these institutional facilities. Residents and project staff claim that teenagers

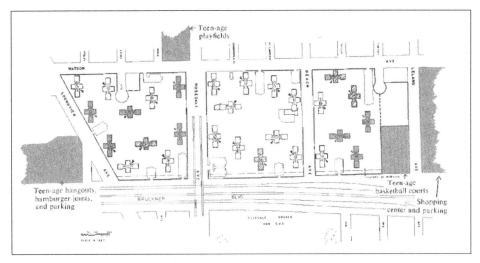

Site Plan of Bronxdale Housing Project. The Bronx, New York, Bronxdale has 1,497 units at 48.6 dwelling units per acre. The shaded areas bordering the project grounds are either commercial or recreational areas. The shaded buildings are the ones experiencing the highest crime and vandalism rates.

View of Bronxdale from teenage hangouts on southwest corner of the project. (Photo by author)

hang out on the public grounds and in the interior stairways and lobbies of adjacent units. They harass and are occasionally involved in the muggings of residents. In New York, Philadelphia, and Cleveland high-rise projects with buildings bordering high schools, the enclosed fire stairs are often used by teenage addicts for selling and using drugs. Where it may not always be possible, or even desirable to intentionally avoid this sort of juxtaposition, it is certainly feasible, to design the site plan of the project so that access to apartment buildings is not from those streets directly opposite schools.

In much the same way, where an area of a project faces on a teenage hamburger joint or game room hangout, the buildings immediately opposite have higher crime rates. The statistics on location and frequency of crime in Bronxdale reinforce the claims of police and residents. The two hamburger joints on the west side of the project, and the teenage play areas on the east, together generate high crime and vandalism rates in the immediately adjacent buildings. The New York City Housing Authority police has found that those of its projects located adjacent to commercial streets suffer proportionally higher crime rates.

This would lead us to conclude that commercial and institutional generators of activity do not, in and of themselves, necessarily enhance the safety of adjoining streets and areas. The unsupported hypotheses of Jane Jacobs, Shlomo Angel, and Elizabeth Wood must be examined more closely for a better understanding of the nature of their operating mechanisms. The simple decision to locate commercial or institutional facilities within a project in order to increase activity and so provide the safety which comes with numbers must be critically evaluated in terms of the nature of the business, the intended users, their identification with area residents, their periods of activity, the nature and frequency of the presence of concerned authorities, and so on.

The policy of HUD and housing authorities across the country of discouraging commercial facilities on project grounds, while initially directed at preventing unfair competitive situations with neighborhood merchants, may have a rationale of another order to it.

JUXTAPOSITION WITH SAFE PUBLIC STREETS

Regardless of variations in the physical configuration of project sites, hundreds of tenants interviewed have consistently identified the public streets bordering their projects as being safer than paths which bisect the interiors of the projects. This view conflicts with the opinion held by the New York City Housing Authority police, who feel that the interior grounds are safer and are perceived as safer. Nevertheless, the buildings and areas of projects which tenants have identified as being most *unsafe* are located in the interior of the project and do not front on any through streets. Consistently, tenants have scale-rated their buildings as safer when the entry, entry grounds, and lobby of the buildings face directly onto city streets. Large superblocks, at various densities, have been found to exhibit systematically higher crime rates than projects of comparable size and density that have city streets continuing through them.

THE DIMENSIONS OF JUXTAPOSED AREAS

From our discussion of the relative merits of juxtaposing housing with other functional facilities, it is evident that a wise evaluation of the problem hinges on an understanding of the thoroughly reciprocal nature of the relationship that exists between the project and the juxtaposed facility.

The success or failure of a particular configuration depends as much on the degree to which residents can identify with and survey activity in the related facility as it does on the nature of the users of that facility and the activities they engage in. This would suggest that the dimensions and nature of the juxtaposition can be significant.

There is little, in this regard, that one can do about the design and location of hamburger joints. But, the size, proportions, and positioning of parks is open to ready manipulation. From experience, the Police Department of the City of St. Louis believes that city parks should be proportioned to facilitate natural surveillance from bordering streets and by adjacent residents. Long thin parks of the same area are therefore preferable to square ones, as they have a longer periphery that can be patrolled. The proportions of a park need not severely limit the facilities placed within it, or the total area provided. The dimensions of a park are equally as important as the proportions. The narrow dimension of the oblong park shown in figure 85 should not be so wide as to prevent

Site Plan of a Park Which Proves Dangerous. The proportions and dimensions of a large square park limit the ability of surrounding residents, vehicles and patrols from observing activity within.

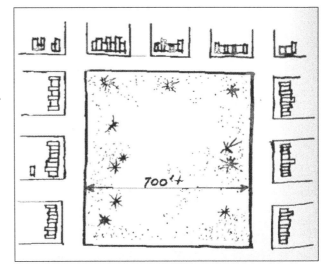

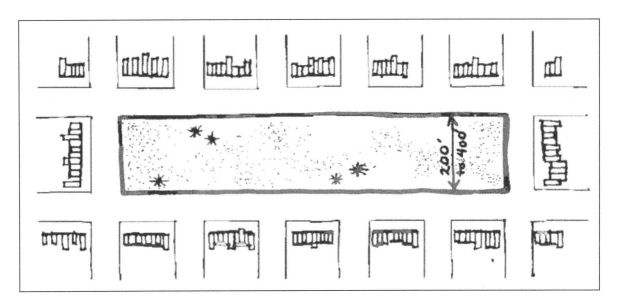

Site Plan of a Park Which Proves Safe. A Long thin Park can provide the same recreation potential while affording ready observation of all internal activity from surrounding buildings and streets.

someone on one side from seeing through to the other side. In residential areas suffering high crime rates, the interiors of large parks which cannot be easily surveyed will go unused. Douglas and Garfield Parks, large internal parks on the West Side of Chicago, are cases in point.

Possibly of all defensible space mechanisms recommended, these last two: the design of the image of the residential environment and its juxtaposition with other activities in the urban setting, will prove most offensive to architects and planners.

There is probably much to the truism that architects are egomaniacs. It is a difficult and demanding profession. From the initial encounters with a client to the final supervision of the construction of a building is a long and, at times, arduous experience. Only those with strong egos can survive it and still be able to look with some pride at the results. But in the process of molding this ego and developing the necessary calluses, architects tend to forget that their clients' experience and judgment of their needs in a building may be vastly superior to that of the architect's. In

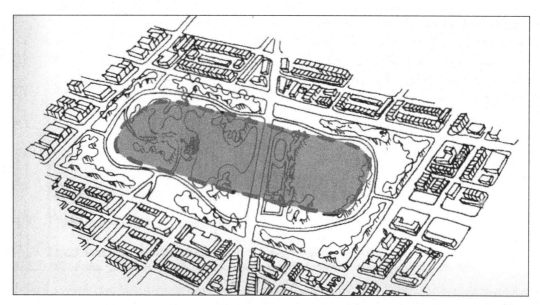

Douglas Park in the Lawndale Area of Chicago. Because of the large size of the park in its present social setting, the interior areas are proving too dangerous to be used.

the process of trying to produce a successfully designed residential building, the architect will be endeavoring to satisfy the aesthetic tastes of his peers—rather than those of his client. If his client is rich and well educated, his tastes may be similar to those of the architect. But if the client comes from a low- or middle-income background, it is most likely that he will aspire to the tastes of the class immediately above him, and probably those in vogue ten and twenty years ago. Architects are chagrined and sometimes express moral indignation when they find their low-income clients rejecting a housing project designed in the most current professional idiom, asking instead for something that looks quaintly middle-class. But this middle-class look is the client's image of arrival—his symbol of status. The well-meaning architect who worked hard at designing buildings, which he knows will please his peers and receive recognition in the professional journals, for some incomprehensible reason, finds himself accused of giving the poor "funny houses."

In a similar way, for decades after the original Utopian physical planners first set down rules for segregating different activities and functions in the design of new cities, urban designers have been fighting for the reintegration of shopping and institutional facilities with housing. Now with this fight almost won, it appears that someone else is again advocating their segregation. The facts however cannot be easily dismissed. The matter is one of scale: at which level is the segregation to occur? It is possible within the frames of our guidelines to juxtapose schools and shops with housing so as to create the desired walking distance milieu, while at the same time providing for the territorially intact residential enclave.

NOTES

1. Adam Walinsky, "Keeping the Poor in Their Place: Notes on the Importance of Being One-Up," *The New Republic* 151 (July 4, 1964): 15.
2. Lee Rainwater, "Fear and the House-as-Haven in the Lower Class," *AIP Journal* 32 (January 1966): 29.
3. "Society has not devised ways for ensuring that all its members have the ability to assume responsibility. It has let too many of them grow up untaught, unmotivated, unwanted. The criminal justice system

has a great potential for dealing with individual instances of crime, but it was not designed to eliminate the conditions in which most crime breeds. It needs help. Warring on poverty, inadequate housing and unemployment is warring on crime. A civil rights law is a law against crime. ... More broadly and most importantly every effort to improve life in America's inner cities is an effort against crime. A community's most enduring protection against crime is to right the wrongs and cure the illnesses that tempt men to harm their neighbors" (*The Challenge of Crime in a Free Society,* The President's Commission on Law Enforcement and Administration of Justice [New York: E. P. Dutton, 1968], p. 69).

3 The Search for Environmental Theory

W. H. Ittelson, H. M. Prohansky, L. G. Rivlin, G. H. Winkel

This historical reading by the founders of environmental psychology serves two purposes. It examines how different theoretical approaches in psychology give rise to radically different methods in understanding how environments affect human experience: gestalt psychology bases study of environmental experiences on internal holistic perceptions while behaviorism examines behaviors resulting from environmental stimuli. By contrast to both, psychoanalysis sees experiences of the building environment influenced by the subconscious, ego, and super ego that are formed in early childhood. Thus, this reading demonstrates that science is far from a single coherent rational system for approaching truth, but can hold highly contradictory points of view with utility as the ultimate measure of scientific value.

The previous chapter looked closely at man's attitudes toward the environment as a function of historical time and cultural setting. Our focus and purpose here narrows considerably as we move from cultural ethos to scientific thought concerning man's environment, from time-related beliefs and attitudes to systematic attempts at theoretical elaborations. If the reader followed the previous discussion closely, then he should have arrived at two conclusions about science in relation to understanding environment and environmental process: first, that science itself is an attitude and means of looking at, understanding, and relating to the environment; and second, that its origins are rooted deeply in those environmental beliefs and attitudes of Western man that began with the demise of medieval conceptions of the earth as the center of the universe.

At root was the view that man was separate from his physical world; that because he was no longer the center of the universe, he could stand apart from his own world, view it and study it with detachment; in the end, he could manipulate it, change it, and make it serve him. This was and is the credo of modern science. Its inexorable search for knowledge is not just to understand, but to control and determine events; and most particularly, those events that are distinguished from man himself, environmental events. If the salvation of man was to be found in God, then science would save him from the awesome, unpredictable, and often catastrophic character of these events.

W. H. Ittelson, H. M. Prohansky, L. G. Rivlin, G. H. Winkel, "The Search for Environmental Theory," from *An Introduction to Environmental Psychology*, pp. 60–79. Copyright © 1974 by Cengage. Permission to reprint granted by the publisher.

Under these circumstances, as one might expect, the nexus for the growth of modern science was the study of the physical and natural settings of men. By the nineteenth century, the efficacy of a scientific empirical approach to knowledge with respect to environmental phenomena had not only been assured but acclaimed. Small wonder, therefore, that by that time burgeoning efforts were being made to treat behavioral man himself as an environmental event and subject him to the same kind of scientific or systematic empirical study being made of other events in the physical world. After all, he too was part of nature and there was no reason why he too could not be viewed with detachment and objectivity. Thus, the more general attempts by philosophers and theologians to resolve such issues as the mind-body dualism, the nature of human thought and perception, and the problem of free will were raised in more precise and empirical terms by physiologists, physicists, and a small but growing group of "psychologists." Depending on approach and the way the new science was conceived, particular problems were formulated and studied in order to answer one or more of the questions of how men learn, think, feel, see, hear, become aroused, and engage in complex behaviors.

These "schools of psychology" will not be considered in a systematic fashion in the present discussion; rather, we will look primarily at some of the more prominent attempts to conceptualize the environment, particularly the physical environment, in relation to human behavior. More detailed and comprehensive accounts of these various approaches that laid the groundwork for modern theory and research in psychology—including some developments in environmental psychology—can be found in Heidbreder (1933), Boring (1942), Wolman (1968), and Woodworth (1948). Of course, none of these schools or approaches to psychology simply emerged. Their origins were rooted not just in developments that led to modern science, but in philosophical, theological, economic, and political conceptions of the nature of man and the universe going back to the time of the Greeks and even before.

From the point of view of environmental psychology, the student who reviews these various schools of psychology will recognize a feature common to all of them. Stated simply, none systematically conceptualized or established a theoretical framework for the description and analysis of the environment per se. Human behavior and experience rather than its setting was the focus of concern. Sometimes directly—although in very general rather than specific terms—but far more often indirectly, these approaches to man's behavior and experience had, at best, implications for his environmental setting. In general this setting was taken for granted and as a result its definition in a theory or an approach was far more implicit than explicit.

The reason for this neglect of the environment is easy to understand. The concern of a science of psychology was man and not his environment. The critical task was to replace metaphysical and other philosophical and theological conceptions of man by empirical descriptions and analyses in a context of reasoned elaborations or theoretical schemas. But there were far more subtle and more sustaining reasons for the failure to describe and conceptualize the environmental context in relation to human behavior and experience.

Not only was psychology concerned almost exclusively with the behavior of the person, but, as was suggested in Chapter Two, the person was not really considered part of his environment so much as an object in the environment. Moreover, this environment was studied as a physical and not a social problem. An understanding of the environment indeed had been established by the newly emerging physical and natural sciences, particularly physics, which easily specified the precise nature and details of many relevant aspects of the physical world.

Of course there was a wide array of complex environmental events—both social and physical—that these sciences did not consider that were conceivably of equal significance in understanding human behavior in natural settings. The natural sciences of that time precluded such an approach. If man was separate from the environment, and if the latter was exclusively a physical problem, then all environmental events of a social nature could be safely ignored.

However, a separate point must be stressed. It was crucial to a beginning psychology that these complex physical and social events be rejected as the legitimate concern of a science of man. And so they were. To be a science—to be guided by the methodological and rational precepts of the already established physical and natural sciences—meant defining human problems and their study in ways that guaranteed that these ways of knowing would be met. The environment had to be dealt with in simple, objective, and verifiable terms, a matter that to a large degree was already being taken care of by the physical and natural sciences. Thus, at the time, the study of how human beings learned meant the presentation of pure learning units (nonsense syllables) each exposed after an exact interval of time, with all other measurable environmental conditions in the room kept constant. The physical environment was treated in atomistic and additive terms. This involved a concern with specific environmental objects, and the environment in general was the collection of all of those objects that could be specified and measured. It has only been in relatively recent times that natural scientists have begun to recognize the environment as a network or system of interrelationships, such that any part or level of structure in it that is studied derives its nature and function from, and in turn has consequences for, the nature and function of all other parts or structures of the environment in which it is embedded. The human body viewed in terms of the origin, nature, and function of any of its parts, for example the heart, illustrates this holistic or systems approach to scientific understanding.

APPROACHES TO MAN: PSYCHOANALYTIC THEORY, BEHAVIORISM, AND GESTALT THEORY

Our discussion begins with three quite different theoretical orientations to man: psychoanalytic theory, behaviorism, and Gestalt psychology. Each of these theories constitutes an historical watershed for the development of still other viewpoints. Indeed, in some instances one finds modern theoretical points of view that have integrated selected aspects of at least two of these different approaches if not all three. It will be helpful if the reader considers these theories as the three points of a triangle with subsequent integrated theories falling between the points of this triangle, or some place inside it when all three theories have been tied together.

Psychoanalytic Theory

Was the environment important in Freud's view of man? Unquestionably so. Did he develop a conceptual scheme for this environment? The answer to this second question is not simply a "no"; rather, it can be said he did not need one. For Freud (1933) put all of his theoretical eggs, so to speak, in one basket. He conceived of man, and all events that followed from his exalted position at the apex of the phylogenetic scale, as rooted in a set of inherited instinctual drives, the life (Eros) and death (Thanatos) instincts. These drives were universal, fixed in an inexorable sequence of development, and ultimately the basis for all human behavior and experience. At the root of Freud's system was the concept of intrapsychic conflicts, for example the Oedipus complex, whose particular form, the ways that they were constrained, and the kinds of consequences they had all depended on the socialization experiences of the individual. To a considerable degree these conflicts, the defense mechanisms made necessary to control them, and indeed the real meaning of what the individual thought, did, and felt remained at an unconscious level. It was at this level that Freud conceived the more conscious and reality-oriented drives and attitudes, which he called the *ego,* that reconciled the demands of the instinctual drives (the *id*) and the physical, social, and cultural mores of organized society.

Freud was an environmentalist in the sense that he felt the social and interpersonal environment shaped and guided the form and consequences of the person's life and death strivings. An inherent succession of psychosexual stages beginning at birth and extending through early adolescence unfolds under the influence of particular people (for example, parents, siblings, friends, and teachers) who are responsible for overseeing the child's basic experiences and activities (eating, playing, sleeping, learning, defecating, and so on) in prescribed human settings (home, playground, school, and so forth). These people, in these settings, establishing the specific form and content of experiences and activities, determine the level, the particular patterning, and ultimate adult consequences of the process of psychosexual development. It is in this sense that Freud can be described as the consummate reductionist. All human events, activities, forms, and concepts, whether of the person, group, or society at large, were manifestations and expressions of the psychosexual system and its development, and therefore could be explained on this basis.

What implications, if any, can be drawn from Freud's psychoanalytic theory about the nature and meaning of the physical environment? At least three major implications can be specified. First, the physical environment is experienced rather than being observed or responded to as if it existed in some objective sense. If all human behavior and experience express the ego–id relationships and intrapsychic conflicts in some modified and disguised forms, then this implies that in meaning, significance, and function the individual's environment itself must be rooted in the underlying intrapsychic system. This implication in turn brings us to still another. Physical environments, their form, content, and meaning, express the unconscious needs, values, and conflicts of the person. In Freud's system the often-referred-to expressive symbolism of man's built environment does not reflect so much the underlying value system of the culture as it does the underlying psychodynamics of individual behavior and experience. In sum, man's cultural, social, and physical systems express a universal basic personality structure that is rooted in the conflicts among and the satisfactions of instinctual drives.

Much of Freud's system of psychosexual development has implications for the design and use of physical settings. The feeding and toilet training of the child, the sexual relations of the parents, the social interactions of siblings, and many other aspects of this developmental approach depend not only on the people involved but also on settings in which these activities occur. Given the centrality of the Oedipus and Electra complexes in Freud's theory, for example, privacy is crucial in the sexual relations of parents. If the small boy has strong sexual attachments for the mother, then what he can see and hear when his parents are involved in any form of "love and romance," either in their bedroom or out, is significant. Given the emphasis on toilet training in Freud's theory, it is not only important how and by whom the child is trained, but where as well. The design of the bathroom, particularly with respect to its privacy aspects, is important. Similar conclusions can be drawn about the design of kitchens in the light of Freud's theory of the oral stage in children and the significance of feeding.

Freud's approach, however, goes well beyond these specific implications. The rationale of man's built environment—regardless of cultural differences—reflects his unconscious desires, his attempts to sublimate these desires, and his ways of both satisfying and restraining his instinctual drives. In its broadest sense and in quite specific terms Freud's theory stands ready to give "underlying" meaning and purpose to modern technology, for example the car or jet plane, regardless of how quickly it progresses in man's attempt to master his physical environment.

Behaviorism

In its origin and development, behaviorism stands in sharp contrast to Freud's psychoanalytic theory. Its setting was the academic animal laboratory rather than the psychiatric treatment room. Unlike Freudian theory it was as much concerned with establishing the precepts for a science of human behavior as it was with understanding man himself. Indeed, our allusion earlier to a "beginning scientific psychology" that used as its model the methodology of the physical and natural sciences, describes a mantle of scientific respectability that was worn more proudly and self-righteously by behaviorists than by any other group of psychologists. Yet the success of behaviorism as a major force in the development of American psychology involved more than its use of this model. It borrowed heavily from the pragmatism of Charles Pierce and William James, and this in turn was consistent with the technocratic, manipulative faith that Americans had in their environment, especially during the decade of the 1920s.

Although classical behaviorism has been modified considerably during the last five or six decades, its basic tenets remain the same. Science, it asserts, is by definition an approach to knowledge in which empirical analysis must be constrained at all times by objectivity. In the case of human behavior only those events that can be observed and empirically specified have any legitimacy for a science of man. The unit of analysis therefore is the S-R or stimulus-response relationship in which observable behavior is elicited by equally observable and measurable stimuli. Some basic S-R units are biologically determined and innately rooted; all other behavior rests upon these essential response systems and is learned through a process of forming new S-R relationships. Wherever problem situations arise in which available S-R units no longer provide an adequate solution to the problem, new responses are evoked and those that lead to satisfaction for the organism become established as new S-R units. Such satisfactions may either be responses that lead to drive-related objects, food or water, for example, that are intrinsically satisfying to the organism (positive reinforcers or rewards), or they may result from responses that help to avoid objects, situations, or events that are threatening or painful to the organism (negative reinforcers or punishments). In one fell swoop behaviorism eliminated consciousness, cognitive activity, and, more generally stated, the "inner life" of the person as the legitimate concern of the psychologist. Behaviorists did not deny that there were internal processes; it was simply that their study and understanding required them to be translated into observable responses. These forms of observed behavior included simple verbalizations tied to equally defined and observable stimulus situations. The individual then becomes a "black box," but a box that can be described in terms of an aggregate of habitual responses (S-Rs) to recurring or similar situations. Whether these were eating, need for privacy, aggressive behavior, sympathy feelings, desire for power, voyeurism, or voting the Republican ticket, what was involved were habitual responses to S-R connected stimuli or stimulus situations. Indeed, such words as "need," "feelings," and "desire" were mentalistic and therefore neither necessary or useful.

It should be apparent that the environment—physical, social, or cultural—does play a crucial role for the behaviorist. Indeed, behaviorism comes close to conceptualizing the environment in the manner of the natural and physical scientist, which means therefore that it is real, measurable, and existing in its own right. But in understanding behavior the significance of the environment as such is not substantive. In other words, the particular objects, things, or people involved does not matter. The significance is structural in the sense that regardless of the nature or complexity of the environment it can be described in the simplest terms, namely, as a stimulus or stimuli which evoke behavior. By understanding the process of human behavior and learning in this way, those responsible for the development or change in the behavior of others (for example, teachers, master craftsmen) would by definition know what the appropriate activities, behaviors, or responses to be learned were, and could even establish the conditions necessary for learning them.

The environments that people create are simply a function of which environments, or objects in the environments, lead to positive or negative reinforcements. Not only are environments assortments of stimuli, but these stimuli determine when, how, where, and with whom we will behave. Even in this respect, behaviorism's conception of the environment, or the stimuli of which it was composed, fell far short of what was needed. Almost all of the attention was given to the response side of the S-R "equation." The nearest approximation to dealing with the environment in any explicit way is the conception of "setting events," that is, certain stimuli (virtually any stimulus will do) become signals for the receipt or nonreceipt of a reinforcer. In this sense the stimulus sets the occasion for the response. Thus, the environment is a complex set of discriminable stimuli signalling the reinforcement possibilities which may occur there. In Chapter Five we consider the limitations of an object-oriented or stimulus-oriented approach to perception of the environment.

Behaviorism's leading spokesman today is B. F. Skinner (1953) whose chief contribution has been his studies of operant behavior, in which environmental stimuli evoke responses which lead to reinforcements, positive or negative. For example, if the child consistently gets candy or some other reward for speaking softly at home, then according to Skinnerian theory he will learn to be a quiet member of the household. According to the Skinnerian approach, environments are often said to gain "meaning" or "value" as a consequence of secondary reinforcement. The quiet house just described takes on reward significance in its own right. The operant behaviorists have reared a formidable theory of culture based on reinforcement, viewing democratic and liberal societies as basically positive (rewarding) reinforcers and authoritarian states as "punitive." Skinner himself, who is a Utopian in his spare time (Skinner, 1971), is decidedly positive in his approach, although this has led him into realms of social engineering which many advocates of democracy find somewhat uncongenial.

Gestalt Theory

Our triangle of major theoretical approaches is completed with Gestalt psychology. Like behaviorism its origin is also the academic research laboratory, but here similarity between the two schools ends. Indeed, Gestalt Psychology and behaviorism stand as the antithesis of each other in purpose, theoretical approach, and subsequent influence on the development of psychology as a science. Its original focus was not behavior but human perception and other cognitive processes, and its setting was the academic research laboratories of German universities, in which the visual perception of movement was the initial problem being considered. Its leaders, Kohler (1929) and Koffka (1935), were essentially protesting all forms of analytic reductionism that attempted to understand complex human psychological processes by establishing their irreducible basic elements. In the case of behaviorism, which developed concurrently with Gestalt psychology, the S-R unit was basic. At an earlier period, but still highly influential when Gestalt psychology emerged, the experimental approach of the psychophysicists attempted to establish functional relationships between measurable stimulus attributes, (intensity of light for instance) and discrete psychological reactions (for example, subjective judgments of the brightness of light) (Boring 1942). Still another experimental approach condemned by the Gestaltists were the German, English, and American association psychologies (structuralism in America). The emphasis here was on human consciousness and experiences with a directed attempt, by means of systematic introspection, to establish the fundamental and irreducible units of human cognitive and affective responses (sensation). All of these analytical reductive approaches seeking the basic units of human behavior and/or experience in relation to measurable and definable stimulus properties assumed that once these relationships were established, the apparent complexities of psychological process and human behavior could easily be described and understood (Heidbreder 1933; Woodworth 1948).

If Gestalt psychology was unalterably opposed to this kind of reductionistic analysis, then what did it stand for? The term *Gestalt* is the obvious clue. The word, which has no exact counterpart in English, suggests "form" or "configuration." The important idea, however, is that what is perceived is the whole, whether an object, a person, an event, or a physical setting. To subject any of these to analysis and study, in terms of its parts, as though these add up to the whole, is to violate the integrity of the phenomenon being studied. Any event, object, behavior, or experience consists of the patterned relationship among the various parts. The now famous Gestalt dictum that "the whole is more than the sum of its parts," is no more mysterious than the belief that because of the patterned interrelationships among parts, properties emerge that cannot be found in the parts themselves.

To use a modern analogy: You do not understand the way a city functions by considering its residences, offices and industries, its transportation system, theaters and other recreation facilities, schools, and hospitals on an individual basis, that is, as distinct and unrelated institutional settings. Only when one sees each of these settings operating in relation to the others does the concept of city make sense. Indeed, it is the city as a total reality which explains the functioning of each of its specific settings. In a later chapter the notion of ambience is introduced to describe one aspect of large-scale environments. In a sense this concept helps to integrate psychologically the various inputs whose continuing interactions make a "city."

The theoretical formulations of Gestalt psychology, despite the focus on perception and other cognitive processes, embrace the study of man in general. Our concern here, however, is its particular significance for the study of man in relation to his physical setting. For environmental psychology at least three of its basic assumptions have very great importance. Whether one accepts them or not, they are crucial, for by either accepting or rejecting them one chooses between vastly different approaches to this new field.

Unlike behaviorism, Gestalt psychology was not rooted in American pragmatism but in German phenomenology. Heidbreder (1933) writes that the Gestaltist "attempts to get back to naive perception, to immediate experience undebauched by learning; and [he] insists that [he] finds these not assemblages of elements but unified wholes; not masses of senses, but trees, clouds and sky." It is in this sense that Koffka (1935) distinguishes between the geographical environment—the environment as it really exists—and the behavioral environment, or the environment as the person experiences it. It is the latter half Koffka sees as the determinant of an individual's behavior. He assumes that in some instances what is actually there and what we perceive to be there may be quite different. (We shall have more to say about this distinction Chapter Five.) However, the Gestaltists believed that the properties of geographical environments, under normal circumstances, become part of the behavioral environment experienced by the individual; in addition, although each individual in principle perceives uniquely, the perception of geographical environments leads to commonalities in the behavioral environments of different people. This is because of common neurological mechanisms that are innate in people and common superimposed socializing experiences.

Finally, explicit in the Gestalt approach was the view that behavior was rooted in cognitive process. It was not determined by stimuli but resulted from and had consequences for the meaning or conceptions that emerged from the perception of some setting, object, person, or event. In this sense environments not only had structure but substance as well. Different environments in effect—or the same environment at different times—could change in meaning and thereby evoke corresponding changes in behavior.

LEWIN'S FIELD THEORY

Perhaps no other theorist has had such varied influence on psychology as Kurt Lewin (1935). Although a Gestalt psychologist, he extended and deepened this approach by turning to such issues, rarely considered by the classical Gestaltists, as child development, personality structure and process, the dynamics of group functions, intergroup conflict, research methodology for the study of man, and the nature of human motivation. In all of these considerations Lewin was acutely aware of the significance of the environment and provided both a broad general approach as well as a very preliminary notation system for conceptualizing this environment. In the main he formulated a broad methodological strategy for the formulation and analysis of problems about human behavior and experience, with the theoretical and empirical details to be filled in by means of continuing systematic research. In this limited review we can only touch upon those significant aspects of Lewin's approach that are relevant to the present concern with attempts to conceptualize the individual's environment.

While the concept of behavioral environment was no less evident in Lewin's approach than in any other Gestaltist's, his interest was not in cognitive process per se but rather in its role in determining behavior. Lewin's field theory represents a formal attempt to provide a set of analytical tools that would take account of all the factors that determined behavior (1951). In essence Lewin believed that the stream of activity we call human behavior resulted from the continuing interaction of factors within the person, for example, needs, values, feelings, and predispositions, with other external factors as they are perceived in a given behavioral setting. Thus, it was neither needs nor stimulus objects that determined how, when, and in what way a person behaves, but the constellation or pattern of inner and outer influences that he experiences. This reasoning was at the nexus of Lewin's concept of the *life space*, which he defined as $B = f(PE)$ in which behavior (B) is seen as a function (f) of the interaction of personality and other individual factors (P), and the perceived environment of the individual (E).

Although Lewin gave no special consideration to the physical world, it is clear that his concept of life space included more than just social and cultural environments. Important at this point are some of the terms he employed to describe the environment generally. Thus, objects, situations, or other people in the person's life space may have positive or negative *valences* depending on their ability to reduce or increase respectively the needs or intentions of the person. *Locomotion,* which could either be social, conceptual, or physical, means a change of position with respect to some goal region. The thirsty man going across the street to get to drink at a water fountain in the park employs physical locomotion toward the goal region "water fountain." By contrast, the young man on a blind date, trying to impress a not-so-interested female companion, is also attempting to locomote toward the socially desirable goal of being liked by her. A *barrier* is a boundary in the life space of the person that offers resistance to locomotion. It may be a physical barrier if the gate to the park is closed, or it may be a social barrier if the young man sees his companion as older and more sophisticated.

We have not done justice to the extensive theoretical framework developed by Lewin in his attempt to conceptualize the content, structure, and dynamics (motivational forces) of the life space. However, as a final comment, Lewin never viewed the life space, or the experienced world of a person, as so supreme in relation to behavior that reality and nonconscious events (for example, a wall the person is unaware of) had no place in his approach. Thus he pointed out that consciousness, or what the person was actually aware of, could not be used as a criterion of what existed psychologically. "There is no question, for instance, that when a person is in a familiar room, the part of the wall which is behind him belongs to his momentary environment." [1936:18] And, we would add, whether he was aware of it or not. In this sense Lewin believed that what was real and therefore to be included in the life space was anything that had effects. Lewin was keenly aware of the fact that beside factors of which the person was unaware, still other factors outside the life space and therefore not subject to psychological laws also influenced behavior. In Lewin's formulation the influence of this kind of reality was not to be denied. Thus, the *foreign hull of the life space* was defined as "facts not subject to psychological laws but which influence the state of the life space." [p. 206] If our thirsty man gets to the fountain and suddenly finds the water discolored and polluted because the city failed to purify its reservoir, we can be sure he will not drink it. The action—or better said, the inaction of the Water Department—clearly had consequences for his behavior.

Barker's Ecological Psychology

Roger Barker (1963a. 1963b. 1968), a colleague of Lewin's, was also trained in the Gestalt tradition. Barker, however, formulated the problem of human behavior in very different terms. His "ecological psychology" can be defined as the psychology of environment, or what he calls a "behavior setting." A behavior setting is bounded in space and time and has a structure which interrelates physical, social, and cultural properties so that it elicits common or regularized forms of behavior. Barker's objective was to determine the relationships between what he calls the extraindividual pattern of behavior—that is, the behavior that all people en masse reveal in a behavior setting—and the structural properties of that setting. Any institutionalized setting such as a church, a school, a hotel terrace, a cocktail lounge, or a playground, is of concern to the ecological psychologist. To take the example of the hotel terrace, it would qualify as a behavior setting in the sense that its physical properties (arrangement of chairs, small tables, railings and so forth) as well as their implicit purpose (relaxation, conversation, drinking, card playing, and so on) impose on those entering it an explicit mode of behavior. The uses of all behavior settings and their objects are to a relatively large extent socially defined.

It is evident from Barker's approach that the environment he is talking about has a reality of its own. This is the objective rather than the psychological environment which is at the core of Lewin's life space. However, if we take a closer look it only seems as if this environment has a reality of its own, for Barker does not come to grips with the social definitions applied to different spaces. Although he speaks of behavior settings in terms of space and place, far more is involved conceptually than a physical setting. He stresses the fact that "behavior episodes" are embedded in a physical framework—tough, highly visible features of the ecological environment—but far more important is the fact that the physical setting itself has a social and cultural definition resulting from the intended purposes of the setting, the kind of people who will use it, and what activities and immediate outcomes will occur. A behavior setting is not simply a space with any set of boundaries and a random array of objects. On the contrary, its physical dimensions, the nature of its objects, where and how they are placed, and so on, are all determined by the socially defined character of the situation.

Given his concern with relating behavioral settings with en masse behavior, Barker's approach can be erroneously conceived of as behavioristic or S-R in character. Such an interpretation is not valid because his theoretical focus is not the psychology of individual behavior but actually aggregates of people responding to physical settings, in which he hopes to establish how non-psychological factors of environment have consequences for typical behaviors in typical behavioral settings. Of course in seeking those relationships he holds in abeyance the inner individual psychological processes that determine by definition all human behavior and experience.

At the core of Barker's definition of behavior setting is a social purpose or meaning involving a set of social rules which unifies or integrates into an orderly system what people do, how they do it, with whom they do it, and when and for what intervals of time. Think of a baseball game, a college prom, a funeral, or a school classroom and the full meaning of Barker's ecological behavior theory becomes evident. What emerges in its own right is that Barker's environment is hardly the geographical environment defined by Koffka. Its reality is not physical but socially defined.

Barker's ecological psychology dictates its own methodology, and it is clearly not that of the laboratory or other kinds of contrived human settings. Behavior is to be observed in everyday, ordinary situations, to be recorded under so-called "free-fall" conditions. "Psychology has been so busy selecting from, imposing upon, and rearranging the behavior of its subjects," he writes, "that it has until very recently neglected to note behavior's clear structure when it is not molested by tests, experiments, questionnaires and interviews." [1963:24]

It might seem that Barker is proposing the obvious: We have defined the purposes of various behavior settings in terms of the behaviors necessary to satisfy these purposes. This may be true, but the fact is that beyond the obvious appropriate behaviors (for example, people eat in dining rooms), we know little else about these settings because we have rarely studied them. There are many questions to ask: What non-appropriate behaviors occur? What happens when behavior settings having the same purposes vary in their physical dimension or in other ways? What consequences does the activity of one behavior setting have on the events in another that is related to it in time and/or space? What occurs when the stable structure of a behavior setting is only partially maintained (for example, sometimes the jukebox in the local school snack shop works and sometimes it doesn't)? We must even ask what the properties of the common en masse behaviors revealed in behavior settings are. Worth quoting in this respect is Barker's own statement:

Both science and society ask with greater urgency than previously: What are environments like? ... How do environments select and shape the people who inhabit them? What are the structural and dynamic properties of the environments to which people must adapt? These are questions for ecological psychology, and in particular, they pertain to the ecological environment and its consequences for men. [1968:3, 4]

Barker's methods for observing the ecological relationship between individuals and their sociocultural setting are discussed in Chapter Eight. The significance of his findings is illustrated by an exhaustive study of schools, in which he was able to show that because smaller schools provide greater opportunities for participation in voluntary activities, students attending them are regulated to a degree that is not possible in large schools, where students are more likely to end up as spectators rather than participants. And since it is from the nonparticipating students that many drop-outs come, the size of the setting may be the critical factor as to whether one graduates.

SOME MICROTHEORETICAL APPROACHES

In considering the major psychological theories of human behavior at least two environmental questions are implicit. What is the environment like, and how do we know the environment? Some theorists have attempted to answer either or both of these questions in specific and direct terms. Important in this respect is the work of Brunswik (1949, 1956), who directed his attention primarily to perceiving or "knowing" the environment. Although Brunswik was Gestalt-oriented, his conception of the individual's psychological environment was quite different from the simple distinction between geographical and behavioral environments made by Lewin and Koffka. Brunswik was concerned with stimuli not as a source of stimulation but as a source of *information* from and about the environment. The view taken by him was simple enough: The cues and other forms of information provided by an object, a constellation of objects, or even a large-scale environment are many and varied. For this reason the information the individual receives from these objects is never perfectly correlated with its source, that is, some information is more valid than other information. This means, in effect, that in the process of getting information from the environment we must also determine the probability of it being correct, to decide whether it is valid information.

Thus Brunswik speaks of "ecological cue validities" and "environmental probabilities," which mean simply that the perceiver becomes part of the perceptual process: given the complexity and the equivocality of his environment, he judges it or gives it meaning by attributing validity to one set of cues rather than another. Given these "educated guesses" or probabilities, the individual then behaves in a way consistent with these judgments. To the extent that these actions confirm the accuracy of his percepts, he builds up particular probabilities about his environment which serve to guide his perceptual judgments in subsequent transactions with his environment. However, since the environment is constantly changing, the hypothesized probabilities we have used in the past may not always be correct; and the organism, if it is not to go under, must acquire new hypotheses. The process of learning, whether in the perceptual system or in the means-end system, is just such an acquiring of new hypotheses.

Although Gibson (1950, 1966) too was concerned with stimuli as sources of information about the environment, his conception of how we perceive it was vastly different. Thus, he distinguished between literal perception and schematic perception. Literal perception refers to the direct experiences of environmental stimuli that all of us have because they are rooted in the basic sensory structures and processes of man. Schematic perception, on the other hand, he defines as "the world of useful and significant things to which we ordinarily attend." This is the environment not only as felt, but as organized into a meaningful universe. In this kind of perception we respond not simply to sensation but to the moods, attitudes, values, and desires that various stimuli induce in us. Thus, hot and cold temperatures, a blinding light, a salty taste, and a fragrant smell will affect nearly all of us in pretty much the same way. But the environmental milieu in which we experience these sensations may be perceived with a wide range of differences, depending upon factors that have nothing to do with the immediate and literal stimuli.

Four factors discussed by Gibson as influencing schematic perception are: previous experience or perceptual set, personal needs, values and attitudes, and social consensus. The latter refers to the fact that our environments have order or make sense because we have imposed such sense or order on them. Through social consensus we group particular objects, apply names to them, and use these names and act accordingly when confronted with them. It is necessary that we recognize the world we move around in not only as being the same world from one day to the next, but the same world that others inhabit. The issues posed by these theorists are explored in greater detail in Chapter Five.

Still other theorists have turned their attention not so much to how we perceive our environment as to what our environment is like. Space limitations compel us to refer generally to these theorists as a group rather than to consider the views of any one of them in detail. Thus, Sells (1966) Fiske and Maddi (1961), and Berlyne (1960) have been concerned with the quality of stimulation with respect to its influence on such factors as personality development, learning capacity, and social competence. Still others, such as Wohlwill (1968), are looking at environment as a source of affect and attitudes which elicit feelings of pleasure and excitement, aversion and boredom. These are seen as a function of certain stimulus attributes such as complexity, incongruity, novelty, familiarity, and variety, to which the organism responds either through arousal or in the form of exploratory activity. Rapoport and Kantor (1967) stress the positive value of ambiguity and uncertainty in "engaging" the individual in his environment, and Wohlwill (1968) has stressed novelty, incongruity, and surprise as these responses are evoked by features of the physical environment. And finally, Fiske and Maddi (1961) emphasize the importance of variation and meaningfulness of stimuli (both internal and external) in arousing the organism neuropsychologically.

Two other theorists, Murray (1938) and Chein (1954), influenced by Lewin, Freud, and Gestalt theory generally, have attempted in a preliminary fashion to conceptualize the person's environment. Murray conceived of environmental objects and situations as positive and negative "presses," depending on whether they facilitated or impeded goal achievement or need satisfaction respectively. The environment he dealt with was Lewin's psychological environment; thus desirable, as opposed to undesirable, environmental goal objects were also identified in terms of positive and negative valences. Chein (1954) in his paper, "The Environment as a Determinant of Behavior," points to the "relative neglect of the environment by many of the most influential theoretical viewpoints." He believes that it is important to put together a schema to provide a more adequate means of conceptualizing the environment. Interestingly enough, in his own preliminary attempt, he turns to Koffka's geographical environment rather than to Lewin's behavioral environment, offering two reasons for doing so. First, he thinks the psychologist's present knowledge of the person is not adequate to conceptualize the behavioral environment, since this environment does not tell us anything at all about how the objective environment influences behavior. Second, Chein stresses the point that things in the objective environment do influence behavior although they are not in the behavioral environment as Koffka conceived of it; that is, the physical setting contains objects, spaces, and qualities which the person usually remains unaware of. As we indicated earlier, Lewin took account of just this problem in his elaboration of the life space, although he never focused on the objective environment in any systematic fashion.

In his formulation Chein defines stimuli as "whatever is capable of initiating a change in the stream of activity." This can be a light source or a complex social situation. But stimuli, he believes, at any level of complexity, may have other functions than to serve as a "release or trigger mechanism." They can also serve in the role of a *goal,* something that satisfies, or as a *noxiant,* something that is unpleasant or produces pain; they can act as *supports,* in that particular features of the environment facilitate certain behaviors, whereas *constraints* either preclude or make the occurrence of such behaviors less likely. Finally, they can serve as directors, which are defined as properties of the environment which "tend to induce specific directions of behavior." Chein further differentiates each of these general types of stimuli, and in the end also provides some dimensions for describing the global features of an environment. Thus, an environment can vary in its degree of *organization,* its degree of *stability,* and finally in the *degrees of freedom* it makes available to the person.

THE VIEW FROM OTHER DISCIPLINES

Physical environmental theory has too many implications to be left just to psychologists. Many other professions and behavioral science fields have also theorized about the nature of the physical environment and man's responses to it. Of course, our discussion in this chapter has been heavily weighted with the views of theoretical psychologists, because, at least within the context of a scientific approach, psychologists either explicitly or implicitly have had most to say about the physical environment in relation to human behavior and experience. Sociologists are by definition dedicated to environmental concepts, but almost exclusive attention is given to the social environment of man. Yet, as Michelson (1970) notes, it was the sociologist Robert E. Park (1952) who first broached the study of human ecology, or that field of sociology that investigates the relationships among a community or group of individuals and its natural environments. With all of the best intentions—and Michelson takes pains to point this out—human ecology was far more a method than a theory, and the investigations that emerged tended to relate the social properties of given areas with the behavioral characteristics of the various groups of people involved. The relationships between the physical properties of urban settings and the corresponding social properties of these settings, or between the urban settings and the behavior of the people living in them, were largely ignored.

On the other hand, some sociologists, such as Gutman and Gans, have taken an interest in the relationships between the design of physical settings—particularly in housing—and the behavior of individuals and groups. Gutman (1966) has considered the general problem of the contribution of sociological thinking to architectural design and the needs of architects. Gans (1962) has considered the design and organization of urban communities in communities. His studies of Boston's West End are discussed in Chapters Eight and Nine. Michelson (1970) himself has posited what he calls an "intersystems congruence theory." This suggests that physical settings by themselves do not determine behavior, but if congruent with the purposes and goals of the individuals who occupy the setting, then they provide supports for the behaviors necessary to realize these goals and purposes. A low-income project, for example, designed for "beauty and expression," but not for meeting the community and "mutual support desires" of its occupants, will be incongruent with the latter's needs.

Anthropologists too have shown interest in physical settings in terms of acquiring a complete understanding of the sociocultural properties of the particular group of people living in a given setting. In dealing with primitive cultures the physical context had to be described and related to the behaviors and experiences of the members in these cultures. Stated differently, the emphasis was on how these people adapted to their physical environment. However, not only did a theory of environment not emerge, but in most instances the emphasis moved from the physical environment itself to an emphasis on the psychological properties of physical settings; that is, what was believed, felt, or valued about the physical setting and how these reactions related to the extant behavior patterns and customs of the groups. The physical environment qua physical environment simply became the backdrop rather than the focus of concern. One anthropologist, however, Edward Hall (1966), has given almost all of his time to the question of national and cultural differences in the organization and use of space, particularly with respect to the psychospatial relationships between individuals during social interaction. His approach is called "proxemics," and it is considered in detail later in Chapter Six.

In recent years the behavioral orientation has evolved in the field of geography. This interest has taken a number of forms. One of the major questions is how the terrain and other geographical factors influence the behavior and experience of aggregates of peoples. Also the reverse: How does man influence his geographical setting? But here too there has been much discussion but little development toward conceptualizing an approach to the physical environment. As we move through the remaining chapters of this book, the reader will have occasion to read about the theory and research of some of the these geographers.

It is true that architects, designers, and planners concerned with the influence of the natural and built environment on behavior and experience have not waited upon developments in the behavioral sciences. Indeed they should not have, because it has been and will continue to be a long wait. Furthermore, as we already suggested, environmental psychology is an interdisciplinary field that will require the integration not only of the conceptions of different behavioral science disciplines but also of those of the architect, designer, and planner.

As one might expect, some architects, designers, and planners have formulated their own microtheories of environment, although these are more orientations to the problems of the physical settings than actual theories. The work of such people as the architect and planner Kevin Lynch (1960) and the architect-psychologist Constance Perin (1970), come to mind in this context. In our discussions in the chapters on methodology (Chapter Eight), the urban setting (Chapter Nine), and the built environment (Chapter Eleven), and in other places in this volume, their particular views are considered. But here it is important to take note of the considerable influence of the environmental conceptions discussed throughout this chapter on the thinking of these individuals. Thus, Lynch (1960), in his *Image of the City*, takes a cognitive approach to the environment in his attempt to get at the visual quality of the American city. By visual quality he means primarily the "legibility" of the city: that is, the ease with which the parts of a city can be recognized and be organized into a meaningful or coherent pattern which exists as an image in our mind.

His colleague Carr (1967) has called this imaged urban form the "city of the mind." We carry with us a picture of the city (or countryside) that is absent from our immediate perception or beyond our perceptual boundaries. Although in many respects this picture may be a distortion of the actual environment on which it is based, it may be as useful in our day-to-day orientations as an accurate map. This cognitive orientation to city planning is taking its place alongside the traditional economic concerns of land use, esthetic quality, traffic problems, and the like. Lynch's work is discussed more fully in Chapters Five, Eight, and Nine.

Alexander (1964), concerned more with design process than environment per se, takes the view that environmental form follows function. Stated more directly, he argues that only by tracing the functional requirements of human needs and activities can we provide the kinds of forms (solutions to problems of designing built environments) that will fit the context (the problem—human need, activity, and so on). In this respect his view followed Kohler's conception of the "good figure," that is, an environmental object, setting, or event designed so that it relates in the most meaningful way or "best fit" to a human activity, function, or need. We will consider Alexander's views again in our discussion of the built environment later in this volume.

The array of theoretical viewpoints presented in this chapter falls short of providing definitive directions. However, at least one important guiding principle does emerge. Each of the viewpoints attacks one aspect of a broad problem. This, in brief, is the problem of conceptualizing man's environment in relation to the fact that he behaves in and experiences it. Our theories do make sense in the light of their particular focuses. What will be needed in the end is a theoretical approach that is eclectic in the sense that it can integrate all of these points of view.

The fact is that there is an objective world that is experienced in very similar ways by all men. On the other hand, it is no less true that there is a subjective environment which, whatever the commonalities of experience, reflects not just differences in men's values, interests, and past experience, but also the uniqueness to be found in the fantasies of the private world of each individual, for we do interpret, fantasize about, and give special meanings to our particular physical settings. Somewhere between these two extremes is a "constructed objective world": Whatever the hard-data information about the environment provided by each physiological sense system, the sheer integration of all this information in the brain—as part of motivational and other directive state influences—undoubtedly provides a "constructed" view of the environment. To this we must add the fact that the behavior of the person himself changes the very environment that in part produced the behavior.

In terms of a systematic and useful conceptualization, the environment, physical or otherwise, remains a vast unknown insofar as we have been able to establish a viable theory of human behavior and experience. On the other hand, it is possible to pull together from some of the theoretical positions discussed above at least a set of working assumptions about the environment which can serve as a guide to research and the analysis of problems. As the reader knows by now, any theory of the environment must articulate and be consistent with a theory of human behavior and experience. Thus, our first task in the next chapter is to sketch some basic assumptions about the nature of man.

REFERENCES

Alexander, C. *Notes on the synthesis of form,* Cambridge, Mass.: Harvard University Press. 1964.

Barker, R. G. On the nature of the environment. *Journal of Social Issues,* 1963a, 19, 17–23.

Barker, R. G. *The stream of behavior.* New York: Appleton, 1963b.

Barker, R. G. *Ecological psychology: Concepts and methods for studying the environment of behavior.* Stanford, Calif.: Stanford University Press, 1968.

Berlyne, D. E. *Conflict, arousal and curiosity.* New York: McGraw-Hill, 1960.

Boring, E. G. *Sensation and perception in the history of experimental psychology.* New York: Appleton, 1942.

Brunswik, E. *Systematic and representative design of psychology experiments.* Berkeley, Calif.: University of California Press, 1949.

Brunswik, E. *Perception and the representative design of psychology experiments.* Berkeley, Calif.: University of California Press, 1956.

Carr, S. The city of the mind. In W. R. Ewald, Jr. (Ed.), *Environment for man: The next fifty years.* Bloomington, Ind.: Indiana University Press, 1967.

Chein, I. The environment as a determinant of behavior, *Journal of Social Psychology,* 1954, 39, 115–127.

Fiske, D. & Maddi, S. *Functions of varied experience.* Homewood, Ill.: Dorsey Press, 1961.

Freud, S. *New introductory lectures on psycho-analysis.* New York: Norton, 1933, (First German edition, 1930).

Gans, H. *The urban villagers.* New York: Free Press, 1962.

Gibson, J. J. *The perception of the visual world.* Boston: Houghton Mifflin, 1950.

Gibson, J. J. *The senses considered as perceptual systems.* Boston: Houghton Mifflin, 1966.

Gutman, R. Site planning and social behavior, *Journal of Social Issues,* 1966, 22, 103–115.

Hall, E. T. *The hidden dimension.* New York: Doubleday, 1966.

Heidbreder, E. *Seven psychologies.* New York: Appleton, 1933.

Koffka, K. *Principles of gestalt psychology.* New York: Harcourt Brace Jovanovich, 1935.

Köhler, W. *Gestalt psychology.* New York: Liveright, 1929.

Lewin, K. *A dynamic theory of personality.* New York: McGraw-Hill, 1935.

Lewin, K. *Principles of topological psychology.* New York; McGraw-Hill, 1936.

Lewin, K. *Field theory in social science.* New York: Harper & Row, 1951.

Lynch, K. *The image of the city.* Cambridge, Mass.: The M.I.T. Press, 1960.

Michelson, W. *Man and his urban environment: A sociological approach.* Reading, Mass.: Addison-Wesley, 1970.

Murray, H. A. *Explorations in personality.* New York: Oxford, 1938.

Park, R. E. *Human communities.* New York: Free Press, 1952.

Perin, C. *With man in mind: An interdisciplinary prospectus for environmental design.* Cambridge, Mass.: The M.I.T. Press, 1970.

Rapoport, A. & Kantor, R. E. Complexity and ambiguity in environmental design. *Journal of American Institute of Planners,* 1967, 23, 210–221.

Sells, S. B. Ecology and the science of psychology. *Multivariate Behavioral Research,* 1966, 1, 133–144.

Skinner, B. F. *Science and human behavior.* New York: Macmillan, 1953.

Skinner, B. F. *Beyond freedom and dignity.* New York: Knopf, 1971.

Wohlwill, J. F. Amount of stimulus exploration and preference as differential functions of stimulus complexity. *Perception and Psychophysics,* 1968, 4, 307–312.

Wolman, B. S. (Ed.) *Historical roots of contemporary psychology.* New York: Harper & Row, 1968.

Woodworth, R. S. *Contemporary schools of psychology.* New York: Ronald, 1948.

SUGGESTED READINGS

Boring, E. G. *Sensation and perception in the history of experimental psychology.* New York: Appleton, 1942.

Heidbreder, E. *Seven psychologies.* New York: Appleton, 1933.

Wolman, B. S. (Ed.) *Historical roots of contemporary psychology.* New York: Harper & Row, 1968.

Woodworth, R. S. *Contemporary schools of psychology.* New York: Ronald, 1948.

4 Understanding Behavior in Conflict

Kenneth W. Thomas and Ralph H. Kilmann

This reading provides a theory of the uses of various modes of resolving differences or conflict. It is has a self-assessment tool that identifies individual propensities in making use of the various modes, recommending that all modes be used appropriately—even the ones that do not come natural to us. This instrument has been used by many Fortune 500 companies as an important tool in supporting teamwork and its value has been demonstrated in practice.

THE FIVE CONFLICT-HANDLING MODES

The *Thomas-Kilmann Conflict Mode Instrument* (TKI) assesses an individual's behavior in conflict situations—that is, situations in which the concerns of two people appear to be incompatible. In conflict situations, we can describe a person's behavior along two basic dimensions: **(1) assertiveness**, the extent to which the individual attempts to satisfy his or her own concerns, and **(2) cooperativeness**, the extent to which the individual attempts to satisfy the other person's concerns. These two dimensions of behavior can be used to define five methods of dealing with conflict. These five conflict-handling modes are shown on the next page:

Kenneth W. Thomas and Ralph H. Kilmann, "Understanding Behavior in Conflict," from *The Thomas-Kilmann Conflict Mode Instrument*, pp. 1–16. Copyright © 1974. Permission to reprint granted by the publisher.

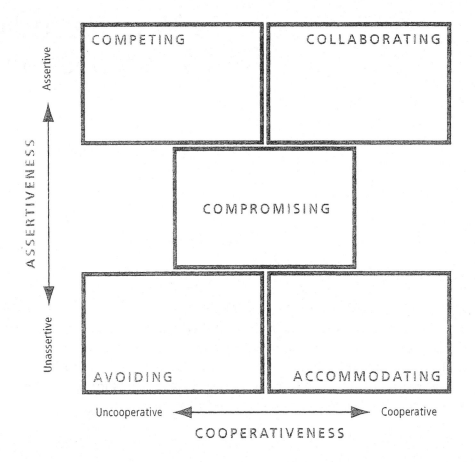

Competing

Competing is assertive and uncooperative, a power-oriented mode. When competing, an individual pursues his or her own concerns at the other person's expense, using whatever power seems appropriate to win his or her position. Competing might mean standing up for your rights, defending a position you believe is correct, or simply trying to win.

Collaborating

Collaborating is both assertive and cooperative. When collaborating, an individual attempts to work with the other person to find a solution that fully satisfies the concerns of both. It involves digging into an issue to identify the underlying concerns of the two individuals and to find an alternative that meets both sets of concerns. Collaborating between two persons might take the form of exploring a disagreement to learn from each other's insights, resolving some condition that would otherwise have them competing for resources, or confronting and trying to find a creative solution to an interpersonal problem.

Compromising

Compromising is intermediate in both assertiveness and cooperativeness. When compromising, the objective is to find an expedient, mutually acceptable solution that partially satisfies both parties. Compromising falls on a middle ground between competing and accommodating, giving up more than competing but less than accommodating. Likewise, it addresses an issue more directly than avoiding but doesn't explore it in as much depth as collaborating. Compromising might mean splitting the difference, exchanging concessions, or seeking a quick middle-ground position.

Avoiding

Avoiding is unassertive and uncooperative. When avoiding, an individual does not immediately pursue his or her own concerns or those of the other person. He or she does not address the conflict. Avoiding might take the form of diplomatically sidestepping an issue, postponing an issue until a better time, or simply withdrawing from a threatening situation.

Accommodating

Accommodating is unassertive and cooperative—the opposite of competing. When accommodating, an individual neglects his or her own concerns to satisfy the concerns of the other person; there is an element of self-sacrifice in this mode. Accommodating might take the form of selfless generosity or charity, obeying another person's order when you would prefer not to, or yielding to another's point of view.

COMPETING

Uses

- When quick, decisive action is vital—for example, in an emergency
- On important issues where unpopular courses of action need implementing—for example, cost cutting, enforcing unpopular rules, discipline
- On issues vital to company welfare when you know you're right
- When you need to protect yourself from people who take advantage of noncompetitive behavior

Questions to Ask

If your score is in the high range, you may wish to ask yourself:
- Are you surrounded by "yes" people?

If so, perhaps it's because they have learned that it's unwise to disagree with you or have given up trying to influence you. This closes you off from information.

- Are others afraid to admit ignorance and uncertainties to you?

In a competitive climate, one must fight for influence and respect, acting more certain and confident than one feels. This means that people are less able to ask for information and opinions—they are less likely to learn.

If your score is in the low range, you may wish to ask yourself:
- Do you often feel powerless in situations?

You may be unaware of the power you have, unskilled in its use, or uncomfortable with the idea of using it. This may hinder your effectiveness by restricting your influence.

- Do you sometimes have trouble taking a firm stand, even when you see the need?

Sometimes concerns for others' feelings or anxieties about the use of power cause people to vacillate, which may result in postponing the decision and adding to the suffering and/or resentment of others.

COLLABORATING

Uses

- When you need to find an integrative solution and the concerns of both parties are too important to be compromised
- When your objective is to learn and you wish to test your assumptions and understand others' views
- When you want to merge insights from people with different perspectives on a problem
- When you want to gain commitment by incorporating others' concerns into a consensual decision
- When you need to work through hard feelings that have been interfering with a relationship

Questions to Ask

If your score is in the high range, you may wish to ask yourself:
- Do you sometimes spend time discussing issues in depth that don't seem to warrant it?

Collaboration takes time and energy—perhaps the scarcest organizational resources. Trivial problems don't require optimal solutions, and not all personal differences need to be hashed out. The overuse of collaboration and consensual decision-making sometimes represents a desire to minimize risk—by diffusing responsibility for a decision or by postponing action.

- Does your collaborative behavior fail to elicit collaborative responses from others?

The exploratory and tentative nature of some collaborative behavior may make it easy for others to disregard your overtures or take advantage of the trust and openness you display. You may be missing some cues that would indicate the presence of defensiveness, strong feelings, impatience, competitiveness, or conflicting interests.

If your score is in the low range, you may wish to ask yourself:
- Is it difficult for you to see differences as opportunities for joint gain, learning, or problem solving?

Although conflict situations often involve threatening or unproductive aspects, approaching all conflicts with pessimism can prevent you from seeing collaborative possibilities and thus deprive you of the mutual gains and satisfactions that accompany successful collaboration.

- Are others uncommitted to your decisions or policies?

Perhaps their concerns are not being incorporated into those decisions or policies.

COMPROMISING

Uses

- When goals are moderately important but not worth the effort or the potential disruption involved in using more assertive modes
- When two opponents with equal power are strongly committed to mutually exclusive goals—as in labor-management bargaining
- When you want to achieve a temporary settlement of a complex issue
- When you need to arrive at an expedient solution under time pressure
- As a backup mode when collaboration or competition fails

Questions to Ask

If your score is in the high range, you may wish to ask yourself:
- Do you concentrate so heavily on the practicalities and tactics of compromise that you sometimes lose sight of larger issues?

Doing so may lead to unintended and costly compromises of principles, values, long-term objectives, or company welfare.

- Does an emphasis on bargaining and trading create a cynical climate of gamesmanship?

Such a climate may undermine interpersonal trust and deflect attention from the merits of the issues being discussed.

If your score is in the low range, you may wish to ask yourself:
- Do you sometimes find yourself too sensitive or embarrassed to engage in the give-and-take of bargaining?

This reticence can keep you from getting a fair share in negotiations—for yourself, your team, or your organization.

- Do you sometimes find it difficult to make concessions?

Without this safety valve, you may have trouble gracefully getting out of mutually destructive arguments, power struggles, and so on.

AVOIDING

Uses

- When an issue is unimportant or when other, more important issues *are* pressing
- When you perceive no chance of satisfying your concerns—for example, when you have low power or you are frustrated by something that would be very difficult to change
- When the potential costs of confronting a conflict outweigh the benefits of its resolution
- When you need to let people cool down—to reduce tensions to a productive level and to regain perspective and composure
- When gathering more information outweighs the advantages of an immediate decision

- When others can resolve the conflict more effectively
- When the issue seems tangential or symptomatic of another, more basic issue

Questions to Ask

If your score is in the high range, you may wish to ask yourself:
- Does coordination suffer because people sometimes have trouble getting your input on issues?
- Does it sometimes appear that people are "walking on eggshells"?

Sometimes a dysfunctional amount of energy is devoted to caution and avoiding issues, indicating that those issues need to be faced and resolved.
Are decisions on important issues sometimes made by default?

If your score is in the low range, you may wish to ask yourself:
- Do you sometimes find yourself hurting people's feelings or stirring up hostilities?

You may need to exercise more discretion and tact, framing issues in nonthreatening ways.

- Do you sometimes feel harried or overwhelmed by a number of issues?

You may need to devote more time to setting priorities—that is, deciding which issues are relatively unimportant and perhaps delegating them to others.

ACCOMMODATING

Uses

- When you realize that you are wrong—to allow a better position to be considered, to learn from others, and to show that you are reasonable
- When the issue is much more important to the other person than it is to you—to satisfy the needs of others and as a goodwill gesture to help maintain a cooperative relationship
- When you want to build up social credits for later issues that are important to you
- When you are outmatched and losing and more competition would only damage your cause
- When preserving harmony and avoiding disruption are especially important
- When you want to help your employees develop by allowing them to experiment and learn from their mistakes

Questions to Ask

If your score is in the high range, you may wish to ask yourself:
- Do you feel that your ideas and concerns sometimes don't get the attention they deserve?

Deferring too much to the concerns of others can deprive you of influence, respect, and recognition. It can also deprive the organization of your potential contributions.

- Is discipline lax?

Although discipline for its own sake may be of little value, some rules and procedures are crucial and need to be enforced. Accommodating on these issues may harm you, others, or the organization.

If your score is in the low range, you may wish to ask yourself:
- Do you sometimes have trouble building goodwill with others?

Accommodation on minor issues that are important to others is a gesture of goodwill.
- Do others sometimes seem to regard you as unreasonable?
- Do you occasionally have trouble admitting when you are wrong?
- Do you recognize legitimate exceptions to the rules?
- Do you know when to give up?

Note: The Thomas-Kilmann Conflict Mode Instrument (TKI) helps you understand how five conflict-handling modes, or styles—competing, collaborating, compromising, avoiding, and accommodating—affect personal and group dynamics and learn how to select the most appropriate style for a given situation. By selecting responses from 30 statement pairs, you discover your preferred style. Based on your particular use of each mode, the TKI report offers specific suggestions to help you understand the pluses and minuses of a particular conflict-handling mode, guidance on the appropriate use of each mode, and tips for learning to work with less preferred modes.

You will find taking the TKI assessment online to be a fast and engaging activity. You will receive immediate feedback as results will be sent directly to you. The TKI assessment is psychologically sound and thoroughly researched, so you can trust the results.

The Thomas-Kilmann Conflict Mode Instrument can be purchased online with an individualized report interpreting your results. For complete information on the TKI and to purchase, visit www.cpp.com/tki.

5 The Anthropology of Space
An Organizing Model

Edward T. Hall

This article gives an overview of how culture—hence history—shapes our environmental experience at all scales of the environment, from the chair to settlement patterns and the architectural spaces in between.

The term proxemics is used to define the interrelated observations and theories of man's use of space. His use of space, however, can only be understood in terms of a multilevel analysis of its manifestations and related determinants. Thus, *infraculture* applies to behavior on lower organizational levels that underlies culture and is rooted in man's biological past. It is a part of the proxemic classification system and implies a specific set of levels of relationships with other parts of the system. A second proxemic manifestation, the *precultural,* refers to the physiological base shared by all human beings, to which culture gives structure and meaning, and to which the scientist must inevitably refer in comparing the proxemic patterns of Culture A with those of Culture B. The *pre*cultural is very much in the present. The third, the *micro*cultural level, is the one on which most proxemic observations are made. Proxemics as a manifestation of microculture has three aspects: fixed-feature, semifixed-feature, and informal.

FIXED-FEATURE SPACE

Fixed-feature space is one of the basic ways of organizing the activities of individuals and groups. It includes material manifestations as well as the hidden, internalized designs that govern behavior as man moves about on this earth. Buildings are one expression of fixed-feature patterns, but buildings are also grouped together in characteristic ways as well as being divided internally according to culturally determined designs. The layout of villages, towns, cities, and the intervening countryside is not haphazard but follows a plan which changes with time and culture.

Even the inside of the Western house is organized spatially. Not only are there special rooms for special functions—food preparation, eating, entertaining and socializing, rest, recuperation, and procreation—but for sanitation as well. *If,* as sometimes happens, either the artifacts or the activities associated with one space are transferred to another space, this fact is immediately apparent. People who "live in a mess" or a "constant state of confusion" are those who fail to classify activities

Edward T. Hall, Thomas Prohansky, ed., "The Anthropology of Space: an Organizing Model," from *Environmental Psychology: People and Their Physical Settings*, pp. 158–169. Copyright © 1976 by Cengage. Permission to reprint granted by the publisher.

and artifacts according to a uniform, consistent, or predictable spatial plan. At the opposite end of the scale is the assembly line, a precise organization of objects in *time* and *space.*

Actually the present internal layout of the house, which Americans and Europeans take for granted, is quite recent. As Philippe Ariès (1962) points out in *Centuries of Childhood,* rooms had no fixed functions in European houses until the eighteenth century. Members of the family had no privacy as we know it today. There were no spaces that were sacred or specialized. Strangers came and went at will, while beds and tables were set up and taken down according to the moods and appetites of the occupants. Children dressed and were treated as small adults. It is no wonder that the concept of childhood and its associated concept, the nuclear family, had to await the specialization of rooms according to function and the separation of rooms from each other. In the eighteenth century, the house altered its form. In French, *chambre* was distinguished from *salle.* In English, the function of a room was indicated by its name—bedroom, living room, dining room. Rooms were arranged to open into a corridor or hall, like houses into a street. No longer did the occupants pass through one room into another. Relieved of the Grand Central Station atmosphere and protected by new spaces, the family pattern began to stabilize and was expressed further in the form of the house.

Goffman's *Presentation of Self in Everyday Life* (1959) is a detailed, sensitive record of observations on the relationship of the façade that people present to the world and the self they hide behind it. The use of the term façade is in itself revealing. It signifies recognition of levels to be penetrated and hints at the functions performed by architectural features which provide screens behind which to retire from time to time. The strain of keeping up a façade can be great. Architecture can and does take over this burden for people. It can also provide a refuge where the individual can "let his hair down" and be himself.

The fact that so few businessmen have offices in their homes cannot be solely explained on the basis of convention and top management's uneasiness when executives are not visibly present. I have observed that many men have two or more distinct personalities, one for business and one for the home. The separation of office and home in these instances helps to keep the two often incompatible personalities from conflicting and may even serve to stabilize an idealized version of each which conforms to the projected image of both architecture and setting.

The relationship of fixed-feature space to personality as well as to culture is nowhere more apparent than in the kitchen. When micro-patterns interfere as they do in the kitchen, it is more than just annoying to the women I interviewed. My wife, who has struggled for years with kitchens of all types, comments on male design in this way: "If any of the men who designed this kitchen had ever worked in it, they wouldn't have done it this way." The lack of congruence between the design elements, female stature and body build (women are not usually tall enough to reach things), and the activities to be performed, while not obvious at first, is often beyond belief. The size, the shape, the arrangement, and the placing in the house all communicate to the women of the house how much or how little the architect and designer knew about fixed-feature details.

Man's feeling about being properly oriented in space runs deep. Such knowledge is ultimately linked to survival and sanity. To be disoriented in space is to be psychotic. The difference between acting with reflex speed and having to stop to think in an emergency may mean the difference between life and death—a rule which applies equally to the driver negotiating freeway traffic and the rodent dodging predators. Lewis Mumford (1961) observes that the uniform grid pattern of our cities "makes strangers as much at home as the oldest inhabitants." Americans who have become dependent on this pattern are often frustrated by anything different. It is difficult for them to feel at home in European capitals that don't conform to this simple plan. Those who travel and live abroad frequently get lost. An interesting feature of these complaints reveals the relationship of the layout to the person. Almost without exception, the newcomer uses words and tones associated with a personal affront, as though the town held something against him. It is no wonder that people brought up on either the French radiating star or the Roman grid have difficulty in a place like Japan where the entire fixed-feature pattern is basically and radically different. In fact, if one were to set out to design two systems in contrasts, it is hard to see how one could do better. The European systems stress the lines, which they name; the Japanese treat the intersecting points technically and forget about the lines. In Japan, the intersections but not the streets are named. Houses instead of being related in space are related in time and numbered in the order in which they are built. The Japanese pattern emphasizes hierarchies that grow around centers; the American plan finds its ultimate development in the sameness of suburbia, because one number along a line is the same as any other. In a Japanese neighborhood, the first house built is a constant reminder to the residents of house #20 that #1 was there first.

Some aspects of fixed-feature space are not visible until one observes human behavior. For example, although the separate dining room is fast vanishing from American houses, the line separating the dining area from the rest of the living room is quite real. The invisible boundary which separates one yard from another in suburbia is also a fixed-feature of American culture or at least some of its subcultures.

Architects traditionally are preoccupied with the visual patterns of structures—what one sees. They are almost totally unaware of the fact that people carry around with them internalizations of fixed-feature space learned early in life. It isn't only the Arab who feels depressed unless he has enough space but many Americans as well. As one of my subjects said, "I can put up with almost anything as long as I have large rooms and high ceilings. You see. I was raised in an old house in Brooklyn and I have never been able to accustom myself to anything different."

The important point about fixed-feature space is that it is the mold into which a great deal of behavior is cast. It was this feature of space that the late Sir Winston Churchill referred to when he said: "We shape our buildings and they shape us." During the debate on restoring the House of Commons after the war, Churchill feared that departure from the intimate spatial pattern of the House, where opponents face each other across a narrow aisle, would seriously alter the patterns of government. He may not have been the first to put his finger on the influence of fixed-feature space, but its effects have never been so succinctly stated.

One of the many basic differences between cultures is that they extend different anatomical and behavioral features of the human organism. Whenever there is cross-cultural borrowing, the borrowed items have to be adapted. Otherwise, the new and the old do not match, and in some instances, the two patterns are completely contradictory. For example, Japan has had problems integrating the automobile into a culture in which the lines between points (highways) receive less attention than the points. Hence, Tokyo is famous for producing some of the world's most impressive traffic jams. The automobile is also poorly adapted to India, where cities are physically crowded and the society has elaborate hierarchical features. Unless Indian engineers can design roads that will separate slow pedestrians from fast-moving vehicles, the class-conscious drivers' lack of consideration for the poor will continue to breed disaster. Even Le Corbusier's great buildings at Chandigarh, capital of Punjab, had to be modified by the residents to make them habitable. The Indians walled up Corbusier's balconies, converting them into kitchens! Similarly, Arabs coming to the United States find that their own internalized fixed-feature patterns do not fit American housing. Arabs feel oppressed by it—the ceilings are too low, the rooms too small, privacy from the outside inadequate, and views non-existent.

It should not be thought, however, that incongruity between internalized and externalized patterns occurs only between cultures. As our own technology explodes, air conditioning, fluorescent lighting, and sound-roofing make it possible to design houses and offices without regard to traditional patterns of windows and doors. The new inventions sometimes result in great barnlike rooms where the "territory" of scores of employees in a "bull pen" is ambiguous.

SEMIFIXED-FEATURE SPACE

Several years ago, a talented and perceptive physician named Humphry Osmond was asked to direct a large health and research center in Saskatchewan. His hospital was one of the first in which the relationship between semifixed-feature space and behavior was clearly demonstrated. Osmond had noticed that some spaces, like railway waiting rooms, tend to keep people apart. These he called sociofugal spaces. Others, such as the booths in the old-fashioned drugstore or the tables at a French sidewalk café, tend to bring people together. These he called sociopetal (1957). The hospital of which he was in charge was replete with sociofugal spaces and had very few which might be called sociopetal. Furthermore, the custodial staff and nurses tended to prefer the former to the latter because they were easier to maintain. Chairs in the halls, which would be found in little circles after visiting hours, would soon be lined up neatly in military fashion, in rows along the walls.

One situation which attracted Osmond's attention was the newly built "model" female geriatrics ward. Everything was new and shiny, neat and clean. There was enough space, and the colors were cheerful. The only trouble was that the longer the patients stayed in the ward, the less they seemed to talk to each other. Gradually, they were becoming like the furniture, permanently and silently glued to the walls at regular intervals between the beds. In addition, they all seemed depressed.

Sensing that the space was more sociofugal than sociopetal, Osmond put a perceptive young psychologist, Robert Sommer, to work to find out as much as he could about the relationship of furniture to conversations. Looking for a natural setting which offered a number of different situations in which people could be observed in conversations, Sommer selected the hospital cafeteria, where 36 by 72-inch tables accommodated six people (1959). As Figure 2–1 indicates, these tables provided six different distances and orientations of the bodies in relation to each other. Fifty observational sessions in which conversations were counted at controlled intervals revealed that: F–A (cross corner) conversations were twice as frequent as the C–B (side by side) type, which in turn were three times as frequent as those at C–D (across the table). No conversations were observed by Sommer for the other positions. In other words, corner situations with people at right angles to each

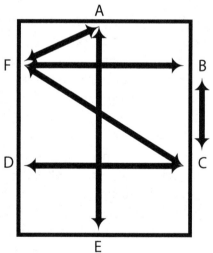

Figure 2–1. F–A, across the corner; C–B, side by side, C–D, across the table; E–A, from one end to the other; E–F, diagonally the length of the table; C–F, diagonally across the table.

other produced six times as many conversations as face-to-face situations across the 36-inch span of the table, and twice as many as the side-by-side arrangement.

The results of these observations suggested a solution to the problem of gradual disengagement and withdrawal of the old people. Both Osmond and Sommer had noted that the ward patients were more often in the *B–C* and *C–D* relationships (side by side and across) than they were in the cafeteria, and they sat at much greater distances. In addition, there was no place to put anything, no place for personal belongings. The only territorial features associated with the patients were the bed and the chair. As a consequence, magazines ended up on the floor and were quickly swept up by staff members. Enough small tables so that every patient had a place would provide additional territoriality and an opportunity to keep magazines, books, and writing materials. If the tables were square, they would also help to structure relationships between patients so that there was a maximum opportunity to converse.

The small tables were moved in and the chairs arranged around them. At first, the patients resisted. They had become accustomed to the placement of "their" chairs in particular spots, and they did not take easily to being moved around by others. The staff kept the new arrangement reasonably intact until it was established as an alternative rather than an annoying feature to be selectively inattended. When this point had been reached, a repeat count of conversations was made. The number of conversations had doubled, while reading had tripled, possibly because there was now a place to keep reading material. Similar restructuring of the dayroom met with the same resistances and the same ultimate increase in verbal interaction.

At this point, three things must be said. Conclusions drawn from observations made in the hospital situation just described are not universally applicable. That is, across-the-corner-at-right-angles is conducive *only* to: (a) conversations of certain types between (b) persons in certain relationships and (c) in very restricted cultural settings. Second, what is sociofugal in one culture may be sociopetal in another. Third, sociofugal space is not necessarily bad, nor is sociopetal space universally good. What *is* desirable is flexibility and congruence between design and function so that there is a variety of spaces, and people can be involved or not, as the occasion and mood demand. The main point of the Canadian experiment for us is its demonstration that the structuring of semifixed features can have a profound effect on behavior and that this effect is measurable. This will come as no surprise to housewives who are constantly trying to balance the relationship of fixed-feature enclosures to arrangement of their semifixed furniture. Many have had the experience of getting a room nicely arranged, only to find that conversation was impossible if the chairs were left nicely arranged.

It should be noted that what is fixed-feature space in one culture may be semifixed in another, and vice versa. In Japan, for example, the walls are movable, opening and closing as the day's activities change. In the United States, people move from room to room or from one part of a room to another for each different activity, such as eating, sleeping, working, or socializing with relatives. In Japan, it is quite common for the person to remain in one spot while the activities change. The Chinese provide us with further opportunities to observe the diversity of human treatment of space, for they assign to the fixed-feature category certain items which Americans treat as semifixed. Apparently, a guest in a Chinese home *does not move his chair* except at the host's suggestion. To do so would be like going into someone else's home and moving a screen or even a partition. In this sense, the semifixed nature of furniture in American homes is merely a matter of degree and situation. Light chairs are more mobile than sofas or heavy tables. I have noted, however, that some Americans hesitate to adjust furniture in another person's house or office. Of the forty students in one of my classes, half manifested such hesitation.

Many American women know it is hard to find things in someone else's kitchen. Conversely, it can be exasperating to have kitchen ware put away by well-meaning helpers who don't know where things "belong." How and where belongings are arranged and stored is a function of micro-cultural patterns, representative not only of large cultural groups but of the minute variations on cultures that make each individual unique. Just as variations in the quality and use of the voice make it possible to distinguish one person's voice from another, handling of materials also has a characteristic pattern that is unique.

INFORMAL SPACE

We turn now to the category of spatial experience, which is perhaps most significant for the individual because it includes the distances maintained in encounters with others. These distances are for the most part outside awareness. I have called this category *informal space* because it is unstated, not because it lacks form or has no importance. Indeed informal spatial patterns have distinct bounds, and such deep, if unvoiced, significance that they form an essential part of the culture. To misunderstand this significance may invite disaster.

Birds and mammals not only have territories which they occupy and defend against their own kind but they have a series of uniform distances which they maintain from each other. Hediger (1955) has classified these as flight distance, critical distance, and personal and social distance. Man, too, has a uniform way of handling distance from his fellows. With very few exceptions, flight distance and critical distance have been eliminated from human reactions. Personal distance and social distance, however, are obviously still present.

How many distances do human beings have and how do we distinguish them? What is it that differentiates one distance from the other? The answer to this question was not obvious at first when I began my investigation of distances in man. Gradually, however, evidence began to accumulate indicating that the regularity of distances observed for humans is the consequence of sensory shifts.

One common source of information about the distance separating two people is the loudness of the voice. Working with the linguistic scientist George Trager, I began by observing shifts in the voice associated with changes in distance. Since the whisper is used when people are very close, and the shout is used to span great distances, the question Trager and I posed was, how many vocal shifts are sandwiched between these two extremes? Our procedure for discovering these patterns was for Trager to stand still while I talked to him at different distances. If both of us agreed that a vocal shift had occurred, we would then measure the distance and note down a general description. The result was the eight distances described in *The Silent Language* (1959).

Further observation of human beings in social situations convinced me that these eight distances were overly complex. Four were sufficient; these I have termed intimate, personal, social, and public (each with its close and far phase). My choice of terms to describe various distances was deliberate. Not only was it influenced by Hediger's work with animals (1955) indicating the continuity between *infra*culture and culture but also by a desire to provide a clue as to the types of activities and relationships associated with each distance, thereby linking them in peoples' minds with specific inventories of relationships and activities. It should be noted at this point that *how people are feeling toward each other* at the time is a decisive factor in the distance used. Thus people who are very angry or emphatic about the point they are making will move in close, they "turn up the volume," as it were, by shouting. Similarly—as any woman knows—one of the first signs that a man is beginning to feel amorous is his move closer to her. If the woman does not feel similarly-disposed she signals this by moving back.

The following descriptions of the four distance zones have been compiled from observations and interviews with non-contact, middle-class, healthy adults, mainly natives of the northeastern seaboard of the United States. A high percentage of the subjects were men and women from business and the professions; many could be classified as intellectuals. The interviews were effectively neutral; that is, the subjects were not noticeably excited, depressed, or angry. There were no unusual environmental factors, such as extremes of temperature or noise. These descriptions represent only a first approximation. They will doubtless seem crude when more is known about proxemic observation and how people distinguish one distance from another. It should be emphasized that these generalizations are not representative of human behavior in general—or even of American behavior in general—but only of the group included in the sample. Negroes and Spanish Americans as well as persons who come from southern European cultures have very different proxemic patterns.

Each of the four distance zones described below has a near and a far phase. It should be noted that the measured distances vary somewhat with differences in personality and environmental factors. For example, a high noise level or low illumination will ordinarily bring people closer together.

INTIMATE DISTANCE

At intimate distance, the presence of the other person is unmistakable and may at times be overwhelming because of the greatly stepped-up sensory inputs. Sight (often distorted), olfaction, heat from the other person's body, sound, smell, and feel of the breath all combine to signal unmistakable involvement with another body.

Intimate Distance—Close Phase. This is the distance of love-making and wrestling, comforting and protecting. Physical contact or the high possibility of physical involvement is uppermost in the awareness of both persons. The use of their distance receptors is greatly reduced except for olfaction and sensation of radiant heat, both of which are stepped up. In the maximum contact phase, the muscles and skin communicate. Pelvis, thighs, and head can be brought into play; arms can encircle. Except at the outer limits, sharp vision is blurred. When close vision is possible within the intimate range—as with children—the image is greatly enlarged and stimulates much, if not all, of the retina. The detail that can be seen at this distance is extraordinary. This detail plus the cross-eyed pull of the eye muscles provide a visual experience that cannot be confused with any other distance. Vocalization at intimate distance plays a very minor part in the communication process, which is carried mainly by other channels. A whisper has the effect of expanding the distance. The vocalizations that do occur are largely involuntary.

Intimate Distance—Far Phase (distance: six to eighteen inches). Heads, thighs, and pelvis are not easily brought into contact, but hands can reach and grasp extremities. The head is seen as enlarged in size, and its features are distorted. Ability to focus the eye easily is an important feature of this distance for Americans. The iris of the other person's eye seen at about six to nine inches is enlarged to more than life-size. Small blood vessels in the sclera are clearly perceived, pores are enlarged. Clear vision (15 degrees) includes the upper or lower portion of the face, which is perceived as enlarged. The nose is seen as over-large and may look distorted, as will other features such as lips, teeth, and tongue. Peripheral vision (30 to 180 degrees) includes the outline of head and shoulders and very often the hands.

Much of the physical discomfort that Americans experience when foreigners are inappropriately inside the intimate sphere is expressed as a distortion of the visual system. One subject said, "These people get so close, you're cross-eyed. It really makes me nervous. They put their face so close it feels like they're *inside you*." At the point where sharp focus is lost, one feels the uncomfortable muscular sensation of being cross-eyed from looking at something too close. The expressions "Get your face *out* of mine" and "He shook his fist *in* my face" apparently express how many Americans perceive their body boundaries.

At six to eighteen inches the voice is used but is normally held at a very low level or even a whisper. As Martin Joos (1962), the linguist, describes it, "An intimate utterance pointedly avoids giving the addressee information from outside of the speaker's skin. The point … is simply to remind (hardly 'inform') the addressee of some feeling … inside the speaker's skin." The heat and odor of the other person's breath may be detected, even though it is directed away from subject's face. Heat loss or gain from other person's body begins to be noticed by some subjects.

The use of intimate distance in public is not considered proper by adult, middle-class Americans even though their young may be observed intimately involved with each other in automobiles and on beaches. Crowded subways and buses may bring strangers into what would ordinarily be classed as intimate spatial relations, but subway riders have defensive devices which take the real intimacy out of intimate space in public conveyances. The basic tactic is to be as immobile as possible and, when part of the trunk or extremities touches another person, withdraw if possible. If this is not possible, the muscles in the affected areas are kept tense. For members of the non-contact group, it is taboo to relax and enjoy bodily contact with strangers! In crowded elevators the hands are kept at the side or used to steady the body by grasping a railing. The eyes are fixed on infinity and are not brought to bear on anyone for more than a passing glance.

It should be noted once more that American proxemic patterns for intimate distance are by no means universal. Even the rules governing such intimacies as touching others cannot be counted on to remain constant. Americans who have had an opportunity for considerable social interaction with Russians report that many of the features characteristic of American intimate distance are present in Russian social distance. However, Middle Eastern subjects in public places do not express the outraged reaction to being touched by strangers which one encounters in American subjects.

PERSONAL DISTANCE

"Personal distance" is the term originally used by Hediger (1955) to designate the distance consistently separating the members of non-contact species. It might be thought of as a small protective sphere or bubble that an organism maintains between itself and others.

Personal Distance—Close Phase (distance: one and a half to two and a half feet). The kinesthetic sense of closeness derives in part from the possibilities present in regard to what each participant can do to the other with his extremities. At this distance, one can hold or grasp the other person.

Visual distortion of the other's features is no longer apparent. However, there is noticeable feedback from the muscles that control the eyes. The reader can experience this himself if he will look at an object eighteen inches to three feet away, paying particular attention to the muscles around his eyeballs. He can feel the pull of these muscles as they hold the two eyes on a single point so that the image of each eye stays in register. Pushing gently with the tip of the finger on the surface of the lower eyelid so that the eyeball is displaced will illustrate clearly the work these muscles perform in maintaining a single coherent image. A visual angle of 15 degrees takes in another person's upper or lower face, which is seen with exceptional clarity. The planes and roundness of the face are accentuated; the nose projects and the ears recede; fine hair of the face, eyelashes, and pores is clearly visible. The three-dimensional quality of objects is particularly pronounced. Objects have roundness, substance, and form unlike that perceived at any other distance. Surface textures are also very prominent and are clearly differentiated from each other. Where people stand in relation to each other signals their relationship, or how they feel toward each other, or both. A wife can stay inside the circle of her husband's close personal zone with impunity. For another woman to do so is an entirely different story.

Personal Distance—Far Phase (distance: two and a half to four feet). Keeping someone at "arm's length" is one way of expressing the far phase of personal distance. It extends from a point that is just outside easy touching distance by one person to a point where two people can touch fingers if they extend both arms. This is the limit of physical domination in the very real sense. Beyond it, a person cannot easily "get his hands on" someone else. Subjects of personal interest and involvement can be discussed at this distance. Head size is perceived as normal and details of the other person's features are clearly visible. Also easily seen are fine details of skin, gray hair, "sleep" in the eye, stains on teeth, spots, small wrinkles, or dirt on clothing. Foveal vision covers only an area the size of the tip of the nose or one eye, so that the gaze must wander around the face (*where the eye is directed* is strictly a matter of cultural conditioning). Fifteen-degree clear vision covers the upper *or* lower face, while 180-degree peripheral vision takes in the hands and the whole body of a seated person. Movement of the hands is detected, but fingers can't be counted. The voice level is moderate. No body heat is perceptible. While olfaction is not normally present for Americans, it is for a great many other people who use colognes to create an olfactory bubble. Breath odor can sometimes be detected at this distance, but Americans are generally trained to direct the breath away from others.

SOCIAL DISTANCE

The boundary line between the far phase of personal distance and the close phase of social distance marks, in the words of one subject, the "limit of domination." Intimate visual detail in the face is not perceived, and nobody touches or expects to touch another person unless there is some special effort. Voice level is normal for Americans. There is little change between the far and close phases, and conversations can be overheard at a distance of up to twenty feet. I have observed that in overall loudness, the American voice at these distances is below that of the Arab, the Spaniard, the South Asian Indian, and the Russian, and somewhat above that of the English upper class, the Southeast Asian, and the Japanese.

Social Distance—Close Phase (distance: four to seven feet). Head size is perceived as normal; as one moves away from the subject, the foveal area of the eye can take in an ever-increasing amount of the person. At four feet, a one-degree visual angle covers an area of a little more than one eye. At seven feet the area of sharp focus extends to the nose and parts of both eyes; or the whole mouth, one eye, and the nose are sharply seen. Many Americans shift their gaze back and forth from eye to eye or from eyes to mouth. Details of skin texture and hair are clearly perceived. At a 60-degree visual angle, the head, shoulders, and upper trunk are seen at a distance of four feet; while the same sweep includes the whole figure at seven feet.

Impersonal business occurs at this distance, and in the close phase there is more involvement than in the distant phase. People who work together tend to use close social distance. It is also a very common distance for people who are attending a casual social gathering. To stand and look down at a person at this distance has a domineering effect, as when a man talks to his secretary or receptionist.

Social Distance—Far Phase (distance: seven to twelve feet). This is the distance to which people move when someone says, "Stand away so I can look at you." Business and social discourse conducted at the far end of social distance has a more formal character than if it occurs inside the close phase. Desks in the offices of important people are large enough to hold visitors at the far phase of social distance. Even in an office with standard-size desks, the chair opposite is eight or nine feet away from the man behind the desk. At the far phase of social distance, the finest details of the face, such as the capillaries in the eyes, are lost. Otherwise, skin texture, hair, condition of teeth, and condition of clothes are all readily visible. None of my subjects mentioned heat or odor from another person's body as detectable at this distance. The full figure—with a good deal of space around it—is encompassed in a 60-degree glance. Also, at around twelve feet, feedback from the eye muscles used to hold the eyes inward on a single spot falls off rapidly. The eyes and the mouth of the other person are seen in the area of sharpest vision. Hence, it is not necessary to shift the eyes to take in the whole face. During conversations of any significant length it is more important to maintain visual contact at this distance than it is at closer distances.

Proxemic behavior of this sort is culturally conditioned and entirely arbitrary. It is also binding on all concerned. To fail to hold the other person's eye is to shut him out and bring conversation to a halt, which is why people who are conversing at this distance can be observed craning their necks and leaning from side to side to avoid intervening obstacles. Similarly, when one person is seated and the other is standing, prolonged visual contact at less than ten or twelve feet tires the neck muscles and is generally avoided by subordinates who are sensitive to their employer's comfort. If, however, the status of the two parties is reversed so that the subordinate is seated, the other party may often come closer.

At this distant phase, the voice level is noticeably louder than for the close phase, and it can usually be heard easily in an adjoining room if the door is open. Raising the voice or shouting can have the effect of reducing social distance to personal distance.

A proxemic feature of social distance (far phase) is that it can be used to insulate or screen people from each other. This distance makes it possible for them to continue to work in the presence of another person without appearing to be rude. Receptionists in offices are particularly vulnerable as most employers expect double duty: answering questions, being polite to callers, as well as typing. If the receptionist is less than ten feet from another person, even a stranger, she will be sufficiently involved to be virtually compelled to converse. If she has more space, however, she can work quite freely without having to talk. Likewise, husbands returning from work often find themselves sitting and relaxing, reading the paper at ten or more feet from their wives, for at this distance a couple can engage each other briefly and disengage at will. Some men discover that their wives have arranged the furniture back-to-back—a favorite sociofugal device of the cartoonist Chick Young, creator of "Blondie." The back-to-back seating arrangement is an appropriate solution to minimum space because it is possible for two people to stay uninvolved if that is their desire.

PUBLIC DISTANCE

Several important sensory shifts occur in the transition from the personal and social distances to public distance, which is well outside the circle of involvement.

Public Distance—Close Phase (distance: twelve to twenty-five feet). At twelve feet an alert subject can take evasive or defensive action if threatened. The distance may even cue a vestigial but subliminal form of flight reaction. The voice is loud but not full-volume. Linguists have observed that a careful choice of words and phrasing of sentences as well as grammatical or syntactic shifts occur at this distance. Martin Joos's choice of the term "formal style" is appropriately descriptive: "Formal texts … demand advance planning … The speaker is correctly said to think on his feet" (1962). The angle of sharpest vision (one degree) covers the whole face. Fine details of the skin and eyes are no longer visible. At sixteen feet, the body begins to lose its roundness and to look flat. The color of the eyes begins to be imperceivable; only the white of the eye is visible. Head size is perceived as considerably under life-size. The 15-degree lozenge-shaped area of clear vision covers the faces of two people at twelve feet, while 60-degree scanning includes the whole body with a little space around it. Other persons present can be seen peripherally.

Public Distance—Far Phase (distance; twenty-five feet or more). Thirty feet is the distance that is automatically set around important public figures. An excellent example occurs in Theodore H. White's *The Making of the President 1960* when John F. Kennedy's nomination became a certainty. White is describing the group at the "hide-away cottage" as Kennedy entered:

> Kennedy loped into the cottage with his light, dancing step, as young and lithe as springtime, and called a greeting to those who stood in his way. Then he seemed to slip from them as he descended the steps of the split-level cottage to a corner where his brother Bobby and brother-in-law Sargent Shriver were chatting, waiting for him. The others in the room surged forward on impulse to join him. Then they halted. A distance of perhaps 30 feet separated them from him, but it was impassable. They stood apart, these older men of long-established power, and watched him. He turned after a few minutes, saw them watching him, and whispered to his brother-in-law. Shriver now crossed the separating space to invite them over. First Averell Harriman; then Dick Daley; then Mike DiSalle, then, one by one, let them all congratulate him. Yet no one could pass the little open distance between him and them uninvited, because there was this thin separation about him, and the knowledge they were there not as his patrons but as his clients. They could come by invitation only, for this might be a President of the United States (1961. p. 171).

The usual public distance is not restricted to public figures but can he used by anyone on public occasions. There are certain adjustments that must be made, however. Most actors know that at thirty or more feet the subtle shades of meaning conveyed by the normal voice are lost as are the details of facial expression and movement. Not only the voice but everything else must be exaggerated or amplified. Much of the nonverbal part of the communication shifts to gestures and body stance. In addition, the tempo of the voice drops, words are enunciated more clearly, and there are stylistic changes as well. Martin Joos's *frozen style* is characteristic: "Frozen style is for people who are to remain strangers" (1962). The whole man may be seen as quite small and he is perceived in a setting. Foveal vision takes in more and more of the man until he is entirely within the small circle of sharpest vision. At which point—when people look like ants—contact with them as human beings fades rapidly. The 60-degree cone of vision takes in the setting while peripheral vision has as its principal function the altering of the individual to movement at the side.

WHY "FOUR" DISTANCES?

In concluding this description of distance zones common to our sample group of Americans a final word about classification is in order. It may well be asked: Why are there four zones, not six or eight? Why set up any zones at all? How do we know that this classification is appropriate? How were the categories chosen?

The scientist has a basic need for a classification system, one that is as consistent as possible with the phenomena under observation and one which will hold up long enough to be useful. Behind every classification system lies a theory or hypothesis about the nature of the data and their basic patterns of organization. The hypothesis behind the proxemic classification system is this: it is in the nature of animals, including man, to exhibit behavior which we call territoriality. In so doing, they use the senses to distinguish between one space or distance and another. The specific distance chosen depends on the transaction; the relationship of the interacting individuals, how they feel, and what they are doing. The four-part classification system used here is based on observations of both animals and men. Birds and apes exhibit intimate, personal, and social distances just as man does.

Western man has combined consultative and social activities and relationships into one distance set and has added the public figure and the public relationship. "Public" relations and "public" manners as the Europeans and Americans practice them are different from those in other parts of the world. There are implicit obligations to treat total strangers in certain prescribed ways. Hence, we find four principal categories of relationships (intimate, personal, social, and public) and the activities and spaces associated with them. In other parts of the world, relationships tend to fall into other patterns, such as the family/non-family pattern common in Spain and Portugal and their former colonies or the caste and outcast system of India. Both the Arabs and the Jews also make sharp distinctions between people to whom they are related and those to whom they are not. My work with Arabs leads me to believe that they employ a system for the organization of informal space which is very different from what I observed in the United States. The relationship of the Arab peasant or fellah to his sheik or to God is not a public relationship. It is close and personal without intermediaries.

Until recently man's space requirements were thought of in terms of the actual amount of air displaced by his body. The fact that man has around him as extensions of his personality the zones described earlier has generally been overlooked. Differences in the zones—in fact their very existence—became apparent only when Americans began interacting with foreigners who organize their senses differently so that what was intimate in one culture might be personal or even public in another. Thus for the first time the American became aware of his own spatial envelopes, which he had previously taken for granted.

The ability to recognize these various zones of involvement and the activities, relationships, and emotions associated with each has now become extremely important. The world's populations are crowding into cities, and builders and speculators are packing people into vertical filing boxes—both offices and dwellings. If one looks at human beings in the way that the early slave traders did, conceiving of their space requirements simply in terms of the limits of the body, one pays very little attention to the effects of crowding. If, however, one sees man surrounded by a series of invisible bubbles which have measurable dimensions, architecture can be seen in a new light. It is then possible to conceive that people can be cramped by the spaces in which they have to live and work. They may even find themselves forced into behavior, relationships, or emotional outlets that are overly stressful. Like gravity, the influence of two bodies on each other is inversely proportional not only to the square of the distance but possibly even the cube of the distance between them. When stress increases, sensitivity to crowding rises—people get more on edge—so that more and more space is required as less and less is available.

REFERENCES:

Ariès, P. *Centuries of childhood*. New York: Knopf, 1962.

Goffman, E. *The presentation of self in everyday life*. Garden City, N.Y.: Doubleday, 1959.

Hall. E. T. *The silent language*. Garden City, N.Y.: Doubleday, 1959.

Hediger, H. *Studies of the psychology and behavior of captive animals in zoos and circuses*. London: Butterworth, 1955.

Joos, M. The five clocks. *International Journal of American Linguistics,* 1962, 28, 127–133.

Mumford, L. *The city in history*. New York: Harcourt, Brace, 1961.

Osmond, H. Function as the basis of psychiatric ward design. *Mental Hospitals* (Architectural Supplement), 1957, 8, 23–29.

Sommer, E. Studies in personal space. *Sociometry,* 1959. 22, 247–290.

White, T. H. *The making of the president 1960*. New York: Atheneum, 1961.

6   Signs of Life: Symbols in the American City

Robert Venturi and John Rauch

This article examines environmental meaning in the American suburb. It examines the physiognomy or exterior appearance of buildings, applied signs, and the location as factors contributing to formation of meaning.

What makes a house look like a house, a school look like a school, or a bank like a bank? What makes a gasoline station look like a good neighbor? *Signs of Life: Symbols in the American City* is intended to show that the elements of architecture have symbolic meaning and give messages about the environment that make it comprehensible and therefore usable by people in their daily lives. For example, the flashing electric sign on Route 66 tells us specifically EAT HERE and its design may suggest the kind of eating available—family dining, soft-light sophisticated, etc.—but off the main highway, suburbia's curving roads and tended lawns, its pitched-roof houses, Colonial doorways and shuttered windows, tell us without need of signs that here is a community that values tradition, pride of ownership and the rural life.

Signs of Life is an attempt to survey the pluralist aesthetic of the American city and its suburbs, and to understand what the urban environment means to people, through an analysis of its symbols, their sources and their antecedents. The focus is particularly on the twentieth-century commercial strip and suburban sprawl because in these environments the tradition of the use of symbolism in architecture has continued from the nineteenth-century city, whereas in areas more directly controlled by architects that tradition has been confused or broken by modern architects' attempts to eradicate historical and symbolic association and decoration from architecture.

Signs of Life argues that:
    —The rich pervasion of symbols and signs that existed in the historical city continues in the city of today, although in different form.
    —There is a ubiquity of symbols and signs in our urban environment that we do not acknowledge.
    —The "ordinary" symbols and signs of the commercial and residential environments are significant in our daily lives.
    —In learning to understand our symbols and signs we come to understand better ourselves and our landscape; this is a necessary prelude to improving that landscape.

Venturi and Rauch, *Signs of Life: Symbols in the American City*. Copyright © 1976 by Aperture, Inc. Permission to reprint granted by the publisher.

82 ✹ Environmental Design Research

Photograph by Stephen Shore

THE HOME

The physical elements of housing—the roads, houses, roofs, lawns and front doors—serve practical purposes such as giving access and shelter, but they also serve as means of self-expression for urban and suburban residents.

Winding roads, romantic roof lines, garden ornaments, colonial front doors and coach lanterns are decorative elements with symbolic overtones that residents use to communicate with others about themselves. The communication is mainly about social status, social aspirations, personal identity, individual freedom, and nostalgia for another time or place. The symbolic subject matter of residential decoration comes from history, rural life, patriotism and the estates of the rich. Suburban neighborhoods and individual houses—and particularly the decorations people add to their houses and yards once they occupy them—directly reflect these preoccupations. The housing content of TV ads, home journals, auto ads, *New Yorker* cartoons and mail-order catalogs echoes the same themes because the mass media attempt to reach their markets by using residential symbols that trigger current social and personal aspirations.

Even with their overall order, row houses show great variation in doorways, windows and siding. Their symbolism may be Colonial, Art Deco, or Mediterranean. Photographs by Venturi and Rauch

Suburban housing symbolism, however, does not tell us why people live in suburbia or much about the problems they experience in suburbia; it merely tells us some of their aspirations while they are there. Moreover, although the mass media are an interesting source of information on group attitudes to housing, they should not be taken as the last word on personal and social values in the United States. Nevertheless, the use of symbolic decoration by Americans in and around their houses is an important clue to American attitudes because it is practiced by almost all social groups, by young and old, rich and poor, renters and owners, urbanites and suburbanites.

THE STRIP

The signs and billboards we see as we drive down Route 1 or Route 66 are mostly commercial advertisements. Their words and symbols attempt to inform and persuade the potential customer in the automobile. To be seen across vast distances and at high speeds, the big sign at the side of the road must leap out at the driver, to direct him or her to the store at the rear of the parking lot. The products in the store are also advertised on the highway, on billboards sponsored by their national manufacturers. On the suburban strip, buildings are small and cheap, signs are large and expensive. The graphic sign in space has become the architecture of the highway landscape.

Most strip signs are composed of "high readers" that communicate eye-catching and evocative images, and "low readers" that give specific information, OVER A BILLION SOLD, and directions, PARK HERE. Seen from afar, the high reader suggests we slow down; then the low reader tells us why we should stop and where to go. The McDonald's arches on the strip and the wagon wheel on the suburban front lawn serve much the same purpose: each identifies its owner and refers symbolically to the owner's aspiration, commercial in one case, personal and communal in the other. However, McDonald's glowing, soaring, parabolic arches have become a national symbol. They signify the same hamburger wherever you are and suggest a familiar location for fast food for the traveler in any town. Other classic strip building types such as the gas station and the motel succeed in the same way by their familiarity and serve to identify their surroundings.

Commercial highway signs and billboards engender in the public a range of feelings from loathing to liking. Few people want neon on their residential streets; most people appreciate the convenience of the local commerce that the signs support and of the vast parking lots and highway systems that require signs to function. If the strip is not "beautiful" in the accepted sense, it is certainly vital, an organized chaos perhaps, and probably more fun to be in than some carefully designed urban plazas that no one visits. Artists may love the strip and preservationists may loathe it, but urban planners and designers have to understand how the strip works if they are to make sensible prescriptions for suburbia.

THE STREET: WELCOME, FREE ASPIRIN, ASK US ANYTHING, STYLISH STOUTS, SURF, CITY HALL, ONE WAY, STOP.

All cities communicate messages—functional, symbolic and persuasive—to people as they move about on the street. Three message systems exist: the heraldic (signs in windows and on buildings), the physiognomic (messages given by the faces of the buildings—the columns and pediments of a Greek Revival bank) and the locational (the *corner* store, the railroad station located at the *end* of Main Street).

These systems are closely related in the city. For example, City Hall has broad stairs, a monumental entrance, a tower and flags to herald its importance and evoke associations with the past. The sign that says CITY HALL evokes a Roman past through the style of its lettering. City Hall may be located on a public square, but it may as easily sit on a city block cheek to jowl with small-scale commercial uses. In either case, City Hall's civic importance will be suggested symbolically through the use of a "civic" architectural style and applied civic symbolic decoration.

Relations and combinations in city streets between signs and buildings, architecture and symbolism, civic pride and honky-tonk, express a messy vitality and produce an unexpected unity. It is not an obvious or easy unity but one derived from the complexity of city life "which maintains, but only just maintains, a control over the clashing elements which compose it. Chaos is very near; its nearness, but its avoidance, gives … force." (August Heckscher, 1962)

This exhibition at the Renwick Gallery endeavors to document sprawl, strip and city in relation to each other and to the nineteenth-century city. It is part of a broader effort among social critics and architects to understand American architectural tastes and to redefine the role of the architect. *Signs of Life* indicates the need to study urban environments, especially unloved "sprawl" environments and to understand the symbolic meanings people ascribe to or invest in them. The exhibition points to a radical discrepancy between the needs, tastes, and preferences of the professionals—the urban designers, architects and planners, and the decisionmakers whose policies they inform—and the people whose lives they influence.

The grandeur that was Rome: the spirit, if not the style, of the strip approaches that of the late Roman Forum with its eclectic accumulations. Photograph by Debora Marum

Decorated house fronts are suburban billboards with flags and eagles, foundation planting, doors, porches, roofs and walls, windows, grills, shutters and ornaments as parts of the symbolic content. Photograph by Stephen Shore

"To own one's own home is a physical expression of individualism, of enterprise, of independence, and of freedom of spirit." Photograph by Stephen Shore

Words and symbols, rather than forms, dominate the urban space. Photograph by John Baeder

Photograph by Stephen Shore

The American bungalow is mainly a Southern and Western phenomenon. It is small, almost rural in scale, and is to the Western city what the row house is to the Eastern. Photograph by Stephen Shore

The rich presence of signs and symbols that existed in the historical city still persists, although in an altered form. Photograph by Stephen Shore

The billboard has become the architecture of the highway and the strip. Photograph by Stephen Shore

On the highway, the symbol is more important than the building. Photograph by Stephen Shore

On Main Street, the buildings of one era are transformed by the signs of the next. Photograph by Stephen Shore

Each man's home is his castle. Photograph by Stephen Shore

The big sign and the little building is the rule of Route 66. Photograph by Stephen Shore

7 Environmental Messages

Franklin Becker

This chapter applies communication theory to interpreting the built environment. Rather than ask about cause and effect models of the relationship between humans and their environments—which cause which?—communication theory joins the theory of symbolic interaction in positing a model of mutual expression and reinforcement.

We all consciously look for nonverbal clues in buildings, landscapes, and interiors, for we know that these clues have something to say about the status, prestige, and other values of those who own them.

J. Ruesch and W. Kees, *Nonverbal Communication*[1]

From fur coats and cars, jewelry and houses, hair styles and hair length, recreation vehicles and cameras, we infer that people are intelligent, warm, creative, wealthy, trustworthy, and solid citizens—or poor, untrustworthy, weak, and immoral. We use these same physical cues to measure our own identity and self-esteem. Initially ice hockey players refused to wear protective head gear because they felt it reflected a lack of courage and diminished the "toughness" of their sport. Elderly persons have preferred uncomfortable chairs to ones designed especially for them because the "better" chairs were institutional looking. Low-income parents have had a playground built by their children with surplus materials razed because it was made of "junk" and symbolized second-class citizenship to them.

Creating buildings and interior spaces that are functional—they meet government codes for safety and sanitation, or they allow certain transactions to be fulfilled with the minimum of effort, or they "work" in the sense that a stove will heat water or brakes will stop a car—is absolutely necessary—and insufficient. To create environments that not only "work" but that *will be used* and are rewarding to those who inhabit and use them, designers must understand the kinds of associations different people make to buildings, furniture, and other design elements and how

Franklin Becker, "Environmental Messages," from *Housing Messages*, pp. 1–14. Copyright © 1977 by Dowden, Hutchinson & Ross. Permission to reprint granted by the publisher.

these associations and interpretations of physical cues affect peoples' feelings of self-esteem, their social standing in the community, and their relationships to their family, friends, and neighbors.

This book explores the social and psychological implications of common physical cues—the kind and quality of materials used in a building, the level of maintenance, the shape of a roof, the arrangement of dwelling units—as symbols of status, competency, respectability, identity, caring, and other everyday concerns.

Design of all types—graphics, interior, architecture, product—has long emphasized the way in which the selection and arrangement of particular images and associations affects people's attitudes and behavior. But design, in the sense of creating images through the manipulation of space, materials, and objects, is not the sole prerogative of experts such as architects. Most people are designers in the sense that they *send* their own environmental messages through their use, selection, and arrangement of objects, furnishings, and space. In a pluralistic society where there is no single unifying set of values, philosophy, or religion (with the possible exception of personal economic gain), the physical environment, as a reflection of an underlying social organization, inevitably presents contrasting and conflicting images. The kinds of conflicts E. T. Hall has described as a consequence of misinterpretation of nonverbal attitudes communicated through body position and distance may be occurring around us every day as a function of misinterpretation of nonverbal messages communicated through the physical environment;[2] or, ironically, as a result of agreement about *what* the environmental messages are, but with the social meaning and impact on the groups or individuals associated with the environmental message being very different than it is for groups who may form their identity by *not* being associated with the same physical cues.

Consciously and unconsciously we interpret our physical environment in a variety of ways. We try to understand the motivations and intentions of those who designed it, the ways in which it affects our behavior and influences our emotional reactions, and what its symbolic meaning is within a particular context. Lee Rainwater describes this type of meta-message with respect to public housing:

> The physical evidence of trash, poor plumbing, and the stink that goes with it, rats and other vermin, deepen their feelings of being moral outcasts. Their physical world is telling them that they are inferior and bad just as effectively perhaps as do their human interactions.[3]

The discrepancy in values between those who authorize, plan, and design the buildings and those who live in and use them is often tremendous in public housing. More affluent segments of the housing market have the opportunity to select from a number of alternatives those that best reflect and enhance their own sense of worth and identity; or, if they buy a home, they can modify it in a way that reflects their own perceived image and self-esteem. Users of public housing and other residential institutions such as dormitories, hospitals, and prisons have many fewer options, and generally they must make do with what they are provided by government or nonprofit private agencies.

Public housing like mental institutions, dormitories, prisons, and other residential institutions managed by one group for the "good" of another can be characterized by the generally paternalistic and negative images they convey to their inhabitants and the occupants' feelings of being neglected, ignored, and treated impersonally. In the context of a therapeutic environment for autistic

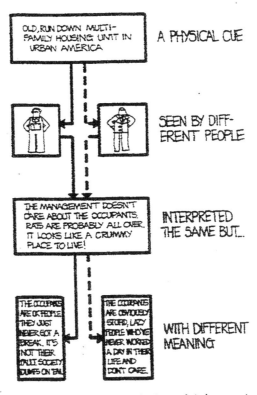

vermin, deepen their feelings of being moral outcasts. Their physical world is telling them that they are inferior and bad just as effectively perhaps as do their human interactions.³

children, Bruno Bettelheim has written of the importance of what he calls "silent messages," which convey through the minute details of the physical environment the staff's concern for the patients' well-being. He makes the point, often overlooked by designers and administrators concerned with the overall design or form of a building, that an institution's intentions are conveyed by the smallest details of the staff's behavior and the physical environment. The occupants spend a great deal of time trying to interpret the staff's attitudes toward them, given in the form of these nonverbal messages. Bettelheim describes autistic children who have a poor opinion of their body and the way it functions and the importance of the bathroom in demonstrating to these patients, nonverbally through its furnishings, the esteem the staff and institutions hold of his or her body. Bettelheim feels that "eventually patients may be able to model their feelings for the body's worthwhileness, and on this basis their self-respect, on the image of it conveyed through the bathroom design and furnishings."⁴

Just as mental patients are often surrounded by conditions and exposed to messages telling them that the administrators of the environment in which they live expect—and hence fear—that they may act destructively (by locked doors, for instance), so do public-housing projects with their hard finishes and supposedly indestructible surfaces and lack of amenities convey the administration's lack of trust in the residents.

Ruesch and Kees have called attempts to influence without words "object language" and defined it as "all intentional and nonintentional displays of material things, such as implements, machines, art objects, architectural structures, and—last but not least—the human body, and whatever clothes or covers it."⁵ The material aspects of words, and the style and substance of the letters and numerals, also function symbolically. Polished bronze numerals on a solid oak door signify something different about the inhabitants of that space, and the way they wish to be perceived than does a scrawled sign on a cracked and peeling plywood door. We use these object symbols to set the scene for social encounters. Ruesch and Kees note that in a democracy, where all individuals are equal, objects have the useful function of announcing inequality that "for reason of taste and conformity, cannot be expressed in words. ... These hazards may be circumvented by the use of object language, which can operate 24 hours a day, is accessible to both rich and poor, literate and illiterate, and may be visible at a considerable distance." Vance Packard became famous chronicling how Americans attempt to differentiate themselves from their neighbors through the purchase of cars, homes, clothes, appliances, and other "extensions of our personality" in a never-ending attempt to enhance status relative to their neighbors, or to at least "keep up with the Joneses."[6]

The way in which the physical environment can symbolically represent management's attitudes toward employees was unexpectedly illustrated in an industrial context many years ago in a study widely known as the Hawthorne study (named after the location where the study occurred). In 1939 Roethlisberger and Dickson studied the effects of different environmental conditions on worker productivity. They found that productivity increased linearly, regardless of the type of environmental change. Increasing lighting increased productivity, as did decreasing lighting. Providing piped-in music increased productivity as did eliminating it.[7] These findings were considered the result of a faulty research design that failed to control for spurious effects, and the term "Hawthorne effect" is now used to describe observed changes in behavior and attitudes that are a function of uncontrolled (and sometimes unknown) variables. Robert Sommer has suggested that rather than demonstrating the spurious effects of environmental changes, the study demonstrated the fallacy of a simple deterministic model of behavior.[8] The environmental changes did make a difference, but their effect was a function of the ways in which individuals interpreted these changes and the significance they attributed to them. Seeing is believing, and the concrete evidence that management was concerned about the employees' environment conveyed positive attitudes of the management toward its employees in a way that words could not. Through the changes in the environmental conditions, management unintentionally reinforced the employees' own sense of worth and value.

SELF-CONCEPT AND PHYSICAL OBJECTS AS SYMBOLS

The notion that individuals define, reinforce, and extend their sense of self through the acquisition and display of physical objects is not new. At the turn of the century, William James, writing about sources of self-esteem, defined the self as

> the sum total of all that he can call his, not only his body and his psychic processes, but his clothes and his house, his wife and children, his ancestors and his friends, his reputation and works, his lambs and horses, his yacht and bank account. All things give him the same emotions. If they wax and prosper, he feels triumphant; if they dwindle and die away, he feels cast down—not necessarily in the same degree for each thing—but in much the same way for all.[9]

Strauss has written that a man's possessions are a fair index of what he is, providing the observers take the trouble to distinguish what a man owns by chance and to what he is really endeared.[10]

He notes that it is no accident that men mark their symbolic movements—from one social class to another, for instance—by discarding old clothes, houses, furnishings, friends, even wives. The significance of possessions and properties is often revealed by reactions to their loss: people not only lose their property but also their sense of direction and purpose in life.

Vance Packard[11] and William H. Whyte[12] have also noted the "object value" that a spouse, cars, homes, and addresses have for corporation executives and how the extent and kind of these "objects" can influence an executive's career and advancement. These possessions become public symbols of and represent one's values, status, and degree of success and, as such, both inform others of one's identity and, at the same time, reinforce one's own sense of self.

Although the judgment of our self-esteem and our identity may be subjective and personal, it develops through our interactions with others and is highly influenced by others' impressions of us and their reactions to our behavior and our values as expressed, often to a large extent, by displays of possessions.

Within the above context, goods of a variety of sorts, from automobiles to homes, can be viewed as "social tools" or symbols that function both as a means of communication among individuals and as a significant reference. Our possessions, as much as our gestures and body orientation and social distance, are a form of nonverbal communication that represents us to others in particular ways. They are symbols, things that stand for or suggest something else. They may do this by reason of relationship, association, convention, even accident; but for any kind of an object to serve as a symbol, it must have a shared meaning for at least two people and for all the people with whom one desires to communicate.

In effect, the process of developing shared meanings is a classification process where objects are placed in relation to other objects. The meaning of things lies in the perspective, not in the thing, and the way in which things are classed together reveals the perspective of the classifier.[13] By defining what the object is, we arouse a set of expectations toward the object and those associated with it, and these expectations function as a guide or prescription for appropriate behavior. Fraternity initiation rites where new members are forced to eat "worms" that are, in fact, cold spaghetti are a vivid example of how our reactions to an object are conditioned by our classification of it. The same object may have very different meanings for different individuals or groups, eliciting negative reactions where positive ones were anticipated. We project our understandings of a meaning of a possession or an activity onto others, and when the definitions of meaning only partially overlap, misunderstanding and conflict are imminent.

SYMBOLS AND ENVIRONMENTAL DESIGN

When symbols have been considered in relationship to environmental design, the discussion has usually been restricted to the analysis of monumental buildings and to special buildings within this tradition, particularly religious and civic. The importance of symbols in the Byzantine church seen as icon, the mosque and its court in Iran as symbol of paradise, and the Roman pantheon as the ideal dome of heaven are well recognized, but we know much less about the symbolism and meaning of ordinary architecture.[14] Most studies of symbolism are distinguished by the focus on a special *place* that is distinguished from the spaces around it. These studies do not attempt to analyze other forms of organized space that are more utilitarian in character than the frequently scrutinized churches and public buildings. Yet artifacts, including buildings and settlements, are one way of making concrete the immaterial nature of values and norms of a society.[15] What becomes significant in a study of building form and function as types of environmental messages is that the buildings may be expressing a set of values and objectives different from and inconsistent with those held by the persons inhabiting the space, however congruent they may be with those held by that part of society responsible for creating these structures.

Given our penchant for studying the past, the distant, and the exotic, it is not surprising that we are more aware of how buildings in primitive culture express underlying values and beliefs than we are about the same processes in our own society. For example, writing about cultural influences on house forms, Rapoport suggests that for the Dogon and Bambara tribes of Mali every object and social event has a symbolic as well as a utilitarian function.

> Houses, household objects, and chairs all have this symbolic quality, and the Dogon civilization, otherwise relatively poor, has several thousand symbolic elements. The frame plots and whole landscape of the Dogon reflect this cosmic order. Their villages are built in pairs to represent heaven and earth, and fields are cleared in spirals because the world has been created spirally. The villages are laid out in the way parts of the body lie with respect to each other, while the house of the Dogon, or paramount sheath, is a model of the universe as a smaller scale. Multi-storied houses are the prerogative of the highest religious and political leaders and are symbols of power, representations of them being used for many purposes; for example, as masks frighten away the soul of the dead.[16]

The forms of buildings become signs that reflect the preconceptions of those who determined them, with these forms reflecting the inner life, actions, and social conceptions of the occupants. The social meaning of a building becomes understandable only within what Gregor Paulsson has described as their "symbol milieu," where all objects gain meaning and are interpreted in the context of their association with human actions and values.[17]

In the earliest civilizations, for example, it was impossible to distinguish between practical and religious (magical) meanings. The first permanent huts in Sumer were built by bending rushes without removing the roots from the ground. The rushes were tied together at the top, and arches formed in this way were connected with horizontal sticks. The resulting hut had its roots in the ground and hence was unified with the element from which life gets its nourishment. These primitive building forms resulted from the need for protection, and physical, as well as social and cultural, aspects were unified in this need. These first huts offered protection against a capricious and dangerous physical environment, provided security by being a visual expression of the group, and at the same time protected against hostile forces by collaborating with the life-giving forces.[18]

The same process of differentiation and cultural symbolization occurs currently, but with the type of meaning of the symbols specific to our culture and particular groups within it. Places of work generally reflect not only their functional purpose but are differentiated according to underlying concepts and values. Hospitals must not only meet certain sanitation criteria; they must also *appear* to be clean and sanitary. The image of the hospital and healing can be as important a healing element as the level of skill and knowledge actually available. A design office that does not appear "architectonic" may lessen a potential customer's confidence in the firm's architectural skills. Our buildings may lack religious symbolism, but we are not a very religious society. We are a consumer-oriented, status-conscious society, and if we look for symbols representing these values, goals, and aspirations, we are likely to find them. Symbolism in environmental design is alive; it simply is so much around us we take it for granted.

SYMBOLISM IN ORDINARY ARCHITECTURE

By ordinary architecture, I mean buildings that are intended for common uses by the general public. These can include institutions, such as schools and dormitories, as well as public multifamily housing developments and single-family detached houses. The definition excludes buildings intended to be monumental, such as museums, civic buildings, and many churches. Most ordinary buildings are designed by nonarchitects, although not all of them. Le Pessac, a housing development designed by Le Corbusier in France, is ordinary architecture by the above definition because it was not intentionally monumental and it is used by common people for ordinary purposes.[19] It is symbolic, however, in that the modern design, typified by the flat roofs uncharacteristic of that region of France, were deliberately representative of a new industrial era and were consciously intended to break with tradition. Levittown is also ordinary architecture within this definition, with as explicit a symbolism as Le Corbusier's but following a very different direction: it attempts to reflect current and traditional values and images of "home" rather than creating new images. Much of ordinary architecture, like schools, incorporates no *deliberate* symbolism and is considered almost purely functional. Yet the most functional buildings and environments can be highly symbolic, often in undesired and unexpected ways.

Interior space planning involving the selection and arrangement of furnishings is another example of how the physical environment is used to reflect underlying social norms and values by conveying messages about status, leadership, and appropriate role behavior. Sommer found that when visitors to a hospital setting were given free choice in sitting at rectangular tables that the leader of the group would take the seat at the head of the table, and the other participants would sit as close to the leader as possible.[20] These results are similar to Strodbeck and Hook's findings in a study of jury behavior that the person who sat at the head of the table was likely to be a person of managerial or executive rank; thus, existing leadership roles were reflected and reinforced by particular seating positions.[21] Sitting at the head of the table or standing at the front of the lecture room may make comfortable conversation difficult and increase the distance between the leader and other participants, but this symbolizes the differences among the participants and can be a positive attribute of the arrangement for those interested in maintaining role and status distinctions. The desire by others to eliminate such arrangements simply reveals how the values and perspectives of the observer affect the interpretation of physical cues.

The possibility of the same symbol, or manifestations of that symbol, being differently interpreted by groups with dissimilar values is, of course, constantly occurring. Architects and non-professionals, respectively, find single-family "ranch" houses either in "poor taste" or the perfect home. As Vance Packard says, the house advertised as "Early American Luxurious Ranch" is in Long Island, not the Texas panhandle.[22] People buy symbols. Most designers do not really quarrel with the symbol but with its lack of authenticity. People *without* recourse to an authentic Italian villa or genuine farmhouse still want a home that reinforces the status image they wish to project of themselves, and they can succeed if their audience consists of other persons like themselves who are, in a sense, also pretending. The accelerating market in "original" oil paintings produced in factories according to formula and available in a choice of colors reflects people's desire to share in the status of being able to patronize the arts.[23]

Those who can afford authentic original art and can recognize the difference between it and what they perceive as "schlock" art may feel that hanging an inexpensive reproduction of a "real" artist may be in better taste than displaying "factory" paintings, but those who buy "schlock" art are pleasing themselves and impressing their friends, not persons they only read about. Packard quotes a *Chicago Tribune* reporter who summed up the attitude toward houses: "You have to *look* successful. A house is a very tangible symbol of success … and the residence is regarded as a goal and a symbol, as well as something to live in."[24]

People who can afford them will buy antiques and original paintings; those who cannot will buy imitations. What becomes symbolic for those with the cash and the training is authenticity itself, and so architects and designers are continually found in restored old farmhouses and gristmills. The spaces are ample and pleasant, and so is the image of understanding quality and being creative and inventive enough to see the beauty in what others may have discarded. Among other groups of people *seemingly* mundane accessories and "features" are employed to help create desired images: air conditioners (when they were a novelty), television aerials (also when they were a novelty), certain types of fences, hedges, circular driveways—the list could go on and on. All of these objects have one characteristic in common: they proclaim to oneself, friends, and passers-by one's status, values, and tastes.

Even the most trivial and mundane objects can acquire the status of meaningful symbols, and they can have an important influence on people's perceptions, attitudes, and behavior. To design homes, or any other type of building, without attempting to understand the kinds of symbols that elicit desired reactions, rather than negative ones, and the range of people for whom these symbols are meaningful is to ignore a fundamental component of people's evaluations of buildings, objects, and urban landscapes. Yet this is what most institutional buildings, including public housing, dormitories, prisons, and offices, do.

In part, the failure of much of modern architecture to incorporate symbols that elicit the intended reactions can be related to the distinction, first made by Gibson, between the perceptual and associational worlds.[25] Gibson proposed a hierarchy of levels of meaning, ranging from concrete meanings—the ground, for instance—to activity-oriented meaning—the ground as something to be walked upon—through value and other meanings to the extreme of symbolic meaning—the ground as homeland. The perception of an object becomes more and more culturally determined as it possesses higher levels of meaning, and these meanings are learned, not given in the object themselves.

While the concrete and use meaning of objects and environments is shared by a wide variety of people, the higher levels of meaning are more personal and less predictable. Manipulating high-level meanings, those in the associations world, is extremely difficult compared to achieving lower-level meanings. We can build walls that everyone will recognize as barriers of sorts, but the meaning of these barriers, or even the association made to particular materials used to construct the walls, may differ considerably among different people. An expensive apartment complex designed by an internationally known architect has "unfinished" poured-concrete ceilings that reveal the framing and nails used to hold them. Some people cannot understand why they should pay high rent for a building that is not, and will never be "finished." Similarly, the housing development Le Corbusier designed in Le Pessac in France has been remodeled almost beyond recognition by successive generations of tenants who found the original flat roofs unsupportive of their notion of a proper house, and so changed them to the sloping roofs traditional in that region.[26] It is conceivable that the architect in both instances could have learned about these particular associations, shared by large segments of the population, before designing the buildings. In other cases it is not so easy. Associations change with time. Americans, in particular, have a tendency to reevaluate the meaning and desirability of buildings and structures rather rapidly. Old factories and warehouses that were considered eyesores and financial liabilities twenty years ago have within the past few years become valued for their strength, beauty of construction, and their history and have been restored and renovated into useful and highly successful shopping and business ventures.

The continuous change in the meaning and use of the same structures, as well as the creation of new buildings whose form expresses no particular function, has resulted in banks that look like colonial homes, restaurants that look like gas stations (and were before they were renovated), gas-stations that look like city halls, and apartment complexes that look like insurance buildings. This state of affairs contrasts sharply with primitive and "vernacular" architecture, where form and symbolic meaning are congruent; as a consequence, the environment is "legible"—it provides cues for expected behavior.[27] People know what behaviors are expected of them—what to wear, what to say, who is allowed in, and what services they can expect.

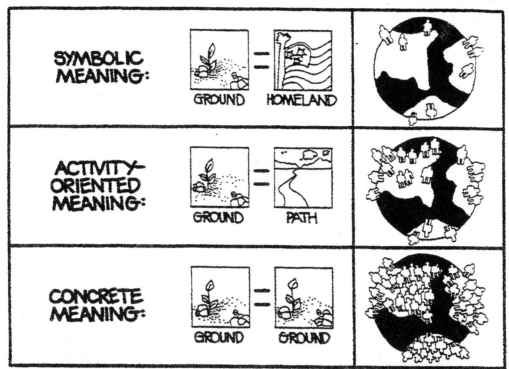

Vernacular architecture is characterized by a standard design "model" in which minor variations are allowed but in which what Boyd has called "featurism"—where the major stress is on differences and "features"—does not exist.[28] Ironically, some of the most despised buildings (by architects) and the most liked buildings by nonarchitects are chain food establishments (for example, McDonald's hamburgers), which are similar to traditional vernacular architecture in that the models used are totally consistent (look for the golden arch). Such building forms may make concrete some ideal (as Rapoport suggests design should), which involves the matching and evaluation of the physical design against an image of what is desirable. Architects such as Robert Venturi and Denise Scott Brown have gone as far as to promote these urban "vernacular" images as a basis for a new design aesthetic.[29]

As a means of avoiding the global implications of a concept like *image* and making its relationship to design more operational, Rapoport suggests dealing with *specifics,* which may allow us to get at differences in images and life-styles by starting with simpler, more molecular concepts, such as activities and (in architecture), functions. Rapoport uses cooking as an example. Any activity—eating, shopping, playing—can be divided into four components: (1) the activity proper; (2) a specific way of doing it; (3) additional, adjacent, or associated activities that become part of an activity system; and (4) symbolic aspects of the activity.

> The activity is one of converting raw food into cooked. The specific way may involve frying, roasting, or other means, the use of special kinds of utensils or ovens, squatting on the floor, etc. Associated activities may include socializing, exchanging information,

listening to music, etc. The symbolic meaning of cooking may be ritual, a way of acquiring status, a way of asserting some special social identity or membership in a group.

> It is the difference in these four aspects of apparently simple activities and functions which lead to specific forms of settings, differences in their relative importance, the amount of time spent in them, who was involved, etc.—in fact, all the kinds of things which affect design and form.[30]

It is the variability of the last two elements of the activity, the associated activities and the symbolic aspect, that leads to different physical forms. Groups may engage in the same activities, but because of the image of these activities and the meanings associated with them, different groups may consider some locations more appropriate than others for these activities and make inferences about people on the basis of *where* they engage in certain activities. For example, many middle-class men repair their own cars as do lower-class men, but middle-class men are generally able to engage in this hobby in the privacy of their garage, invisible to the public. Lower-class men generally do not have garages and so work on the street, in full public view and often with associated social activities being an important component of the activity. Use of public areas for such hobbies/social gatherings has different meanings for middle-class groups who feel such activities are appropriately done out of public view and may lead to negative labeling of one group or area by the other—"lower class," "slums"—and social conflict among groups.

Tenants in architect-designed apartments who personalize exterior spaces like porches and backyards with the materials and artifacts of their choosing (linoleum with brick pattern, for instance) may incur the wrath of management or disdain of nonresidents for whom such displays convey images of "bad taste" and "lower class." For the resident, they may convey completely opposite images of "home," "pride," and "belonging."[31]

We need to understand the meaning and associations different groups attach to different materials, artifacts, and physical arrangements and how these meanings support their own sense of self and identity. The design professions and the public generally have different images and evaluate environments differently, and within the public there are an almost infinite number of groups with different images. Yet although there are different images held by different groups, we need to explore the possibility that there are some basic images that are central to all groups. Pitched roofs, front and back distinctions, and extensive landscaping may be concepts that are universally accepted as desirable even if particular expressions are different. If the validity of such concepts can be established and incorporated into any design solution that is created, leaving the particular embellishment or "style" of the expression to the individual tastes of the occupants, the design may be more successful than it has been in the recent past.

The following chapters examine some of the images and associations different groups, particularly low- and moderate-income residents in public multifamily housing, hold of their environment and how their interpretation of "environmental messages" affects their sense of self-esteem and their attitudes toward their neighbors and management. It should become clear that people are not passive recipients of messages sent to them by others. They are active participants in structuring their own worlds. They use the physical environment to express their own values, attitudes, tastes, and identity.

REFERENCES

1. J. Ruesch and W. Kees, *Nonverbal Communication: Notes on the Visual Perception of Human Relations* (Berkeley, Calif.: University of California Press. 1956).
2. E. T. Hall, *The Silent Language* (New York: Doubleday & Company, 1959). See also V. Packard, *The Hidden Persuaders* (New York: Pocket Books, 1957).
3. L. Rainwater, "Fear and the House-as-Haven in the Lower Class," *Journal of the American Institute of the Planners* 32 (1956): 23–37.
4. B. Bettelheim, *Home for the Heart* (New York: Bantam Books, 1974).
5. Ruesch and Kees, *Nonverbal Communication.*
6. V. Packard, *The Status Seekers* (New York: David McKay Co. 1959).
7. J. F. Roethlisberger and W. J. Dickson, *Management and the Worker* (Cambridge: Harvard University Press, 1939).
8. R. Sommer, "Hawthorne Dogma," *Psychological Bulletin* 70 (1958): 582–598.
9. W. James, *Principles of Psychology* (New York: Holt, 1890). cited by S. Coopersmith. *The Antecedents of Self-Esteem* (San Francisco: W. H. Freeman and Company, 1967).
10. A. Strauss, *Mirrors and Masks: The Search for Identity* (Glencoe, Ill.: The Free Press, 1959).
11. Packard, *The Status Seekers.*
12. W. H. Whyte, *Organization Man* (New York: Doubleday & Company, 1956).
13. Strauss, *Mirrors and Masks.*
14. See A. Rapoport, "Symbolism and Environmental Design," *International Journal of Symbology* 1 (1970): 1–9. See also A. Rapoport, "Images, Symbols, and Popular Design," *International Journal of Symbology* 4 (1973): 1–12.
15. P. A. Sorokin, *Society Culture and Personality* (New York: Harper, 1947), Cited by Rapoport, *House Form and Culture.*
16. A. Rapoport, *House Form and Culture* (Englewood Cliffs, N J.: Prentice-Hall, 1969).
17. G. Pauisson, *The Study of Cities* (Kobenhavn, 1959), cited by C. Norberg-Schulz, *Intentions in Architecture* (Rome: Universitetsforiaget, 1963).
18. C. Norberg-Schulz, *Intentions in Architecture* (Rome: Universitetsforiaget, 1963).
19. P. Boudon, *Lived-In Architecture,* (Cambridge: The MIT Press, 1969).
20. R. Sommer, "Small Group Ecology," *Psychological Bulletin* 67 (1967): 145–152.
21. F. L. Strodtbeck and L. Hook, "The Social Dimensions of a Twelve Mart Jury Table," *Sociometry* 24 (1961): 397–415.
22. Packard, *The Status Seekers.*
23. D. Black, "Schlock Art 'For $2.50 You Don't Get Dewdrops,'" *The New York Times,* May 11, 1975.
24. Packard, *The Status Seekers.*
25. J. J. Gibson, *The Perception of the Visual World* (Boston: Houghton Mifflin, 1950), cited by Rapoport, "Symbolism and Environmental Design."
26. Boudon, *Lived-In Architecture.*
27. Rapoport, *House Form and Culture.*
28. Ibid.
29. R. Venturi, D. Brown, and S. Izenour. *Learning from Las Vegas* (Cambridge: The MIT Press, 1972).
30. Rapoport, *House Form and Culture.*
31. F. D. Becker, *Design for Living: The Residents' View of Multifamily Housing* (Ithaca, N.Y.: Center for Urban Development Research, Cornell University. 1974).

8 Does Post-Modernism Communicate?

Linda Groat and David Canter

Two environmental psychologists set out to test scientifically claims made by post-modernist architects that their architecture succeeds in communicating better than modernist architecture. They used photographic elicitation by selecting published buildings in the United States and England. While the detailed discussion of methods is very useful, their finding that twenty architects and twenty accountants recognized different meanings in the photographs used to interview them may result from factors that they did not control for, including whether the architects were already familiar with these well publicized buildings.

In a research study, 20 architects and 20 accountants of similar backgrounds were tested on what the images of Modern and "Post-Modern" architecture meant to them—with intriguing results.

Times of radical change tend to be promising and invigorating—but also treacherous. So it is, too, with architecture at the threshold of the 1980s. Some of the most promising work in design—and the riskiest—is being done by those architects who are making a conscious attempt to manipulate not only form but also the meanings evoked by that form. Any number of architects and critics have already put forward numerous arguments for considering the role of meaning in architecture. And although the key words in their arguments, semiotics, the language of architecture, architectural or visual meaning—may vary, the general principle is the same: an essential aspect of people's interaction with buildings is the meanings they associate with those buildings; therefore, good design should encompass a conscious manipulation of intended meanings.

This is a necessary and significant contribution to the theory of architecture, but it is not an easy one to put into practice. Do we really know, for instance, that combined references to Palladio and Art Deco will not be perceived as a confusing, jumbled eyesore? The assumption that historical allusions will be understood and appreciated may be little different from the Modernist faith that purity of form would be appreciated as such. Serious mistakes are inevitable if the assumptions

Linda Groat & David Canter, "Does Post-Modernism Communicate?," from *Progressive Architecture*, Vol. 60. Copyright © 1979 by Penton Media. Permission to reprint granted by the publisher.

made about meanings conveyed by particular formal elements are wrong. We could end up in 10 or 20 years with a lot of white elephants, in much the same way that we have now inherited some much-disparaged relics of the Modern Movement.

This set of concerns led us to undertake in 1978 an empirical study of the meanings perceived in Modern and Post-Modern buildings. The specific intent of our study was to test two salient points of the Post-Modernist argument: 1, that architects and laypeople have different sensibilities toward architecture, and 2, that Post-Modern building having been designed to appeal to these two sensibilities, do in fact manipulate meanings successfully. These two issues, which ultimately set the structure of our research procedures, were identified through a careful review of the relevant literature, particularly the work of Charles Jencks, who has written the most extensively on the subject.

To put this research study into proper perspective, we should mention that it is the first reported study to investigate assumptions of perceived meanings in specific architecturally "significant" buildings. It is also the first architectural research to test the responses of practicing professionals—in this case, a group of 20 architects and a group of 20 accountants—rather than students.

SORTING FOR MEANING

Since we wanted to test the Post-Modernist argument that different meanings might be important to different groups of people, we tried to find a way to discover which concepts or ideas were important to each participant. Rather than develop a questionnaire or checklist based on concepts of importance to us, we devised what we call a multiple sorting task, which allowed each respondent to sort a set of building photos into groups according to any criterion. There was no restriction as to the number of groups formed, the number of buildings in a group, or how many times the set of photos could be sorted. After each sort, the participant was asked to label both the criterion by which the buildings had been sorted and the categories that had been formed. Thus the criterion given was taken to be a concept of importance for that individual, and the category labels were taken to be the meanings associated with all the buildings in that group.

One advantage of the sorting technique is that the resulting data can be analyzed at various levels of sophistication. On a very basic level, the task provides an effective way of structuring participant interviews. People who normally find it difficult to articulate their ideas on architecture often find it helpful, even revealing, to be asked to categorize buildings. Usually even their casual comments provide insights of great potential value to the architect. And, in addition, more sophisticated statistical analyses can help to reveal less obvious, but equally significant issues of relevance to design.

Our results, as it turns out, provide a potentially stimulating challenge for the practice of a truly non-Modern architecture. The major findings can be summarized as follows: The argument for designing buildings to appeal to different architectural sensibilities is a valid one, but only a small proportion of Post-Modern buildings manage to do that successfully. Both aspects of these results—the existence of both professional and popular codes and the failure of certain Post-Modern buildings to manipulate them well—have significant ramifications for architectural practice and are therefore important to consider in some detail.

Reactions to Post-Modern Buildings

In the authors' investigations, 24 modern buildings were selected to be analyzed through photographs by accountant and architect subject groups. Buildings were selected to fit three categories: Modern, Transitional, and Post-Modern. While reactions to those of each category were sought, the investigators were particularly interested in determining whether or not the subjects viewed Post-Modern buildings as fulfilling their intentions of being multivalent, accessible, and enjoyable to a wide range of tastes. They also wanted to know which works were good models of Post-Modern buildings. A listing of the Modern and Traditional buildings follows this summary of reactions to the Post-Modern buildings.

Lang House

Guild House

Brandt House

Byker Wall

La Muralla Roja

Lang House. This private residence was the least successful as a Post-Modern building. Its historical references were not perceived by the accountants, most of whom seemed to dislike it actively, and who as a group ranked it last (24th). The architects were more charitable: although they did not seem to find the house multivalent, in the end they ranked it 15th.

Guild House. This housing for the elderly achieved some success in that its conventional style was appreciated by the lay group, and it was appreciated by both groups as being relatively unique. Its function was consistently misread by the accountants and sometimes even by the architects. In the end, however, the accountants ranked it in 22nd place and the architects in 19th.

Brant House. This private residence was not well understood by the nonprofessionals nor was it appreciated by the professionals. Its historical allusions were not perceived, and its function as a residence was infrequently understood. Neither group found in it a unique or complex set of meanings. It was ranked 19th by the accountants and 23rd by the architects.

Byker Wall. This government housing scheme in England achieved only limited success. Although its function was generally understood, and it seemed successfully multivalent with both groups, in the end it was ranked 23rd by the accountants and 14th by the architects.

La Muralla Roja. This apartment complex in Spain assumed a rather ambiguous relationship to the requirements of Post-Modernism. While the accountants understood its function, they neither seemed to find any particular value in it nor did they completely reject it by ranking it in 14th place. The architects found it more successful as a Post-Modern building and ranked it 6th, but this in itself would still not make the complex a particularly successful model of Post-Modernism.

Credits: Lang House, Washington, CT, 1975, Robert A.M. Stern and John S. Hagmann, architects. Photo: Ed Stoecklem. Guild House, Philadelphia, PA, 1960–63, Venturi & Rauch, architects. Photo: courtesy Venturi & Rauch. Brant House, Greenwich, CT, 1976, Venturi & Rauch, architects. Photo: courtesy Venturi & Rauch. Byker Wall. Newcastle-upon-Tyne, England, 1974–78. Ralph Erskmes Arkitektkontor. Photo: Roger Trancik. La Muralla Roja, Sitges. Spain, 1975, Taller de Arquitectura. Photo: Geoffrey Broadbent.

ARCHITECTS AND NONARCHITECTS

The most obvious point to make about the differences between architects and nonarchitects in their interpretations of the built environment is simply that the differences are so consistently evident. The many and complex ways in which the architects' conceptions differed from those of the accountants practically oozed out of our research results in all directions. For example, architects and accountants frequently tend to use different criteria in evaluating buildings and often hold very different opinions of the same building; also, architects seem to employ a greater range of evaluative criteria and a more complex set of specific judgments. Most likely, as the results of previous research suggest, these differences are due primarily to the architects' specialized training and professional experience. But the impact of these different sensibilities is the same no matter what the source, architects are not likely to design effectively if they rely only on their own experience of environments as a model.

Given the number of significant differences between architects and nonarchitects, it should not be surprising that some notable Post-Modern buildings do not actually seem to operate on both the professional and the popular levels. This conclusion is derived from comprehensive analyses of the 40 participants' responses to single color photos of 24 buildings ranging from Modern to Post-Modern—as labeled by recognized architectural critics. Previous studies have already established the validity of simulating environments in this way, so there is every reason to believe that these responses to representative photos can be taken as approximating the responses to the real thing. We therefore feel confident in suggesting that there seem to be some common patterns in the way that the eight Post-Modern buildings in our study have been interpreted by the nonarchitects.

NONARCHITECTS AND POST-MODERNISM

The first point—and this is the good news for Post-Modernists—is that these buildings do seem to be more successful than Modern buildings in evoking unique sets of associations. But the bad news is that these associations are not necessarily the ones intended by the architects. In some instances, the perceived meanings are contradictory to the original intent, just as critics have claimed is the case for Modern buildings. A specific example of this tendency is represented by Venturi & Rauch's Guild House. This building stood out from the others on the basis of meanings attributed to it. Yet one of the more typical comments about it was it "must be transient housing or a motel with a sign like that." References to brick row houses or any other intended allusions were never considered by the nonarchitects. It is probably fair to say that for some of the participants this building was interpreted as "ugly and ordinary" (as Venturi intended), but without any redeeming complex or contradictory meanings.

Second, we also found that Post-Modern buildings are not necessarily preferred over Modern buildings. In fact, the set of Post-Modern buildings in our study tended to be categorized toward the extremes, being either the most-liked or, more often, the least-liked buildings. Another related pattern, of even more significance for the practitioner, was the tendency for the participants to disagree strongly in their preferences for and/or dislike of certain Post-Modern buildings: there was considerable disagreement among individual accountants as well as between the accountant group and the architect group.

The potential of Post-Modern buildings to engender controversy and extremes of judgment suggests that designing with an intent to manipulate meaning can be risky business. To be sure, there are outstanding successes: Hillingdon Civic Centre and the Butterworth house were revealed by our research as such. But there is as well considerable likelihood for failure, and, unfortunately, those who are most likely to suffer from that are not the architects. Several buildings, including Guild House, Byker Wall, the Lang house, and the Brant house, seemed to be considered unsuccessful in some respects.

One way of at least minimizing failure in future attempts to design meaning into buildings is to generate, and subsequently design in accordance with, some basic principles regarding the perception of meaning in architecture. The three principles described below are offered only as a starting point. However, even with future additions and revisions, they must remain general rather than specific: for the goal is not to develop prescriptive rules for form, but to provide aids to the design process.

THREE DESIGN PRINCIPLES

A major concern of nonarchitects is that a building design seem appropriate to the building type and use. Among nonarchitects, the most common and immediate response to a building seems to be: what is it? This prevalent concern for identifying building type was not shared by the architects, however, and is therefore one of the most significant differences between the two groups. At face value, this suggests that it would be preferable to design buildings to ensure that the type is easily identifiable; but in reality the appropriateness of a building form to its actual use seems to be more important. For example, one accountant, who remarked "How sad, what an uninviting city hall," identified Boston City Hall as a civic building, but nevertheless obviously considered it a failure. In this case, in order to be considered appropriate as a city hall the building needed to be seen as inviting.

Interestingly, a particular form may be viewed either favorably or unfavorably depending on the appropriateness of its function. A number of accountants reacted positively to the Johnson Glass House while assuming it was a park pavilion or an information booth. One who inquired about its use, however, responded. "Who'd want to live in a glass house?" Another telling example is the response to Hillingdon. Many accountants responded positively to it without knowing whether it was a college building, shops, or housing. Still, the building appeared to them to be so eminently appropriate for any of these purposes that it seemed hardly to matter whether they could identify the precise use.

The point of these three examples is simply that if a building is interpreted as being appropriate to its purpose, then it has a good chance of being considered successful.

A building in the historic mode is more likely to be appreciated and understood by nonarchitects if it can be interpreted as relating to a single stylistic tradition. The only buildings which attained almost unanimous appreciation, even fascination, among the nonarchitects were Hillingdon and Butterworth. And this was not due to the mistaken belief that they were genuinely old buildings. Rather, they seemed to be appreciated for relating to a specific stylistic tradition that could be understood, if not labeled.

A contrasting example is that of the Lang house, which was almost unanimously rejected by the nonarchitects. Although the reasons for this antipathy are not entirely clear, it was evident that the combination of the moldings, proportions, color, and general appearance did not evoke any pleasing associations relating to any particular architectural style. It would seem, then, that subtlety of eclecticism may be missed by, and frequently alienating to, the general public.

The buildings nonarchitects find most appealing may be those that many architects consider the least serious architecture. Hillingdon and Butterworth convey intended meanings and a richness of associations to the nonarchitect group, however, those architects who isolated the two as being significantly similar in some respect described them in the following terms: perverse, purposefully irrational, contextual and whimsical. The two other buildings frequently rated highly by the accountant—Frank Lloyd Wright's Marin County Civic Center and Alvar Aalto's church at Vuoksenniska—were described in combination with the first two by another architect as being "an emotional response to architecture."

These three principles, it seems, offer the practitioner some insight into the layperson's interpretation of contemporary architecture, yet their potential as effective design guidelines is evidently very limited. Scores of issues—from the relation of interior to exterior, interior spatial arrangements, color, materials, and so on—remain beyond the scope of these few points. And, as stated earlier, to develop rules of form would be not only impossible, but completely undesirable. Ideally, then, how can the sensitive practitioner act to moderate the tension between the architect's desire for poetic license and the need for consistency in architectural language? We are suggesting an interactive process, such as the sorting task, whereby the discourse between people (architects and nonarchitects) ultimately modifies the conceptions originally held by the individuals concerned.

In summary, we would argue that the chief value of the Post-Modernist position lies in its exploration of the meanings and associations inherent in architecture, but continued experimentation with formal vocabularies, though important, is not enough. What is necessary, as well, is a realization of the conceptual contribution that clients, users, and the public—as well as architects—can make in the process of giving buildings (or all places for that matter) meaning.

The Modern Buildings Surveyed

Chapel, Illinois Institute of Technology, Chicago, IL, 1952, Mies van der Rohe, architect. Kneses Tifereth Israel Synagogue, Port Chester, NY, 1956, Philip Johnson, architect. Lake Shore Apartments, Chicago, IL, 1949–51, Mies van der Rohe, architect. Unité d'Habitation, Marseilles, France, 1946–52, Le Corbusier architect. City Hall, Tokyo, Japan, 1952–57, Kenzo Tange, architect. Civic Center, Chicago, IL, 1964, C. F. Murphy, architects. Glass House, New Canaan, CT, 1947–49, Philip Johnson, architect. Breuer House, New Canaan, CT, 1947, Marcel Breuer, architect.

The Transitional Buildings Surveyed

City Hall, Boston, MA, 1964–69, Kallman McKinnell Knowles, architects. Senate, Secretariat, and Assembly Building, Brasilia, Brazil, 1958–60, Oscar Niemeyer, architect. Crawford Manor, New Haven, CT, 1962–66, Paul Rudolph, architect. House VI, Cornwall, CT, 1977, Peter Eisenman, architect. Unitarian Church, Rochester, NY, 1959–62, Louis Kahn, architect. Marin County Civic Center, San Raphael, CA, 1959–64, Frank Lloyd Wright, architect. Air Force Academy Chapel, Colorado Springs, CO, 1959, Skidmore Owings & Merrill, architects. Church of Vuoksenniska, Imatra, Finland, 1957–59, Alvar Aalto, architect.

Butterworth House

Hillingdon Civic Centre

Notre Dame du Haut

Butterworth House. This was an extremely successful house in the eyes of the accountants, who generally liked its traditional style, understood its function, found a unique pattern of meaning in it, and thus ranked it in 2nd place. In ranking the house 9th, the architects liked it only moderately and were less inclined to see complex meanings in it. However, if they would be more willing to emphasize the lay code in their approach to design, this house would be a very successful model for Post-Modernism.

Hillingdon Civic Centre. This borough hall outside London was the only building in the Post-Modern group to be well-liked and appreciated by both subject groups. It was ranked 1st by the accountants and 4th by the architects. The building's references to traditional styles seemed to work so well that even a few architects thought it was an older building. It also seemed to evoke a relatively unique pattern of meanings, although its correct function was not always perceived. (It is believed that this is due more to the photograph used, which does not show the building's most "telling" signs of contextual and whimsical. Two other buildings frequently rated highly by the accountants—Frank Lloyd Wright's Marin County Civic Center and Alvar Aalto's church at Vuoksenniska—were described in combination with the first two by another architect as being "an emotional response to architecture."

Notre Dame du Haut. This classic by Le Corbusier was the architects' unanimous favorite, but its position with the accountants was more ambiguous. Its function was frequently misunderstood, and its meaning was not considered particularly unique, which finally put it in 9th place. Nevertheless, some of the accountants truly loved it, while others were troubled by it. This suggests that if the context of the building were understood, it might be considered more favorably, and that it might provide a potential model for Post-Modernism, but perhaps only in special circumstances.

Credits: Butterworth House, Starksboro, VT, 1973, Turner Brooks, architect. Photo courtesy of Turner Brooks. Hillingdon Civic Centre, London Borough of Hillingdon, England, 1974–77, Robert Matthew, Johnson-Marshall & Partners, architects. Photo courtesy of Linda Groat. Notre Dame du Haut, Ronchamp, France, 1950–54, Le Corbusier, architect.

9 The Social Life of Small Urban Spaces

William H. Whyte

This classic study uses observation to discover what makes some plazas and mini-parks more popular than others. Hint: seating has a lot to do with it, and after that, several other variables. This research is also among the very influential because it directly influenced landscape architecture as well as the building codes of New York City. From a theoretical point of view it demonstrated that absence of density could be a bigger problem than high density, contradicting earlier social sciences studies influenced by animal studies of density, which were treating high density as a problem.

In their use of plazas, New Yorkers were very consistent. Day in, day out, many of them would sit at certain plazas, few at others. On the face of it, there should not have been this variance. Most of the plazas we were studying were fairly comparable. With few exceptions, they were on major avenues and usually occupied a block front. They were close to bus stops and subway stations and had strong pedestrian flows on the sidewalks beside them. Yet when we rated plazas according to the number of people sitting on them at peak time, there was a very wide range—from 160 people at 77 Water Street to 17 at 280 Park Avenue (see chart 1).

How come? The first factor we studied was the sun. We thought it might well be the critical one, and our initial time-lapse studies seemed to bear this out. Subsequent studies did not. As I will note later, they showed that the sun was important, but did not explain the difference in the popularity of plazas.

Nor did aesthetics. We never thought ourselves capable of measuring such factors, but did expect our research to show the most successful plazas would tend to be the most pleasing visually. Seagram's seemed very much a case in point. Here again, the evidence proved conflicting. Not only was clean, elegant Seagram's successful; so was the fun plaza at 77 Water Street, which some architects look on as kitsch. We also noticed that the elegance and purity of a building's design seems to have little relationship to the use of the spaces around it.

The designer sees the whole building—the clean verticals, the horizontals, the way Mies turned his corners, and so on. The person sitting on the plaza may be quite unaware of such matters. He is more apt to be looking in the other direction: not up at other buildings, but at what is going on

William H. Whyte, "Sitting Space," from *The Social Life of Small Urban Spaces*, pp. 24–39, 121. Copyright © 1980 by Project for Public Spaces. Permission to reprint granted by the publisher.

Above: The ledge at St. Peter's Church, part of the Citicorp complex, has become one of the most used sitting places on Lexington Avenue.

at eye level. To say this is not to slight the designer's eye or his handling of space. The area around Seagram's is a great urban place and its relationship to McKim, Mead & White's Racquet Club across the street is integral to it. My personal feeling is that a sense of enclosure contributes to the enjoyment of using the Seagram plaza. But I certainly can't prove this with figures.

Another factor we considered was shape. Urban designers believed this was extremely important and hoped our findings might support tight criteria for proportions and placement. They were particularly anxious to rule out "strip plazas"—long narrow spaces that were little more than enlarged sidewalks, and empty more often than not. Designers felt a developer shouldn't get bonuses for these strips, and to this end they wanted to rule out spaces the length of which was more than three times the width.

Our data did not support such criteria. We found that most strip plazas were, indeed, empty of people most of the time. But was the shape the cause? Some square plazas were empty, too, and several of the most heavily used places were, in fact, long narrow strips. One of the five most popular sitting places in New York is essentially an indentation in a building—and long and

Left: **Another popular place to tarry is a simple round bench at Rockefeller Center, just across the street from St. Patrick's Cathedral.**

narrow. Our research did not prove shape unimportant or designers' instincts misguided; as with the sun, however, it did prove that other factors were more critical.

If not shape, could the *amount* of space be the key factor? Some conservationists were sure this would be it. In their view, people seek open spaces as a relief from the overcrowding they are normally subjected to, and it would follow that places affording the greatest feeling of light and space would draw the most. If we ranked plazas by the amount of space, there surely would be a positive correlation between the size of the plazas and the number of persons using them.

Once again, we found no clear relationship. As can be seen in chart 2, several of the smaller spaces had lots of people, several of the larger had lots of people, and several of the larger had very few people. Sheer space, it appears, does not draw people. In some circumstances, it can have the opposite effect.

What about the amount of *sittable* space? Here we begin to get close. As chart 3 shows, the most popular plazas tend to have considerably more sitting space than the less well-used ones. The relationship is rough. For one reason, the amount of sitting space does not include any qualitative factors: a foot of concrete ledge counts for as much as a foot of comfortable bench space. We considered weighting the figures on a point basis—so many points for a foot of bench with backrest, with armrests, and so on. This would have produced a nicer conformance on the chart.

We gave up the idea, however, as too manipulative. Once you start working backwards this way, there's no end to it.

There was no necessity. No matter how many variables we checked, one point kept coming through. We at last saw that it was the major one:

People tend to sit most where there are places to sit.

This may not strike you as an intellectual bombshell, and, now that I look back on our study, I wonder why it was not more apparent to us from the beginning. Sitting space, to be sure, is only one of the many variables, and, without a control situation as a measure, one cannot be sure of cause and effect. But sitting space is most certainly prerequisite. The most attractive fountains, the most striking designs, cannot induce people to come and sit if there is no place to sit.

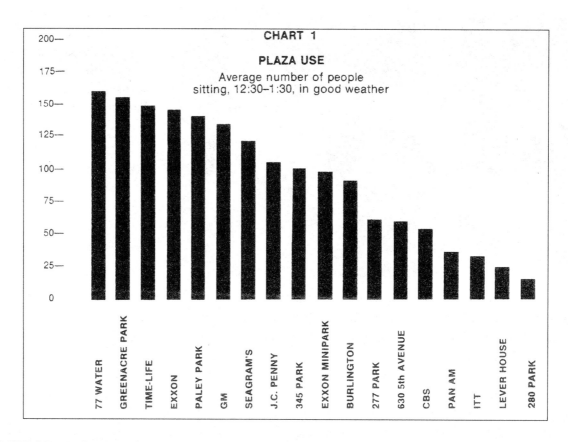

INTEGRAL SITTING

Ideally, sitting should be physically comfortable—benches with backrests, well-contoured chairs. It's more important, however, that it be *socially* comfortable. This means choice: sitting up front, in back, to the side, in the sun, in the shade, in groups, off alone.

Choice should be built into the basic design. Even though benches and chairs can be added, the best course is to maximize the sittability of inherent features. This means making ledges so they are sittable, or making other flat surfaces do double duty as table tops or seats. There are almost always such opportunities. Because the elevation changes somewhat on most building sites, there are bound to be several levels of flat space. It's no more trouble to make them sittable than not to.

It takes real work to create a lousy place. Ledges have to be made high and bulky; railings put in; surfaces canted. Money can be saved by not doing such things, and the open space is more likely to be an amenable one.

This is one of the lessons of Seagram's. Philip Johnson recounts that when Mies van der Rohe saw people sitting on the ledges, he was quite surprised. He had never dreamt they would. But the architects had valued simplicity. So there were no fussy railings, no shrubbery, no gratuitous changes in elevation, no ornamentation to clutter spaces. The steps were made easy and inviting. The place was eminently sittable, without a bench on it. The periphery includes some 600 feet of ledge and step space, which is just right for sitting, eating, and sunbathing. People use all of it.

So ledges ought to be sittable. But how should this be defined? If we wanted sittable ledges in the New York City zoning amendments we thought we would have to indicate how high or low ledges should be, how deep, and, since there were adversary proceedings ahead, be able to back up the specifications with facts.

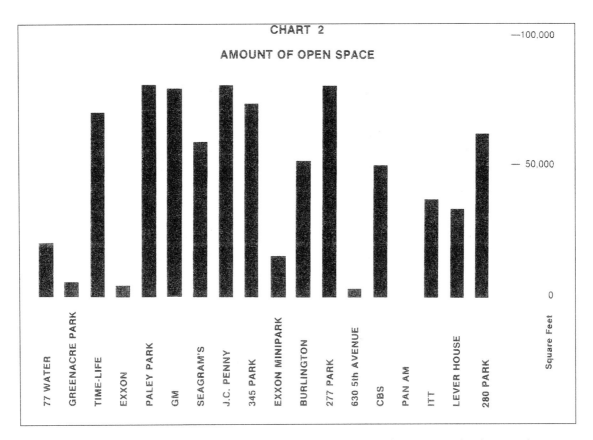

The proceedings turned out to be adversary in a way we hadn't expected. The attack came on the grounds that the zoning was *too specific*. And it came not from builders, but from members of a local planning board. Rather than spell out the requirements in specific detail, the board argued, the zoning should deal only with broad directives—for example, make the place sittable—leaving details to be settled on a case-by-case basis.

Let me pause to deal with this argument. It is a persuasive one, especially for laymen, and, at the inevitable moment in zoning meetings when someone gets up and says, "Let's cut through all this crap and get down to basics," everyone applauds. Be done with bureaucratic nitpicking and legal gobbledygook.

But ambiguity is a worse problem. Most incentive zoning ordinances are very, very specific as to what the developer gets. The trouble is that they are mushy as to what he is to give, and mushier yet as to what will happen if later he doesn't. Vague stipulations, as many cities have learned, are unenforceable. What you do not prescribe quite explicitly, you do not get.

Lack of guidelines does not give builders and architects more freedom. It reinforces convention. That is why so few good plazas were built under the 1961 zoning resolution. There was no law preventing builders from providing better plazas. There weren't any guidelines either. And most builders do not do anything far out of the ordinary. A few had sought special permits for amenities not countenanced by existing regulations. But the time-consuming route to obtain special permits makes the builder and architect run a gauntlet of city agencies, with innovation as likely to be punished as rewarded.

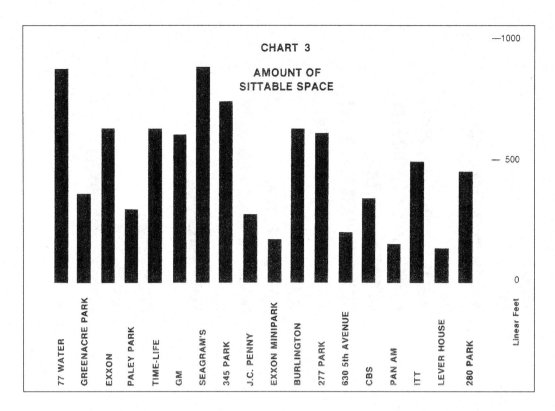

SITTING HEIGHTS

One guideline we expected to establish easily was the matter of sitting heights. It seemed obvious enough that somewhere around 17 inches would probably be near the optimum. But how much higher or lower could a surface be and still be sittable? Thanks to the slope of sites, several of the most sat-upon ledges provided a range of continuously variable heights. The front ledge of Seagram's, for example, started at 7 inches at one corner, rising to 44 at the other. Here was a dandy chance, we thought, to do a definitive study. By repeated observation, we could record how many people sat at which point over the range of heights; as cumulative tallies built, preferences would become clear.

They didn't. At a given time there might be clusters of people on one part of the ledge, considerably fewer on another. But correlations didn't last. When we cumulated several months of observation, we found that people distributed themselves with remarkable evenness over the whole range of heights. We had to conclude that people will sit almost anywhere between a height of one foot and three, and this is the range specified in the new zoning. People will sit on places higher or lower, to be sure, but there are apt to be special conditions.

Another dimension is more important: the human backside. It is a dimension architects seem to have forgotten. Rarely will you find a ledge or bench deep enough to be sittable on both sides; some aren't deep enough to be sittable on one. Most frustrating are the ledges just deep enough to tempt people to sit on both sides, but too shallow to let them do so comfortably. Observe such places and you will see people making awkward adjustments. The benches at General Motors plaza are a case in point. They are 24 inches deep and normally used on only one side. On Sundays, however, a heavy influx of tourists and other people will sit on both sides of the benches. Not in comfort: they have to sit on the forward edge, erectly, and their stiff demeanor suggests a tacit truce.

Thus to another of our startling findings: ledges and spaces two backsides deep seat more people comfortably than those that are not as deep. While 30 inches will do it, 36 is better yet. The new

zoning provides a good incentive. If a ledge or bench is 30 inches deep and accessible on both sides, the builder gets credit for the linear feet on each side. (The 30-inch figure is thoroughly empirical; it is derived from a ledge at 277 Park Avenue, the minimum-depth ledge we came across that was consistently used on both sides.)

For a few additional inches of depth, then, builders can double the amount of sitting space. This does not mean that double the number of people will use the space. They probably won't. But that is not the point. The benefit of the extra space is social comfort—more room for groups and individuals to sort themselves out, more choices and more perception of choices.

Steps work for the same reason. The range of space provides an infinity of possible groupings, and the excellent sight-lines make virtually all the seats great for watching the theater of the street. The new zoning ordinance does not credit steps as sitting space. It was felt that this would give builders too easy an out and that some plazas would be all steps and little else. But the step principle can be applied with good effect to ledges.

Corners are functional. You will notice that people often bunch at the far end of steps, especially when an abutting ledge provides a right angle. These areas are good for face-to-face sitting. People in groups gravitate to them.

One might, as a result, expect a conflict, for corners are also the places where pedestrian traffic is heaviest. Most people take short cuts, and pedestrian flows in plazas are usually on the diagonals between the building entrance and the corners of the steps. We see this at Seagram's. As mentioned previously, the main flow to and from the building cuts directly across the step corners, and it is precisely there that you will find the heaviest concentration of people sitting, sunbathing, and

Most ledges are inherently sittable, but with a little ingenuity and additional expense they can be made unsittable.

Some places, like Liberty Plaza in Washington, D.C., combine good sitting heights and bad sitting heights.

picnicking. But, for all the bustle, or because of it, the sitters seem to feel comfortable. The walkers don't seem to mind either, and will carefully negotiate through the blockages rather than detour around them.

We find similar patterns at other places. All things being equal, you can calculate that where pedestrian flows bisect a sittable place, that is where people will most likely sit. And it is not so perverse of them. It is by choice that they do. If there is some congestion, it is an amiable one, and a testimonial to the place.

When ledges are two backsides deep, choice is greatly enlarged and more people can use the ledges without feeling crowded.

Circulation and sitting, in sum, are not antithetical but complementary. It is to encourage both that the zoning stipulates the plaza not be more than three feet above or below street level. The easier the flow between street and plaza, the more likely people are to move between the two—and to tarry and sit.

This is true of the handicapped, too. If circulation and amenities are planned with them in mind, the place is apt to function more easily for everyone. Drinking fountains that are low enough for wheelchair users are low enough for children. Pedestrian paths that are made easier for the handicapped by ramps, handrails, and steps of gentle pitch are easier for all. The new zoning makes such amenities mandatory, specifying, among other things, that all steps along the main access paths have treads at least 11 inches deep, closed risers no higher than 7.5 inches, and that ramps be provided alongside them. For the benefit of the handicapped, the zoning also requires that at least 5 percent of the seating spaces have backrests. These are not segregated for the handicapped, it should be noted. No facilities are segregated. The idea is to make all of a place usable for everyone.

Except on very beautiful days, the steps of the New York Public Library are underused. These steps could become one of New York's great gathering spots.

BENCHES

Benches are artifacts the purpose of which is to punctuate architectural photographs. They're not so good for sitting. There are too few of them; they are too small; they are often isolated from other benches or from whatever action there is on the plaza. Worse yet, architects tend to repeat the same module in plaza after plaza, unaware that it didn't work very well in the first place. For example, Harrison and Abramowitz's plazas at Rockefeller Center are excellent in many respects, but the basic bench module they've stuck to is exquisitely wrong in its dimensions—7.5 feet by 19 inches. A larger rectangle would be proportionately as good but work vastly better, as some utilitarian benches in the same area demonstrate.

The technological barriers to better bench design are not insuperable. The prime specification, that benches be generously sized, is the easiest to meet. Backrests and armrests are proved devices. The old-fashioned park bench is still one of the best liked because it provides them; of the newer designs that also do, some of the stock ones of the play- and park-equipment manufacturers are

The steps at Seagram's are well used, particularly at the corners where pedestrian flows are highest.

best. Architects have had a way with chairs; for some reason they seem to come a cropper with benches.

They do worst when they freeze their bench designs in concrete permanence. If some of their assumptions prove wrong—that, say, people want to sit away from the action—it will be too late to do much about it. This has been a problem with a number of pedestrian malls, where all design bets were made before the mall was opened. If some of the sitting areas go unused, there's no easy way of heeding the lesson, or, indeed, of recognizing that there is one.

Why not experiment? Some features, like ledges and steps, will be fixed, but benches and chairs don't have to be. With sturdy wooden benches or the like, some simple market research can be done to find out where and in what kind of groupings they work best. People will be very quick to let you know. We have found that by the second day the basic use patterns will be established, and these won't change very much unless the set-up is changed. And it will be clear in what direction the changes should be made.

If one looks. This is the gap. Rarely will you ever see a plan for a public space that even countenances the possibility that parts of it might not work very well: that calls for experiment and testing, and for post-construction evaluation to see what does work well and what doesn't. Existing spaces suffer a similar fate. There are few that could not be vastly improved, but rarely is an evaluation undertaken. The people responsible for the place are the least likely of all to consider it.

Left: Benches at Mechanics Plaza in San Francisco face the action of Market Street.

Below: Benches put right in the middle of the sidewalk outside 747 Third Avenue draw heavy use.

Forced choice is rarely chosen.

The impulse to move chairs, whether only six or eight inches, is very strong. Even where there is no functional reason for it, the exercise of choice is satisfying. Perhaps this is why the woman above moved her chair a foot—neither into the sun or out of it.

CHAIRS

Now, a wonderful invention—the movable chair. Having a back, it is comfortable; more so, if it has an armrest as well. But the big asset is movability. Chairs enlarge choice: to move into the sun, out of it, to make room for groups, move away from them. The possibility of choice is as important as the exercise of it. If you know you can move if you want to, you feel more comfortable staying put. This is why, perhaps, people so often move a chair a few inches this way and that before sitting in it, with the chair ending up about where it was in the first place. The moves are functional, however. They are a declaration of autonomy, to oneself, and rather satisfying.

Small moves say things to other people. If a newcomer chooses a chair next to a couple or a larger group, he may make some intricate moves. Again, he may not take the chair very far, but he conveys a message. Sorry about the closeness, but there's no room elsewhere, and I am going to respect your privacy, as you will mine. A reciprocal move by one of the others may follow. Watching these exercises in civility is itself one of the pleasures of a good place.

Fixed individual seats are not good. They are a design conceit. Brightly painted and artfully grouped, they can make fine decorative elements: metal loveseats, revolving stools, squares of stone, sitting stumps. But they are set pieces. That is the trouble with them. Social distance is a subtle measure, ever changing, and the distances of fixed seats do not change, which is why they are rarely quite right for anybody. Loveseats may be all right for lovers, but they're too close for acquaintances, and much too close for strangers. Loners tend to take them over, placing their feet squarely on the other seat lest someone else sit on it.

Fixed seats are awkward in open spaces because there's so much space around them. In theaters, strangers sit next to each other without qualm; the closeness is a necessity, and convention makes it quite tolerable. On plazas, the closeness is gratuitous. With so much space around, fixed-seat groupings have a manipulative cuteness to them. The designer is saying, now you sit right here and you sit there. People balk. In some instances, they wrench the seats from their moorings. Where there is a choice between fixed seats and other kinds of sitting, it is the other that people choose.

To encourage the use of movable chairs, we recommended that in the zoning amendment they be credited as 30 inches of sitting space, though most are only about 19 inches wide. The Building

People outside the Metropolitan Museum of Art move their chairs close to the sidewalk to enjoy the passersby on Fifth Avenue.

Department objected. It objected to the idea of movable chairs at all. The department had the responsibility of seeing that builders lived up to requirements. Suppose the chairs were stolen or broken and the builder didn't replace them? Whether the department would ever check up in any event was a moot point, but it was true that the fewer such amenities to monitor, the easier the monitoring would be. Happily, there was a successful record at Paley and Greenacre parks to point to, and it was decisively persuasive. The chairs stayed in. They have become a standard amenity at new places, and the maintenance experience has been excellent. Managements have also been putting in chairs to liven up existing spaces, and, even without incentives, they have been adding more chairs. The most generous provider is the Metropolitan Museum of Art. Alongside its front steps, it puts out up to 200 movable chairs and it leaves them out, 24 hours a day, seven days a week. The Met figured that it might be less expensive to trust people and to buy replacements periodically rather than have guards gather the chairs in every night. That is the way it has worked out. There is little vandalism.

HOW MUCH SITTING SPACE?

A key question we had to confront was how much sitting space should be required. We spent a lot of time on this—much too much, I now realize—and I'm tempted to recount our various calculations to demonstrate how conscientious we were. The truth is that almost any reasonable yardstick would work as well as ours. It's the fact of one that is important.

This said, let me tell how conscientious we were. We measured and remeasured the sitting space on most of the plazas and small parks in midtown and downtown New York. As sitting space, we included all the spaces meant for people to sit on, such as benches, and the spaces they sat on whether meant to or not, such as ledges. Although architects' plans were helpful, we did most of the measuring with a tape, on the ground, in the process stirring inordinate curiosity from passersby and guards.

Next, we related the amount of sitting space to the size of the plaza. As chart 3 shows, the square feet of sitting space on the best-used plazas ran between 6 and 10 percent of the total open space. As a ballpark figure, it looked like somewhere around 10 percent would be a reasonable minimum to require of builders.

For other comparisons we turned to linear feet. This is a more precise measure of sitting space than square feet, and a more revealing one. As long as there's some clearance for one's

Exxon minipark.

When ledges are two backsides deep, choice is greatly enlarged and more people can use the ledges without feeling crowded.

back, the additional square inches behind one don't matter very much. It is the edges of sitting surface that do the work, and it is the edges that should be made the most of.

For a basis of comparison, we took the number of linear feet around the total site. Since the perimeter includes the building, the distance is a measure of the bulk of the project and its impact on the surrounding environment. Amenities should therefore be in some proportion to it. On the most popular plazas, there were almost as many feet of sitting space as there were perimeter feet. This suggested that, as a minimum, builders could be asked to provide that amount of sitting space.

Even on the best plazas, the architects could have done better. To get an idea of how much better, we calculated the additional space that could have been provided on various plazas rather easily, while the original plans were being made. We did not posit any changes in basic layout, nor did we take the easy way of adding a lot of benches. We concentrated on spaces that would be integral to the basic design.

In most cases, it was possible to add as much as 50 percent more sitting space, and very good space at that. The Exxon plaza, for example, has a fine pool bordered by two side ledges that you can't sit on. You can sit on the front and back ledges, but only on the sides facing away from the pool. With a few simple changes, such as broadening the ledges, sitting capacity could have been doubled, providing some of the best poolside space anywhere. All in all, these examples indicated, builders could easily furnish as many feet of sitting space as there are feet around the perimeter of the project.

The requirement finally settled on was a compromise: one linear foot of sitting space for every thirty square feet of plaza. This is reasonable, and builders have been meeting the requirement with no trouble. They could meet a stiffer one. The exact ratio is not as important, however, as the necessity of considering the matter. Once an architect has to start thinking of ways to make a place sittable, it is virtually impossible not to surpass any minimum. And other things follow. More thought must be given to probable pedestrian flows, placement of steps, trees, wind baffles, sun traps, and even wastebaskets. One felicity leads to another. Good places tend to be all of a piece—and the reason can almost always be traced to a human being.

10 What Would a Non-Sexist City Look Like?

Dolores Hayden

Architectural historian Dolores Hayden argued that the suburbs had become the site of urban growth, so she focuses on redesigning them to support a wider range of family types and economic activities than the strictly residential nuclear family.

"A woman's place is in the home" has been one of the most important principles of architectural design and urban planning in the United States for the last century. An implicit rather than explicit principle for the conservative and male-dominated design professions, it will not be found stated in large type in textbooks on land use. It has generated much less debate than the other organizing principles of the contemporary American city in an era of monopoly capitalism, which include the ravaging pressure of private land development, the fetishistic dependence on millions of private automobiles, and the wasteful use of energy.[1] However, women have rejected this dogma and entered the paid labor force in larger and larger numbers. Dwellings, neighborhoods, and cities designed for homebound women constrain women physically, socially, and economically. Acute frustration occurs when women defy these constraints to spend all or part of the work day in the paid labor force. I contend that the only remedy for this situation is to develop a new paradigm of the home, the neighborhood, and the

---

1. There is an extensive Marxist literature on the importance of spatial design to the economic development of the capitalist city, including Henry Lefebre, *La Production de l'espace* (Paris: Editions Anthropos, 1974); Manuel Castells, The Urban Question (Cambridge, Mass.: MIT Press, 1977); David Harvey, *Social Justice and the City* (London: Edward Arnold, 1974); and David Gordon, "Capitalist Development and the History of American Cities," in *Marxism and the Metropolis,* ed. William K. Tabb and Larry Sawyers (New York: Oxford University Press, 1978). None of this work deals adequately with the situation of women as workers and homemakers, nor with the unique spatial inequalities they experience. Nevertheless, it is important to combine the economic and historical analysis of these scholars with the empirical research of non-Marxist feminist urban critics and sociologists who have examined women's experience of conventional housing, such as Gerda Wekerle, "A Woman's Place Is in the City" (paper for the Lincoln Institute of Land Policy, Cambridge, Mass., 1978); and Suzanne Keller, "Women in a Planned Community" (paper for the Lincoln Institute of Land Policy, Cambridge, Mass., 1978). Only then can one begin to provide a socialist-feminist critique of the spatial design of the

Dolores Hayden; Susan S. Fainstein & Lisa Servon, eds., "What Would a Non-Sexist City Look Like?: Speculations on Housing, Urban Design, and Human Work," from *Gender and Planning: A Reader,*. Copyright © 1980 by Rutgers University Press. Permission to reprint granted by the publisher.

city; to begin to describe the physical, social, and economic design of a human settlement that would support, rather than restrict, the activities of employed women and their families. It is essential to recognize such needs in order to begin both the rehabilitation of the existing housing stock and the construction of new housing to meet the needs of a new and growing majority of Americans—working women and their families.

When speaking of the American city in the last quarter of the twentieth century, a false distinction between "city" and "suburb" must be avoided. The urban region, organized to separate homes and workplaces, must be seen as a whole. In such urban regions, more than half of the population resides in the sprawling suburban areas, or "bedroom communities." The greatest part of the built environment in the United States consists of "suburban sprawl": single-family homes grouped in class-segregated areas, crisscrossed by freeways and served by shopping malls and commercial strip developments. Over 50 million small homes are on the ground. About two-thirds of American families "own" their homes on long mortgages; this includes over 77 percent of all AFL-CIO members.[2] White, male skilled workers are far more likely to be home-owners than members of minority groups and women, long denied equal credit or equal access to housing. Workers commute to jobs either in the center or elsewhere in the suburban ring. In metropolitan areas studied in 1975 and 1976, the journey to work, by public transit or private car, averaged about nine miles each way. Over 100 million privately owned cars filled two and three-car garages (which would be considered magnificent housing by themselves in many developing countries). The United States, with 13 percent of the world's population, uses 41 percent of the world's passenger cars in support of the housing and transportation patterns described.[3]

The roots of this American settlement form lie in the environmental and economic policies of the past. In the late nineteenth century, millions of immigrant families lived in the crowded, filthy slums of American industrial cities and despaired of achieving reasonable living conditions. However, many militant strikes and demonstrations between the 1890s and 1920s made some employers reconsider plant locations and housing issues in their search for industrial order.[4] "Good homes make contented workers" was the slogan of the Industrial Housing Associates in 1919. These consultants and many others helped major corporations plan better housing for white male skilled workers and their families, in order to eliminate industrial conflict. "Happy workers invariably

---

American city. It is also essential to develop research on housing similar to Sheila B. Kammerman, "Work and Family in Industrialized Societies," *Signs: Journal of Women in Culture and Society* 4. No. 4 (Summer 1979): 632–50, which reviews patterns of women's employment, maternity provisions, and child-care policies in Hungary, East Germany, West Germany, France, Sweden, and the United States. A comparable study of housing and related services for employed women could be the basis for more elaborate proposals for change. Many attempts to refine socialist and feminist economic theory concerning housework are discussed in an excellent article by Ellen Malos, "Housework and the Politics of Women's Liberation," *Socialist Review* 37. (January–February 1978): 41–47. A most significant theoretical piece is Movimento di Lotta Femminile, "Programmatic Manifesto for the Struggle of Housewives in the Neighborhood," *Socialist Revolution* 9 (May–June 1972): 85–90.

2. *Survey of AFL-CIO Members Housing 1975* (Washington, D.C.: AFL-CIO, 1975). p. 16. I am indebted to Allen Heskin for this reference.
3. *Transit Fact Book*, 1977–78 ed. (Washington, D.C.: American Public Transit Association, 1978), p. 29; *Motor Vehicle Facts and Figures* (Detroit, Mich.: Motor Vehicle Manufacturers Association, 1977), p. 29, 31, 53.
4. Gordon, p. 48–50, discusses suburban relocation of plants and housing.

mean bigger profits, while unhappy workers are never a good investment," they chirruped.[5] Men were to receive "family wages," and become home "owners" responsible for regular mortgage payments, while their wives became home "managers" taking care of spouse and children. The male worker would return from his day in the factory or office to a private domestic environment, secluded from the tense world of work in an industrial city characterized by environmental pollution, social degradation, and personal alienation. He would enter a serene dwelling whose physical and emotional maintenance would be the duty of his wife. Thus the private suburban house was the stage set for the effective sexual division of labor. It was the commodity par excellence, a spur for male paid labor and a container for female unpaid labor. It made gender appear a more important self-definition than class, and consumption more involving than production. In a brilliant discussion of the "patriarch as wage slave," Stuart Ewen has shown how capitalism and anti-feminism fused in campaigns for homeownership and mass consumption: the patriarch whose home was his "castle" was to work year in and year out to provide the wages to support this private environment.[6]

Although this strategy was first boosted by corporations interested in a docile labor force, it soon appealed to corporations who wished to move from World War I defense industries into peacetime production of domestic appliances for millions of families. The development of the advertising industry, documented by Ewen, supported this ideal of mass consumption and promoted the private suburban dwelling, which maximized appliance purchases.[7] The occupants of the isolated household were suggestible. They bought the house itself, a car, stove, refrigerator, vacuum cleaner, washer, carpets. Christine Frederick, explaining it in 1929 as *Selling Mrs. Consumer*, promoted homeownership and easier consumer credit and advised marketing managers on how to manipulate American women.[8] By 1931 the Hoover Commission on Home Ownership and Home Building established the private, single-family home as a national goal, but a decade and a half of depression and war postponed its achievement. Architects designed houses for Mr. and Mrs. Bliss in a competition sponsored by General Electric in 1935; winners accommodated dozens of electrical appliances in their designs with no critique of the energy costs involved.[9] In the late 1940s the single-family home was boosted by FHA and VA mortgages and the construction of isolated,

---

5. Industrial Housing Associates, "Good Homes Make Contented Workers," 1919, Edith Elmer Wood Papers, Avery Library, Columbia University. Also see Barbara Ehrenreich and Deirdre English, "The Manufacture of Housework." *Socialist Revolution* 5 (1975): 16. They quote an unidentified corporate official (ca. 1920): "Get them to invest their savings in homes and own them. Then they won't leave and they won't strike. It ties them down so they have a stake in our prosperity."
6. Stuart Ewen, *Captains of Consciousness: Advertising and the Social Roots of the Consumer Culture* (New York: McGraw-Hill Book Co., 1976).
7. Richard Walker, "Suburbanization in Passage," unpublished draft paper (Berkeley, University of California, Berkeley, Department of Geography, 1977).
8. Christine Frederick, *Selling Mrs. Consumer* (New York: Business Course, 1929).
9. Carol Barkin, "Home, Mom, and Pie-in-the-Sky" (M. Arch, thesis, University of California, Los Angeles, 1979), p. 120–24, gives the details of this competition; Ruth Schwartz Cowan, in an unpublished lecture at M.I.T. in 1977, explained GE's choice of an energy-consuming design for its refrigerator in the 1920s, because this would increase demand for its generating equipment by municipalities.

overprivatized, energy-consuming dwellings became commonplace. "I'll Buy That Dream" made the postwar hit parade.[10]

Mrs. Consumer moved the economy to new heights in the fifties. Women who stayed at home experienced what Betty Friedan called the "feminine mystique" and Peter Filene renamed the "domestic mystique."[11] While the family occupied its private physical space, the mass media and social science experts invaded its psychological space more effectively than ever before.[12] With the increase in spatial privacy came pressure for conformity in consumption. Consumption was expensive. More and more married women joined the paid labor force, as the suggestible housewife needed to be both a frantic consumer and a paid worker to keep up with the family's bills. Just as the mass of white male workers had achieved the "dream houses" in suburbia where fantasies of patriarchal authority and consumption could be acted out, their spouses entered the world of paid employment. By 1975, the two-worker family accounted for 39 percent of American households. Another 13 percent were single-parent families, usually headed by women. Seven out of ten employed women were in the work force because of financial need. Over 50 percent of all children between one and seventeen had employed mothers.[13]

How does a conventional home serve the employed woman and her family? Badly. Whether it is in a suburban, exurban, or inner-city neighborhood, whether it is a split-level ranch house, a modern masterpiece of concrete and glass, or an old brick tenement, the house or apartment is almost invariably organized around the same set of spaces: kitchen, dining room, living room, bedrooms, garage or parking area. These spaces require someone to undertake private cooking, cleaning, child care, and usually private transportation if adults and children are to exist within it. Because of residential zoning practices, the typical dwelling will usually be physically removed from any shared community space—no commercial or communal day-care facilities, or laundry facilities, for example, are likely to be part of the dwelling's spatial domain. In many cases these facilities would be illegal if placed across property lines. They could also be illegal if located on residentially zoned sites. In some cases sharing such a private dwelling with other individuals (either relatives or those unrelated by blood) is also against the law.[14]

Within the private spaces of the dwelling, material culture works against the needs of the employed woman as much as zoning does, because the home is a box to be filled with commodities. Appliances are usually single-purpose, and often inefficient, energy-consuming machines, lined up in a room where the domestic work is done in isolation from the rest of the family. Rugs and carpets

10. Peter Filene, *Him/Her/Self: Sex Roles in Modern America* (New York: Harcourt Brace Jovanovich, 1974), p. 189.

11. Betty Friedan, *The Feminine Mystique* (1963; New York: W. W. Norton & Co., 1974), p. 307, somewhat hysterically calls the home a "comfortable concentration camp"; Filene, p. 194, suggests that men are victimized by ideal homes too, thus "domestic" mystique.

12. Eli Zarelsky, *Capitalism, the Family, and Personal Life* (New York: Harper & Row, 1976), develops Friedman's earlier argument in a more systematic way. This phenomenon is misunderstood by Christopher Lasch, *Haven in a Heartless World* (New York: Alfred A. Knopf, 1977), who seems to favor a return to the sanctity of the patriarchal home.

13. Rosalyn Baxandall, Linda Gordon, and Susan Reverby. eds., *America's Working Women: A Documentary History, 1600 to the Present* (New York: Vintage Books, 1976). For more detail, see Louise Kapp Howe, *Pink Collar Workers: Inside the World of Woman's Work* (New York: Avon Books, 1977).

14. Recent zoning fights on the commune issue have occurred in Santa Monica, Calif.; Wendy Schuman, "The Return of Togetherness," *New York Times* (March 20, 1977), reports frequent illegal down zoning by two-family groups in one-family residences in the New York area.

which need vacuuming, curtains which need laundering, and miscellaneous goods which need maintenance fill up the domestic spaces, often decorated in "colonial," "Mediterranean," "French Provincial," or other eclectic styles purveyed by discount and department stores to cheer up that bare box of an isolated house. Employed mothers usually are expected to, and almost invariably do, spend more time in private housework and child care than employed men; often they are expected to, and usually do, spend more time on commuting per mile traveled than men, because of their reliance on public transportation. One study found that 70 percent of adults without access to cars are female.[15] Their residential neighborhoods are not likely to provide much support for their work activities. A "good" neighborhood is usually defined in terms of conventional shopping, schools, and perhaps public transit, rather than additional social services for the working parent, such as day care or evening clinics.

While two-worker families with both parents energetically cooperating can overcome some of the problems of existing housing patterns, households in crisis, such as subjects of wife and child battering, for example, are particularly vulnerable to its inadequacies. According to Colleen McGrath, every thirty seconds a woman is being battered somewhere in the United States. Most of these batterings occur in kitchens and bedrooms. The relationship between household isolation and battering, or between unpaid domestic labor and battering, can only be guessed, at this time, but there is no doubt that America's houses and households are literally shaking with domestic violence.[16] In addition, millions of angry and upset women are treated with tranquilizers in the private home—one drug company advertises to doctors: "You can't change her environment but you can change her mood."[17]

The woman who does leave the isolated, single-family house or apartment finds very few real housing alternatives available to her.[18] The typical divorced or battered woman currently seeks housing, employment, and child care simultaneously. She finds that matching her complex family requirements with the various available offerings by landlords, employers, and social services is impossible. One environment that unites housing, services, and jobs could resolve many difficulties, but the existing system of government services, intended to stabilize households and neighborhoods by ensuring the minimum conditions for a decent home life to all Americans, almost always assumes that the traditional household with a male worker and an unpaid homemaker is the goal to be achieved or simulated. In the face of massive demographic changes, programs such as public housing, AFDC, and food stamps still attempt to support an ideal family living in an isolated house or apartment, with a full-time homemaker cooking meals and minding children many hours of the day.

By recognizing the need for a different kind of environment, far more efficient use can be made of funds now used for subsidies to individual households. Even for women with greater financial resources the need for better housing and services is obvious. Currently, more affluent women's problems as workers have been considered "private" problems—the lack of good day care, their lack

15. Study by D. Foley cited in Wekerle (see n. 1 above).
16. Colleen McGrath, "The Crisis of Domestic Order," *Socialist Review* 9 (January–February 1979): 12, 23.
17. Research by Malcolm MacEwen, cited in *Associate Collegiate Schools of Architecture Newsletter* (March 1973), p. 6.
18. See, for example, Carol A. Brown, "Spatial Inequalities and Divorced Mothers"(paper delivered at the annual meeting of the American Sociological Association. San Francisco, 1978); Susan Anderson-Khleif, Research report for HUD on single-parent families and their housing, summarized in "Housing for Single Parents." *Research Report, MIT-Harvard Joint Center for Urban Studies* (April 1979), p. 3–4.

of time. The aids to overcome an environment without child care, public transportation, or food service have been "private," commercially profitable solutions: maids and baby-sitters by the hour; franchise day care or extended television viewing; fast food service; easier credit for purchasing an automobile, a washer, or a microwave oven. Not only do these commercial solutions obscure the failure of American housing policies, they also generate bad conditions for other working women. Commercial day-care and fast-food franchises are the source of low-paying nonunion jobs without security. In this respect they resemble the use of private household workers by bourgeois women, who may never ask how their private maid or child-care worker arranges care for her own children. They also resemble the insidious effects of the use of television in the home as a substitute for developmental child care in the neighborhood. The logistical problems which all employed women face are not private problems, and they do not succumb to market solutions.

The problem is paradoxical: women cannot improve their status in the home unless their overall economic position in society is altered; women cannot improve their status in the paid labor force unless their domestic responsibilities are altered. Therefore, a program to achieve economic and environmental justice for women requires, by definition, a solution which overcomes the traditional divisions between the household and the market economy, the private dwelling and the workplace. One must transform the economic situation of the traditional home-maker whose skilled labor has been unpaid, but economically and socially necessary to society; one must also transform the domestic situation of the employed woman. If architects and urban designers were to recognize all employed women and their families as a constituency for new approaches to planning and design and were to reject all previous assumptions about "woman's place" in the home, what could we do? Is it possible to build non-sexist neighborhoods and design non-sexist cities? What would they be like?

Some countries have begun to develop new approaches to the needs of employed women. The Cuban Family Code of 1974 requires men to share housework and child care within the private home. The degree of its enforcement is uncertain, but in principle it aims at men's sharing what was formerly "women's work," which is essential to equality. The Family Code, however, does not remove work from the house, and relies upon private negotiation between husband and wife for its day-to-day enforcement. Men feign incompetence, especially in the area of cooking, with tactics familiar to any reader of Patricia Mainardi's essay, "The Politics of Housework," and the sexual stereotyping of paid jobs for women outside the home, in day-care centers for example, has not been successfully challenged.[19]

Another experimental approach involves the development of special housing facilities for employed women and their families. The builder Otto Fick first introduced such a program in Copenhagen in 1903. In later years it was encouraged in Sweden by Alva Myrdal and by the architects Sven Ivar Lind and Sven Markelius. Called "service houses" or "collective houses," such

---

19. Patricia Mainardi, "The Politics of Housework," in *Sisterhood Is Powerful*, ed. Robin Morgan (New York: Vintage Books, 1970). My discussion of the Cuban Family Code is based on a visit to Cuba in 1978; a general review is Carollee Bengelsdorf and Alice Hageman, "Emerging from Underdevelopment: Women and Work in Cuba," in *Capitalist Patriarchy and the Case for Socialist Feminism*, ed. Z. Eisenstein (New York: Monthly Review Press, 1979). Also see Geoffrey F. Fox, "Honor, Shame and Women's Liberation in Cuba: Views of Working-Class Emigré Men," in *Female and Male in Latin America*, ed. A. Pescatello (Pittsburgh: University of Pittsburgh Press, 1973).
20. Erwin Muhlestein, "Kollektives Wohnen gestern und heute," *Architese* 14 (1975).

projects (figs. 1 and 2 [not included]) provide child care and cooked food along with housing for employed women and their families.[20] Like a few similar projects in the USSR in the 1920s, they aim at offering services, either on a commercial basis or subsidized by the state, to replace formerly private "women's work" performed in the household. The Scandinavian solution does not sufficiently challenge male exclusion from domestic work, nor does it deal with households' changing needs over the life cycle, but it recognizes that it is important for environmental design to change.

Some additional projects in Europe extend the scope of the service house to include the provision of services for the larger community or society. In the Steilshoop Project, in Hamburg, Germany, in the early 1970s, a group of parents and single people designed public housing with supporting services (fig. 3 [not included]).[21] The project included a number of former mental patients as residents and therefore served as a halfway house for them, in addition to providing support services for the public-housing tenants who organized it. It suggests the extent to which current American residential stereotypes can be broken down—the sick, the aged, the unmarried can be integrated into new types of households and housing complexes, rather than segregated in separate projects.

Another recent project was created in London by Nina West Homes, a development group established in 1972, which has built or renovated over sixty-three units of housing on six sites for single parents. Children's play areas or day-care centers are integrated with the dwellings; in their Fiona House project the housing is designed to facilitate shared baby-sitting, and the day-care center is open to the neighborhood residents for a fee (fig. 4 [not included]). Thus the single parents can find jobs as day-care workers and help the neighborhood's working parents as well.[22] What is most exciting here is the hint that home and work can be reunited on one site for some of the residents, and home and child-care services are reunited on one site for all of them.

Fig. 3. [not included]—"Urbanes Wohnen" (urban living) Steilshoop, north of Hamburg, Germany, public housing for 206 tenants, designed by the tenant association in collaboration with Rolf Spille, 1970–73. Instead of seventy-two conventional units they built twenty multifamily units and two studios. Twenty-six mental patients were included in the project, of whom twenty-four recovered. Partial floor plan. Units include private bedrooms (br), living rooms (lr), and some studies (s). They share a collective living room, kitchen, dining room, and playroom. Each private apartment can be closed off from the collective space and each is different. (1) storage room; (2) closets; (3) wine cellar; (4) *buanderie;* (5) fire stair.

21. This project relies on the "support structures" concept of John Habraken to provide flexible interior partitions and fixed mechanical core and structure.

22. "Bridge over Troubled Water." *Architects' Journal* (September 27, 1972), p. 680–84; personal interview with Nina West, 1978.

23. Dolores Hayden, *A "Grand Domestic Revolution": Feminism, Socialism and the American Home, 1870–1930* (Cambridge, Mass.: M.I.T. Press, 1980); "Two Utopian Feminists and Their Campaigns for Kitchenless Houses," *Signs: Journal of Women in Culture and Society* 4, no. 2 (Winter 1979): 274–90; "Melusina Fay Peirce and Cooperative Housekeeping," *International Journal of Urban and Regional Research* 2 (1978): 404–20; "Challenging the American Domestic Ideal," and "Catharine Beecher and the Politics of Housework," in *Women in American Architecture*, ed. S. Torre (New York: Whitney Library of Design, 1977), p. 22–39, 40–49; "Charlotte Perkins Gilman: Domestic Evolution or Domestic Revolution," *Radical History Review*, vol. 21 (Winter 1979–80), in press.

In the United States, we have an even longer history of agitation for housing to reflect women's needs. In the late nineteenth century and early twentieth century there were dozens of projects by feminists, domestic scientists, and architects attempting to develop community services for private homes. By the late 1920s, few such experiments were still functioning.[23] In general, feminists of that era failed to recognize the problem of exploiting other women workers when providing services for those who could afford them. They also often failed to see men as responsible parents and workers in their attempts to socialize "women's" work. But feminist leaders had a very strong sense of the possibilities of neighborly cooperation among families and of the economic importance of "women's" work.

In addition, the United States has a long tradition of experimental utopian socialist communities building model towns, as well as the example of many communes and collectives established in the 1960s and 1970s which attempted to broaden conventional definitions of household and family.[24] While some communal groups, especially religious ones, have often demanded acceptance of a traditional sexual division of labor, others have attempted to make nurturing activities a responsibility of both women and men. It is important to draw on the examples of successful projects of all kinds, in seeking an image of a non-sexist settlement. Most employed women are not interested in taking themselves and their families to live in communal families, nor are they interested in having state bureaucracies run family life. They desire, not an end to private life altogether, but community services to support the private household. They also desire solutions which reinforce their economic independence and maximize their personal choices about child rearing and sociability.

Fig. 4. [not included]—*A.* Fiona House, second-floor plan, main building, showing corridor used as playroom, with kitchen windows opening into it; first-floor plan, rear building, showing nursery school. *B.* Axonometric drawing. Fiona House. Nina West Homes, London 1972, designed by Sylvester Bone. Twelve two-bedroom units for divorced or separated mothers with additional outdoor play space, and neighborhood nursery school facility. Flats can be linked by intercom system to provide an audio substitute for baby-sitting.

What, then, would be the outline of a program for change in the United States? The task of reorganizing both home and work can only be accomplished by organizations of homemakers, women and men dedicated to making changes in the ways that Americans deal with private life and public responsibilities. They must be small, participatory organizations with members who can work together effectively. I propose calling such groups HOMES (Homemakers Organization for a More Egalitarian Society). Existing feminist groups, especially those providing shelters for battered wives and children, may wish to form HOMES to take over existing housing projects and develop services for residents as an extension of those offered by feminist counselors in the shelter. Existing organizations supporting cooperative ownership of housing may wish to form HOMES to extend their housing efforts in a feminist direction. A program broad enough to transform housework, housing, and residential neighborhoods must: (1) involve both men and women in the unpaid labor associated with housekeeping and child care on an equal basis; (2) involve both men and women in the paid labor force on an equal basis; (3) eliminate residential segregation by class, race,

---

24. Dolores Hayden, *Seven American Utopias: The Architecture of Communitarian Socialism, 1790–1975* (Cambridge, Mass.: M.I.T. Press, 1976), discusses historical examples and includes a discussion of communes of the 1960s and 1970s, "Edge City, Heart City, Drop City: Communal Building Today." p. 320–47.

and age; (4) eliminate all federal, state, and local programs and laws which offer implicit or explicit reinforcement of the unpaid role of the female homemaker; (5) minimize unpaid domestic labor and wasteful energy consumption; (6) maximize real choices for households concerning recreation and sociability. While many partial reforms can support these goals, an incremental strategy cannot achieve them. I believe that the establishment of experimental residential centers, which in their architectural design and economic organization transcend traditional definitions of home, neighborhood, city, and workplace, will be necessary to make changes on this scale. These centers could be created through renovation of existing neighborhoods or through new construction.

Suppose forty households in a U.S. metropolitan area formed a HOMES group and that those households, in their composition, represented the social structure of the American population as a whole. Those forty households would include: seven single parents and their fourteen children (15 percent); sixteen two-worker couples and their twenty-four children (40 percent); thirteen one-worker couples and their twenty-six children (35 percent); and four single residents, some of them "displaced homemakers" (10 percent). The residents would include sixty-nine adults and sixty-four children. There would need to be forty private dwelling units, ranging in size from efficiency to three bedrooms, all with private fenced outdoor space. In addition to the private housing, the group would provide the following collective spaces and activities: (1) a day-care center with landscaped outdoor space, providing day care for forty children and after-school activities for sixty-four children; (2) a laundromat providing laundry service; (3) a kitchen providing lunches for the day-care center, take-out evening meals, and "meals-on-wheels" for elderly people in the neighborhood; (4) a grocery depot, connected to a local food cooperative; (5) a garage with two vans providing dial-a-ride service and meals-on-wheels; (6) a garden (or allotments) where some food can be grown; (7) a home-help office providing helpers for the elderly, the sick, and employed parents whose children are sick. The use of all of these collective services should be voluntary; they would exist in addition to private dwelling units and private gardens.

To provide all of the above services, thirty-seven workers would be necessary: twenty day-care workers; three food-service workers; one grocery-depot worker; five home helpers; two drivers of service vehicles; two laundry workers; one maintenance worker; one gardener; two administrative staff. Some of these may be part-time workers, some full-time. Day care, food services, and elderly services could be organized as producers' cooperatives, and other workers could be employed by the housing cooperative as discussed below.

Because HOMES is not intended as an experiment in isolated community buildings but as an experiment in meeting employed women's needs in an urban area, its services should be available to the neighborhood in which the experiment is located. This will increase demand for the services and insure that the jobs are real ones. In addition, although residents of HOMES should have priority for the jobs, there will be many who choose outside work. So some local residents may take jobs within the experiment.

In creating and filling these jobs it will be important to avoid traditional sex stereotyping that would result from hiring only men as drivers, for example, or only women as food-service workers. Every effort should be made to break down separate categories of paid work for women and men, just as efforts should be made to recruit men who accept an equal share of domestic responsibilities as residents. A version of the Cuban Family Code should become part of the organization's platform.

Similarly, HOMES must not create a two-class society with residents outside the project making more money than residents in HOMES jobs that utilize some of their existing domestic skills.

The HOMES jobs should be paid according to egalitarian rather than sex-stereotyped attitudes about skills and hours. These jobs must be all classified as skilled work rather than as unskilled or semiskilled at present, and offer full social security and health benefits, including adequate maternity leave, whether workers are part-time or full-time.

Many federal Housing and Urban Development programs support the construction or non-profit, low and moderate-cost housing, including section 106b, section 202, and section 8. In addition, HUD section 213 funds are available to provide mortgage insurance for the conversion of existing housing of five or more units to housing cooperatives. HEW programs also fund special facilities such as day-care centers or meals-on-wheels for the elderly. In addition, HUD and HEW offer funds for demonstration projects which meet community needs in new ways.[25] Many trade unions, churches, and tenant cooperative organizations are active as nonprofit housing developers. A limited-equity housing cooperative offers the best basis for economic organization and control of both physical design and social policy by the residents.

Many knowledgeable nonprofit developers could aid community groups wishing to organize such projects, as could architects experienced in the design of housing cooperatives. What has not been attempted is the reintegration of work activities and collective services into housing cooperatives on a large enough scale to make a real difference to employed women. Feminists in trade unions where a majority of members are women, wish to consider building cooperative housing with services for their members. Other trade unions may wish to consider investing in such projects. Feminists in the co-op movement must make strong, clear demands to get such services from existing housing cooperatives, rather than simply go along with plans for conventional housing organized on a cooperative economic basis. Feminists outside the cooperative movement will find that cooperative organizational forms offer many possibilities for supporting their housing activities and other services to women. In addition, the recently established national Consumer Cooperative Bank has funds to support projects of all kinds which can be tied to cooperative housing.

In many areas, the rehabilitation of existing housing may be more desirable than new construction. The suburban housing stock in the United States must be dealt with effectively. A little bit of it is of architectural quality sufficient to deserve preservation; most of it can be aesthetically improved by the physical evidence of more intense social activity. To replace empty front lawns without sidewalks, neighbors can create blocks where single units are converted to multiple units; interior land is pooled to create a parklike setting at the center of the block; front and side lawns are fenced to make private outdoor spaces; pedestrian paths and sidewalks are created to link all units with the central open space; and some private porches, garages, tool sheds, utility rooms, and family rooms are converted to community facilities such as children's play areas, dial-a-ride garages, and laundries.

To convert this whole block and the housing on it to more efficient and sociable uses, one has to define a zone of greater activity at the heart of the block, taking a total of one and one half to two acres for collective use (fig. 5B [not included]). Essentially, this means turning the block inside out. The Radburn plan, developed by Henry Wright and Clarence Stein in the late 1920s, delineated this principle very clearly as correct land use in "the motor age," with cars segregated from

---

25. I am indebted to Geraldine Kennedy and Sally Kratz, whose unpublished papers, "Toward Financing Cooperative Housing," and "Social Assistance Programs Whose Funds Could Be Redirected to Collective Services," were prepared for my UCLA graduate seminar in spring 1979.

residents' green spaces, especially spaces for children. In Radburn, New Jersey, and in the Baldwin Hills district of Los Angeles, California, Wright and Stein achieved remarkably luxurious results (at a density of about seven units to the acre) by this method, since their multiple-unit housing always bordered a lush parkland without any automobile traffic. The Baldwin Hills project demonstrates this success most dramatically, but a revitalized suburban block with lots as small as one-fourth acre can be reorganized to yield something of this same effect.[26] In this case, social amenities are added to aesthetic ones as the interior park is designed to accommodate community day care, a garden for growing vegetables, some picnic tables, a playground where swings and slides are grouped, a grocery depot connected to a larger neighborhood food cooperative, and a dial-a-ride garage.

Large single-family houses can be remodeled quite easily to become duplexes and triplexes, despite the "open plans" of the 1950s and 1960s popularized by many developers. The house in figure 6A [not included] becomes, in figure 6B [not included], a triplex, with a two-bedroom unit (linked to a community garage); a one-bedroom unit; and an efficiency unit (for a single person or elderly person). All three units are shown with private enclosed gardens. The three units share a front porch and entry hall. There is still enough land to give about two-fifths of the original lot to the community. Particularly striking is the way in which existing spaces such as back porches or garages lend themselves to conversion to social areas or community services. Three former private garages out of thirteen might be given over to collective uses—one as a central office for the whole block, one as a grocery depot, and one as a dial-a-ride garage. Is it possible to have only twenty cars (in ten garages) and two vans for twenty-six units in a rehabilitated block? Assuming that some residents switch from outside employment to working within the block, and that for all residents, neighborhood shopping trips are cut in half by the presence of day care, groceries, laundry, and cooked food on the block, as well as aided by the presence of some new collective transportation, this might be done.

What about neighbors who are not interested in such a scheme? Depending on the configuration of lots, it is possible to begin such a plan with as few as three or four houses. In Berkeley, California, where neighbors on Derby Street joined their backyards and created a cooperative day-care center, one absentee landlord refused to join—his entire property is fenced in and the community space flows around it without difficulty. Of course, present zoning laws must be changed, or variances obtained, for the conversion of single-family houses into duplexes and triplexes and the introduction of any sort of commercial activities into a residential block. However, a community group that is able to organize or acquire at least five units could become a HUD housing cooperative, with a nonprofit corporation owning all land and with producers' cooperatives running the small community services. With a coherent plan for an entire block, variances could be obtained much more easily than on a lot-by-lot basis. One can also imagine organizations which run halfway houses—for ex-mental patients, or runaway teenagers, or battered women—integrating their activities into such a block plan, with an entire building for their activities. Such groups often find it difficult to achieve the supportive neighborhood context such a block organization would offer.

I believe that attacking the conventional division between public and private space should become a socialist and feminist priority in the 1980s. Women must transform the sexual division

---

26. See also the successful experience of Zurich, described in Hans Wirz, "Back Yard Rehab: Urban Microcosm Rediscovered," *Urban Innovation Abroad 3* (July 1979): 2–3.

of domestic labor, the privatized economic basis of domestic work, and the spatial separation of homes and workplaces in the built environment if they are to be equal members of society. The experiments I propose are an attempt to unite the best features of past and present reforms in our own society and others, with some of the existing social services available in the United States today. I would like to see several demonstration HOMES begun, some involving new construction following the program I have laid out, others involving the rehabilitation of suburban blocks. If the first few experimental projects are successful, homemakers across the United States will want to obtain day-care, food, and laundry services at a reasonable price, as well as better wages, more flexible working conditions, and more suitable housing. When all homemakers recognize that they are struggling against both gender stereotypes and wage discrimination, when they see that social, economic, and environmental changes are necessary to overcome these conditions, they will no longer tolerate housing and cities, designed around the principles of another era, that proclaim that "a woman's place is in the home."

School of Architecture and Urban Planning
University of California, Los Angeles

11 Perception and Awareness: What Is This Setting?

Fritz Steele

Steele gives a vivid description of how perception is active, resulting from acculturation of our senses, so that we only see what we are programmed to see. Different meanings are not only the result of different interpretations, but also, more fundamentally, environmental evaluation takes place at the very instant of sensation, before we even know the nature or origin of what we experience. This perspective helps set up the somatic point of view.

Because a sense of place is the result of interplay between a person and a setting, an important determinant of that sense is the means of connecting the two. This connection process can be roughly divided into two general parts: (1) perceiving what is there in the setting and organizing it into usable categories of information, and (2) becoming aware of particular features or combinations of features in a setting at a particular moment.

In this chapter we will consider some basic aspects of the human experiences of perception and awareness. My purpose is not to go into the kind of detail that would be contained in a book on the psychology of perception, but simply to provide a basis for discussing the more central ideas regarding our own roles in experiencing a sense of place.[1]

PERCEPTION: CREATING OUR OWN SCENARIOS

Perception is an information-receiving process wherein a person (1) receives a signal from the immediate setting (sees a bird fly by, smells an oil slick, hears another person utter a sound); and (2) organizes these incoming signals in such a way as to give them meaning within a personal view of the world (identifies the moving object as a "bird" or "seagull," registers the smell as oily, decodes the other person's sounds as speech and understands its meaning, and so on).

In playing its linking function, perception helps us organize external information so that we can feel that we "know" something about what surrounds us and what is likely to happen to us. Having this information provides us with some control over our own fate, so that we are not always at the whim of unpredictable events. The importance of this sense of control is brought home to

---

Fritz Steel, "Perception and Awareness: What Is This Setting?," from *The Sense of Place*, pp. 21–31. Copyright © 1981 by CBI Publishing Company. Permission to reprint granted by the publisher.

us when we lose it, as in the experience of diving into murky water where sights and sounds are suddenly cut off.

A second major function of human perception is to deal with the fact that there is always too much to tune into. In almost any setting at any time there are more potential signals than we can receive or process. We are not only limited in the amount of information we can process; we also need to retain some energy (and attention) for activities other than perception. A major problem is how to select what to receive and what to screen out. In relatively safe situations the quality of our decisions may not make much difference. In others, such as passing through a dangerous jungle area, the ability to focus on subtle cues (the rustle of a leaf, a flash of movement ahead) can mean the difference between living and dying. People naturally acquire selection patterns that work best for them in the settings in which the patterns were developed: a resident of the Amazon jungle can perceive the reflection from a snake's skin that would be "invisible" to most New Yorkers; and a New Yorker may be able to hear the "inaudible" sounds of a mugger's crepe soles tip-toeing along a Central Park bicycle path.

This view of perception as a selective process helps to illuminate what was meant in Chapter 2 about persons helping to create their own sense of place. There are many signals in any given setting, but which ones we pick up and how we interpret them shape how we actually experience both the setting and ourselves in it.

A writer named Serge Boutourline has described the difference between an "object-oriented" and "signal-oriented" view of the environment.[2] The object-oriented view says that people are surrounded by articles that have specific properties; the person's ability to perceive the environment is measured by the ability to tune into these properties and use them. The signal-oriented approach says that the environment is made up of an infinite number of signals being sent out by the objects (and lack of objects) surrounding a person. Perception is thus determined by the points on the person's "envelope of space" that receive these signals, and in what order they are received. This theory suggests the analogy of the cinema: we are like directors putting together movie scenarios (our own experiences), using sets and props (our surroundings, including various aids such as other people, transport vehicles, communications devices, drugs) that help us to collect and order signals in some quantity and sequence (the editing process), which then becomes our perception of the "world." We usually think of this experience as simply a function of what's "out there," downplaying our own role in the creation of the scenario.

This view is consistent with the theme of this book, which is that much of our experience of place is determined by how we perceive, organize, and react to signals from our settings, rather than any objective qualities of the settings themselves. Perception is therefore an active contributor to shaping our world, rather than a passive receiver of whatever is around us.

PERCEPTUAL STYLES

The preceding comments have referred to the general process of human perception that is shared by most people. There are also specific styles of perceiving that vary from person to person and group to group. The particular locale and culture in which one is raised will favor some views of the world and discourage others. For example, people who grow up in the United States plains states are more aware of the horizon than those who grow up in city settings where one usually only can see for short distances.

The degree of contrast among parts of our regular settings can determine what we are able to see, as well as our preferences and what we consider to be "beautiful." People who grow up in the Barrens area of the North American Arctic can see the beauty that eludes those who are familiar with more "upholstered" or lush settings.

> Staring out over the limitless brown expanse I at first saw only a rolling world of faded brown, shot through with streaks and whorls of yellow-greens, for when I tried to see it all, the individual colors merged into anonymity. It *was* a barren sight, and yet that desert face concealed a beauty that rose from a thousand sources, under the white sun. The deep chocolate bogs, laden with rich sepia dyes that stain the streams and pools, were bounded by wide swales of emerald sedges and tall grass. On the sweeping slopes that rose above these verdant meadows, the dark and glossy greens of dwarf birch scrub formed amorphous patches of somber vitality that were illuminated by broad spaces where the brilliance of ten million minute flowers drew themselves small butterflies as gorgeous as any in the world.
>
> (Farley Mowat, *People of the Deer*)

While as a visitor it took Mowat some time to see the variations and the beauty in the Barrens, natives of this area would quite naturally see these features, having spent their lives making such distinctions.

Another factor that attunes our perceptual style is our pattern of personal interests. For example, when college president John Coleman took a sabbatical to work as a manual laborer laying sewer lines, he started seeing waste systems that had been invisible to him before. When visiting an art museum on his days off, instead of speculating about the place of art in the world's history, he wondered who had laid the museum's underground pipes.[3] Thus we tend to notice those items that interest us—they become the main figures that we pick out of the larger number of potential signals, and the rest are left as background.

The kind of detail that has considerable variety if you look for it: the suburban fireplug.

PHYSICAL PROPERTIES AND PERCEPTION

Of course, not all factors that shape a person's particular pattern of perception are qualities of the person. There are some features of physical setting that have been found to have consistent effects on perception. For one, our view of the sizes of objects is influenced by the overall scale of the setting in relation to ourselves. We overestimate sizes when we are small, as is shown in William Saroyan's views of Sunday church services as a child:

> When I sat upstairs to listen to Reverend Knadjian's sermon and looked down at the benches, every place taken, I imagined that there were a great many people there, a multitude, in short. The fact is that the church could scarcely contain two hundred people. The balcony ran around the auditorium. There were two rows of benches on the sides, and four at the back of the balcony. Still, I had always imagined that a great multitude was inside the Church.
>
> (William Saroyan, *Places Where I've Done Time*)

This relative perception also explains why we can go back to the settings of our childhood, but we can never go back to our childhood places, which were experiences that were mixtures of ourselves and those settings. The large woods we explored are revealed to the adult as a patch of trees in a vacant lot, the kitchen that seemed so formidably vast as Mother's domain now looks tiny and cramped, and so on.

Another important physical property is the degree of closure in a structure. We see spaces as "things" as long as any closure at all provides a boundary that defines an area and gives us something to work with. Nan Fairbrother described this in her wonderful discussion of landscape design for human enjoyment:

> Human vision seems naturally inclined to create enclosures in space even when the actual physical barriers are extremely slight, and given the merest suggestion of enclosure we ourselves supply the rest. A widely spaced row of lamp standards, for instance, arched over a road creates a continuous tunnel in space; half a dozen bollards will close off the side of a square for the eye as well as the motor car.
>
> (Nan Fairbrother, *The Nature of Landscape Design*)

People who understand this can create a strong spirit of place for a modest house and front yard simply by placing a few stones, posts, or pieces of fence in strategic spots. Later we will return to the sense of place that can be enriched by contrast, scale, and enclosure, especially when we open ourselves to perceiving settings in new ways.

AWARENESS OF SETTINGS

As noted earlier, perception is only one-half of the process of linking a person to a setting. After perception comes awareness, where the person uses incoming information as raw material for thoughts and feelings about the setting. Awareness can be about specific elements in the setting (colors, floors, walls, trees, odors, and so on), or about patterns and relationships among elements such as distances, relative locations, or contrasting textures.

What Stimulates Our Awareness?

Sights: Most people are probably familiar with the ways in which the things they see shape their awareness of their setting. That which is seen is partly determined by elements that stand out as "figures," and those that remain in the background; this relationship can be reversed, as when we suddenly become aware of a single detail in a room. In order to see a range of possible sights in a setting, however, we must allow what exists to come into our awareness. People often do the opposite, which is to say, they shape their perception of the setting based on what they are accustomed to seeing or expect to see. This habit leads to what the Gestalt psychologists call staring, rather than seeing. Edwin Way Teale observed two experienced starers on the breathtaking crest of the Continental Divide in Colorado's Rocky Mountains:

> As we stood discussing such things (as the joy of such a spot), two business men struck up an acquaintance nearby. They talked endlessly, loudly, always on the same subject: the clubs they had belonged to, how one had presided over a grand conclave, how the other had headed a committee that brought in twenty-two new members. All the while the great spiritual experience of the mountains was passing them by. Unseen, unfelt, unappreciated, the beauty of the land unfolded around them. The clubs of the world formed their world entire. It enclosed them like the home of a snail wherever they went. For them, the scene would have been just as moving if they had been hemmed in by billboards.
>
> (Edwin Way Teale, *Journey into Summer*)

One wonders why the men were there to begin with; they were probably "doing" the Rocky Mountains in a day or two.

Not only businessmen have trouble with staring, of course. For many years, explorers who visited the inner gorge of the Grand Canyon in Arizona saw a barren environment because they had been told that the gorge had no plant life except at one area called Vasey's Paradise. This has recently been shown to be quite false; there are many plants that grow in the Canyon, and the barrenness was mostly in the eyes of the beholders.[4]

Because people tend to see in settings what they expect to be there, they often fail to be aware of beauty in unconventional sites that are not labeled "beautiful" by prevailing values. Seeing beauty along the banks of the Seine in Paris fits with what one is supposed to see there; but seeing beauty in the rundown dockside areas of the Thames in London requires one really to look at what is there, and to allow the special patterns of light, texture, reflection, and contrast to be seen for their own beauty, in spite of the fact that many of the elements are old, broken, or derelict.

There is an interesting problem in the English language with the way we describe awareness: we use almost entirely visual terms, such as "seeing," and "looking," to give our sense of place awareness. In fact, western European civilizations do rely on sight to the detriment of the other senses, but not as greatly as our vocabulary would suggest.

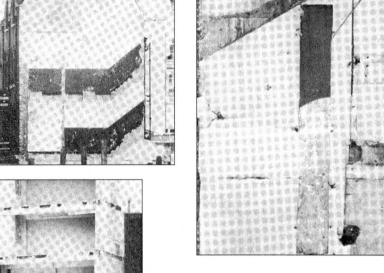

Three building ends that can be seen as dilapidation or beautiful abstract forms, depending on your point of view.

Smells: For impact on our awareness of settings, smells are at least a close second to sights. For instance, farmers generally sense the changing seasons of the year first through changing smells, not through visual cues. Each season has its own distinctive smells, but so do the transition periods, so that a "country smells calendar" would have many more than four recurring seasons on it.

> What a world of the nose the country can be from the cidery smell of apples rotting in the brown, frosty grass under a wild apple tree to the honorable aroma of freshly dug onions spread on sacking in the autumn sun. There are plenty of others, hearty enough, some of them, but all, somehow or other, fit into a country world.
>
> (Henry Beston, *Northern Farm*)

Smells are also an important part of city awareness, but with different patterns. The changes of seasons produce fewer new odors because they are masked by activities such as vehicle traffic and its exhaust fumes that are continuous throughout the year. The variations in smell are sensed from section to section of a city, such as the gamey smells of a market area on a warm day, or tarry smells of soft streets. Cities as a whole may also have characteristic smells: there is a certain whiff of diesel exhaust fumes that always means "London" to me as they are belched throughout the city by the taxis and buses; while New Haven, Connecticut's odors often seem for some reason to remind me of vegetable soup.

A very special corner that looks like nothing. Your nose tells you that you're next to a spice company.

Given such patterns, it was inevitable that there would be attempts to design settings with smells to make people more or less aware of setting. In the United States, consumer products companies spend millions in advertising ("Oh, you had fish for dinner? Ughh.") to convince Americans that they should cover all traces of their home life (cooking smells, furniture odors, and so forth) with some anonymous scent such as "green trees," which had nothing to do with activities in the house. In the opposite direction, Vita Sackville-West and Harold Nicolson reportedly designed the gardens at Sissinghurst Castle in Kent to use smells to enhance immediate awareness of the setting. They did this by using mixtures of plantings that provided a succession of fragrances throughout the year, and by planning the relative locations of plants with different scents, so that visitors experienced special fragrance sequences as well as visual sequences while walking through the gardens.[5]

Sounds: Although we may notice a particular sound if it is unusual, such as a siren suddenly screaming in the night, our basic reception is made up of a mixture of sounds of different sources, intensities, and degrees of pleasantness (a learned taste except at extremely high, painful levels) that are received more or less together and create an overall "auditory atmosphere." Two settings can have different atmospheres, as Coleman describes so nicely:

> It suddenly hit me today how very noisy the kitchen [of the Union Oyster House Restaurant in Boston] is. The world I am used to [the President's office] at Haverford is such a quiet one. In my office, the only sounds through the day are the IBM typewriter next door, the loud gong of the grandfather clock each hour, the periodic ring of the telephone outside followed by my secretary's warm hello, and whatever quiet conversation there is within. In the Oyster House kitchen, it's a different world entirely. Muzak is constantly playing above my head, with music from my generation or from Broadway hit shows of one or two decades ago. One of the cooks has his radio going still louder, tuned to sports broadcasts, soul music, or what seems like an hourly replay of the hit of the day, "Killing Me Softly." In the busy hours, there is a steady shout of orders, and a reshout of lost orders; and there is the constant flow of social banter. Cooler and range doors bang, frying pans drop, and the steamer lets off steam. And over it all, there is the clatter of china and glassware being sorted into trays and the shoosh and swoosh of water in the dish machines. I know I am where the action is.
>
> (John Coleman, *Blue-Collar Journal*)

While visual cues on the average make us think verbally of what we see, both smells and sounds have their greatest impact subliminally, that is, not necessarily on the consciousness. A certain smell can change our mood, and the pattern of sounds can affect our mood or our view of the setting without our thinking about it. This was illustrated by an incident in a company whose building was redesigned as an "office landscape," complete with plants and a so-called "white noise generator" to produce an ambient noise level (gentle hum) that would mask conversations and provide privacy. One day the white noise generator broke down, and complaints about the temperature in the office area immediately began. Later discussions showed that the workers had unconsciously associated the hum of the generator with air conditioning noise, which it did, in fact, resemble. When the noise stopped, the office staff made the assumption that the air conditioning had gone off, so therefore it must be getting warmer in the office.

Heightened Awareness

There are certain times when one's awareness of settings suddenly increases dramatically. An example is the situation in which a decision is required, such as a driver arriving at a major junction or crossroad and having quickly to scan the nearby surroundings (buildings, signs, natural features) for cues as to the correct route. This is one reason why the distance seems longer when one is going to a destination for the first time than it does when making the return trip, especially when driving in an automobile. When trying to find the destination initially, one is aware of more elements of the route while looking for potential guide posts and points at which one might be required to make a decision. More details are carefully observed, therefore, and more experience packed into the first trip, making the return trip seem shorter by comparison.

Awareness of our immediate surroundings is also heightened by strangeness. Being "out of our element" often makes us notice features that can be seen (but are seldom noticed) in our home territories; this can open up new possibilities or pleasures within our surroundings. The striking cleanliness of certain European cities tends to jog American tourists' vision so that they notice details such as porches, stoops, steps, and fences that are invisible (but often just as interesting) elements in their own home towns.

Last, changes in body state can lead to greater awareness of surroundings. The most familiar instance is the one when we feel physically ill. At such times we become more sensitive to subtle cues in the setting: currents of moving air, slight sounds, small changes in temperature, hardness of surfaces, increases in light intensity, and so on. At such times we have less energy and attention to devote to simple adaptations to environmental variations that are, in fact, happening all the time, but that are usually screened out of our awareness. Instead, we are more attuned to our body and its relationship to the immediate surroundings. The old-fashioned hangover is a classic case of heightened settings awareness.

My purpose with these points has not been to tout constant awareness of settings, but to show that there are identifiable factors that enhance this sensitivity, and to suggest that to some degree it can be personally controlled. For example, you can make the conscious choice to look for certain features, which generally leads to seeing many new qualities that had previously gone unnoticed. A sculptor friend once started me looking at tin roofs of Vermont barns, and I saw varieties of style, construction, and beauty that had always been there but that had been invisible to me before. Similarly, if you were especially to look at the doorway of every building you entered over the course of a chosen week, you would never again take doorways for granted or be oblivious to their different qualities.

AWARENESS THROUGH CERTIFICATION

In closing this chapter, I want to touch on a special process that can increase awareness of settings in modern urban areas. This process, called "certification," results in a person feeling that his or her setting is somehow special, legitimate, or more real, as it has been certified by some reliable outside source.

As far as I know, the process of certification was first described by American novelist Walker Percy.[6] He suggested that when one sees one's own neighborhood in a movie that personal setting has been authorized as a real someplace, not just anyplace. This serves as an antidote to the modern urban trend toward undifferentiated settings that encourage alienation and disconnection from one's immediate surroundings. Through certification, the person is helped to see them as having distinctive features and a spirit of place.

When certification is considered this way, it can obviously happen in other ways besides seeing one's familiar territories in a commercial film. A similar effect occurs when someone sees the home area on a television news program, or reads about it in a newspaper, magazine, or book. In a study of Parisians' views of their city's special spots, Stanley Milgram found that they accent those international symbols (such as the *Arc de Triomphe*) that have been repeatedly certified by schools and public officials.[7] These choices are to some extent arbitrary social definitions, as they are in any city's school system, but they still shape citizens' views of the "important" locales in their cities.

My last example has been with us for many hundreds of years: it is the impact of visual arts. To take a modern instance, Cezanne changed the way many people saw the countrysides he painted, as did the other Impressionists and Post-Impressionists. Even today, many visitors to Paris see

City locations are often certified by being major stops in the transport system (Boston's Park St. Subway station).

it less for itself and more as a confirmation of the Paris they "know" through painting. The Ash Can School of painters in New York helped people to see beauty in the mundane underside of a large city's life. In a sense, the rough settings were certified as having value because people were bothering to do paintings of them without cleaning them up or idealizing them.

NOTES

1 For readers who would like more information on human perception, I would recommend J. J. Gibson, *The Senses Considered as Perceptual Systems* (Boston: Houghton Mifflin Co., 1966); the section on "Basic Psychological Processes and the Environment," in H. Proshansky, W. Ittelson, and L. Rivlin (eds.), *Environmental Psychology* (revised ed.) (New York: Holt, Rinehart and Winston, 1976); and Chapters 3 and 4 of David Canter, *The Psychology of Place* (London: The Architectural Press, 1977).

2 Serge Boutourline, "Notes on 'Object-oriented' and 'Signal-oriented' Approaches to the Definition of the Physical World Which Surrounds Individual Human Beings," unpublished paper prepared for Department of Architecture, University of Washington, 1969.

3 John R. Coleman, *Blue-Collar Journal: A College President's Sabbatical,* Philadelphia: J. B. Lippincott, 1974, p. 51.

4 Virginia McConnell Simmons, "Vasey's Paradise Lost?" *National Parks and Conservation Magazine,* Vol. 50, No. 10, 1976.

5 Ann Scott-James, *The Making of Sissinghurst,* London: Michael Joseph Publishers, 1973.

6 Walker Percy, *The Moviegoer,* New York: Alfred A. Knopf, 1961.

7 Stanley Milgram with Denise Jodelet, "Psychological Maps of Paris," in H. Proshansky, W. Ittelson, and L. Rivlin (eds.), *Environmental Psychology* (revised ed.).

12 The Homeless in Urban Parks: Is Exclusion the Solution?

Louise Mozingo

What principles of planning could accommodate homeless in public parks?

The concept was simple and laudable: Create a small park in the Tenderloin, a district of San Francisco woefully lacking in open space. City landscape architect Walter Kocian designed McCauley Park as a "social sidewalk" with a choice of seating, trees, a lawn panel and night lighting. After a thorough public review, Kocian saw the park through to completion in 1982.

The sunny, wind-sheltered park worked well, according to Kocian, and was used by all segments of society. But by 1987, word came down from the office of then mayor Dianne Feinstein that the park be fenced and closed at night. Though Kocian objected, the city put up the high fence without the review process required in the initial design. Prison-like and abandoned by most former users, McCauley Park quickly became the turf of local drug dealers who controlled access through the two gates. Now the park is frightening. But the impetus behind the fencing was behavior that, if socially unacceptable, was non-threatening: the use of the park by the homeless.

Such use now challenges most landscape designers working in urban communities. The homeless are far greater in number than the "undesirables" that William Whyte, in *The Social Life of Small Urban Spaces* (1980), contended would just go away if other people intensively used a public space. We know now that they will not go away. For those who are hungry and destitute, as Clare Cooper Marcus and Carolyn Francis state in *People Places* (1990), public space is "a place to eat, sleep and call home."

Drug dealers twice prevented landscape architect Walter Kocian from photographing prison-like McCauley Park in San Francisco's Tenderloin district, even at mid-day on a crowded street. Finally, Kocian hurriedly snapped this photograph in the early morning.

An important step in understanding this issue is to recognize that homeless people who use public landscapes are not homogeneous. While developing a master plan for Runyon Canyon, an urban wild-land in Los Angeles, Randy Hester, ASLA, found three types of homeless people: relatively permanent residents, transient criminals and runaway teenagers. To help the community decide how to deal with the issue, Hester interviewed on video most of the canyon's homeless. After viewing the video, the community decided to accept the permanent homeless as part of the park, but expel the criminals and runaways. Hester manipulated the master plan accordingly,

---

Louise Mozingo, "The Homeless in Urban Parks: Is Exclusion the Solution?," from *Landscape Architecture* Vol. 84, No. 2. Copyright © 1984 by University of Wisconsin Press. Permission to reprint granted by the publisher.

siting trails away from the shelters of permanent residents of the park. Here collective, informed decision-making struck a balance between the need for control and the needs of the homeless.

Other communities also accept the homeless in their public spaces. In San Francisco's Buena Vista Park, surrounded by housing ranging from mansions to modest rental units, the chemically dependent homeless frequent a very visible, sunny, wind-protected slope during the day; some sleep in the park. Nonetheless, other neighborhood people, including children, intensively use the park for recreation without significant problems. The common characteristic of public open spaces where these tacit compromises exist is that they are large, topographically complex and vegetated. This allows space enough for distinct territories defined by visual and physical buffers between the homeless and others—while making it impossible for one group to dominate the park.

This is not to say that the homeless in public spaces do not present a challenge in urban open spaces. Most of the urban homeless are alcoholics or mentally ill or both. In 1981, Glide Memorial Church, an activist congregation in San Francisco, tried to provide an open space designed for and run by homeless alcoholics: People's Park or, more colloquially, Wino Park. It was opened with much fanfare and notable community and political support. Three years later the church, with the help of the homeless themselves, shut it down. It had been taken over by drug dealers, the sleeping shelters used for shooting galleries, crime in the area markedly worse. Clearly segregating the alcoholic homeless in their own special landscapes is not the answer to this issue.

At McCauley Park, the presence of the homeless in an open, street-side park provided, literally, no space for compromise. "Negative design to control social behavior," as Kocian calls it, negates the design intent, serving no one well.

The design of the new much-heralded Yerba Buena Gardens likewise discourages the homeless with gated entrances and security guards on continuous patrol. While some may see exclusion as a solution, it is not. If we are concerned about the increasing numbers of homeless people the public landscape is expected to absorb, then we must work for solutions where they really exist—in public policy regarding education, jobs, housing and mental health. Those who have bothered to study and talk to homeless people tell us that they, like all of us, need a place in this world to connect, to find refuge. Most often public space is the only place this can happen. Landscape architects must be advocates of true "publicness" in our public places.

Louise Mozingo is assistant professor of landscape architecture at UC Berkeley and a practicing landscape architect in San Francisco.

13 Models of Design in Studio Teaching

Stefani Ledewitz

In the process of discussing two models of teaching studio, the two-stage "Analysis—Synthesis" and the reiterative "Concept—Test," the author exposes the folly of separating programming as a standalone process independent from architectural design.

Stefani Ledewitz *is an assistant professor of architecture at Carnegie-Mellon University, where she has taught for four years. She received her education in architecture at Princeton and Yale.*

Implicit Content of Studio Teaching

The purpose of the studio in architectural education, as it is generally described, is to teach architectural design. But we know from recent research on studio teaching that this means different things to different people. Julian Beinart has pointed out fundamental disagreements among teachers over what is meant by both "architecture" and "design."[1] This is evidenced in the tremendous diversity of content and methods in studio teaching in different schools and even within one department. As a teaching vehicle, the studio has been both praised and condemned. It has been held up as a highly sophisticated means of teaching creative problem-solving. With equal conviction, though, it has been criticized for its lack of rigor: as merely "training" without intellectual discipline or as "a personal indulgence" in which "knowledge comes not from an assimilation of external information, but wholly from an internal dialogue between the individual and his inner self."[2]

The lack of clarity over the purpose and effectiveness of the design studio reflects its complexity as a teaching/learning setting. It is characterized by multiple and sometimes contradictory goals, implicit theories, and inherent conditions of "inexpressibility, vagueness, and ambiguity."[3] It

---

Stefani Ledewitz, "Models of Design in Studio Teaching," from *Journal of Architectural Education*, Vol. 38, No. 2, Pp. 2–8. Published by Blackwell Publications, 1985. Copyright by John Wiley & Sons. Permission to reprint granted by the rights holder.

also reflects the heavy pedagogical responsibility the studio carries in architectural education. The studio is the primary means of teaching at least three basic aspects of design education. It is where students learn and practice a number of new skills, such as visualization and representation. It is also where students learn a new language. Schön describes design as a "graphic and verbal language game," in which drawing and talking are complementary and inextricably linked.[4] Words like "form" and "scale" have new and complex meanings that are not easy to internalize. Learning to explore and communicate ideas through drawing is a new experience for most students. Thirdly, and most significantly, the studio is where students learn to "think architecturally." In architecture, as in other fields, this "way of thinking" refers to a particular domain of problems and solutions that characterize, and are fundamental to, professional performance. Despite the fact that we do not define it precisely, we can easily distinguish those students who have learned to "think architecturally" from those who have not.

The educational experience in studio involves not only learning all three of these aspects, but learning them all at the same time. Integrating the skills, the language, and the approach to problems is, in fact, a large part of learning to design. Each becomes a means of learning the others. Drawing skills, for instance, are essential to learning to communicate spatial concepts. Likewise, learning to recognize architectural issues can inform and aid the development of visualization skills. In teaching studio, therefore, it is both difficult and ineffective to isolate these aspects of design education. This complicates the formulation of explicit teaching objectives. And for this reason, the attempt to articulate such objectives often seems artificial and perhaps even contrary to the ultimate purposes of the studio.

There is also another reason why the content of teaching in studio is not generally made more explicit. All the aspects of design education—the skills, the language, and the approach to problems—are more effectively taught indirectly through experience than taught directly by explanation. "The learner cannot really understand ahead of time what it is he needs to learn, nor can he understand the meaning of what his teachers tell him, until he has immersed himself in various experiences that those who do understand make available to him."[5] In fact, what we consider most essential—the ability to "think architecturally"—is the most difficult to explain directly to a student who lacks such experience.

As a result, only a fraction of the content of most studios is articulated explicitly and taught directly. The content is largely implicit in the nature and organization of the projects we give. Students learn much about what "architecture" is and what "design" is even in the type of problems we select, in the questions we ask (and don't ask), and in the schedule we plan. Likewise, we read into what our students say or do much about what we think they understand.

Because so much of the content of studio teaching is implicit, we should be aware of what we are communicating so that we can be intentional about it. Contradictions between what we say explicitly and what we convey implicitly, or between different implicit messages, can be very confusing to students. Implicit communication is especially difficult for students to deal with, since it may make it impossible to pinpoint the source of a contradiction.

Moreover, there is great danger of what Schön calls "learning binds," in which teacher and student are each acting on implicit cognitive schemes the other doesn't understand. In an extreme learning bind, the teacher, failing to communicate, gives up on the student and/or the student, unable to be understood, gives up on the teacher. In order to avoid the dilemma of mutually-reinforced misunderstandings, Schön argues that we should try to build a series of agreements with our students on the nature of architecture and design.[6] This requires that we try to make more explicit the objectives, standards, and assumptions that underlie our teaching, which, in turn, demands that we develop a greater awareness of the implicit messages we convey to students.

Some of the most confusing messages for students concern the nature, purpose, and process of designing.[7] Taken together, these can be considered the "model of design" we present, although such "models" are often neither coherent nor internally consistent. It may be for this reason that discrepancies between implicit and explicit messages in studio are common. Some design instructors present explicitly a version of the design process that contradicts what is communicated implicitly in the studio. Far more frequently, design instructors claim to be "pluralistic" about the design process: "imposing" a model of design is considered too doctrinaire. Nevertheless, these instructors do communicate implicitly—and unintentionally—their attitudes about design, and therefore may be imposing them without recognizing it.

I would like to discuss here some of the ways that models of design are conveyed implicitly in the studio. In particular, I would like to suggest that many of our common practices in teaching studio derive from a model of design (the analysis-synthesis model) that we do not necessarily subscribe to and that has been challenged as "theoretically untenable ... and practically confusing."[8] Moreover, I would add that another model of design (the concept-test model) would lead to some different teaching methods that might enable students to learn more effectively.

Analysis-Synthesis Model and Its Consequences

Design has long resisted description because of its unpredictable and intangible character, marked by moments of insight, imagination, and "flights of fancy." It is difficult to document because "although outsiders can directly observe behavioral and representational parts of designing, they cannot directly observe cognitive design processes taking place inside someone's head."[9] Early research into design aimed to derive "systematic" design methods by defining more explicit processes of decision-making.[10] This work was founded, as Hillier, Musgrove, and O'Sullivan pointed out in 1972, on rationalist-empiricist assumptions about the necessity of objectivity in problem-solving: "the notion that science can produce factual knowledge, which is superior to and independent of theory; and the notion of a logic of induction, by which theories may be derived logically from an analysis of facts."[11]

The model of design derived from this paradigm of knowledge "would characteristically and necessarily proceed by decomposing a problem into its elements, adding an information content to each element drawn as far as possible from scientific work, and 'synthesizing' (i.e., inducting) a solution by means of a set of logical or procedural rules."[12] It was assumed that non-quantifiable and intuitive aspects of design would have an important role in the process, but would be differentiated as much as possible from its rational aspects. The process is thereby divided into a rational, systematized "analysis" (problem-defining) stage and a creative, intuitive "synthesis" (problem-solving) stage. The educational consequences of this model are that "students would be taught to analyze problems and to synthesize solutions."[13]

Certainly not all design instructors subscribe to this model of design. There are those, on the one hand, who see design as mysterious artistic inspiration (non-problem-solving) and, on the other hand, those who see design as a far more complex intellectual activity (meta-problem-solving). Yet, it is the analysis-synthesis model that is most widely reflected in design studio teaching. Some common practices illustrate the prevalence of the model.

Two-Stage Analysis-Synthesis Organization

Although not necessarily formally entitled "analysis" and "synthesis," a studio project is often divided into two discrete and identifiable parts. The first part, which might take from a few days to many weeks, is the analysis phase, in which site, program, building type, context, and other investigations are carried out. Analytic sketches, diagrams (e.g., bubble diagrams), and reports are produced, but preconceived design concepts are discouraged as premature. This is perceived as a "pre-design" phase by students, who tend after a while to become impatient to "get into designing."

At some point, the studio shifts in focus to the design concept, and assignments change from analytic exercises to design proposals. During this stage, references are made "back" to analysis work, but no new analysis assignments are made. This continues to reinforce the segregation of synthesis activities from analysis activities.

Emphasis on Design Methods in Analysis

The analysis stage of a studio project is commonly characterized by well-defined, explicit procedures, while the synthesis stage is relatively unstructured. During the early weeks of a studio project, analytic assignments of short duration (three weeks is a long assignment) are often given to the class as a whole, conveying the expectation that there are certain prescribed procedures that everyone should undertake and in the same sequence. Sometimes these are group exercises, to which each individual is expected to contribute to a team effort. Group assignments in themselves entail negotiating agreed-upon objectives and methods for design, which through that process are made more explicit than in individual work.

When synthesis begins, studio teaching becomes more responsive to student-initiated moves. It is far less typical of design instructors in this stage to impose on a student pre-defined external (to the student) procedures. And it is even less likely that such procedures will be imposed on the class as a whole. This does occur to a very limited extent when one-day sketch problems are assigned late in a project, but even these are often designed to take students "out" of a problem, as a kind of relief. The general mode of synthesis teaching is the individualized board crit, with or without interim group reviews. Students have the primary responsibility for finding their way through the problem, and the instructor's role is to see that they do not stray too far off-course. Advice concerning a student's process of design often consists of periodic reminders of presentation requirements or suggestions to "draw a section," or "consider how it will stand up," or "begin looking at elevations," generally leaving students a great deal of latitude in how they work on a problem.

One-time Distribution of Project Information

The major pertinent information about the project is generally given to students (or assigned for them to acquire) at the outset of the project. On a typical first day of a project, students are given the problem statement, program, site maps, context maps, photographs, etc. It may be no more than a few pages or it may be a deluge of material, but it is generally all the problem information students will be given. Material that is provided once the project is underway is more likely to be supplemental (and optional) reference material. In fact, if new or contradictory information is introduced into the studio (e.g., by an outside reviewer) later in the project, it is often hard for students to digest, and may even create a crisis of "indigestion" in the studio, in which students question or reject the given parameters and assumptions for a project.

The Analysis-Synthesis Model and Learning Difficulties

Without respect to the validity of this model of design, which will be discussed in the next section, I believe its consequences in studio teaching can be criticized on pedagogical grounds. These criticisms are echoes of dissatisfactions often expressed about studio experiences by students or teachers. I would like to suggest, however, that there is a relationship between each of these learning difficulties and the underlying analysis-synthesis model of design.

Discontinuity Between Analysis and Synthesis

One dissatisfaction frequently voiced by design teachers is that the analysis of problems by students is not incorporated into their synthesis. Jurors sometimes comment on the discontinuity of thought between early analytic diagrams and the final design proposal. This discontinuity is, of course, fundamental to the analysis-synthesis approach.[14] Learning to overcome it is part of what the studio is perceived to teach, and some students are more successful at learning it than others. In some cases, major inconsistencies between a problem definition and its solution are not even recognized by the student, much less reconciled. The dichotomy is even more serious when students begin to see form-making as entirely separate and different from problem-solving.

Intentions Confused with Solutions

Many students' final presentations are disappointing because the physical form consequences of their design intentions have not been explored. Although there are, of course, many reasons why a design proposal is not fully developed, it is not uncommon to find that it occurs because a student mistakes elaboration of analytic diagrams for a design solution. This is the assumption Colquhoun calls the "onomatopoeic relationship between forms and their content."[15] In such a case, the design intentions expressed by the diagrams a student draws may be thoroughly documented, but the physical form to realize those intentions has not been developed beyond a preliminary "layout" of functions. Characteristic of this "preoccupation with the program"[16] is a set of well-worked-out plans, but very little development in section or elevation. In some instances, students with very good analytical capabilities do not see the difference between a diagram of intentions and a well-developed design concept, and may not even engage in a truly synthetic process. The segregation of analysis from synthesis enables them to continue investigating the problem and to keep deferring the commitment to a solution in three-dimensional form.

Inappropriate Closure

It is unusual for students, even in their fifth year, to bring their designing to closure at an appropriate time: more often, they are either frustrated by not "completing" a design or stop designing prematurely. Students who are taught (even implicitly) the analysis-synthesis model are led to expect that theoretically, given sufficient information and a systematic process, they should reach an optimal design solution. But, short of reaching such a solution, this model of design does not provide any way to know when to stop designing. As a result, project deadlines may be perceived as arbitrary and totally unrelated to the design process; and students have little guidance in pacing their work toward the final presentation. For most students, this means just "calling quits" at the last possible minute to draw it up. For others, the response is almost the opposite: to hold fast to their design at an early stage and "tinker" with it. In either case, students may be unrealistically looking to their evolving design proposal itself to define the endpoint of its evolution.

Fear of Designing

Students, even very capable students, often feel they have no control over the design process and are fearful of it. This is one of the most serious difficulties we face in teaching students to design, and it can be attributed, in part, to the emphatic distinction between analysis and synthesis. When this distinction is perceived as a wide gap, it demands a "leap in the dark." Summerson describes the dilemma of making the leap from program to form: "The conceptions which arise from a preoccupation with the program have got, at some point, to crystallize into a final form and by the time the architect reaches that point he has to bring to his conception a weight of judgment, a sense of authority which clinches the whole matter, causes the impending relationships to close into a visually comprehensible, expressive whole."[17] Dreading this leap, students often hope for "the big idea" that will bridge the gap for them.[18] If the big idea, or the "right" design concept, is seen as an unpredictable inspiration, it may become the source of anxiety, oppression, and a loss of self-confidence. Students who are conscious of the need for a strong design concept may therefore hold fast to an inconsequential idea or an irrelevant metaphor, no matter how much difficulty they have in working it out. These students are caught in the grip of a design process they do not control and consequently cannot apply purposefully to solve design problems.

The Concept-Test Model and Its Consequences

Developments in the fields of cognitive psychology,[19] information science and artificial intelligence,[20] and philosophy of science,[21] have raised serious questions about the foundations of the analysis-synthesis model. Hillier, Musgrove, and O'Sullivan argue that the analysis-synthesis model is theoretically untenable because "factual (perceptual) knowledge" cannot exist outside a theoretical (cognitive) framework and because the logic of induction, as demonstrated by Popper, is "both unattainable and unnecessary."[22] Problem-solving, as we understand it today, is not the aggregation of objectively-derived facts, but a dialectic between pre-conceived solutions and observed facts.

Zeisel, Simon, Korobkin, and others have also criticized the analysis-synthesis model for creating a confusing and inaccurate picture of what designers actually do. It does not account, for example, for the observed sequence of documents that architects in practice produce (schematic design, design development, construction documents) in which the design ideas become more specific and more refined at each stage. The model is also unrealistic in characterizing that process as an aggregation of solutions, whereas designing tends to deal primarily with holistic issues.

In practice, the analysis-synthesis model is unwieldy; and the more closely a designer adheres to the model, the more unwieldy the process of designing becomes. The dilemma is that the optimization of aggregated solutions on which the eventual design solution depends is unattainable for any problem complex enough to warrant it. In the first place, that kind of detailed information about person-environment relationships is generally unavailable. Secondly, even when it is available, the process of analyzing it is very complicated and costly. But even more fundamentally, the increased information and complexity generated with this model actually makes the task of synthesis more difficult, not easier. "Far from helping the designer escape from his preconceptions, the effect of proliferating technology and information is to force the designer into a greater dependence on them."[23] The more articulated, systematized, and segregated from the synthesis process the analysis is, the worse the "leap in the dark" becomes.

Another important objection to the model is that the segregation of analysis from synthesis denies the validity of any preconceptions in design.[24] Yet as Colquhoun points out, the impact of design precedents, typologies, and other knowledge we carry with us is not only inescapable but essential to creative problem-solving. "If … forms by themselves are relatively empty of meaning, it follows that the forms which we intuit will, in the unconscious mind, tend to attract to themselves certain associations of meaning. This could mean not only that we are not free from the forms of the past and from the availability of these forms as typological models but that, if we assume we are free, we have lost control over a very active sector of our imagination and of our power to communicate with others."[25]

From these theoretical and practical difficulties with the analysis-synthesis model, the concept-test model of design emerged as an alternative that is both more tenable in theory and more useful in practice. The concept-test model conceives design as a developmental process that interconnects the activities of "conjecturing" and "testing," or as Korobkin and Zeisel defined them, "imaging, presenting, and testing." These activities occur in a cyclical pattern that Zeisel describes as a spiral converging on a "domain of acceptable responses."[26] By conjecturing, or imaging, a designer conceives of a "solution in principle" early in the design process, which is progressively developed and refined (or discarded). The representation of the conjecture by drawing or making models is a means of elaborating it and communicating it back to the designer or to others for evaluation, or "testing." "Testing is a feed-back and feed-forward process, adjusting the relation between a design product as it develops and the many criteria and qualities the product is intended to meet."[27] The activities of conjecturing and testing, intuition and rationality, creative leaping and rigorous analysis, thrive on each other; oscillating or cycling between them is what enables the designer to learn from his or her work and progressively improve the design.

From this rough sketch of the concept-test model, which is already familiar to many, I would like to discuss its consequences for teaching by describing some pedagogical methods for studio that I believe follow from adopting it. These methods are illustrative rather than definitive. They were selected because I have some experience with them, particularly in several studios I taught with Louis Sauer to upper level undergraduate students. My purpose here is not so much to recommend this particular set of techniques as to demonstrate their relationship to an underlying model of design that provides them a theoretical framework. In each case I will describe briefly the method and then discuss its relationship to the concept-test model.

Multiple Design Cycles

Studio projects are each subdivided into a series of design encounters with a problem. Each cycle, or stage in the project, concludes with a design proposal for the project as a whole. The first cycle is short (perhaps only a few days) and produces a very schematic proposal. The cycles are successively longer and the proposals successively more developed as they become closer and closer approximations of an acceptable solution. On a small project there might only be two cycles (the minimum); a more complex project might have four or five.

The subdivision of a project into a series of design cycles gives recognition to the process of successive approximations in design. Although it is not intended to be the literal representation of a design process, which includes much more cycling, searching, and blind alleys, it is clearly a non-linear progression. The important feature of the multiple cycles is that, while their products change, their internal structure remains constant: that is, each cycle represents the designer's best effort to solve the problem in terms of what he or she understands at that point. It is a method that emphasizes the resolution of many issues simultaneously, since it structures a problem holistically rather than by focusing on individual issues. The repeated cycles through the problem, and especially the shorter cycles, call on students' abilities to "juggle" many aspects of a design problem, rather than to concentrate on only one or one at a time.

Beginning Backwards

The starting point of a project that begins backwards is its solution: students are asked to conceive of a solution to a problem before they are asked to analyze it. For example, a first-day sketch problem is assigned in which, given only a brief problem statement, students produce a design solution in a very short time. The purpose of the sketch problem is to stimulate an initial design concept, or parti, that, however inadequate it may be as a "solution in principle," can be "tested" (developed or discarded). Students are often surprised at their own ability to produce a coherent proposal so quickly. This is important: the ability to generate a design concept is necessary in order to get into the cycle of concepts and tests. The sketch problem works best, therefore, if it is a kind of problem familiar to students in the class. The least successful sketch problem I have given involved site planning at a scale (a city block) that most of the class had not faced before.

The amount of time and information given for the sketch problem can be significant. Having varied the duration from three hours to three days, I have found the twenty-four hour version most successful in the studios I have taught. If the sketch problem is too long and informative, students can get caught up in (and intimidated by) the tangible requirements of the problem. On the other hand, if students are given too little to work with, they have a hard time relating their sketch problem proposals to the problem later on.

Approaching a project this way is sometimes thought to fixate students on a premature and potentially inappropriate concept. But I would contend that it is no more a problem at the outset of a project than at any point in its development, particularly if such preconceptions are allowed to remain latent during the design process. The "backwards" approach recognizes and gives value to these preconceptions, including the knowledge of "solution types" and "instrument sets" that students bring to the problem. This is the "prestructuring" that Hillier, Musgrove, and O'Sullivan argue is essential to designing. Their argument, in fact, is that better design can be achieved only by "restructuring the cognitive schemes which designers bring to bear on their task."[28] Instead of ignoring the way students prestructure their problems, beginning with a "pre-solution" is a way of trying to understand—and help students understand—what they bring to a problem that will enable them to solve it better.

The pedagogical purpose of beginning backwards can also be seen as helping create for students the perception of a need for knowledge. Perceived need, as we know from studies of the learning process, is a critical motivating factor.[29] This suggests that students who begin by trying out the knowledge they have (synthesis) might see more value in acquiring additional knowledge they need (analysis) and therefore learn more in the process.

Incremental Information

Instead of a comprehensive package of project information that is presented to students at the outset of a project, information about the project is broken into a series of packages that students acquire as the project progresses. The incremental information is prepared to correspond with multiple design cycles: at each cycle, information relevant to that level of design is provided.

In organizing the information for a project, my approach has been to emphasize diversity in the information at each design cycle: to introduce from the start a full array of the kinds of information students will need, based on the issues they are expected to address. The information typically ranges, for example, from occupancy requirements and client goals to codes and materials. It is skeletal at first and becomes increasingly detailed. In this way, only as the need for new and more detailed information arises in the design process, are students asked to deal with it.

One of the goals of decomposing the information is to teach students how to differentiate relevant from irrelevant information at each stage—that is, to acquire information strategically. In later design cycles, therefore, students are encouraged to take the initiative in identifying and acquiring the information they need to test their ideas, though only a few very capable students have attempted to do this. It may be that if information were incrementalized in a structured way for students in early studios, they would be better able to do it for themselves in later studios.

Acquiring information as a means of testing design ideas is a fundamental aspect of the concept-test model. In order to design, students have to understand the difference between external sources of knowledge and their own perceptions, the necessity for external knowledge as a means of evaluating their own ideas, and the importance of that evaluation in every cycle of their design. As the need for information is seen to arise from the design (or specifically from the design conjectures), so can the nature of the information that is needed.

Solution Type Studies

Projects include a solution type study in which form-generating strategies relevant to the project are derived from analyzing architectural precedents. The purpose of studying solution types is to enable students to see alternative form organizations, or design concepts, that suggest approaches to the problem-at-hand. This is not a functional building type study, which defines programmatic requirements, but an examination of the characteristics and implications of different form organizations.

Familiarity with solution types is useful because it not only gives recognition to the cognitive scheme a student brings to a problem, but builds on it by relating it to a larger set of similar (or dissimilar) solutions. In addition to creating an inventory of relevant form strategies, the development of an understanding of "the part that modifications of type-solutions play in relation to problems and solutions that are without precedent in any received tradition" can give rise to more radically inventive solutions.[30] A study of solution types can provide a model for identifying appropriate precedents to a problem and for differentiating the significant characteristics of those precedents from what is simply appealing about them. It can not only challenge superficial notions of originality and the value of uniqueness for its own sake, but it can also discourage unthinking adoption of prior solutions. The key is to help students distinguish the pertinent characteristics of the precedents (including the "prototypical" characteristics) from what is irrelevant or inappropriate.

An investigation of solution types also demonstrates what is meant by a "solution," which is not at all obvious to novice designers. Examples of worthy architectural solutions provide a point of reference to which students can aspire and by which they may evaluate their own work. Moreover, they can be a means of articulating and clarifying the formal issues in a problem, which otherwise can be very difficult for students to see, yet are fundamental to generating form.

Form Experiments

Short design exercises, or "experiments," are assigned either individually or to the entire class to help students increase their design facility. In each case, the idea of physical form as the realization of specific design intentions is emphasized. In-class (one-day) exercises have included, for example, increasing the area requirements in the program, adding an adjacent lot to the site, diagramming two different structural systems (steel and concrete) for the building, and changing a major client goal. Longer assignments require students to design for multiple conditions (such as a housing unit for two occupant groups) or to develop alternative proposals.

The intent of these form experiments is to develop "contingent thinking" abilities. This is the designer's capacity for detached commitment—to propose an idea with full commitment, then to evaluate it as a detached critic—that is the core of the concept-test model. It is an ability that is essential to what we mean by "thinking architecturally." An indication of contingent thinking in the studio is the difference between exploring design experiments (contingent commitment) and defending design statements (absolute commitment) in the presentation of proposals.

Self-Evaluation

Students are encouraged in board crits and in group reviews to take initiative in evaluating their own work. I try, for example, to structure reviews to serve as models of self-evaluation for students. Participating critics are asked to take on the role of the designer of the project and to communicate to students their "self"-evaluation. In turn, the students attempt to understand the vicarious "self"-evaluation so that they can write their own self-evaluation after the review. These experiences in crits and reviews are intended to enable students to see that the development of their design skills entails developing self-criticism skills. This is a reinforcement of the role of evaluation, or "testing," in the design process, which must eventually become second nature to a designer.

A last-day sketch problem is sometimes assigned to correspond to the first-day sketch problem in scope and issues, in order to help students evaluate their own progress in the studio. Its purpose is to make students more aware of the way their cognitive schemes are developed through their studio experience. By setting out comparable problems and requirements in a situation designed to focus on the way students prestructure a problem, the growth (or not) of that prestructuring capability can be seen. This is particularly significant if we take the restructuring of those cognitive schemes as one of the goals of architectural education.

Self-evaluation is fundamental to the concept-test model because, according to this conception of design, as Schön suggests, the object of the designer is not rationality but "reflexivity": the ability to reflect on and learn from one's work.[31] He suggests that this must be taught by discussion and by example, where the instructor shares with the student reflections on the student's work and the instructor's own expectations. Such shared reflections afford the opportunity to address not only the current status of the student's project, but the design intentions it reveals and the underlying cognitive scheme from which it evolved.

Articulated Criteria for Evaluation

Both informally throughout the studio and formally at key points along the way, explicit criteria for evaluation are discussed that are derived from the concept-test model of design. As teaching tools, the criteria are used with the intention of reinforcing a coherent understanding of design through their content and through the way they are applied. Their purpose is to assess students' progress in developing their design process. They address such capabilities as generating a comprehensive design concept and identifying and responding to diverse issues in the design problem.

Talking with a student about the progress he is making in a problem in relation to a particular model of design can help him to see more clearly what he is doing, to be more purposeful about it, and to gain better control of it. Formal criteria discussed at the beginning of the term and at the end of a project or project cycle can serve these same functions, enabling students to know what is expected of them and to direct their performance to meet those objectives.

Schön has proposed a set of "design subcompetences" that derive specifically from a concept-test model.[32] They emphasize, for example, the cyclical process of decision-making, the dialectic between conception and observation, and the contingent nature of design decisions. A loose adaptation of Schön's subcompetences suggests a set of criteria that can be used to evaluate students' design capabilities and might be applied with some modification to different levels of experience.

Students should be able:

- To demonstrate an appreciation for the givens of site and program, and their implications for design.
- To articulate their design intentions.
- To construct a conceptual framework for design within which to evaluate different design decisions.
- To make appropriate use of precedents; to demonstrate an understanding of the relevance of particular solution-types to the problem.
- To apply to design the consideration of a rich variety of design factors, such as climate, lifestyles, context relationships, materials, etc.; to recognize an appropriate set of factors for a given problem; and to be aware of priorities among those factors.
- To make choices among alternatives with an appreciation for their consequences.
- To detect and follow through the implications of earlier moves.
- To recognize the connections among the implications of design moves in terms of various different design factors.
- To evaluate the consequences of design moves: to relate design decisions to design intentions.
- To work out coherent patterns of design decisions, consequences, implications, and evaluations.

I am not suggesting that such process-oriented criteria should be the only basis for evaluation in studio. An understanding of what a "good" design process is must be part of and consistent with an understanding of what constitutes "good" architecture. The purpose of learning how to make design decisions, after all, is only to learn how to make better decisions.

Evaluation of a student's total performance in studio must therefore be based on a broader set of criteria. Those that focus specifically on the design process are of value because through them we acknowledge that learning how to design is an intrinsic and important part of the content of the studio.

Some Conclusions

If we think of teaching studio as designing learning experiences, we might consider the "models of design" that underly our practice of teaching as well as our practice of architecture. By conceiving of teaching as itself a process of design, we may be able to inform the way we teach through our understanding of the design process. In particular, if we understand design to be a cyclical process of concepts and tests, then teaching might be considered a process of developing concepts and testing them.

A "concept-test" approach to teaching suggests that we should be engaged in "reflection-in-action," a process of trying to articulate and evaluate our understandings of design and architecture. As designers of learning experiences, we should expect as much of ourselves as of our students: to be able to construct a conceptual framework for our teaching, to understand its implications for the way we teach, and to evaluate its consequences for our students. Just as the restructuring of the cognitive schemes our students bring to designing enables them to become better designers, so the restructuring of the cognitive schemes we bring to studio teaching should enable us to become better designers of our students' learning experiences.

NOTES

1 Beinart, Julian "Analysis of the Content of Design," *Architecture Education Study* Volume 1, 1981.

2 Balfour, Alan "Captive of Love and Ignorance: Architecture Education and Practice," *Architecture Education Study* Volume 1, 1981, p. 797.

3 Schön, Donald "Learning a Language, Learning to Design," *Architecture Education Study* Volume 1, 1981, p. 426.

4 *Ibid.*, p. 349.

5 *Ibid.*, p. 414.

6 For a thorough discussion of the problem of "learning binds," see Don Schön's "Learning a Language, Learning to Design" *Architecture Education Study* Volume 1, 1981.

7 Argyris, Chris "Teaching and Learning in Design Settings," *Architecture Education Study* Volume 1, 1981.

8 Hiller, Bill, Musgrove, John, O'Sullivan, Pat "Knowledge and Design," in Mitchell, William (ed.) *EDRA-3: Proceedings of the Third Annual Conference* Dowden, Hutchinson, and Ross (Stroudsburg, Pa) 1972, reprinted in Proshansky, Ittelson, and Rivlin (eds.) *Environmental Psychology: Man and His Physical Setting* (2nd ed.) Holt Rinehart and Winston (New York, NY) 1976, p. 74.

9 Zeisel, John *Inquiry by Design* Brooks/Cole Press (Monterey, CA) 1981, p. 5.

10 The most thorough and influential elaboration of design process was Christopher Alexander's *Notes on the Synthesis of Form* Harvard University Press (Cambridge, MA) 1964. Other design research is described in Gregory, S. A. *The Design Method* Butterworths (London) 1966, and Jones, J. C. *Design Methods: Seeds of Human Futures* John Wiley and Sons (New York, NY) 1970.

11 Hillier et al., *op.cit*, p. 73.

12 *Ibid.,* p. 73.
13 *Ibid.,* p. 70.
14 "It is easy to bring out the contrast between the analytical nature of the program and the synthetic nature of its realization … (T)he tree of sets (analysis) is obtained by successive division and partition. The tree of diagrams (synthesis) … is made by successive composition and fusion." Alexander, *Notes on the Synthesis of Form,* p. 93–94.
15 Colquhoun, Alan "Typology and Design Method" in Gutman, Robert (ed.) *People and Buildings* Basic Books (New York), 1972, p. 404.
16 Summerson, John "Case for a Theory of Modern Architecture" *The Builder* Volume 192 (May 24, 1957), p. 947.
17 Summerson, *ibid.,* p. 947.
18 Summerson sees the gap between analysis and synthesis as the "missing architectural language" *ibid.,* p. 947.
19 See, for example, Bruner, Jerome *Beyond the Information Given: Studies in the Psychology of Knowing* Norton (New York, NY) 1973.
20 Two major works are Newell, Allen and Simon, Herbert *Human Problem Solving* Prentice-Hall (Englewood Cliffs, NJ) 1972, and Reitman, Walter *Cognition and Thought: An Information-Processing Approach* John Wiley and Sons (New York, NY) 1965.
21 See Karl Popper's work, especially *Conjectures and Refutations* Oxford University Press (New York, NY) 1963 and Simon's later book *The Sciences of the Artificial* MIT Press (Cambridge, MA) 1969.
22 Hillier *et al., op. cit.,* p. 72.
23 Hillier *et al., op. cit.,* p. 77.
24 In *Notes on the Synthesis of Form,* Alexander's purpose is to eliminate the role of personal prejudice in design. In his later work, especially *A Pattern Language,* his emphasis shifts to reconfiguring those preconceptions from personal prejudices into universally valid patterns.
25 Colquhoun, *op. cit.,* p. 403.
26 Archer, L. Bruce "The Structure of the Design Process" in Broadbent, Geoffrey and Ward, Anthony, (eds.) *Design Methods in Architecture* Architectural Association (London) 1969.
27 Zeisel, *op. cit.,* p. 9.
28 Hillier *et al., op. cit.,* p. 71.
29 See Bruner's *Beyond the Information Given* Norton (New York, NY) 1973.
30 Colquhoun, *op.cit.,* p. 405.
31 Schön, Donald "The Design Studio as Education for Reflection in Action" Paper presented at ACSA Northeast Region Conference (October 1982), revised version in *Journal of Architectural Education* Fall 1984, Volume 38 Number 1.
32 Schön, Donald "Learning a Language, Learning to Design" *Architecture Education Study* Volume 1, 1981, p. 406ff.

REFERENCES

Alexander, Christopher, *Notes on the Synthesis of Form* Harvard University Press (Cambridge, MA) 1964.
Alexander, Christopher, Sara Ishikawa, Murray Silverstein with Max Jacobson, Ingrid Fiksdahl-King, Shlomo Angel, *A Pattern Language* Oxford University Press (New York, NY) 1977.
Archer, L. Bruce, "The Structure of the Design Process" in Broadbent and Ward (eds.), *Design Methods in Architecture* Architectural Association (London) 1969.

Archer, L. Bruce, "Systematic Method for Designers" Series of articles in *Design* Volumes 172–188, April 1963–August 1964.

Argyris, Chris, "Teaching and Learning in Design Settings" *Architecture Education Study* Volume 1, 1981, p. 551–660.

Balfour, Alan, "Captive of Love and Ignorance: Architecture Education and Practice" *Architecture Education Study* Volume 1, 1981, p. 771–801.

Beinart, Julian, "Analysis of the Content of Design" *Architecture Education Study* Volume 1, 1981, p. 3–157.

Broadbent, Geoffrey, "A Plain Man's Guide to Systematic Design Methods" *Royal Institute of British Architects Journal* Volume 75, May 1968, p. 223–227.

Broadbent, Geoffrey and Ward, Anthony (eds.), *Design Methods in Architecture* Architectural Association (London) 1969.

Bruner, Jerome S., *Beyond the Information Given: Studies in the Psychology of Knowing* Norton (New York, NY) 1973.

Bruner, Jerome S., *The Process of Education* Harvard University Press (Cambridge, MA) 1960.

Colquhoun, Alan, "Typology and Design Method," *Arena* Volume 83 (June 1967), reprinted in Robert Gutman (ed.) *People and Buildings* Basic Books (New York, NY) 1972, p. 395–405.

Gregory, S. A. (ed.), *The Design Method* Butterworths (London) 1966.

Hillier, Bill and Leaman, Adrian, "How is Design Possible?" in *Journal of Architectural Research* Volume 3, Number 1 (January 1974).

Hillier, Bill, John Musgrove, and Pat O'Sullivan, "Knowledge and Design" Mitchell, William (ed.), *EDRA-3: Proceedings of the Third Annual Conference* Dowden, Hutchinson, and Ross (Stroudsburg, PA) 1972, reprinted in Proshansky, H. M., Ittelson, W. H., and Rivlin, L. G. (eds.), *Environmental Psychology: Man and His Physical Setting* (2nd ed.) Holt Rinehart and Winston (New York, NY) 1976, p. 69–83.

Jones, J. Christopher, *Design Methods: Seeds of Human Futures* John Wiley and Sons, Inc. (New York, NY) 1970.

Korobkin, Barry J., *Images for Design* Harvard School of Design (Cambridge, MA) 1976.

Kuhn, Thomas S., *The Structure of Scientific Revolutions* (rev. ed.) University of Chicago Press (Chicago, IL) 1970.

Moore, Gary T. (ed.), *Emerging Methods in Environmental Design and Planning* MIT Press (Cambridge, MA) 1970.

Newell, Allen and Simon, Herbert A., *Human Problem Solving* Prentice-Hall, Inc. (Englewood Cliffs, NJ) 1972.

Popper, Karl, *Conjectures and Refutations* Oxford University Press (New York, NY) 1963.

Reitman, Walter R., *Cognition and Thought: An Information-Processing Approach* John Wiley and Sons, Inc. (New York) 1965.

Schön, Donald, "Learning a Language, Learning to Design" *Architecture Education Study* Volume 1, 1981, p. 339–471.

Schön, Donald, "The Design Studio as Education for Reflection in Action." Paper presented at ACSA Northeast Region Conference (October 1982); revised version in *Journal of Architectural Education* Fall 1984 Volume 38 Number 1.

Simon, Herbert A., *The Sciences of the Artificial* (rev. ed.) MIT Press (Cambridge, MA) 1969.

Summerson, John, "Case for a Theory of Modern Architecture" *The Builder* Volume 192 (May 24, 1957), p. 947–948.

Zeisel, John, *Inquiry by Design* Brooks/Cole (Monterey, CA) 1981.

14

Territoriality

Barbara B. Brown

Territoriality is historically an important concept to emerge out of environmental psychology. This excellent example of a thorough literature review considers to what extent our human experience of the physical environment differs from animals that also have been observed to exhibit territorial behavior. It demonstrates that biological explanations are inadequate and helps argue for the cultural basis of understanding human experience. The article also examines many factors that affect human territoriality and applications in architecture, though it fails to examine how architectural form is important to a full understanding of territoriality.

13.1. INTRODUCTION

A student at work in a library carrel leaves briefly to find another reference. The student is dismayed to find an interloper seated at the carrel 10 minutes later and asks for the seat back. Two navy recruits enter an isolation chamber for a 10-day isolation experiment. The two men immediately divide the small room in half. Although the division reduces the amount of space available for each, the men respect the invisible boundary line. A new college student is decorating her dormitory room. She tapes up her collection of family photos and displays her consuming passion for ballet by hanging up 17 ballet posters, ticket stubs from recent performances, and a well-worn pair of practice shoes.

Despite the variety of the examples, they all illustrate the operation of territoriality. The first example is perhaps the most prototypical in that it focuses on the demarcation and defense of space, a reflection of the biological roots of the concept of territoriality. Biologists first employed the concept to describe the behavior of nonhuman populations. Popularized applications of these concepts suggested that humans were similarly predisposed to be aggressive defenders of turf. Ironically, although many social scientists still link biological determinism with territoriality, many biologists no longer do so. Nevertheless, the biological heritage has made a lasting imprint on the field. This imprint is evident in definitions of territoriality, in anthropological investigations of its human origins, and in demonstrations of the resource control functions. In tracing these

Barbara B. Brown; Daniel Stokols & Irwin Altman, eds., "Territoriality," from *Handbook of Environmental Psychology*, pp. 505–531. Copyright © 1987 by John Wiley & Sons. Permission to reprint granted by the publisher.

influences, it becomes clear that a strict biological interpretation of territoriality, while useful, is inadequate.

The newer and more social perspective on territoriality is apparent in the final two examples. Although the biological approach demonstrated that territoriality can regulate host-intruder encounters, territoriality can also be involved in the regulation of more sustained social interactions. In the example of the isolated recruits, territoriality helps to maintain the viability of the dyad under stressful conditions. Finally, the college student's dormitory personalizations demonstrate that territoriality can be a vehicle for the display of identity.

Unlike the biological approach, the social approach to territoriality really cannot claim a unified intellectual heritage. Instead, its proponents come from the fields of biology, anthropology, humanistic and behavioral geography, and environmental and social psychology. Some of these proponents have grown dissatisfied with the limitations of their biological approach, while others do not even consider their work to be within the scope of territoriality. Yet they all focus on the ways in which places and things are inherently a part of social processes and human identity.

Major reviews of the field of environmental psychology reveal the emergence of the second, more social perspective. Craik accurately labeled the field's bias by assigning territorial research in 1973 to the *human spatial behavior* approach and in 1977 to the *functional adaptation* paradigm. But by 1978 Stokols noted that "recent analyses have emphasized the cognitive and social-organizational functions of human territoriality rather than its biological (reproductive and survival-related) aspects" (p. 271). Finally, in 1982 Russell and Ward continued the trend by claiming that cognitive and affective aspects of territoriality were becoming popular.

Yet on closer examination the studies that represented this new direction in 1978 still restrict their attention to the abilities of territory holders to resist intrusions or influence attempts. Although these studies provide novel applications of the concept of territoriality to the topics of gang conflict, crime, and home-owner defensiveness, territorial functions still appear quite utilitarian. By 1982, half of the six cited studies continued to deal with territorial intrusion.

Thus although it is clear that research in territoriality is broadening it is also clear that the bulk of empirical support reflects active behavioral components of territoriality. Studies of territorial marking and intrusion are common; studies of cognitive and affective psychological ties to territory are rare. This bias in research distorts the picture of human territorial functioning by suggesting that territories become important only when they are violated or threatened. Their potential for contributing to identity expression and social system functioning has not been realized.

The interplay of the two major perspectives on territoriality will be addressed in the present chapter. The biological perspective will be shown to emphasize the control of resources via the demarcation and defense of space. The social perspective will show how a territory can enter into social processes and reveal itself in dominance patterns or as a promoter of system viability. The social perspective also reveals how territories engage cognitive and affective ties and serve to support the possessor's identity.

The basis for the two perspectives appears in the shades of difference among various definitions of territoriality. Although the biological perspective on demarcation and defense is still prevalent, a review of both the biological and the anthropological literature reveals the limitations of such a focus and the shift toward a more social perspective on territoriality. The unique qualities of human territoriality are taken into account in an outline of the structural variations among human territories. Finally, empirical support for the role of territoriality in resource control, system viability, and identity is presented and research directions designed to strengthen the social approach to territoriality are discussed.

13.1.1. Definitions of Territoriality

In Table 13.1 two clusters of definitions of territoriality are offered. The clusters differ not so much in terms of major concerns as in subtle shifting of attention to one or more of the common themes of territoriality. The first cluster, characteristic of the biological approach, directs attention to the demarcation, control, and defense of space; the owner's feelings about or valuation of the space receives little attention.

The second set of definitions attend more to the organizational benefits of territoriality. Here we get some notion of why a territory might be useful.

Table 13.1 Definitions of Territoriality

Definitions That Emphasize Occupation and Defense

Altman & Haythorn (1967), Altman, Taylor, and Wheeler (1971), and Sundstrom and Altman (1974): "Territoriality involves the mutually exclusive use of areas and objects by persons and groups" (Altman, 1975, p. 106).

Ardrey (1966): "A territory is an area of space—water, earth, or air—that an animal or group defends as an exclusive preserve primarily against members of their own species" (p. 3).

Davies (1978): "Whenever individual animals or groups are spaced out more than would be expected from a random occupation of suitable habitats" (p. 317).

Dyson-Hudson & Smith (1978): "We define a territory as an area occupied more or less exclusively by an individual or group by means of repulsion through overt defense or some form of communication" (p. 22).

Eibl-Eibesfeldt (1970): "I propose that any space-associated intolerance be called territoriality, where a 'territory owner' is that animal before which another conspecific must retreat" (p. 309).

Goffman (1963): "Territories are areas controlled on the basis of ownership and exclusiveness of use."

Hall (1959): "The act of laying claim to and defending a territory is called territoriality" (p. 146).

Sommer (1969), Sommer & Becker (1969), Becker (1973), and Becker and Mayo (1971): "Territories are geographical areas that are personalized or marked in some way and that are defended from encroachment."

Van den Berghe (1974): "*Territoriality* means the defense of a relatively fixed space against occupation and/or use by co-specifics."

Definitions That Emphasize Organizational or Attachment Functions

Altman (1975): "Territorial behavior is a self-other boundary regulation mechanism that involves personalization of or marking of a place or object and communication that it is 'owned' by a person or group. Personalization and ownership are designed to regulate social interaction and to help satisfy various social and physical motives. Defense responses may sometimes occur when territorial boundaries are violated" (p. 107).

Austin & Bates (1974): "Possession of valued objects and of space" (p. 448).

Bakker & Bakker-Rabdau (1973): "Territoriality ... will indicate *the inclination toward ownership*. ... Territory will refer to *the object of ownership*, be it a stretch of land, a particular object, an idea, or anything else that holds an individual's fancy to such a degree that he seeks to own it" (p. 3).

Brower (1980): "The relationship between an individual or group and a particular setting, that is characterized by a feeling of possessiveness, and by attempts to control the appearance and use of the space" (p. 180).

Edney (1976): 'Territoriality in humans is largely a passive affair ... defined by the criterion of continuous association of person or persons with specific place. ... (It) is an important organizer in human life and behavior" (p. 33).

Malmberg (1980): "Human behavioural territoriality is primarily a phenomenon of ethological ecology with an instinctive nucleus, manifested as more or less exclusive spaces, to which individuals or groups of human beings are bound emotionally and which, for the possible avoidance of others, are distinguished by means of limits, marks, or other kinds of structuring with adherent display, movements, or aggressiveness (p. 10–11).

Pastalan (1970): "A territory is a delimited space that a person or group uses and defends as an exclusive preserve. It involves psychological identification with a place, symbolized by attitudes of possessiveness and arrangements of objects in the area."

Sack (1983): "By human territoriality I mean the attempt to affect, influence, or control actions and interactions (of people, things, and relationships) by asserting and attempting to enforce control over a geographic area" (p. 55).

These definitions do not contradict the first set; they just bring to mind the fact that territories endure over time and their owners are not perpetually involved in demarcation and defense. These definitions also focus on the idea of psychological identification with spaces. Territories are not only organizational devices; they may be important and valued in their own right due to their symbolic value. These definitions shift attention to the feelings and thoughts of the owners and the symbolic value of the personalizations, not just their mere presence.

Given the preponderance of definitions of the first type, one might question whether a broader definition of territoriality that incorporates social system functioning and identity issues is useful. In order to answer that question the next two sections will review animal territoriality and the anthropological debate on the historical origins of human territoriality. Surely, if territorial occupation and defense for the purposes of resource control provide a sufficient framework for the study of territoriality, then such will be the case in anthropological and biological studies where the biological definitions first emerged.

13.1.2. Animal Territoriality

Earlier summaries (Edney, 1975a; Sundstrom & Altman, 1974) of human and nonhuman territoriality (hereafter called *animal* territoriality) identified the following eight differences. In animals, uses of space are stereotyped, suggesting a biologically based mechanism; human uses of space are variable, suggesting a learned mechanism. In animal territories, there is a link between aggressive defense and territoriality; this link does not hold for humans. Animal territories are intact; human territories are geographically dispersed. Animals claim exclusive ownership of territories; humans have both exclusive and time-shared ownership. Total invasion by another group is uncommon for animals; it is common for humans. Animals must invade the territory in an intrusion; humans can use weapons to invade territories without trespass. Animals exclude all other co-specifics from their territories; humans entertain co-specific visitors.

Thus it appeared that a biological basis for territoriality could only be applied to animals. Since the time of that conclusion, growth in the field of sociobiology and an increase in experimental studies of animal territories (in, e.g., *The Journal of Animal Ecology*) led to a more complex view of territoriality. Now, even biologists question whether the original biological framework is appropriate for animal populations and early human societies. Currently, although some still claim a biological origin for animal territoriality, the notion of a territorial instinct that was unresponsive to learning and driven to expression is less accepted. The major change instigated by this research was to focus on territoriality as an adaptive mechanism that is responsive to different ecological demands.

The learned component of animal territoriality received support from studies that demonstrate that animals are less stereotyped in their use of territories and exhibit a greater variety of territorial signals than previously believed. For example, some animals alternate between territorial systems and dominance systems in a way that allows them to adapt to fluctuating ecological conditions (Freedman, 1979). Some species have been observed to maintain geographically dispersed territories, for instance, birds who use different trees for nut storage. Timesharing of territories among animals has also been noted. Squirrels that have different peak activity times will share a territory; nocturnal and diurnal lizards share the same space (Ferguson, Hughes, & Brown, 1983). Animals also have the ability to in-trade on other territories without entering them: their birdcalls or colorful throat displays serve as vocal and visual "weapons."

Even the link between territoriality and aggressive defense is not clear. Some researchers have emphasized that the possession of territory actually decreases the likelihood of aggression, at least when territorial claims are clear. Others note that territories may be claimed with nonaggressive means such as chemical smell secretions or visual displays that defend the territory by preventing intrusion.

In sum, animal territorial behaviors are flexible and can often vary across the life span of the animal and across different types of resources.

13.1.3. Early Human Territoriality

Further drawbacks to a strict biological interpretation of territoriality are found in anthropological literature. A biological interpretation of human territoriality could be appealing if early human societies possessed territories. Consequently, anthropologists search for the presence of territoriality in hunter-gatherer societies, the forerunners to contemporary settled agricultural or industrial societies. To the extent that present-day hunter-gatherer groups mirror earlier ones, demonstration of territoriality among current hunter-gatherers may argue for historical continuity of and possible biological basis of human territoriality.

One problem with this approach is that many anthropologists looked to kinship rather than territoriality to provide social organization (Gold, 1982). Furthermore, anthropologists may limit their search to the resource control functions of territoriality; other functions might be ignored.

These problems have created some confusion in the literature, Lee (1968), for example, argued that territoriality is neither universal nor biologically impelled because he could find no evidence of it among the !Kung bushmen. In contrast, Eibl-Eibesfeldt (1974) found several sources of evidence that support the existence of territoriality among the !Kung. Such contradictions may stem from differences among researchers in their definitions of territoriality—whether it exists at the individual or group level (Godelier, 1979), whether it is defined by active defense or by regular use (Altman & Chemers, 1980), or whether it changes with fluctuations in resource availability (Trigham, 1972).

However, the same trend away from biological determinism that was observed in biologists' accounts of animal territoriality can be seen in anthropologists' investigations of the parameters of human territoriality. Dyson-Hudson and Smith (1978) argued that territorial systems would be present only when benefits outweighed costs and that ecological conditions influence the balance of benefits and costs. Benefits may include more efficient harvesting of resources (Cass & Edney, 1978) and greater familiarity with and access to territorial resources. Costs include the time, energy, and risks associated with territorial defense, and the spatial limitations imposed. Conditions of resource availability and abundance are the two ecological conditions that they propose will affect cost-benefit ratios and the social forms in a culture. They argued on the basis of anthropological accounts that a territorial group will be chosen over dispersed-isolated groups, dispersed information-sharing groups, or home-ranging groups when the resources are predictable (temporally and spatially) and abundant (in patches or over the entire territory). The other three exploitation systems were found to develop under other combinations of resource predictability and abundance.

Even though Dyson-Hudson and Smith's theory appeared to deviate from strict biological interpretations of territoriality, it was criticized by Cashdan (1983) for remaining too firmly rooted in the animal model. She argues that the "cognitive and cultural capacities of our species alter the ways in which territories can be defended" (p. 47). Animals' costs of territorial defense increase with increases in the size of the territories because the larger the territory, the more time and energy spent in patrolling and defending territorial boundaries. In contrast, humans have sophisticated communication and memory systems that allow potential intruders to teach their children or others to avoid the rival group's claim to territory. Thus potential confrontations may be less frequent among humans than among animals because humans have more ways of learning to avoid territorial intrusions.

Cashdan also proposed that social boundary defense is a second, uniquely human form of territorial defense whereby a group perimeter is defended instead of a geographic one. Social boundary territories, characteristic of some Australian and Eskimo groups, arise when territories are very large due to sparse or unpredictable resources. These groups adapt by cultivating social and political ties with other dispersed groups so that information concerning the location of food resources may be exchanged. A group that desires to forage in another group's territory can attain foraging rights by enacting a series of greeting rituals. The costs of territorial access across the social boundaries involve the time and energy devoted to greeting rituals themselves and the long-term cultivation of reciprocal social and political ties.

Other anthropological accounts of territoriality have also deviated from the biological focus in emphasizing the social, cultural, or religious meanings that become intertwined with territories. For example, the Tiv "viewed their land as an extension of their geneology [sic]" (Gold, 1982, p. 51) and had a complex system of shifting territories that maintained their juxtapositions to other lineage groups' territories. The Australian aborigines maintained "dreaming space" territories that were symbolically connected to the ancestors (Tuan, 1977). In fact, one researcher views territory as "a set of ideas" and studies the ways in which these "cognitive models are expressed on the ground" (Blundell, 1983, p. 58). Clearly, even nomadic groups who do not accumulate property view their territories as more than devices to protect resources such as food.

Although the debate concerning hunter-gatherer territoriality still continues, it demonstrates some trends evident in more recent treatments of territoriality. First, there is less adherence to the view that territoriality is a biologically determined drive or impulse among humans. Some deviate from the biological position by concluding that human ancestors were not territorial (Suttles, 1972) while others are content to point out the variability in the form and expression of territoriality (Wilson, 1975). Without denying that territories serve biological needs, the new approach is to consider the situations in which territoriality provides flexible adaptation to certain ecological conditions. And, finally, there is recognition that territoriality serves cultural purposes in providing tangible symbols to reinforce a common cultural heritage.

But despite this growth and diversity in the field, the term *territoriality* still conjures up images of aggressive, instinctual defense systems. For example, in a comment on Cashdan's work, Ehrenreich (1983) states:

> I have only one misgiving about the work. It seems regrettable that the analysis is tamed in reference to the issue of "territoriality." No matter how carefully or broadly this concept is defined, it conjures up a biological imperative. Like the idea of the "naked ape," territoriality is a concept "we could live without." (p. 58–59)

Because Cashdan had explicitly opposed a wholesale application of animal models to human territoriality, the stigma attached to the word can be strong indeed.

13.1.4. Unique Qualities of Human Territoriality

The research reviewed previously offers two conclusions. First, the original biological approach has been modified by biologists themselves. They observed that an exclusive emphasis on demarcation and defense was inappropriate. The revised biological perspective points out that human and animal uses of territory are much more flexible, much less biologically impelled than first believed.

Although the research advances show that human and animal uses of territory differ quantitatively rather than qualitatively, the boundaries between the two types of territory are not completely blurred. Social and cultural concerns are more prominent in human territoriality than in animal territoriality. Consequently, humans exhibit more territorial behavior toward significant objects, for example, than do animals. A pet dog's territorial claim to a toy does not compare with a human attachment to a family heirloom. Human attachments to objects are much more frequent and appear to be based on an object's symbolic evocations of cultural, family, and individual histories (Csikzentmihalyi & Rochberg-Halton, 1981).

This ability to confer cultural meanings onto objects is only one example of the larger role that culture plays in the regulation of territoriality (Cashdan, 1983). For example, human cultures have laws that maintain over time the abstract rights to possession of territory. Consequently, human territorial defense does not depend on the occupant's physical strength or cunning in defeating potential claimants to the territory. Instead, the culture provides laws that become proxy defenders of territory.

Perhaps the most general difference between human and animal territories is that human territories serve different needs. "Whereas animal territoriality is rooted in physiological needs connected with survival, human territoriality may also embrace 'higher' needs for, say, status, recognition by others, and achievement or self-image" (Gold, 1982, p. 48). Territories also facilitate the achievement of certain human psychological processes including needs for privacy, intimacy, and solitude (Altman, 1975; Taylor & Ferguson, 1980; Westin, 1970). In contrast, the principal function of territoriality in animal populations is to provide clear and predictable ways of regulating access to resources, thereby clarifying the animal's exchanges with the environment and decreasing moment-to-moment conflicts over the use of space. Thus one difference between human and animal territoriality is that human territories project identities to visitors.

Another difference is that animals rarely engage in social visits across territorial borders. Some species will habituate to the presence of (Wilson, 1975) or even synchronize breeding schedules with their neighbors (termed the Fraser Darling effect). These conditions of social stimulation clearly do not approach the sociability that humans have with visitors.

Humans, in contrast, often use their territories to entertain legitimate visitors. Although visitors are not allowed the same use of space as owners, they are allowed access to otherwise well-protected territories such as living rooms. The existence of territorial visits among humans underscores the role of territoriality as a social system regulator and conveyer of symbols of identity. Yet these more central functions of identity are not equally supported in all types of territories. The following review suggests how structural differences among territories may correlate with their functions.

13.2. STRUCTURAL CHARACTERISTICS OF TERRITORIES

13.2.1. Occupancy and Centrality

Altman (1975) proposed that three different types of territory exist that differ along dimensions of the duration of occupancy and psychological centrality. Primary territories such as homes or bedrooms are typically occupied for long periods and are central to the lives of their owners. Secondary territories are somewhat more accessible to a greater range of users, but regular occupants exert some control over who may enter the territory and what range of behaviors may take place. Although there may be regular users such as bar "regulars" or members of a country club, the time spent within a secondary territory is usually somewhat more limited than the time spent in a primary territory. The limits of occupancy are determined not solely by the users, but by collective owners of secondary territories. Furthermore, secondary territories, while important, are generally not as central to the lives of their occupants as are primary territories. Public territories such as seats on a bus or at a library table are usually occupied for short stretches of time and are not very central to the lives of their occupants. Occupancy of public territories is open to almost everyone and is usually determined on a "first come, first served" basis.

Because the type of territory is not defined strictly by any physical feature, conflicts may arise over the ownership of a space. For example, a graduate student may come to define a certain regularly used library table as a secondary territory. An infrequent user of the library may not recognize this claim and may become puzzled when the graduate student overreacts on finding the seat taken. Or a student who has been used to living in a single-room primary territory may resent the college roommate who invites strangers into the room. Home owners who have joined a Neighborhood Watch anticrime group may come to define the residential block as a secondary territory and react defensively to strangers who use the block as a public territory.

Despite these potentials for misperception on the part of competing users, Taylor and Stough (1978) found, via a repertory grid methodology, that individuals can distinguish between territories on the basis of psychological centrality and duration of use. The differences parallel the sociological distinctions between primary and secondary groups. Primary groups involve face-to-face interactions and affective relations while secondary group relations may be more distant or segmental (Litwak & Szelenyi, 1969). In keeping with these distinctions, Taylor and Stough's respondents perceived that greater comfort, control, privacy, and familiarity with others are available in more primary territories. Consequently, additional dimensions, beyond duration and centrality, draw attention to the more social qualities of the distinctions among primary, secondary, and public territories.

13.2.2. Marking, Markers, and Intrusion

These additional distinctions serve to reinforce a more social perspective on territoriality, whereby territories promote identity display and social system regulation. A third distinction, described in Table 13.2, concerns the motivations underlying territorial marking. A resident of a home may intend a name-plate to be a decorative self-expression; yet the nameplate may have the effect of conveying a primary territorial claim (Brown & Altman, 1981, 1983). The act of personalization is more of a conscious claim for space in other territories; users of public or secondary territories are much more aware of the need to defend their turf by conspicuous placement of books or other markers. Consequently, the functions of territorial markers may be more self-expressive for primary territories and more utilitarian for secondary or public territories.

A fourth dimension depicted in Table 13.2 concerns the range, type, and mix of markers that are used in various territories. Marker characteristics may reveal the owners' marking intentions as well as the territory's durability and psychological centrality. For example, primary territories, because of their centrality and durability, often contain markers reflecting personal characteristics of their occupants. The markers themselves may appear to reflect more central values, may be more durable, and may portray highly personal qualities of the owners. For example, primary territory markers can include permanent nameplates, artworks, and furnishings. Because such territories are long term, the markers need not be portable and can vary in size, permanency, and attachment to the territory itself.

In secondary territories, markers may be valuable, yet they may be specially protected when the regular users are absent. For example, the trophy case in a country club may be kept locked due to the vulnerability of the territory when it is not occupied by the regulars. Other markers may be more explicit statements of territorial boundaries such as "members only" or "keep out" signs.

Table 13.2. Dimensional Variations Between Public, Secondary, and Primary Territories

Dimension	Public	Secondary	Primary
Duration	Short	Short, but regular usage common	Long
Centrality	Not central	Somewhat central	Very central
Marking intentions	Intentionally claiming territory	Often claiming territory	Usually personalizing or decorating
Marking range	Few physical markers or barriers; much bodily and verbal marking	Some reliance on physical markers; bodily and verbal marking common	Heavy reliance on a wide range of markers and barriers; bodily and verbal marking usually not necessary
Responses to invasion	Can relocate or use immediate bodily and verbal markers	Can often relocate, use immediate bodily and verbal markers, as well as some re-emphasis of physical markers	Cannot relocate easily, can use legal recourse, reestablishment of physical markers and barriers, as well as bodily and verbal markers

Source: "Territoriality and Residential Crime: A Conceptual Framework" by B. Brown and I. Altman, 1981, in *Environmental Criminology* by P. J. Brantingham and P. L. Brantingham, Beverly Hills; Sage Publications. Copyright 1981 by Sage Publications. Reprinted by permission.

Public territories are almost always defended with occupancy and/or minimal physical or nonverbal markers. Physical markers are often limited to items that are convenient and available such as books or umbrellas. In recognition of the ephemeral nature of these territories, owners do not risk using valuable markers such as purses to protect the territory.

A fifth dimension along which territories vary involves reactions to territorial intrusion. In general, both the strength of territorial defenses and the impact of territorial intrusions increase from public to secondary to primary territories. Intrusions of primary territories appear intentional, because the intruder has had to ignore salient markers or boundaries such as closed doors. Owners have a wide range of territorial defenses available in such cases, including legal defenses and physical retaliation. The owners may react strongly to an intrusion for a number of reasons: The place symbolizes the personal identity of the owner; valuable territorial markings may be ruined or taken by intruders; the owners may have no territory to retreat to after the most central territory has been intruded on (Brown, 1983). Thus for economic, physical, and psychological reasons intrusions into primary territories are serious matters.

Secondary territories, with their mix of public and private use, lesser importance to owners, and less clear-cut evidence of marking and personalization, may be more susceptible to intrusion. The motives for invasions may be variable, ranging from a deliberate attempt at intrusion to an accidental invasion. Similarly, the reactions to invasion may vary considerably, depending on the extent to which the occupants feel that the territory is central and that they have adequately marked it. Reactions to an invasion will also be affected by the motives that owners attribute to the intruders.

When a public territory is invaded, the owner has some but only minimal "rights" to the territory. Because such territories assume the least importance to owners, owners or invaders are likely to respond by retreating. If a user wants to reclaim an invaded territory, verbal request or nonverbal signals may be the only recourse.

13.2.3. Structural-Functional Relationship

With respect to all five dimensions, it is apparent that different types of territories are used for different functions. The primary territory is the most multifunctional. It allows for a great deal of order, organization, predictability, and control. But it also allows for the expression of a sense of identity. It is likely that these two functions are related. Control can promote a sense of efficacy that becomes incorporated into the self-identity. Similarly, a certain amount of control ought be a prerequisite to the development of deep psychological investments in a place. One would not develop a sense of identification with something that cannot be relied on to express the self.

The type of control available will also be likely to influence the type of identity displayed in a territory. Primary territories are often controlled by an individual who can choose to display unique aspects of personal identity. Secondary territories are often associated with groups such as neighbors, co-workers, the regulars at the bar, or members of a street gang, and they are therefore more likely to be controlled by a group than an individual. The type of identity displayed may be a group identity and thus may emphasize only one role within the repertoire of its owners.

In public territories, where control is fleeting, displays of identity are typically restricted to the occupants' immediate appearance and belongings. Any sense of control the users have may derive from the predictability of behavior in the setting rather than the ability to create and enforce one's choice of rules. For example, occupants may not be able to erect a "no smoking" sign, but they can predict that others present will obey the rules for the use of the territory.

One exception to the association between identity functions and primary territories occurs in what Stokols and Jacobi (1984) call *commemorative environments* such as the Statue of Liberty, a mosque, or the Lincoln Memorial. Although these places may have the same limitations on demarcation and occupancy as most public territories do, they also support aspects of individual or group identity the way primary territories do. While such religious, ethnic, or historical attachments are important, they are not derived in the same manner as territorial attachments. That is, territorial attachments are usually forged through a combination of activities (such as occupying, personalizing, and defending space) and psychological transformations (such as developing feelings of territorial attachment, ownership, and identification) that emerge from experience with a place. Attachments to commemorative environments do not qualify as territorial attachments because they can be created independently of actual experience with a place.

A second form of person-place relationship that is not considered territorial is one that involves exclusive ownership. For example, legal ownership of a piece of investment property does not constitute territorial ownership if the territorial cognitions and feelings do not accompany the ownership. That is, unless the owner develops a feeling of ownership, attachment, or identification, mere legal ownership does not constitute a territorial relationship. Similarly, an absence of legal ownership does not imply an absence of territoriality. A child can become territorial about his or her toys without legally owning them.

The present conceptualization and the bulk of the empirical work focus on territories where attachments are forged through actual use, not vicariously. Activities such as occupancy, defense, and personalization and psychological ties such as feelings of ownership, attachment, or identification are assumed to be necessary to constitute a territorial relationship. Admittedly, the bulk of the research in public territories has assumed the presence of territoriality simply by demonstrating behavioral components of territorial demarcation and defense. Nonetheless, it is assumed that such behaviors indicate a psychological claim to the space as well.

Furthermore, it is argued that primary territories allow for the greatest degree of control and the greatest potential for individualistic identity displays. Secondary territories have a moderate degree of control: identity may be that of a role within a group. Finally, public territories emphasize order, organization, and control; identity displays are more limited, deriving from the appearance of the owner or objects carried by the owner.

13.3. TERRITORIAL DEMARCATION AND DEFENSE OF SPACE

13.3.1. Physical Territorial Markers

Most studies of territoriality emphasize the demarcation and defense of public territories. Public territories are often self-consciously marked to reserve space; owners realize that their claims to space are tenuous. Consequently, public territorial marking is especially geared toward preventing intrusions rather than providing cues that facilitate interactions or express identity.

Limiting conditions for the effectiveness of public territorial markers in settings such as libraries include the duration of absence of the owner, the availability of alternative spaces, and the desirability of the territory. All markers appear to prevent intrusions when the other users of the library have plenty of alternative spaces available. However, as population density increases and alternative spaces decrease, a marker will lose its effectiveness (Sommer & Becker, 1969).

Although it has been claimed that personal markers provide better protection than impersonal ones (Sommer & Becker, 1969), the impersonal quality of the marker is likely to be confounded with its functional ambiguity. A marker is particularly susceptible to intrusion if it can be mistaken for litter such as racing forms in racetrack seats (Arenson, 1977), school newspapers on snack bar tables, and scattered journals on library tables (Sommer & Becker, 1969). Markers such as notebooks and jackets are typically not abandoned permanently, so that could account for their greater effectiveness. The functional ambiguity of certain markers may explain their limited effectiveness better than their personal or impersonal nature does.

In line with this interpretation, it was found that a half-empty beer mug is a more effective deterrent to intrusion of a table at a bar than a more personal marker such as a sports jacket (Hoppe, Greene, & Kenny, 1972). The authors reasoned that prospective customers realize that patrons may forget their jackets when leaving the bar but that they (or the bartenders) seldom leave half-empty beer mugs. Prospective customers assume that the bartender expects the patron to return. Similarly, it is possible to think of situations in which not only would personal markers provide less protection than impersonal markers, but they themselves would be at risk in the setting. For example, in bus stations or airports where thievery is frequent, individuals avoid using their luggage or jackets as objects to defend a territory in their absence. Thus rather than concluding that personal markers are superior to impersonal ones it is appropriate to take into account the local norms and customs that govern the use and protection of territory.

13.3.2. Social Defenders of Territory

Perhaps because of the limited effectiveness of public territorial markers, users sometimes enlist the aid of neighbors to save seats at a game or movie theater when temporarily vacating the seat. Sommer and Becker (1969) observed that neighbors were more likely to defend an adjacent space when the user had been absent a relatively short time (e.g., 15 min vs. 60 min). Likelihood of defense was unrelated to the user's prior duration of occupancy (5 vs. 20 min) or degree of personalized contact with the neighbor (no contact vs. asking for the time vs. chatting informally, all for 5 min). However, when neighbors are explicitly asked to defend a territory, a large proportion (71%) will do so, and many will put their own territorial markers on the claimed space (Hoppe *et al.*,1972).

13.3.3. Nonverbal Territorial Markers

In public territories, there are instances in which the shape and extent of the territory are not marked or bounded by physical markers. For example, Goffman (1963) contends that museum visitors claim the space encompassed by their apparent path of gaze toward an art object. Less anecdotal evidence has supported the use of nonverbal markers in public territories. For example, restaurant diners appear to touch their plates of food in two ways (Truscott, Parmelee, & Werner, 1977). They reposition the plate of food to achieve better placement of the food or they touch the plates without moving them. This second, nonutilitarian form of plate touching appeared to serve territorial functions because it was more likely to occur when the diner had more need to establish a territorial claim. That is, the touching was more likely to occur after service by a waiter or waitress than by the self and when the plate was served with food rather than empty.

The validity of the role of touch as a territorial marker was extended by examination of the phenomenon in another locale—the pinball parlor. In this study (Werner, Brown, & Damron, 1981), the roles of two other nonverbal behaviors—body orientation and closeness—were examined for their ability to protect a territory from intrusion. In the game arcade, as was not the case in Goffman's museum example, merely gazing at a pinball machine did not protect it. (However, Lindskold, Albert, Baer, & Moore, 1976, demonstrated that gazing at a store window does deter passersby from intervening.) But standing close to or touching the machine did deter intrusion. Similarly, individuals who were engaging in play would touch the machine more frequently when approached by a stranger than when playing in isolation. Thus touch is an easy, dynamic marker used to establish a public territory and to protect it from an impending intrusion.

Interactional or *portable territories* arise when territorial claims are made to protect an ongoing interaction rather than the space itself. Goffman (1963) has described these as "line of talk" territories. These spaces are not bubble shaped like personal spaces but are elongated to encompass the space that connects two or more interactants. These territories are also protected by nonverbal signals. For example, they are defended better when the interactants are relatively close together (Efran & Cheyne, 1973) are interacting (Cheyne & Efran, 1972), are in large groups (four vs. two individuals) or are high status (e.g., older vs. younger; Knowles, 1973), or are mixed-sex dyads (63% vs. 49% for same-sex dyads, Cheyne & Efran, 1972). Thus a variety of both static and dynamic nonverbal signals protect interactional territories.

13.3.4. Characteristics of Territorial Occupants

Investigators have examined the effect of group size, culture, and gender on territorial occupancy, intrusion, and defense. As occupancy time increases, same-sex groups claim larger spaces and mixed-sex groups use more markers. It was suggested that the mixed-sex groups used markers to keep territorial boundaries intact while same-sex groups on these beach territories kept boundaries unmarked in order to socialize across boundaries. Generally, as group size increases, the average space per person decreases (Edney & Jordan-Edney, 1974), although this may be true only for groups of friends, not strangers (Edney & Grundmann, 1979).

A cross-cultural study of beach territories, while failing to replicate effects of group size for either French or German samples, found a greater clarity of territorial boundaries for Germans than for French (Smith, 1983). A comparison of American and Greek reactions to territorial contaminations also yielded more differences than similarities. While both groups were quick to remove a garbage sack from their lawns, Greeks were not as quick to remove one from the sidewalk or street in front of their house (Worchel & Lollis, 1982). These two samples of cross-cultural territories suggest that culture plays a role in the way in which territorial spaces are claimed and regulated.

Sex differences have appeared in some studies but not in others. French and German males use fewer markers on beach territories than females (Smith, 1983), while U.S. males claim larger beach (Edney & Jordan-Edney, 1974) and dormitory room territories (Mercer & Benjamin, 1980). A comparison of female and male markers in a bar showed that male markers are intruded on on fewer trials and, when intruded on, protect the territory for a longer amount of time. Male territories were never invaded by a lone intruder (Shaffer & Sadowski, 1975). As if to underscore this point, Haber (1980) instructed confederates to intrude on male and female students' classroom desk territories. She had to abort her plans when her confederates could not bring themselves to complete all the planned invasions; however, they completed twice as many invasions for females.

The reluctance to intrude on male territories is well founded; when fraternity and sorority tables in a cafeteria were invaded the males were more likely to say unfriendly things to the intruders (Calsyn, 1976). Other studies show that males and females who find their library seats taken are equally likely to withdraw (McAndrew, Ryckman, Horr, & Solomon, 1978), or to ask the intruder to leave (Taylor & Brooks, 1980). Thus anticipated negative reactions by intruded-on males may only materialize when their rights to space are established via occupancy rather than marking. These findings stand in contrast to observations of interactional territories. These territories are best defended from interlopers by mixed-sex dyads rather than male (or female) dyads. Thus the perceived intimacy or strength of the bond between territorial owners may provide more deterrence than does fear of male retaliation.

13.3.5. Styles of Territorial Occupancy and Intrusion

Despite the fact that public territories appear to be easily violated, many intruders do not invade these spaces lightly. For example, if intruders must sit at occupied tables, they tend to choose the most distant seat possible and they leave earlier than control subjects who seat themselves at unmarked tables (Becker, 1973).

Some intruders appear more comfortable with their role than others. Consistent findings suggest that there are both deferential and offensive styles of intrusion. Sommer labeled the styles he observed *avoidant* and *offensive* (1967). When students wanted to establish a territory that would allow them to avoid distractions by others, they chose end chairs at six-person tables (Sommer, 1967) or spaces near the wall or facing away from the door (Sommer & Becker, 1969). Offensive claimants, ones who desire a territory by themselves, tended to select the middle seats of a six-person table (Sommer, 1967) or seats facing the door and center or aisle seats (Sommer & Becker, 1969).

Sommer and Becker (1969) observed the effects of three different styles of intrusion by a confederate—verbal requests, nonverbal requests, and nonverbal aggressiveness. Only the direct verbal query led to frequent defense by the neighbor; both nonverbal approaches—barging into the territory or hesitantly approaching the seat—decreased the neighbor's defense of space. In the game arcade naive intruders also adopted deferential or assertive styles of claiming a video game that was guarded but not used by a confederate (Werner, *et al.*, 1981). Other studies have noted that intruders apologize, avert their eyes, purse their lips, or stare at the intruded-on individuals: again this supports the existence of intrusive and apologetic styles of intrusion (Efran & Cheyne, 1974). Why intruders select a particular style is not yet known; however, Lavin (1978) found that apologetic or deferential styles are more frequent when intruders can see the territory holder and are not blocked by physical barriers protecting the territory. Thus relative openness of the current occupant may elicit a more deferential approach.

If occupants of public territories are intruded on, their most frequent reaction is to abandon the territory. All individuals who found their marked seats invaded on returning from a cafeteria line retreated and most individuals retreated when an invader had taken the adjacent seat (Becker & Mayo, 1971) or when the owner's markers had been brushed aside and replaced with a different set of markers (McAndrew *et al.*, 1978). When occupants do try to reclaim their territories, acts of surprise or intimidation may precede the request. For example, invaded owners of carrel spaces in the library walk past the intruder before returning to demand their space (Taylor & Brooks, 1980). Intruded-upon owners of classroom seats stop and stare at the intruder before requesting their space (Haber, 1980).

13.3.6. Architectural Features and Territorial Claims

Certain architectural features appear to encourage the development of territoriality in public spaces. Students are more likely to make territorial claims for library tables that are close to a wall, facing away from the distractions of the main entrance, and toward the rear of the room (Sommer & Becker, 1969). Passersby are more likely to drink from a water fountain if it is shielded from the spatial proximity of others by a physical barrier (Baum, Reiss, & O'Hara, 1974).

Territorial claims are clearer for well-demarcated carrel sites in a library than for unbounded tables (Taylor & Brooks, 1980). The private nature of the carrels was confirmed by descriptions of carrel intruders. They were more likely to be seen as more pushy and rude (65%) than table intruders (22%). In an experimental test, a female confederate invaded a marked but recently vacated table or carrel space. All of the carrel owners asked for their spaces back while half of the table owners did so, suggesting that the salient boundary line of the carrels enhanced the legitimacy of the user's claim.

In sum, strength of territorial ownership and defense has been shown to vary according to characteristics of the setting such as territorial markers, architectural features, and social defenders and characteristics of the occupants such as their gender, cultural background, or group size. The implications these variations have for other ongoing social processes are not apparent; the emphasis to this point has been on the ways in which territories create "keep out" messages. The following section reviews ways in which territories involve group processes such as dominance displays, communication of status, and social system maintenance.

13.4. TERRITORIALITY AND SYSTEM VIABILITY

13.4.1. Dominance and Territoriality

Among animals, dominance hierarchies and territorial systems interact in complicated ways. Dominance hierarchies may substitute for or exist within territorial systems. When they coexist, the individual on home turf may actually be able to dominate others who are higher in the hierarchy (Wilson, 1975). Or the dominance rankings can overrule individual territorial claims. For example, an overlord male lizard may have free access to female lizard territories although the females defend their borders against encroachment by other females.

In human populations, dominance and territoriality are related in complex ways, and empirical studies often yield inconsistent results. Altman (1975) suggests that the inconsistency of results may be due to variations in measures of dominance, to the social dynamics within the sample, and to characteristics of the samples studied.

Dominance is sometimes measured as the amount of social contact and other times as powerful or directive behaviors. When the first definition is used, highly dominant individuals in mental hospitals act as overlords who claim territories that encompass the territorial borders of lower-status members of the group (Esser, 1968; Esser, Chamberlain, Chappie, & Kline, 1965; lack of confirmation was provided by Esser, 1973). When dominance is defined in terms of behaviors such as name-calling, issuing orders, and physical attack, then more dominant individuals occupy the more desirable territories (Austin & Bates, 1974; Sossin, Esser, & Deutsch, 1978).

The influence of social dynamics on the relation between dominance and territoriality was illustrated in a study of 17 boys in a rehabilitation center (Sundstrom & Altman, 1974). According to the boys' own judgments of dominance ranks and desirable territories, the most dominant boys early on had the most desirable spaces such as those near the television. But when two highly dominant boys were replaced by two newcomers, the group renegotiated the division of territories through fights and disturbances, a process often observed in animal territories (Wilson, 1975). For 3 weeks the number of fights and disturbances increased and the boys showed no fixed territories. In the third phase, the low- and medium-dominant boys began to carve out individual territories, while the high-dominant ones were struggling with the other boys. This study along with others (cf. DeLong, 1970, 1973) demonstrates that a relationship between dominance and territoriality may or may not exist depending on fluctuations in group structure and process.

13.4.2. Territoriality and Status Relations

Studies of settings other than residential treatment facilities illustrate the more diverse and subtle connections between territoriality and influence. These situations differ from previous studies of dominance in that individuals are not aiming for rights to exclusive use of space. Visitors are accepted into the territories, yet the owners still draw on their territorial resources to shape and guide interactions within those territories.

In sports encounters, the opposing team is allowed access to the home turf, yet the hosts attempt to dominate the game. In these encounters, the home team has the "home court advantage" (Altman, 1975; Schwartz & Barsky, 1977). A home team advantage may be partially due to greater familiarity with idiosyncratic court conditions or the absence of travel fatigue. Schwartz and Barsky (1977) reasoned that the noisy support by home crowd fans was an advantage because the effect is stronger for indoor games such as basketball than for outdoor games such as football.

Other studies examine the ability of territory owners to dominate visitors when the domination does not involve physical superiority. It has been found that individuals believe they have more control in the more central primary territories than in secondary or public territories (Taylor & Stough, 1978) and they actually are more likely to influence decisions made there (Taylor & Lanni, 1981). Several studies have examined the advantages that college students have over visitors to their dormitory room. Hosts have the advantage in negotiation tasks (Martindale, 1971) and can dominate a cooperative task when visitors are dissimilar to the residents (Conroy & Sundstrom, 1977).

In that last study it was revealed that territories could facilitate pleasurable exchanges as well as contentious ones. The territorial dominance effect reversed itself when the visitor had similar opinions to the host. Thus territories can also facilitate prosocial encounters when conditions favor good treatment of visitors. In addition, hosts may have greater psychological comfort on their home turf. Edney (1975) found that dormitory residents evaluated their room more positively and appeared more relaxed and secure than visitors.

In many settings status rankings also correlate with territoriality in work environments. Offices comprising the more desirable territories are expected to be assigned to those who have greater status or power within the organization. Indications of high status in an office include low accessibility, large floor space, high-quality furnishings (i.e., wood is higher status than metal, carpeting is higher status than bare floor). A study of 529 office workers indicated that, especially for high-status individuals, the presence of high-status markers correlated positively with employees' beliefs that the work space accurately reflected their rank within the organization (Konar, Sundstrom, Brady, Mandel, & Rice, 1982). This study did not examine whether status markers were related to dominant behaviors, but it does suggest that the visitors to the offices could gauge the statuses of the officeholders via their territorial cues and adjust strategies of interaction accordingly.

The role of territorial claims in ongoing interactions was pinpointed more precisely in a symbolic interactionist's investigations of role-played negotiations between a boss and an employee (Katovich, 1986). The conversations took place in either the employee's or the boss's office. Territorial claims entered into the conversation in quite subtle ways. For example, the officeholder rather than the visitor assumed the right to initiate a handshake. But the power to designate visitor space within the office depended upon rank. In the boss's office, the boss appeared to direct the person to a visitor's space (e.g., "Have a seat") or to question his or her right to space ("What can I do for you?"). When the boss entered the employee's space, the boss sat without invitation, presuming the power to claim visiting space without permission. In this case, according to Katovich, the "turf master" is relegated to the role of "turf guardian." The subtle ways in which an employer's status and territorial ownership become entwined in the interaction with an employee illustrate that territories can enhance system viability by clarifying interactions and making them predictable. Territories also can enhance the functioning of systems in ways that have nothing to do with dominance or power.

13.4.3. System Maintenance

At the level of the primary territory, studies of living environments demonstrate that the long-term stability of the residential environment system is related to the establishment of territoriality. For example, U.S. Navy volunteers who are isolated in pairs inside one room for extended lengths of time are more likely to maintain their compatibility with each other and elect to complete the isolation experiment if they quickly develop and maintain individual territories (Altman & Haythorn,

1967; Altman, Taylor, & Wheeler, 1971). Although the volunteers were in temporary quarters and had little ability to personalize the room, the territorial provision of control appeared to help them withstand the isolation. Even in less stressful environments, married couples (Rosenblatt & Budd, 1975) and families (Altman, Nelson, & Lett, 1972) develop territorial systems that promote smooth functioning within the social units.

In secondary territories, Suttles (1968) investigated the division of territorial groupings among Chicago gangs and found that they enhanced both the members' sense of group identity and their ability to control entry into certain areas at certain times. Separate gangs existed for ethnicity (black, Italian, Mexican-American, and Puerto Rican) and, within those groups, for age gradations. A more recent study of ethnic gangs in Los Angeles (Moore, Vigil, & Garcia, 1983) corroborates these findings and further demonstrates that cohesive gangs may even import members who do not live in the area to take a proprietary interest in and identify with a neighborhood. Less formally defined neighborhood groups may also feel a high degree of security and community, may experience fewer incidents of residential burglary (Brown, 1983), and may more effectively fight proposed zoning changes in the neighborhood (Smith, 1975). A more extensive treatment of the relationship between territoriality and the functioning of social systems, especially with reference to residential settings and crime, is found in Taylor, Chapter 25, this volume.

13.4.4. Personalization and Social Interaction

The very act of personalizing may enhance system viability by facilitating certain interactions. For example, some researchers have noted that gardening, yard work, or other upkeep tasks are ways of personalizing territory that create opportunities for neighbors to become acquainted with one another. The social ties may increase the owners' commitments to the individual territory as well as the neighborhood territory (Beck & Teasdale, 1978; Bush-Brown, 1969; Lewis, 1979; Newman, 1972). Backyard gardeners have also reported better ability to distinguish between neighbors and strangers as well as fewer problems with intruders on the street (Taylor, Gottfredson, & Brower, 1981).

The effects of environmental personalizations on actual interactions between strangers have also been demonstrated. Visitors to a waiting room have been shown to affiliate more when there are easily understood conversation pieces decorating the room (Mehrabian & Diamond, 1971). Thus the mere presence of certain environmental personalizations may enter into social processes even when the interactants have no role in the personalization process itself.

Personalization may enhance system viability partially by clarifying the personal qualities of the territory owners, as illustrated in a study of personalizations in dormitory rooms (Vinsel, Brown, Altman & Foss, 1980). It was found that the students' choice of personalizations in the freshman year related to the students' likelihood of remaining in school. Two themes distinguished between those who dropped out (for reasons other than academic failure) and those who chose to remain. First, the diversity of interests displayed via the decorations was much narrower in scope for the future dropouts. Whereas a "stay-in" might display interests in sports, abstract art, statements of values, personal relationships, and theater, a dropout would display fewer of such decorative categories. A second difference was found in the pattern of commitments displayed. Stay-ins appeared to be committing themselves to the university environment by displaying such things as university club or Greek insignia, maps of the campus and local area, and mementos of local events such as concerts. The dropouts appeared to have maintained their commitments to hometown people and places. Their decorations included items such as letters from younger siblings, dried prom flowers, and posters of hometown attractions. Thus the type of identity conveyed through the decorations was quite different for the two groups. It is possible that the decorative differences actually contributed to and shaped the students' interactions in the room and the impressions received by others. Certain types of identity messages may prove dysfunctional in the students' attempts to adjust to the new living environment. This study illustrates how processes involved in maintaining a viable system may involve the presentation of certain types of identity displays, a theme elaborated below.

13.5. TERRITORIALITY AND IDENTITY

The space-claiming and system viability functions of territoriality are relatively easy to observe in concrete behaviors involving occupancy, dominance, demarcation, or defense of space. The provision of identity is more difficult to study because it is manifested more in cognitions and affective ties to places or things. Nonetheless, the substance of self-identity may be studied through owners' choices of personalizations. Furthermore, the very act of personalizing or caring for one's territory may create strong bonds of attachment to the territory. Finally, identity functions can be revealed through the psychological states that accompany occupancy, demarcation, or personalization of space. Although claiming and identifying with space are two different activities, they are actually intertwined. That is, activities that control space also provide feedback relevant to the individual's sense of identity, as illustrated in the following section.

13.5.1. The Development of Control and Identity Functions

The best research available on the beginnings of territorial behavior is found in cross-cultural studies of the acquisition of concepts of possessiveness, typically involving objects. Furby (1974, 1978, 1980, 1982) argues that among humans objects play a complex role in social coordination and identity display. When a child learns cultural rules governing possessions, the child begins to develop a sense of self and a sense of competence in the world. In all societies children acquire a sense of control and competence partially by manipulating objects around them. When adults interfere with the child's attempts to touch and play with certain objects, children learn boundary conditions for ownership. Thus the child's early identity development involves experiences with feeling competent and in control with regard to objects. Consequently, the first encounters with objects appear to establish a link between ownership, identity, and competence.

In a later stage of development, the manipulation of objects becomes important for social interaction. For example, possessing a toy draws the attention of other age mates. Or simultaneous play can lead to social interchanges when two toddlers are attracted to the same toy. Furby notes that peers respond to each other more when showing, giving, or taking an object than when interacting without an object. Consequently, concepts of ownership are immediately linked to social interaction experiences. This connection is maintained through adulthood. Furby's older respondents reported not only that ownership implies social power and status, but that ownership helps to define individuality when possessions can be viewed as extensions of the self, as discussed in the following section.

13.5.2. Personalizations and Identity Messages

Illustrations of the identity functions of territoriality rarely come from territory researchers themselves. Although definitions of territoriality from the social approach (Table 13.1) referred to feelings of attachment or valuations of space, the bulk of research comes from other disciplines. Table 13.3 summarizes some of the ways these researchers describe the identity aspects of the possession of things. Although territory researchers refer to the actual territory only incidentally as a space that is staked out and defended, place attachment researchers emphasize the symbolic contents that make the territories worth defending.

Personalizations may enter into territorial functioning in several ways that have little to do with an intentional claim to or defense of territory. First, onlookers may form impressions of occupants based upon the personalizations. Second, territorial personalizations allow the territory owner to foster certain impressions that may or may not be accurate reflections of the owner. Third, the very act of personalizing may create or intensify bonds of attachment between owner and territory.

Table 13.3. Identity Functions of Places and Objects

Tuan (1980): "Likewise with our houses, streets, and buildings: the constraints that they put on us focus our energies and intentions; the clear images that the structures present to us sharpen our sense of self" (p. 465). "[Artifacts] stabilize experience, support our sense of a perdurable self, and confirm our belief in a comprehensible universe. The house in many societies is a microcosm that encapsulates with clear and graspable detail what the larger world is like and how we should behave in that world. The house imparts lessons implicitly, without demands on conscious thought" (p. 471). "Our fragile sense of self needs support, and this we get by having and possessing things because, to a large degree, we are what we have and possess" (p. 472).

Hayward (1977): "What people call 'home' serves as a symbol of how they see themselves and how they want to be seen by others" (p. 3).

Kimber (1973): "Gardens … represent social territories in which persons define their own places and express their self-images" (p. 7).

Dovey (in press): "To accuse someone, their possessions or 'home' of being inauthentic implies a strong moral judgment and arouses righteous indignation" (p. 1).

Sadalla, Burroughs, & Quaid (1981): "The design of a house may be construed as a symbol or a set of symbols which communicate something of the owner's identity and social status" (p. 201).

Csikszentmihalyi & Rochberg-Halton (1981): "A home is much more than a shelter; it is a world in which a person can create a material environment that embodies what he or she considers significant. In this sense the home becomes the most powerful sign of the self of the inhabitant who dwells within" (p. 123).

A number of studies have revealed links between personalizations of a place and perceived characteristics of the occupants. Maslow and Mintz (1956) had judges rate pictures of individuals when seated in beautiful or ugly rooms. The judges in beautiful rooms rated the pictures higher on dimensions of energy and well-being than judges in ugly rooms. In a follow-up study, Mintz (1956) found that experimenters who conducted interviews in both types of rooms actually stayed longer in and reported more positive mood states in the beautiful rooms. Another study revealed that the judged levels of formality and friendliness of rooms were also believed to characterize their occupants (Canter, West, & Wools. 1974). Judges have also been shown to agree on inferences of residents' personality, occupational type, and occupational prestige from pictures of residents' houses (Cherulnik, 1982).

Finally, several studies demonstrate that the choice of personalizations creates impressions of social, not just personal, identity. For example, the styles of gardening surrounding Puerto Rican households have been described as representing "social territories in which persons define their own places and express their self-images" (Kimber, 1973, p. 7). Six distinct styles were identified that represent the degree of allegiance the resident showed to two contrasting traditions: the vernacular and high style. Gardens in the vernacular tradition were treated as a utilitarian source of work space, food source, and waste receptacle. High-style gardens were used to "create artificial landscapes, to decorate the dwelling, and to express the esthetic taste of the owner or of the local landscape architect" (p. 23).

Personalizations do not always create positive images of occupants. Personalizing may also be considered a form of deviance by the larger society, as in the case of vandalism or graffiti. Use of vandalism or graffiti can symbolize individual identity (Ley & Cybriwsky, 1974), group identity, or dominance over another's territory (Pablant & Baxter, 1975). Graffiti wars may take place where territorial boundary lines are disputed. Vandalism may be a symbolic form of personalization that restores the vandal's feelings of control over the space (Allen & Greenberger, 1980).

13.5.3. Personalizations and Actual Identity

Many researchers assume that personalizations are accurate reflections of some aspects of the owners' identity. For example, Cooper (1972), using Jungian theory, suggested that houses are sacred symbols of the self. Rapoport (1969) emphasizes that house form may demonstrate the owner's tie to cultural identity. Altman and colleagues (Altman & Chemers, 1980; Altman & Gauvain, 1981; Gauvain, Altman, & Fahim, 1983) noted that houses may reflect an individual's need simultaneously to establish individuality from and communality with the culture.

In more traditionally empirical studies, it has been demonstrated that personalizations do reflect individual or family characteristics. Artifacts found in living rooms correlate with the owner's social status (Laumann & House, 1972). Similarly, the decorative complexity of housing interiors correlates with materialistic values espoused by the owners (Weisner & Weibel, 1981). Using the concept of front region from Goffman (1959), one study examined whether living rooms served as front regions by conveying desirable images of the occupants. Naive judges could accurately infer the residents' idealized self-images by scrutinizing the living room (Sadalla, Burrough, & Quaid, 1981).

Social group memberships are also reflected in personalizations. Duncan (1973) found that two distinct social clusters in one village were identifiable by personalization styles. One group preferred the "English upper-class style of studied seediness," (p. 343) complete with colonial houses and bucolic landscapes. The second group preferred a prosperous neighborly style evoked by newer colonial reproduction houses personalized with Americana symbols and unfenced yards. The environmental differences reflected social differences with the first group belonging to different churches and clubs and preferring less contact with neighbors than the second. Similar group identities were revealed by Pratt (1982), who focused on house interior personalizations. In his study, one social group decorated to convey uniqueness while the other strove to follow decorative standards of the group.

Ethnic identities may also be reflected in choices of territorial personalization. Mexican-American houses in Tucson are much more likely to have chain link fences than Anglo houses in the same area (Arreola, 1981). Slavic-American houses in Kansas City are personalized differently from the houses of their non-Slavic neighbors (Greenbaum & Greenbaum, 1981). The Slavic households had more potted plants, better sidewalk and house maintenance, more extensive landscaping, and more attractive yards. Interviews revealed the Slavs to be more involved in neighborhood sociability, suggesting that they had formed a secondary neighborhood territory.

Home interiors contain a wide variety of objects that hold special meanings for identity. Interviews with 315 members of 82 lower- and upper-middle-class families revealed that 1,694 objects were cited as special or meaningful (Csikszentmihalyi & Rochberg-Halton, 1981). The objects could be grouped into 17 categories to reflect the object's use, meaning, personal significance, or mode of acquisition. Some objects were meaningful because they invoked the past such as family reunions or travels; others were symbols of ethnic or religious identities. Emotional qualities such as feelings of enjoyment or accomplishment were also conveyed through objects. Thus objects served to embody a wide range of emotional meanings, social ties, or other aspects of authentic identity.

The role of exterior personalization in reflecting ties to the local community has been corroborated in other studies. In a neighborhood that generally encouraged neighborliness, neighborly behaviors and attitudes were related to the likelihood and value of home improvements made by the residents (Galster & Hesser, 1982). Within a middle-class neighborhood the presence of temporary personalizations in the form of Halloween decorations was associated with both reports of neighborhood cohesiveness and cul-de-sac street designs (Brown & Werner, 1985). Thus territorial personalizations can symbolize a wide range of affect-laden identity commitments.

13.5.4. Place Attachments

Conceptual work on attachment to place has rarely been the focus of traditionally trained psychologists. While the feeling of being "at home" may be commonly experienced, it is difficult to capture the essence of this feeling in concrete instances of behavior. Even when psychologists consider the verbal responses to interviews or questionnaires as legitimate data, they tend to concentrate their efforts on measuring beliefs or reports of behavior. Affective concerns may be tapped in attitude questionnaires, but it is typical to conceive of affective states very globally in terms of a general evaluative dimension whereby something is judged to be good or bad (Fishbein & Ajzen, 1975).

Because traditionally trained psychologists are not very fluent when assessing the experiential components of emotional or affective bonds (De Rivera, 1984), various phenomenological and philosophical works prove more informative when examining place attachment (cf. Buttimer & Seamon, 1980; Relph, 1976; Rowles, 1978, Seamon, 1979). The special feeling of attachment to place was described by Eliade (1957) as an attitude toward the "sacred" as contrasted with the "profane." Heidegger (1971) formulated the concept of *dwelling* that describes an active, caring process by which individuals transform a house into a home. This work has been continued by European scholars who examine the *appropriation* of space, whereby places become meaningful due to the activities, work, and attachments embedded within them (Barbey, 1982; Korosec-Serfaty, 1985). Bachelard (1964) argues that the house serves as a place to study attachments, but that "all really inhabited space bears the essence of the notion of the home" (p. 5). Along with an emphasis on activities that make the house meaningful, Bachelard argues that the "house is one of the greatest powers of integration for the thoughts, memories, and dreams of mankind" (p. 6). Finally, Tuan (1974) discusses *topophilia,* an affective bond between people and place that may vary in strength from ephemeral sensory delight to deeply rooted attachment. Thus conceptual approaches from outside of psychology emphasize that sensory experiences, memories, cognitive integration, affective concern, and activities all contribute to the bonds between people and place.

More traditionally empirical researchers have recently been attracted to these conceptions of affective bonds between people and places. Rather than using concepts such as dwelling or appropriation that appear to evolve experientially, Stokols and colleagues (Stokols, 1981; Stokols & Shumaker, 1981) describe the state of *place dependence,* a perceived association between persons and the environment. Dependence results when the occupants perceive that an available space meets their needs better than alternative spaces. The dependence is greater when a greater variety of needs or more basic needs are met. A subset of place dependence experiences could be related to territoriality. In many cases, a high degree of place dependence corresponds to primary territorial ties. An exception to this linkage would exist when a place is very dissatisfying, yet no satisfactory alternatives exist (Stokols, Shumaker, & Martinez, 1983). In this example, the occupants are place dependent but unlikely to establish the identification with and concern for the place that are necessary for primary territorial attachments. The emotional and cognitive experiences might involve alienation, helplessness, or destructive impulses that are inconsistent with primary territorial ties.

Another conceptualization that could involve territoriality is the construct of *place identity,* a substructure of self-identity. It contains "memories, ideas, feelings, attitudes, values, preferences, meanings, and conceptions of behavior and experience which relate to the variety and complexity of physical settings that define the day-to-day existence of every human being" (Proshansky, Fabian, & Kaminoff, 1983, p. 59). This conceptualization emphasizes the role of places in organizing memory as well as providing expressive opportunities. Territorial attitudes and cognitions can serve similar functions of displaying identity. Because territories also play a role in system maintenance, it is likely that they promote the organization of memory, too, although this possibility has yet to be investigated. In sum, concepts such as dwelling, topophilia, and place identity may point to areas of territorial functioning that have yet to be articulated.

Empirical work on the more elusive qualities of place attachment is limited. Some research considers the positive emotional states that accompany territoriality among home owners. For example, home personalizations made by residents of low- to moderate-income housing developments made the home feel "comfortable and home-like" (Becker & Coniglio, 1975). Furthermore, "the emotional connotations of objects were very important to their owners—objects used to personalize an interior carried emotional meaning to their owners beyond their territorial marking function" (p. 62). However, if one defines territory more broadly than a defended turf, it is clear that these personalizations, more than the geographical area of the territory, help to create the feeling of territorial ownership and the blending of personal and environmental identities.

Results of interviews with home owners have helped to illuminate the psychological processes involved in creating primary territorial ties. Respondents reported that transforming a house into a "home" involves more than just liking a place or admiring its beauty: "A variety of places may have emotional and aesthetic significance to a person, yet no place feels like home" (Horwitz & Tognoli, 1982, p. 337). One way respondents turned a house into a home was through active personalization or shaping of the environment. These results corroborate the traditional territory literature in that qualities of the physical environment per se do not determine the possession of territory. Some type of cognitive and affective transformation process is a prerequisite to a place becoming a territory. Empirical research on home owners suggests that females and the elderly may forge stronger territorial attachments than others.

13.5.5. Sex Differences in Attachment to Territory

Sex differences in affective ties to territories appear to be most prominent in primary territories such as the home. Although males are often home owners in a financial sense, women are often the ones to decide on home personalization style, to care for daily upkeep, and to spend more time there. In terms of territorial feelings and attitudes, women appear to have more intimate associations with the home environment. Men are more frequently mentioned as intruders and defenders of territories and they appear to occupy larger territories.

A study of middle-class Israeli apartment owners illustrates the differing territorial investments of men and women (Sebba & Churchman, 1983). An interview of 90 residents revealed that, while few (20%) of the women felt that the entire apartment "belonged" to them, a majority (53%) felt that it "represented" them. In contrast, the men felt they owned the home more frequently than they felt represented by it (31% vs. 17%). These territorial feelings of identity appeared to be engendered by the activities of personalization and upkeep, duties more likely to be performed by women. Similarly, Tognoli (1980) found in intensive interviews of 10 adults that women were more likely to feel that their first abode after leaving the family home was truly their own "home." He speculated that the greater homemaking experiences for females allowed them to convert a new house into a home more easily.

Saegert and Winkel (1980) note this blend of home activities and self-identity for females. "The home is both a physical space where certain activities are performed and a value-laden symbol. Both meanings of the word are closely linked to definitions of the female sex role in our culture" (p. 41). In fact, a content analysis of the meanings of home reveals that women more often reported the home to be a source of affection, a secure family place, and a personalized place (Hayward, 1977). There was a trend for men to report that *home* meant an impersonal structure of their own childhood home. Yet even the one personal association to home by males was not confirmed in a later study (Holahan, 1978). In that study, women reported more personal and social associations for both their present and childhood homes.

Even when females are not performing roles such as homemaker and mother, they personalize their environments in a more intimate manner. Women students chose to personalize their college dormitory walls, for example, with more numerous symbols of personal relationships such as photos of or letters from friends and family (Vinsel *et al.*, 1980). Males were more likely to personalize with sports themes, or with entertainment equipment such as stereo speakers.

13.5.6. Age Differences in Attachment to Territory

Rowles (1980) contends that one's attachment to home territories intensifies with age. He has examined elders' attachment to place through a phenomenological perspective. From interviews of elders in an Appalachian community he proposed that attachment to home engenders the feeling of physical, social, and autobiographical *insideness* based on contemporary and historical levels of involvement. A *physical* insideness is generated from the "immediacy of everyday activity" (1980, p. 158) and the rhythmical or routine patterns of travels around the community. A *social* insideness involves a continuing role in various social networks.

The deepest level of place attachment is reflected in an *autobiographical* insideness, a condition in which the elders make a "heavy historical investment in this place. Each has created an environment richly differentiated as an array of places laden with personal meaning in relation to a life history. Over the years, each one of them has become more a part of the place to the point where it becomes an autobiography—literally an extension of the self" (1980, p. 162). When one is returning from a long sojourn, the sense of autobiographical insideness must be reestablished by reacquainting oneself with the environmental cues that serve as symbols for the incident memories. Rowles contends that feeling "inside" a place can actually help individuals cope with the stresses of growing old. But, because a past relationship with a place is needed in order to create insideness at a deep level, relocation of the elderly can deny them this source of participation in a place (p. 165).

13.6. RESEARCH DIRECTIONS

13.6.1. Territorial Cognitions and Affect

In order to develop a complete explanation of the identity functions of territoriality, it will be necessary to give further attention to the ways in which humans are affectively and cognitively bonded to territories. These bonds are implicit in the concept of centrality that distinguishes among public, secondary, and primary territories (Altman, 1975). Seamon (1979) noted that "research in territoriality has defined attachment to place and space largely in terms of fear, protection, exclusiveness, and preservation" (p. 70). He calls for greater attention to qualities of "at-homeness" that allow for warmth, "at-easeness," roots, regeneration, and appropriation.

One possible reason for the absence of work on territorial attachments and cognitions, beyond the methodological difficulties, is a cultural reluctance to admit to the importance of owning places and things. Although psychologists' discussions of territoriality often focus on the benefits of possessing a territory, scholars from other fields view the existence of ownership and possessiveness as a pessimistic comment on basic human nature. For example, within the Judeo-Christian heritage, Belk (1982) has noted that four of the seven deadly sins (greed, pride, gluttony, and envy) counsel against indulging in possessiveness. Within sociological thought, both Marx and Veblen condemned those who seek happiness, power, or prestige through the possession of objects (Belk, 1982). Others (Malthus, 1836; Schumacher, 1973) contend that humans' insatiable appetites for possessions drain the planet of limited resources. Despite these criticisms, humans continue to value and identify with certain possessions. The cultural heritage of derogatory comment on possessiveness may explain the relative absence of research on the topic.

Current attempts to assess place attachments via traditional questionnaire formats have shifted from simple, unidimensional assessments toward more complex and multidimensional ones (Brown & Werner, 1985; Fischer, Jackson, Stueve, Gerson, Jones, & Baldassare, 1977; Kasarda & Janowitz, 1974; Riger & Lavrakas, 1981). Nevertheless, these measurements are limited to variables such as home ownership, duration of residence, evaluations of space, and reports of social activities. They do not tap the richness of concepts such as topophilia or dwelling that are more apt measures of the ways in which environments support memories, cognitive integrations, and affective ties.

13.6.2. Impression Formation

Despite the lack of good operational measures of place attachment, the experiential provisions of attachments to place may underlie the more "visible" indications of territoriality such as personalization and defense. Although the phenomenological approach is counter to some researchers' conceptions of acceptable scientific practice, the place attachment interpretation of territoriality is not inherently phenomenological. To illustrate, there are several research possibilities intrinsic to conceptions of place attachment that can be pursued via a more traditional methodology.

The expressive function of place attachment (Proshansky, Fabian, & Kaminoff, 1983) can easily mesh with other impression formation research, for example. Borrowing from attribution theorists, it has been established that firm attributions concerning personal qualities of an individual depend especially on nonnormative or unexpected behaviors (Jones & Davis, 1965). Similarly, visitors to a territory may gain firmer (though not necessarily more accurate) impressions of inhabitants from the expressive qualities of their environments than from their required attributes. These impressions may then shape and guide interactions between owners and visitors.

13.6.3. Dysfunctional Territorial Stability

An emphasis on the social and identity aspects of territories suggests that future research can examine territorial dysfunctions in this light. Possible angles of approach involve the temporal qualities of territories and the evaluative meaning of territories that fail to support the owners' territorial needs. Some temporal features of territories are flexible, in that window shades may be pulled and doors opened and closed or books placed on library tables to indicate desires for openness and closedness. But many more features of the territory are less changeable—housing styles are difficult and costly to alter, neighborhood traffic flows are stable, and walls are a constant thickness.

The stability of the territory may create dysfunctions when the owner undergoes a major change in identity but the territory remains stable. For example, a recently divorced couple is presented with a problem due to the inflexible nature of their territorial stability. Both members of the couple may desire to shed their old, intertwined identities but the house continues to reinforce their old identities as marriage partners. Changing the old territory or finding a new one will require tremendous amounts of time and effort. Similarly, individuals who relocate may regret having to relinquish their old territorial ties. Along these lines, it has been found that individuals who have clear plans for relocation also exhibit themes of *preparatory detachment* in cognitive maps of their current environment (Wolfsey, Rierdan, & Wapner, 1979). Thus future research needs to examine both the personal problems and the coping mechanisms that evolve when territorial contexts fail to change in synchrony with personal aspects of identity.

The stability of territories may also create problems at the societal level. The old allocation of territories may not accurately reflect new societal values, for example. New laws and social values may support equal opportunity while existing land use patterns conform more to old racist values. Or the spatial dimensions of the single-family home may be poorly adapted to many families' needs for space (cf. Hayden, 1981). The time required for the environment to catch up with changing social values may adversely affect certain groups in their attempts to control or identify with their territories.

13.6.4. Dysfunctional Territorial Identity

Territories may become dysfunctional when they communicate damaging information about the personal identity of the owner. Goffman (1963) noted that places can communicate stigmas, morally reprehensible aspects of identities. For example, a mental patient cannot hide the identity of the building in which he or she lives. Visitors cannot be prevented from acquiring this aspect of the individual's identity. Newman (1972) had the same observation of the design of most public housing projects. He noted that the typical institutional design of a public housing project makes its identity unmistakable. This has the effect of injuring the residents' pride and self-esteem and also communicates openness to criminal activity. Territories then may be dysfunctional when the owner cannot disguise damaging information about his or her financial circumstances or other undesired characteristics.

Territoriality theory can also help to illuminate some of these reasons why true identities may not be displayed in a territory. First, the individual may not feel enough security in a place to risk revealing to others important elements of the self. It is known that feelings of security increase from more public to more primary territories (Taylor & Stough, 1978). Given greater control and protections afforded by primary territories, it is likely that the most personally revealing expressions of the self will be created in settings where the owner has secure knowledge of who will be admitted and how they will behave.

In some circumstances, territories give off undesirable information even when the territory owner has complete control and choice over territorial appearances. For example, new college students may decorate their dormitory rooms in keeping with the style used back home. However, in a new environment with new potential friends, the decor may appear unsophisticated or unattractive. The students may come to realize that aspects of their identity may require change in order to fit in at college; meanwhile, the territory only serves to reinforce their lack of fit. These undesirable meanings may be communicated through territories either wittingly or unwittingly. In Goffman's terms, impressions may be given or they may be given off, pointing to the role that a lack of awareness may play in territorial personalization.

13.6.5. Dysfunctional Territorial Commitments

Trade-offs among one's territories may create dysfunctions that affect one's time commitments or even one's identity. Some (Edney & Uhlig, 1977; Mithun, 1973) note that commitments must sometimes follow a hydraulic model whereby the time put into one territorial commitment lessens the time available for others. Thus limited time and energy can be invested in primary territories when the secondary ties in the neighborhood are very demanding. Edney and Uhlig (1977) suggested that the particular problem of investing in both group and individual territories is due to more than just scarce time resources. They speculated that a territorial investment in a group territory might lead to "a forfeiture of identity for the sake of group unity" (p. 458).

On the other hand, different territorial commitments may solidify attachments to a range of territories. For example Rivlin (1982) describes how the secondary territorial commitments within a Lubavitcher Jewish neighborhood complemented and strengthened the individual identities of members of the community. The identities supported in the primary territory of the home may grow stronger when supported by a congruent neighborhood identity. Thus commitments to different types of territories may have a synergetic effect when the demands across territories are congruent; different territorial commitments may become stressful when the demands across territories are incongruent.

13.6.6. Social Interactions and Territoriality

Finally, greater emphasis on the role of social functions is likely to highlight the implications territoriality holds for social interaction—including interactions between co-owners of a territory. Sharing a territory has been found to help foster a sense of security and identity and to be associated with lower risk of territorial intrusion for block territories (Brown, 1983). Yet researchers have not examined the processes involved in sharing territories. Of course, group members may solve the problem of sharing by carving out individual territories within the group territory. This territorial division has been found to take place within families (Laufer & Wolfe, 1977; Sebba & Churchman, 1983) and between individuals who share rooms (Altman & Haythorn, 1975; Rosenblatt & Budd, 1975). However, the physical separations (walls, room dividers, etc.) that can be provided by territorial boundaries may not be available in the group setting. In those territorial groups, some other form of interaction regulation must evolve. Altman's privacy regulation theory would point to norms, rules, and personal spacing as likely sources of management within a territory. Other mechanisms would include dominance hierarchies, turn-taking norms, scheduling (Rapoport, 1975), or developing an interpersonally reserved style (Westin, 1970).

A second domain where research is needed involves the way in which territorial contexts shape social interactions with visitors themselves. Katovich (1986) found that territorial claims enter into role-played conversations between bosses and employees. Similarly, in the study of student dormitory territories it was suggested that personalizations might help to encourage certain types of social encounters and discourage others (Vinsel *et al.*, 1980). However, it is not clear what general processes underlie the ways in which territorial claims facilitate or constrain interactions with co-owners, visitors, or intruders to the territory and how these interactions would differ if they took place in oilier territorial contexts.

Concepts of territoriality offered by sociologists Lyman and Scott (1967) may prove helpful in this area. Their definitions of territories, intrusions, and defenses are often referenced, but rarely used, within the psychological literature. They emphasize the ways in which social roles and statuses of territory owners affect the management of a territory. Consequently, Lyman and Scott's territorial encroachments involve disruptions of the social roles or statuses of the owners rather than the violation of spatial boundaries.

Similarly, their typology of territorial defenses downplays physically aggressive defenses in favor of defending social interactions and meanings. For example, *insulation*—the erection of a barrier to indicate that interaction is unwelcomed—might include wearing uniforms or sunglasses to convey impenetrability symbolically. In the *linguistic collusion* defense the territory owners flaunt their territorial identities so clearly that any outsider will be made to feel unable to take over the territorial program. For example, professors may escalate their use of academic jargon to keep undergraduates at bay and blacks may play "the dozens" to communicate inaccessibility to whites. While these examples of interactional defenses of territories may enhance group identity and aid territorial organization, they have not received recognition within psychology as legitimate territorial regulators.

13.6.7. Identity Management

A uniquely human aspect of territoriality that deserves more attention is what biologists term *intraspecific deceit* (Dawkins & Krebs, 1978). Deceitful territorial displays are common interspecifically, for example, when insects elude predators by taking on the appearance of twigs. But intraspecific examples of deceit are rare because fake territorial signals must be indistinguishable from true territorial signals to be effective. Fake signals are often difficult to produce because many territorial signals correspond to the animal's true ability to protect a territorial claim. For example, deer may use roaring contests as signals of their intent to claim territories. Because their vocal pitch corresponds to their size, it is likely that the winners of a roaring contest are larger than the losers. Thus there is a veridical basis for the territorial signals.

In contrast, the notion of intraspecific deceit could have wide applicability to human territoriality, although it too is a neglected area of research. The concept of deceitful places has been described but not fully researched by the sociologist Goffman. He describes a *back region* as "a place, relative to a performance, where the impression fostered by the performance is knowingly contradicted as a matter of course" (1959, p. 112). Social psychologists also study a variety of ways in which individuals make strategic use of social behaviors such as impression management (Schlenker, 1980), ingratiation (Jones, 1964), self-monitoring (Snyder, 1979), and script-enactment (Zanna & Pack, 1975) to gain social goals. All of these processes may be used strategically with little or no correspondence between the actor's true feelings and identity. However, social psychologists typically study these processes without reference to the strategic use of the environment to develop or maintain certain impressions. Research within territoriality needs to be attuned to territorial sociability and impression management for a well-rounded understanding of human territoriality.

In sum, this chapter has argued that territoriality should expand past its biological origins. The behaviors that are involved in claiming spaces have received more attention than other important aspects of territoriality. Territoriality is more than just claiming and defending space; even biologists and anthropologists have started to abandon the original emphasis on demarcation and defense. Now the attention needs to shift to the positive benefits of territoriality for the psychological and social life, including its role in social interaction and identity maintenance.

In particular, future research needs to articulate the more "hidden" cognitive, affective, and social interactional features of territoriality. Primary territories afford the best opportunity to study the ways in which places become central to individuals and groups. It has been suggested that these territories serve cognitive functions by supporting memories and integrating cognitions. Expressive functions are served by territorial personalizations—important symbols that may strategically or actually communicate aspects of individual and group identities. Researchers should strive for more sophisticated assessments of the ways in which territories and their personalizations serve social and affective concerns. Similarly, concepts such as appropriation need to be investigated to discover how activities can cultivate affective and cognitive bonds. Finally, the ways in which territories enter into and guide social interactions deserve investigation.

REFERENCES

Allen, V. L., & Greenberger, D. B. (1980). Destruction and perceived control. In A. Baum & J. E. Singer (Eds.), *Advances in environmental psychology: Vol. 2. Applications of personal control* (p. 85–109). Hillsdale, NJ: Erlbaum.

Altman, I. (1975). *Environment and social behavior: Privacy, personal space, territory and crowding.* Monterey, CA: Brooks/Cole.

Altman, I. & Chemers, M. M. (1980). *Culture and environment.* Monterey, CA: Brooks/Cole.

Altman, I. & Gauvain, M. (1981). A cross-cultural and dialectic analysis of homes. In L. Liben, A. Patterson, & N. Newcomb (Eds.), *Spatial representation and behavior across the life span: Theory and application.* New York: Academic.

Altman, I. & Haythorn, W. W. (1967). The ecology of isolated groups, *Behavioral Science, 12,* 168–182.

Altman, I., Nelson, P.A. & Lett, E. E. (1972). The ecology of home environments. *Catalog of Selected Documents in Psychology.* Washington, D.C.: American Psychological Association.

Altman, I., Taylor, D. A., & Wheeler, L. (1971). Ecological aspects of group behavior in social isolation. *Journal of Applied Social Psychology, 1,* 76–100.

Ardrey, R. (1966). *The territorial imperative.* New York: Atheneum.

Arenson, J. (1977). Reactions to invasions of marked seats at a racetrack. *Social Behavior and Personality, 5,* 225–228.

Arreola, D. D. (1981). Fences as landscape taste: Tucson's barrios. *Journal of Cultural Geography, 2,* 96–105.

Austin, W. T., & Bates, E. L. (1974). Ethological indicators of dominance and territory in a human captive population. *Social Forces, 52,* 447–455.

Bachelard, G. (1964). *The Poetics of space.* New York: Orion.

Bakker, C. B., & Bakker-Rabdau, M. K., (1973). *No trespassing! Explorations in human territoriality.* San Francisco: Chandler and Sharp.

Barbey, G. (1982). The appropriation of home space. In P. Korosec-Serfaty (Ed.), *Appropriation of space* (p. 215–217). Strasbourg, France: Louis Pasteur University.

Baum, A., Reiss, M. & O'Hara. J. (1974). Architectural variants of reaction to spatial invasion. *Environment and Behavior, 6,* 91–100.

Beck, R. J., & Teasdale, P. (1978). Dimensions of social lifestyle in multiple dwelling housing. In A. Esser & B. B. Greenbie (Eds.), *Design for communality and privacy* (Based on a workshop convened at the Sixth Annual Conference of the Environment Design Research Association, Lawrence, Kansas), New York: Plenum.

Becker, F. D. (1973). Study of spatial markers. *Journal of Personality and Social Psychology, 26,* 439–445.

Becker, F. D. & Coniglio, C. (1975). Environmental messages: Personalization and territory. *Humanitias, 11,* 55–74.

Becker, F. D. & Mayo, C. (1971). Delineating personal space and territoriality. *Environment and Behavior, 3,* 375–381.

Belk, R. W. (1982). *Acquisitiveness and possessiveness: Criticisms and issues.* Paper presented at the meeting of the Association for Consumer Research. San Francisco.

Blundell. V. (1983). Comments. *Current Anthropology, 24,* 58.

Brower, S. (1980), Territory in urban settings. In I. Altman, A. Rapoport, & J. Wohlwill (Eds.), *Human behavior and environment.* New York: Plenum.

Brown, B. B. (1983). *Territoriality, street form, and residential burglary: Social and environmental analyses.* Unpublished doctoral dissertation, University of Utah.

Brown, B. B., & Altman, I. (1981). Territoriality and residential crime: A conceptual framework. In P. J. Brantingham & P. L. Brantingham (Eds.), *Environmental criminology* (p. 55–76). Beverly Hills, CA: Sage.

Brown, B. B. & Altman, I. (1983). Territoriality, street form, and residential burglary: An environmental analysis. *Journal of Environmental Psychology, 3,* 203–220.

Brown, B. B., & Werner. C. M. (1985). Social cohesiveness, territoriality, and holiday decorations: The influence of cul-de-sacs. *Environment and Behavior, 17,* 539–565.

Bush-Brown, L. (1969). *Garden blocks for urban America.* New York: Scribners.

Buttimer, A., & Seamon, D. (1980). *The human experience of space and place.* London: Croom Helm.

Calsyn, R. (1976). Group responses to territorial intrusion. *Journal of Social Psychology, 40,* 51–58.

Canter, D., West, S., & Wools, R. (1974). Judgements of people and their rooms. *British Journal of Social and Clinical Psychology, 13,* 113–118.

Cashdan, E. (1983). Territoriality among human foragers: Ecological models and an application to tour bushman groups. *Current Anthropology, 24,* 47–66.

Cass, R., & Edney, J. J. (1978). The commons dilemma: A simulation testing the effects of resource visibility and territorial division. *Human Ecology, 6,* 371–386.

Cherulnik, P. D. (1982). Impressions of neighborhoods and their residents. *Proceedings of the 13th International Conference of the Environmental Design Research Associates, 13,* 416–423.

Cheyne, J. A., & Efran, M. G. (1972). The effect of spatial and interpersonal variables on the invasion of group controlled territories. *Sociometry, 35,* 477–489.

Conroy, J., & Sundstrom, E. (1977). Territorial dominance in a dyadic conversation as a function of similarity of opinion. *Journal of Personality and Social Psychology, 35,* 570–576.

Cooper, C. (1972). The house as a symbol of self. In J. Lang, C. Burnette, W. Moleski, & D. Vachon (Eds.), *Designing for human behavior: Architecture and the behavioral sciences.* Stroudsberg, PA: Dowden, Hutchinson, & Ross.

Craik, K. (1973). Environmental psychology. *Annual review of psychology, 24,* 403–422.

Craik, K. (1977). Multiple scientific paradigms in environmental psychology. *International Journal of Psychology, 12,* 147–157.

Csikszentmihalyi. M., & Rochberg-Halton, E. (1981). *The meaning of things.* New York: Cambridge University Press.

Davies, N. B. (1978). Ecological questions about territorial behavior. In J. E. Krebs & N. B. Davies (Eds.). *Behavioral ecology: An evolutionary approach.* Sunderland, MA: Sinauer.

Dawkins, R., & Krebs, J. R. (1978). Animal signals: Information on manipulation. In J. R. Krebs & N. B. Davies (Eds.), *Behavioral ecology.* (p. 282–309), Sunderland, MA: Sinauer.

De Rivera, J. (1984). Emotional experience and qualitative methodology. *American Behavioral Scientist, 27,* 677–688.

Delong, A. J. (1970). Dominance-territorial relations in a small group. *Environment and Behavior, 2.* 190–191.

Delong, A. J. (1973). Territorial stability and hierarchical formation. *Small Group Behavior, 4,* 56–63.

Deutsch, R. D., Esser. A. H., & Sossin, K. M. (1978). Dominance, aggression, and the functional use of space in institutionalized female adolescents. *Aggressive Behavior, 4(4),* 313–329.

Dovey, K. (in press). The quest for authenticity and the replication of environmental meaning. In D. Seamon & R. Mugerauer (Eds.), *Dwelling, place and environment.* The Hague, Netherlands: Martinus Nijhof.

Duncan, J. S. (1973). Landscape taste as a symbol of group identity. *Geographical Review, 63,* 334–355.

Dyson-Hudson, R., & Smith, E. A. (1978). Human territoriality: An ecological reassessment. *American Anthropologist 80,* 21–41.

Edney, J. J. (1974). Human territoriality. *Psychological Bulletin, 81,* 959–975.

Edney, J. J. (1975). Territoriality and control: A field experiment. *Journal of Personality and Social Psychology, 31,* 1108–1115.

Edney, J. J. (1976). Human territories: Comment on functional properties. *Environment and Behavior, 8,* 31–47.

Edney, J. J. & Buda, M. A. (1976). Distinguishing territoriality and privacy: Two studies. *Human Ecology, 4,* 283–295.

Edney, J. J. & Grundmann, M. J. (1979). Friendship, group size, and boundary size: Small group spaces. *Small Group Behavior, 10,* 124–135.

Edney, J. J. & Jordan-Edney, N. L. (1974). Territorial spacing on the beach. *Sociometry, 37,* 92–104.

Edney, J. J. & Uhlig, S. R. (1977). Individual and small group territories, *Small Group Behavior, 8,* 457–478.

Efran, M. G. & Cheyne, J. A. (1973). Shared space: The cooperative control of spatial areas by two interacting individuals. *Canadian Journal of Behavioral Science, 5,* 201–210.

Efran, M. G., & Cheyne, J. A. (1974). Affective concomitants of the invasion of shared space: Behavioral, physiological, and verbal indicators. *Journal of Personality and Social Psychology, 29,* 219–226.

Ehrenreich, J. (1983). Comments. *Current Anthropology, 24(1).* 58–59.

Eibesfeldt, I. (1970). *Ethology: The biology of behavior.* New York: Holt, Rinehart & Winston.

Eibesfeldt, I. (1974). The myth of the aggression-free hunter and gatherer society. In R. L. Holloway (Ed.), *Primate aggression, territoriality, and xenophobia* (p. 435–458). New York: Academic.

Esser, A. H. (1968). Dominance hierarchy and clinical course of psychiatrically hospitalized boys, *Child Development, 39,* 147–157.

Esser, A. H. (1973). Cottage fourteen, *Small Group Behavior, 4,* 131–146.

Esser, A. H., Chamberlain, A. S., Chappie, F. D., & Kline, N. S. (1965). Territoriality of patients on a research ward. In J. Wortis (Ed.), *Recent advances in behavioral psychiatry, 7,* 36–44.

Ferguson, G. W. Hughes, J. A., Brown, K. A. (1983). Food availability and territorial establishment of juvenile sceloporus undulatus. In R. B. Huey, E. R. Pianka, & T. W. Schroener (Eds.), *Lizard ecology: studies of a model organism* (p. 134–148). Cambridge, MA: Harvard University Press.

Fischer, C. S., Jackson, R. M., Stueve, C. A. Gerson, K., Jones. L. M., & Baldassare, M. (1977). *Networks and places: social relations in the urban setting.* New York: Free Press.

Fishbein, M., & Ajzen, I. (1975). *Belief, attitude, intention, and behavior: An introduction to theory and research,* Reading, MA: Addison-Wesley.

Freedman, D. G. (1979). *Human sociobiology.* New York: Free Press.

Furby, L. (1974). Socialization practices with respect to possession and ownership: A study using the Human Relations Area Files. *Oregon Research Institute Research Bulletin, 14,* 20.

Furby, L. (1978). Possessions: Toward a theory of their meaning and function throughout the life cycle. In P. B. Baltes (Ed.), *Life Span development and behavior* (Vol. 1, p. 297–336). New York: Academic.

Furby, L. (1980). The origins and early development of possessive behavior. *Political Psychology, 2,* 30–42.

Furby, L. (1982). *Some aspects of possessive behavior during the second year of life.* Paper presented at the meeting of the Association for Consumer Research, San Francisco.

Galster, G. C., & Hesser, G. W. (1982). The social neighborhood: An unspecified factor in homeowner maintenance? *Urban Affairs Quarterly, 18,* 235–254.

Gauvain, M., Altman, I., & Fahim, H. (1983). Homes and social change: A cross-cultural analysis. In N. R. Feimer & E. S. Geller (Eds.), *Environmental psychology: Directions and perspectives.* New York: Praeger.

Godelier, M. (1979). Territory and property in primitive society. In M. von Cranach, K. Foppa, W. Lepenies, & D. Ploog (Eds.), *Human ethology.* Cambridge, England: Cambridge University Press.

Goffman, E. (1959). *The presentation of self in everyday life.* New York: Doubleday.

Goffman, E. (1963a). *Behavior in public places.* New York: Free Press.

Goffman, E. (1963b). *Stigma.* Englewood Cliffs, NJ: Prentice-Hall.

Gold, J. R. (1982). Territoriality and human spatial behavior. *Progress in human geography, 6,* 44–67.

Greenbaum, P. E. & Greenbaum, S. D. (1981). Territorial personalization: Group identity and social interaction in a Slavic-American neighborhood. *Environment and Behavior, 13,* 574–589.

Haber, G. M. (1980). Territorial invasion in the classroom: Invadee response. *Environment and Behavior, 12,* 17–31.

Hall, E. T. (1959). *The silent language.* New York: Double-day.

Harrington, M. (1965). Resettlement and self-image. *Human Relations, 18,* 115–137.

Hart, R. (1978). *Children's experience of place.* New York: Halstead.

Hayden, D. (1981). *The grand domestic revolution: A history of feminist designs for American homes.* Cambridge, MA: MIT Press.

Hayward, D. G. (1977, April). An overview of psychological concepts of "home." *Proceedings of the Meeting of the Environmental Design Research Association, 8,* 418–419.

Heidegger, M. (1971). *Poetry, language, and thought.* (Albert Hofstadter, Trans.). New York: Harper & Row.

Holahan, C. (1978). *Environment and behavior: A dynamic perspective.* New York: Plenum.

Hoppe, R. A., Greene. M. S., & Kenny, J. W. (1972). Territorial markers: Additional findings. *Journal of Social Psychology, 88.* 305–306.

Horwitz, J., & Tognoli, J. (1982). Role of home environment in adult women: Women and men living alone describe their residential histories. *Family Relations, 31,* 335–341.

Jones, E. E. (1964). *Ingratiation.* New York: Appleton-Century Crofts.

Jones, E. E., & Davis, K. (1965). From acts to dispositions: The attribution process in person perception. In L. Berkowitz (Ed.), *Advances in experimental social psychology* (Vol. 2). New York: Academic.

Kasarda, J., & Janowitz, M. (1974) Community attachment in mass society. *American Sociological Review, 39,* 328–339.

Katovich, M. (1986). Ceremonial openings in bureaucratic encounters: From shuffling feet to shuffling papers. In N. K. Denzin (Ed.), *Studies in symbolic interaction* (Vol. 6). Greenwich, CT: JAI Press.

Kimber, C. T. (1973). Spatial patterning in the door yard gardens of Puerto Rico. *Geographical Review, 63,* 6–26.

Knowles, E. S. (1973). Boundaries around group interaction: The effect of group and member status on boundary permeability. *Journal of Personality and Social Psychology, 26,* 327–331.

Konar, E., Sundstrom, E., Brady. C., Mandel, D., & Rice, R. W. (1982). Status demarcation in the office. *Environment and Behavior, 14,* 561–580.

Korosec-Serfaty, P. (1985). Experiences and uses of the dwelling. In I. Altman & C. M. Werner (Eds.), *Home environments.* New York: Plenum.

Laufer, R. S., & Wolfe, M. (1977). Privacy as a concept and as a social issue: A multidimensional developmental theory. *Journal of Social Issues, 33,* 22–42.

Laumann, E. O., & House, J. S. (1972). Living room styles and social attributes: The patterning of material artifacts in a modern urban community. In E. O. Laumann, P. M. Sigel, & R. W. Hodges (Eds.), *The logic of social hierarchies* (p. 189–203). Chicago: Markham.

Lavin, M. W. (1978, August). *Cognitive and nonverbal responses to boundaries of territorially controlled spaces.* Paper presented at the 86th annual meeting of the American Psychological Association, Toronto, Canada.

Lee, R. B. (1968). What hunters do for a living, or how to make out on scarce resources. In R. B. Lee & I. DeVore (Eds.), *Man the hunter* (p. 30–48). Chicago: Aldine.

Lewis, C. A. (1979). Comment: Healing in the urban environment. *Journal of the American Institute of Planners, 45.* 330–338.

Ley, D., & Cybriwsky, R. (1974). The spatial ecology of stripped cars. *Environment and Behavior, 6,* 53–68.

Lindskold, S., Albert, K. P., Baer, R., & Moore, W. C. (1976). Territorial boundaries of interacting groups and passive audiences. *Sociometry, 39,* 71–76.

Litwak, E., & Szelenyi, I. (1969). Primary group structures and their functions: Kin, neighbors, and friends. *American Sociological Review, 34,* 465–481.

Lyman, S. M., & Scott, M. B. (1967). Territoriality: A neglected sociological dimension. *Social Problems, 15,* 236–249.

Malmberg, T. (1980). *Human territoriality.* New York: Mouton.

Malthus, T. R. (1836). *Principles of political economy.* London: Kelley.

Martindale, D. A. (1971). Territorial dominance behavior in dyadic verbal interaction. *Proceedings of the 79th Annual Convention of the American Psychological Association, 6,* 306.

Maslow, A., & Mintz, M. (1956). Effects of aesthetic surroundings: I. Initial effects of three aesthetic conditions upon perceiving "energy" and "well being" in faces. *Journal of Psychology, 41,* 247–254.

McAndrew, F. T. Ryckman, R. M., Horr, W., & Solomon, R. (1978). The effects of invader placement of spatial markers on territorial behavior in a college population. *Journal of Social Psychology, 104.* 149–150.

Mehrabian, A., & Diamond, S. G. (1971). Effects of furniture arrangement, props, and personality on social interaction. *Journal of Personality and Social Psychology. 20,* 18–30.

Mercer, G. W., & Benjamin, M. L. (1980). Spatial behavior of university undergraduates in double-occupancy residence rooms: An inventory of effects. *Journal of Applied Social Psychology, 10,* 32–44.

Mintz, H. (1956). Effects of aesthetic surroundings: II. Prolonged and repeated experience in a "beautiful" and an "ugly" room. *Journal of Psychology, 41,* 459–466.

Mithun, J. S. (1973). Cooperation and solidarity as survival necessities in a black urban community. *Urban Anthropology, 2,* 247–259.

Moore, J., Vigil, D. & Garcia, R. (1983). Residence and territoriality in Chicano gangs. *Social Problems, 31,* 182–194.

Newman, O. (1972). *Defensible space: Crime prevention through urban design.* New York: Macmillan.

Pablant, P., & Baxter, J. C. (1975). Environmental correlates of school vandalism. *Journal of the American Institute of Planners, 41,* 270–279.

Pastalan, L. A. (1970). Privacy as an expression of human territoriality. In L. A. Pastalan & D. H. Carson (Eds.), *Spatial behavior of older people.* Ann Arbor: University of Michigan.

Pratt, G. (1982). The house as expression of social worlds. In J. S. Duncan (Ed.), *Housing and identity: Cross-cultural perspectives.* New York: Holmes & Meier.

Proshansky, H. M., Fabian, A. K., & Kaminoff, R. (1983). Place identity: Physical world socialization of the self. *Journal of Environmental Psychology, 3,* 57–83.

Rapoport, A. (1969). *House form and culture.* Englewood Cliffs, NJ: Prentice-Hall.

Rapoport, A. (1975). Towards a redefinition of density. *Environment and Behavior, 7,* 133–158.

Relph, E. (1976). *Place and placelessness.* London: Pion.

Riger, S., & Lavrakas, P. (1981). Community ties: Patterns of attachment and social interaction in urban neighborhoods. *American Journal of Community Psychology, 9,* 55–66.

Rivlin, L. G. (1982). Group membership and place meanings in an urban neighborhood. *Journal of Social Issues, 38,* 75–93.

Rosenblatt, P. C., & Budd, L. G. (1975). Territoriality and privacy in married and unmarried cohabiting couples. *Journal of Social Psychology, 97,* 67–76.

Rowles, G. (1978). *Prisoners of space?* Boulder, CO: Westview.

Rowles, G. D. (1980). Growing old "inside": Aging and attachment to place in an Appalachian community. In N. Datan & N. Lohmann (Eds.), *Transition of aging* (p. 153–172). New York: Academic.

Russell, J. A., & Ward, L. M. (1982). Environmental psychology. *Annual Review of Psychology, 33,* 651–688.

Sack, R. D. (1983). Human territoriality: A theory. *Annals of the Association of American Geographers, 73,* 55–74.

Sadalla, E. K., Burroughs, J., & Quaid, M. (1980). House form and social identity. In R. Slough (Ed.), *Proceedings of the 11th International Meeting of the Environmental Design Research Association, 11,* 201–206.

Saegert, S., & Winkel, G. (1980). The home: A critical problem for changing sex roles. In G. Wekerle, R. Peterson, & D. Morley (Eds.), *New space for women.* Boulder, CO: Westview.

Schlenker, B. R. (1980). *Impression management: The self-concept, social identity, and interpersonal relations.* Monterey, CA: Brooks/Cole.

Schumacher, E. F. (1973). *Small is beautiful: Economics as if people mattered.* New York: Harper & Row.

Schwartz, B., & Barsky, S. F. (1977). The home court advantage. *Social Forces, 55,* 641–661.

Seamon, D. (1979). *A geography of the lifeworld.* London: Croom Helm.

Sebba, R., & Churchman, A. (1983). Territories and territoriality in the home. *Environment and Behavior, 15,* 191–210.

Shaffer, D. R., & Sadowski, C. (1975). This table is mine: Respect for marked barroom tables as a function of gender of spatial marker and desirability of locale. *Soriometry, 38,* 408–419.

Smith, H. W. (1983). Estimated crowding capacity, time, and territorial markers: A cross-national test. *Sociological Inquiry, 53.* 95–99.

Smith, R. A. (1975). Measuring neighborhood cohesion: A review and some suggestions. *Human Ecology, 3,* 143–160.

Snyder, M. (1979). Self-monitoring processes. In L. Berkowitz (Ed.), *Advances in experimental social psychology* (Vol. 12, p. 85–128). New York: Academic.

Sommer, R. (1967). Sociofugal space. *American Journal of Sociology, 72,* 654–659.

Sommer, R., & Becker, F. D. (1969). Territorial defense and the good neighbor, *Journal of Personality and Social Psychology, 11,* 85–92.

Sossin, K. M., Esser, A., & Duetsch, R. D. (1978). Ethological studies of spatial and dominance behavior of female adolescents in residence. *Man-Environment Systems, 8,* 43–48.

Stokols, D. (1978). Environmental psychology. *Annual Review of Psychology, 29,* 253–295.

Stokols, D. (1981). Group x place transactions: Some neglected issues in psychological research on settings. In D. Magnusson (Ed.), *Toward a psychology of situations: An interactional perspective* (p. 393–415). Hillsdale, NJ: Erlbaum.

Stokols, D., & Jacobi, M. (1984). Traditional, present oriented, and futuristic modes of group-environment relations. In K. Gergen & M. M. Gergen (Eds.), *Historical social psychology.* Hillsdale, NJ: Erlbaum.

Stokols, D., & Shumaker, S. A. (1981) People in places: A transactional view of settings. In J. Harvey (Ed.), *Cognition, social behavior, and the environment* (p. 441–488). Hillsdale, NJ: Erlbaum.

Stokols, D., Shumaker, S. A., & Martinez, J. (1983). Residential mobility and personal well-being. *Journal of Environmental Psychology, 3,* 5–19.

Sundstrom, E., & Altman, I. (1974) Field study of territorial behavior and dominance. *Journal of Personality and Social Psychology, 30,* 115–124.

Suttles, G. D. (1968). *The social order of the slum: Ethnicity and territory in the inner city.* Chicago: University of Chicago Press

Suttles, G. D. (1972). *The social construction of communities.* Chicago: University of Chicago Press.

Taylor, R. B., & Ferguson, G. (1980). Solitude and intimacy: Linking territoriality and privacy experiences. *Journal of Nonverbal Behavior, 4,* 227–239.

Taylor, R. B., & Brooks, D. K. (1980). Temporary territories?: Responses to intrusions in a public setting. *Population and Environment, 3,* 135–143.

Taylor, R. B., Gottfredson, S. D., & Brewer, S. (1981). Territorial cognitions and social climate in urban neighborhoods. *Basic and Applied Social Psychology, 2,* 289–303.

Taylor, R. B., & Lanni, J. C. (1981). Territorial dominance: The influence of the resident advantage in triadic decision making. *Journal of Personality and Social Psychology, 41,* 909–915.

Taylor, R. B., & Stough, R. (1978). Territorial cognition: Assessing Altman's typology. *Journal of Personality and Social Psychology, 36,* 418–423.

Tognoli, J. (1980). Differences in women's and men's responses to domestic space. *Sex Roles, 6,* 833–842.

Trigham, R. (1972). Territorial demarcation of prehistoric settlements. In P. J. Ucko (Ed.), *Man, settlement, and urbanism* (p. 463–475). London: Duckworth.

Truscott, J. C., Parmelee, P., & Warmer, C. (1977). Plate touching in restaurants: Preliminary observations of a food-related marking behavior in humans. *Personality and Social Psychology Bulletin, 3,* 425–428.

Tuan, I. F. (1974). *Topophilia.* Englewood Cliffs, NJ: Prentice Hall.

Tuan, Y. (1980). The significance of artifact. *Geographical Review, 70,* 462–472.

Van Den Berghe, P. L. (1974). Bringing beasts back in: Toward a biosocial theory of aggression. *American Sociological Review, 39,* 777–788.

Vinsel, A., Brown, B. B., Altman, I., & Foss, C. (1980). Privacy regulation, territorial displays, and effectiveness of individual functioning. *Journal of Personality and Social Psychology, 39,* 1104–1115.

Weisner, T. S., & Weibel, J. C. (1981). Home environment and lifestyles in California. *Environment and Behavior, 13,* 417–460.

Werner, C. M., Brown, B. B., & Damron, G. (1981). Territorial marking in the game arcade. *Journal of Personality and Social Psychology, 41,* 1094–1104.

Westin, A. (1970). *Privacy and freedom.* New York: Atheneum.

Wilson, E. O. (1975). *Sociobiology.* Cambridge, MA: Harvard University Press.

Wolfsey, E., Rierdan, J., & Wapner, S. (1979). Planning to move: Effects on representing the currently inhabited environment. *Environment and Behavior, 11,* 3–32.

Worchel, S. & Lollis, M. (1982). Reactions to territorial contamination as a function of culture. *Personality and Social Psychology Bulletin, 8,* 370–375.

Zanna, M. P., & Pack, S. J. (1975). On the self fulfilling nature of apparent sex differences in behavior. *Journal of Experimental Social Psychology, 11,* 583–591.

15

Observation: The World Under a Glass

Robert B. Bechtel and John Zeisel

This methodological chapter examines a constellation of techniques that could be used when carrying out behavior observation. It demonstrates the rigor required in designing all the phases of a research instrument.

Observation is the most fun of any of the methods in environment behavior research. This is because every person enjoys watching other humans and then, to compound the enjoyment, delights as much or more in telling someone else about it. Yet it is an expectation of enjoyment that can sometimes stand in the way of getting useful results. A long observation can become boring. The fact that observation has become a high-technology method can increase or decrease the enjoyment, depending on one's viewpoint.

Everyone watches and therefore "knows" what people do at the beach on a Sunday afternoon. But what about funerals? How do people sit, stand, move about, and otherwise behave at a funeral? Most people are too emotionally involved in the funerals they attend to watch the behavior of others or feel self-conscious about observing the bereaved. Yet the answer to this question is vital to the design of churches and funeral parlors.

And what about the everyday behavior that nobody bothers to watch? How do people sit on buses, work in offices, live in houses, throw money away at gambling casinos, or wait in line at shopping centers? All these are important questions to answer in the behavior-environment equation, but people tend not to observe the commonplace. The observer, then, becomes the poet laureate of the ordinary. A good observer not only records what people do in these everyday circumstances, but presents the findings in such a way as to help people understand their behavior in situations they would not ordinarily think about.

Observation has developed into a highly technological field, yet it remains the one method that people can use with minimal training. Some sort of training, however, must take place before observation can be useful in research. It is useful to describe observation as having five dimensions: the behavior, the environment, the time, the observer, and the record of observation. These five dimensions will be explored and the issues and specialized methods of observation will be described.

Robert B. Bechtel & John Zeisel; Robert B. Bechtel, Robert W. Marans, & William Michelson, eds., "Observation: The World Under a Glass," from *Methods in Environmental & Behavioral Research*, pp. 11–40. Copyright © 1987. Permission to reprint granted by the publisher.

BEHAVIOR

What one watches other people do is referred to loosely as *behavior*. People cannot stop "behaving" unless they are dead. Behavior is what an organism is doing at any moment. The words we use to describe behavior may be simple, like "standing," "sitting," "talking," or "sleeping." In environment behavior research, however, another element is introduced: the behavior must always be seen within an environmental context. People sleep in beds or on the floor. They converse in restaurants or on sidewalks. In the same sense that people cannot stop behaving, they cannot get away from the environment. There is always a surrounding environment and thus always a behavior-environment relationship.

The span of behavior goes from *molar*, or global, to molecular. Molar behavior consists of the larger units of behavior. These do not include very large numbers of people, however, because an observer cannot watch very many people at once. Instead, molar units of behavior refer to more complex activities, such as going to the store or working in an office. *Molecular* units are smaller in the sense that they involve quantitatively less behavior. The distinction is relative, however. What is a molar unit to one researcher may seem like a molecular one to another. Birdwhistell (1970) watches minute facial gestures, but these may be too small to be mentioned by Barker (1968), who describes behavior settings, which are units of behavior containing several people and many molecular units. The divisions of behavior, then, are on a continuum and are arbitrarily designated by the observer.

Most environment behavior research deals with molar behavior, while the molecular is more often given to *human factors* research (McCormick and Sanders 1982). Human factors research most often deals with man-machine interactions or person-furniture units. These involve finer distinctions than most environment and behavior research. The observer must clearly define the kind of units of behavior being observed so that someone else using the same unit can *count* them. Ultimately, it is the goal of observation to record units of behavior. Yet, to insist that this is the only goal of behavioral observation is to miss a significant amount of what observation can accomplish. For example, observation can serve as *orientation*. When first encountering an environment or a new design, the observer may want to walk around the environment and/or watch others in a casual fashion.

For example, smelling the air in an office building gives a researcher an indication of air quality. Looking at windows from different places in a room at different times of the day gives a researcher a sense of how much glare users of the space experience. Listening to conversations and noise gives a researcher a picture of the acoustic environment. Sensing the dryness or humidity in the air gives a researcher an idea of how users of a space experience the atmosphere. And eating the food in a building's cafeteria can provide a perspective on what it is like to eat there on a daily basis. Observation, therefore, can mean using all of ones senses.

By such informal sampling of the environment and its related behavior, the observer can derive several hypotheses about what environmental factors may influence behavior. However, the same observations may serve merely to orient one to the general structure of the environment, to identify actors, count rooms, experience the size and shape of the buildings, and establish reference points. This orientation should really precede any other form of observation, for the observer must always have at least a superficial familiarity with any environment before beginning observation.

The ultimate goal of observational methods in environment behavior research is primarily to gain insight into research questions and problems. This may, in fact, be the purpose of using any or all research methods. To probe a research question in an actual research setting means focusing on the problem, the question, and the setting, rather than on the definition of the method itself. In other words, if a researcher has overly much concern for defining and circumscribing the method too early in the study, it is possible to overlook the ultimate goal.

An example of gaining insight in a research situation will clarify what this can mean to a research project. Zeisel and Drake (1984) were writing a guidebook on how to evaluate emergency departments for the Department of Health and Welfare, Canada, first, in order to help the department determine where redesign of particular emergency departments should be of priority, and second, to develop a knowledge base of design and management decision to help achieve the results desired by hospital staff, administrators, and patients. The project began with the researchers analyzing available methods—both observational and interviewing—and determining for each method what data could be gathered. Interviews can assess users' attitudes and perceptions, inventories can be taken of wear and tear on materials in the department, behavior maps can be accumulated to describe where people spend time, photographs can record instances of effective and ineffective design, and so on. But rather than begin the research project with a case study in which to test this methodological outline, the researchers decided to spend some time observing several emergency departments that had not been part of the research plan. The first department observed was three years old. There it was found that an entire observation room had been redesigned since the facility opened. It also appeared the methods would be quite useful in discovering the data expected. In the second emergency department, only one year old, it was found that other major physical redesigns were being planned for. In both these hospitals, administrators and staff explained that they had difficulties in planning for the emergency department because, contrary to the prevailing policy, the emergency rooms were a convenient place to tell emergency patients to return for check-ups rather than send them to outpatient departments. In both of the case study hospitals it was also found that major changes had been made or planned, but that the problem of confusion between emergency and outpatient use was not a problem. In one of the case study hospitals, the staff sometimes answered the telephone "Emergency Department" and sometimes "Outpatient Department." Signs in one facility said "Emergency Department," while staff and the rest of the hospital often directed potential patients to the "Outpatient Department" at the same location, where they found no signs indicating such a department. The insight gained from these planned observations was that change was an essential and ongoing part of the life of an emergency department but, more importantly, that the medical and local culture in which a hospital finds itself determines the nature of treatment and the service boundaries in any emergency department. In some areas, casual walk-in patients to the emergency department are considered to be legitimate users and these departments are set up to handle them. In other hospitals, the distinction between outpatient and emergency patients is much more distinct and any confusion between the two is seen as an administrative problem. These general insights helped to frame the evaluation methods guidebook in a way that enabled local authorities to tailor the way they should use particular research methods to reflect the culture and the definition of an emergency department in their own hospitals. In concrete terms, the most visible evidence of this was that a description of the relationship between emergency and outpatient cases was seen as a given variable, defining the situation within which the emergency department was to be evaluated, rather than an evaluative variable where a greater outpatient-to-emergency patient ratio was assumed to be negative.

This lesson gained from an unstructured observation reveals the *behavior-environment paradox*. This paradox takes the form of a misperception of the "true" environment-behavior relationship. In many cases the research problem is presented to the researcher as a need for a physical change, when a little observation can reveal that the change is not necessarily needed if behavior (a cheaper and less permanent commodity) is changed. The paradox is the assumption of environmental dominance over behavior. In simple terms: "The environment makes us behave this way, therefore, if the environment is changed a certain way, our behavior will change accordingly."

The behavior-environment paradox underlies the "common sense" thinking of many designers and their clients. Observation can often reveal mistaken assumptions and prevent the research from getting off on a false start.

Defining the Problem

The loosest use of observation comes about when one simply wants to know what is happening in an environment. This can happen when a designer asks, "How does my building work?" or when a designer or social scientist wants to know what it is like to live in a certain place.

To answer such a question, the observer uses his or her full range of abilities and tries to cover the widest range of behavior in an environment. Sights, sounds, smells, temperature, lighting, subjective moods, objective actions. All these are noticed—but not necessarily recorded—and processed into a slowly forming impression of what is happening.

In a local county office Bechtel observed the activities in the reception room. One secretary acted as receptionist in a large space also used by staff for coffee breaks and as a gathering place. At the same time it served as a waiting room for clients. The staff-client conflict was immediately obvious. Clients could overhear staff talking about other clients. In addition, clients sometimes brought children who had to be supervised by a second secretary in an adjoining room. At such times chaos was at a maximum. The lack of order created a less than businesslike image of the office and created doubts in both staff and clients. It did not take much observation to recognize that a clear separation of spaces was needed as a first step. Here, several methods of observation—visual, aural, and participatory—were required, but the observer did not need to record specific categories because a more general familiarization was first necessary.

Gans (1970) moved to a suburban development to find out what it was like to live there. White (1980) walked down Manhattan streets to find out what was happening. Many designers enter buildings to observe "how they work." In these circumstances the observer is looking for some way to organize the chaos of activity so that it can be understood. A variety of concepts may be tried and abandoned. An observation may lead to puzzlement—why is everybody hurrying? And this may lead the observer to ask a passing pedestrian that question. Thus, the most open form of observation is a constant seeking to comprehend what is being observed. This may lead to many questions and to many more observations.

And sometimes observation can also answer more specific questions that interviews and questionnaires cannot reveal. In the Arrowhead project (Dumouchel 1971) broken windows were a serious economic problem but questioning did not reveal the source. Residents attributed these acts to "outsiders." Observation revealed, however, that children in the residences (and some adults) would often get locked outside and break the windows to get in. The cold of the Cleveland winter was a highly motivating force. Therefore, the problem was not one of outside "invaders," but of lack of control over one's own living space. This illustrates an observation followed by a query through other methods, followed by more observations—that is, the observation "sandwich" design.

Interviews and questionnaires are the most frequent methods used, with observation in the middle of the sandwich. The first layer of the sandwich is made by conducting enough observation to get the question or questions properly formulated for application to other methods. For example, the Arrowhead project revealed that while the elderly constituted 11 percent of the population, they were only 1 percent of the observed population out of doors. Interviews were then designed to solicit reasons why the elderly did not leave their apartments. Several reasons became apparent. The elderly found it difficult to move about the grounds when there was ice and snow. Furthermore, they feared exploitation from younger people who often robbed older people while on the street or who would sometimes push open the doors while they were entering and rob their homes. Later observation of street activity showed these reports to be accurate. Thus, the first layer of the sandwich poses the question from observation data. The second layer attempts to answer by more causal methods, while the final layer of the sandwich confirms the answer by additional observation.

THE ENVIRONMENT

The environmental end of the behavior-environment equation does recognize that an environmental context provides cues to the proper behavior expected. Often, the environment will determine the kind of observation that takes place. A setting that is too dark may prevent photography, or, with increasing technology, require either a high-speed film or infrared nightscopes for observation. Similarly, some environments allow an observer to become unobtrusive because of sheer numbers, while in other environments, lack of numbers makes the observer conspicuous.

Perhaps the most frequent observation that assumes the environment is a prime variable is that which measures environmental change.

Testing for Change

One of the most frequent kinds of studies done in environmental behavior research is to test for an expected difference in behavior that design or a change in environment is assumed to have produced. An astute reader will recognize that this is a direct test of the environment-behavior paradox: hence, the need to understand how the original behavior was related to the change. This observation may be an attempt to measure a change by comparing measures after construction with measures taken before a building was built; it may be an attempt to determine the form a design should take *before* a building is produced, or it may be an attempt to measure whether a change in behavior was successful *after* a building has been lived in. In all these cases observation is a critical tool because it can document how people respond naturally to environmental changes.

Trites *et al.* (1970) observed the amount of walking nurses did in three kinds of hospital designs and demonstrated that the least amount of walking occurred in a radial design. These data led to the popular radial design of intensive care units that has become a standard.

Howroyd (discussed in Bechtel, Ledbetter, and Cummings 1976) studied traditional and modern middle eastern desert communities and observed how important a wall was in defining the separation of community from the harsh environment. The wall served both as a psychological comfort and as a physical provider of shade. This led Howroyd to select a townsite for his community that was naturally surrounded by hills on three sides. Research showed that the residents of the town felt safer and more protected from the environment by the hills. The original hypothesis was confirmed.

Much of the observational testing for change follows a pre-post-measure model, where the effect of design is determined by the observed difference in behavior in the post design observation. A classical POE paradigm (see chapter 9) occurs when the designer works from data in the pre-measure; this is *not* an experimental design. Many maintain that it should really involve a control group that does not experience the new design. Nevertheless, studies continue to involve the simpler pre-post-measures in an attempt to determine whether a design has had the effect intended. One might dub these kinds of studies the *design-change paradigm*. What is important is to obtain comparable observations between the pre-post-measurement periods. For example, if one wants to measure the effect of a renovation in a cafeteria, the most *obvious* observation periods are mealtimes before and after the design period.

In a follow-up to the Arrowhead study (Dumouchel 1971), the observation of children's play before and after the installation of new playgrounds showed that the children's play had changed from solitary and fragmented to healthier group play centered around the playgrounds.

THE TIME

It should be perfectly obvious that any observation covers a slice in time and can never cover the full life history of an environment. The time scale of observation ranges from one year in the classical ecological psychology studies (see chapter 6) to a few minutes in a classical time-motion study of human factors. The best framework to use in approaching the time-sampling dilemma is to ask: What is the time frame surrounding the behavior as it naturally occurs in the environment? Does the behavior begin repeating itself every twenty-four hour period? Or, does the behavior take a weekly cycle? Unfortunately (in the sense of time sampling), many environments show marked differences in seasons critical for indoor environments when requirements change from heating to cooling or from wet to dry.

Strictly speaking, if it is thought that seasons will make a critical difference, observation should be made on a time period representative of each season—for example, periods in May, July, October, and February. In practical terms, this is almost never done because few clients are willing to wait a year for results. More often, the most critical season is chosen for observation and the other seasons are asked about in a retrospective questionnaire.

Deciding on a critical season is not always easy, however. For example, in a cold regions study (Bechtel and Ledbetter 1976), it first seemed obvious that winter would be the most critical season in Alaska. Yet, observations in summer demonstrated that the constant daylight had as much of a disruptive effect as the extremes of winter. Some people were unable to sleep for days at a time. Blackout curtains were a necessity for many homes. Children were especially susceptible to the interruption of diurnal rhythms. Thus, had there been no measures taken during the summer, important design information would have been missed.

It is becoming obvious that any time measure of less than a year incurs the danger of missing critical information. Therefore, although it must be recognized that very few studies will collect annual data, an attempt must be made to try to compensate by gathering detailed information about seasonal differences.

Within the season chosen various times must be sampled, to give a representative picture of behavior. An important question is, what takes place at night? Does the place being studied close down? If so, does some kind of activity such as cleaning or maintenance take place?

Another major question is whether to study weekends. Can it be assumed that weekdays are the same as weekends? Or do weekends see a complete absence of behavior? For public places, weekends become the prime time for behavior observation, while for factories, weekends may hold a complete absence of behavior.

Within each day the time sample becomes more precise. Does one observe during the entire day? Wright (Barker and Wright 1955) discovered that intense observation tires the observer within about twenty minutes. Should observation therefore be spaced so as to increase observer accuracy? The answer is that most observation is adapted to a time interval schedule to allow the observer to rest.

Observation can take place every five minutes or ten minutes, but the intervals cannot be purely arbitrary. Time intervals must be pre-tested to determine whether they miss a significant amount of data. This is usually done by having one team do intensive observation simultaneously with a second team that records only at the selected time interval.

In summary, the process of deciding on time intervals is a continuous narrowing of focus from seasonal to weekly, to daily, and, finally, to a selection of an appropriate time interval between observations.

THE OBSERVER

So far little has been said about the observer. The most obvious requirement is that the observer always appear to blend with the crowd, since an observer who is observed performing this task becomes an obtrusive presence. A matching of dress and demeanor is therefore a first necessity. In other respects the observer has a wide choice of approaches to making observations.

The Naive Observer

The simplest, and yet probably the most difficult stance to take, is that of naive observer. Ideally, this kind of observer comes as if from a distant planet and knows absolutely nothing about the customs and practices of the human race. The value of such a stance is that it makes no assumptions about behavior and reports behavior as literally as possible. The disadvantage is that it is difficult to take on this degree of naivete and free oneself of assumptions about behavior. Yet, like any other skill, it can be learned. The advantage of using a naive observer is that often persons living in a particular culture are the last to realize obvious facts about themselves.

A naive observer stance is especially effective in observing children, the elderly, or the handicapped because these groups offer a rich field of discovery for the uninitiated. The inability of arthritic patients to use common doorknobs, or the inability of children to see over adult height barriers can open up new vistas to the naive observer. After just a short period of exposure, the naive observer can see that the normal world is filled with barriers to wheelchair access, how some door jambs can be insurmountable, how wrinkled carpets and soft deep carpets become an obstacle course, and how the strewn objects of a child's room can help account for many home accidents.

Participant Observation

The most common of all observation roles, and the one that has the longest history, is participant observation (Jacobs 1970). This technique, which is the principal method of anthropology, has been used for over a hundred years. With this method, a single observer becomes a member of a society or group and attempts to observe and record every aspect of behavior in that culture. Typically an anthropologist becomes a member of the society for several years and then writes up the observation in book length format. Primary data are a daily journal and conversations with *informants.* Informants are natives of the culture who become teachers and interpreters of what the observer sees. Informants are necessary to provide a cultural perspective on what is observed. The goal of participant observation is to become familiar with the culture or the rules of behavior of the entire group rather than to study the behavior of any individual.

Long-term participant observation has several distinct problems relating to the acceptance by the people observed, the feelings of the observer, and entry and exit from the place of observation. The first task of a participant observer is to be accepted by the people who will be observed. The observer has a "cover" story, for example: "I am an anthropologist, and I want to learn your ways." Sometimes the observer does not reveal his/her true identity because this would interfere with the behavior to be observed. For example, when Caudill (1958) went to a mental hospital to observe patients, he pretended to be a patient or attendant. If the patients had learned his true identity they would very likely not have behaved "naturally" in his presence. This kind of deception raises ethical issues. Does the investigator have the right to observe under false pretenses, given the need for behavioral data (Redlich and Brody 1955)?

Since no single participant observer is able to participate in all roles in a society, any observation is somewhat biased by being limited to the points of view obtained in the roles penetrated. Thus, for example, Bechtel (1965) pointed out that a participant observer in a mental hospital would have very different reports on behavior depending on whether the observer was posing as an attendant, a patient, or an accountant. While every good observer will attempt to report on all roles in a given society or situation, it is not possible to participate in all roles. Liebow (1970) also raises the point that a participant observer is never fully a part of the society being observed.

Anthropologists have developed techniques for being accepted in societies. One of these is the withdrawal-and-return method. First the anthropologist arrives, sets up housekeeping, and goes about his or her business. People are suspicious, not eager to converse and shy with the stranger. After a time the anthropologist leaves. In a week or so, he or she returns. Now the neighbors, fellow shoppers, or passers-by have a reason to talk. "Oh," they say, "you've been away." Conversation naturally follows, and with it, acceptance into the group.

Not so easily handled is the entry-exit problem. This involves an internal adjustment on the part of the observer. Being a member of another culture, the observer brings values, beliefs, and behaviors that are out of place in the new society. Holding those values and customs in abeyance may require a severe personal adjustment. Neophyte anthropologists have been known to leave the field because of the emotional difficulties this situation presents. These problems can range from severe depression and loneliness to identity crises. And even when the entry adjustment is made and the observer can feel comfortable in the new society, the same problems can arise all over again when the observer leaves. In some cases, adjustment to an American lifestyle after living among peasants can be just as severe. Overcoming these emotional and value conflicts is a major part of learning to make accurate observations. Liebow (1970, 273) concludes: "In retrospect, it seems as if the degree to which one becomes a participant is as much a matter of perceiving oneself as a participant as it is being accepted as a participant by others."

For most environment behavior research, the observation attempted will not be as long and intensive as an anthropological study, but with increasing international involvement, the need for cross-cultural data on environment behavioral issues is becoming more imperative. Thus, much existing anthropological data are used as background material to prepare for observation and questionnaire combinations for shorter-term participant observation. For example, in studies of mental hospitals in Peru (Bechtel and Gonzales 1971) and housing in Iran (Tadjer, Cohen, Shefferman, and Bigelson, Inc. 1975), anthropological observations were very helpful in identifying the particular behaviors on which to concentrate observations. In Peru the interaction between doctor and patient was closer and far more paternal than in the United States. In Iran, larger spaces for visiting were a critical design factor in supporting the extended families that were the primary basis of Iranian culture.

Participant observation as it is practiced in most environment behavior studies today will typically be a short-term observation of particular places or life-styles to determine both the global patterns of behavior-environment linkages and some easily observable specifics. Participant observation is also useful as a method of acquainting designer and researcher with the lifestyles of the people for whom a design is intended. A good example of the unexpected things observation can turn up is provided in the Arrowhead (Dumouchel 1971) project, where it was found that a number of salespeople and visitors could not find their way around the housing estate. This led to recommendations for a more comprehensible pathway system.

The Hidden Observer

Many times when it is necessary to observe behavior in a naturalistic setting, it becomes imperative that the behavior not be influenced in any way by the knowledge that there is an observer about. This is often true in public places where one wants to observe the embarrassment and awkwardness of getting lost, or in mother-child interactions where one wants to see whether parents will take part in child's play in public or private, and in many other circumstances where it is especially important to keep observation secret.

The most common laboratory form of secret observation is through the one-way mirror—a large half-silvered glass that prevents subjects seeing anything but their own reflection while the observer can see everything the subjects do through the glass.

In the field, hidden observation is most often achieved by moving away from the subjects and viewing from a nearby building with a vantage point above eye level. Here the observer can observe with the naked eye, with a telescope or field glasses, or with a photographic long lens without being detected by the subjects. A possible problem with increased distance from the subjects is the loss of detail, but with modern optics the lenses can often reveal more detail than would be available to the naked eye even at close range.

With secret observation there is again an ethical issue—does the observation constitute an invasion of privacy? It is commonly accepted that behavior in public can be observed secretly as long as anonymity is preserved, but if pictures are to be published, either written permission must be obtained or the faces of the subjects must be blocked out.

The Professional Observer

The role most often played in observing is that of the professional, armed with social science knowledge and techniques, knowing that information on time and behavior must be categorized and recorded before it can be turned into useful data. Experience as a professional observer cuts down the time needed for defining problems and deriving hypotheses and enables the researcher to develop and test categories more quickly. After taking part in a number of observational studies, an observer learns how and where to look to define critical behavior in relation to designs. The professional role is largely one of developing and using the categories in the section that follows.

RECORDING OBSERVATION

Categories of Observation

Several methods have been developed for working out the behavioral and time categories necessary before observation can take place for data gathering. Up to this point most of the observation described has been relatively loose and impressionistic. This is fine for the definition of problems or for participant observation, but when scientific data are needed, a category system must be developed that deals simultaneously with behavior and time categories. These techniques range from the most global, like *behavior specimen recording,* to the most specific, like Bale's *interaction process analysis,* which is a fully developed instrument.

Developing categories involves a stage of reconnaissance similar to the problem definition stage, followed by a trial of categories, or a pre-test, then a reliability testing stage, followed by data collection and analysis.

Behavioral Specimen Records

A particular global method of observation developed by Wright (1967) originally involved watching children. Wright's technique is to have an observer write down every behavior in common-sense language. Traditionally this observation lasts a full day (Barker and Wright 1953), but more often it involves much shorter periods.

The behavior specimen record is written by the observer, typically by hand on a lined 8½ by 11-inch tablet on a clip board with a stop watch attached. The observer writes down the behavior as it occurs and marks the time in a margin at specified intervals. Since

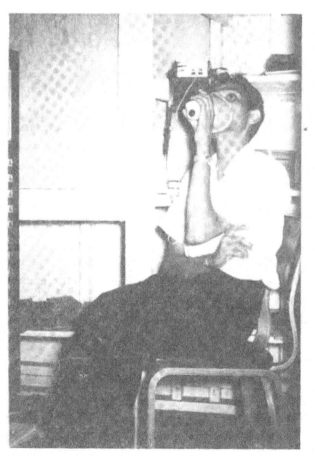

1-1. Steno mask being used by observer.

this form of recording is very exhausting, a team of observers is used so that each one observes for only fifteen or twenty minutes.

An alternative to the constant writing is to record the observation by speaking into a microphone. If one is close to the person being observed, however, the sound of the voice will be very obtrusive. This particular form of obtrusiveness can be overcome by the use of a device called a *steno mask* (fig. 1-1), which is placed over the face and spoken into. The rubber surrounding the face successfully masks the sound of the voice. Unfortunately, since the device resembles a gas mask, it is itself obtrusive when used in public! It is only appropriate when the observer can be well hidden. It must also be remembered that tape recordings relieve the observer from the need to record in writing but involve added expense and time for transcription.

Behavior specimen records become primary data that are scored into *episodes*—actions that have a beginning and an end. Two or more observers mark episodes and must reach a reliable agreement on their definition and scoring (fig. 1-2[not included]) (from Barker and Wright 1955, 237).

At this point we pause in our review to consider the importance of behavioral categories. Even in largely undifferentiated types of observation, such as behavior specimen records, it is necessary to agree on categories of behavior. Episodes, as we have noted, are categories derived from a transcript of behavior. In figure 1-2 [not included], an environmental transition is observed, which involves coming into the house, taking off wraps, and putting things away. Typically, these episodes also involve smaller episodes like taking off mittens and commenting on the cold. Still smaller observable events would be the father admonishing the child to come along, opening the door, entering, and closing the door. Note that not all of these actions were recorded but are assumed to have taken place (in this instance, the closing of the door was not included). Since the person being observed is the small boy Chuck, the father's activities are recorded only as they relate to the boy. There is a virtual infinity of small events going on that are not recorded such as eye blinks, gestures of hands, and interruptions of walking. *Molar* observation ignores these small aspects and concentrates on a larger level of behavior. The researcher defines an episode for this type of observation by deciding how inclusive he or she wants it to be. Looking at figure 1-2 [not included], it could be decided that the whole observation from beginning to end would be one episode called "coming into the house." It began with the decision to come in and ended with getting the last wrap off and settling into a new activity. Or, still being molar, but on a lower scale, one could call it three episodes: going inside, taking off wraps, and putting wraps away. The decision is purely arbitrary and depends on the purposes served by recording the episodes. For example, one could use the three smaller episodes to demonstrate the need for a closet near the doorway to allow coats to be put away most conveniently. An interesting question that could be answered by observations would be: Do children in houses with closets near the door put their clothes away more often than children in houses with closets further from the door, and how do parental admonitions affect the situation?

BEHAVIOR MAPPING

A behavioral map is actually an observational tool. The researcher takes a drawn-to-scale map of an environment and then notes behavior as it occurs in its true location on the map. Usually the notation is made in some code with a specific time frame adhered to. For example, *the number of times* people speak to each other may be noted on the map *every two minutes*. Often the maps indicate one-square-foot grids on the floor. An example of behavioral categories is given in figure 1-3, which breaks down patient behaviors observed in a hospice, a special home for terminally ill cancer patients (Koff *et al.* 1980). Figure 1-3 shows the same categories parcelled into an observation format. A critical point in behavioral mapping is to decide on the categories of behavior needed and to pre-test these in an actual environment.

Behavioral mapping was developed by Ittelson *et al.* (1970) to record behavior as it occurred in the design. In this way design features and behavior were linked in both time and space. It is usually used on a microscale for an environment such as a room because it is a convenient space for one person to observe. It can, however, be used on a wider scale with proper techniques for observation.

1-3. Categories for behavioral mapping of hospice patients.
1. A *graphic* rendering of the area(s) observed
2. A clear *definition* of the human behaviors observed, counted, described, or diagrammed
3. A *schedule* of repeated times during which the observation and recording take place
4. A *systematic procedure* followed in observing
5. A *coding* and *counting* system, which minimizes the effort required in recording observations.

In other words, to do behavioral mapping it is necessary to obtain an accurate scale map of the area to be observed, to decide clearly on the behaviors to be observed, schedule specific times for observation, agree on a system for recording the behavior, and then analyze the data in relation to how it has accumulated on the map. The purpose of behavioral mapping is to locate behavior on the map itself, to identify kinds and frequencies of behavior, and to demonstrate their association with a particular design feature. By associating the behavior with a design feature it is then possible to both ask questions and draw conclusions about the behavior and its relationship to design. For example, in a mental hospital it was possible to show how patients' standing behaviors related to the nurse's office and how social conversation related to the TV area. Lack of activities was associated with poorly planned lounges. See figure 1-4 for an illustration of categories and mapping (in this case a map was not used).

Behavioral mapping was used in the post-occupancy evaluation of a hospice, a nonhospital institution whose purpose is to make terminally ill patients feel comfortable in their last hours. It minimizes institutional requirements and emphasizes the comfort of the patient. The purpose of the design was to make the environment feel more homelike. The behavioral mapping was carried out by recording categories of patient and staff behavior at five-minute intervals over a twenty-four-hour period. The researchers discovered (1) that patients spent 84 percent of their time in the rooms, making the room the most important design feature from that standpoint, and (2) that auxiliary rooms such as the chapel and viewing room for deceased patients were used very little. This latter finding did not mean that these features were useless, however, because questionnaire and interview data showed that these rooms served an important purpose in affirming that the hospice was not a hospital.

For behavioral mapping to be useful, procedures and categories must be standardized for each specific location to establish the reliability of observers.

Behavioral mapping is also used with other methods such as interviews and questionnaires. Once the behavior has been associated with a design feature, people are questioned in order to confirm or disprove the initial finding.

PRESELECTED CATEGORY SCALES

Once it becomes necessary to select units of behavior that are below the molar level, one has a choice of trying to find an instrument with pre-tested categories, which is difficult, or developing one's own categories, which is also difficult. An example of a scale that has been used extensively is the Bales Interaction Process. While this scale was developed to score the social behavior of interaction, it has obvious relevance as a measure of how the environment, or specific variables, influence social interaction. It can be used to study the design process as it unfolds in a design team, or the effects of environmental variables on board meetings, discussions, and so on. The interaction process analysis, which was developed over thirty years ago (Bales 1950), has since been modernized (Bales and Cohen 1979). Both versions can be used depending on researcher preference. An example of the older scale is given in figure 1-5 (from Bales 1950, 18). Note the twelve categories on which subjects are scored: "shows solidarity," "shows tension release," and so on. Note also that a partial explanation of each category is given on the chart itself so that the observer does not always have to rely on memory.

Observation with the Bales scale requires a period of practice with a trained observer until a high degree of reliability is obtained. The modernized version, called SYMLOG, is shown in figure 1-6 (from Bales and Cohen 1979, 413). Note that the categories have increased to twenty-six, and are given in abbreviated form. Much more training is required to learn these categories, but more detailed data are obtained.

FROM PROXEMICS TO KINESICS

One of the earliest types of observation in environment behavior research came from Edward Hall's (1960) studies of the social distances people try to maintain in different cultures. Hall observed that these distances often relate to the senses: whether we can smell the other person, feel body heat, reach out and touch, or see facial features. The distances also vary according to social situations—friends stand closer in conversation than do strangers. Hall called the study of these distances *proxemics*. "Proxemic patterns" are the spatial patterns that constitute the norm for a culture in specific types of situations. Hall's manual (1974) has a series of proxetic codes for recording behavior. Figure 1-7 shows examples of proxetic codes for posture, body orientation, and lateral displacement of bodies (from Hall 1974, 57).

Proxemics continues to be a viable method in cross-cultural studies. Sussman and Rosenfeld (1982), for example, found that bilingual people use different distances when speaking different languages. They "jump back" to speak English and move closer together to speak Spanish. De Long (1976) found that proxemic distances were maintained when he asked subjects to simulate behavior with dolls in a one-twelfth-scale model building.

Kinesics is undoubtedly the most minute of all the observational categories. Developed by Albert Scheflen, Jacques van Vlack and Ray Birdwhistell at the Eastern Pennsylvania Psychiatric Institute (but chiefly by Birdwhistell), this system of observation concentrates on the nonverbal motions of the body as a language. Symbols are used called kinographs (fig. 1-8, from Birdwhistell 1970, 260). Macrokinesic (larger categories) and microkinesic (smaller categories) are recorded, usually from films. It is much more difficult to record from "live" observation because of the large number of kinesic activities going on. Birdwhistell is fond of saying that "a lot goes on in twenty seconds." While this system has had its widest application in the field of psychotherapy, it has obvious uses as a measure of discomfort under various environmental conditions. Le Compte (1981) used a kinesic observation of gestures to rate discomfort under crowded conditions in Turkey. He observed that despite its potential, kinesics has been applied very little in environmental studies.

Observer ______________ Day __________ Date __________ time begun am pm

time completed am pm

KITCHEN	ZONE 1					KITCHEN					MEDICAL RECORDS					PUBLIC BATH-ROOMS					STORAGE				
	P	V	Ch	S	V1	P	V	Ch	S	V1	P	V	Ch	S	V1	P	V	Ch	S	V1	P	V	Ch	S	V1
1. prof duty w/o ptnt																									
2. prof duty with ptnt																									
3. meeting																									
4. smoking																									
5. talking																									
6. eating & drinking																									
7. food prep																									
8. hygiene																									
9. telephone																									
10. lying in bed																									
11. sitting																									
12. standing																									
13. pacing																									
14. TV-radio																									
15. reading & writing																									
16. recreation																									
17. traffic																									
Interaction																									
Patient wheelchair																									
sitting																									
standing																									

1-4. Recording format for hospice patients' behaviors.

PHOTOGRAPHIC TECHNIQUES AND SOUND RECORDING

A particularly useful method for observing molar behavior has been developed in film (Cook and Miles 1978). Time-lapse photography offers a way of speeding up time in motion picture filming by shooting a single frame every thirty seconds or so. When the film is played at normal speeds, the action is time-compressed—a day's behavior can be seen in fifteen or twenty minutes of viewing. This method is especially effective for outdoor spaces such as plazas, patios, shopping malls, and even indoor areas, where crowd activity can be effectively condensed into a short viewing period. New high-speed film makes indoor and night photography practical.

The film itself can act as an educator and salesman. Projects for Public Spaces, Inc., a research organization, has very effectively sold social science to businessmen merely on the basis of their viewing such films. It becomes immediately obvious that the behavior fits or does not fit the environment. It is easy to identify, for example, the places where no one sits or where crowds gather and obstruct traffic. Indeed, many design research projects for public spaces can be effectively accomplished by filming activity on a busy weekend.

Time-lapse filming can also be used as a primary data source in the following ways. Slowed down, it can score particular behaviors for peak periods. (Photographing a clock in the corner of each frame counted provides a record of the time period.) Not only can numbers of people be counted but sexes can be differentiated and children counted separately from adults; and unlike "live" observation, the film can be run again and again to check reliability of observation. Categories of observation can be defined and observed with a precision that is not possible with live observation. The time-lapse technique has become an outstandingly successful method for studying behavior in public spaces.

Photography, video tapes, and sound tape recordings of behavior are new and rapidly developing techniques that are fast becoming a part of established observation methodology. The lure of gadgetry, however, often leads to inappropriate use and disappointment with results. The time-lapse camera is useful for molar behavior but progressively more limited as scale is reduced. *Molecular* behavioral categories such as facial expressions are often not discernible in the normal format used for studying a public area. Graininess of film presents a problem, especially with video, because one often cannot see the direction of a subject's glance or discern nuances of expression without an obtrusive close-up of the face.

Sound tapes are another tempting approach, as a substitute for taking notes. With tapes one expects to obtain the same clarity of speech we find in motion pictures and on television. As every filmmaker knows, however, clarity of sound is often achieved by "dubbing over" the visual film in the studio where the sound can be completely controlled. The actor gets in a sound booth and tries to match voice to the lip movements in the film. In "live" recording, several people often speak simultaneously, producing an unintelligible garble, and background noises may overwhelm the words. People who are not trained actors may speak too softly to be heard or they may not pronounce words very well and depend on hand gestures instead of words to express ideas. It is normal for at least 10 to 20 percent of the words spoken in everyday conversation to be lost in a recorded conversation, and in a meeting with several people present the percentage may go much higher. In meetings where all spoken words are needed as data, researchers have found that employing court recorders with stenographic machines is necessary to insure accuracy (Conway 1973).

RECORDING TRACES

When researchers want to know how people behave or have behaved in places they cannot observe, we enter the realm of reconstruction. Behavior that has taken place in the past leaves many kinds of traces behind. From these, researchers reconstruct the behaviors that produced them.

Archeology

Anthropologists in archeology were the first to recognize that ancient traces are a useful source of data about human behavior (Rathje 1979). Archeology, which is the science of inferring human behavior from such traces, has become very sophisticated with carbon, argon, and tree-ring dating, pollen analysis, and even the diagnosis of diseases in fossil skeletons and mummies. Few give a thought, however, to the fact that the fossils of tomorrow are the garbage dumps of today. The *Project du Garbage* (Rathje and Hughes 1978; Rathje and Ritenbaugh 1984) counted, dated,

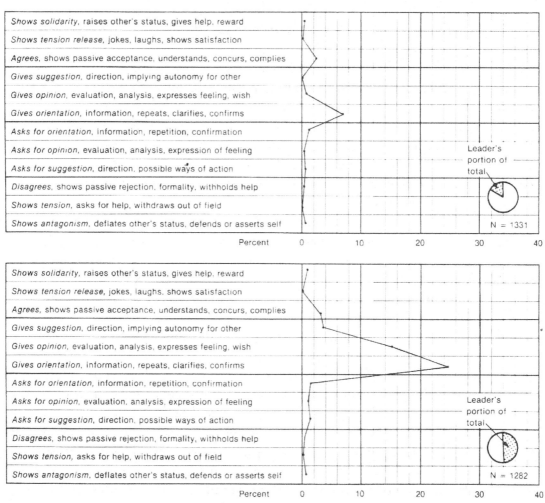

1–5. Older Bales' interaction scale. Reprinted with permission from Interaction Process Analysis *by R. F. Bales (Chicago: University of Chicago Press, 1950).*

cataloged, and weighed the garbage of urban America to explore what the material traces in garbage can reveal about human behavior. The study demonstrated that the United States has undergone a significant dietary change between 1981 and 1985, eating less meat and more fruits and vegetables. In addition, the garbage studies documented increased waste of sugar and beef during wartime sugar and beef shortages (Rathje 1977).

Other Surface Recordings

Zeisel (1981) has described traces as they are more commonly used in environment behavior research. He divides traces into four categories: by-products of use, adaptations of use, displays of self, and public messages. *By-products* are created by erosion of surfaces, leftovers, and missing traces.

Erosion is a relative term. Trained Indian scouts of pioneer days regarded a broken blade of grass as evidence that a person had passed by. For the average observer, however, erosions must be more obvious. Worn pathways in the grass are an indication of traffic. More subtle are the worn control surfaces in an automobile or airplane cockpit that indicate frequency of use of those controls. Another example of traces occurs in institutions for the handicapped, where areas that

1-6. Modernized Bales* interaction scale called SYMLOG. Reprinted with permission from SYMLOG: A System for the Multiple Level Observation of Groups *by R. F. Bales and S. Cohen (New York: The Free Press, 1979).*

are difficult to traverse are heavily marked by bumps from wheelchairs. Evidence of erosion may be seen everywhere, but great caution must be taken in interpreting it. In judging that a pathway through the grass indicates that a cement sidewalk should have been placed there, one may have failed to consider how the particular environment is managed. The buildings and grounds managers may prefer the appearance of the dirt path to a gleaming white sidewalk that would conflict with the landscape design. Another approach is to allow pathways to form first as a guide to where sidewalks should be placed.

Erosions can be used to uncover hidden pathways and unexpected uses. In the Arrowhead study (Dumouchel 1971), tracks in snow were an effective erosion measure because they indicated how a centrally located playground acted as a barrier to neighborhood traffic.

INSTRUCTIONS	CODE		
	Column No.	Variable	Description
62 *Posture* See Coding Scale opposite.	62	Posture	0 1 2 standing 3 leaning 4 sitting 5 squatting 6 prone 7 8 9
63 *Body orientation* This scale describes the orientation of the subjects' bodies to each other, beginning with back-to-back orientation (0) and opening out through side-by-side (5) and right-angle (7) to face-to-face orientation (9). The shoulders are the reference points to observe in deciding orientation. The most common positions for interacting are 5 through 9, although two persons standing "in line" (4) or backed up to each other (0) in crowds will also be aware of and interact with each other to some extent. Be sure that both subjects in an interaction are rated the same on this scale. (See Coding Scale opposite.)	63	Body orientation	0 1 2 3 4 5 6 7 8 9
64 *Lateral displacement of bodies* Refers to the amount of displacement on the body orientation scale (63). Records the degree to which the subjects are removed from the base positions. The displacement spectrum is amplified by adding increments of space to the basic displacement of the subjects; this space is indicated by the "plus" in the coding scale opposite.	64	Lateral displacement of bodies	0 (two arms extended—plus) 1 (two arms extended) 2 (one arm extended—plus) 3 (one arm extended) 4 (two elbows extended) 5 (one elbow extended—plus) 6 (one elbow extended) 7 (line up of opposite shoulders) 8 (shoulders overlap) 9 (facing directly)

1-7. Examples of proxetic codes. Reprinted with permission from Handbook for Proxemic Research *by Edward T. Hall (Philadelphia: Society for the Anthropology of Visual Communication, 1974).*

Leftovers are the most ubiquitous kind of traces, most often constituting what we commonly call "trash"—paper cups, beer cans, cigarette butts. Several researchers have used photographs of trash scatter to measure effectiveness of anti-litter campaigns (Geller *et al.* 1982). Others have randomly sampled and weighed trash. A good observation training exercise is to reconstruct a party from its

FACE

−◯−	Blank faced	⊙ ●	Stare
− ⌒	Single raised brow indicates brow raised	ⓢⓢ	Rolled eyes
− ⌢	Lowered brow	ɸ ɸ	Slitted eyes
╲	Medial brow contraction	◌ ◌	Eyes upward
∴∵	Medial brow nods	−◌ ◌−	Shifty eyes
⌒ ⌒	Raised brows	◌ ◌	Glare
◯ ◯	Wide eyed	◠ ◠	Inferior lateral orbit contraction
− ◯	Wink	△ₛ	Curled nostril
⟩ ⟨	Lateral squint	ₛ△ₛ	Flaring nostrils
⟩⟨ ⟩⟨	Full squint	ˌ△ˌ	Pinched nostrils
A or B	Shut eyes: with A—closed, pause 2 count; Blink B—closed, pause 5 plus count	△	Bunny nose
		𝔸	Nose wrinkle
		⌢	Left sneer
◡ ◡	Sidewise look	⌣	Right sneer
ҩ ҩ	Focus on auditor	◯	Out of the side of the mouth (left)

1-8. Kinographs.

leftovers. How many people smoked? How much liquor was consumed? Where did most of the party take place? Did the party stay together as a group or split up into subgroups? What were the favorite places? In a more systematic study, researchers would establish traces to observe by watching several parties first and recording traces as they occurred to build up a statistical basis for later behavioral inferences. For example, how many cups per person are normal use, how many napkins, and so on.

Missing traces indicate a lack of use in areas where erosion and leftovers are expected but do not occur. Lawton (1968) discovered that many social areas in high-rise buildings were not used. Very frequently outdoor places are not used; these are the "nondefensible spaces" described by Newman (1972) (nondefensible in that they are claimed by no one). The cues that Newman used to determine this were a failure to clean up the area and the fact that no one watched the space informally. Also significant are the many balconies that show lack of use in the United States compared to similar spaces in other countries. It is possible to count physical traces of use on balconies by viewing the side of a building. A series of photographs can document use over a year.

Zeisel's *adaptations for use* (1981) are clear indications that a change has been made in the environment because it did not serve its original intention. These would include all additions to buildings, renovations, redecorating, and "improvements." It is hard to detect adaptations when they were intended to fit into an existing structure but others like solar units and windmills are easily recognized. *Repairs* as a general class are sometimes easy to detect, often not. Zeisel calls many additions (such as solar units) *props*. He also looks for deliberate barriers, which he calls *separations*. Newman (1972) recommends separations as a way of creating defensible space. Arches over entryways, railings, fences, and other forms of separation act to keep intruders out and to convey the message that the separated area is someone's property. *Connections,* according to Zeisel, are created by occupants between two spaces when the design intended a separation that should have been a connection. Figure 1-9 shows a "connection" made through a basketball court fence at Project Arrowhead because it blocked a well-used pathway.

Zeisel's category *displays of self,* similar to what biologists call territorial marking, conveys a message of ownership. Decorative lettering on mailboxes, name plates on doorways, and the display of personal possessions are examples. Such displays become important for families and individuals who move often from place to place because the mementos seem to symbolize home. For older people, mementos represent ties with the past. The mantelpiece or the top of a bureau or coffee table is made into the shrine of the house, where the pictures of family and souvenirs of trips are displayed.

Zeisel defines *personalization* as a further step in identifying a place as belonging to a specific person. A desktop is adorned by pictures of family and by trophies or awards. Office walls contain personal photos or mementos. The child's room has souvenirs of special occasions, school, and travel. The college dormitory room displays posters that express the personal taste of the student. Personalization seems to be a basic need of workers. When the Lever Brothers building in New York City was first constructed, it had been designed to eliminate all personalization. Management forbade the hanging of any personal pictures or display of personal objects because they would conflict with the integrity of the design. The workers rebelled by vandalizing the building so severely that management relented and allowed personalization. When observing management policy, which either allows or tries to discourage personalization, it should be treated as a separate variable, unrelated to whether the design itself seems to encourage or make personalization difficult.

In the Cold Regions study (Bechtel and Ledbetter 1976) airmen at remote airbases preferred older barracks to new ones because the older ones were so run down that it did not matter how highly they were personalized. The new buildings had fancy vinyl wall coverings in which one was forbidden to place nails or tacks. Thus, how the design provides for the display of personal items is extremely critical to personalization. Figure 1-10 shows a single narrow shelf provided for each house in new housing for Iranians. It is loaded nearly to the bursting point. Ironically, nearby housing was being demolished that had provided countless niches in the walls for displays.

Clare Cooper-Marcus (1970) claims that each house is to some extent an expression of self, both in its selection and the way it is arranged. An environmental inventory of display is suggested to analyze the quality of self-presentation.

So important is furniture and other living room objects that Laumann and House (1970) and Davis (1955) created living room scales to measure social class. While these scales are now outdated, they can be brought up to date by inclusion of VCRs, home computers, and other devices.

Zeisel also uses *identification* and *group membership* as definite messages in the environment. Marking articles with one's name is identification, while group membership is often expressed in bumper stickers and jacket and sweatshirt labels.

Public messages are another form of traces. These range from official signs to public bulletin boards to graffiti. The PBS film *Style Wars* (Silver and Chalfant 1983) chronicled the state of high art to which graffiti has been carried in the New York City subways. The film takes a cinema verité tour of the graffiti gangs as they go about "writing" on subway cars and buildings. Their pride in their work is an unintended satire on more highbrow art forms. The young artists show a concern for the mortality of their work and its artistic excellence and keep scrapbooks filled with photos of their best work. In New York graffiti became a vehicle for artistic competition. In other cities (Suttles 1968) graffiti serves as a territorial marking for neighborhood gangs.

Whatever classification one applies to personalized traces, it is important to attempt to understand the purpose of the trace and its potential conflict or blending with the surrounding environment. A high degree of personalization indicates a corresponding degree of ease with the environment but not necessarily comfort. The prevalence of graffiti can signal areas of social conflict.

Archives

Official records of various kinds constitute another category of traces. They differ from the types discussed thus far in that they are formal, organized, and stored in archives.

Census data and other public records are an important resource. The U.S. Bureau of the Census began counting citizens in 1790 and has continued to do so every ten years since. As the country grew, so did the number of questions asked. In addition, state and local governments as well as branches of the federal government began to collect their own data. Marriages, births, property exchanges, tax records, service and employment records, and credit records have become part of the enormous data banks that exist today and are readily available to researchers. Census and early military records are stored at the national archives in Washington D.C. Federal employment records are stored in a warehouse in St. Louis, Missouri. Most of these records are microfilmed for preservation and ease of use.

Institutional records are also useful but more difficult to obtain. If a researcher is asked to study an organization, he or she quickly finds out that the records of organizations and businesses tend to be widely scattered and incomplete. Records of meetings and sales transactions are kept locally, but many other sets of data may be systematically destroyed or kept in separate locations.

Individual records comprise another category of traces. Each individual carries an increasing array of credit cards, a social security number and voter registration card, cards for membership in organizations and auto clubs, a driver's license, and I.D. for place of employment and leaves a trail of records of purchases, rents and mortgages paid, debts, contributions, traffic tickets, library books borrowed, bank deposits, checks written, taxes paid at various levels, hospital and doctor visits, dental records, and school grades. These constitute an endless source of data for an equally endless number of purposes.

Health records are an important source for studies relating physical aspects of the

1-9. Broken fence indicates blockage of a pathway

environment to physical and mental health (Wilner *et al.* 1962; Faris and Dunham 1939; Kaplan 1971). At one time it was believed that providing a clean, physically attractive environment would improve health. Now it is recognized that the causal chain to health is influenced by many more variables. Nevertheless, the many health archives are useful in ascertaining environmental relationships.

Condon (1983) used health records to show a critical link between illness and seasonal changes among the Copper Eskimos. Those uninitiated to cold climate studies would expect health to be linked closely to the cold. Actually, the disorienting effects of constant daylight in summer are greater than the constant dark and cold of winter. Yet, the greatest number of sick calls is in January because of the pressures of interrupted diurnal rhythms and the relatively crowded conditions of the settlement. The Eskimos disperse for hunting in the summer and are less likely to communicate diseases. Local archives of this kind are an invaluable source for determining environment-behavior interactions. In earlier studies it was revealed that merely gathering the population into a settlement increased the incidence of tuberculosis, and measures were needed to curb the further spread of the disease.

Crime statistics are a form of archival data that are used for a variety of purposes. Wilkinson and Bechtel (1970) were able to reconstruct the Kansas City riot of 1968 from police calls. Evidence from this study showed many areas of spontaneous activity as opposed to the unsupported concept of a single group of leaders. Many studies have been done with crime data to discover whether there is any truth to the popular belief that the moon influences criminal behavior (Campbell and Beets 1978). So far, although the debate continues (Garzino 1982: Campbell 1982) there does not seem to be much evidence for such an influence.

The theory that weather influences crime and violence, however, does seem to have some support (Harries and Stadler 1983; De Fronzo 1984; Atlas 1984), and the builders of prisons are well advised to consider frequent showers and air-conditioning as useful preventatives of violence.

The use of archival data is increasing and the view of what constitutes archival data is increasing as well. A popular new form of recycling data from old studies is called *meta analysis*. This form of analysis takes a series of studies done on a given subject and re-analyzes the data from a new viewpoint. For example, Mullen (1983) examined studies on helping behavior to determine effects of group size. While there is some debate about the various conclusions drawn from meta analysis, it seems to be a new form of archival use that is well established (Glass, McGaw, and Smith 1981).

1-10. *Narrow shelf in room of government (pre-Khomeini) housing in Iran, piled with possessions.*

Personal documents are a resource that may be overlooked. Many people have been moved by *The Diary of Anne Frank* (Frank 1952), yet do not readily see the diary as a valid document for historical and environmental research. Its historical value as a document of Nazi persecution during World War II is obvious, but it also documents an attempt to remain civilized in extremely close quarters and during a very tense time. Descriptions of how toilet and bathtub use had to be scheduled and how noise and eating were carefully controlled are important data on the basic requirements for living under such environmentally constrained circumstances. Diaries, letters, and other personal documents are important sources for obtaining data concerning how people reacted to and felt about observational conditions. A good example of diary use is Zube's (1982) compilation of how Arizona pioneers responded to the landscape of the nineteenth century. The diaries and letters of pioneers contain comments on their observations of the landscape as they encountered and lived with it. These observations can be compared with contemporary responses using present-day research methods to measure historical change.

Post-occupancy evaluations (POEs) are an important archival source for both designers and researchers (see chapter 6). Since relatively few of these are being published, it becomes a challenge to accumulate a sufficient personal archive. A good designer will want to acquire as many POEs as possible in his or her own specialty areas and this may mean personally conducting POEs. In many cases POEs are done by students as class exercises, theses or dissertations. Governmental agencies such as the General Services Administration have a number of unpublished studies on office buildings. To find out about these POEs, one must establish an extensive network of colleagues that will share information. The Environmental Design Research Associates maintain such a network with a list of researchers and practitioners interested in POEs.

The POE study on housing conducted by Bechtel and Srivastava in 1978 uncovered over 1,300 POE studies; many more have been performed since then. However, the quality of many of these studies is a problem. Of the original 1,300 less than 300 reported enough information to determine what methods they used. Many simply did not report "data" as such but gave impressionistic opinions. Thus, the discerning collector of POE information has to exercise a great deal of judgment in selecting those that provide the most useful information. Despite these difficulties in uniformity, reporting, and accessibility, POEs remain the largest source of information on how completed buildings and design projects actually function. In fact, they comprise the largest archive of environment behavior research.

ISSUES

How Not to Obtrude

The classic study on how being studied affects behavior is the famous Hawthorne project (Roethlisberger and Dickson 1939). The original purpose of the Hawthorne studies was to improve production at an electronics plant by increasing available lighting. It was discovered, however, that the control group, which was not exposed to the new lighting (and, in fact, where lighting decreased) also improved in production. Thus, the finding of the control group improvement became more famous than the original study because it illustrated that just being studied may make people feel special and stimulate a desire to please the experimenter or observer, in this case, by producing more. Since that time, the Hawthorne study has become a classic example of observer and experimenter effects on subjects.

Of course, not all observer effects are attempts to please the observer. Often the effect is to avoid or eject the observer from the scene. The question of how much an observation influences what is observed is a problem that pervades all scientific measurement. Heisenberg's uncertainty principle (Price and Chissick 1977) is a dictum that says that nothing in nature can be measured without interfering with it in some way. Thus, the attempt to measure itself introduces an irreducible error. Although no less an authority than Einstein could not accept Heisenberg's principle, it is commonly accepted today.

Translated into social science methodology and observation as a specific method, Heisenberg's uncertainty principle means that behavior will be influenced if the subjects know they are being watched. In short, the Hawthorne effect is social science's counterpart of the uncertainty principle. How can this be overcome? There are at least two somewhat polarized responses to this important question. One answer is never to let the subjects of a study know they are being observed. The other and opposite extreme is to require the informed consent of any subjects being observed. The objection to the first extreme is that it violates the privacy and civil rights of people if they are observed without their knowledge. The "informed consent" alternative is objected to because it maximizes the Hawthorne effect and negates the very purpose of studying "natural" behavior. Evidence for this effect abounds. Bechtel (1967) found that when visitors to a museum knew they were in an experiment, they spent three times the amount of time in a room looking at prints as the uninformed visitors (220 versus 71 seconds).

Thus, the ethical dilemma of observation is whether to gain consent and thus risk invalidation of the behavior to be observed. Most researchers solve this dilemma by assuming that any public behavior observed is not a violation of privacy and do not ask for consent. When it comes to observation in a school or institution, however, or a clearly private situation such as therapy, consent is obtained. Observation must be made for a time to determine whether researcher effects occur, and the principal measurement is made once effects seem to wear off. Also, if any pictures are to be published of people in public settings, consent must be obtained. While this solution may not meet the approval of all researchers, it is consistent with published ethical procedures.

Reliability of Categories

Perhaps the most critical issue in the use of observation is obtaining proper reliability among judges when recording categories. Since it is seldom that all behavior is observed, the selection of categories of behavior is critical to the success of observation, yet without reliability, the data become useless. A few scales, such as Bales (1950 and Bales and Cohen 1979), have high reliability, but most have to establish reliability among judges before they are used. This is a difficult task that is often overlooked in the desire to obtain quick results. Every research project should report reliability of judges as being .90 or better to elicit confidence in the data.

Inference of Causality

The main issue, once observation has taken place and reliability has been established, is the problem of determining why the observed behavior occurs and what it means. In participant observation this is overcome by asking informants about purpose and meaning and by living with the behaviors as a participant. In briefer methods of observation, other means such as interviewing, questionnaires, and archives are used independently to verify interpretations. Even when interviews or questionnaires are used to ask subjects directly about observed behavior, it is not a simple two-step process. Both observations and questionnaires need to be pre-tested so that both are found to be reliable and valid before the main data collecting in the field. Most often a third method is employed to obtain three sets of data, converging on the findings related to causality (Campbell and Fiske 1959).

REFERENCES

Atlas, R. 1984. Violence in prison: Environmental influences. *Environment and Behavior* 16:275–306.

Bales, R. 1950. *Interaction Process Analysis: A Method for the Study of Small Groups.* Reading, Mass.: Addison-Wesley.

Bales, R. and S. Cohen. 1979. *SYMLOG: A System for the Multiple Level Observation of Groups.* New York: Free Press.

Barker, R., and H. Wright. 1951. *One Boy's Day.* New York: Harper Brothers.

———. 1955. *Midwest and Its Children.* Evanston, Ill: Row, Peterson.

Bechtel, R. 1965. Participation and observation in the mental hospital. *Kansas Journal of Sociology* 1:166–74.

———. 1967. Hodometer research in museums. *Museum News,* March 1967. p. 23–25.

Bechtel, R., and A. Gonzales. 1971. A comparison of treatment environments between North American and Peruvian mental hospitals. *Archives of General Psychiatry* 25:64–68.

Bechtel, R., and C. B. Ledbetter. 1976. *The Temporary Environment.* Hanover, N.H.: U.S. Army Cold Regions Research and Engineering Laboratory.

Bechtel, R., C. B. Ledbetter, and N. Cummings. 1980. *Post-occupancy Evaluation of a Remote Australian Community: Shay Gap, Australia.* Hanover, N.H.: U.S. Army Cold Regions Research and Engineering Laboratory.

Bechtel, R., and R. Srivastava. 1978. *Post-occupancy Evaluation of Housing.* Washington, D.C.: Dept. of Housing and Urban Development.

Birdwhistell, R. 1970. *Kinetics in Context: Essays on Body Motion Communication.* Philadelphia: Univ. of Pennsylvania Press.

Campbell, D. 1982. Lunar-lunacy research: When enough is enough. *Environment and Behavior* 14:418–24.

Campbell, D., and J. Beets. 1978. Lunacy and the moon. *Psychological Bulletin* 85:1123–29.

Campbell, D., and D. Fiske. 1939. Convergent and discriminant validation by the multi-trait-multi-method matrix. *Psychological Bulletin* 56:81–105.

Caudill, W. 1958. *A Psychiatric Hospital as a Small Society.* Cambridge, Mass.: Harvard Univ. Press.

Chapin, F. 1974. *Human Activity Patterns in the City.* New York: Wiley.

Condon, R. 1983. *Inuit Behavior and Seasonal Change in the Canadian Arctic.* Ann Arbor: UMI Research Press.

Conway, D. 1973. *Social Science and Design: A Process Model for Architect and Social Scientist Collaboration.* Washington, D.C.: American Institute of Architects.

Cook, R., and D. Miles. 1978. *Plazas for People: Seattle Federal Building Plaza A Case Study.* New York: Project for Public Spaces, Inc.

Cooper-Marcus, C. 1974. The house as symbol of the self. In *Designing for Human Behavior,* ed, J. Lang, C. Burnette, W. Moleski, and D. Vachon. Stroudsburg, Pa.: Dowden, Hutchinson and Ross.

Davis, J. 1955. Living Rooms as Symbols of Status: A Study in Social Judgment. Ph.D. diss., Harvard University.

De Fronzo, J. 1984. Climate and crime: Tests of an FBI assumption. *Environment and Behavior* 16:185–210.

De Long, A. 1976. Architectural research and design: The art and architecture building project. *Free Flow* 1:1–11.

Dumouchel, J. R. 1971. *Arrowhead: Final Recommendations.* Kansas City. Mo.: Environmental Research and Development Foundation.

Dunham, H. W., and Paris, R. 1939. *Mental Disorders in Urban Areas.* Chicago: Univ. of Chicago Press.

Frank, O. 1952. *Anne Frank: Diary of a Young Girl.* New York: Doubleday.

Gans, H. 1970. *The Levittowners.* New York: Pantheon.

Garzino, S. 1982. Lunar effects on mental behavior: A defense of the empirical research. *Environment and Behavior* 14:395–417.

Geller, S., R. Winette, and P. Everett. 1982. *Preserving the Environment.* Elmsford, N.Y.: Pergamon.

Glass, G., B. McGaw, and M. Smith. 1981. *Meta Analysis in Social Research.* Beverly Hills, Cal.: Sage.

Guetzgow, H. 1950. Unitizing and categorizing problems in ending qualitative data. *Journal of Clinical Psychology* 6:47–58.

Hall, E. 1960. *The Hidden Dimension.* New York: Doubleday.

———. 1974. *Handbook for Proxemic Research.* Philadelphia: Society for the Anthropology of Visual Communication.

Harries, K., and S. Stadler. 1983. Determinism revisited: Assault and heal stress in Dallas, 1980. *Environment and Behavior* 15:235–56.

Ittelson, W., L. Rivlin, and H. Proshansky. 1970. The use of behavioral maps in environmental psychology. In *Environmental Psychology,* ed. H. Proshansky, W. Ittelson, and I. Rivlin, New York: Holt, Rinehart & Winston.

Jacobs, G. 1970. *The Participant Observer.* New York: Braziller.

Kaplan, B. 1971. *Psychiatric Disorder and the Urban Environment.* New York: Behavioral Publications.

Koff, T., W. Ittelson, R. Bechtel, D. Monahan, D. Lupu, K. Bursal, and E. Gerrity. 1980. *A Post Occupancy Evaluation of Hillhaven Hospice.* Tucson, Ariz.: Long Term Care Gerontology Center.

Laumann, E., and J. House. 1970. Living room styles and social attributes: The patterning of material artifacts in a modern urban community. *Sociology and Social Research* 54:321–42.

Lawton, M. P. 1968. Social and Medical Services in Housing for the Aged. Philadelphia: Philadelphia Geriatric Center. Mimeo.

Le Compte, A. 1981. The ecology of anxiety: Situational stress and the rate of self stimulation in Turkey. *Journal of Personality and Social Psychology* 40:712–21.

Liebow, E. 1970. A field experience in retrospect. In *The Participant Observer,* ed. G. Jacobs, 260–73. New York: Braziller.

McCormick, E., and M. Sanders. 1982. *Human Factors in Engineering.* New York: McGraw-Hill.

Mullen, B. 1983. Operationalizing the effect of the group on the individual: A self-attention perspective. *Journal of Experimental Social Psychology* 19:295–322.

Newman, O. 1972. *Defensible Space.* New York: Macmillan.

Price, S., and S. Chissick, eds. 1977. *The Uncertainty Principle and Foundation of Quantum Mechanics: A Fifty Years' Survey.* New York: Wiley.

Rathje, W. 1977. In praise of archeology. In *Historic Archeology and the Importance of Material Things,* ed. L. G. Ferguson. Columbia, S.C.: Society for Historical Archeology.

———. 1979. Trace measures. *New Directions for Methodology of Behavioral Science* 1.

Rathje, W., and W. Hughes. 1978. *Final Report, Project du Garbage* Washington, D.C.: National Science Foundation.

Rathje, W., and C. Rittenbaugh. 1984. Household refuse analysis. *American Behavioral Scientist* 28 (special issue).

Redlich, R., and E. Brody. 1955. Emotional problems of interdisciplinary research in psychiatry. *Psychiatry* 18:233–39.

Roethlisberger, F., and W. Dickson. 1939. *Management and the Worker.* Cambridge, Mass.: Harvard University Press.

Rosenfeld, H. 1960. Instrumental affiliative functions of facial and gestural expressions. *Journal of Personality and Social Psychology* 4:65–72.

Silver, T., and H. Chalfant. 1983 *Style Wars.* New York: Public Art Films, Inc.

Sussman, N., and H. Rosenfeld. 1982. Influence of culture, language, and sex on conversational distance. *Journal of Personality and Social Psychology* 42:66–74.

Suttles, G. 1968. *The Social Order of the Slum.* Chicago: Univ. of Chicago Press.

Tadjer, Cohen, Shefferman, & Bigelson, Inc. 1975. *Studies and Planning Services to Develop and Apply Performance Specifications in Procurement and Evaluation of Housing.*

Trites, D., F. Galbraith, M. Sturdavant, and J. Leckwart. 1970. Influence of nursing unit design on the activities and subjective feelings of nursing personnel. *Environment and Behavior* 3:303–34.

Wilkinson, C., and R. Bechtel. 1970. *The Social History of a Riot.* Washington, D.C.: National Institutes of Mental Health, Metropolitan Mental Health Problems Division.

Whyte, W. 1980. *The Social Life of Small Urban Spaces.* Washington. D.C.: The Conservation Foundation.

Wilner, D., R. Walkley, R. Pinkerton, and M. Tayback. 1962. *The Housing Environment and Family Life.* Baltimore: Johns Hopkins Univ. Press.

Wright, H. 1967. *Recording and Analyzing Child Behavior.* New York: Harper & Row.

Zeisel, J. 1981. *Inquiry by Design.* Monterey, Cal.: Brooks/Cole.

Zeisel, J., and P. Drake. 1984. Post-Occupancy Evaluation Methodology for Emergency Departments. A report prepared by Building Diagnostics, Inc., for the Department of Health and Welfare, Health Facilities Design Division, Ottawa.

Zube, E. 1982. An exploration of landscape images. *Landscape Journal* 1:31–40.

16 Ethnicity and Urban Recreation: Whites, Blacks, and Hispanics in Chicago's Public Parks

Ray Hutchison

Variation in recreational behavior in urban parks by Hispanic, Afro-American, and Anglo-American supports the American Cultures perspective that American life expresses multiple experiences, not a singular one. Additionally, the article provides an example of survey research done for social scientists but that designers could use to tease out design implications. In general, designers want to be able to make use of others' findings even if the researchers did not consider design implications in the publication of their works.

Field observations of white, black, and Hispanic groups in thirteen neighborhood and regional parks in Chicago were made to determine ethnic and/or racial variations in leisure and recreation activities. Significant differences were found not only in the types of activity, but also in the age, sex, size, and social composition of activity groups. These results suggest that meaningful social and cultural differences between ethnic and racial subgroups produce distinctive patterns of recreation behavior. While earlier studies relate black-white differences to the influence of ethnicity, these studies have failed to adequately conceptualize or operationalize the origins of black-white (race) and Hispanic-white (cultural) differences; the social forces responsible for differences between black and white groups in this study appear to be of different origin than those between whites and Hispanics. This study illustrates the advantage of an observation technique in supplementing data generated from surveys of recreation participation.

Keywords: Race, Ethnicity, Hispanics, Urban Recreation

Leisure and recreation activities are a fundamental part of the informal social organization, social activity, and cultural norms of population subgroups and social life in the urban community (McMillen, 1984; Hutchison and Fidel, 1985). Differences in recreation activity may be a consequence of distinctive ethnic subcultures, the social class positions of a particular group, or a more complex interplay between the two (Edwards, 1981; Stamps and Stamps, 1985). Studies of black-white recreation differences reflect the longstanding societal goal of providing equal opportunity for participation in American culture (Washburne, 1978; Washburne and Wall, 1979),

Ray Hutchinson, "Ethnicity and Urban Recreation: Whites, Blacks, and Hispanics in Chicago's Public Parks," from *Journal of Leisure Research*, Vol. 19, No. 3, pp. 205–222. Copyright © 1987 by National Recreation & Park Association. Permission to reprint granted by the publisher.

while research on Hispanics, the most rapidly growing subgroup in the U.S. population, indicates a pragmatic concern with the assimilation of the large numbers of Hispanics across the United States (Hutchison and Fidel, 1985).

Our approach to the study of urban recreation views the activities of whites, blacks, and Hispanics as a reflection of the normative structure and value systems of the respective subgroups. We believe that it is the social composition of recreation groups—rather than the specific activity—which is most important in understanding possible differences and similarities between ethnic and racial groups. This approach emphasizes the meaning of recreation activities to the group involved, as suggested by Buchanan *et al.* (1980) and Kelly (1978).

Field observations of thirteen neighborhood and regional parks in Chicago, conducted during the summer months of 1981 and 1982, recorded information on the type, size, age, and sex composition of activity groups to test predictions of differences in recreation activity. This study is concerned with behaviors actually observed within the public recreation setting, rather than responses of individuals or households to a survey questionnaire. This behavioral data allows for a more detailed analysis of the social organization of leisure activities among racial and ethnic groups than has been possible in earlier studies.

Subgroup differences are indicated by the social organization of recreation groups and social interaction between groups, even when particular activities (such as picnicking) are the same. In the Chicago data, the recreation activity of whites and blacks are strongly associated. The largest differences are found when comparing whites and Hispanics. While white-black differences have sometimes been explained by the "ethnicity" perspective, these results suggest that important social and cultural (ethnic) differences distinguish Hispanic recreation activity from that of both whites and blacks.

Review of Literature

Ethnicity and Social Class. Recent studies have compared the recreation and leisure behavior of blacks (Cheek, Field, and Burdge, 1976; Edwards, 1981; Kelly, 1980; Stamps and Stamps, 1985; Washburne, 1978) and Mexican-Americans (Hutchison and Fidel, 1985; McMillen, 1984) to the white population. Explanations of group differences in these studies have focused on the social class (or marginality) and ethnicity perspectives.

According to the social class or marginality perspective, variations in participation rates are explained by differences in social status rather than by cultural factors (Williams and Babchuk, 1973; Yancey, Ericsen, and Juliani, 1976). The extent of participation is related both to socialization patterns and opportunities for exposure to particular types of activities among different social class groups. Because of the unequal provision of recreation facilities, segregation of residential housing markets, and unequal distribution of incomes, minority groups are expected to have value orientations and social activities which differ systematically from those of the dominant society.

The ethnicity perspective, on the other hand, focuses on cultural differences in ethnic leisure styles (Washburne, 1978; Washburne and Wall, 1979) and the desire of minority groups to reconstruct their ethnic status in succeeding generations by socializing with those of similar backgrounds (Antunes and Gaitz, 1975). Several recent studies have adopted the concept of emergent ethnicity (Yancey, Ericksen, and Juliani, 1976), which suggests that ethnic subcultures will develop in groups spatially and occupationally segregated from the dominant society.

The two theoretical positions suggest very different policies for meeting the recreation needs of urban groups. The marginality perspective requires a commitment toward continued development of similar recreation facilities for ethnic groups, based on the idea that these groups do share a common orientation toward recreation activities. Special compensatory programs, facilities, and learning programs would be developed for those groups which have been excluded in the past. The managerial implications of the ethnicity perspective involves the more difficult choice of deliberately maintaining different facilities for ethnic groups corresponding to their specific recreation preferences (Dwyer, Hutchison, and Wendling, 1982).

It should be noted that emergent ethnicity is not conceptually distinct from the marginality perspective emphasized in earlier studies. By definition, groups which are most marginal (isolated from dominant groups by residence or occupation) are also most likely to have developed ethnic subcultures. The value of this approach is to emphasize the dynamic and ongoing processes which create and/or maintain ethnic subcultures.

While many studies document differences in white and black leisure and recreation activity, it is not clear if these patterns are due to social class or ethnic differences. A sampling of results from quality studies supporting each theoretical position is presented below; for a more complete overview of additional studies in this area see Benjamin and O'Leary (1978), Stamps and Stamps (1985), and/or Wendling (1981).

White-Black Comparisons. Numerous studies have compared black and white leisure activities, frequently producing contradictory findings (Cheek, Field, and Burdge, 1976; Edwards, 1981; Kelly, 1980; Meeker, Woods, and Lucas, 1973; Washburne, 1978; Washburne and Wall, 1979). Meeker *et al.* (1973) note that blacks are more group oriented and more likely to make use of urban recreational facilities, while whites are more individualistic and more likely to participate in outdoor wildlife recreation activities. Kelly's (1980) national sample of more than 4,000 individuals supports these results, finding that whites were more likely to participate in outdoor and winter recreation activity. Washburne (1978) found substantive differences in his sample of low income black and white families and asserted that these variations in leisure activities are due to ethnicity.

Other studies, however, have found only small differences in black-white recreation activity (e.g., Cheek, Field, and Burdge, 1976) or have attributed those differences to social class rather than race or ethnicity. Edwards (1981), for example, found that black-white differences disappear among blacks living in white areas. Studies of the black family have generally made an assumption that social class is more important than race in determining lifestyles (Blackwell, 1975; Kronus, 1971; Wilson, 1980). This literature strongly suggests that middle class blacks are more like middle class whites in their family patterns, fertility rates, religious behavior, educational aspirations, political beliefs, and the like, than they are to lower class blacks or whites.

The recreation literature has neglected the numerous ethnographic studies of black neighborhoods which emphasize the prevalence of peer group activity and street corner life among working- and lower-class groups (Anderson, 1978; Hannertz, 1969; Liebow, 1969). While peer groups are obviously found among whites and Hispanics as well, they appear to be especially important in the black community.

Researchers remain divided as to whether observed differences are due to race (emphasized in Washburne, 1978), social class (Kelly, 1980), or to the combined factors of race and class (Edwards, 1981). If there is a consensus to be drawn from these studies, it is that black-white differences, if they exist, are due not to the simple influence of either class or race, but to a more complex (and not well understood) interaction between these two factors.

White-Hispanic Comparisons. The social science literature comparing Hispanic groups with the white population documents systematic cultural differences in family structure (Mirande, 1977; Penalosa, 1968), social values (Rubel, 1966), and social participation (Antunes and Gaitz, 1975; Babchuck and Williams, 1973). Alvirez and Bean (1976) note three characteristics which distinguish the Mexican-American family. These include familism (the importance of the family and extended family), male dominance (where the father and male children exercise authority over female members of the household), and segregation by age groups (involving respect for elders and the subordination of younger persons). They also note a consistent segregation of activities by sex, where male children are accorded greater freedom while female children are protected from contact with those outside the family.

The consequences of these patterns is noted by Pi-Sunyar (1973, p. 49) in his description of social activities in a Mexican town:

> Entertainment and relaxation, indeed the whole field of recreation (apart from spectator sports, going to the movies, and so forth) is virtually a family preserve ... such gatherings bring together both sexes and all ages, but polarize along sexual and generational lines, married women gravitating to a specific corner, adult men congregating to discuss local problems of business and politics, adolescent girls monopolizing parts of the patio. Only young children are free of restraint, while in contrast adolescents and even married adults behave more as spectators than as participants. At no time do unmarried men and women mingle freely together.

The organized and ritual nature of leisure activity in Hispanic culture is frequently noted in travel descriptions and in scholarly work as well. Charles Flaundrau (1964) writes in Viva Mexico:

> There are city parks and squares in other countries, but in none do they play the same intimate and important part in the national domestic life that they do in Mexico ... The Plaza is in constant use from morning until late at night. Ladies stop there on their way home from church, "dar una vuelta" (to take a turn), as they call it, and to see and be seen ... By eleven o'clock the whole town will, at various hours, have passed through it, strolled in it, played, sat, rested, or thought in it ...

The leisure and recreation activity of specific ethnic (as opposed to racial) groups has not received much attention. Only two published studies directly compare the recreation activities of Mexican-Americans and the general population, and these provide very different results. McMillen (1984) measured the extent and intensity of participation in 32 activities through personal interviews with 130 Mexican-American households in Houston. These responses were then compared with the "general" population as measured by a national (NORC) household sample. He concluded that there was no difference in the leisure participation patterns of Anglos and Hispanics.

Hutchison and Fidel (1984), using observational data of white (Anglo) and Mexican-American groups in Chicago, reported evidence of differences in recreation patterns, and in the social organization of groups involved in recreation activities. These studies do not provide definitive evidence for either differences or similarities between white and Hispanic groups: both studies concern only Mexican-Americans, rather than the total Hispanic population, and the very different methodologies used in the studies may account for a large part of the difference in reported outcomes.

Hypotheses

This summary of recent research concerning race and ethnic differences leads us to propose a set of hypotheses which predict differences between white, black, and Hispanic groups observed in Chicago. In contrast to the importance of primary groups in Hispanic culture, as noted above, increasing individuality resulting from the dissolution of primary groups is recognized as a feature of modern industrial societies (Reissman, 1950). The emphasis on the individual (in American society) and the family group (in Hispanic culture) leads to the first hypothesis:

> H1: Individual activities (representative of the dominant culture) will predominate among white and black groups; family activities (representative of a traditional culture) will predominate among Hispanics.

Ethnographic studies of black neighborhoods note the importance of the male peer group. This produces the second hypothesis:

> H2: Peer groups will be observed more frequently among black groups than among whites or Hispanics.

Previous research has documented white-black differences in recreation activity. As long as blacks and other minority groups occupy social positions marginal to that of whites, we may expect to observe differences in recreation activities. This results in the final hypothesis:

> H3: Systematic differences are expected in the activities observed for white vis a vis black and Hispanic groups.

Methodology

The data reported in this study are based upon field observations completed during the summer months of 1980 and 1981. The purpose of the project was to study ethnic and racial differences in recreation activity through the direct observation of white, black, and Hispanic groups in public recreation sites.

In 1980 the Chicago population was approximately 43 percent white, 40 percent black, and 16 percent Hispanic and Oriental. The selection of research sites was determined by a two level sample which reflects the major population groups (whites, blacks, and Hispanics) and recreation settings available to the public (neighborhood, regional, and lakefront parks). While this does not represent a probability sample per se, our sampling procedure suggests a stratified sample which accounts for the major sources of variation in the control variables (population groups and park setting).

The location of the thirteen parks selected for detailed study is shown in Figure One. Because the Chicago public park system was centrally planned, neighborhood and regional parks in different areas of the city are largely comparable in the size and type of facilities provided. For example, Humboldt, Marquette, Riis, and Washington Parks are regional parks of comparable size; each location has sports facilities, large amounts of open space, playground areas, and walks and benches under large shade trees. The population characteristics of the local neighborhoods and of the dominant user groups for each of the thirteen parks is shown in Table One. Each research site was divided into four subareas, and hourly observations recorded all activities taking place within the park boundaries.

Observation forms were specially designed to collect detailed information on the number of persons and social composition of each activity group observed in the park, including age, sex, race, and type of social grouping. Observations were made during daylight hours on both weekdays and weekends, and represent a minimum of four complete days for each location. This procedure produces results similar to "instant-count samples" and "typical user distribution patterns" found in other studies [c.f., Tyre and Siderelis, 1979, Routledge, 1985].

The unit of analysis in this study is the activity group, rather than individuals or households (as typical of survey data). Activity groups were defined as those naturally occurring social groups observed within the public recreation site. An activity group may represent an individual, couple, family, or other social grouping. It should be noted that while there is a rough correspondence between the size of the social group and the type of activity (jogging and bicycling is frequently an individual activity, tennis necessarily involves two or more persons, and softball requires a larger group), there may also be a good deal of variance between the type of group and activity observed (picnic groups may be made up of couples, family groups, an extended family group, or an organized group of unrelated individuals).

TABLE ONE

Community Location, Type of Facility, Population Characteristics, and Primary User Groups for Chicago Public Parks Included in Study

Park Name	Park Type	Location	Neighborhood Population	User Population
Cornell	Neighborhood	Hyde Park	Mixed	Mixed
Oz	Neighborhood	Lincoln Park	White	Mixed
Brainerd	Neighborhood	Brainerd	Black	Black
Fernwood	Neighborhood	Fernwood	Black	Black
Harrison	Neighborhood	18th Street	Hispanic	Hispanic
Pietrowski	Neighborhood	26th Street	Hispanic	Hispanic
Marquette	Regional	Marquette Park	White	White
Riis	Regional	Hermosa	White	Mixed
Washington	Regional	Washington Park	Black	Black
Humbolt	Regional	Humbolt Park	Hispanic	Hispanic
Diversey	Lakefront	Lincoln Park	White	White
Lawerence	Lakefront	Uptown	Mixed	Mixed
Burnham	Lakefront	Prairie Shores	Black	Black

Research personnel were trained during visits to each field site. We recorded winter-observer reliability coefficients of .90 or higher during a series of pretests with the field staff. In addition, the senior researcher met with staff members at each location during the summer, and made independent observations to insure accuracy of the data collected.

Research personnel were matched to the dominant user groups in each park (i.e., a black observer in black parks, a Mexican-American observer in Hispanic parks, white observers in white and mixed parks). Observations were completed while the field staff positioned themselves on benches and other unobtrusive locations. This allowed for a close view of activities within specified areas while preserving the naturalness of the research setting (Golden, 1979).

Over the course of the summer we completed 3,072 observations, providing detailed information on the behavior of more than 18,000 activity groups. Data provided by these observations answer not only the basic question of what kinds of activities different racial/ethnic subgroups participate in, but also how they participate—as individuals or as part of a family unit, in groups segregated by age and sex or in mixed social groups.

Research Findings

The data yielded information on some 18,000 groups engaged in more than 300 different activities ranging from the commonplace (bicycling and walking) to the exotic (catching frogs and watching parrots), as well as deviant activities. The full range of activities were divided into three categories: mobile, stationary, and sports activities. Most sports activities occur in facilities designed for specific activities (tennis courts, baseball diamonds, basketball courts, and the like). The distinction between mobile activities (characterized by bicycling, walking, and jogging) and stationary activities (picnicking, lounging in the grass, sitting on park benches) is important to resource managers because of (1) the amount of time spent in the park and (2) the size and type of participating groups, and (3) the degree of utilization of public facilities. Clearly, a family using the public park for a picnic is making more intensive use of public space than is the individual who jogs through the park.

Activities Observed. Important differences in white, black, and Hispanic activities are found in Table Two. If we examine the three summary categories, there is a strong correspondence between white and black activities: more than 50 percent of the white and black activity groups were observed in mobile activities, and an equal number of black and white groups (37 percent) in stationary activities. Hispanic activity groups are markedly different from both whites and blacks, as the majority (56 percent) were observed in stationary activities, and only 25 percent in mobile activities. Only a small number of activity groups were observed in sports activities, indicating the importance of the public park as a setting for informal social activities as well as outdoor recreation.

Examining the complete list of twenty-three activities, just three or four activities predominate for whites; bicycling and jogging alone account for more than 40 percent of all groups observed during the course of the summer. A similar pattern exists for blacks, where more than a third of all groups were observed walking or bicycling. Among Hispanics, six activities should be noted. While two of these (walking and bicycling) also rank high for whites and blacks, the remaining four—use of playgrounds, picnicking, watching sports events, and lounging in the grass—occur with much greater frequency among Hispanics.

The chi-square statistic computed for the full table is significant at the .001 level, although the large number of cases makes this result inconclusive (with an n of more than 15,000 observations, even small differences in the table will produce a significant chi-square value). Differences in the Spearman rank-order correlations between the three groups are shown at the bottom of Table Two.

TABLE TWO

Recreation Activities of White, Black, and Hispanic Recreation Groups Observed in Chicago Public Parks

Activity	White	Black	Hispanic
Mobile	52.5	50.2	24.6
Walking	15.7	19.3	9.5
Bicycling	16.0	15.0	9.3
Jogging	14.7	7.6	2.1
Walking dog	3.6	2.7	0.3
General play	1.3	3.7	3.2
Other	1.2	1.9	0.2
Stationary	37.4	37.4	55.9
Playground	5.7	7.9	12.8
Benches	11.7	9.5	6.8
Ground	3.9	4.7	11.5
Picnic	1.7	3.7	8.7
Spectator	0.9	1.0	10.3
Sunbathing	6.4	0.8	0.4
Automobiles	0.6	3.8	0.6
Board Games	2.2	0.1	0.0
Food Vendors	0.1	0.7	1.8
Other	4.2	5.2	3.0
Sports	10.2	12.3	19.6
Tennis	4.3	2.4	4.7
Basketball	0.3	5.2	3.9
Baseball	1.3	1.7	5.7
Softball	1.1	0.9	3.0
Soccer	0.7	0.1	1.9
Golfing	1.2	0.4	0.1
Other	1.3	1.6	0.3
Total N Observed	8860	2881	4519

Rank-order correlations:
- white-black   .660 **
- white-Hispanic   .346
- black-Hispanic   .629 **

Note: Table shows n of activity groups; number of individuals may differ. Results for mixed-race and ethnic groups are not included. Total may not add to 100.0 due to rounding error. Chi-Square for this table is significant at the .001 level but the large number of cases makes this result inconclusive. (**) denotes .01 significance level.

As in the case of the Pearson correlation (r), the rank order correlation may range from -1 (indicating complete discordance) to +1 (complete concordance; see Snedecor and Cochran, 1967, p. 193–195). Significance levels for the Spearman correlations, computed by Kendal (1955), are also shown. The coefficient of .66 between white and black groups indicates a strong and statistically significant association between activities for these groups; the much weaker coefficient of .35 between white and Hispanic groups shows little association between activities of these two groups. The correlation for blacks and Hispanics (.63) shows a strong and statistically significant association for these two groups.

Size and Type of Social Group. The type of recreation activity is only the surface level of leisure and recreation; equally important is the social setting and type of social group within which the activity takes place. Even if leisure activities are identical, the social organization of the activity group may result in a qualitatively different leisure episode.

As noted earlier, there is a rough correspondence between particular types of activity and the size and type of the activity group. Jogging and bicycling are usually individual activities, while picnics involve larger family or peer groups. The average size of all white groups was 2.5 persons, compared to 3.8 persons for blacks, and 5.7 persons for Hispanics. The relative size of activity groups is also indicated by the data in Table Three, which examines the social organization of white, black, and Hispanic activity groups.

Fully half (51.7 percent) of all white activity groups were comprised of individuals; peer groups form the second largest category. Family groups rate very low, accounting for no more than 10 percent of the total. The black pattern is somewhat similar: individuals account for nearly forty percent (38.7) of all activity groups, while peer groups account for another 38 percent of the total. Families accounted for only 1 in 10 of the black activity groups.

This pattern is reversed for the Hispanic population, where individuals account for less than ten percent of all activity groups observed and family groups account for nearly a quarter (24.3 percent) of the total. Mixed groupings indicate persons of different ages who come to watch sporting events, gather around playgrounds to meet with neighbors and watch the children, and picnic with groups of friends. The large number of mixed activity groups reflects in part the difficulty of disaggregating the large communal groups observed in Hispanic parks—rather than recording these groups as corporate bodies of six or seven family groups, we considered them as multiple family groups or simply as mixed groups. Nearly 55 percent of all Hispanic activity groups appear in the nuclear family, other family, and mixed group categories; no such comparable grouping is found in either the white or black population. The rank order correlations emphasize these differences: while white and black groups are strongly associated with one another, the correlation between blacks and Hispanics was not statistically significant, and the white-Hispanic correlation shows no relationship.

Age and Sex Composition. Further differences in the social composition of groups appear in the age and sex structure of activity groups, shown in Table Four. The number of young adult and adult activity groups is substantially greater among both whites and blacks, accounting for more than half of the total (the comparable figure for Hispanics is 33.4 percent); mixed age groups make up nearly half of the Hispanic groups. The difference in age composition may be explained in part by the large number of family and kin groups involved in recreation activities in the Hispanic parks, so that specific age groupings within the Hispanic population occur with less frequency than among the other groups.

TABLE THREE

Social Composition of White, Black, and Hispanic Activity Groups Observed in Chicago Public Parks

	White	Black	Hispanic
Individual	51.7	38.7	9.6
Couple	7.1	8.7	2.8
Peer Groups	27.1	37.9	20.8
Nuclear Family	6.1	4.4	14.5
Multiple	3.3	5.7	9.8
Mixed Groups	1.3	1.5	29.8
Sports Teams	0.3	1.4	12.5
Other Groups	1.0	1.7	0.2
Total N Observed	8196	2886	4514
Rank order correlations:	white-black	.952 *	
	white-Hispanic	.000	
	black-Hispanic	–.226	

Note: Table shows n of activity groups; number of individuals may differ. Results for mixed-race and ethnic groups are not included. Total may not add to 100.0 due to rounding error. Chi-Square for this table is significant at the .001 level but the large number of cases makes this result inconclusive. (*) denotes .05 significance level.

Nearly a third of all Hispanic activity groups were female; figures for whites and blacks are 17 and 22 percent. This reflects the child care functions of mothers and older female children in watching over younger children. Male groups appear more frequently among both whites and blacks—indeed, more than half of all groups are males for both groups. While the number of mixed-group combinations (mixed, predominantly male, and predominantly female groups) are nearly equal for all three groups, there is a noticeably smaller number of mixed groups (mixed-sex or couple) for the Hispanic population.

As in Table Two, the chi-square statistics for Tables Three and Four are significant at the .001 level, but the large number of cases makes this result inclusive. Due in part to the small number of comparisons in the tables, the rank order correlations are not statistically significant. For the sex composition of activity groups, the black-white correlation is very strong, while the age composition of activity groups produces the highest correlation (.643) for whites and Hispanics in any of the tables.

Discussion

The data analysis generally supports the hypotheses discussed at the beginning of the paper: individual activity groups are more common among whites than Hispanics, where family groups predominate; peer groups are more common among blacks; and there are differences in the types of activities observed between whites, blacks, and Hispanics. One unexpected result stands out: black groups more closely resemble whites in the type of activity, type of group, and sex composition of social groups, than do Hispanic groups.

TABLE FOUR

*Age and Sex Composition of White, Black, and Hispanic Activity Groups
Observed in Chicago Public Parks*

Sex Composition	White	Black	Hispanic
Male Groups	51.8	55.0	34.2
Predominantly Male	8.3	7.3	18.6
Mixed Groups	17.4	11.7	5.2
Predominantly Female	5.1	4.2	11.3
Female Groups	3.3	5.7	9.8
Age Composition			
Children	8.4	17.6	12.0
Teen Groups	6.6	10.2	6.1
Young Adults	34.4	26.1	16.7
Adult Groups	21.1	18.9	16.7
Elderly	14.1	2.3	0.8
Mixed Age Groupings	15.4	14.9	47.8
Total N Observed	8260	2944	4519

Rank-order correlations:	Sex	white-Hispanic	.900
		white-Hispanic	.400
		black-Hispanic	.300
	Age	white-black	.714
		white-Hispanic	.643
		black-hispanic	.643

Note: Table shows n of activity groups; number of individuals may differ. Results for mixed-race and ethnic groups are not included. Total may not add to 100.0 due to rounding error. Chi-Square for this table is significant at the .001 level but the large number of cases makes this result inconclusive.

Differences in recreation behavior between population subgroups may reflect a distinctive ethnic subculture, the marginal social status of particular minority groups, or a more complex interplay between these factors. In analyzing the results of this study, a complex pattern of interaction emerges. While distinctive differences in activity patterns and composition of activity groups are observed, the social composition of white and black groups are more similar to one another than to Hispanics. This suggests that the social forces responsible for differences between white and black groups may be of different origin from those between whites and Hispanics. The possible causes of those patterns are discussed in this section.

To some degree differences between groups may be an artifact of demographic patterns specific to each group. The large number of elderly white groups results from the relative concentration of older whites in the city, and, more specifically, the concentration of these persons in communities adjacent to several of the research sites. The resulting difference in age groups between whites and blacks and Hispanics should not be attributed to social class or ethnic differences, but to residential patterns, birth-rates, and periods of settlement for each group. Similarly, the relatively larger number of family groups among Hispanics in part reflects the younger age structure and age-at-marriage of this group (although these demographic features also reflect an ethnic difference; see Jaffe, Cullen, and Boswell, 1980). In interpreting this recreation data, we must be sensitive to the age structure and demographic patterns common to each group.

In addition to demographic variables, we should direct attention to the nature of the data included in the study. The observational study presented here, for example, does not include information concerning participation in indoor leisure time activity (watching television, visiting with relatives, reading books and magazines) or outdoor recreation (camping, hunting, boating). Were these activities included we might observe different results. Due to their shared marginal status in the white dominated society, for example, both blacks and Hispanics may be under-represented in outdoor activities more commonly measured in recreation studies.

On the other hand, the study of informal social activities in leisure surveys may well highlight ethnic differences between Hispanics and blacks (such as using Spanish-language media). But our approach to studying the possible ethnic and social class bases of recreation behavior emphasizes the importance of the social group, rather than the specific activity, and for this reason the differences observed in the Chicago data seem especially salient.

While the observational data do not provide a direct measure of social class, there is much evidence of intragroup variation. While both blacks and whites participate in more individualistic activities than Hispanics, we also observed differences between black groups in different areas of the city. In lakefront parks in more affluent neighborhoods we observed many blacks jogging, sunbathing, playing volleyball, and engaging in other more cosmopolitan and perhaps unexpected activities. These activities were not observed among blacks in neighborhood parks in other areas of the city. These observations follow Edwards (1980), who noted that black residents of predominantly white neighborhoods may participate in different activities than those living in predominantly black neighborhoods.

Conclusions

The results of this study indicate systematic differences in the types of activities, and in the size, type, age, and sex composition of recreation groups. The Hispanic recreation pattern is distinguished from both whites and blacks in a greater emphasis in family activities, mixed age groups, and a more intensive use of park facilities. Indeed, the very character of Hispanic parks, particularly in the Mexican-American neighborhoods, is very different from that observed in other areas of the city. The neighborhood park itself has become an integral part of Hispanic leisure activity: teens gather around benches to talk and watch young girls walk through the park with their sisters or friends; at the playground areas large numbers of young families mingle in the shade and visit with friends; at the baseball diamonds teams from local leagues play while family members—including not only wives and children but also other relatives and friends—gather to watch. Vendors pass through the park selling helados (frozen fruit and ice cream bars) and crushed ice drinks from pushcarts. While these activities may be similar to those observed in other locations, the atmosphere of the Hispanic park is very different from that observed in white and black neighborhoods in the city.

Parks in white and black neighborhoods experience much less intensive use. Indeed, the predominance of individual, mobile activities among both groups insures that the parks will be occupied only fleetingly by the majority of park users. There are peaks of activity in these parks, to be sure, since these activities are more likely to take place in the early morning or late afternoon hours. We relate the pattern of activity and the emphasis of individual groups to the greater influence of the dominant culture of individualism among both the white and black population.

It is important to note the larger number of peer groups and relative under-utilization of parks in the black population. These results conform to the ethnographic studies of black neighborhoods noted earlier. The presence of male peer groups, hanging-out inside the park, may also explain why the parks are under-utilized by other groups.

Systematic differences between Hispanics and whites and blacks, observed in the present study, appear to be the result of a distinctive ethnic subculture rooted in a more traditional family structure which stresses the importance of the group (rather than the individual) and reinforces specific roles between age and sex groups. This pattern may be emphasized or reinforced by the social class distinctions and marginal position of the minority group in American society, but it is none-the-less rooted in an ethnic subculture. While there are distinct differences between white and black groups, they are more similar to one another than are blacks and Hispanics, indicating the complex interplay between ethnic and social class as categories of analysis.

These conclusions suggest three important conditions for future research. First, those studies which have attributed black-white differences in recreation activity to ethnic differences must be reevaluated. We will find little support in the race and ethnicity literature to support the contention that black-white differences are due to ethnic or cultural differences (see Berger, 1970; Blauner, 1969; Wilson, 1980). Although the evidence is indirect, as noted above, the Chicago data suggest that black-white differences may be more strongly related to social class than to "ethnicity."

Interest has been shown in the study of ethnic differences in recreation activities, and it seems useful to direct our attention to specific ethnic groups in American society. In this regard, the study of Hispanics in Chicago immediately suggests that distinctions must be made between different Hispanic groups in future research. Soccer is common to South Americans and Mexicans, while baseball is more common in the Caribbean and in Mexico but is relatively unknown in South America. Although these groups share characteristics which distinguish them from whites and blacks, there are different patterns of activity particular to each ethnic subgroup.

Finally, the results of the present study have direct implications for resource managers in central cities. The Chicago parks included in the study were by and large constructed at the same point in time and provide comparable facilities for the neighborhood populations—but they are utilized very differently by specific population subgroups. Significant here is the more intensive use of public recreation facilities by the rapidly growing Hispanic population. While Hispanics may have access to the facilities comparable to those provided other groups, it is incumbent upon resource managers to insure that additional maintenance be provided to compensate for greater wear. There may also be a need to provide additional park facilities in Hispanic neighborhoods to prevent crowding in existing areas. At the opposite extreme, we found parks located in black neighborhoods to be greatly under-utilized by the surrounding community, and it is up to resource managers to determine the causes of such under-use and develop appropriate strategies to insure that the facilities become more available to local populations.

REFERENCES

Alvirez, D., & Bean, F. D. (1976). The Mexican American family. In Mindel, C. H., & Habenstein, R. W. (eds.), *Ethnic families in America.* New York: Elsevier.

Anderson, E. (1978). *A place in the corner.* Chicago: University of Chicago Press.

Antunes, G., & Gaitz, C. M. (1975). Ethnicity and participation: a study of Mexican-Americans, whites, and blacks. *American Journal of Sociology, 80,* 1192–1221.

Benjamin, P. J., and O'Leary, J. T. (1980). Comparison of the outdoor recreation behavior of urban blacks and whites. Paper presented at the 1980 SPRE-NRPE Annual Meeting, Phoenix, Arizona.

Berger, B. (1970). Black culture or lower-case culture? p. 117–128 in Rainwater, L. (ed.), *Soul.* Chicago: Aldine.

Blackwell, J. (1975). The black community: diversity and unity. New York: Oxford University.

Blauner, R. (1969). Black culture: myth or reality? In Whitten, N., and Szwed, J. (eds), *Afro-American anthropology.* New York: Free Press.

Buchanan, T., Christensen, J. E., and Burdge, R. J. (1980). Social groups and the meaning of outdoor recreation activities. University of Illinois, Institute for Environmental Studies and Department of Leisure Sciences, Research Paper #321.

Cheek, N. H., and Field, D. R. (1976). *The social organization of leisure in human society.* New York: Harper and Row.

Cheek, N. H., Field, D. R., & Burdge, R. J. (1976). *Leisure and recreation places.* Ann Arbor: Science Publishers.

Cheek, N. H., and Burch, W. R. (1976). The social organization of leisure in human society. New York: Harper and Row.

Dwyer, J. F., Hutchison, R., & Wendling, R. C. (1982). Participation in outdoor recreation by white and black Chicago households. Chicago: U.S. Forest Service, North Central Experiment Station, mimeo.

Edwards, P. K. (1981). Race, Residence, and Leisure Style: Some Policy Implications. *Leisure Sciences, 4,* 95–112.

Flaundrau, C. (1964). *Viva Mexico.* Champaign: University of Illinois Press.

Golden, P. (1976). Choices and constraints in social research. p. 1–32 in Golden, P., (ed.), *The research experience.* Itasca, Illinois: Peacock Publishers.

Hannertz, Ulf. (1967). *Soulside.* New York: Columbia University Press.

Hutchison, R., and Fidel, K. (1984). Mexican American Recreation Activities. *Journal of Leisure Research, 16,* 344–349.

Jaffee, A. J., Cullen, R. M., & Boswell, T. D. (1980). *The changing demography of Spanish Americans.* New York: Academic Press.

Kelly, J. R. (1978). A revised paradigm of leisure choices. *Leisure Sciences, 3,* 129–154.

Kendall, M. G. (1955). *Rank order correlation methods* (Second Edition), London: Charles Griffin.

Kronus, S. (1971). *The black middle class.* Columbus, Ohio: Charles E. Merril Publishing Co.

Liebow, E. (1967). *Talley's corner.* New York:

McMillen, J. B. (1983). The social organization of leisure among Mexican-Americans. *Journal of Leisure Research, 15,* 164–173.

Meeker, J. W., Woods, W. K., & Lucas, W. (1973). Red, white, and black in the national parks, *North American Review,* 3–7.

Mirande, A. (1977). The Chicago family: a reanalysis of conflicting views. *Journal of Marriage and the Family, 27,* 680–689.

Penalosa, F. (1968). Mexican family roles. *Journal of Marriage and the Family, 27,* 680–689.

Pi-Sunyar, O. (1973). *Zarnora: change and continuity in a Mexican town.* New York: Holt, Rinehart, and Winston.

Reissman, L. (1950). *The lonely crowd: a study of the changing American character.* New Haven: Yale University Press.

Rubel, A. J. (1968). *Across the tracks: Mexican Americans in a west Texas city.* Austin: University of Texas Press.

Rutledge, A. J. (1985). *A visual approach to park design.* New York: John Wiley.

Snedecor, G. W., and Cochran, W. G. (1967). *Statistical Methods*. Ames, Iowa: Iowa State University. (Sixth Edition), (19).

Stamps, S. M., and M. B. Stamps. (1985). Race, Class, and Leisure Activities of Urban Residents. *Journal of Leisure Research, 17,* 40–56.

Tyre, G. L., and Siderelis, C. D. (1979). Instant count sampling: a technique for estimating recreation use in municipal settings. *Leisure Sciences, 2,* 173–184.

Washburne, R. (1978). Black under-participation in wildland recreation: alternative explanations. *Leisure Sciences, 1,* 175–189.

Wall, P. (1979). Cities, wild areas, and black leisure: in search of explanations for black/white differences in outdoor recreation. St. Paul, Minnesota: U.S. Forest Service.

Wendling, R. C. (1981). Black-white differences in outdoor recreation behavior: state-of-the-art and recommendations for management and research. p. 106–107, *Proceedings of the Conference on Social Research in National Parks and Wildland Areas.*

Williams, J. A., and Babchuk, N. (1973). Voluntary associations and minority status: a comparative analysis of anglo, black, and Mexican-Americans. *American Sociological Review, 38,* 637–646.

Wilson, W. J. (1980). *The declining significance of race.* Chicago: University of Chicago.

Yancey, W., Ericksen, and Juliani, R. (1976). Emergent ethnicity: a review and reformulation. *American Sociological Review, 41,* 391–403.

17 Inside Spatial Relations

Ellen J. Pader

This theoretical article discusses how environmental meaning results from the process of enculturation, the socialization that makes a person a member of a society, and acculturation, the process of becoming a member of a culture other than the culture one grew up in. The article provides examples of cultural change in traditional societies thus adding the important historical dimension to environmental meaning.

ABSTRACT

This paper explores the interaction between domestic spatial organization and the process by which individuals learn by the patterns of their society. Drawing from Humphrey's (1974) study of Mongolian nomads and Okely's (1983) ethnography of Gypsies in England, and using Giddens' theory of structuration as a theoretical under-pinning, it is argued that social and spatial relations play an active part in the creation, maintenance and transformation of conceptual frameworks used by the social actor to understand and organize the world. As such, spatial relations are seen not only as integral to social reproduction, but also as a subtle and powerful ethnic boundary.

1. INTRODUCTION [1]

"Space itself may be primordially given, but the organization, use, and meaning of space is a product of social translation, transformation and experience" (Soja, 1980, 210).

1.1 Spatiality

Spatial relations, the interplay of the organization, distribution and categorization of objects and people in space, are an integral part of the study of the social dimensions of the environment. For the spatial appropriation of a locale incorporates the structures and principles of a society or group.

Ellen J. Pader, "Inside Spatial Relations," from *Architecture Behaviour*, Vol. 4, no. 3, pp. 251–267. Copyright © 1988 by Architecture Behaviour. Permission to reprint granted by the publisher.

The study of spatial relations has as its base the study of the most commonplace, everyday actions of everyday people as well as less frequently performed activities. It tracks the movements and the concrete products which people negotiate in the performance of these movements. These products consist of mundane physically bounded locales, such as the home, as well as the more extraordinary, such as a religious edifice. They also include geographical areas—villages and towns—whether or not they are bounded physically by a wall, and areas less visibly bounded, such as a nation or the seating arrangements around a table. The study of spatial relations, as represented in any given context, leads to a deeper understanding of the social relations of the society of which they are an active part. In this paper I am concerned primarily with delving into spatial relations, or spatiality[2]—the arrangement of concrete entities in space with the concomitant, interdependent social relations of individuals and groups—as an essential element of social relations, including relations of power, and social change. In particular, I examine the role of spatiality in the enculturation process, a generative process which both enables and constrains social relations and reproduction.

1.2 Enculturation

Enculturation refers to the lifelong

> "process by which the individual, through informal and non-formal modes of cultural transmission, learns the language, the technological, socioeconomic, ideational, as well as the cognitive and emotional patterns of culture" (Wilbert, 1979, 8).

Non-formal modes of education include non-institutional, but systematic forms of learning for selected groups, such as explicitly being taught the skills appropriate to one's status. Informal education is acquired and accumulated

> "knowledge, skills, attitudes and insights from daily experiences and exposure to the environment" (Coombs & Ahmed, 1974, quoted in Wilbert, 1979, 8).

It is the informal mode of education which is emphasized here. All modes of education, however, are entwined in the production, maintenance and transformation of society.

1.3 Naturalization

An important aspect of enculturation is the concept of "naturalization". Naturalization is the process of making culture appear natural. We do this by organizing, categorizing and interpreting our world so as to make it appear universal, as part of a timeless and inevitable established or

---

1. Thanks to Arza Churchman and Denise Lawrence for commenting on an earlier draft of this paper. Thanks also to Edward W. Soja for support, comments, and setting space in its proper place. The interpretation remains my own. Both the Graduate School of Architecture and Urban Planning and the Institute of Archaeology at UCLA have continued to back my research endeavours.
2. I use "spatiality" interchangeably with "spatial relations". Soja defines spatiality as existing "in both substantial forms (concrete spatialities) and as a set of relations between individuals and groups" (1985, 92). Both terms connote not only the relation between objects and space, but also the objects which define any space.

natural order rather than as the cultural construct that it is (Barthes, 1972, 141–42). This is not a neutral manipulation of the physical environment but, as will be discussed in a later section, is actively implicated in the transformation of nature into a means by which relations of power may be masked and legitimated.

> "The space of physical nature is ... *appropriated* in the social production of spatiality—it is literally made social" (Soja, 1985, 93).

Material culture objects and their location in space are fundamental to this process (e.g., Hodder, 1982, 1987; Moore, 1986; Pader, 1982).

The major underlying presuppositions about the social dimensions of space upon which this paper is predicated are:

1. Spatiality is socially produced (see for example the articles in Gregory & Urry, 1985, and in particular the article by Soja);
2. Objects are neither randomly nor arbitrarily selected or positioned in space;
3. Space, objects and people give meaning to each other.

Using Giddens' theory of structuration (1979, 1981, 1984, 1985) as the theoretical underpinning, I argue that the organization of space is an integral part of the structuration of social life, that is, the process by which societies continually reproduce and reinterpret social relations across space and time. Spatial relations are inextricably intertwined with a society's underlying principles of organization, or structural principles (Giddens, 1979, 1984). These concepts will be discussed in a subsequent section of the paper.

The specific context, or locale, which is analyzed here is the home. As Giddens argues, to understand the rules and practices of a society, one must first understand the individuals who comprise that society and their routinized, daily behaviour as integral parts of the "social settings which they confront in their day-to-day lives" (1984, 117). The home setting is the ideal forum for the unselfconscious, everyday behaviour that is required, and for the learning of that behaviour (Goffman, 1959; Okely, 1983). The home is a prime and primary local for enculturation and hence for the reproduction and transformation of society (Bourdieu, 1977; Donley, 1982).

It is in the home that we develop many of our conceptual frameworks. It is largely here that we develop our sense of order and learn how to categorize our world. As Saegert noted,

> "The way we live in our homes reflects, expresses and forms the social relationships among household members, kin, neighbors and even more distant social partners" (Saegert, 1985, 292).

For these reasons, the home is often considered a microcosm of the sociopolitical environment, an important means by which to bridge the gap between the analysis of atomistic individual behaviour and the analysis of the extra domestic, social world (Schminck, 1984; Yanagisako, 1979). Following Kuper's (1972) concepts, the home, as the physical base for much family interaction, contains a "condensation of values"; it is through the mediation of the individual household members that the "politics of space" are played out. Yet because of the routinized, everyday and taken-for-granted nature of the organization of people and actions within the physical home, the inhabitants are often unable to verbalize the meaning of their spatial organization (Bourdieu,1979, 134, note 3; Okely, 1983, 78). Nor is there a single, "real" or "true" set of meanings and values embedded in the home; but rather a multitude of interrelated interpretations depending on the perspective of the individual (Churchman & Sebba,1983; Hodder, 1986).

2. SOCIAL AND SPATIAL RELATIONS

People produce space in an image of themselves and of their place in society. They create physically and/or symbolically bounded areas, organize people and objects within them and allocate uses to those areas which make sense within their general conceptual framework—a culturally constructed, ordered framework. Any concrete object or concept which disrupts the framework by which people classify matter falls into Douglas' definition of dirt as "matter out of place" (1966, 35). That which is out of place, which makes no sense within one's categorizations of the world, appears dirty and polluting. Such "dirty" matter comes to connote danger and, as such, is powerful and becomes a powerful taboo (Douglas, 1966, 94). With respect to western homes, this perhaps explains why we are hesitant to put kitchen items in the bathroom. Is it truly dangerous to one's health to eat in the bathroom—or only to one's culturally constructed sense of propriety, and therein lies the danger? And why, as will be discussed later, do Gypsies in England not only refuse to eat in a room containing a toilet, but won't even allow a toilet and food in the same physical structure? What is the purpose of this ordering and re-ordering of experience and the environment? And what are the implications of the fact that one person's or society's dirt is another's order?

To understand and explain the organizational principles and the symbolic order underlying spatiality and other facets of society, be it industrialized western or non-industrialized non-western society, I turn to Giddens' theory of structuration for a conceptual framework (Giddens, 1979, 1981, 1984, 1985). His perspective provides insight into the processes by which people, objects and space give meaning to one another and enable a cohesive system of social relations and social change, with transformational properties. This discussion of structuration is not a critique of the theory, but a discussion of the points most relevant for understanding the role of domestic objects and spatial relations in the enculturation and naturalization processes.

Giddens asserts that space and time cannot be treated as "mere environments of action" (Giddens, 1985, 265). The organization and use of space is not a reflector or by-product of culture/environment, but is inextricably and actively intertwined with the fabric of social life. Society functions as a dynamic, chronic and spatial symbolic system which can only be understood in a spatial-temporal context.

In order to clarify this perspective and explore the enculturative aspect of the physical domestic environment, I draw from and develop two primary ethnographies. These are Caroline Humphrey's short, but insightful, article "Inside a Mongolian Tent"(1974) based on the research of Russian ethnographers and Judith Okely's study of Gypsies in England, "The Traveller-Gypsies" (1983). These studies deal with the normative forces underlying individual action, but the authors present an historical perspective which enables a greater depth of understanding of the conglomerate.

Both the Mongolians and the Gypsies are nomads. The Gypsies move within the realm of, and in opposition to, the dominant industrialized English culture and society, while retaining their separate identity. The Mongolians live on the Asian steppes and, until the early 1920s were part of a feudal mode of production. Unlike the Gypsies, they do not live in opposition to a larger geographically determined society, but have become part of it, adapting many of the latter's values and actions to a new mode of life. Both studies demonstrate that when a subordinate group adapts aspects of the dominant society's culture, the adaptation is not haphazard, but is incorporated into their material representation of the sociopolitical world, with the home as a major focus of that world.

3. THE MONGOLIAN *GER*

> "It is because the practice of categorising social relationships by manipulating objects in the space of the tent still occurs, that we can know certain social changes are taking place" (Humphrey, 1974, 275).

The 1921 socialist revolution in Mongolia changed the traditional way of life for the pastoral, nomadic population. The government named progress as the first order of business; with progress defined in part as egalitarian gender relations, greater emphasis on the rights and upbringing of children in their role as the hope of the future, and a move from a religious (Buddhist) society to a state society. According to Humphrey, there is evidence of continuing success of material and administrative goals in the transition from a pre-revolutionary feudal state to a socialist one, but less is known about the success in another, less easily measurable goal—the transformation of social relations.

In order to analyze the progress of social transformation, travellers' records dating back to the 13th century were examined by Russian ethnographers. These show a consistency over time and across the steppes in where objects are positioned in the *ger*, or tent—the parents' bed is always along the centre of the eastern part of the tent—and how objects and people are categorized by the Mongolians according to their positioning. Not only does each object have its prescribed position, but its categorization also helps define social relations through establishing who is associated with the object and whether it is in the part of the tent deemed male and ritually pure (the western half); female, dirty and impure (the eastern half); *xoimor* or honorific and upper (the back half); or junior, lower status (the front half near the entrance). The male section has higher status than the female section, and the upper quadrant formed by the intersection of the male and honorific halves is the highest status area of all (See Figure 1)[3].

A system of categorization still persists in Mongolian *gers*, which led ethnographers to realize that one could learn about current social relations, and by extension, about changing dynamics since the pre-1921 era by comparing the patterns of the old and new systems. Of particular interest were deviations from the traditional pattern and additions to it—or, in other words: to what degree has the overall form remained stable while the contents changed, and what is the significance of any such change, or lack there of? For example, portable sewing machines are now commonly found in *gers*. Consistently, they are found firmly ensconced on the female side, among

---

3. Vreeland's (1954) study of the Mongolians, although based on the memories of three Mongolians from different communities who had lived in the United States for between three and 20 years, shows a remarkable similarity (1954, 57). There are certain variations from Humphrey's descriptions, more in the seating arrangements than in the object positioning. However it is not always clear whether Vreeland's informants were talking about the pre- or post-1921 arrangements, nor how accurate their memories were.

the woman's domestic implements, "merged into traditional categories" (Humphrey, 1974, 275). Here, the form is clearly retained while a new object is merged into the pre-existing symbolic order.

Similarly, with the revolution came a new status for children. This too is manifested in the categorization of objects and space: no longer do children sleep on the floor at the head of their parents' bed, the latter perhaps symbolizing the children's lack of individual identity separate from their parents. They now have a bed on the male side of the tent, in the position previously reserved for male guests of junior status. There might even be a curtain around the bed for privacy, a new concept. Thus, by relocating the children within the well-defined categorization system, the new role and higher status of children is objectified, while concurrently helping to change the meaning of that area. Concomitantly came a state emphasis on hygiene and washing oneself: for the first time, a washstand and bucket appeared in the front near the door. This is the first instance of an area equally accessible to all. These objectifications of the social and cultural context are more than a reflection or description of the old and new orders but, I would argue, are essential for the successful implementation of the new order via their participation in the processes of structuration.

4. THE THEORY OF STRUCTURATION

A major facet of Giddens' theory of structuration is that any symbolic system must be considered as inextricably related to ideology as a means by which sectional interests of a group are presented as universal interests and legitimated. Unlike traditional structural and semiotic perspectives, but like post-structural and "second-wave" semiotic ones (Hebidge, 1979), signs are not considered to be arbitrary nor of fixed meaning. They can only be interpreted from the perspective of the total social context, with that interpretation being biased by the perspective of whomever is doing the interpreting. An individual's interpretation is influenced by her/his place within the society that produced the signs, or from her/his relations to the society as an outsider. Thus, the methodological starting point of this approach, like that of other generative theories (such as Bourdieu, 1977) is to remove the emphasis from the end point, from the sign, and transfer it to the act of sign formation itself, to the rules by which signs are generated.

4.1 Terminology

Like many theorists, Giddens refines and redefines some key terms in order to develop a specific connotation (see Giddens, 1984, for a glossary of his terminology). The *locale* in which any interaction occurs sets

> "boundaries which help to concentrate action in one way or another" (Giddens, 1984, 375).

Signification is the theory by which individuals code signs as part of the symbolic order. *Signs* such as language, objects or the placement of objects in space, are the main elements of signification, while codes are the "structural properties of social systems" (Giddens, 1979, 99). That is, codes are part of the normative forces by which rules are generated and society reproduced, with examples of structural properties being family patterns and economic units (1984, 165). *Rules* are not the same as norms, in that rules are not formalized prescriptions such as the rules that guide a game. Rather, rules form the basis of meaning and sanctioning of social conduct from which individuals draw in their daily actions by putting boundaries on actions. They both enable and constrain action, but do not function as an absolute, inviolable edict. Through the repeated and routinized actions and interpretations of individuals, rules are created and reproduced, but not necessarily in the same form as they started (1984, 18). As in the game of operator ("Chinese whispers" in England), in which a phrase is whispered from person to person, the phrase that starts and the phrase that ends is never the same, yet the players think that they're reproducing the phrase exactly. The implication is that there is a recursive relationship between rules and practice, between the ways in which, for example, the family pattern is manifest and reproduced and the pattern itself. The following example will clarify these points.

In the Mongolian case, part of the theory of coding/signification by which the family pattern (the structural property) is reproduced includes appropriate seating of individuals according to socially significant positions and relations. The seating arrangements become the rules by which practice becomes, in essence, institutionalized in their seeming "everydayness" or "naturalness." When the locale of the children's sleeping area (the sign) moved from the impure, lower status female side on the floor by the parents to the pure, higher status male side (in some "radically modern" families, the children's bed replaces the Buddhist altar in the *xoimor*, the sacred part of the *ger*), the signification of each of the areas and roles also changed. As a sign's meaning changes, they do not do so in isolation; as an integral part of the symbolic order, the other signs with which it interacts also undergo alteration. In this case, while the children's status rises, the relative, official power position relegated to adult males lessens.

Corresponding to the emphasis on children as "the future", female and male children are no longer distinguishable according to seating position; they are now treated as one category, not two categories, female child and male child. Inherent in these changing seating positions are changing social relations and thereby changing relations of power. Thus, embedded in any structure of signification and the rules underlying it are hierarchies such as gender/age relations or economic inequalities—as well as the mechanism of their legitimation.

4.2 Social Systems

Central to this theory is the concept of the knowledgeable agent, the individual as capable of reflexively monitoring action, as opposed to the concept of person as a robot, glued to a matrix of action which they can know only implicitly and from which they cannot readily depart. Following from this, Giddens' concept of *social system* includes the individuals who form a group. Social systems are the

> "patterning of social relations across time-space, understood as *reproduced practices* ... (they are) widely variable in terms of the degree of 'systemness' they display and rarely have the sort of internal unity which may be found in physical and biological systems" (1984, 377, my emphasis).

4.3 Structure

Structure is used in this theory as a "memory trace" (1984, 377) which exists

> "paradigmatically, as an absent set of differences, 'present' only in their instantiation, in the *constituting moments* of social systems" (1979, 64, my emphasis).

As with rules, this is a notion connected to a chronic, dynamic movement in space and time; to an existence which is both dependent on individual action and knowledge, but which recursively is also enmeshed within that knowledge.

4.4 Signs, Meaning, and Change

Each of these elements—locale, signification, signs, coding, social systems and structures—is actively engaged in the definition of the other elements. The corollary of this is that signs and the rules by which they are formed are generative, they could not be static. The transformational possibilities are ever present in that they are socially produced and reproduced; they exist only inasmuch as they are used and reused by people—they cannot exist in a vacuum. Something has no meaning on its own, but only acquires meaning by use and by its relation to other things, by what it is not, by difference. The implication is that meaning depends on context and interpretation (this will be discussed in more detail later).

Something as common to us as books become a powerful sign of social change in the context of the Mongolian nomads. As Humphrey states (1974, 275):

> "In former times, books were appropriate only for lamas and senior men, since they were seen as holy receptacles for truth and sacred history. They were kept in the senior male part of the *xoimor*, if not on the Buddhist altar itself; and, wrapped in several layers of silk, they were read only on special occasions. Women were forbidden to read them. There was a saying, 'For a woman to look at a book is like a wolf looking at a settlement'. But since the revolution, literacy has been one of the most important government policies and now virtually all families possess some books. These are kept together on a shelf by the head of the parents' bed on the woman's side."

Here then, there is a change in the value and meaning of books (the sign), and the locales in which they were and are now positioned. With the same action, there is a simultaneous raising of women's position and a greater interaction of women with the world outside the family (this is only one of several indications of such a change; also see Vreeland, 1954, 55, on the changing status of women). Previously, the head of the parents' bed was used for the children to sleep and to store the women's hats. Here the social system is seen as being in flux by reference to the new practices, and recursively, it is by virtue of such actions as the repositioning of the material object/sign that the system is able to change successfully.

4.5 Duality of Structure

With the emphasis put on action in this theory, signs cannot be viewed as merely passive conveyors of communication, a sort of shorthand, as in conventional structuralism and semiotics. Rather, a sign, in being an element of signification, takes on the property of referring

> "to the structural features of social systems, drawn upon and reproduced by actors in the form of *interpretative* schemes" (Giddens, 1979, 98, my emphasis).

Thus, since signs are fundamental aspects of signification, there is a constant interplay between individual action and the theory of coding. In terms of the Mongolians, it is on account of this generative, interpretative property of signs that the structure is sufficiently flexible to enable new meanings that correspond with changing external conditions.

This recursive property of signification—the interdependency of action, sign formation and structure—in conjunction with the communicative aspect of signs, is what Giddens labels the *duality of structure*. This concept is at the core of the theory of structuration and, as will be seen, forms part of its definition. Structure, as in the duality of structure, is both

> "the medium and the outcome of the conduct it recursively organizes"(1984, 374).

As stated earlier, rules and practices can only exist in conjunction with one another. This means that the actors act and react, they interpret the codes or rules according to the situation (the context), individual predilection and understanding of the rules. For example, it is commonly recognized that one knows to act a certain way in one's own home, and in different ways in a close friend's or a superior's home, or a religious edifice. Yet exactly how one acts will depend on many factors, including the desire to obey or deviate from the rules to demonstrate one's attitude toward and about the situation. This is no different for the Mongolians who know their place, literally and figuratively; the books and seating arrangement in the *ger* also gain their effectiveness by virtue of the duality of structure. As stated earlier, where a child sits is both part of the message, the medium, as well as being the message, the outcome.

4.6 Rules and Practice

If people alter their behaviour in a given situation and, say, find it permissible to sit in a different area, the rules are in the process of reinterpretation. Not all change is intentional; the unintended consequences of action and varying degrees of competence on the part of individuals also can implement social transformations. The implication is that

> "Social systems are not constituted of roles, but of (reproduced) practices; and it is practices, not roles, which (via the duality of structure) have to be regarded as the 'points of articulation' between actors and structures" (Giddens, 1979, 118).

4.7 Structural Principles

The codes by which meaningful interaction can occur are possible because they are embedded in the enculturation process, in the processes of informal and non-formal learning. Understanding comes not just from the end results, for example from the particular object itself or the positioning of objects, but from the principles of organization which underlie the use and signification of those objects and their organization, and which thereby legitimate them. These principles of organization of society are *structural principles*. Some examples of structural principles which might be active in the organization of society are progress, individuality, communality, sedentarism, nomadism, urban and rural. All these principles of organization engender relations of power and domination. Different societies demonstrate different degrees of interest in any particular principle of organization, with the specific mode of manifestation being both culturally specific and affecting all levels of the societal totality. Structural principles can be known either tacitly, as what Giddens refers to as practical consciousness, or explicitly, as discursive consciousness. These principles of organization are indeed open to studied, conscious alteration by the participants of a society. The exploration of the structural principles and the results of action, together, make it possible to move beyond the superficial inconsistencies and into the motivating forces.

4.8 Structuration Defined

To finally get to the term which gives Giddens' theory its name, *structuration* refers to the process by which societies constantly reproduce themselves, re-producing and re-presenting the structural principles, as if in a spiralling motion, never quite returning to the place where they started. Giddens defines structuration as

> "The structuring of social relations across time and space, in virtue of the duality of structure" (1983, 376).

Structure, it will be remembered, is not a grid or pattern limiting action, it is a set of rules and resources from which individuals "draw" in some manner in the moment of its utilization. Again, this points to the notion that the substance of social codes, such as a family pattern, has a normative force, although the codes themselves are not normative. In this way rules, which form the basis of meaning and are routinized and reinterpreted by individuals in daily life, are both constitutive and regulating, enabling and constraining.

Within the theory of structuration, objects and spatiality must be interpreted in their own contexts. The same object may have different meanings in different locales: a certain bench style becomes a pew in the context of a religious edifice and causes a different reaction than the same bench—no longer a pew—in a train station. Signs and symbolic systems must then be considered within their contextual setting and be open to multiple interpretations and meanings. Symbolism and the theory of sign coding function as a means of communication but, more, they have a constitutive function by which they are interwoven with the ideological dimension. While often appearing and "feeling" neutral and devoid of deeper sociopolitical consequences, the very fact that coding systems are produced within social contexts means that they interact with the structures by which relations of power are enabled and reproduced:

> "Whenever a sign is present, ideology is present too" (Volosinov, 1973, 10).

How does this relate to the study of spatiality? In the Mongolian example, social relations are a motivating force underlying the spatial organization within the *ger*. The people, objects and specific locations become the signs, the pattern of positioning the theory of coding. The rules governing the spatial organization envelop the social relations. They include and legitimate relations of power, while hiding their cultural origins. The physical organization of people according to gender exemplifies the concept of duality of structure: it is the medium by which conduct is organized while simultaneously being the outcome of that conduct. Through an understanding of the rules—be it implicit or explicit—through the process of enculturation, the individuals know how to set up their home. It is one of the important ways they learn to categorize their world and their place in it. This point was illustrated when the children of both sexes, as the hope of the future in an atmosphere of progress, moved from the traditional mother's side to the father's side, with the changing connotations embedded in each side. Thus, the organization and categorization of space in the home is a fundamental part of the structuration of social life.

Concomitantly, if a particular organization of space is seen as valid, proper and appropriate, it is because it represents the expected behaviour, based on previous experience. Over time, the structuring "feels" right because it meshes with other signs within the total symbolic order, while recursively and cyclically being the medium of its own signification. Hence, the physical and the conceptual structurings come to appear as part of an established and natural order, reinterpreting and reproducing the entire system of signification.

The Gypsies in Britain have a different interpretation of the world and of their place in it. The following ethnographic study presents a second case, with the emphasis being on the structural and symbolic underpinnings which interact with spatial choices.

5. THE TRAVELLER-GYPSIES

> "The sedentary society seems to need to identify Gypsies in terms of spatial location. Defining persons who travel is among other things an attempt to pin them down in space. The trouble is, Gypsies are moving through space" (Okely, 1979, 82).

The Gypsies not only have a different concept of spatial organization than the dominant British in whose physical territory they dwell, but that difference is one of their most outstanding structural principles. Many of those differences relate to the home and are

> "allied to daily, often commonplace practices (which are) concerned, for example, with eating, washing, the use of space and the placing of objects in that space" (Okely, 1983, 78).

The particular aspect of the coding system which will be explored is that which relates to their concepts of cleanliness and pollution. Unless otherwise specified, all data derive from Okely (1983).

Until the mid-nineteenth century most Gypsies traveled with pack horses and tents. From then until the 1950s most used horse-drawn wagons, built by *gorgios*, or non-Gypsies. There are five basic styles of wagons, plus an additional sleeping cart used by some families (Huth, 1940; Ward-Jackson & Harvey, 1986). Interestingly, but not surprisingly, the interior organization is essentially identical in all types.

Now most Gypsies live in trailers pulled by a motor vehicle, enabling greater mobility through the British landscape. The trailers are either bought with ready-made interiors or, preferably, are custom designed. When ready-made, certain alterations are made immediately in order to avoid polluting behaviour: the sink is covered with formica and replaced by two bowls which can be distinguished easily from one another, one for washing dishes and dish towels and the other for personal washing. The bowl for personal washing is kept physically separate from dish washing and cooking. If a family can afford two trailers, the activities related to eating—cooking and dish washing—are relegated to a different trailer than the activities related to personal washing. In the theory of structuration, the bowls and their placement are elements of signification, and function as part of a complex of normative forces through which rules can be generated and society reproduced; the bowls do more than just differentiate two types of washing.

Following this sense of ordering, toothbrushes and hand soap are never kept near the dish washing area. It is interesting that soap, which Gorgios see as the ultimate source of cleanliness, is to the Gypsies potential dirt when out of its appropriate categorical location. In Douglas' terms, it becomes "matter out of place" (1966, 35) and hence taboo. In the Gypsy signification system, in the context of the personal washing area, hand soap is clean, while in the context of the dish washing area, it is dirty; there a different type of soap is clean.

Within their emic categorization, in ready-made trailers the bathing/toilet area is converted to a closet to avert polluting behaviour (Okely, 1983, 86).[4] Other activities are allocated to specified areas, following from the same underlying principles of organization and as part of the same system of signification. Conflicting constructs, or "structural contradictions" (Giddens, 1984, 198) between Gypsies and Gorgios, that affect attitudes toward hand soap and proper toilet location, toward what is considered to be "naturally" right and appropriate, together demonstrate to the Gypsy the inherent dirtiness of Gorgios (Okely, 1983, 82).

Okely argues that

"the primary pollution taboos (are) associated with the symbolic separation of the inside of the body. The other taboos follow from this" (1983, 83).

Hence, a major structural principle which enables the maintenance of the structural property of Gypsy ethnicity is the separation of inside and outside. Anything which goes into the body must be clean, what is outside is less important. Clothes washing takes place outside the trailer, for clothes, which touch the outside body, must not be conceptually nor literally mixed with food preparation which takes place inside the trailer. The inside of the trailer is kept spotless, while the periphery of the Gypsy encampment might be strewn with rubbish and debris from metal scrapping. The trailers are organized in a radiating pattern with the central, communal area of the "star" being

---

4. In a recent book, *English Gypsy Caravans,* Ward-Jackson & Harvey (1986) discuss the "deficiencies" of the horse-drawn wagon (and by extension, the trailer), from a thoroughly ethnocentric perspective: "Compared with the house dweller, the inmates of a van do suffer two deficiencies—the privy is external, and a bath may be had only by friendly invitation, resort to a public bath house, or by opportunistic improvisation. But there are compensations, and no domicile is perfect" (1986, 74). From an emic perspective, these are hardly "deficiencies," but matters of carefully considered choice. It is also interesting to note that the Gypsies use the term "trailer" in contradistinction to the English term "caravan."

an extension of the trailer, of Gypsy ethnicity; hence it is also kept spotless. Gorgio planners once designed a permanent Gypsy site with toilets located in the centre; not surprisingly it was rather unsuccessful (Okely, 1983, 88). The food which goes into the body and that which comes out are appropriately separated by space and physical boundaries.

The Gypsies often comment on how the Gorgios have beautifully tended gardens outside, but despair of the condition inside the home and refuse to drink from a cup in a Gorgio home. One sign of the "dirtiness" of Gorgio homes is that they keep rubbish of all types in the home. Even when they move into houses, Gypsies tend not to keep waste baskets inside the house. As argued earlier, to do otherwise would be to confuse categories, to violate the coding system and thereby to cause all havoc to organizational principles, creating an environment of danger.[5]

Within the Gypsy categorization system, privacy from neighbouring Gypsies is not an important issue. Despite the proximity of trailers, curtains are usually kept open day and night (Okely, 1983, 88). One exception is that when a woman breastfeeds she might close the curtains so that no man can see (ibid., 298). The trailer consists of only one "room", making it impossible for individuals to retire to their own bedrooms. This is yet one more way in which the structural principle of sharing with one's kin is continually recreated and reinforced. Such a structural principle might make it more difficult, even incomprehensible, to put an elderly parent into a home with strangers when all your life your system of enculturation has emphasized constant interactions and sharing rather than the individuality implied by owning a room. Elderly Gypsies are taken care of by families, although recently more are moving onto permanent sites, in opposition to the fundamental principle of nomadism (ibid., 160).

Concepts of clean and dirty are coded into the Gypsies' notion of women as potentially polluted and polluting; their underwear, which touch their body, cannot be hung on the line in the open to dry nor washed in the same bowl as men's clothes, for a dress could pollute them. The gender relations are further seen in that women and men use separate bowls for washing, the women's having the potential of polluting the male, and that one of the most common reasons for preferring segregated toilets was to prevent men from possible pollution by seeing a woman exposed (Okely, 1983, 208).

Death and birth are also polluting activities, relegated to areas outside the trailer complex. In earlier times, birth took place in a tent on the periphery of the encampment and all utensils therein were burnt, as was the wagon or trailer in which death occurred (ibid., 210). Nowadays the Gypsies consign these activities to Gorgio-run hospitals, thereby maintaining the symbolic order, albeit through a reinterpretation of the details. Having the Gorgios deal with death reinforces their attitudes towards both death and the Gorgios.

Although I have simplified a complex conceptual framework in this discussion, it should be clear that spatial relations in the Gypsy material life are integrally intertwined with the process of enculturation and the naturalization of the cultural environment. To keep scrap paper inside the home would be as "uncomfortable" and "unnatural" as to have the toilet, cooking and washing facilities within one structure. The structural principles and the symbolic order underlying spatial

---

5. Similarly, Kent found that when Navajos moved from traditional ramadas to tract houses, they continued to organize space according to their own conceptual framework, not according to that of the Euro-American house builders (1984, 185); while Pader found a similar interplay of spatial and social relations among rural Mexicans moving to Los Angeles (1987). Conversely, Moore found that when young Marakwet (Kenya) men explicitly want to break with tradition, they consciously reorganize space (1986, 131).

relations in and around the home are integral elements of how Gypsies learn the importance of ethnic identity. Spatial relations are part of the Gypsies' self-ascribed identity, a fundamental means of differentiating themselves from the Gorgio and intrinsic part of the structuration of their daily life.

6. RECAPITULATION

The preceding discussion on the theory of structuration formed the basis for interpreting the social meaning and production of spatiality amongst the Mongolian nomads and the Gypsies in England. The following are some of the basic properties and key points underlying this interpretation:

There is an inextricable, recursive relationship between ideology, action and spatiality—including objects, the organization of objects and the relations between the individual responsible for the selection and organization of objects. Spatiality is not merely a residue of action, but, by virtue of the duality of structure, spatiality is an integral part of social action and ideology, as medium and outcome.

1. Signs are not arbitrary; they are appropriate within their context of use.
2. Symbolic meanings are only interpretable by reference to their context of use. Hence, form and content are inseparable.
3. The same object, or combination of objects, may have a different meaning depending on the context and the person doing the interpreting.
4. The entire structure of signification is important for interpreting structural principles: the specific object/sign used, how it is used and the fact that something is positioned in a specific way are all essential elements in the categorization of the world.
5. The structuration of social life exists within a spatial-temporal context.

The implications of these points is that, when examined from the perspective of structuration, spatiality is an integral part of the total societal context and as such plays a critical role in the formation and reformation, interpretation and reinterpretation of society.[6] As Soja states (1985, 92):

"Spatiality is portrayed as a social product and an integral part of the material constitution and structuration of social life. Above all else, this means that spatiality cannot be appropriately understood and theorized apart from society and social relationships and, conversely, that social theory must contain a central and encompassing spatial dimension."

---

6. Not included in the discussion are the relations of the family's life cycle to spatial relations nor the need to delve into class differences when appropriate for the society in question. These are areas requiring further research.

7. CONCLUSION

Any initial ambiguities concerning the title of the paper, "Inside Spatial Relations," should now be resolved. In the exploration of the structural principles by which the Mongolian nomads and Gypsies in England organize and reproduce their societies, and as a means of exploring the structuration of their social lives, I have concentrated on the following:

1. The primary data are the organization and use of the internal domestic arena, that is, of the home;
2. I am looking inside spatial relations to discover their deeper socio-political meanings and their correlations with social relations; and
3. because spatial relations are a powerful form of enculturation "inside" also connotes delving into the process by which people, as individuals and as part of a larger socio-cultural process, learn, use, interpret and reinterpret the values and codes of their culture—whether or not they adhere to them or use them as a base from which to deviate is another matter.

Spatial relations are an integral part of the process by which people "naturalize" their environment, legitimate power relations through masking cultural constructions and making their own social life appear timeless, inevitable and proper in contradistinction to people from different backgrounds. Like other non-verbal actions, spatial organization reinforces culture by seeming to be naturally determined, rather than socially produced. Objects and their spatial organization within the domestic dwelling are active and integral elements in the lifelong process of enculturation. By continually repeating and thereby transforming these behaviours in everyday actions, members of a group are actively part of the spatial-temporal process by which individuals enable society to reproduce itself, affecting and being affected by how people perceive themselves and their place in the world. In the home, the recursive relationship between ideology, action and spatial relations is intensified, with each giving meaning to the other, as both the medium and outcome of social reproduction.

BIBLIOGRAPHY

BARTHES, R. (1972), "Mythologies" (Paladin, London).
BOURDIEU, P. (1977), "Outline of a Theory of Practice" (Cambridge University Press, Cambridge).
BOURDIEU, P. (1979), The Kabyle House or the World Reversed, in Bourdieu, P., Ed., "Algeria 1960" (Cambridge University Press, Cambridge).
COOMBS, P. H. & AHMED, M. (1974), "Attacking Rural Poverty: How Nonformal Education can Help" (Johns Hopkins University Press, Baltimore).
CHURCHMAN, A. & SEBBA, R. (1983), Women's Territoriality in the Home, in Safir, M., Mednick, M.T., Israeli, D. & Bernard, J., Eds., "Women's Worlds" (Praeger, New York).
DONLEY, L. (1982), House Power: Swahili Space and Symbolic Markers, in Hodder, I., Ed., "Symbolic and Structural Archaeology" (Cambridge University Press, Cambridge).
DOUGLAS, M. (1966), "Purity and Danger" (Ark, London).
GIDDENS, A. (1979), "Central Problems in Social Theory: Action, Structure and Contradiction in Social Analysis" (Macmillan, London).
GIDDENS, A. (1981), "A Contemporary Critique of Historical Materialism" (University of California Press, Los Angeles).

GIDDENS, A. (1984), "The Constitution of Society" (University of California Press, Los Angeles).

GIDDENS, A. (1979), "Central Problems in Social Theory: Action, structure and contradiction in social analysis" (Macmillan, London).

GIDDENS, A. (1985), Time, Space and Regionalisation, in Gregory, D., & Urry, J., Eds., "Social Relations and Spatial Structures" (St. Martin's Press, New York).

GOFFMAN, E. (1959), "The Presentation of Self in Everyday Life" (Anchor Books, New York).

GREGORY, D. & URRY, J., Eds., (1985), "Social Relations and Spatial Structures" (St. Martin's Press, New York).

HEBIDGE, D. (1979), "Subculture: The Meaning of Style" (Methuen and Company Ltd., London).

HODDER, I. (1982), "Symbols in Action" (Cambridge University Press, Cambridge).

HODDER, I. (1986), "Reading the Past: Current approaches to interpretation in archaeology" (Cambridge University Press, Cambridge).

HODDER, I. (1987), The Contextual Analysis of Symbolic Meanings, "The Archaeology of Contextual Meanings" (Cambridge University Press, Cambridge).

HUTH, F. G. (1940), Gypsy Caravans, *Journal of the Gypsy Lore Society,* 19 (1940).

HUMPHREY, C. (1974), Inside a Mongolian Tent, *New Society,* 30 (1974), 273–275.

KENT, S. (1984), "Analyzing Activity Areas: An Enthnoarchaeological Study of the Use of Space"(University of New Mexico Press, Albuquerque).

KUPER, H. (1972), The Language of Sites in the Politics of Space," *American Anthropologist,* 74 (1972), 411–425.

MOORE, H. (1986), "Space, Text and Gender: An Anthropological Study of the Marakwet of Kenya"(Cambridge University Press, Cambridge).

OKELY, J. (1979), An Anthropological Contribution to the History and Archaeology of an Ethnic Group, in Burnham, B., Ed., "Space, Hierarchy and Society" (BAR International Series 59, Oxford).

OKELY, J. (1983), "The Traveller-Gypsies" (Cambridge University Press, Cambridge).

PADER, E. J. (1982), "Symbolism, Social Relations and the Interpretation of Mortuary Remains" (BAR International Series 130, Oxford).

PADER, E. J. (1987), Social Construction of Domestic Space: A comparison of Mexican-American households. (Presented at the American Anthropological Association, Chicago).

SAEGERT, S. (1985), The Role of Housing in the Experience of Dwelling, in Altman, I. & Werner, C. M., Eds., "Home Environments" (Plenum Press, New York).

SCHMINCK, M. (1984), Household Economic Strategies: Review and research agenda, *Latin American Research Review,* 19 (1984), 87–101.

SOJA, E. W. (1980), The Socio-Spatial Dialectic, *Annals of the Association of American Geographers,* 70 (1980), 207–225.

SOJA, E. W. (1985), The Spatiality of Social Life: Towards a Transformative Retheorisation, in Gregory, D. & Urry, J., Eds., "Social Relations and Spatial Structures" (St. Martin's Press, New York).

VOLOSINOV, V. N. (1973), "Marxism and the Philosophy of Language" (Seminar Press, London).

VREELAND, H. H. in (1954), "Mongol Community and Kinship Structure" (Human Relations Area Files, New Haven).

WARD-JACKSON, C. H. & HARVEY, E. D. (1986), (2nd. ed.), "The English Gypsy Caravan: Its Origin, Builders, Technology and Conservation" (David & Charles, London).

WJLBERT, J. (1979), Introduction, in Wilbert, J., Ed., "Enculturation in Latin America: An Anthology"(UCLA Latin American Center Publications, Los Angeles).

YANAGISAKO, S. J. (1979), Family and Household: The Analysis of Domestic Groups, *Annual Review of Anthropology,* 8 (1979) 161–205.

18 Vernacular Architecture as an Expression of Its Social Context in Eressos, Greece

Eleftherios Pavlides and Jana E. Hesser

This chapter demonstrates the power of photographic elicitation in connecting architectural form with emic understandings, cultural perceptions, and historical meanings of the built environment by examining the changes of environmental meaning over hundred and fifty years in Eressos, Greece.

Anecdotes abound of architect-designed buildings in culturally foreign contexts that have gone unused, or that have been used in surprising and "unconventional" ways, or that have been extensively transformed by the inhabitants. Why does this happen? It is presumed that an understanding of the local cultural context, the local patterns of space use, or the local meaning attached to the visual forms of built objects could have prevented or ameliorated some of these architectural misadventures. We believe such understanding is possible and with this premise in mind, we set about to examine the built environment of a Greek island village. Our objective was to "see" that environment through the eyes of its inhabitants and to arrive at an understanding of its use and meaning as defined by those inhabitants.

We believe that the approach we adopted in studying this vernacular architectural setting represents a significant departure from much previous work. Most important, we sought to define significant visual categories and to understand the meaning attached to visual variation, as defined and understood by the inhabitants. We visually documented the environment as it appeared to us only as a necessary take-off point into this other reality. Second, we made an effort to document how the village architecture had changed through time, in a departure from many earlier studies which attribute a timeless quality to vernacular built form. Third, we collected detailed comparative data on a sample of buildings in order to describe variation, instead of describing a representative archetype as is often done. This chapter discusses the results of this study and identifies how these results can be of value to designers.

CULTURAL SETTING: ERESSOS, LESBOS

The island of Lesbos lies seven miles from the west coast of Asia Minor (Turkey). Eressos is located on the northern side of a fertile valley on the slopes of three hills which command a view of

Eleftherios Pavlides & Jana E. Hesser; Setha M. Low & Eric Chambers, eds., "Vernacular Architecture as an Expression of Its Social Context in Eressos, Greece," from *Housing, Culture and Design: A Comparative Perspective*, pp. 357–374. Copyright © 1988 by University of Pennsylvania Press. Permission to reprint granted by the publisher.

the Aegean Sea to the south. Like other settlements on Aegean islands, Eressos is located several miles inland from the sea which, in the past, was a source of pillagers. Most of its fifteen hundred inhabitants engage in pastoralism and agriculture and produce primarily for commercial markets but also for partial subsistence. A small percentage of men are in white-collar occupations (for example, the civil service or teaching), and some run small businesses (for example, stores, taxi services, coffee shops, or metalworks).

The village is ninety kilometers from Mytilini, the major port and city of Lesbos, and is connected to it by a road paved in the early 1970s. Taxis make frequent trips to Mytilini and there is a daily bus between the two places. Electricity was introduced into most homes in the 1960s, although some houses still exist without this amenity. Although interior plumbing is now being installed, most houses still obtain water either from a neighborhood spigot or from a spigot in the yard.

The village forms a compact settlement with well-defined borders and is surrounded by open fields and pasturage. Houses and yards, located immediately adjacent to one another, are clustered in residential islands separated by narrow cobblestone streets. Tall walls surround these residential islands and subdivide them into lots containing a yard and one or more buildings. Each lot with its yard and buildings belongs to a nuclear family, or a nuclear family and one set of grandparents.

The house, the yard, and the street in front of the house are the domain of women, their female friends, the elderly, and children. They are places of work, socializing, and child rearing. With the exception of going to work in the fields and going to church, women spend most of their time in their own homes and neighborhoods. By contrast, men spend little time at home or in their neighborhoods. For them, the house is a place to wash, eat, change clothes, sleep, and receive company. Only on formal occasions such as their namedays, an engagement, or a marriage will men stay home to participate in the celebration.

The residential islands surround a large open space, the central public square. While the public square is the heart, or nucleus, of the village which spreads out around it, there are other smaller squares and open spaces distributed throughout the village. Each one is a focal point for a neighborhood where neighbors (usually women and older people) may gather during the day. These neighborhoods are named and their general boundaries are known by the villagers.

The central square provides the focus for the men's primary place of social interaction. A large part of the central square is shaded by an enormous plane tree during the summer. The edges of this space are occupied by shops and public offices and by cafes that serve their customers on outdoor tables when the weather is good. The public square is occupied almost solely by men, and at times by children at play, usually boys. When not working, men spend as much of their time as possible in the public square and in the cafes. There they find entertainment, exchange information, conduct deals, seek employment, or hire laborers.

Women only timidly venture into this public space and only if they must. They recognize the public square as the domain of men. Rather than enter the public square themselves, women will send children to do errands or deliver messages to their husbands. If they must enter a shop or office on the public square, they will not cross the street to reach it, but will approach it by way of the skirting streets. Only when public events or festivities such as a wedding celebration are held in the public square do women freely enter it, but then, only accompanied by their husbands and families.

While recently there has been some "loosening" of this separation of public and private, male and female domains, in certain rural villages, by and large it characterizes the social structure of Greek village life.[1] It meant that we spent much of our time in those areas that are primarily the domain of women, and that women became our most numerous and most important informants.

METHODS

Theoretical Approach

Our theoretical approach was based on a sociolinguistic model. We considered this an appropriate model because our basic premise was that built form constitutes a system that depicts and conveys information for its community of users—it is a kind of communication system, or a kind of "language."

Sociolinguists strive for a study of language that depicts the full complexity of its actual use in society (Hymes 1974, 19). Sociolinguists examine language in the context of a speech community which shares rules for the conduct and interpretation of speech (Hymes 1974, 31). To understand the meaning of language in a particular community, it is studied in the context of actual communicative events (Hymes 1974, 16, 133).

Sociolinguistic research utilizes ethnographic methods and constructs both "emic" and "etic" accounts of Speech events. In anthropology, emic accounts of behavioral events are defined as those representing the insider's or actor's point of view, and etic ones represent an outsider's point of view. The etic account is considered useful as a preliminary grid which can be related to emic accounts and which can provide a framework for comparing different emic accounts. It is the emic account, however, that validates information by revealing, for example, how phonological features are relevant to the identification of cultural behavior (Hymes 1974, 11, 22).

To obtain the insider's point of view the sociolinguist conducts ethnographic research of speech events which includes simultaneous study of the circumstances of their occurrence, identity of participants, and features of few utterances themselves (Hymes 1974, 199). Sociolinguists also value a diachronic study of language, in the belief that understanding the way language has changed through time is an important aspect of understanding an existing speech community.

Sociolinguistics, or what might also be termed "socio-semiotics," provides a paradigm for combining ethnographic fieldwork with a detailed study of the form of meaningful sound (morphemes) in its social context. The same approach, when applied to a study of architectural form, generates "architectural semiotics," in the original sense of the word. As initially defined by De Saussure, semiotics meant the "empirical study of systems of signs within systems of use in actual communities," in contrast to its more common recent usage as the "study of systems of signs as codes alone" (Hymes 1974, 6).[2]

Taking the same approach that the sociolinguist takes to the study of language, we hypothesized that when vernacular architecture is examined from the point of view of an insider (the emic account), socially significant information known and shared by the inhabitants will be revealed. The etic account of a house (i.e., a description of its appearance, features, construction, and so on), though constituting necessary preliminary information, can only be assigned meaning through the collection of emic data.

To test the hypothesis, detailed documentation of house features and their variation (the etic account) had to be supplemented with information on how the members of the community perceive, categorize, and value house features. To achieve these objectives the anthropological methodology of participant observation and interview was combined with traditional architectural visual documentation of houses through measured drawings and extensive photography, and with interviews that included the use of slides as an eliciting device.

Drawing on the sociolinguistic model, we also felt it was vital to add a historical dimension to our study. In our view, social pressures are continually operating upon vernacular architectural form and decoration, not from some remote point in the past, but as an immanent social force acting in the living present (to paraphrase Labov [1983]), and so the meaning of architectural form for its inhabitants is also a dynamic changing one. As a result we added a diachronic element to our data collection to discover how the present built environment was created.

Data Collection

We studied Eressos during a continuous residence in the village from October 1977 to August 1978.[3] We spent the first three months obtaining census data and walking through the entire village identifying and making notes on a map about the visual diversity of houses. We frequently encountered residents and solicited from them information about village life and social structure, building practices, and the history of particular buildings and people. We documented visual observations with photographs and sketches, and we recorded and later transcribed the conversations and interviews we had with people who invited us into their homes. We became familiar with the local dialect which proved to be invaluable for our work. Using certain words from the local dialect indicated to informants that we did not have the prejudice against village life that is common among urban Greeks.

During the next five months of our stay, we studied thirty houses intensively. Although the sample was gathered by convenience, we attempted to include in it the full range of visual variation identified in our preliminary work. (In a subsequent survey of house types in the village, we found that our sample did contain representatives of each type in roughly the same proportion as they occurred in the village.) We systematically documented these houses with photographs, sketches, and drawings based on detailed measurements of all features of the house, including, for example, the dimensions of grooved moldings around wall cavities, the components of windows, and the size of door hinges. It usually took us two days to complete documentation of a single house. Throughout these months, we continued collecting information through unstructured interviews and participant observation, especially with the families whose houses we measured.

During our last months in Eressos, we conducted systematic interviews with the owners and residents of those houses we had measured. Using slides to elicit information, we showed each family pictures of its own house, as well as of the variety of house types and features found in the village. These interviews provided information about past and present construction practices, uses of the house, and village history; they also elicited revealing value-laden responses.

In this way we obtained explicit information about the use and meaning of particular spaces or architectural features for a particular group, in the present as well as in the past. At other times inferences about use and meaning could be made by relating characteristics of the people being interviewed, such as age, socioeconomic standing, gender, or gender of offspring, to their responses. The focus of our interest in these interviews was the respondent's familiarity with and associations elicited by the presented images; ability to name features, rooms, or elements and definition of appropriate uses or activities associated with the space. We reconstructed the present and past meaning of house form and decoration, and variations thereof, by looking for consistencies between reactions of respondents.[4]

RESULTS

In considering the results of our study, which are described below, we want to emphasize that these are findings that emerged from analysis of the data and which became accessible only because we approached our study of the built environment through the eyes of its inhabitants. We did not anticipate these results. We set out to determine only if the built environment possessed meaning for its users and if so, what that meaning was.

Time and Change

While vernacular architecture has most commonly been regarded as having a timeless, unchanging quality (Glassie 1968, 33; Dorson 1973, 13), the diachronic emphasis of our study revealed constant transformation through time in the architecture of Eressos. The existing buildings, and the memories of the inhabitants, allowed us to reconstruct the changing form and meaning of the village's architecture over the past 130 years. Within this time, we discerned three periods salient for the inhabitants which were also manifest in house form and decoration. We did not specify the periods according to our knowledge of history; instead, they emerged from the data and reflect the inhabitants' sense of time. These periods provide the context for other findings to be discussed.

Period I, from 1850 to 1889, is the earliest time for which we can decipher any information about houses, either from oral accounts or from securely dated existing buildings. During that time Eressos was part of the Ottoman Empire, and a small Turkish minority lived harmoniously with the predominantly Greek population of the village. A great earthquake in 1889 caused considerable destruction in Eressos and stimulated extensive construction and renovation. The earthquake now serves as a convenient marker of time: the villagers still refer to it in their conversations by pinpointing events as having occurred before or after it. They also identify houses that pre- and post-date the earthquake.

Period II bridges the time between the great earthquake of 1889 and the end of World War II in 1945. This was a time of rising nationalism as well as increasing identification with the Western world. During the last decade of the nineteenth century and the first decade of the twentieth, the idea that Greek political authority should replace Ottoman rule spread through the Greek populations of the Ottoman Empire including Lesbos. In 1912, the idea was realized and Lesbos became part of Greece. In the Balkan Exchange of 1922, an agreement was made between Greece and Turkey to exchange the Greek and Turkish populations within their borders. The Turkish minority of Eressos left and was replaced by Greek refugees from Asia Minor.

Period III extends from the end of World War II to the present. After the civil war, which was fought at the conclusion of World War II and which ended in 1949, there began a massive exodus from many rural areas of Greece, including Eressos, to major urban centers. A changing national economy has supported this abandonment of rural villages which has only now begun to wane. In the past thirty years Eressos has dwindled from 3,500 to its present size of 1,500 people.

Sensitivity to Distant Influences

Most commonly the stylistic inspiration for vernacular architecture has been said to derive from strictly indigenous sources (Jenkins 1973, 505; Evans 1973, 530).

However, we found primarily nonlocal sources inspiring or stimulating stylistic change in Eressos. The village has not existed in a vacuum—it has experienced the currents of social, political, economic, and architectural developments occurring elsewhere. While the loci generating these currents and the nature and degree of their impact on Eressos have changed over time, their influence has been persistent and significant.

During Period II, the source of influences upon Eressos shifted from the East to the West. Inspiration for prestigious visual form was derived more and more from the Greek mainland and Western Europe and less from Asia Minor, where economic and cultural ties had been maintained for centuries. These stylistic influences and changes anticipated and accommodated the new political, economic, and cultural order that followed the incorporation of Lesbos into the Greek state in 1912.

These new stylistic elements were derived from the neoclassic architecture of Athens and other mainland cities influenced by nineteenth-century European Greek revival architecture.[5] For example, plaster decorations of the fireplace and sacred corners began to incorporate neoclassical motifs such as triglyphs, corinthian columns, and dentines. Eastern decorative motifs, such as the heart shape, or Byzantine floral and leaf shapes, were eliminated. Neoclassic influences were also evident on the house exterior. Triglyphs and dentile decorations appeared under the eaves of some houses,[6] and allusions to a pediment on the frontal facade of other houses were suggested by the framing of the tiled roof to form a triangle. In one house, the stucco on the exterior corners was etched to resemble pilasters. Creating precise symmetry on the facade, rarely seen in earlier buildings, was another expression of this new sensibility.

The iconography of women's handiwork changed too, paralleling changes in the architecture. Patterns reflecting Greek national identity began to appear in carpets and other textiles. Figurative subjects depicting Greek folk tales, and the meander motif of ancient Greece, replaced abstract Eastern designs.

In Period III buildings have been modernized according to standards set by the architecture and life-style of Athens and other large cities. In earlier times, distant influences inspired new forms and decorative motifs in already existing elements (such as fireplaces). Now totally new elements and new spatial arrangements are being introduced as well, and old elements eliminated.

The new stylistic criteria adopted are largely derived from international modernist architecture, which rejected both interior and exterior decoration. This movement has heavily influenced architecture in Athens and through Athens, all of Greece. In the context of Eressos it translates into a desire to simplify and smooth the house surfaces, often by using concrete; to remove features considered old fashioned such as narrow rectangular windows, wall protrusions, and cavities. "Modernity" also means furnishing the interior with appliances and furniture, and decorating walls with paint and patterned paper or plastic.

The Expression of Status Consciousness

Although vernacular architecture has often been presumed to be vigorously utilitarian (Roberts 1973, 282–83) and totally unselfconscious (Megas 1968, 3–12), we found evidence to the contrary.

The inhabitants of Eressos, far from being unselfconscious about their houses, interpret small differences in house form and decoration as important status indicators.

In Period I, Eressos had a highly stratified society based on a system of ascribed status dependent on one's family of birth. The highest status members of this society were referred to as "aristocracy." The only way of bettering one's status in society was through the system of arranged marriage. This social stratification in Periods I and II was expressed architecturally by the overall type of house (there were seven house types) (Pavlides 1985, 158–96) and by particulars of its features which were always congruent with the status expressed by the house type. Specific dimensions of spaces, combinations of features, and degree of decoration could also indicate status. Small houses were simple and had few relatively unadorned wall elements, while large houses were more complex and had more spaces, more wall elements, and more elaborate decoration. Wood was particularly scarce and its interior use was prestigious. Degree of elaborateness was another criterion used to identify status. The more elaborate and complex a decoration, the greater its prestige. The adjective *vari* (heavy) was used to describe a highly elaborate plaster mantel (*phari*) or icon corner (*iconostassi*). Dimensions could also indicate status. The larger the dimension, the better, whether of an entire house, of a room, of a wall cavity, or of a window. Dimensions were not continuous, however, but instead were clustered around a few standard dimensions for the particular feature, for example, in all the rooms we measured in our thirty-house sample there were only five room heights: 180, 255, 290, 310, and 350 centimeters.

Eressos houses continue to express status in Period III, but it is through degree of modernization rather than through a well-defined hierarchical system of size and features as in Periods I and II. House type, size, and features have become secondary to the use of modern materials such as cement and paint, the presence of furniture and appliances, the removal of old-fashioned features, the piping of water, and electrification. Status is determined by the extent of modernization and smaller, fully modernized houses are more highly valued than larger, nonmodernized ones.

Dowry as a Stimulus for Construction and Renovation

In any society, house construction and renovation do not happen randomly. In Eressos, the need to provide daughters with a house and its furnishings as part of their dowry has been and remains the primary stimulus for house construction and renovation.[7] The changing expression of status in the Eressos house, throughout the three periods, has been due to changing perceptions of what constitutes an appropriate dowry.

In Period I, the erection of a new house or the renovation of an older one was undertaken to make up part of a dowry. Although young women and men had some say in spouse selection, family negotiations (*proxenio*) were primary. A girl's dowry figured prominently in these negotiations and its size and quality were vital factors in attracting a desirable husband. Providing a dowry house was accomplished either by constructing a new one or by renovating the family house and securing another smaller one for the parents. A family was often aided in its task by other villagers in exchange for produce or labor. Only wealthy villagers had cash to pay for labor to construct grand houses for their daughters.

The preparation of a house entailed not only building the walls, roof, ceilings, doors and windows, and built-in benches and cupboards but also producing furnishings for it. The design and size of a house were decisively influenced by the need for storage and display of the "furnishings," which included the material accoutrements of daily life (clothing, bedding, food, utensils, rugs) as well as prestige and decorative items (embroidery and crochet work, photographs, rugs). All of these material and decorative accoutrements, except for food utensils, were exclusively produced by women as part of their dowry. In Period I, these furnishings defined the appearance of the house interior, and anything of value in a house, especially in the less affluent ones, was the result of women's labor.[8]

During Period II, a fully equipped house remained a primary part of the dowry. House construction and renovation continued to be stimulated by the presence of a daughter approaching marriageable age. The introduction of neoclassical stylistic elements in architecture (especially among the wealthier villagers) and in furnishings reflected changing tastes and ideas about the type of dowry most likely to attract potential grooms.

In Period III the institution of dowry has remained strong and is still the primary factor stimulating renovation and stylistic modification of existing buildings, and the occasional construction of new ones. There is pressure to provide a totally modernized house in Eressos even though the possibility exists that the house will not be lived in, or might be abandoned after several years, when the young family emigrates to Athens. An even better dowry is considered to be a condominium apartment in Athens.

The Distinction Between Furniture and Furnishings

In discussions of the house interior, furniture is commonly subsumed under the heading "furnishings." It became clear to us, however, that furniture and furnishings ought to be treated as two distinct categories when considering their meaning for the house interior and its users in Eressos.

All houses on Lesbos during Periods I and II lacked furniture. The absence of furniture and the multiple uses of space characteristic of this period (see "Division of the House into Rooms," below), had important implications. Without furniture it was necessary for all activities to take place on the floor or on built-in benches. Various portable items were used for activities which today call for relatively immovable furniture. For example, a thin mattress was used for sleeping, a small low table was used for preparing food and for eating. These were stored after use. Since the floors were used for both sitting and sleeping, they had to be well covered with carpets for protection and insulation, and since they were highly visible without furniture, they also became a significant visual element of the house.

The absence of furniture also affected the appearance of the walls. All storage was accommodated in niches and other cavities embedded in them or on protrusions from them. All the house was in some sense public and all areas were "on display." Consequently wall cavities were frequently "closed" with a diaphanous cloth drape, not only to protect the objects stored inside from dust and sunlight, but also to visually enhance them and sometimes to attract attention to their contents. Horizontal surfaces of wall protrusions and cavities were invariably draped with a decorative cloth and shelves edged with crochet-work *dandeles*. The process of covering and decorating the floor and wall surfaces was referred to as "dressing" the house (*to spiti ine dimeno*) and constituted the total furnishing of it.[9]

In Period III the house interior has been radically redefined with the use of relatively immovable furniture and appliances. Beds, tables, chairs, sofas, a refrigerator, and a bottled-gas stove are crowded into the small rooms of houses built for use with a few small movable objects. Since storage functions of built-in cupboards and niches are now served by furniture, they are no longer needed. Their removal also frees up wall surface and makes furniture placement easier. Hairline cracks provide evidence of where these wall elements used to be. The only wall element not removed in the process of a complete modernization is the *iconostassi* in the sacred corner of the house.

Division of the House into Rooms

We are accustomed to dividing the interior space of houses into function-specific rooms or areas, but Eressos houses during Periods I and II were not divided this way. Instead, they were divided into "formal" and "informal" areas. Any given activity could take place in various parts of the house, depending on the character of the activity or the status of its participants. For example, entertaining a guest could take place in any one of several rooms depending on the status of the visitor or the formality of the occasion. By the same token many different activities could take place in the same space, as circumstances dictated. Thus, for example, the same room could be used for informal socializing, women's craft activities, eating, sleeping for the whole family, and food preparation exclusive of cooking, or it could be turned into a "formal" area by the use of appropriate carpets and other furnishings.

The introduction of furniture, which became widespread in Period III, has resulted in the function-specific naming of rooms. In the modernized house, tables, chairs, and sofas define "dining rooms" (*trapezeria*) and "living rooms" (*salone*), rooms specifically associated with entertaining. The introduction of beds define one or two rooms as "bedrooms" (*krevatokamera*). The desire to have rooms for particular activities often led to the building of additions or the subdividing of an existing room to create a house with a room assigned for each activity. The subdivision of existing spaces into more rooms, combined with the introduction of furniture, has resulted in extremely crowded interior spaces. The resulting inconvenience is well tolerated, however, because of the symbolic value of the newly created and furnished rooms.

Paradoxically, actual patterns of space use have changed only modestly. Sitting still occurs on the floor during informal events, and sleeping can still occur in various places in the house or in the yard. The modern "kitchen" (*kouzina*), while still used for many activities previously associated with the renovated space, is rarely used for cooking or dishwashing. These activities still take place in the yard or in a utility room separated from the rest of the house.

Age of Occupants, House Features, and Decoration

Two factors affect house features in such a way that they signify the age of the occupants. The first factor is the continuous stylistic change that has characterized house form and appearance over the last 130 years. A house prepared as dowry at a particular time reflects the style in vogue at that time and thus the age of the occupants. The second factor is the custom of passing on to a new couple, as dowry, any valuables or decorative items, such as carpets or embroideries, owned by the parents. With this transference of material goods, the interior of older couples' houses takes on an impoverished look. In the past, this impoverished look was reinforced by the custom of using black coverings over all interior surfaces of the house for a prolonged period after a family death, more likely to be experienced by older people. Although in Period III this dramatic altering of interior decor is no longer practiced during mourning, avoidance of decoration is considered appropriate. Thus, because older people have given their best as dowry and because they express mourning by avoiding decoration, rather stark house interiors were correctly identified during the slide interviews as belonging to older people.

House Form and Gender of Offspring

In Period III, the extent to which a house has been modernized is commonly related to the presence of a daughter in the family. A house that still has the stigmatized features of plaster decorations over the fireplace, wall cavities and protrusions, uncovered ceiling beams, and unplastered exterior surfaces is likely to be the house of a daughterless family. In some instances, such houses are not even provided with electricity or piped water. Without a daughter who requires a dowry, there is less incentive to spend money and expend effort to change the house.

Summary of Findings

The following major points emerged from our study of the architecture of Eressos: (1) There is a sense of time and change that is specific to the locality. (2) Local styles are sensitive to distant influences and are composed of elements gathered from diverse sources. Local architecture is sensitive and responsive to social, political, and economic pressures, and to architectural developments occurring elsewhere. (3) There is a high degree of status consciousness expressed in the built environment, in contradiction to the notion of a "natural" or "unselfconscious" architecture. (4) The primary stimulus for construction of new houses or renovation of old ones is the need for families to provide dowry for their daughters. (5) A distinction can be made between furniture and furnishings of a house, and these have important implications for the use of space in the house interior. (6) Interior space is not divided according to function specificity, but instead according to the formal or informal character of an activity. (7) Age of the occupants is expressed in stylistic features of the house and its interior decoration. (8) The gender of offspring is expressed in the degree of modernization a house exhibits.

DESIGN AND PLANNING IMPLICATIONS

The type of research reported here can be useful to architectural practice and education and is relevant to establishing appropriate governmental policy on the preservation of vernacular architecture.

Designing for the Newly Urbanized

The rapidity of urbanization experienced everywhere in the world today annually uproots millions of people who leave their vernacular built habitats to seek new shelter in architect designed housing. Knowing something about the newly urbanized—their original habitats, patterns of space use, and reading of visual form—could prove useful to the planners and designers of new housing. Anecdotes about new housing being inappropriately used by its new inhabitants are sometimes amusing, often tragic, in the misallocation of the limited resources available to impoverished people. They also point to the great need to understand the cultural background of migrants to urban centers.

The division of the Eressos house into "formal," "everyday," and "utility" zones according to the character of activity is an example of information about the social context of architecture that could be useful to designers. This information provides insight into the way activities are structured in the house. It sheds light on why fully equipped kitchens are not used as such in Eressos and has implications for the way these people are likely to perceive their surroundings when they move to urban areas. Kitchens in Eressos are zoned as "everyday" zones, and there is a strong taboo against the presence of food odors generated by cooking in areas used for socializing. Modern apartments and houses that we are accustomed to, with cooking areas often integrated into the living areas, would be unacceptable to Eressiotes. It is of interest that some Athenian housewives explicitly express the importance of physically separating the cooking area from the living areas of a house or apartment.

Designing in Vernacular Settings

A second possible application of studies like ours is to the design of new structures in vernacular settings. Not knowing local codes of social meaning—for example, whether and how social stratification is expressed—could elicit unexpected reactions from local people. This point can be illustrated by the example of a house built in Eressos that was an architect's interpretation of the local vernacular. While this house was very successful from an outsider's point of view, local residents were ambivalent since its prototype was one of the least prestigious local house types. In this particular case local reaction mattered little to the Athenian who built the house. However, use of local vernacular for its visual qualities without understanding its social connotations could present difficulties if the building being constructed were for local use. Knowledge of the code could help, either to observe it, for example, through the conscious use of prestigious design elements or avoidance of stigmatized building types, or to anticipate and offset confusion through appropriate public education.

Defining Government Policy on Historic Preservation

In many countries, including Greece, governmental regulations provide guidelines for architectural preservation and for the construction of new buildings in vernacular settings. Government policy and the definition of appropriate regulations for new construction could benefit from social contextual studies of vernacular architecture. We witnessed an example during our stay in Eressos. A traveling exhibit of drawings and models of vernacular architecture was brought to Eressos, sponsored by the Ministry of Housing. Regional architectural stereotypes were presented in an effort to reeducate the peasants to build in the old vernacular. There was one type which supposedly represented the entire island of Lesbos. It was an artificial construct based on some building features found on Lesbos but had nothing to do with the houses of Eressos, or with the actual houses found in other villages.

Another example is provided by the following experience we had while doing research in Eressos. While there we sometimes expressed our views on the value of preserving the old buildings and tried to convince people not to destroy them. In one particular instance a local man asked for drawings for a modern cinder block building to replace a lovely (in our view) older stone house. In spite of persuasive reasons for saving the old building and renovating it, he was fixed in his plans to destroy it. Perplexed by our persistence and concern, he finally inquired whether we knew someone who would be a good husband for his daughter who preferred old-fashioned houses. We were ignoring the supreme social function of the house in Eressos, which is to serve as dowry. What mattered was not cost or practicality, but the image of modernity that would most likely attract a desirable groom for his daughter. The old house was torn down and its stone walls used to construct the foundation for a new cinder-block house. Local perceptions like these clearly can block efforts to preserve vernacular environments. Preservation efforts can be most effective when they address local needs, perceptions, and concerns.

CONCLUSIONS

In examining the architecture of Eressos over the last 130 years, we documented continuous changes in architectural form involving extensive renovations, and dramatic alterations in furnishing the house interior. These changes were related to social contextual factors including political authority, economy, means of production, and social stratification. During all three periods the primary stimulus to change remained the need to provide appropriate dowry. Often architectural changes served no purpose other that to satisfy changing perceptions of acceptable and desirable architecture used to express the social position and aspirations of house owners. Functional or utilitarian concerns served by these architectural changes were secondary. Changes in the architecture of Eressos occurred primarily as a response to its changing social meaning.

The kind of anthropological research that coincided with our collection of visual data requires lengthy stays in a community. The collection of etic and emic data is costly and takes a lot of time and effort. *A priori* there is no obvious reason for expending the extra energy that is needed to study the visual environment in its social context in this way. However, a purely visual approach to the architecture of Eressos would never have revealed the richness of information that the inhabitants read in it. Coherent patterns of meaning emerged only by understanding the inhabitants' point of view.

Further studies of the nature involving anthropologists as well as architects are essential for our understanding of vernacular environments. They can also provide information relevant for our schools of architecture, which are seeking ways to sensitize students to the social aspects of design; for environmental designers who increasingly are confronted with designing for users who are both geographically and culturally far removed from themselves; for governments interested in passing regulations and laws to help preserve their national architectural heritage.

NOTES

1. A similar division between male and female domains and places of activity has been described as existing in other parts of Greece, for example, in Vasilika (Freidl 1962, 12) in northern Greece (du Boulay 1974, 31), on Tinos (Dubisch 1976. 321–22), on Ios (Currier, 1976, 309–10), and on Kalymnos (Bernard 1976, 295). It has been the subject of extensive analysts and a film by Hoffman working on Thira (1976, 331–82).

2. Amos Rapoport (1982, 43) also raises this point:

    In linguistics itself, there has been increasing criticism of the neglect of pragmatics (see Bates, 1976)—the "cultural premises about the world in which speech takes place" (Keesing 1979, 14). The development of sociolinguistics is part of this reevaluation, the point is made that the nature of any given speech event may vary depending on the nature of the participants, the social setting, the situation—in a word the context (see Gumprerz and Hymes, 1972; Giglioli, 1972). In any event, it appears that the neglect of pragmatics and the concentration on syntactics almost to the exclusion of everything else are serious shortcomings of the semiotic approach.

3. One of the authors (Pavlides) is a native Greek and has maternal relatives residing in Eressos. Linguistic fluency and established ties with inhabitants through the network of kinship greatly facilitated entry into the village, access into people's houses, and flow of communication.
4. Much of the preceding description of setting and methods is drawn from a previously published work by the authors (Pavlides and Hesser 1986, 68–71) and is used here by permission of Princeton University Press.
5. Radford and Clark (1974, 67), who have documented a similar shift in motif to neoclassicism on Thira at this time, also see it as the introduction of forms "not direct from ancient Greece, but by way of Genoa, Venice and Germany."
6. Tzakou (1974) has documented a similar transformation of the house exterior on the island of Siphnos.
7. The process of arranging marriage contracts and the role played by dowry in Eressos is similar to that described for other areas of Greece. The father everywhere bears the primary responsibility, but he is aided by his wife and sons. The wife's major contribution is the weaving and decoration of carpets and linens for the house interior (Papaharalambos 1968, 43; Friedl 1962, 53–54; du Boulay 1974, 95–96; Bialor 1976, 232). However, the house is not invariably a part of the dowry. It is mandatory in other villages on Lesbos (Zourou 1974, 85) and is mentioned as a common part of the dowry by Peristiany (1976, 217), Hoffman (1976, 332), Dubisch (1976, 321), Bernard (1976, 296), Allen (1976, 185–86), Kenna (1976, 349), and Pasadaiou (1973, 12). However, on Cyprus (Papaharalambos 1968, 5) and on Chios (personal communication) it was customary for the groom to build the house. In Karpofora inclusion of a house in the dowry is a recent phenomenon (Aschenbrenner 1976, 214). In Vasilika, the family house goes to the sons of the family (Friedl 1962, 214).
8. Sinos (1976, 15) reports that in simple houses on Cyprus the only items of value were those made by the women for their dowries. These items were used not only in daily life but also for decoration of the walls and doorways.
9. These storage areas also have been noted by Papaharalambos (1968, 44) in the houses on Cyprus and by du Boulay (1974, 23–26). Our experience in other parts of Greece suggests that the building of houses with a similar variety of storage features was typical in rural areas and probably reflected an absence of furniture. That people today, even when they have furniture, commonly sit on the floor for informal gatherings or for work is indicative of the significance of furniture as objects of prestige and show, rather than as totally utilitarian and necessary parts of the house.
10. The same pattern of use and equipping of the house described here is described, with some variations, by du Boulay for a contemporary village in northern Greece (1974, 23–24).

REFERENCES

Allen, P. S. 1976. Aspida: A depopulated Maniat community. In *Regional variation in modern Greece and Cyprus Towards a perspective on the ethnography of Greece*, ed. M. Dimen and E. Friedl, 168–98 New York: New York Academy of Science.

Aschenbrenner, S. E. 1976. Karpofora: Reluctant farmers on a fertile land. In *Regional variation in modern Greece and Cyprus*, 207–21. See Allen 1976.

Bates, E. 1976. *Language and Context: The acquisition of pragmatic*. New York: Academic.

Bernard, H. R. 1976. Kalymnos. This island of the sponge. In *Regional variation in modern Greece and Cyprus*, 291–307. See Allen 1976.

Bialor, P. A. 1976. The northwestern corner of the Peloponnesos: Mavrikion and its region. In *Regional variation in modern Greece and Cyprus*, 222–31. See Allen 1976.

Currier, R. 1976. Social interaction and social structure in a Greek island village. In *Regional variation in modern Greece and Cyprus*, 308–13. See Allen 1976.

Dorson, R. M. 1973. Concepts of folklore and folklife studies. In *Folklore and folklife: An introduction*, ed. R. M. Dorson, 1–50. Chicago and London: The University of Chicago Press.

Dubisch, J. 1976. The ethnography of the islands: Tinos. In *Regional variation in modern Greece and Cyprus*, 314–27. See Allen 1976.

du Boulay, J. 1974. *Portrait of a Greek mountain village*. Oxford: Clarendon Press.

Evans, E. E. 1973. The cultural geographer and folklife research. *In folklore and folklife*, 517–32. See Dorson 1973.

Friedl, E. 1962. Vasilika: *A village in modern Greece*. New York: Holt, Rinehart and Winston.

Gigliolo, P. P., ed. 1972. *Language and social Context*. New York: Penguin.

Glassie, H. 1968. *Patterns in the material folk culture of the Eastern United States*. Philadelphia: University of Pennsylvania Press.

Gumpertz, J. J., and D. Hymes. 1972. *Directions is sociolinguistics: The ethnography of communication*. New York: Holt, Rinehart and Winston.

Hoffman, S. M. 1976. The ethnography of the islands: Thira. In *Regional variation in modern Greece and Cyprus*, 328–40. See Allen 1976.

Hymes, D. 1974. *Foundations in sociolinguistics*. Philadelphia: University of Pennsylvania Press.

Jenkins, J. G. 1973. The use of artifacts and folk art in the folk museum. In *Folklore and folklife*, 497–516. See Dorson 1973.

Keesing, R. M. 1979. Linguistic knowledge and cultural knowledge. Some doubts and speculation. *American Anthropologist* 81:14–34.

Kenna, M. 1976. Houses, Fields, And Graves: Property and ritual obligation on a Greek island. *Ethnology* 15:21–34.

Labov, W. 1973. *Sociolinguistic patterns*. Philadelphia: University of Pennsylvania Press.

Megas, G. A. 1968. Skopoi kai methododia tin erevnan tis Laikis Oikodomis: Horotaxia, poleodomia, architectoniki. *Laographia* 16:3–12.

Papaharalambos, G. H. 1968. *I Kypriaki Oikia, Leukosia*.

Pasadaiou, A. 1973. *I Laiki architectoniki tis Imbrou*. Athens: Academia Athinon.

Pavlides, E. 1985. Vernacular architecture in its social context: A case study of Eressos, Greece, Ph.D. diss., University of Pennsylvania.

Pavlides, E., and J. F. Hesser. 1986. Women's roles and house form and decoration in Eressos, Greece. In *Gender and power in rural Greece*, ed. J. Dubisch, 68–96. Princeton: Princeton University Press.

Peristiany, J. G. ed. 1965. *Honor and shame: The values of Mediterranean society*. London: Weidenfeld and Nicolson.

Radford, A., and G. Clark. 1974 Cyclades: Studies of a vernacular environment. In *Shelter in Greece*, ed. B. Doumanis and P. Oliver, 431–44. Greece: Architecture in Greece Press.

Rapoport, A. 1969. *House form and culture*. Englewood Cliffs, N.J.: Prentice-Hall.

———. 1982. *The meaning of the built environment*. Beverly Hills, Calif.: Sage.

Roberts, W. E. 1971. Folk architecture. In *Folklore and folklife*, 281–94. See Dorson 1973.

Sinos, S. 1976. *Anadromi sti Laiki architektoniki tis Kyprou*. Athens.

Tzakou, A. 1974. *Central settlement on the Island of Siphnos: Form and evolution in a traditional system*. Athens.

Zourou, F. M. 1974. *O gamos sti Voria Lesbo*. Mytilne.

19 Fengshui: Its Application in Contemporary Architecture

Teh Tien Yong

Fengshui theory is summarized (chi, yin-yang, bagua, 5 elements) and applied to the layout of villages and houses in this article. Fengshui can be viewed as a preindustrial form of design guidelines that combined ecology, psychology, social awareness, health and safety before the division of labor characteristic of modernism. It is still practiced today.

Interested readers might also want to find Kim, Mintai and Erin Lynch, 2004, "Site Planning Here and There: Comparing Western Site Planning and Design and Eastern Feng Shui," *Landscape Review*, 9(1), June 2004, which shows the similarity between contemporary criteria for good design and ancient feng shui criteria in regard to actual parks and plazas in the U.S. Similarly, we direct readers to Michael Y. Maka, and S. Thomas Ngb, "The art and science of Feng Shui—a study on architects' perception," *Building and Environment* 40 (2005) 427–434.

The principal philosophy that has greatly influenced Chinese thought and culture over the ages is the *Yijing: The Book of Changes*, believed to have originated from the legendary Emperor Fu Xi in the year 3322 B.C.[1] It represents symbolically, the organised, rhythmic and purposeful Universe, allowing the reader to infer relationships between himself and the Cosmos beyond normal perceptual levels.

It has been this understanding of the environment that has bred the natural sciences of acupuncture and Fengshui, two departments of the same science concerned with the flow of subtle energies (*qi*) in the human body and in the earth respectively.[2]

It was not until the Sung Dynasty (during the 10th century A.D.) however, that all the elements of Fengshui were gathered methodically and built firmly on a philosophical basis into one system, combining every form of influence which heaven may be said to exercise on earth.[3]

Time and the human propensity for developing superstition however has not left the theories of Fengshui untouched over the past millennium. What the layman understands today as being Fengshui is a science infused with numerous myths and superstitions and where its primary use is the attraction of good fortune to individuals and business enterprises. A resurgence of interest by the Chinese in the *Yijing*, acupuncture and Fengshui, and an increased interest in the West, augurs

Teh Tien Yong; Hasan-Uddin Khan, ed., "Fengshui: Its Application in Contemporary Architecture," from *Mimar 27: Architecture in Development*, pp. 27–33. Copyright © 1988 by Concept Media Ltd. Permission to reprint granted by the publisher.

the beginnings of its acceptance as an ecological science that studies the symbolic relationship between the Cosmos, Nature and Man.

Fengshui, or the art of placement and urban orientation practiced by the Chinese over the past millennia suffered a set-back at the turn of this century when the western-educated Chinese elite grew in numbers and brought back with them the reactionary movements that have swept across the whole of Europe. The impact was devastating and almost overnight, age-old Chinese practices inexplicable in terms comprehensible to the western-educated mind were debunked as superstition and pseudo-sciences. Such attitudes were prevalent in writers like Eitel[4] and more recently E. Lip[5] and Low[6] who both hold rather ambivalent opinions. The practice has, nevertheless, survived till today due primarily to a Chinese preoccupation with the accumulation of wealth. This has, albeit, been kept to superficial levels, limited to projects ranging from the realignment of doors, tomb siting, interior layouts and occasionally a house design.

Lately, there has been a resurgence of interest in Fengshui amongst the decision-making elite and projects like the Hong Kong and Shanghai Bank Building and the Competition for the Peak, both of which are in Hong Kong, attest to this new concern for the integration of Fengshui with modern architecture. Unfortunately, the lack of understanding of the logical basis for Fengshui has inadvertently retarded its application in larger projects like town planning and urban design.

Recent discoveries by biologists on the impact of the Earth's magnetic field on certain kinds of bacteria and by geographers in the field of plate tectonics[7] may perhaps induce scientific investigations into certain key ideas held by Fengshui.[8]

What is Fengshui? One definition that has been put forward is: "the art of perceiving the subtle energies that animate nature and the landscape, and the science of reconciling the best interests of the living earth and those of all its inhabitants."[9] This definition from John Mitchell perhaps spells out most accurately the original intents behind the concept of Fengshui. Literally, the term means wind-water which may have been derived from the necessity to seek shelter from the loessial winds from the north and from the torrential river floods.

According to Skinner[10] the term "Geomancy" is a misnomer, and more properly refers to an Arab form of divination which spread north into Europe and south into Africa at the end of the first millenium.

The term most consistently used in place of Fengshui in classical Chinese texts is "*dili,*" i.e, land patterns, or in modern terms, geography. This, therefore, indicates that Fengshui was *not* intended as superstition but as an integral part of the study of the land itself and the patterns on it, both natural and man-made.

QI AND SYMBIOSIS

The concept of *qi* or life-force (breath of life), runs through Fengshui as much as it does in acupuncture, the practice of which relies on the location of acupuncture meridians for the modification of the flow of *qi* through these points. Similarly, the practice of Fengshui is the modification of the flow of *qi* along the surface of the earth.

The whole universe is seen as a living organisation. Landscape and all nature were interdependant and part of an irrevocable symbiotic relationship: "Everything depended on everything."[11]

Herein we see how Fengshui, formed as an arm of the Chinese philosophy, actually implants Man as one of the components of the natural cycle of events into the landscape. So successful were the Chinese in their ability to dwell in the environment that the Chinese landscape appears as the epitome of harmonious composition—each practitioner of Fengshui literally became a friend of the environment. This perhaps is the reason why Chinese landscape is highly identifiable. C. Norberg-Schulz puts it across most succinctly when saying in a different context that, "Dwelling above all presupposes identification with the environment. And in this context, 'identification' means to become 'friends' with the environment."

The environmental image formed through such a system of placement as Fengshui perhaps imparts on its inhabitor and beholder an "important sense of security" and draws our attention to Lynch's theory on the relationship between environmental image, systems of orientation and natural structure.[12]

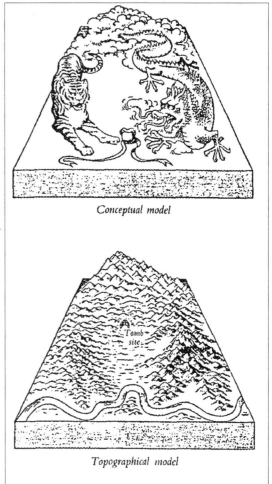

Conceptual model

Topographical model

FACTORS INFLUENCING THE DEVELOPMENT OF FENGSHUI

Fengshui's development was influenced by China's geographical configuration. To its north and west, central China is surrounded by ranges of mountains. The rivers mainly originate from the west, run through the low-lying areas, providing water for its agriculture and run into the sea. This configuration of natural land forms became a model for almost every type of Chinese architecture.

Climatic conditions have also had an impact on Fengshui. China is situated in the northern hemisphere. In winter bitterly cold winds blow from the northwest. From the opposite direction the south-east prevailing wind brings in warm air, and in the summer, cool air. The warm sun is from the east and the southeast; the western sun is usually hot. As a result the ideal building form is high and solid towards the north to shear off the cold wind. Facing the south it is low and open in order to capture light, warmth, and the summer breeze.

Confucianism, one of the most influential philosophies in China, defines the Chinese morality and social order. It predominately deals with man to man relationships. This belief system also profoundly affected Chinese architecture and city form. The traditional Chinese social and political hierarchy is clearly reflected in physical form.

The city of Chang-An, for example, was planned in accordance with the traditional principles of order and hierarchy. The city was laid out in a grid-pattern. The Emperor's palace was in the north, the highest position. The grid squares were the largest in the north, gradually decreasing in size as they decreased in importance to the south.

The idea of a well-disciplined society also manifests itself through the form of the traditional Chinese courtyard house. The northern end of the home is higher and inhabited by the parents. The son's bedroom is located just south of the parents' rooms. The southernmost area of the house is the servants' quarters. The roof of the southern end is generally lower than the north.

The elemental forms of the mountains

Shape		Planet	Element
Conical		Mars ♂	FIRE
Round head, long body		Jupitor ♃	WOOD
Square		Saturn ♄	EARTH
Round, ablong mound		Venus ♀	METAL
Alive, crooked moving		Mercury ☿	WATER

FORM SCHOOL

Different schools of thought emerged concerning Fengshui.

"Heaven requires the aid of Man to carry out its scheme of justice. Earth requires the aid of Man to bring its products to absolute perfection. Neither Heaven nor Earth are complete in themselves, but leave the last finish of everything to Man. Consequently, as regards the natural outlines of the Earth's surface, there is much room left to the active interference of Man."[13]

Mankind therefore has, to a certain degree, the capacity to influence his destiny, and historical times often bear the products of man in such attempts. Hills not quite high enough have been raised, waterways have been diverted to take tortuous courses and railway lines thought to be harbingers of malevic *qi* have been uprooted and discontinued, amongst a host of other examples.

The "Form" School of Fengshui first started with Yang Yunsong and Zeng Wendi of Kanchou, and its doctrine refined especially by Lai Dayu and Xie Zhuyi. Its theory emphasises land formations and terrain, taking them where they arise to where they terminate, and thereby determining position and orientation. Fengshui *xiansheng* give their whole attention to the mutual appropriateness of dragons, sites, eminences and waters with a stubborn refusal to discuss anything else.[14]

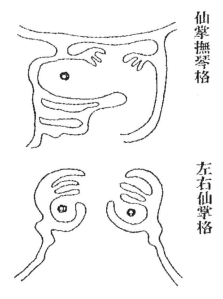

River formations and Fengshui application.

Unlike the "Compass" School, the "Form" School relies heavily on intuition for the analysis of a placement but is surprisingly regarded as being the less subjective of the two. The basic rules of the "Form" School are elaborated at great lengths in standard texts like those of Yang Yunsong. These rules apply at any level from the siting of a city to the orientation of a room. The following is a summary of the basic rules[15]:

- Buildings, be they tombs or towns, should if possible be constructed on sloping or well drained land.
- The north of any built site should possess a mountainous shield or screen of trees protecting it from malevic *qi*.
- The dead should be buried on the south facing slope of the above-mentioned shield, facing the town and the living.
- Entrances to the town or the home should always be from the south and be given a clear view of this orientation to harvest beneficial *qi*.
- In the landscape, dragon and tiger forms denote the presence of *yang* and *yin qi* respectively and are most happily placed when they form a complete horseshoe with the dragon in the east and the tiger in the west. The point of transition is seen as the point of greatest concentration of beneficial *qi*.
- Boldly rising formations are termed *Yang* whilst gentle, undulating elevations are termed *Yin*. On ground where male characteristics prevail, the best site is on a spot having female characteristics and otherwise on a predominantly female site.
- Flat land is not propitious from a Fengshui point of view.
- The ideal proportion determined by the Taoists is three-fifths male and two-fifths female for the active concentration of the beneficial *qi* on the site.

Using the Fengshui compass in the Ch'ing dynasty.

IDEAL FENGSHUI LANDSCAPE

Mountains

Mountains, volcanoes and other hilly features are easily the youngest features on the surface of the earth. The Himalayas for example, are still growing, formed out of an enormous collision between what is now the Indian peninsula and Asia. Not surprisingly, the Chinese viewed them as virile and powerful manifestations of the pristine forces, a "fit lair for the dragons."

The Elemental Forms of the Mountains

It is inevitable therefore, at this stage to see how mountain forms came to be associated with the "five elements" and consequently with the five governing planets. Suffice to say, in the hilly areas,

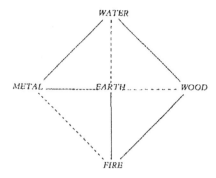

Composite diagram of the relationships between the elements.

it is imperative that Fengshui sites be located in places where mountain forms exist in complete compatibility as in accordance with the constructive cycle of the five elements.

In addition to the elemental categorisation of mountains, there is a separate series owing their influences on a site to the "nine moving stars," seven of which belong to Ursa Major and pertains more to their astrological influences on specific individuals. For example, the sloping shoulders of the broken army (Pojun) would be a disastrous configuration if within sight of a house of a professional soldier.

Water

Contrary to the western preference for straight water courses, the Chinese town planner is involved in earnest attempts to introduce "natural" curves into a water course at first opportunity.

Water courses are the most obvious flow lines of *qi* and the general rule is that water flowing fast and in straight lines are rapid conductors of *qi* and are therefore undesirable. Slow, sinuous, deep water courses on the other hand, are conducive to the accumulation of *qi* especially if they form a pool in front of the site in consideration.

River Formations and Fengshui Application

The confluence is considered a key dragon point and should form a graceful curve rather than a union of conflict. Generally, stream confluences are beneficial because of the concentration of *qi*, whilst the branching of a stream through coarse sedimentation, or at the delta of a river is dispersive of *qi*.

Sharp bends, like straight lines are unfavourable, as they act like "secret arrows" capable of removing *qi* accumulations. Skinner states from a geographical standpoint that water flowing through areas of uniform sediment would automatically meander and that straight streams of rivers indicate inherent faults in the structure of land, dangerous physically and in the case of Fengshui, psychically.

Even artificial confluences or branches can be created and preferably, the "dragon lair" should be nestled amongst branches of the river rather than directly on the main trunk watercourse.

Westward or eastward flowing streams are considered auspicious if they flow directly towards the site and meander around it. Such a configuration ensures beneficial *qi* accumulation.

Water, being the main instrument of landscape sculpture, not only carries mountains and valleys physically but is also a conveyor of *qi*. From the surfacial water, dragons rise as the water evaporates. Wind or *feng*, distributes the water vapour as clouds which, taking the form of dragons in the air, consolidate finally to precipitate life-giving rain into mountains which are the traditional lair of these dragons.

Such picturesque imagery of the flight of dragons demonstrates a systematic knowledge of the connection between evaporation, cloud formation and rain. What appears to be three different kinds of dragons are three continuous interlocking parts of a natural cycle.

The flow of *qi* seems interminably linked with fluid mechanics and it is said that in a site to which the wind has access from all directions, *qi* will scatter before it had any time to accumulate. If, however, the wind is more mellow, then the vital health, *qi*, is retained.

Compass School

The "Compass" School, or Song Miao Zhifa, began first in Fujian and gained popularity with Wang Ci of the Song Dynasty. Its theory of application emphasizes the planets and the diagrams; a *yang* hill should face in a *yang* direction and a *yin* hill should face in a *yin* direction so that they are not at odds. Complete reliance is put on the eight trigrams and the five planets instrumental in determining the principles of generation and destruction. More mechanical in the nature of its application than the "Form" School, its principles however lack the clarity of the latter.

The use of the compass for Fengshui pre-dates its maritime employment, and its application primarily as a land instrument for divination in all probability retarded the introduction of the maritime compass till circa 10th century A.D.

Using the Fengshui Compass in the Ch'ing Dynasty

The ancient Chinese displayed knowledge of the impact of the earth's magnetic field on life, and in fact noted that "certain maggots which arise from fish and meat, placed on the ground, move northwards."[16] Biological work done in the late 1970's does confirm that certain bacteria swim northwards in the northern hemisphere and southwards in the southern hemisphere. The earliest formal recognition of the effect of the earth's field upon organic life is found in writings of the Fujian School of Fengshui. The Chinese have always thought of the compass as south pointing, hence the term *zinanzhen* or south-pointing needle.

The Compass and Its Divisions

The analysis of the Chinese Fengshui compass by the successive halving of divisions to be found in its western counterpart is totally unsatisfactory.

The compass is divided into 12 earthly branches at intervals of thirty degrees, and in addition, has a number of "Rings" divided according to different classifications.[17] Whilst the European compass point refers specifically to a particular direction, the Chinese compass bearings refer to a segment of the circle, not a specific point on its circumference.

The compass is used by the Fengshui practitioner to take bearings or points where various landscape formations, dragons or rivers appear to terminate, disappear, enter or leave the landscape from the point of view where the reading is taken. Thus, the direction of the dragon "veins," especially where they come to a head (which may be a cliff or end of a line of prominent natural features, drainage lines, intersection of rivers, railway tracks and existing architectural lines etc.), must be taken into account as each may carry some part of the flow of *qi* through the site.

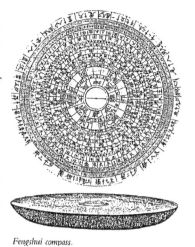

Fengshui compass.

Fengshui Compass

On flat land, woods, boulders or large trees may mark the passage of *qi* through the earth though such sites may not possess as much of the primal *yang* energy present in sloping or mountainous areas. The three plates of the compass indicate different facets of the site:

a) the outer or Heaven plate governs among other things the potency of the *qi* flow;

b) the earth plate is used in divining the "dragon's pulse" and in locating the veins and arteries of earth *qi*, measuring the relative health of the area surrounding the point under analysis;

c) the middle plate, or main plate, is to be used to discover the influence of Heaven and Earth on those living at the site under scrutiny.

Five Elements

This world-outlook was systematized by yet another group of thinkers, the proto-scientific school of naturalists (Ying-Yang Jia), headed by Zou Yan 320–270 B.C., oldest of the Chi-Xia academicians. The naturalists elaborated the theory of the two fundamental natural forces, *yin* and *yang*, and the theory of the five elements, and the system of the symbiotic correlations in which a great number of objects were classified by fives in correspondence with the elements WOOD, FIRE, EARTH, METAL and WATER.[18]

The five elements of the Chinese are similar to the ancient Greek elements FIRE, AIR, EARTH and WATER, with the exception of the exclusion of air and the inclusion of wood and water. Wood, which is organic matter, signifies the whole vegetative cover of the earth while metal symbolises to a certain extent things fabricated or purified from the earth.

Composite Diagram of the Relationships Between the Elements

Air is left out because it consists substantially of water vapour and clouds, which are already included under water.

In a way, the Chinese elemental view of the universe is more ecologically oriented and dynamic than the Greek model, as it stresses the mutual creation and destruction of the elements. Herein the fundamental differences between the early philosophical formulation of the Chinese and that of the Greeks reveal the basic differences between Chinese and European culture.

It is a little misleading however to use the term "elements." *Xing* indicates movement and therefore the term "five moving agents" may be more appropriate as, like the trigrams and hexagrams of the *Yijing*, these are also symbols of change and transformation.

There exist two cyclic relationships among the five elements. In the Former Heaven sequence their *yang* aspect is especially applicable to the waxing half of the year. It may be seen that wood burns to produce fire, which results in ash (earth) in which metal may be found. Metal is also found in the veins of the earth from which springs the underground streams (water) which nourish vegetation and produce wood.

On the other hand, the Later Heaven sequence indicates the destructive order of the elements and portrays the waning half of the year, the *yin* aspect. Each element destroys another, as in Fengshui theory, the destroyer is inimical to the destroyed element.

The cycles however cover a wide arena of things and Feuchtwang explains it most clearly by saying:

"Wood is understood to be all vegetation, which is fed by water, and swallows, covers, binds earth, is cut down by metal implements and ignites; water is understood to be all forms of fluid including the liquefaction of metal by fire, and which can be solidified by being staunched with earth and earth is understood to mean all mixed, impure and inanimate substances including the ash produced by fire."

In the above, Feuchtwang seems to imply that the five elements refer not only to the qualitative aspect of things but also to their compositional characteristics. It may therefore be conjectured at this point that some sort of physical-relational diagram may be drawn up as an aid to harmonious architectural compositions.

Manifestation of the 5 Elements

The 5 elements which figure prominently in Chinese cosmology and the practice of Fengshui is a classification system for all things occurring in the universe.

For the purposes of architectural application they may be categorized according to:

- Form
- Orientation
- Placement
- Colour
- Material
- Texture
- Numbers

Decreasing Order of Perception

Such an order gives the planner/architect a high degree of flexibility in conforming with the 5-element aspect of Fengshui, allowing the application of another manifestation down the hierarchy if the most preferred one is inadmissible owing to the urban and planning constraints or otherwise, i.e. if ideal form cannot be fulfilled then colour follows and so forth.

The Lo-shu Grid

Numbers also figure prominently in Fengshui, being associated with the Lo-shu grid, a nine-gridded N-S square used to categorise areas within a site or dwelling into its component elements. All numbers add up vertically, horizontally and diagonally to 15, a number of significance to the Chinese as it represents the number of days in each of the 24 phases of the lunar year.

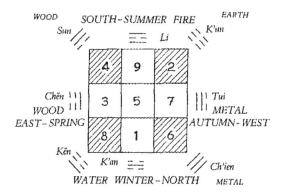

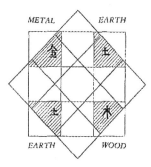

The Lo-shu grid.

The numbers 5 and 10 are never used, being numbers of completion, since Fengshui stresses the dynamic nature of the universe. Completion has a finality to it incompatible with the notion of constant flux and change.

Applying the Lo-shu grid to a site or dwelling, one can use it as a device for determining the appropriate position for various uses provided for in the architectural program.

The following Fengshui guidelines (see overleaf) lay out the principles of the subject on form and planning. There are basically two areas into which most effort was put:

a) the interpretation of a Fengshui model first put forward by Professor Winston Yeh; (a U-shaped model developed in his Master's thesis at Harvard University);
b) the manifestation of the five elements.

Guidelines on these two aspects may be said to be universally accepted by all practitioners irrespective of dialect groups. It was precisely for this reason that oft-considered Fengshui beliefs that are related to numbers have been ignored, they being heavily linked with the Cantonese, a dialect group whose subculture has woven a great deal of superstition into Fengshui.

Proportions, or rather a system of measurement based on the geomancer's ruler, is not given mention in the guidelines as there was insufficient data for arriving at some conclusion on its origins. It was conjectured that it may have its roots in rudimentary anthropometry based on the Chinese physique, but pursuit of this came to naught.

Indeed, proportions would have made a fitting accompaniment to the Fengshui model and 5-element guidelines. All three do not come under the realm of superstition and are instead,

Fengshui Guidelines

Basic form as has been exemplified in case studies takes a U-shaped pattern with a high back. This back generally faces North or if that is inadmissable owing to geography or topography, is up against a hill or backed by trees.

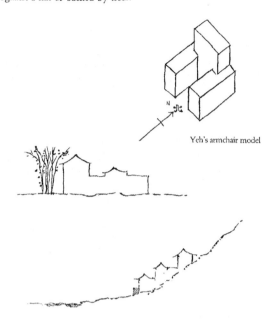

Yeh's armchair model

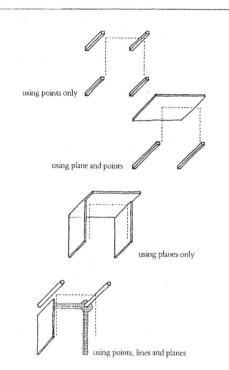

using points only

using plane and points

using planes only

using points, lines and planes

The widespread association of this with good Fengshui may be due to the fact that it effectively contains space, defining an enclave that is sufficiently protected, yet possessing an open aspect.

Modern city planning however, may not always permit such a connected linear interpretation of this U-shaped pattern. Devices such as points, lines and planes may be put into use to overcome any restrictions.

Landscape:

Landscape forms an integral part of Fengshui and should be carefully considered in planning. The principle components in good Fengshui landscape are:
i. Water
ii. Trees
iii. Hilly features.

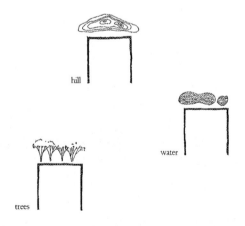

hill

water

trees

Orientation:

While a generally north-south attitude is preferred, the NW-SE orientation appears to be superior as it conforms favourably with the cosmological conditions of the Universe. NW-SE being locations of the Gates to Heaven.

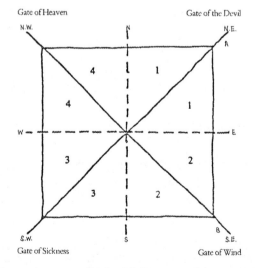

Generally, meandering and undulating features are preferred so as to reduce the amount of malevic *qi* in the site and also as a means of containing good *qi*. All three landscape components (water, trees and hilly feature) are often employed as shields against *sha qi* and should therefore be located in the rear of any U-shaped pattern or in the direction most likely to harbour malevic forces.

Conversely, entrances in the NE-SW are avoided as much as possible for the Gates of Hell and Gates of Illness are harbingers of ill fortune. The Hongkong and Shanghai Bank represents a prominent case in point where the escalators to the main banking hall take a N.E. aspect.

The following diagrams, digested from Low Wai Lang's extraction from the Imperial Encyclopedia, puts down in graphic form some Fengshui guidelines which I consider to have greatest direct impact on architecture. They exist on the level of general application and in no way takes into account astrological compatibility between specific individuals and the buildings or sites which they inhabit. Such an exercise dwells beyond the scope of this thesis. The diagrams are divided into 2 sections: Good (吉) and bad influences (凶) and should provide a fair idea of the overlay of cosmology onto the rational in general Fengshui practice.

GOOD

Room facing south

Depth of the enclosure is greater than its width

Living room in the centre

Master bedroom at the head of the living area

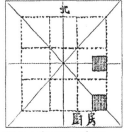
Kitchen in the east or south-east

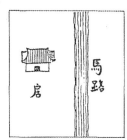
Road to the east

BAD

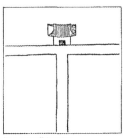
House at a T-junction

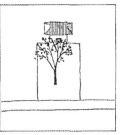
A tree in front of the house

Small building overshadowed by a tall building

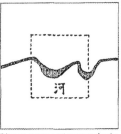
River or stream cutting across the site

High boundary walls

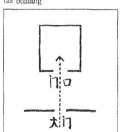
Alignment of main door with subunit door

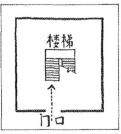
Staircase facing the maindoor

A tree growing through the roof

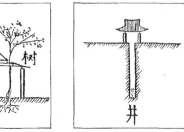
House over a well

19. Fengshui 295

abstractions of the Chinese view of the world (micro environment) and the universe (macro environment).

The guidelines stipulated are applicable throughout all levels of planning. This is consistent with the *Yijing's* theory of infinite progression and regression.

NOTES

1. *Foreword by Robert van Over:* I-Ching; *publ.* The New American Library, Inc. *1971.*
2. *Afterword by John Mitchell,* Fengshui; Ernest J. Eitel, *Synergetic Press 1984.*
3. *The Living Earth Manual of Fengshui, Stephen Skinner, ch.1 p.9; Graham Brash (Pte) Ltd, Singapore.*
4. *At a time when the British Empire had control over a large portion of the globe and being a member of the clergy, Eitel's British supremacist attitude is evident and he was to conclude that Fengshui was "the blind gropings of the Chinese mind after a system of natural science and was marked for decay and dissolution."*
5. *It was in one of her earlier books,* Chinese Geomancy, *Singapore 1979, that she came to term Fengshui as pseudo-science.*
6. *Low's attitude is the epitome of ambivalence, saying, "If you believe it, it exists. If you don't, it doesn't."*
7. *Geological research into plate tectonics reveal cyclical thermal and movement patterns within the earth's crust. Startling discoveries include the switching of the earth's polarity over regular intervals millions of years apart.*
8. *The key idea being the concept of Qi.*
9. *John Mitchell, (afterword* Feng Shui: *Eitel).*
    Other definitions:
    "*The art of living in harmony with the land and deriving the greatest benefit, peace and prosperity from being in the right place at the right time is called Fenghui."—S. Skinner,* The Living Earth Manual of Feng Shui.
    "*This well-known word (Fengshui) means wind-water, but in its wider sense stands for the relations to the surrounding nature, the influence of the landscape, the beauty of the buildings and the happiness of the inhabitants." Ernst Borschmann,* Picturesque China.
10. *Skinner, etymological note on Fengshui,* The Living Earth Manual of Fengshui.
11. *Sarah Rosebach,* Fengshui, the Chinese Art of Placement.
12. *A good environmental image gives its possessor an important sense of emotional security. Accordingly, all cultures have developed "systems of orientation." That is, "spatial structures" which facilitate development of a good environmental image, these systems of orientation being often based or derived from a natural structure.*
13. Fengshui: *Ernst J. Eitel, p. 48. Here Eitel expounds on the Chinese belief in Man's capacity to influence Fengshui and hence to a limited degree, his destiny.*
    Linyun, a noted practitioner of Fengshui in Hong Kong also agrees that Man's influence is limited. The general course of events cannot be altered.
14. *Stephen Skinner's opinion on the segregation of the two schools. General practice however, seems to amalgamate the two modes of thought.*
15. *A more thorough exposition of the basic rides are provided in S. Skinner's* Living Earth Manual of Fengshui *and in Low Wai Lang's* Chinese Geomancy and Architecture, *a fourth year B. Arch, elective,* NUS.
16. *Transl. Needham, 1962, vol. 4, part 1, p. 262. cf. S. Skinner.*

20 Overview of Collective and Shared Housing

Karen A. Franck

This text describes alternatives to the single-family suburban land use pattern.

Collective housing, as defined in this book, is housing that features spaces and facilities for joint use by all residents who also maintain their own individual households. These spaces and facilities form a central characteristic of the housing and not simply an added amenity. Today in collective housing, the shared facilities supplement complete, self-sufficient dwelling units so that each household has its own kitchen even though there also is a larger, shared kitchen. In the past, shared facilities in collective housing often replaced facilities conventionally placed in individual dwelling units; thus individual units often lacked private kitchens, but the individuality and separateness of the households was acknowledged, both socially and spatially, in other ways.

Today's collective housing can be distinguished from shared housing, in which unrelated individuals share single dwelling units, forming joint or group households.[1] In shared housing, spaces or facilities that usually are part of the "private domain of individual households, such as kitchens, bathrooms, and living rooms, are placed in the shared domain of the joint household. Shared housing differs from collective housing in the degree of autonomy and privacy of the occupants. In this overview both collective and shared housing are discussed, while the subsequent chapters in this section focus primarily on collective housing."[2]

While shared and collective housing differ in the degree of autonomy of the households and in the types of spaces that are shared, they are similar in other respects. In both types of housing, sharing means at the very least the joint use of common facilities and spaces by unrelated persons or households. Sharing may also mean social interaction between residents, group activities, and coordination and cooperation in pursuit of common tasks. Both are intended for long-term occupancy; they are not intended exclusively for special user groups; and they are not intentional communities where residents hold a common set of philosophical or religious beliefs that guide their everyday lives. In these different ways shared and collective housing can be distinguished from other types of housing with shared spaces and facilities—such as military barracks, dormitories, congregate housing for the elderly, community group homes for people with mental or

Karen Franck; Karen Franck & Sherry Ahretzen, eds., "Overview of Collective and Shared Households," from *New Households, New Housing*, pp. 3–19. Copyright © 1989 by Karen Franck. Permission to reprint granted by the author.

other disabilities, convents, monasteries, and Utopian communities. Several of these other types, however, are precursors of contemporary shared and collective housing.

HISTORY OF HOUSING WITH SHARED SPACES IN THE UNITED STATES

In the nineteenth and early twentieth centuries there was a great variety of housing with shared facilities and spaces. Utopian communities, both religious and nonsectarian, located in rural areas, were particularly numerous between 1820 and 1850 (Hayden 1976) and some still exist, such as the Hutterite communities in New York State and elsewhere. Other forms of cooperative living, including cooperative living clubs and early cooperative apartment buildings, were not intentional communities but were based on the premise that joint use of spaces and facilities by unrelated individuals or households had economic, practical, and social advantages.

One cooperative living club was the Jane Club, organized by Mary Kenney in Chicago for young, single female workers and managed by the residents. The building for the Jane Club that opened in 1898 included 30 private bedrooms, a social room, a dining room, a kitchen, a laundry-room, and a bicycle and trunk storage room (Hayden 1981). From 1885 to 1920, women in other cities organized cooperative boarding clubs. In an exhibition in the Woman's Building at the Columbian Exposition, Mary Coleman Stuckert displayed her drawings and model of a proposed new community with cooperative housekeeping facilities. Facilities in her plan included a meeting hall, library, kindergarten, kitchen, dining room, and laundry. In 1916 Alice Constance Austin planned an entire cooperative colony to be built in Llan del Rio, California. Hot meals were to arrive at each house from a central kitchen and dirty dishes were to be returned to the kitchen via an underground tunnel. The dwellings themselves had no kitchens at all (Hayden 1981). While the Jane Club depended on cooperation and exchange among residents and Stuckert's plan expected residents to eat together, in Austin's plan the individual households would eat in their own houses. The advantage of the central kitchen was practical rather than social: to save the time and energy that individual households spend preparing their own meals.

The first speculative cooperative apartment buildings in New York also contained extensive common facilities. Hudson View Gardens—built in 1924—contained a restaurant, a staff of maids, a commissary, a supervised playground, a beauty shop, and a barber shop (Hayden 1981). In 1925 the United Workers Cooperative Association built in the Bronx the Workers' Cooperative Colony, consisting of 750 units, an auditorium, a library, a kindergarten and nursery, and, nearby, other commercial facilities and a cafeteria. In addition to family apartments, private rooms were clustered around a shared kitchen: these were intended for single people and the elderly, whose relatives also sometimes lived in the project. A cooperative restaurant and then, in 1937, a cooperative dining club did develop. Early rental apartment houses and apartment hotels for the well-to-do in New York and Boston also were frequently equipped with extensive common facilities, as were residences for single men and single women (see chapter 2).

Experiments with collective living in the United States declined significantly following the 1930s, particularly after World War II, when the single-family detached house, long an American ideal, became affordable to many more families. Prime among its characteristics are spatial and social privacy and self-sufficiency: ideally it is to be occupied only by members of a single household who are related to each other by blood or marriage; no spaces or faculties are to be shared with other households; and all household tasks are to be performed by each household, separately (Franck 1987). With growing economic prosperity and increases in retirement benefits after World

War II, both young single adults and elderly people were able to afford to live as independent households (Glick 1984). And they were expected to live in dwelling units, often apartments, that approximated the ideal of the social and spatial privacy of the single-family house even when these dwellings were occupied by single adults. Alternatives that entailed the sharing of a single-family house by several unrelated adults often were forbidden by local zoning ordinances, as they still are. Both the dwelling unit (house or apartment) and the household occupying it became increasingly privatized and isolated (Slater 1970).

At present the types of housing in the United States that do have shared facilities as a central defining feature tend to be exclusively for students, the elderly, or other particular types of residents. Moreover, the housing segregates these different types of residents from each other and from other kinds of households. In congregate housing for the elderly, residents' complete private apartments are supplemented by communal dining rooms and other common spaces and by recreational and health services. In retirement communities the elderly have individual houses that are supplemented by club houses or community centers and other facilities that provide a great variety of recreational activities. Security, assistance in case of emergency, and lack of maintenance responsibilities are additional benefits. Life-care communities also provide private apartments and shared spaces, offering residents increasing levels of health-care and housekeeping services as they become increasingly frail. Dormitories and other forms of housing exclusively for students are examples of housing with shared facilities for short-term residence. Students may have single rooms and share bathrooms or they may share apartments; in either case these units are supplemented by additional shared spaces for studying or relaxing. Community group homes are supportive housing for people with mental disabilities or other handicaps; they provide bedrooms, shared bathrooms, shared kitchens, and additional common social spaces. Residence in these may be short or long term.

The predominance in the United States of housing with shared spaces and facilities for particular groups indicates how much contemporary American society tends to view such housing as appropriate for people with specialized needs. This assumes that those who are not in school, not elderly, and not handicapped do not desire, and would not benefit from, more sharing of spaces and facilities than is currently available in conventional housing, in which a high degree of social and spatial separation is the norm.

It is hard to tell whether other types of households in the United States would in fact appreciate more opportunities to share spaces and facilities in the residential setting since there are so few cases for them to see or experience. One survey, conducted by Leavitt and Saegert, of readers of *Ms.* magazine indicated a strong willingness among women to share living spaces (Van Gelder 1986). Twenty-six percent were willing to share a kitchen or a living room (18 and 17 percent already did so); 19 percent were willing to share a bathroom (15 percent already did so). One reason for sharing living space is to share housing costs. Of those with annual household incomes under $10,000, 53 percent would like to share housing costs. But even among those with incomes over $75,000, 21 percent said they would like to share housing costs. Respondents also drew their own plans of ideal homes and mentioned other advantages of sharing. When describing her plan one woman mentioned "the opportunity for group work and play." Another, who saw an advantage in service professionals living together, referred to a "place where life and living blur into an unsegmented whole" (Van Gelder 1986, 40). While the questions in the survey referred to being "willing" to share spaces, respondents also seemed to express a desire to do so.

ADVANTAGES OF SHARED AND COLLECTIVE HOUSING

Shared housing—housing in which a single dwelling is occupied by independent and unrelated adults who use the same kitchen within the unit—has economic, practical, and social advantages. Cost savings from sharing facilities can significantly lower the rent or the mortgage payments for each individual. The sharing of costs also allows for amenities that no resident could afford alone, such as a large living room, a garden, or an excellent location (Raimy 1979). Practical advantages can result from sharing household responsibilities, such as grocery shopping, preparing meals, and cleaning, which can give residents more time for other activities. Taking advantage of this potential, however, requires coordination and cooperation.

The social benefits of shared housing include the increased security and support provided by the simple presence of others; possibilities for social interaction, companionship, and friendship between residents; and organized group activities. One form of shared housing that has developed in the United States is the purchase or rental of large houses by nonprofit organizations for occupancy by unrelated individuals who are often, but not exclusively, elderly. In her research on eight cases of such housing, occupied primarily by elderly people, West (1981) makes a clear distinction between the support and security of co-presence and other more active forms of sharing. West found that a primary reason for moving to these group residences is "not to be alone." Sometimes a move followed a frightening event such as fainting or a criminal attack. These residents may be seeking the security of shared presence rather than more frequent social interaction. And, indeed, the degree of actual sharing of activities was relatively low. Most residents, 60 percent, reported that they spent most of their time in their own rooms. Almost half of the residents interviewed reported that they had imagined that group living would generate a lot of enjoyable group activities, but it had not. Except for group meals that were served to residents, the kinds of sharing that occurred most frequently were between a few residents and were part of a brief, unplanned encounter.

Significantly those residents in West's research who were most satisfied with group living were living in groups of 6 to 10 members; those least satisfied were in groups of 16 to 20. Building form contributed significantly to the amount of active social sharing among residents. The greatest amount of social interaction occurred in buildings of several stories, such as townhouses, and the least amount occurred in sites with detached, horizontal layouts. Residents in the former also were more satisfied with the amount of privacy they had. Since these were older houses, West speculates that the townhouses may have had more transition spaces and niches (stair landings and breakfast nooks) that allowed casual exchanges between residents when they were on their way somewhere.

Contemporary collective housing, in which shared spaces and facilities supplement complete dwelling units, is very rare in the United States (when collective housing is distinguished from housing for special groups). The advantages of such housing, as demonstrated by research on collective housing in Denmark and Sweden, are somewhat different from the advantages of shared housing (see chapters 4 and 5). The economic advantage of collective housing is primarily the opportunity to have amenities that might be difficult for single households to afford, such as darkrooms, workshops, one or more guest rooms, or very large living rooms. The actual cost of a dwelling unit is not likely to be reduced in collective housing; in many cases it is the same as or higher than the cost of conventional apartments or houses. The practical and social advantages are considerable, but many of them, as in shared housing, depend on coordination and cooperation among residents to perform tasks. The regular sharing of meals saves individual households the time and effort of preparing every evening meal on their own (and of the related efforts of grocery shopping and cleaning up). This can be particularly desirable for working parents. The shared spaces also provide greater opportunity for sharing child-care responsibilities. Beyond the security and support extended by the presence of others, there is the social interaction and companionship generated by joint activities, particularly the sharing of meals and their preparation, which make for a richer domestic life for adults and for children. In this way collective housing offers advantages over the separation of conventional single-family houses.

Interaction and independence, community and privacy are significant issues in the design and use of shared and collective housing. In shared housing the single common kitchen reduces the independence and the privacy of each resident; however, the provision of private baths and private entrances in shared housing can enhance independence. Social interaction and the development of community can be enhanced by having a social space large enough to accommodate all residents for a meal. Day-Lower, West, and Zimmers (1985) recommend that seating areas, such as window seats or breakfast nooks, be placed near circulation paths or adjacent to transition spaces such as doorways and stair landings. Similarly, a variety of spaces for sitting, both indoors and outdoors, that have a sense of intimacy can invite private conversations between residents.

In collective housing the presence of complete dwelling units *and* common spaces allows for a greater balance of community and privacy, but whether social interaction and the development of community actually occur depends on the residents, just as it does in shared housing. Thus many of the same design features suggested for shared housing are useful in collective housing. These include a space to accommodate the entire community for a meal, additional shared spaces and facilities, and spaces indoors and outdoors that offer residents an opportunity to linger and chat. (For more suggestions see chapters 4 and 5.)

In both types of housing the shared spaces can only accommodate and encourage interaction between residents; they cannot ensure that it occurs. When the common spaces are truly used, especially when they are used for regular common meals, the potential social benefit of such housing for generating active social sharing is realized. Simply having the spaces for such activities is not enough to realize this potential; a high proportion of the residents must be committed to reorganizing and performing the tasks that regular group activities require. A lack of regular group activities does not, however, diminish the other advantages—enjoying shared amenities and the support and security provided by the simple presence of other residents.

The range of economic, practical, and social advantages of shared and collective housing is apparent in the following contemporary American cases and in the historic and contemporary American and European cases described in subsequent chapters in this section. The American cases of shared housing include mingle units, quads, GoHomes, and sponsored group residences. Two cases of American collective housing also are presented.

MINGLE UNITS

Mingle units are apartments or single-family houses that are purposely designed for occupancy by two people who wish to share housing costs without sacrificing too much privacy or independence. The motivation for sharing is thus largely economic rather than social or practical, although the simple presence of another person offers the kind of comfort and security offered by other types of shared housing. The distinguishing design characteristic of mingle units is the floor plan: it contains two "master," or principal, bedroom suites of comparable size and amenities, each with its own bathroom. Only two people share the dwelling; they often are co-purchasers and therefore share a mortgage and the financial and legal responsibilities it entails.

One of the hallmarks of the post-World War II American single-family house has been the social and spatial hierarchy of the bedrooms; a single master bedroom that is relatively large and private and often has its own bathroom with one or more subsidiary bedrooms that are smaller and less private and may share a bath. The underlying assumption is that the master bedroom will be shared by mother and father and the subsidiary bedrooms will be occupied by children, preferably one for each child. The desirability of this arrangement may be questionable even for the traditional nuclear family. It is, however, not at all suitable for a household that is not hierarchically organized, such as one consisting of two independent single persons, a single parent and a grown child, or two couples. The mingles plan, by virtue of the equal size and amenities of the two bedroom suites and their privacy, can better meet the needs of these other household types.

The term *mingles* was most likely coined by developers who began using the plan in the late 1970s as a way of attracting buyers who could not afford to buy a house or an apartment without sharing the costs. In 1981 about 20 percent of the homes built by Berkus Group Associates were designed for this "tandem living style," as were one third of the units built by Fisher Friedman (Gottschalk 1981). Visits to new developments in southern California in 1984 indicated that the mingles plan was routinely included in new tract housing of single-family detached and attached homes, comprising from 10 to 30 percent of all units.

One type of mingles plan, illustrated in the plan from Tierra Vista in Serrano Highlands, California, shows bedrooms of equal size with comparable bath and storage space (Fig. 1-1). Moreover, the suites are separated by the shared living/dining spaces, giving each bedroom some privacy. While the dining space is somewhat separated from the living space, it is not separated enough to constitute a second, distinct social space. While all the two-bedroom plans at Tierra Vista feature two complete and separate bedroom suites, only this plan was described in the sales brochure as "the perfect plan for sharing singles." Of the 12 two-bedroom units sold as of June 1984, three had been sold to tandem buyers, in all cases to women who work together.

Another mingles plan, from a development built by Lewis Homes in Upland, California, provides two social spaces—the living room and the kitchen (Fig. 1-2). These are separate and more distinct than the comparable spaces at Tierra Vista. This plan allows each resident to use a space outside of his or her own suite without intruding on the other resident.

In many essential features the mingles house is no different from the traditional single-family house. What is different is the expectation of who will live there, the nature of their relationship, and their need for two social areas and for equal and complete bedroom suites that are as private as possible. Privacy and equality of members within the unit have thus become more important than in the traditional single-family house, where hierarchy of members is the rule. Indeed, privacy, independence, and equality seem to be more significant design issues than sharing in the mingles plan.

QUADS

Quads are a type of rental housing built by private owners, for profit, to house students, single working people, or elderly people who are willing to share a kitchen and

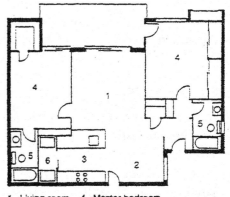

1. Living room 4. Master bedroom
2. Dining area 5. Bathroom
3. Kitchen 6. Washer / dryer

Figure 1.1. Mingles unit at Tierra Vista in Serrano Highlands, California: floor plan.

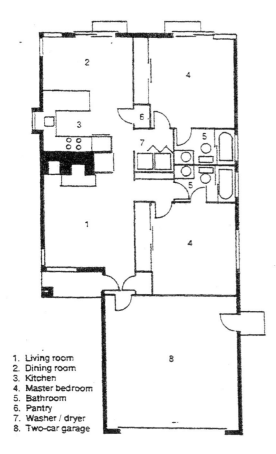

Figure 1-2. Mingles unit at Las Flores in Upland, California: floor plan.

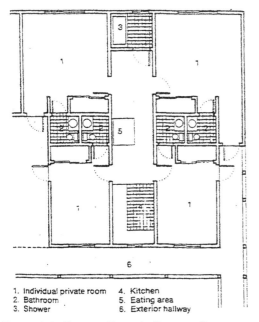

Figure 1-3. Campus Court in Eugene, Oregon: floor plan of a quad.

a bathtub/shower with other residents. Each room has its own toilet and sink. Each kitchen is shared by four persons, hence the term *quad*, which seems to be a local term in Eugene, Oregon, where 10 or 15 quad complexes were built in the early 1970s. Some cater to students and others to single working people and the elderly.

The site I visited, Campus Court, has 26 quad units, or a total of 104 bedrooms. The bedrooms range from 130 to 190 square feet; rents range from $215 to $235 a month with a lease that extends from September to June. The striking characteristic of the quad is a floor plan that allows each bedroom to have its own door to an exterior corridor, creating a private entry and exit for each resident (Fig. 1-3). A bed, a dresser, and a refrigerator are provided in each room. Four bedrooms are grouped around a kitchen to which each room has access. The kitchen, narrow and rather uninviting in layout, serves a purely utilitarian function (Fig. 1-4). There are no other gathering spaces except the roof, which is used for sunbathing.

The physical appearance of Campus Court is more like a motel than a college dormitory. The intention is to provide affordable housing at a profit to the owner. At the same time aspects of dormitory life are present. A live-in manager interviews new residents and tries to place them with people they will get along with. Housekeeping services, including weekly vacuuming, are provided; residents provide their own linen. The manager has found it preferable to restrict residency to students because of their common lifestyle; the habits of working people tend to conflict with those of students.

The intentions behind quads are economic and practical: to give students and other single persons housing that has a high degree of privacy and security and is affordable by virtue of the single-room accommodations, the shared kitchens, and the shared shower and tub. The social benefits of sharing—such as social interaction, group activities, and performance of common tasks—may develop among residents, but these are not explicit objectives. Nor does the design of the kitchen appear to encourage such activities.

GOHOMES

GoHomes are the invention of architect Ted Smith. The first one was built in 1983 in Del Mar, outside San Diego (Fig. 1-5). It was built as a four-unit cooperative house that combines work space with living space in each unit and provides private bathrooms, private entrances from the outdoors, and a shared kitchen.[3] Smith's intentions were to provide affordable housing, with work spaces, within walking distance of the beach and to meet the local zoning requirements for a single-family house (by having only one kitchen). The building is cooperatively owned by shareholders, who each paid $10,000 per share and then paid for or did most of the interior and facade work for his or her unit. Each shareholder pays $350 a month in carrying costs. Of the four original residents, one is a professional musician who gives music lessons; another uses his work space for drafting; a third does stained-glass work; and a fourth is a computer buff.

Each unit has two levels—the second a loft space—and each has its own very small bathroom (one is only 3 feet by 8 feet). Most of the units have a little less than 500 square feet of floor space on the two levels. Each unit has two entrances from the outdoors, one for professional use and one for residential use, and one entrance to the shared kitchen (Fig. 1-6).

In this GoHome Smith wanted to maximize the individuality and the independence of the units and to limit the connectedness between them. In his observations of housesharing among his friends, he noticed how much they prized their privacy: to be able to come and go without passing through common areas and to eat in their own spaces. Therefore the kitchen is primarily utilitarian. Smith reported in 1984 that this GoHome "was not meant to be a beautiful communal living space. … It is missing the thing that makes a place feel like a home—the kitchen. Most of the GoHome is workspace." Privacy and independence more than shared use were the guiding concerns in the design of the first GoHome.

Two subsequent GoHomes, also built in Del Mar, follow the same principles of providing affordable living and working spaces near the beach, with a shared kitchen, private baths, private entrances from the outdoors, and private entrances from the units to the kitchen. Like the first GoHome these are designed to allow for possible future conversion to a single-family house in order to increase their flexibility. The number of units, or what Smith calls "suites," has been increased to six and the shared kitchens are larger. Rents or carrying charges for suites in the latest GoHomes are $450 to $500, while rents for newly built efficiency apartments in Del Mar are about $650.

In the second GoHome one of the six suites is used as an office/workshop by three of the residents—two architects and a furniture maker. This work space is contiguous with the shared kitchen/dining area. Smith reports that there is much more active sharing between residents here than in the first GoHome, with sharing of meals and assignment of tasks. "There is less independence," he says. "It's more like a big family and less like independent houses." In the third GoHome a domed ceiling graces the 20-by-14-foot kitchen, which opens onto a deck. A pair of units joined together provides a place for a couple to live. Smith is keen to encourage a mixture of households—both singles and couples.

Smith adopted the term *GoHome* from the lyrics of a song written by a friend. According to Smith, the word refers to getting back to basics and returning to an earlier, "sweeter time." The concept reflects his desire to see a more integrated city, based on combinations of uses instead of separations. As a model the GoHome is a way "to put the city back together" (Katkov 1984, 51). The basic model remains constant: affordable living and working spaces that support privacy as well as community and that have various sizes and shapes, where ceiling height is as important as

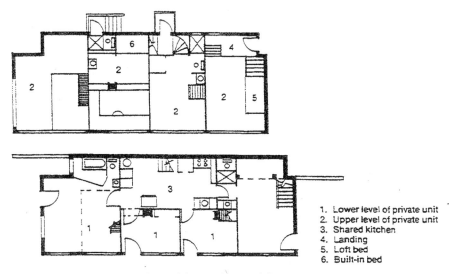

Figure 1-6. First GoHome: plans of first and second floors.

amount of floor space. Possible variations are numerous, including the incorporation of varying amounts of shared space and the integration of GoHomes with other dwelling units. A combination of GoHomes and row houses is to be built on a site in downtown San Diego.

SPONSORED GROUP RESIDENCES

Sponsored group residences are houses purchased (or leased) and managed by nonprofit organizations for occupancy by unrelated individuals or small households such as couples or single-parent families. These and other organizations also operate services to match renters with homeowners. The National Shared Housing Resource Center in Philadelphia, which provides technical assistance, resource development, and training for shared housing and matching programs, estimates that there are 400 such programs nationwide (Damiani 1988).

One such program is the Boston Aging Concerns (BAC), which owns and manages one of the earliest intergenerational group residences in the country, the Shared Living House in Boston's Back Bay. It was established in 1979 in what had originally been a private home and then a lodging house. Currently the Victorian building contains 14 bedrooms and one complete apartment in addition to a common kitchen, living room, and dining room. The bedrooms vary in size; some are as small as 80 square feet. In 1985 rents ranged from $165 to $312 a month. In August 1985, 12 of the 13 tenants in residence were women and 9 of them were age 50 or over.

Residents are expected to share household maintenance chores and to contribute to the purchase of food staples for the kitchen. Once a week residents have dinner together and hold a meeting that is attended by a facilitator from BAC. Although the intention of BAC is for additional meals to be shared, residents tend to cook individually, with two or three sometimes cooking jointly. The original goal was to create a strong sense of community where there would be frequent group activity, but residents' strongest reason for living there is economic rather than social; people choose to live there for its desirable location in the Back Bay, its pleasant atmosphere, and its low rent rather than for the opportunity to interact with others. As in the group residences studied by West (1985), sharing primarily takes the form of common use of facilities and informal, unplanned contacts rather than frequent group activities or coordination and exchange among residents. Several residents are frustrated by the lack of social interaction and the infrequency of group activities.

Innovative Housing, a shared housing program in Mill Valley, California, sponsors and manages 100 shared houses. Their activities include leasing or purchasing houses for sharing and aiding the operation of these houses through workshops and other support activities, facilitating shared homeownership, developing living and working spaces for sharing, and designing and developing small cooperative communities of shared houses. One example of the last activity is a vest pocket community of seven group residences, designed by Dan Solomon, to be built on two adjacent sites in Fairfax, California (Fig. 1-7). Each of the seven houses will have a study, a shared kitchen, and a spacious living/dining area with a fireplace (Figs. 1-8 and 1-9). Two of the houses also will have community rooms that residents from all the house rooms will be decided by the residents, with funding for furniture or equipment from Innovative Housing. Possibilities include a library, an exercise room, and a computer room. To enhance privacy, the bedrooms, with the exception of the bedrooms for handicapped residents, will be placed on the second floor. Two rooms will share a bathroom but each will have its own sink. House Three also will have sleeping porches on the second floor, which can be furnished with a desk, a window seat, or an additional bed, depending on residents' wishes (Fig. 1-9). Each cluster of houses will have its own outdoor space, and there also will be a trellis and a barbecue pit for use by the entire community.

All together the houses can accommodate 30 people, with single parents having the option of renting one of the rooms with an adjoining sleeping porch to give them more space. Innovative Housing encourages residents to share meals, but the decision to do so is left up to each household. Initially, core groups of two to three residents for each house will participate in a series of workshops conducted by Innovative Housing. These core groups will then set up the houses, make decisions on sharing arrangements and the final interior design and furnishings, and interview additional residents for the house. Rents are projected to be $350 to $400 a month.

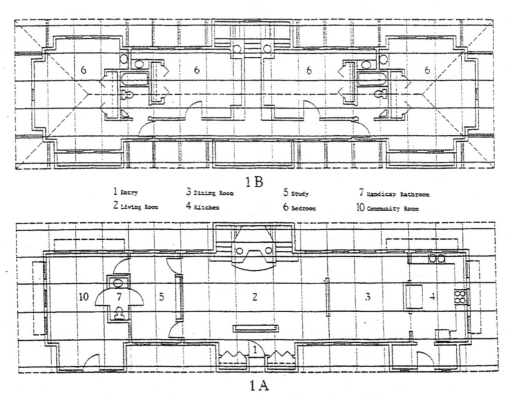

Figure 1-8. Innovative Housing Vest Pocket Community: plans of first and second floors, House 1.

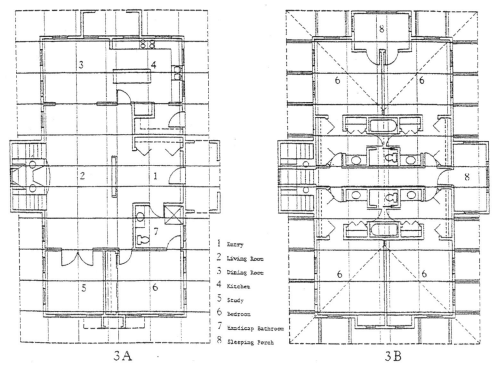

Figure 1-9. Innovative Housing Vest Pocket Community: plans of first and second floors, House 3.

COLLECTIVE HOUSING

338 Harvard Street in Cambridge, Massachusetts, and Sunlight in Portland, Oregon, are cases of collective housing where a common kitchen and living space are provided in addition to private dwelling units that have their own kitchens, baths, and living spaces. 338 Harvard Street is a former Lutheran rectory that has been renovated by developer/architect Gwen Rono (Fig. 1-10). The house, with a new addition, now contains ten complete one- and two-bedroom apartments and several shared spaces: a large living/dining room served by an adjacent kitchen (with laundry), a study, a garden, a sun deck, and a guest room and bath (Fig. 1-11). The condominium apartments cost between $130,000 and $220,000 and range in size from 556 to 935 square feet. Details are planned to create a "sense of gracious living." These include hardwood floors, a fireplace in the shared living room, a large and elegant entry hall, and terraces for five of the apartments.

Rono's goal was to provide housing for empty-nesters that would encourage social interaction between residents and a strong sense of community while removing the cost and burden of maintaining a private home. She aimed to achieve an age mix, with 80 percent age 60 or over. The original sales brochure emphasized "an ongoing opportunity for residents to participate in the evolution and development of their own supportive community; ten attractive apartments designed to preserve privacy and independence; gracious common spaces to encourage the community life of the house."

As it turned out, the age range of residents is wider than expected; 60 percent are over 50, and three owners do not live in their units but lease them to students or young professionals. People's reasons for living in the house are thus more diverse than originally expected, with less of a central focus on the creation of a supportive community. Nonetheless, monthly potluck dinners and house meetings are held in the common living room and several residents gather there for coffee on Saturday mornings. Residents also use the living room for their own parties.

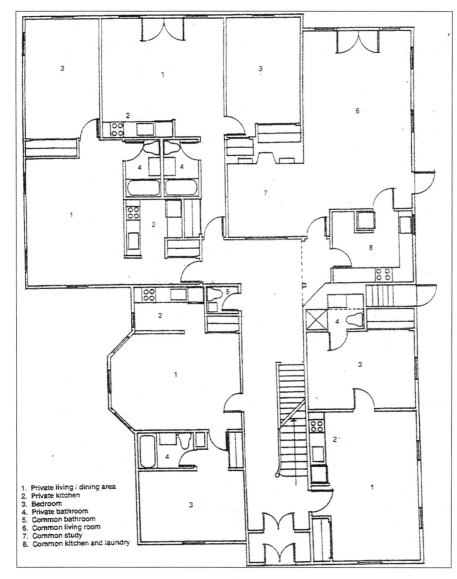

Figure 1-11. 338 Harvard Street: plan of first floor. *(Gwen Rono, Architect)*

The guest-room was so heavily used that another room, intended to be an office, was converted to a second guestroom. Although the common living room and study are not heavily used, the residents appreciate these rooms very much: they provide a sense of space and present additional options. Since the condominium association was established, residents have taken on more responsibility for common household tasks, such as sorting the mail, and as more of the owners begin to live in their apartments, the use of common areas and the sense of community are likely to increase.

While 338 Harvard Street was created by an outside sponsor, Sunlight in Portland is a community created by the residents themselves. Beginning in the early 1970s, a group of six families, including Bill Church, a local architect and planner, held regular potluck suppers in their neighborhood in northwest Portland, sometimes two or three times a week. They also shared a sailboat. In 1976 they decided to buy and share an apartment building but later decided against it because of the lack of privacy between apartments. The group grew to eight families who met regularly; all decisions were made by consensus. Eventually the group decided to build on land that was suitable for solar design, on a bus line, and 20 minutes from downtown Portland. A site was found and purchased, and construction of 15 single-family detached houses and one community building began in 1977 on a 6 ½-acre sloped, wooded site.

The group also agreed on a number of design restrictions by which all would abide: parking in one location separated from all the houses; houses built above the shadow line, using passive solar heating; and houses made of weathered cedar only one story in height and unobtrusive in the landscape. Each family contributed an equal amount to the purchase price of the land and to the cost of the community building, but the cost of the construction of the individual houses varied. Each family owns its own house and the ground beneath it; all other land is owned in common.

Church and another architect in the group served as planners and advisors. Each family designed its own house within the restrictions. The houses range from 800 to 2,400 square feet; there are no garages or basements. The result is, indeed, unobtrusive houses of different sizes tied into the slope, surrounded by trees and reached by winding lanes. The community building contains a large gathering/dining space that can seat 75 people for a meal, a kitchen, a guest room/study with bath, and a workshop with tools donated by residents (Fig. 1-13). A potluck dinner is held every Wednesday evening and usually is attended by about 20 people. Outside groups can rent the community space for gatherings. An athletic field was added in 1984. Decisions are still made by consensus.

In collective housing, unlike in shared housing, the comfort and security of co-residence are offered without sacrificing the privacy and independence created by complete individual dwelling units (Table 1-1). The luxury of having community *and* privacy with spaces designed for both extremes should a be more frequent design consideration in all kinds of housing. Even households happy with the privacy and independence of traditional dwellings may desire, in addition, common spaces that support shared activities between households and between households of different ages and lifestyles. The chapters in this section present additional cases of communities that offer these opportunities.

Table 1-1. Characteristics of Contemporary Shared and Collective Housing in the United States[1]

	No. of People or Households Sharing	Bathrooms	Kitchens	Entrances from Outdoors
Shared housing Mingle units	2 people	1 per person	1	1 for 2 people
Quads	4 people	1 sink/toilet per person 1 tub/shower for 4 people	1	4 people
GoHomes	4–6 people	1 per person	1	1 per person
Group homes	4–20 people	Sometimes 1 per person	1	1 for whole house
Collective housing[2]	10–1 households	1 or more per household	1 per household and 1 for all households	Sometimes 1 for each household

1. In shared housing unrelated individuals share a single dwelling unit and thus constitute a single household. In collective housing each household has its own complete dwelling unit and then all the households share additional spaces and facilities.
2. This is based on only two examples, which are described in the text.

OVERVIEW OF CHAPTERS

Nineteenth- and early-twentieth-century collective housing is the topic of chapters 2 and 3. In "Apartments and Collective Life in Nineteenth-Century New York," Elizabeth Cromley describes the development of a variety of accommodations that offered various combinations of individual rooms, suites, or apartments with shared spaces and facilities. The apartment hotel or family hotel offered permanent residence in private suites of living rooms and bedrooms, supplemented by shared dining rooms and parlors. Middle-class families with children and young couples often lived in such buildings. Buildings also were designed for other groups, including single working women and bachelors. Cromley reviews the kinds of design and occupancy issues architects, developers, and residents faced during this time. What should be private and what might be shared was not a foregone conclusion but rather a question to be debated and explored.

In "Early European Collective Habitation: From Utopian Ideal to Reality," Norbert Schoenauer describes the rich array of early-collective housing that was built or proposed in England, Denmark, Germany, Austria, Switzerland, Sweden, and the Soviet Union. In these examples, as in those described by Cromley, meal preparation and other housekeeping tasks were performed by building staff, and the buildings were designed for various types of households, including families with children. Collective housing in Europe, however, was more often part of a larger political or social agenda than it was in the United States.

Chapters 4 and 5 chronicle contemporary efforts in Sweden and Denmark to develop collective housing and describe the results of these efforts. In "Communal Housing in Sweden: A Remedy for the Stress of Everyday Life?" Alison Woodward focuses primarily on rental housing built by public authorities. A variety of shared spaces and facilities supplement complete apartments. The buildings house a mixture of residents, including many families with children. In some of her examples meal preparation and other tasks are done by the residents themselves; in others this service is provided by a staff hired by the management. Woodward gives detailed history of the recent development of collective housing in Sweden and presents findings from a survey of residents in four projects.

In "Cohousing in Denmark," Kathryn McCamant and Charles Durrett outline the development and the essential social, design, and management characteristics of Danish collective housing. These communities supplement complete individual dwellings with a community house that contains a common kitchen, a dining/living area, and various other shared spaces and facilities. Significantly, these communities are planned, designed, and managed by the residents themselves. Community life centers most directly on regular, shared evening meals prepared by the residents. The authors suggest how the Danish collective housing model can be adapted in the United States.

In "The Party Wall as the Architecture of Sharing," Jill Stoner proposes a cultural and architectural transformation of the party wall into a membrane that connects as much as it separates households. This transformation would require changes in the structure, program, and regulations for multifamily housing in the United States. The changes in program center on the idea of larger, more inclusive households, each composed of several smaller subgroups. Examples include two-generation households, households of single-parent families, and households of single adults. The households would occupy "suites" consisting of private and shared spaces. The design and function of the shared spaces, which are generated by the redefined party wall, would vary according to the particular composition of the household.

ADDITIONAL INFORMATION

For additional information on nineteenth- and early twentieth-century collective housing in the United States, see Hayden's *The Grand Domestic Revolution* (1981). For a more complete description of collective aspects of early apartment buildings and apartment hotels in New York, see Cromley's *Alone Together: A History of New York's Early Apartments* (1989). Suggestions for designing group residences are given in Day-Lower, West, and Zimmers' *Designing Shared Residences for the Elderly* (1985). Additional detail and analysis of Danish collective housing are given in McCamant and Durrett's *Cohousing: A Contemporary Approach to Housing Ourselves* (1988).

NOTES

1. This definition of shared housing seems to have been widely accepted in the United States following the development of shared housing programs in the 1970s (Streib 1984; Day-Lower 1983; Raimy 1979), but this particular distinction between collective and shared housing has not been made before, as far as I know. Collective housing as defined here also has been called *communal housing* (see chapter 4) or *congregate housing* (see chapter 8). The latter term, however, tends to refer primarily to housing for the elderly.

2. This overview is based in large part on research conducted by the author on social and spatial innovations in American housing with funds from the National Science Foundation (Grant CE-839721-13). I am grateful to Jerry Finrow for drawing the quad floor plan, to Stephanie Kidd for drawing the mingles units and the GoHome, and to Daniel Solomon and Associates for providing drawings of the Fairfax Vest Pocket Community project.

3. Two units have since been added to the first GoHome.

REFERENCES

Cromley, E. 1989. *Alone Together. A History of New York's Early Apartments*. Ithaca, NY: Cornell University Press.

Damiani, D. M. 1988. Shared lives—Shared experiences—Shared resources. *Shared Housing Quarterly: Special Issue* 5 1:1–3.

Day-Lower, D. 1984. *Shared Housing-for Older People: A Planning Manual for Group Residences*. Philadelphia: Shared Housing Resource Center.

———. Sheree L. West, and H. Zimmers. 1985. *Designing Shared Housing for the Elderly*. Philadelphia: National Shared Housing Resource Center.

Franck, K. A. 1986. Together or apart: Sharing and the American household. In *Discipline of Architecture*, 79–89. Washington D.C.: Association of Collegiate Schools of Architecture.

———. 1987. Shared spaces, small spaces, and spaces that change. In *Housing and Neighborhoods*, ed. W. Van Vliet, H. Choldin, W. Michelson, and D. Popenoe, 137–172. Westport, CT: Greenwood Press.

Glick, P. 1984. American household structure in transition. *Family Planning Perspectives* 16: 305–211.

Gottschalk, E. C. 1981. Doubling up. *The Wall Street Journal* (Apr. 17):18.

Hayden, D. 1976. *Seven American Utopias*. Cambridge, MA: MIT Press.

———. 1981. *The Grand Domestic Revolution: A History of Feminist Designs for American Homes, Neighborhoods and Cities*. Cambridge, MA: MIT Press.

Katkov, R. 1984. The GoHome. *Arts & Architecture* 3:48–51.

McCamant, K. and C. Durrett. 1988. *Cohousing: A Contemporary Approach to Housing Ourselves*. Berkeley, CA Habitat Press.

Raimy, E. 1979. *Shared Houses, Shared Lives*. Los Angeles: J. D. Tarcher.

Slater, P. 1976. *The Pursuit of Loneliness*. Boston: Beacon Press.

Streib. G., F. Folte, and E. and M. A. Hilher. 1984. *Old Homes—New Families*. New York: Columbia University Press.

Van Gelder, L. 1986. Special *Ms.* Poll: Dream houses. *Ms.* (April):34–36, 40, 88.

West, S. 1981. *Sharing and privacy in shared housing for older people*. Ph.D. dissertation. New York: City University of New York.

21 Women and Downtown Open Spaces

Louise Mozingo

Based on observation of where people sit in public parks, Mozingo reports a tendency for women to sit towards the back and men toward the front.

A variety of users participate in the public life of downtown open spaces: the employed and the homeless, young and old, shoppers and tourists, and men and women. My interest is in how men and women perceive and use public space differently; my focus here is on issues designers should consider in order to make downtown open spaces more acceptable to women users.

I shall examine these issues in three ways: by reflecting on the historic division of the city into separate sexual realms, by reviewing the literature discussing psychological factors that effect the perception and behavior of women in public settings, and by reporting on survey and observational research designed to reveal any differences in men's and women's attitudes towards downtown open space.

THE SEXUALLY DIVIDED CITY

To appreciate the cultural context of women in downtown public environments, we must look first at the forces that have shaped the American city—a city divided into male and female realms. Women in downtown public spaces are in the midst of a cultural environment that is the product of a powerful historic dichotomy.

In the late nineteenth century the orientation of American society and economy changed from rural and agrarian to urban and industrial. Cities of a few square miles, "walking cities," evolved into cities of 20 to 50 square miles or larger. As cities grew, land uses became specialized into residential, commercial, and industrial zones.

One by-product of this sorting out was the central business district, which was the center of the new industrial economy. An equally specialized area was the residential district, or suburb. Homogenous residential neighborhoods were built at the edge of the city, initiating a housing pattern that remains dominant to this day.

Louise Mozingo, "Women and Downtown Open Spaces," from *Places*, Vol. 6, No. 1, pp. 38–47. Copyright © 1989 by Design History Foundation. Permission to reprint granted by the publisher.

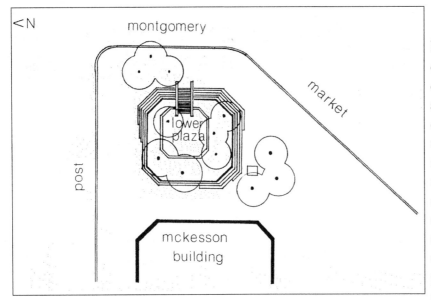

A perhaps unconscious but not (to nineteenth century Americans) unwelcome result was the sexual segregation of the American city. In the walking city, the jumble of commercial, residential, and industrial uses, all proximate to each other, did not establish clear definitions of separate sexual realms. But the central business district, public, and powerful, was a place by and for men.

Moreover, the growth of the suburbs coincided with societal and institutional support for what Rothman calls the concept of "educated motherhood."[1] A myriad of social reformers, municipal agencies, and settlement houses, armed with new knowledge of germ theory and nutrition, set out on a crusade to ensure the well being of the urban mother and child. The gist of this social movement is the cliched but apropos phrase, "a mother's place is in the home"—a home that was in the suburbs, away from the germs, congestion, and moral corruption of the central city.

The 1950s and 1960s suburban explosion and reciprocal "Manhattanization" of the central business district built walls where there had been fences of sexual segregation. Even the one enclave of women downtown—the department store—moved to the suburban shopping mall.

Seagert states: "Urban life and men tend to be thought of as more aggressive, assertive definers of important world events, intellectual, powerful, active, and somewhat dangerous. Women and suburbs share domesticity, repose, closeness to nature, lack of seriousness, mindlessness, and safety."[2] The downtown and the suburb became more than manifestations of sexual segregation and a male-empowered society; they became sexual symbols.

THE PSYCHOLOGY OF WOMEN IN OPEN SPACES

Little research on people's behavior in or reactions to public space has used sex as a primary differential, and specific studies on women and environments are limited. Nevertheless, some general conclusions have been made: women have smaller personal space bubbles than men do (people stand closer to women), women find crowded situations less stressful than men do (and may even find some crowded situations pleasant), and groups of women have smaller territories than groups of men do.

Henly, researching women's personal space, noted that women move out of the way of other pedestrians more often than men. Women in public environments are touched more often than men, and, quite predictably, usually do not reciprocate the touching when it is initiated by men.[3]

Nager and Nelson-Shulman found that women's personal space and anonymity are invaded twice as often as men's. Moreover, men are approached with requests for information (what time is it?) while women most often are encroached upon with intrusions of a sexual nature. They found that "gaze aversion, stiff carriage, susceptibility to invasion, and the tendency to condense space

Crocker Plaza, San Fransisco. A rise with steps provides an area for viewing the action on the street. This row of steps is favored by men.
Photos by Louise Mozingo.

by holding one's arms close to the body are signs of deference and submission communicated non-verbally" by women.[4]

These results make it difficult to say whether women indeed have smaller personal space bubbles and territories, or whether, through constant violations of these psychological boundaries, women learn to adapt while remaining fundamentally uncomfortable. Their personal psychological boundaries are uneasy and undefined.

Proshansky, Ittelson, and Rivlin propose that comfort in regard to these boundaries involves maximizing people's "freedom of choice"—that is, environments with a range of physical settings can provide varying degrees of privacy, territoriality, and crowding.[5]

The small numbers of women in downtown open spaces suggests these environments do not provide women with range of settings that make them psychologically comfortable.

This research leads to two questions about sexually integrating downtown open spaces: How do we manipulate the physical environment to acknowledge appropriate degrees of privacy, territoriality, and crowding? What kind of environments reinforce the psychological boundaries of women?

Case Study: Crocker Plaza and Redwood Park

To understand the factors critical to women's use of downtown parks and plazas, I studied two specific places: Crocker Plaza and TransAmerica Redwood Park, both in San Francisco's Financial District. Skyscrapers are the dominant building type in this area, with concomitant high density and crowding.

Crocker Plaza,[6] situated in an odd, leftover wedge of space created by the intersection of north San Francisco's grid system and diagonal Market Street, is very much part of the street. The main feature is a forty by forty foot octagonal arrangement of sitting steps, which surround a sunken plaza that functions as a Bay Area Rapid Transit station entrance. Because of a slope on the site, there are six steps along the Market Street side and only one step on the side nearest the McKesson Building (which defines the plaza's western edge).

Redwood Park, six blocks north of Crocker Plaza and at the base of the TransAmerica pyramid, is a mid-block open space enclosed by skyscrapers and surrounded by large, mature redwood trees. The principal entrances lead from Washington and Clay streets, although the little-used

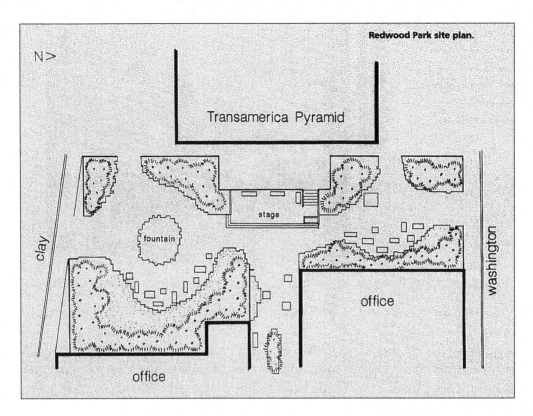

Redwood Park site plan.

Merchant Street alley, which terminates in the park, also serves as an entryway. The entire park is unobtrusively fenced with gates at each entrance.

Twenty-three backless benches, three park benches, steps, and an irrigated lawn provide places to sit within a backdrop of tall redwood trees. A splashing fountain is located at the south end of the park and a raised stage is located in the middle, at the base of the pyramid. The edges of the park are densely planted with redwood trees, which soften the visual impact of the surrounding high rises, provide human scale elements, and add visual richness to the-park.

The combination of gated entrances, dense vegetation, and mid-block siting removes Redwood Park from the street, unlike Crocker Plaza, which accepts the street as part of its essence. This lends Redwood Park a more intimate quality than Crocker Plaza, even though it is considerably larger—23,850 square feet, compared to 3,725 square feet.

I casually observed the users of Redwood Park and Crocker Plaza numerous times over a year and a half. Two things became very obvious after spending time there. First, women tended to come in groups, rather than alone, and if they did come alone they clustered together. Second, women had an extremely difficult time sitting comfortably and modestly on the steps.

I also systematically observed and surveyed users of Redwood Park and Crocker Plaza. At each of these open spaces I conducted detailed behavior observation (15 minute behavior mapping, noting sex, location, and activity of each user) between 11 a.m. and 2 p.m. on two warm, sunny weekdays in October (San Francisco's "summer"). I also distributed questionnaires during warm and sunny weekday lunch hours in October and the following March. The questionnaire included both multiple choice and open-ended questions to obtain as wide a range of responses as possible.

Finally, I surveyed 32 men and 47 women employees of one of the corporate office towers of downtown San Francisco, some of whom used downtown spaces, some of whom did not.

Redwood Park, San Fransisco. Trees create a physical barrier between the park and the street while the rumble of the fountain overwhelms the noise of traffic. This secluded place is favored by women.

These observations and surveys yielded the following results:

Number of users: These spaces differed dramatically in their use by women. At best, 20 percent of the people using Crocker Plaza were women, compared to at least 40 percent, and sometimes 70 percent, of the people using Redwood Park. Peak use at Crocker Plaza was at 12:45 p.m., but at Redwood Plaza there was a double peak. During the first peak, at 12:15 pm., there were one third more men than women in the park; however, during the second peak at 1:30 p.m., there were twice as many women as men in the park.

User distribution and location: People filled Crocker Plaza from its southeast corner back towards the north side and the McKesson Building. The southeast corner of the plaza is what one might call the "100 percent corner," the area where pedestrian traffic is heaviest and which (designers might say) is the most desirable sitting space. However, this is a male "100 percent corner." Women distribute themselves evenly around the plaza and, if anything, seem to have a separate "100 percent corner" of their own towards Montgomery Street.

At Redwood Park, behavior mapping showed no "100 percent corner," no discernable center of people and activity for either men or women. People sprinkled themselves throughout the benches and steps.

Liked areas: Users of Crocker Plaza, asked to circle their preferred areas of the plaza on a map, reinforced the results of the behavior observation. Men more often

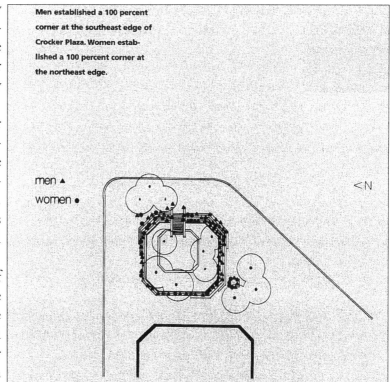

Men established a 100 percent corner at the southeast edge of Crocker Plaza. Women established a 100 percent corner at the northeast edge.

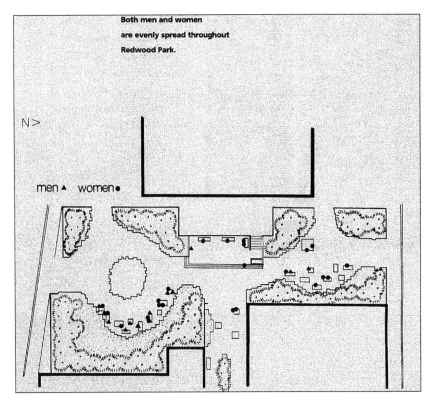

Both men and women are evenly spread throughout Redwood Park.

chose the "100 percent corner" near Market Street, and women more often chose the corner towards Montgomery and Post. Explaining their reasons for choosing this area, women stated "sun, not too windy" "quieter," "great view," and "fewer weirdos on this side." The men consistently stated that they chose their corner because it was the best place to watch people.

Women users of Redwood Park revealed preferences that were not manifested in the behavior observation. They clearly preferred sitting near the fountain, stating reasons such as "the fountain," "come watch people, yet private, kind of secluded," and "partial sun, some seclusion." Women may prefer the plaza's combination of noise mitigation, sun, and the chance to watch people from a secluded vantage point. Men at Redwood chose areas all over the park and consistently stated what they liked about the park was the sun.

Disliked areas: At Crocker Plaza, both sexes disliked the side nearest the McKesson Building, and each disliked the area corresponding to the "100 percent corner" of the opposite sex. To a more subtle extent, this was the case at Redwood Park. Men disliked the fountain area, considering it noisy. Women disliked the raised stage with park benches, declaring it "too conspicuous" and "uncomfortable," even though behavior observation showed they sat there regularly. This is the only place with park benches, so women may be trading off psychological comfort for the physical comfort afforded by benches with backs.

Catchment areas: In both open spaces, the catchment areas of women were significantly smaller than those of men. Women, apparently, are unwilling or unable to travel as far as men.

Preferred activities: Users of both open spaces indicated their principal activities there were eating, talking, and watching other people. However, more men than women said they preferred watching people, and more women than men said they preferred eating and talking. This seems to support the results of the behavior observation, which indicate that women tended to come in groups with whom they socialized.

Disliked factors: Male and female users expressed clear differences about factors they disliked in and around Crocker Plaza. Women were more annoyed by noise, traffic, litter/dirt, and crowded conditions than men were. Men, however, were more annoyed by the presence of derelicts than women were. At Redwood Park, both men and women cited far fewer disliked features, indicating a higher degree of satisfaction with their experience there.

Lacked features: Both men and women using Crocker Plaza said they would have wanted more trees, sun, and grass there. Most of the women noted the lack of benches while only about one of four men did. A similar number of men even said the plaza was "just right," while no women did, and in general had fewer responses to the question, indicating men had a higher degree of satisfaction with the plaza. At Redwood Park, the most frequent answer for both sexes was "just right," indicating again that the park provided a great deal of satisfaction for people of both sexes who use it.

Alternative lunchtime destinations: Women at Crocker Plaza, asked where they went when they did not come there during lunch hour, said they either stayed in their office, went to restaurants, or went to other open spaces. Women at Redwood Park said they either stayed in the office or went to restaurants. Men in both spaces said they went to restaurants or to other open spaces; none opted to stay in their office.

A common assumption is that women do not go to downtown open spaces at lunch because they have errands to run. But women said this was the least of their reasons for not coming. In fact, more men than women stated this as a reason for not coming to the plaza. The primary reason all users gave for not coming to the spaces was weather.

OFFICE SURVEY

The results of the survey of office workers reiterated many of the behavior observation findings and the survey of open space users.

More men said they were habitual users of open spaces than did women. Fewer women went to open spaces alone, and more went to an open space with a friend or a group.

Women said the primary reason they did not go to open spaces during their lunch hours was that their jobs (generally lower-echelon) allowed them only short lunch breaks. They do not have time to travel as far as men do.

Women said they preferred to use open spaces for eating, talking, and, to a lesser extent, watching others. Men said they preferred watching others and, secondarily, talking. Again, women tended, more than men, to say they use open spaces as places to interact socially with friends. These results are similar to the results of the surveys of open space users.

Both men and women said litter and dirt were the most annoying characteristic of open spaces, but they differed about other factors they did not like. Men expressed annoyance at derelicts, crowding, pigeons, lack of sun, and too much concrete. For women, annoyances were crowding, no comfortable seating, and, to a lesser extent than men, derelicts. Many more women than men thought San Francisco needed more downtown open space.

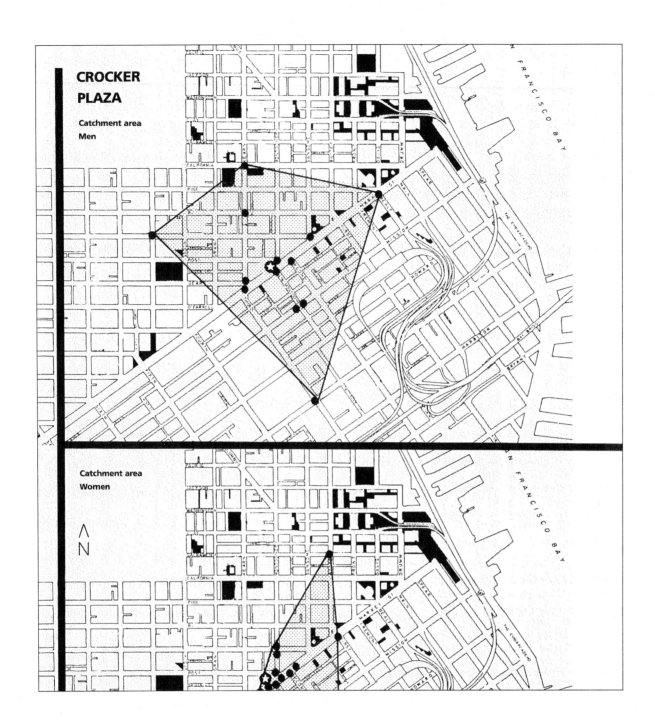

CONCLUSION

To begin creating downtown open spaces that are more woman-friendly, designers and planners must consider what experiences women are seeking in open spaces, and they must determine which design features support these sought-after experiences. While the scope of this study is limited, it does indicate that men and women perceive and appreciate public open space in different ways. The differences suggested by the results of this research are indicative of other areas for study and exploration.

The difference in character of Crocker Plaza and Redwood Park may be a paradigm for the different kind of open space experiences women and men accept and prefer. Crocker Plaza overwhelmingly accepts the dynamic yet inherently noisy and distracting urban environment. To be there means to appreciate and want to be a part of this type of urban expression. Redwood Park rejects the dominant urban environment, its stress, and its ever-changing, unpredictable nature. Crocker Plaza is outward reaching, socially interactive, and enmeshed in urban life. Redwood Park is enclosed and self-contained, inwardly oriented and far less interactive.

Men and women may have not only different preferences in downtown open spaces but also different concepts of optimum open space experiences. Men may be seeking environments that provide intense and unpredictable social interaction, connectedness to the street and its activity, urban stimuli, and publicness. They are not as bothered by stresses that usually accompany such an environment, and, perhaps, consider such stress as part of the exciting urbanness they seek.

Women may be looking for relief from environmental stress, and view downtown plazas and parks as places that should be removed from but not isolated from the dominant urbanness of downtown. Women seem to prefer open spaces that emphasize a filtering or mitigation of negative factors, psychological familiarity and comfort, places to socialize with friends, and spatial control. In a sense, women may be seeking "back yard" experiences and men may be seeking "front yard" experiences.

Although this study confirms some of Whyte's findings in *The Social Life of Small Urban Spaces*,[7] it raises some fundamental differences. Whyte's model of urban open space advocates business, activity, and connection to the street. It is steeped in the historic precedents of the male-dominated downtown. The model creates forums for stranger interaction, where it is more likely that women's psychological boundaries would be violated.

I would suggest this model represents only one part of a range of valid and successful forms of open space. Although Whyte states, "A good plaza starts at the street corner" and advocates designs in which "it is hard to tell where one ends and the other begins," the results of this study suggest otherwise: spaces that are distinctly removed and oriented away from the street can be particularly successful for women. By their less public and less connected nature, these spaces help women more easily maintain their vital psychological boundaries.

This research suggests several specific issues designers and planners must consider if downtown open spaces are to become more woman-friendly:

The assumption that women use downtown open spaces less frequently because they are not interested is not true. For both men and women, going to an open space is important—it can provide relief from the office environment and a chance to be outside.

Women are more sensitive to urban annoyances and environmental stresses—noise, crowding, dirt, and traffic—than men are. Features that mitigate these stresses will make downtown open spaces more amenable and attractive to women.

Women often go to downtown open spaces with friends with whom they socialize. People-watching forums suitable for strangers sitting side by side, such as Crocker Plaza, are not well suited for the experiences women tend to seek in open spaces.

Women do not prefer to be "on display" in downtown open spaces. They probably perceive that their personal or psychological boundaries may be more easily violated in such a situation.

The perception of both physical and psychological safety is important to women. Women may perceive safety not merely as a lack of "undesirables" (an issue that has risen to the forefront because of Whyte's work) but also in the degree of spatial control they feel: the maintenance of territoriality, lack of crowding, and degree of group control.

Getting to an open space is a problem for women. People of lower employment status, mostly women, are unable to travel as far during their lunch breaks as men are. Providing access for women will mean a re-evaluation of the usefulness of larger open spaces intended to serve larger catchment areas. Clearly, open spaces need to be distributed much more frequently throughout downtown.

Steps, sculptures, and sitting blocks of other than standard height will produce in many women an unsolvable conflict between standards of propriety, physical comfort, and the desire to be in open space. For whatever historical and cultural reasons, women wear skirts; therefore, considering a six-inch riser and 14-inch tread as adequate seating space is an insult to them.

By building downtown open spaces that are woman-friendly we would go much further in building spaces that are people-friendly. The key is viewing preferred open space experiences of women and men as taking place not in separate spheres but on a continuum. Designers and planners tend to classify types of downtown open spaces into rigid categories that imply uniform degrees of publicness. For example, the San Francisco Downtown Plan equates plazas with being "very public" and parks with being "less public." We need to re-evaluate such classifications in favor of more integrated concepts.

Such concepts would permit design flexibility and allow people to choose the comfort level they prefer in urban settings. Such concepts recognize that both men and women have preferences along a *continuum*, and allow for the transformation of stereotypical sexual roles as socialization patterns change. The next generation of women may well move farther into the "front yard" of downtown open spaces.

The downtown environment is, by and large, a grim, alienating place. Open spaces are so vital to rehumanizing downtown that it is essential they be places for all people. Designers and planners must become aware of the "mass of social images and symbols" that are imbued in our culture and which pervade the process by which our cities, and the open spaces within them, are built. We must look forward to environments that accept and acknowledge both men and women.

NOTES

1. Sheila M. Rothman, *Women's Proper Place* (New York: Basic Books, 1978).

2. Susan Saegert, "Masculine Cities, Feminine Suburbs," in *Women and The American City* (1981).
3. Henly, from Anita Nager and Yona Nelson-Shulman, "Women in Public Places," *Centerpoint* (New York: City University Graduate Center, 1979).
4. Anita Nager and Yona Nelson-Shulman, "Women in Public Places," *Centerpoint* (New York-City University Graduate Center, 1979).
5. Harold M. Proshansky, William H. Ittelson, and Leanne Rivlin, *Environmental Psychology* (San Francisco: Holt, Reinhart and Winston, 1976).
6. Since this study, Crocker Plaza has been given an official name, McKesson Plaza, reflecting the name of the building in front of which it sits. Many people still use the name Crocker Plaza to refer to the plaza.
7. William H. Whyte, *The Social Life of Small Urban Spaces* (Washington, D.C.: The Conservation Foundation, 1980).

22 Designing to Orient the User

Gerald Weisman

How architects can take advantage of what is known about cognitive mapping in the design of buildings and urban districts.

Large, complex buildings such as hospitals, transportation facilities, and shopping centers present many challenges both to the architects responsible for their design and to the people who use them. Not the least of these challenges is designing such environments to be maximally legible so that users know where they are within the building or complex and are able to proceed confidently and correctly to desired destinations and means of egress.

Increased understanding of the problem of environmental legibility has accompanied recent growth in architectural research, particularly research that examines relationships between the built environment and the behavior of people. One's inability to find his or her way within a building, this research suggests, is not a mere inconvenience. Users' response to, satisfaction with, and even safety within a building all may be influenced by the building's legibility. Furthermore, one doesn't make wayfinding easier simply by mounting more signs. Buildings provide many different forms of information—both graphic and architectural in character—that may be employed for effective wayfinding. The creation of truly legible environments requires an awareness of the wayfinding problems people can and do experience, an understanding of the key components of the wayfinding process, and the development of complementary architectural and graphic approaches to the resolution of these problems.

DISORIENTATION AND ITS COST

A dozen studies of wayfinding, conducted over the past decade by investigators in a range of settings, clearly indicate that many environments are—at least for a substantial minority of their users—far from legible. Among office employees questioned by the Buffalo Organization for Social and Technical Innovation (BOSTI), 15 percent still found wayfinding difficult after two months in a new work setting. Data gathered by this writer from more than 70 university students indicates that 8 percent became regularly and seriously lost in classroom buildings on their own campus; more than one-quarter of the students using the most confusing of these buildings reported

Gerald Weisman, "Designing to Orient the User," from *AIArchitect*, Vol. 78, No 10; October 1989. Copyright © 1989 by The American Institute of Architects. Permission to reprint granted by the publisher.

becoming lost. In a study of the Dallas-Fort Worth Airport, 25 percent of the travelers interviewed by Texas A&M researcher Andrew Seidel characterized the signage as less than clear and 12 percent found the terminal confusing. These percentages may seem relatively modest until one recognizes the numbers of users potentially involved. For example, 75,000 or more people move through this airport daily. Thus, upwards of 10,000 of these travelers may be having problems with wayfinding. Dallas-Fort Worth is also the airport immortalized a number of years ago in a news story about a college professor who, upon becoming lost within the terminal building, began gibbering mathematical equations and tearing off his clothes.

As the story of the unfortunate professor suggests, illegible environments can exact significant costs from both building occupants and operators. Staff time may be lost as a consequence of having to direct or even personally escort building users to destinations that they are unable to find by themselves. At one Canadian hospital studied by Robert Dewar of the University of Calgary, almost a third of staff members queried indicated that they were approached at least once each day with wayfinding questions. As part of the planning and programming for a major hospital at the University of Michigan, Carpman, Grant, and Simmons interviewed visitors. Their findings indicate that the single most important predictor of stress experienced by visitors was the degree of difficulty in finding their way within the hospital. Wayfinding was rated more important than such other stress-related variables as the length of the patient's stay or the visitor's desire for privacy.

A MODEL OF WAYFINDING BEHAVIOR

An awareness of the problem of disorientation, while important, is but a first step toward the creation of more legible environments. Even if one recognizes that a building presents severe problems, it still is necessary to determine what forms of environmental information will resolve or at least ameliorate these difficulties. Such a determination is far from simple. Human behavior is influenced by many factors, and the architectural environment by itself never has totally predictable and unvarying effects. However, based on an understanding of the psychological principles and mechanisms by which people take in and organize information from their environment, it is possible to build a conceptual model of the wayfinding process and to formulate guidelines for the design of more legible environments.

Central to this model of wayfinding behavior is the concept of a mental image (cognitive map) of the environment, which people develop with time and experience in a place. The cognitive map is a mental representation of key landmarks or regions in one's environment and the spatial relationship between them. Cognitive mapping is a concept most familiar to environmental designers through Kevin Lynch's classic work, *Image of the City* (MIT Press, 1960). Because most buildings, like the cities Lynch studied, cannot be perceived in their entirety from any one location at one time, effective wayfinding requires that a person know the locations of places now out of sight and how to get to them. In short, wayfinding is a cognitive as well as a perceptual task. It depends on what one knows of an environment as well as what one sees.

Thinking of wayfinding as cognitive as well as perceptual broadens our understanding of the kinds of information that an environment might usefully provide. Such information can be divided into four categories: (1) signs and numbers, (2) architectural differentiation, (3) perceptual access, and (4) plan configuration. Most buildings, of course, have multiple categories of information; thus attention must be given to both graphic and architectural variables and the ways they relate to and can reinforce one another.

Signs and numbers. These are the most common and conscious forms of information for wayfinding in the architectural environment. While signs can facilitate both wayfinding and a sense of comfort and confidence, they are not without their limits. Particularly in buildings with exceedingly complex floor plans, it may not be possible—no matter how many signs are used—to achieve wayfinding performance as good as that in simpler buildings without any signage whatsoever. Furthermore, too many signs, or an effort to convey too much information on any one sign, can contribute to information overload for building users. In *Wayfinding in Architecture* (Van Nostrand Reinhold, 1984), R. Passini emphasizes how important it is that building users be able to take in information from signs at a glance.

Architectural differentiation. For many building users, wayfinding is facilitated primarily by elements other than formal signage systems. In this author's study of a nursing home, more than three-fourths of the aids to orientation mentioned by residents were not signs but rather distinctive elements within the environment, such as plants, a grandfather clock, or the elevator. Such features served to differentiate one space and corridor from another and thus to facilitate wayfinding.

Perceptual access. Where it is possible to see through or out of a building—as with an atrium or open gallery—wayfinding is simplified. It is not necessary to construct a cognitive map of a building if desired destinations are within one's field of vision. Similarly, views to the exterior from key decision points such as corridor intersections and elevator lobbies permit identification of one's present location by relating it to landmarks in the larger environment.

Plan configuration. Research suggests that it is far easier to find one's way in some buildings than in others. What often differentiates more legible buildings from those that thwart effective wayfinding is the configuration of their floor plans. In general, it appears that legibility is enhanced and wayfinding is facilitated when building plan configurations can be visualized easily and described readily. One can think, for example, of L-, T-, or I-shaped buildings. Right-angle corridor intersections are more readily noted and remembered than are oblique relationships. Clarity of plan configuration is most important when an environment provides only limited information through signs, differentiation, or access.

ASSESSING ARCHITECTURAL LEGIBILITY

In summary, the design of more legible settings involves providing and systematically organizing complementary forms of environmental information. No single aid to wayfinding is likely to solve the problem. Indeed, the boundaries quickly blur between forms of information that might be viewed as solely graphic or as architectural in character. Both must be considered in concert and in the context of the wayfinding process. Research has clearly demonstrated that signs can rarely if ever solve problems created by an illegible and confusing building.

While it is neither possible nor desirable to formulate definitive answers to all wayfinding problems, one can assess the legibility of proposed or existing environments. The following questions for design review can both heighten awareness of potential problems and suggest possible directions for enhancing architectural legibility.

- Does the building possess some correspondence between exterior and interior? Are primary entries and destinations apparent? Is the visual access provided from exterior to interior?
- Are views to the exterior provided at key decision points such as corridor intersections? Are primary destinations within the building made visible through an atrium or open gallery?

- Does the building provide clear identification of regions (such as wings or organizational departments)?
- Do architectural features (such as artwork, lighting, color, and finishes) reinforce signage in the identification of key locations?
- Are long, unbroken corridors with many identical elements along their length (such as office doors) kept to a minimum?
- Is the plan of the building one that can be visualized and described readily (such I-, T-, and L-shaped plans)? Are corridor intersections at right angles rather than oblique angles?
- Are key services and amenities (such as elevator lobbies) placed at distinctive locations, such as the intersection of major corridors?
- Is the signage system treated as supplemental rather than the primary form of wayfinding information? Is information on signs presented in manageable chunks? Is information prioritized in terms of importance? Are all signs treated as components of a system with consistency in design and placement? Do signs recognize the potential for first-time or non-English-speaking users?
- Are directories and "you are here" maps located in highly visible places and oriented to correspond to the environment they represent (for instance, north to the top and straight ahead)? Is typography large enough to be legible? Is the user's present location clearly indicated? Can users access map or directory information in multiple ways (for example, by store name, category of merchandise, and location)?

It must be recognized that a legible environment is by no means a boring one. Quite the contrary, it is often the simplest of settings—such as institutional buildings that provide little or no environmental information—that cause the greatest problems in wayfinding. Legible buildings, much like the most satisfying of the cities Lynch studied, can be rich and complex within a comprehensible structure. Well designed environments can and should support stimulation and exploration as well as orientation.

23 A New Look at the Person in Person–Environment Relations: Theoretical Assumptions About the Body

Galen Cranz

This working paper summarizes the theoretical points that shaped the EDRA award-winning book *The Chair: Rethinking Culture, Body and Design* (Norton, prbk 2000). It can be used to amplify what is meant by sensation, perception, and cognition or to introduce somatic theory—the idea that body and mind including culture operate as a whole system. We did not include a chapter from *The Chair* in this reader because we assign the entire book; it's an affordable paperback.

This paper reevaluates theoretical assumptions in the field of person-environment relations from the point of view of the human body. I have taught architecture from a social and cultural point of view for twenty years, and for the last fifteen years, I have also been studying practices popularly called "bodywork."[1] In this paper, for the first time, I seek to integrate these two arenas by asking myself if the models of human body and mind implicit in each are congruent or not. This unusual perspective challenges the field in the hopes of stimulating a higher order transformation of basic theory. Such higher order transformations might be expected to establish linkages to other aspects of architecture; for example, if person-environment relations roughly corresponds to "commodity," we could expect stronger links to "firmness" and "delight."

Assumption 1. Our field shares with the rest of Western Civilization the belief that *the mind and the body are two separate things.* In the field of person-environment relations, we assume that the person is a psychological entity. Designers and social scientists alike typically study behavior or attitudes, feelings, opinions, and beliefs toward the environment—all internal, subjective states. Even where behavior is involved, the physical qualities are downplayed. This paper is an attempt to redress that imbalance.

Why is it worthwhile to think about the mind and the body as one or as at least closely related? Psychology, at one point, tried to limit itself to the study of only that which can be directly observed, hence, behavior rather than inferior subjective matters like feelings, judgments, beliefs, etc. But when psychology decided that it was safe to embrace the realm of the subjective experience, sensuality was lost. The field went beyond mere perception and behavior to cognition, imagination, inner conflict, etc. But the field of person-environment relations has turned its back on the human

Galen Cranz, *A New Look at the Person in Person-Environment Relations: Theoretical Assumptions About the Body.* Copyright © 1991 by Center for Environmental Design Research. Permission to reprint granted by the publisher.

as a sensate being. When we put the mind into the body, we respect its needs and by implication respect others. When we separate mind and body, environments can become extremely repressive physically because we no longer think about the sensate beings that are using them. We think only about people in social structure—the workers go here, the bosses go there—and we forget physical discomfort that may be involved. In so far as we remember it, it reinforces social hierarchy: We give pleasurable environments to the top and less pleasurable ones to the bottom. Uniting mind and body is no guarantee that we would move towards a more equitable environment, but it is one step in that direction. It is harder to be cruel, authoritarian, or even hierarchical when we respect the physical experience that we all have in common, rather than the status differences that separate us.

Assumption 2. A related assumption is that *cognition is separate from perception*. One of the things first experienced in bodywork is that the line between knowing-through-perception and knowing-through-cognition is blurred. I have come to think that cognition is a form of perception, which may be heretical, but I would like to entertain that as a proposition. Cognition is mental processing, it occurs in the third part of the brain—the cerebral cortex. Cognition involves analysis, comparing things, saying this is like that, this is a sub-case of that, this is bigger than that. Supposedly, cognition puts things in a mental structure, unlike "pure" perception. However, psychologists themselves admit that there is no such thing as pure perception: for example, one feels that which one has been trained to expect. Psychologists themselves already know that cognition affects perception. But bodyworkers have experienced the way one "knows" through their hands and so are even less comfortable than psychologists about accepting the conventional split between sensation and conception. If cognition and perception are more continuous than the existence of the linguistic categories suggests, then the body as a whole, as already suggested, is the more relevant unit of analysis. If the mind-body is the unit of analysis, then giving mental delight without sensory pleasure is a contradiction in terms. Design for both sensation and conception might be dubbed "Sensual Rationality," order based on intelligent stimulation and orchestration of the senses.

Moreover, how we number our senses is also open to question. Most Westerners believe there are five senses, but at least a sixth and seventh have been recognized. Proprioception is the body's ability to sense itself, and how we sense that our bodies are moving is related to kinesthesia—our perception of movement through space. These senses have been exploited by our very best designers, like Frederick Law Olmsted.

Assumption 3. Many people from journalists to M.D.s believe that *anatomically humans have an evolutionary problem, especially in the back*. Some speculate that we are really four-legged animals who are tottering around on two legs, so the reason we have back problems is because of something evolutionarily inadequate about our structure. Multi-millennia from now everything will be fine, but until then suffering is inevitable.[2] But the practice of and theory latent within bodywork allows us to understand what we are actually designed quite perfectly. As a culture we misuse ourselves, specifically we distort the dynamic equilibrium of the body by tightening and locking some muscles and joints while overworking others, and thereby damage the otherwise perfect structure that we have. One consequence of this view is that industrial design should not be in the business of creating prosthetic devices for a "flawed" back. Rather than design for "support," it could design for movement, option, stimulation, and equal distribution of effort throughout the body.

Assumption 4. A fourth assumption is that *gravity is the enemy,* because it pulls us down. Actually, we cannot function properly without gravity. In outer space we can float around, which feels wonderful, but after three months without gravity osteoporosis sets in. In order to have long duration (over 90 days) space missions, centrifugal force is necessary to produce artificial gravity, and people must do very vigorous exercises, or they must be brought back to Earth every ninety days. This suggests that gravity is important to our well-being, not a detriment. Indeed, the structure and function of our upright posture have been analyzed to show that mechanically we depend on it.[3] Aesthetically and architecturally, this suggests that observing the play of gravity should be a delight for humans since their own bodies enjoy it. Revealing structure would be preferable to concealing it. Posts come to mind as an instance of our being able to experience forces pushing up as well as being channeled down.

Assumption 5. From a mechanical point of view, most people think that *the body is a stacked structure.* Instead, we are closer to a tensegrity structure. Humans are not like arches, primarily compression structures, nor like balloons which are tension structures. We are a combination of tension and compression structures—hence Buckminster Fuller's term, tensegrity.

This model entails the interaction of an entire system, so that changes in one part can be expected to create changes in its other parts. Proper posture and movement allow humans to use gravity constructively within this tensegrity model. A tensegrity structure keeps all parts in dynamic opposition equal and opposite throughout the whole system. The structure is impaired as a system when one part freezes, forcing other parts of the system to do more than their original share of work.

Common places where this occurs in the body are the neck, the waist when it is all too often inappropriately used as a hinge, the sit bones when not in secure contact with the seat, and the legs when seated without having one's feet on the ground. Design can help rectify these problems: To relieve the static locking or the excessive stress of the neck, slanted reading surfaces are a must in order to help people keep the spine working as a whole, to retain its double curve and not fall into a C-shaped stoop, designers and office managers should create and use more standup work stations. In order to allow everyone to sit with their feet on the ground, we need to order multiple-sized chairs or invest in adjustable chairs or footstools. We could routinely order two, three, or four different chair sizes at fifteen, seventeen, nineteen-inch heights from the floor.

If humans are buoyant, as the tensegrity model implies, then they expand in and through space. They are not static statues which merely punctuate designed space. This provides us with a new criterion for evaluation, admittedly a bit abstract in its most general form; does a space narrow people or allow them to pulsate, that is to expand and contract alternately?

Assumption 6. Understanding the body as a static structure rather than a dynamic one uncovers a related assumption that *one can constrain part of the body without consequence.* Most people constrain their feet markedly. It is actually a demonstrable health hazard to constrain the toes and cripple the feet as we do.[4] In the early 20th century women pinched in their waists with whalebone corsets in order to have an hour glass figure, going so far as to surgically remove the lower rib in order to intensify the effect. We think of that with horror, and we look at Chinese foot binding as unthinkable. But pinching our toes into a point thereby narrowing the metatarsals; or throwing the back and foot into stress via the use of high heels, although it is not as gross, is also damaging to the overall welfare of the body system.[5] If we think of the body as a tensegrity structure, restricting movement in one part overuses and stresses the rest of the system. In some ways this raises the old mitten-vs.-glove issue in design: In this case I maintain that a chair is better treated like a mitten rather than a glove because over-designing the chair restricts the body's movement within it.

Assumption 7. Another assumption is that *comfort means external support,* whereas in the original Latin the term to comfort meant to strengthen.[6] Eastern culture traditionally has viewed comfort as control from within.[7] By the end of the 19th century the word comfort came to mean "support" or to make easier by providing outside external support. At the same time that the concept changed, furniture makers started padding furniture heavily with springs and deep cushioning.

Thinking that we need high top shoes to support the ankles, arch supports to support the foot, or lumbar support for the back assumes that comfort is external support. Rudofsky has stated that there is no arch in the human foot. Technically he means that it is not a compression structure. Like the rest of our body, it is closer to a tension structure. In the long run, we may be tiring ourselves by walking around with "arch" supports, which may stress and therefore weaken the "arched" part of the foot. Probably we should be barefoot a lot more than we are. Such a behavioral shift has implications for floor surfaces, thermal and textural, and for the design of transition space between indoors (shoeless) and outdoors (shoes).

The prominent ergonomics researcher Etienne Grandjean working in Switzerland assumes that the most comfortable posture is one where muscles do the least work. Thus, according to him, sitting is more comfortable than standing, and stooping is more comfortable than sitting up straight. He notes that back muscles work less when the entire torso stoops forward. He acknowledges that the front edges of the spinal vertebrae put extra pressure on the disks when the spine is in this C-shaped stoop, and so concludes that back comfort and disk health contradict one another! His remedy is lumbar support to retain the lumbar curve while the upper body continues its stoop! A preferable idea is for muscular effort to be distributed equally throughout the body, rather than absent altogether along the spine![8]

We may want to reverse this trend toward providing more external support and instead strengthen the torso in the older Asian or Latin sense. If so, we would need to sit less, which, in turn, suggests designing for a wider variety of postures: standing, lying, sitting cross-legged. When we do use chairs, they should not be overdesigned, that is, they should not curve around the body. They should not mimic anatomical shape. Chairs that envelope the body and curve around the torso turn the rib cage in on itself; they do not give the rib cage the opposition to open, needed in turn to give room to the lungs, the heart and the organs of digestion. One design implication is to return to simple forms of chairs, composed of very simple planes. Perhaps Reitveld's early 20th century chair is not as theoretical or intellectual as it appears to most of us today. Another implication is to find alternatives to chairs altogether as discussed below.

Assumption 8. Much furniture design assumes that *we can find a perfect position.* We assume that there must be a way that human beings can be structurally comfortable and if only we could find that position, then we could design environments, chairs particularly, around this perfect position. But there is no perfect position. Bodyworkers and ergonomic researchers agree on this point.[9] Thinking about the structure of our joint, notice that the roundness of the ball joint means that the head of a bone can sit anywhere in relation to its socket. The ball and socket design accommodates a wide variety of movements and positions. There is no facet in the joint where finally it locks in and—click—the person is at rest. Only lying down can provide true rest. Otherwise, humans are designed for movement.

The anthropologist Gordon Hewes described the numerous postures in cultures around the world—all considered comfortable and natural.[10] Culture limits and shapes this variety in large part through the design of the near-environment. Chairs, for example, reinforce the sitting behavior of the 2/3 of the world's population who use them. Westerners seldom squat or sit cross-legged (tailor fashion) because the chair directs them to do otherwise.

For environmental design professionals this point of view has implications for evaluating the near-environment. It suggests that external support, rather than being comfortable by trying to stabilize the body in fixed positions, actually stresses and ultimately weakens the body.

<u>Assumption 9</u>. *Chairs are a technological extension of our physiology,* therefore, "natural." Actually, chairs (like the high rise) are a potent symbol of westernization, modernization, and industrialization. Japanese people are using chairs more and more these days to show their progressive, western thinking. Instead of physiology, chairs really represent, in varying proportions, social status, aspirations regarding art, explorations about technology and production, and only to some extent concerns about efficient work and physiological well-being.[11]

The chair is said to have originated in Egypt about 5,000 years ago.[12] It was developed further in Greece and then it was lost socially in Roman times. It was reinvented in the Middle Ages. The medieval chair was an extension of the chest. In feudal times life was politically unstable, so people had to be able to pack their things and retreat to another castle quickly. The halls in these castles were filled with chests lined up along the edges of the wall available for sitting. The first chairs were literally extension of the chests, mimicking the wall they had been pushed against. Carving and height elaborated this same form for royal or religious uses. Over time, the angle between the seat and back was increased from 90 degrees, requiring sophisticated engineering, recognizing physiology, offering sculptural play. This change was accompanied by molded seats and front rails, culminating in what may be the optimization of the conflicting demands for status, sculptural integration and anatomical ease in 18th century chair designs like Sheffield, Chippendale, and the like.[13] From an ergonomic point of view, the thighs and muscles are not supposed to do any load bearing, but deep padding, a 19th century contribution, spreads the load away from the sit bones (ischial tuberosities) over the muscles. When muscles carry weight, blood vessels are compressed and circulation is cut off. Firm padding had already been introduced in the 18th century, but the 19th century exaggerated it and softened it—to our detriment. During the late 19th century and into 20th century new technological processes allowed designers to manipulate materials in new ways. Baldly stated, 20th century chair design is the history of what can be done with materials. For example, the ability to steam wood and bend it generated the Thonet chair. This chair breaks all the ergonomic rules: the raised edge cuts the thighs, and the back offers no plane for opening the rib cage against. But from the point of view of mass production these chairs were wonderful because they are light, cheap, and have visual flair—qualities that contribute to their appeal still today. The excitement of working with steel and later plastic generated the ensuing 50 years of chair design: chairs by Breuer, Van der Rohe, Corbusier, and Eames explore the potentials of new materials and new production processes.

Sitting is natural, but chair sitting is not. The feature that distinguishes a chair from a stool is its back. Leaning back onto the chairback while sitting down is virtually impossible to coordinate. Leaning back drives the spine down and forward, so that people end up in a C-shape. When that becomes uncomfortable, people sit up, now at the edge of the chair, but in a few minutes they tire, so they push back into the seat in order to lean back, but once there the same down and forward forces set in again, driving the pelvis forward, producing a C-shaped spine—in a vicious cycle. This is what some critics have analyzed as the inherent instability of the sitting position.

Assumption 10. After fifteen years of bodywork, I realized that a cultural bias or assumption is built into the inherent instability argument—namely, that *sitting up without support makes one tired*. After teaching my first two seminars on the history of the chair, I began to see that no matter how carefully one designs the chair, something is always wrong with it. For example, by countering the fact that people slide forward, some other problems emerge. Namely, a backward cant of the seat pushes the thigh bone into the socket and creates too acute an angle between thigh and trunk. To compensate for this, the back must be tipped backwards, but this new slanted back rest puts stress on the neck, and so on and so forth. I began to suspect that the chair could never have been well-designed because of problems with the sitting-and-leaning-backward posture itself. An incident crystallized that into a hypothesis.

A British friend with whom I had been to university and who later went on to do Volunteer Service Overseas, the equivalent of the Peace Corps in Africa, was showing me snapshots from her time there in 1966. I saw nothing special about these people, who looked more or less like us: some skinny bodies, some collapsed spines and chests, some necks and heads jutting forward, rounded shoulders. In the context of all these pictures, two people were special. They were very grand specimens. My friend knew I had been studying posture, but she did not know that I had been studying the chair, so when she volunteered that the two that I picked out as being special grew up in villages without missionary schools so that they never sat in a chair, you can imagine my excitement. All the others had gone to missionary schools and learned to sit in chairs! By not sitting in chairs the bodies of the two had developed fully and evenly. I felt confident in concluding that chair sitting is neither natural nor healthy, but rather inherently compensatory. Designers try to make up for stress and contradictions in the posture itself. Seeing these Africans made me realize that the "inherent instability" argument was part of the "biological defect assumption." We have four major overlapping sets of muscles in the torso that are designed to keep us upright, but in the West, years of chair sitting have weakened them so that as adults our torsos have become weak. Sitting upright is not any more unstable than any other human activity; when we use our muscles, they interact with one another to produce a dynamic equilibrium; the system works well if we use it!

What are the design implications of believing that chair sitting is not natural, is inherently compensatory and ultimately damaging to the torso? It means, among other things, that the search for the perfect chair is impossible[14] which in turn means that we should rely on other postures—standing, squatting, sitting cross-legged, and lying down—for as many tasks and social occasions as possible. It does not necessarily mean that we have to or could, abandon or prohibit the chair. Rather designers can legitimize the use of other postures by designing for them. Other cultures offer many examples.

In a traditional Indian banquet everyone sat on carpets on the ground. In *Now I Lay Me Down to Eat* Rudofsky exposes our rewriting of Western history to change the Last Supper from a Roman banquet lying down to a chair-sitting event. The Roman banquet facility was a horseshoe-shaped stone platform with an empty space for a serving person or table in the center. The surrounding stone surface was covered with rugs and cushions. Each person laid his head toward the center, propped up on pillows to eat and talk.

Both the Turkish and Chinese use multipurpose platforms which offer a place to sit and allow more than one person to sit on it at a time. Children like these very much, and specialists tell me that when free to design their own environments in school, for example, British and American children create platforms to sit beside or on, as occasion and task require.[15] I had been thinking about replacing all the furniture in my living room with platforms for several years, but since I did not act, I suspected some unconscious resistance. Finally, I discovered the source of my reluctance; it is not high status to have multi-function furniture. In this culture the highly evolved object that serves one function is sophisticated and desired. Adults, successful ones, achieve the ability to buy or commission refined objects. We feel that we will be judged as either cheap or childish imagining only multipurpose platforms or module systems.

Assumption 11. *We assume that we can change the body, relatively mute and dumb by simply by changing the environment.* Simple determinism lingers in this arena. For example, if we redesign the chair we can shape behavior. But people will resist using a "reformed" flat, planar chair or use it badly if they do not understand how to sit for their best anatomical functioning. If they think "sitting up straight" is just good manners or evidence of good breeding, they will continue to reject it as snobbish and stiff. Conversely, people cannot change years of bad posture without environmental change. Better chairs are important not only physiologically, but also symbolically to support the new idea as well as the new behavior. In other words, person-environment relations are not about persons or environment, but about the relation between them. The interaction is intangible (and therefore hard to photograph), but let us remind ourselves of what we are really studying. Phenomenologists, pragmatists, symbolic interactivists, qualitative methodologists, and students of "place" have been trying to study relationships and interactions, but they are still the minority. As Kevin Lynch noted in *Good City Form,* "Environmental design means shaping objects but it also means educating people and thereby changing consciousness. We can't re-form things without changing our minds and bodies."[16]

Assumption 12. *The body is part of nature, free from culture, society and psychology.* The body is also a cultural artifact, its form, posture and movement being culturally shaped and regulated. Some view it as culture's most significant "work of art."[17] As a field, person-environment relations needs to take a new look at the body in the person part of this equation.

CONCLUSIONS

What model of human-environment interaction do we have if we restate all the these assumptions in their corrected form?

The mind and body are interconnected, and, therefore, perception and cognition may not be qualitatively different. The body is designed perfectly for upright posture, sitting, and movement in gravity. It works with gravity's downward pull, creating uprightness somewhat like a tensegrity structure. It works as an entire system, so that no one part of it can be constrained—or freed from any work whatsoever—without maldistribution of effort, culminating in stress at some point in the body. Where it works as a system, it is strong and comfortable in itself. But it is a moving system, never comfortable in any one position for long. Chair sitting is an overused position, creating its own health detriments. Sitting upright, without back support, as on a stool, is probably better for long term well-being. We cannot reform seating habits by eliminating chairs, but rather through a combination of education and provision of environmental alternatives. The body, like the mind within it, is part of culture, society, and psychology and should be incorporated into person-environment research.

NOTES

1. Chiefly, the Chinese martial art, Tai chi, and the Western "Alexander Technique." Both fit within Juhan's definition of bodywork as the body being manipulated therapeutically with accompanying shifts in emotions and mental attitudes. Deane Juhan, *Job's Body: A Handbook for Bodywork,* Station Hill Press: Barry town, N.Y., 1987, p. xix.
2. The upright posture is actually older than previously assumed. C. Owen Lovejoy, "Evolution of Human Walking," *Scientific American,* Nov. 1988, p. 118–125.
4. Kirby, Ph.D., "The Probable Reality Behind Structural Integration; How Gravity Supports the Body," unpublished manuscript, 11 pp. (ca. 1980).
5. Kormer, Melvin, M.D., "Kick Off Your Heels," *New York Times Magazine,* 1988. Not only women deform their feet through high heels, but they account for 95% of podiatrists' patients. Some men also wear shoes which are too narrow, but in general men's are designed wider than women's.
5. Rudofsky, Bernard, *The Unfashionable Human Body.*
6. Gideon, Sigfried, *Mechanization Takes Command.*
7. Rudofsky, op. cit.
8. Grandjean, Etienne, "The Design Of Work Places," *Fitting the Task To the Man: An Ergonomic Approach,* Taylor & Francis Ltd., London, 1980, pp. 51–62.
9. Ergonomic researchers study work and the relationship between human physical movement and the immediate, touchable environment. Bodyworkers seek therapeutic change and see the body as a whole system. Consequently, even if they were research-minded, they would not be willing to study one joint, nor to model the human mechanically nor to study dead parts of the body. Thus, a study which takes vertebrae from a corpse and puts them under pressure to watch what happens to them would be virtually useless from their viewpoint. Despite their substantial differences, the two groups concur that human beings do not have a perfect static posture.
10. Hewes, Gordon, "World Distribution of Body Postures," *Scientific American.*
11. Just as the home is more a locus for status display than a place of simple shelter from natural elements: Witold Rybzcynski, *Home: A Short History of an Idea,* N.Y.: Viking, 1986.
12. Sigfried Gideon, *Mechanization Takes Command,* N.Y.: Oxford, 1948 and John Gloag, *The Englishman's Chair—Origin, Design, & Social History of Seat Furniture in England,* London: Allen & Unwin, 1964.
13. Greenberg, Alan, "Eighteenth Century Design Paradigms," *Via,* Philadelphia: University of Pennsylvania, 1977.
14. Stewart, Doug, "Modern Designers Still Can't Make the Perfect Chair," *Smithsonian,* April 1986, pp. 97–105, could not answer the question, only raise it.
15. Hart, Professor Roger, Director, City University of New York, Program in Environmental Psychology, Center for Research on Children in the Environment, March 16, 1989.
16. Lynch, Kevin, *Good City Form,* Cambridge, Mass., The MIT Press, 1981.
17. Johnson, Don, "The Body: Which One? Whose?," in *Whole Earth Review,* Summer 89, No. 63, pp.4–8.

24 Missing Dimension in Environmental Research: Detailed Visual Documentation

Eleftherios Pavlides

This article argues that environmental design research has failed to influence architectural practice because of its inadequate recording and analysis of the physical environment whose impact on behavior and perception it ostensibly measures. It recommends grounding social science investigation of built form on architectural analysis and evaluation and proposes photographic elicitation interviews as a way of linking the physical to the social and cultural.

ABSTRACT

Environmental Psychology has had minimal impact on architectural practice despite extensive research and the adoption of environmental psychology in architectural curricula. One explanation for architects' disinterest or inability to utilize the results of environmental research results is proposed here: environmental research would impact the design professions if the research process included the collecting and analysis of detailed visual information and the publications reporting research results were profusely illustrated. One theoretical and methodological framework which addresses this issue, termed sociosemiotics, combines ethnographic and archeological methodologies to the study of visual form. The approach is analogous to sociolinguistics which combines ethnographic fieldwork with a detailed study of the form of sound in its social context. The theoretical framework proposed above can be operationalized in a four phase research process:

1. Photographic documentation of several buildings to determine the visual variation present in a particular architectural environment or type;
2. Detailed visual documentation through drawing and photography of a few buildings representing the visual variation discovered in phase one;
3. Observation to discover use and meaning of the environment under study by various subgroups inhabiting it;
4. Photoelicitation interviews to confirm and expand the findings of phase three and to produce emic interpretations of the researched environment.

Eleftherios Pavlides, "Missing Dimension in Environmental Research: Detailed Visual Documentation," from EDRA 22, 1991: *Healthy Environments*, pp. 279–283. Copyright © 1991 by Environmental Design Research Association. Permission to reprint granted by the publisher.

This research method has been used successfully by the author in a variety of settings. The detailed visual information produced in phase one and two allow the production of research reports with extensive illustrations, which are an integral part of the information presented. The inclusion of extensive illustration makes the material more meaningful to the architectural design process.

INTRODUCTION

During the past thirty years, significant research on the social aspects of architecture has been accomplished, much of it under the aegis of the Environmental Design Research Association. However, the considerable literature produced from these efforts has had minimal impact on architectural practice. Some think this disparity between research and practice is the result of architects' inability to utilize research findings. Architectural professionals are thought either to lack interest in this area or to lack the training to use it because of their education's visual emphasis. Courses on Environmental Psychology that have been established for a number of years in architectural curricula have failed to increase the impact of environmental research on architectural practice.

In this paper, I will argue that environmental research will become more relevant to architectural design if more visual information is used during the conduct of research and in the presentation of research results. In much of environmental design research, social aspects of the environment are contrasted to formal visual qualities of the environment. An implicit assumption is that in order to complement the formal concerns considered the domain of the architects, social scientists are to provide the hidden social dimension, i.e., the (non) visual. This assumption often results in verbal or diagrammatic (non) visual research protocols and minimally or non illustrated research reports. Presenting a setting in strictly verbal or diagrammatic terms limits the usefulness of the findings.

This paper discusses one theoretical and methodological framework for addressing the impoverished visual documentation of the physical environment, the "Achilles heel," of environmental design research. The proposed approach combines the visual sophistication of architecture with the cultural and contextual sensitivity of ethnography.

Photography and detailed drawings are used to document the visual variability of an environment and this provides the starting point for subsequent research. The visual (indeed all sensory) qualities of an environment are thoroughly investigated before attempting to identify the social and psychological aspects of that environment. Analysis of the photographic record by the researcher, utilizing the art/historic/archeological methodology of studying visual form through similarity and contrast of proportion, color, decoration, scale, etc., is used to generate an etic reconstruction of the built environment under investigation. Participant observation and informant interviews provide baseline information about use and interpretation. Finally, photoelicitation provides emic information by revealing how various groups of inhabitants view, interpret, and use the visual variability of their environments.

I developed this method, which is based on a theory I have termed sociosemiotics (Pavlides, Hesser, 1989: 360), in 1977 in order to test the hypothesis that the conventionalized form of a vernacular architecture constitutes a language useful to the inhabitants' social life. (Pavlides, 1985). The method was applied during fieldwork carried out over nine months in Eressos, Greece, where I was assisted by Jana Hesser, an anthropologist. Since then I have supervised students using this method during several field studies in 1985 in Marysville, Kansas, in collaboration with sociolinguist Harriet Ottenheimer; in 1986 in San Isidoro, New Mexico, in collaboration with David Stea, an environmental psychologist; and in Epidaurus, Greece, in 1987, in collaboration with Jana Hesser. I have also supervised students who have applied this approach to the study of emergency rooms, churches, bars, etc. All these studies yielded significant information.

THEORETICAL BACKGROUND: SOCIOSEMIOTICS

The theoretical framework for this method was derived from three of anthropology's four subfields, namely cultural anthropology, archeology, and linguistics.

Cultural Anthropology

A cardinal assumption of cultural anthropology is that no single cultural construction of reality is absolutely better than others (Johnson, Allen, 1978: 8) and there is great emphasis on avoiding ethnocentrism when studying a culture different from one's own. That is, the culture should be examined on its own terms. This means that the proposed research uses the inhabitants' perceptions to define salient environmental features and relevant social variables.

The matrix of environmental forms is associated with particular social groups, meanings, or activities through ethnographic fieldwork: participant observation, informal interviews, and ethnographic interviews based on photoelecitation. By identifying the social variables (such as ethnicity, age, rank, social class, gender, etc.) which are common to the inhabitants who hold the same understanding, use, or interpretation of a specific environment, culture appropriate social categories are derived rather than imposed by the researcher.

Archeology

"Place" is one of three parameters defining a social situation in ethnographic research, along with "actors" and "activities" (Spradley, 1980:40). "Place," however, in ethnographic research is usually a verbal or diagrammatic category and its visual features are not described or represented in significant detail. The standards in sociosemiotics for describing "place" or the built form defining a social situation are derived from archeology (and its twin field, from a theoretical point of view, art history).

Archeology draws inferences from material artifacts and architectural remains to reconstruct earlier societies. Detailed examination of visual form is critical to archeology. Archeology and art history have developed sophisticated methods for recording and analyzing subtle variations of visual form to decipher social and cultural meaning. In the approach proposed here, detailed examination and documentation of buildings and their context through scaled drawings and extensive photography provides a starting point and a baseline for all subsequent research.

Discovery of social meaning and use of the environments being studied, e.g., expressions of social categories such a gender, social class, or age, follows the visual analysis. Thus, as in archeology and art history, visual form is analyzed first and then given social interpretation instead of starting with social categories and seeking visual manifestations of them in material artifacts or architectural form. Photographic elicitation validates, modifies, expands, and enriches with multiple meanings original interpretations based on architectural form alone.

Archeology and art history also stress the relationship between visual form and chronology and my approach shares with them a diachronic organization of the material. Environmental design studies frequently ignore the chronology of processes resulting in existing visual form. Many studies on important concepts such as territoriality, personal space, and architectural meaning have been conducted without regard for historical context. However, pressures are continually operating upon architectural form and decoration, not from some remote point in the past, but as an imminent social force acting in the living present, to paraphrase Labov, and so the meaning of architectural form for its inhabitants is also a dynamic and changing one. (Labov, 1973) Consequently, diachronic depth is needed in data collection. In order to discover how and why the built environment is used and valued today by various groups, we have to reconstruct its history in relation to social and environmental change.

Linguistics

Sociolinguistics provides a paradigm for combining ethnographic fieldwork with a detailed study of form, as exemplified by the work of Del Hymes and William Labov. Sociolinguists study the form of sound in its social context. In an analogous approach, visual form can be studied in its social context. The theoretical framework generated by this approach has been termed sociosemiotics (Pavlides, Hesser, 1980).

Sociolinguists have yearned for a study of language which depicts the full complexity of its actual use in society (Hymes, 1974:19). By contrast to structural linguistics, which seeks to discover invariant properties of language across various languages and through time, sociolinguistics examines language in the context of a speech community, which shares rules for the conduct and interpretation of speech (Hymes, 1974:31). In an effort to generate a theory that accounts for the meaning of language in a particular community the study of language is carried out in the context of actual communicative events rather than as description of grammatical and syntactical rules (Hymes, 1974:16, 133).

In order to achieve this goal sociolinguistic research utilizes both "emic" and "etic" accounts. "Emic" accounts of behavioral events are defined as those representing the insiders' or actors' point of view, while "etic" ones represent an outsiders' point of view. The "etic" account is considered useful as a preliminary grid to be related to "emic" accounts and to serve as a framework for comparing different "emic" accounts.

In sociosemiotics an "etic" account of the built environment is constructed through detailed documentation of architectural form employing the archeological/art/historic methodologies, as discussed above. The detailed documentation of architectural features and their variation serves as a "preliminary grid" that has to be supplemented with information on how the members of a community perceive, interpret, and value those features.

In sociolinguistics, it is the "emic" account that validates information, for example, by revealing how phonological features are relevant to identification of cultural behavior (Hymes 1974:11, 22). In order to examine a speech community and construct an "emic" account of language, ethnographic research is applied to the study of language. Ethnographic research is also required in sociosemiotics in order to construct "emic" accounts of built form, by investigating the activity patterns and social significance that architectural form and decoration holds for various groups of inhabitants.

Finally, sociolinguistics has a diachronic dimension, as does sociosemiotics as I have already discussed above.

METHODOLOGY

The theoretical framework proposed above can be operationalized in a four phase research process: 1. orientation to determine the visual variation present in several buildings representing a particular architectural environment or type; 2. detailed visual documentation through drawing and photography of several buildings representing the visual variation discovered in phase two; 3. observation to discover use and meaning of the environment under study by various subgroups inhabiting it; 4. photoelicitation interview.

Phase I. Orientation: Identification of Physical and Social Parameters

During an initial phase of orientation the range of existing variation of features is established and recorded by visiting several buildings of a particular "type," i.e., hospitals, offices, buildings, schools, houses, etc. This is possible because despite the conventional assertion that architects are trained to design unique buildings, in reality, the variation in form that exists within a particular building type, such as hospitals, offices, museums, or houses of a certain region at a particular period, results from a combination of only a few features arranged by a few rules. Architecture history identifies seminal buildings, which introduced new architectural features as well as changes in the organization of the building to support new activity patterns. The investigation of a building type through time identifies how morphological diversity developed over time.

During the orientation phase informal interviews and observation provide the first layer of information in identifying relevant user groups, salient issues, and "natural" time periods in terms of changes in design as well as its use and interpretation. Expert informants are sought and contacts are made at this time for future systematic interviews.

Phase II. Detailed Visual Documentation Through Drawings and Photographs

A sample of buildings are then selected to represent the variability of physical features of the building type, as identified in phase I. These are then systematically documented in detailed scale drawings, (plans and sections) and in extensive architectural photographs of interior and exterior spaces.

The visual recording taking place during this phase, is similar to two aspects of the visual recording that archaeologists perform on a site. First, the data collected by archaeologists are extraordinary both in the amount of visual detail and in the precision with which information is located in chronological and spatial contexts. Second, archaeologists document visual information without knowing whether the collected information is relevant. A priori, it is not possible to determine what visual information communicates to inhabitants of a certain environment.

Phase III. Observation

Detailed visual documentation with drawings and photographs is a time consuming activity. However the time spent in occupied homes or buildings offers the opportunity for observation and conversation, which can produce significant information about the use of space, the history of the building, and users' interpretation of visual features. Recording and analyzing this information is an essential part of the research process. Participant observation provides a basis for formulating preliminary ideas about use and meaning of the built environment. For example, when this methodology was used to study churches, the researchers attended several services; when it was used to study houses, the researchers experienced the spectrum of informal to formal socializing in people's homes; and when it was used to study nature centers the researchers spent time as users of those centers.

Phase IV. Photoelicitation

The final research phase is based on interviews, which are structured by presenting a variety of users with an extensive sample of photographs depicting a wide variety of the environments they are familiar with. For those who have never experienced firsthand an actual environment depicted in the photographs, photographic images are limited in their ability to evoke significant responses. It is impossible to discuss realistically the experience of an environment one has only seen as a photograph. However, for those already familiar with a particular environment through use, photographs are very effective as aids in recalling the specific characteristics and qualities (both visual and non visual) of an environment as well as the ways it is used.

Furthermore, photographic documentation often includes information which may have not even been perceived by the researchers. When a photograph is used as an eliciting device during an interview, it often reveals visual information new to the researcher because the informant remarks on aspects of the photograph which were not noticed by the researcher at the time the photograph was taken.

The researcher does not ask the respondent to rate or rank the photographs, sometimes according to criteria defined by the researcher as sometimes is done in photoelicitation research (Groat, Canter 1979:84–87). Rather, general questions are asked such as "What activities take place in this area and when?"; "Who takes part in these activities?" "What can you say about somebody using this area?"; "Has this area changed in either its use or its physical features?", etc. These questions elicit specific information which may include respondent evaluations of the represented environments based on criteria salient to the respondents.

As extensive a variety of people are selected for the interviews as possible, without any a priori firmly defined categorization of cultural subgroups. Relevant social and cultural subgroups or categories are derived by identifying those who respond in similar ways to the photographs used during interviews. Common social characteristics of those with common responses during photoelicitation help identify them as a distinct cultural subgroup. For this purpose, a detailed inventory of social characteristics such as gender, occupation, age, ethnicity, social rank, socioeconomic class, etc. is taken from every person interviewed with photographs.

Sometimes an unanticipated social characteristic emerges requiring the collection of additional information from those already interviewed. For example, an unanticipated social category encountered in a Greek village was "families with female offspring." These were the families who modernized their dwellings. A house, provided by a girl's family, was a major component of a girl's dowry and a modernized house was considered to be attractive to prospective grooms (Pavlides, 1983).

CONCLUSION

This method reveals how various user groups perceive or use a specific environment. Sociosemiotic research reveals how a majority of people respond, but also and perhaps more significantly, identifies a range of possible responses. Often, the most interesting findings for an architectural designer are the infrequent responses of a minority of respondents (i.e., the handicapped) members of outlier groups.

Presentation of results includes the rich visual material gathered in phases one and two and used in the interviews of phase four. The illustrations are not mere elaborations of the text but an integral part of the information presented. Photographs, scaled plans, and sections enable an architectural audience to comprehend the qualities of a built environment and to evaluate it for these physical characteristics, as well as to gain insight on user's perceptions, interpretations, and expectations of it. Combining this extensive visual information with an analysis of the way various groups of users interpret and use an environment provides an architectural designer with information, which is useful in the architectural design process. The transdisciplinary research approach proposed here is best carried out by a team of researchers rather than by a single researcher.

The different modes of data collection (photography, measuring, drawing, interviews, and participant observation) and the logistics of applying them, require diverse skills and knowledge best obtained through team effort. All the examples cited in this paper involved collaboration between architects and social scientists.

REFERENCES

Johnson, Allen W. (1978) *Quantification in Cultural Anthropology: An Introduction to Research Design.* Stanford University Press.

Hymes, Dell. (1974) *Foundations in Sociolinguistics.* University of Pennsylvania Press, Philadelphia.

Groat, Linda and Canter, David. (1979) "Does Post-Modernism Communicate?" in *Progressive Architecture* Dec 1979: 84–87.

Labov, William. (1973) *Sociolinguistic Patterns.* Philadelphia, University of Pennsylvania Press.

Pavlides, Eleftherios. (1983) "Modernization and the Fireplace in Eressos, A Greek Rural Town," in *Oz*, 5:20–3.

Pavlides, Eleftherios. (1985a) "Architectural Change in a Vernacular Environment." *A Case Study of Eressos, Greece, in EDRA* 16: 57–65.

Pavlides, Eleftherios. (1985b) *Vernacular Architecture in its Social Context. A Case Study of Eressos Greece.* Ph.D. Architecture, University of Pennsylvania, Ann Arbor, University Microfilms.

Pavlides, Eleftherios and Hesser, Jana E. (1986) "Women's Roles and House Form and Decoration in Eressos, Greece." in *Gender and Power in Rural Greece,* edited by Jill Dubisch, Page 1568–96, Princeton University Press, Princeton.

Pavlides, Eleftherios and Hesser, Jana E. (1989a) "Sacred Space, Ritual, and the Traditional House." in *Dwellings, Settlement and Tradition,* edited by Nezar Elsayyad and Jean Paul Bouldier, 278–293, Univ. Press of America, Lanham, NY.

Pavlides, Eleftherios and Hesser, Jana E. (1989b) "Vernacular Architecture in its Social Context." in *Current Perspectives on Housing and Culture,* edited by Setha Low and Erve J. Chambers, Philadelphia, Univ. of Pennsylvania Press.

Spradley, James. (1980) *Participant Observation,* New York, Chicago, San Francisco, Dallas, Montreal, Toronto, London, Sydney: Holt, Rinehart and Winston.

25 The Park and the People

Roy Rosenzweig and Elizabeth Blackmar

Archeological research shows that a primarily African-American and Irish village on the site of what would become Central Park was demolished, even though official park documents and newspapers said that only a few "shanties and bone-boiling establishments" were displaced.

In September 1825 cartman John Whitehead and his wife Elizabeth began selling off parcels of the farmland they owned, which lay roughly between 83rd and 88th streets and Seventh and Eighth avenues. The first purchaser was Andrew Williams, a twenty-five-year-old African-American bootblack, who bought three lots for $125. Epiphany Davis, a black laborer and a trustee of the African Methodist Episcopal Zion church, purchased twelve lots for $578 that same day. (AME Zion had been organized in New York in 1796; a contemporary described it as the "largest and wealthiest church of the coloured people in this city, perhaps in this country.") Within a week of Williams's and Davis's purchases, AME Zion bought six lots from the Whiteheads. Over the next three years three or four other church leaders—trustees, deacons, and preachers—purchased lots in the Whitehead tract. Between 1825 and 1832 the Whiteheads sold fifty land parcels, no fewer than twenty-four of them to black families.

By 1829 at least nine houses dotted this landscape, including one belonging to Andrew Williams. The other houses also seem to have been owned by African Americans. We might, then, suspect that black settlement of Seneca Village began in 1825 with these initial purchases, but it may have begun even earlier in this general area. By the second decade of the nineteenth century, free African Americans had apparently developed a community on York Hill, an elevation located almost precisely in the middle of the future Central Park, on the blocks just west of the Whitehead tract, between 79th and 86th streets and Sixth and Seventh avenues. It gave its name to the village of Yorkville, then being settled in that vicinity and farther north and east. One account describes Bill Dove, a young runaway slave from Virginia (and later a family retainer for Boss Tweed), who spent 1819 hiding out among black families who lived in this vicinity. In the early 1830s, St. Michael's Episcopal Church briefly conducted a mission Sunday school "among the colored people" on this site. Although the city owned most of York Hill, by the late 1830s William Matthews, a young black man from Delaware, may have held almost five acres.

Roy Rosenzweig & Elizabeth Blackmar, *The Park and the People: A History of Central Park*. pp. 65–77. Copyright © 1992 by Cornell University Press. Permission to reprint granted by the publisher.

The building of the first reservoir in the late 1830s and early 1840s disrupted York Hill's black community. In 1838 New York acquired the thirty-seven-acre York Hill tract as a receiving basin for the new Croton water system. Some families probably moved directly west and joined those who had begun to settle the Whitehead tract, where ten more houses were added between 1835 and 1839. In the late 1830s the African Union church, which William Matthews served as minister and trustee, bought land in Seneca Village. By 1840 the former Whitehead tract was home to more than a hundred people. By the next decade, Seneca Village (reflecting the virulent racism of the day) was known as "Nigger Village." But as the neighborhood more than doubled in population, its composition changed; by 1855 when at least 264 people lived there, Irish Americans made up about 30 percent of the community.

Among the earliest Irish residents of the area was its most famous native. In 1842 Sara Plunkitt, wife of Irish immigrant laborer Pat Plunkitt, gave birth to twin sons, one of whom grew up to be the celebrated West Side Tammany boss George Washington Plunkitt. Years later Plunkitt recalled that he was born on "Nanny Goat Hill," just "twenty feet inside the Central Park wall at [West] Eighty-fourth Street" and right on the edge of what he called "Nigger Village." Within the next seven or eight years, the Plunkitts moved farther south, although still perhaps within the borders of the future park. Plunkitt may not have been the only future Tammany boss to spend his early years on the western edge of Seneca Village. In 1846 the Croker family—including three-year-old Richard—fled famine-ridden Ireland and took up residence, according to one biographer, "in a dilapidated dwelling in what is now the western portion of Central Park." Young Richard's father plied his trade as an itinerant veterinarian among the horses, cows, and pigs of the park dwellers. Although some other white residents—police officer William Evers and milkman Philip Dunn, for example—settled in Seneca Village in the 1840s, most came after 1850, seeking cheap housing in an increasingly crowded and expensive city.

Seneca's white population generally faced the same contempt leveled at their black neighbors. The commingling of whites and blacks sparked fears and fantasies of miscegenation and "amalgamation." Working from the notes of his father, a missionary to the Seneca Village residents in the 1840s and 1850s, John Punnett Peters of St. Michael's described the park in the late 1840s as a "wilderness" filled with "the habitations of poor and wretched people of every race and color and nationality." "This waste," he continued, contained "many families of colored people with whom consorted and in many cases amalgamated, debased and outcast whites. Many of the inhabitants of this village had no regular occupation, finding it easy to replenish their stock of fuel with driftwood from the river and supply their tables from the same source, with fish."[16]

Were the residents of Seneca the "wretched" and "debased" floating population that Peters and other observers described? The origins of the village in purchases from the Whitehead tract as well as in the earlier settlement at York Hill suggests that this community had a much longer and more continuous history. Three-quarters of those residents (or their families) who were taxed in 1840 were still there fifteen years later. Virtually every black family in Seneca Village recorded by the 1850 census was still there five years later. Such figures acquire special significance when we consider that 40 percent of Boston's population moved in those same five years, that other cities had similarly high mobility rates, and that African Americans, in general, showed significantly less residential stability than other city residents.

Other evidence reinforces this picture of unusual stability. Although few Seneca Village black heads of household were New York City natives, by 1855 they had been in the city an average of twenty-two years, a sharp contrast to the area's Irish residents. Some black residents had much deeper roots specifically in Seneca Village; at least nine individuals or families could trace their ties back more than two and a half decades. Over those years they developed dense webs of interconnection.

Between 1825 and 1827 Diana and Elizabeth Harding (probably mother and daughter) purchased land in Seneca Village from the Whiteheads. Sometime before 1835 Elizabeth Harding married Obadiah McCollin, a cook born in Westchester County, who had already acquired at least two lots of Seneca Village land from James Newton, who had purchased it from the Whiteheads in 1825. Despite her marriage (and in seeming contravention of the common law of married women's property rights that prevailed in New York until 1848), Elizabeth Harding McCollin continued to hold some Seneca Village land in her own name. In the course of the next three decades, the McCollins forged ties and alliances with other families. In 1855 their household included six-year-old Frederick Riddles; Frederick's parents, Peter and Angelina Morris Riddles, are not listed in that year's census, but they were present five years earlier when they buried his nineteen-month-old brother and his grandmother, Nancy Morris, in the AME Zion graveyard. Nancy Morris had purchased land in Seneca Village back in 1827, and her daughter Angelina remained a landowner there thirty years later, even after she and her husband had moved out (and left their young son in the care of their neighbors, the McCollins). Also still present in Seneca Village was Nancy Morris's other daughter, Charlotte, who had married William Godfrey Wilson.

Such examples of intermarriage and interconnection can be multiplied even on the basis of the limited surviving evidence. Elizabeth Harding McCollin's father, Samuel Harding, for example, boarded for a time with his daughter and previously with Elizabeth and James Thompson, the son of Ada Thompson, another long-standing resident. And William Godfrey Wilson (Nancy Morris's son-in-law) may have been the son of Sarah Wilson (also a longtime Seneca Villager), who later adopted Catherine Treadwell, daughter of another of the original purchasers of the Whitehead land. These instances of kinship and neighborhood ties stretching over at least four decades may seem unexceptional; yet they defy the stereotype of the park dwellers as a drifting population of criminals. So does information on their housing, jobs, property holdings, and community institutions.

Most observers described the humble dwellings of Seneca Village residents as "shanties." In part, the word accurately describes small, one-story, six-to-ten-foot-high dwellings usually built out of unpainted rough board and not professionally constructed. Ishmael Allen, for instance, shared his nine-by-eleven-foot dwelling on 83rd Street with his wife, four children, and a boarder. Yet the word *shanty*, as a cultural term, often describes (and demeans) a building's occupants as well as the building itself. Although many lived in crowded circumstances, their conditions were often significantly better than thousands of other poor immigrant and black families living downtown in cellars, garrets, or eight-by-ten-foot tenement rooms. Park dwellers' also had considerable outdoor space, an amenity in short supply in the downtown tenement districts. Given what we know about the length of residence of so many Seneca Village black families, it also seems unlikely that their shanties were the rickety structures described by outside observers. Some perhaps more closely resembled rural cabins. Certainly park dwellings were valuable enough to cause disputes over ownership when the city took over the land. In seeking permission to remove a two-room "little house" he had erected at his own expense, Irish Seneca Village resident John Wallace pointed out that it "is to me of considerable importance having a wife and four little children to support." The quality of housing, moreover, varied considerably. Not too far from the Allens lived the four-person

McCollin household in an ample, nine-hundred-square-foot, two-story frame house, which the census taker valued at four thousand dollars.

One should not exaggerate the wealth of even the McCollins, one of the best-off Seneca Village families, whose substantial dwelling no doubt reflected savings accumulated over more than one generation as well as perhaps their own construction labor. Obadiah McCollin could not have earned a very large weekly salary as a cook, one of the few occupations open to African Americans in antebellum New York. Like their counterparts elsewhere in the city, virtually all black Seneca Villagers earned their living in the service trades—as domestics or waiters, for example—or as unskilled laborers. The same could be said of their Irish neighbors, most of whom were laborers earning perhaps a dollar per day. Among Seneca residents, only German grocer Henry Meyers, black grocer William Pease, and New York-born innkeeper John Haff could even loosely be considered occupationally "middle class."

The economic activities of women and children supplemented the earnings of male household heads. Many black women worked as domestics or laundresses. Wives also contributed to the household economy through housework: sewing, economizing on meal preparation, and especially scavenging for food, clothing, fuel, and implements that could be used by their own households or traded in New York City's extensive secondhand market.

Such activities throw a different light on the repeated references to "living off the refuse of the city," gathering "rubbish of all description," and denuding the park's forests for firewood. For contemporary commentators, the scavenging of the park dwellers was a mark of sloth, of lack of "regular occupation." Yet it might as easily have signified the reverse—the energy and resourcefulness with which park dwellers supplemented paltry wages with food, fuel, furniture, and clothing that could be obtained without cash. On the urban fringe in upper Manhattan trees offered a free source of fuel for warmth and cooking. It was only a short walk to the river, where driftwood and fish could be gathered much more easily and with less competition than downtown. There were economical uses for refuse that could not be recycled for human consumption: unused garbage fed the pigs and goats that some park dwellers raised: the bones of dead animals fueled the two bone-boiling plants located at 66th and 75th streets, a short walk south of Seneca Village. A few residents had fairly extensive gardens as well as their own stables and barns. Others—such as eighty-eight-year-old Henry Garnet—kept small gardens out of which they supplemented their diets. The ability to raise at least some of their own food and to take advantage of the larger urban and natural ecology were among the advantages Seneca Village residents had over downtown poor families.

Most important, many of the black Seneca residents had something denied to most of their compatriots elsewhere in the city: security of tenure based on landownership. Throughout the city, few black New Yorkers owned land because of the barriers imposed by limited financial resources, a state law that prohibited black inheritance as late as 1809, informal racial bars on land sales, and the high price of downtown Manhattan real estate. In 1850 census takers counted only seventy-one black property owners; ten years later the number had grown only slightly to eighty-five. In this context, Seneca Village, where the Whiteheads willingly sold land to African Americans and where land was cheap by New York standards, offered an unusual opportunity for blacks who had some savings and wanted to become landowners. At least some black Seneca Village landowners actually lived downtown. Joseph Marshall, a hardworking house painter and AME Zion church member, owned five lots in Seneca Village as well as his house on Centre Street in lower Manhattan.

Among black Seneca Village residents, landownership rates were extraordinarily high. With more than half the black households in Seneca Village in 1855 owning property, African-American residents there had a rate of property ownership five times as great as New Yorkers as a whole. In 1850 black Seneca Villagers were thirty-nine times as likely to own property as other black New Yorkers. Seneca Village's Irish households were not equally fortunate: only three of twenty-one owned property, and none of the recent Irish arrivals did. Irish immigrant settlers of Seneca Village in the 1850s faced some of the same problems as did black migrants to the north a century later: a narrowing of opportunities, in this case, less available land and higher prices.

The high levels of property ownership and residential stability among black Seneca Villagers allowed them to reinforce and develop their own community institutions, particularly churches. A settlement centered on four city blocks and comprising around sixty households included two African-American Methodist churches (AME Zion and African Union) and one racially mixed Episcopal church (All Angels', an affiliate of St. Michael's). AME Zion church had purchased land from the Whiteheads in 1825 and 1827, and in 1827 when the city transformed the Potters Field into Washington Square, thereby eliminating the burial ground used by AME Zion, it began to use some of its Seneca Village lots as a cemetery. Not until 1853 did AME Zion begin construction of a church, although a congregation—with a hundred weekly worshipers—predated that building by as much as five or six years. In downtown Manhattan, where most black New Yorkers lived, AME Zion had faced competition from three other Methodist churches, and one of those rivals now competed with AME Zion in Seneca Village. The trustees of African Union Methodist Episcopal church had purchased land only a hundred yards from AME Zion in 1837, although in 1855 they claimed to have "been in possession of said lots and meeting house thereon for more than twenty years." The African Union Church also housed another important local institution, Colored School No. 3, set up in the 1840s, one of only a handful of black schools in New York City.

St. Michael's at Broadway and 99th Street created Seneca Village's third church in 1846 as a mission to the poor residents of the park. First, it set up a Sunday school and then held services in the home of a white policeman, William Evers. Thomas Peters greatly expanded the missionary work, and by 1848 he arranged to build a wooden church on West 84th Street with subscriptions raised among wealthy white parishioners of St. Michael's and other philanthropic New Yorkers—Robert Minturn, for example. Known as All Angels' Church when it opened in 1849, it ministered to an unusual congregation. Black parishioners came largely from Seneca Village, white parishioners from Irish and German settlements located within a mile of the church.

African Americans numbered about two-thirds of the names in All Angels' register and were some of its most loyal and active members. Ishmael Allen, who lived next door, not only served as church sexton but named his first son after the Reverend Mr. Peters. The widow Ada Thompson, a domestic worker born in Virginia in 1796, lived just across "old lane" from the church. In September 1849 Peters came to her small house to baptize her first grandchild, who was named (like four other black Seneca Villagers) after the late president William Henry Harrison. Over the next six years, Peters baptized three more of Thompson's grandchildren and buried her son and a fourth grandchild. Four children of ragpicker and sailor John White were baptized through All Angels'. A fifth was buried in the graveyard in Astoria, Queens, that Peters established for the church after burials were banned below 86th Street in Manhattan. But although All Angels' was the best-endowed and largest of Seneca Village's three churches, only about thirty people seem to have attended its weekly services. Many black residents may have preferred to worship in all-black churches. African Union, with only half the capacity of All Angels', had fifty regular congregants, and AME Zion seems to have been twice as large as that. In a community of perhaps only 260 inhabitants, 180 people attended church each week. Even allowing for some exaggeration and for the attendance of some people from outside Seneca Village, this community was exceptionally devoted to its churches.

The community involvement suggested by these high levels of church attendance was reflected in politics as well, although here the evidence is somewhat sketchier. In the mid-nineteenth century, black New Yorkers faced formidable and unique obstacles to voting: a $250 freehold estate and three years of residency in the state were required. As late as 1845 (the last time citywide statistics were collected) only 91 of 13,000 black New Yorkers had the franchise, and ten years later, with the city's black population just below 12,000, the number of voters was still under 100. Of that tiny cadre of black voters, 10 lived in tiny Seneca Village; thus, that community's residents were several times more likely to have voting privileges than black New Yorkers in general. Some black men who lived downtown had also qualified to vote based on landownership in Seneca Village; indeed, land purchases there may have been a deliberate stratagem to meet the property qualification. At least three of those "absentee" owners took a prominent role in New York politics. Timothy Seaman, who owned a lot on 87th Street, and James N. Gloucester, a minister who held a lot on 88th Street, were both leaders in the campaign for unrestricted black suffrage. Charles B. Ray, who owned three lots a half mile south of Seneca Village, was a well-known abolitionist clergyman and president of the New York Society for the Promotion of Education among Colored Children. Ironically, a settlement that contemporary and historical accounts depict as disorganized and degraded may have been one of the pillars of New York's antebellum black community.

PIG KEEPERS, GARDENERS, SISTERS, BONE BOILERS, AND SQUATTERS

Other, less-established settlements clustered through the area of the future park. The southeastern corner, which the *Journal of Commerce* called "Pigtown," was home to about fourteen households, roughly three-quarters of them Irish. A larger concentration of Irish families could be found farther north and west (between 68th and 72nd streets and between Seventh and Eighth avenues) with about thirty-four households, two-thirds of them Irish. Although these Irish-American park dwellers did not develop the same sorts of institutions within the boundaries of the future park as did black Seneca Villagers, they did join in the community life of surrounding Irish-Catholic settlements. Some attended St. Lawrence O'Toole Roman Catholic Church in Yorkville built in 1851 (now Church of St. Ignatius Loyola). Others apparently walked to the slightly more distant Catholic churches on 50th and 117th streets.

The park site allowed Irish immigrants, many of whom came from rural areas, to grow food or keep hogs and goats as they had back home. Immigrants who wanted to tend animals were much more likely to live uptown when restrictions tightened on such activities downtown after the 1849 cholera epidemic. Most kept pigs or raised food to supplement their wages as day laborers on the road gangs building uptown streets. German immigrants lived alongside the Irish in these areas but developed distinctive settlements. One dominated the northern end of the park, the other the southwestern corner between 69th and 79th streets and Sixth and Seventh avenues, below the reservoir. One 1855 census taker, apparently referring to Germans who lived in the middle of the park, noted that "a majority of the deaths that are recorded on this page are among the children of the 'German' population who have been in the Country but a short time, very poor, having no visible means of support except picking rags, gathering cinders, etc., located in a 'Swamp,' which is continually wet, and subject to 'Fever and Ague.'" Counting the population farther north in the park, a different census taker wrote: "Germans cultivate small patches for gardens and make out to raise enough to live upon in their way. But nothing more."

Compared with Seneca Villagers, as the census takers' comments show, the German ragpickers and gardeners were even more closely tied to the park land for their subsistence. Many of the thirty-nine gardeners—all but six of them German immigrants and the second largest occupational group in the park after laborers—eked out a marginal existence, but a few had modestly prosperous spreads. A German-born music teacher with the colorful name of Jupiter Zeuss K. Hesser began cultivating seven lots near Seventh Avenue and 100th Street around 1852, which he called "Jupiterville." By 1855 he had erected a "neat two story house … with fine hard walls," a chimney, a "very nice cellar," and a "good sewer 4 or 5 feet deep"; he had cleared the ground of stones, bushes, and woods, laid down manure, dug a ten-foot well with the "most excellent water," fenced in his gardens, and built a barn, chicken coop, and goat stable. Within five blocks of Hesser lived Henry Ellerman, who had arrived from Germany in the late 1840s. Assisted by his father-in-law and three German immigrant boarders, Ellerman cultivated eight acres and produced two thousand dollars worth of crops in a year.

Though most German and Irish park dwellers had been in New York City considerably less time—twelve years on average—than their black neighbors, at least some could claim longer tenures within the park. In 1836 Catherine and William Coggery, for example, arrived in New York well in advance of the famine-driven wave of Irish immigrants in the 1840s, and within nine months, they settled on 93rd Street near Seventh Avenue. Several other Irish families joined them in the next ten years. When asked in an 1857 court case about her familiarity with a tract of land in the upper park, Catherine Coggery replied: "I … have been looking at it for 20 years."

The area of the park under longest continuous settlement was probably the northeast corner, where the old Boston Post Road made its way between two rocky ridges. By the 1750s Jacob Dyckman had built a tavern on a hill in the vicinity of 105th Street and Fifth Avenue. It soon passed into the McGown family, which owned the tavern and the surrounding land for most of the next century. During the Revolutionary War, Hessian mercenaries occupied McGown's Pass, as it had come to be called, and in 1814 sixteen hundred militiamen guarded the area against a threatened British invasion. (The stone blockhouse at West 109th Street, the oldest building in the park today, is a surviving relic of the chain of fortifications built then.) In 1847 the Sisters of Charity of New York purchased a dilapidated frame house surrounded by pools of water on the site of the abandoned tavern; they took turns cooking their meals on a small coal stove and carried water from the nearest spring. "I have heard of poverty, but I never saw such a picture of it before," a young candidate for the order said to herself when she arrived in 1849. Within a few years, the sisters had constructed a flourishing religious community on what they called Mount St. Vincent. By the mid-1850s, their convent, with seventy sisters (half of them Irish-born), eleven Irish female servants, and nine Irish male employees, encompassed several substantial buildings including a laundry, a large brick chapel, a boarding academy for two hundred "young ladies," and a free school for fifty or sixty children from surrounding areas.

The religious buildings at McGown's Pass were not the only impressive structures within the proposed park boundaries. In 1848 the State of New York had erected the Arsenal on ten acres of land at 64th Street and Fifth Avenue. About fifteen blocks north the wealthy Wagstaff family maintained an old farmhouse at Fifth Avenue and 79th Street, one of the few paved streets in the area. And at around 68th and Sixth, the broker Peter B. Amory and his family of ten occupied the Amory family homestead.

On the western side of the park, a world away from the Amorys and the Wagstaffs, were the bone-boiling plants of George Moller and William Menck. Such "nuisance" industries were being driven out of lower Manhattan by ordinances, restrictive covenants, and public pressure. Leather dresser Benjamin Beaman, butcher Ludwig Sheff, and soap boiler Charles Lucke also faced fewer restrictions on their trades here than downtown. Some park dwellers helped to gather the thirty-four thousand bushels of animal bones that Moller and Menck required each year; others found the dollar-a-day wages offered at the plants attractive; and the rest were willing to tolerate (or at least lacked the resources to complain about) the noxious odors released when bones were boiled to produce fuel for sugar refining. (The current occupant of the site of the Menck bone-boiling works at West 66th Street—the swank Tavern on the Green—posts no commemoration of its distinguished predecessor.)

Others in the future park engaged in businesses that were conventionally viewed as illegal. Most of the evidence on such crime comes from observers with little understanding of and still less sympathy for the park dwellers. The press repeatedly accused them of "theft" between 1855 and 1857, but such charges often recorded their removal of their own property from the park before the onset of construction. Other charges reflected differing perceptions of customary rights. "Some of the people living in that vicinity," the *Journal of Commerce* reported on June 28, 1856, "are in the *habit* of cutting small limbs from the few remaining trees" to use in drying hops for beer. That being said, it would hardly come as a surprise that people who did steal food, fuel, furniture, or clothing (or whose scavenging sometimes crossed the thin line separating it from theft) found the park a convenient place to avoid legal scrutiny, particularly given the scarcity of police in upper Manhattan. This same absence of close police surveillance probably encouraged other illegal pursuits. Some Irish widows with no visible means of support may have operated illegal liquor outlets, or *shebeens*—a traditional trade for such women in their native Ireland. In March 1855 when a police officer broke up a Sunday morning boxing match at a location just south of the park, the participants reassembled in "Pigtown" near 65th Street. And when police first arrived in Central Park in 1856, they cracked down on "disorderly" (and presumably unlicensed) dance houses, which had probably operated for years.

Of course, the most common charge against park residents was that they illegally occupied the land by "squatting" there. As a broad generalization, the term *squatters* could not apply to the one-fifth of the residents who owned their own land and who as a group had a level of property ownership 50 percent above the average for the city. Of the four-fifths who did not own property, nine families appear in the city tax lists, indicating that they held ground leases requiring them to pay the taxes. The majority of park dwellers appear in neither land nor tax records, but some "squatters" probably had formal or informal arrangements with landowners that permitted use of the land. In the early 1840s, for example, landowner Abraham Higbe allowed Nicholas Ray and John Donnelly to settle their families and grow corn, potatoes, and other vegetables on his land in return for their clearing it of brush. After the mid-1840s, Donnelly apparently began to pay a cash rent of twenty-five dollars per year, but the landlord's agent did not always make the annual collection, perhaps because the sum seemed so small to him. Donnelly, meanwhile, collected rents from subtenants on the same land. When Donnelly moved from the area, rent collection became even more casual. One resident, widow Mary O'Donnell, had to enlist the help of a local policeman to locate the current landlord. When they found him, he was willing to accept whatever cash she offered as that year's rent.

The *New York Sun,* one of the few newspapers even mildly sympathetic to the so-called squatters, noted on May 6, 1857, that of the "many persons who have erected shanties in the swamps and on the rocks" of northern Manhattan, "most … seek the permission of the owners of the land before erecting their shanties, or they squat on lands whose owners are unknown. Not a few of them have been paying a small ground rent, and raising fruit and vegetables on patches of land which would otherwise have been unproductive." In other words, most New York landlords, even of marginal lands in the future Central Park, kept track of who lived on their property, even if they did not always collect regular rents from them. Thus, the park dwellers most accurately called squatters were the few who made their homes on lots whose owners were listed as "unknown." Like the word *shanty*, in mid-nineteenth-century New York the term *squatter* was more of a cultural category than a formal legal description, a convenient shorthand for the sort of poor people more affluent New Yorkers preferred to remove from their neighborhoods.

Eviction of all these people—landowners and squatters alike—would begin when the commission of estimate finally issued its Central Park report in the fall of 1855.

26 The Enacted Environment of East Los Angeles

James T. Rojas

Mexican-Americans in Los Angeles use their front yards and sidewalks as active living space.

One planning report on East Los Angeles found that the area "lacks a physical identity … therefore needs a plaza." Funny they should say that. As everyone in Los Angeles knows, and as visitors can perceive, East L.A. has a very strong identity that is created by the way its Mexican and Mexican-American residents use its spaces. East L.A. is an animated and extroverted environment that confronts the viewer; no space is left unmarked or unused.

By working, playing and "hanging out" in spaces like streets, front yards and driveways, East L.A. residents create a spontaneous, dynamic and animated landscape that is unlike any other in Los Angeles. These spaces, which often isolate residents in other communities, bring the residents of East L.A. together. The identity of the place is created through the culturally related behavior patterns of the residents. It is not built; it is enacted.

SELLING ON THE STREET

Street vendors are one of the most noticeable elements in the East L.A. landscape. They flow in and out of commercial and residential areas and attract crowds wherever they go.

Los Moscos (flies), as they have been called,[1] are day laborers who use the streets to sell their menial labor. From 10 to as many as 50 men station themselves at strategic locations (near hardware stores and major traffic arteries), positioning themselves on the street so they can confront drivers with their eyes. If a driver shows any kind of interest and slightly slows down, he will be swarmed by work-hungry men.

Mariachis (Mexican musicians) walk from bar to bar in their black uniforms and instruments looking for work. They station themselves at one particular corner, where prospective employers go to hire them for events.

"Carriers," who sell anything they can carry, are the simplest form of vendor because they do not have much overhead. For example, one man carries around a box of tapes while another carries a long pole with wicker baskets of silk flowers hanging from each end.

James T. Rojas, "The Enacted Environment of East Los Angeles," from *Places*, Vol. 8, No. 3, pp. 42–53. Copyright © 1993 by Design History Foundation. Permission to reprint granted by the publisher.

Mariachis, murals, yard sales and social fences help activate the environment of East Los Angeles.

"Asphalt vendors" stand by strategic freeway off-ramps and on median strips at major intersections. They keep their wares on the ground, in shopping carts, or in plastic bags tied to chain link fences. These vendors approach cars as they stop at intersections and try to sell the occupants a bag of oranges or peanuts for a dollar.

"Pushcart vendors" roam the streets selling exotic fruit cocktails, tamales, ice cream and vegetables. One resident said, "In the morning a man comes around selling bread and vegetables and later in the day different vendors come selling other eatable items." The pushcart vendors almost look out of place on the suburban streets of East L.A., dodging moving cars as they push their small carts.

"Tent vendors" sell odds and ends from their front lawns and sidewalks, mainly on Saturdays, much like a garage sale. Fences are an important part of this composition because they hold up items and easily delineate the selling space. One boy had sacks of peanuts tied to the fence in front of his house and conducted business from a small table on the sidewalk.

"Auto vendors" are a spontaneous sort who drive around to different locations to find the right market. They conduct business from their truck or car by parking on the roadside and setting up shop. Some will set up tents on vacant lots, while others prefer street corners. Some trucks have been converted to elaborate roving bazaars with things attached everywhere.

"Roach coaches," or food trucks, have long been part of the American vending fabric. In East L.A., these stainless steel trucks have been redesigned with long windows on the side to serve customers and personalized with names like "Maritita's." They have become very popular and follow Mexicans all over the city, from West Side construction sites to *discotecas* in Hollywood.

NO BLANK WALLS

In East L.A., blank wall space has become a tableau for cultural expression for *cholos* (gang members), political groups and shop owners. Very few walls are left untouched by graffiti, store signs, or murals. Even garage doors, fences, sidewalks, benches, buses and freeway signs have become displays of personal expression. All this expression creates a new reality of visual stimulation, "fills in" the landscape and reveals the different sorts of order in a place.

Graffiti, the most prolific form of visual communication, can be found just about everywhere. To the outsider none of these markings make any sense, but to the people that make and read them, they do. *Cholos,* for example, use graffiti as territorial indicators. Most residents do not like graffiti and are constantly painting over it.

Stores and buildings are kinetic because of their flamboyant use of graphics and words. The use of both pictures and words is very common. Certain pictures indicate the type of store. A large pig's head or jersey cow indicates a butcher shop. Cornucopias indicate vegetable and fruit stands.

Murals, the most celebrated form of public decoration, express many different values. They add an element of public art and local culture to otherwise dull buildings and streets by saluting pedestrians and motorists, and they make otherwise marginal spaces very tolerable. Many buildings are painted from top to bottom, which changes the character of these sometimes rather plain structures.

Religious murals of Our Lady of Guadeloupe are popular because she is the patron saint of Mexico. Murals from the '70s often express social

**Above: Pushcart vendors sell their wares on the street.
Below: Vendors congregate for weekly street market.**

Pushcart vendors seem out of place in suburban scale East L.A.

concerns. However, the most common murals are those commissioned by shop owners for advertisements; these can be whimsical and animated. On one corner, a bar with an aquatic theme is covered with an ocean-blue mural; Neptune's eyes gaze out with a mischievous look. On another corner, another bar is covered with a mural of a woman in a bathing suit smoking a cigarette and having some fun.

Most murals are painted on the large walls on the side of corner buildings. They "wrap" the commercial activity from a busy street into otherwise quiet streets and forgotten areas. These transitional corner spots are important places. Often, vendors will hang out in these locations, further activating the space.

PROPS

Props add a layer of architecture to the landscape and help make spaces usable. Props produce a sense of security in a place by acting as territorial markers: they are apparent and aggressive; they can be seen, heard, felt and smelled.

A parked car can become the center of a day's activities just by shifting its location. A pushcart selling ice cream occasions a fleeting moment of social exchange between eager children. A sofa under a tree or on a porch can be a place for residents to wallow away the afternoon. A barbecue pit can generate revenue and be a place to swap neighborhood gossip.

Music is used as a prop because sound can control and define a space. Spanish and disco music are aggressive to some, normal to others. *Mariachis* and car stereos add to the ambiance through their music; each appeals to a different audience. The music adds an extra layer to the landscape.

Many shop owners have replaced the fronts of their stores with glass walls that can be opened during the day; these "opened ends" connect indoor and outdoor spaces. Inexpensive wares, placed in front of the store, serve as a three-dimensional display that adds a tactile quality to the pedestrian experience and advertises what's inside.

Olympic Boulevard, otherwise a no-man's land, has been "pedestrianized" by the use of props. Gas stations have been converted into taco stands by the heavy use of props and only minor changes to the structure. Pumps are replaced with tables and chairs, which make a bold attempt to capture and reenforce street activity; people can sit here and have direct visual access to the street. Wrought iron sheds are sometimes added in an attempt to enclose some of the seating areas. The thirty-foot sign that advertised the gasoline company now announces the taco stand.

Murals adorn a front yard wall.

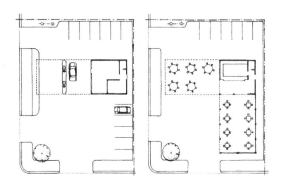

[Above and bottom-right] Gas stations have been turned into pedestrian-oriented restaurants.

[Diagram] How a typical conversion works.

26. The Enacted Environment of East Los Angeles ✹ 359

The front yard is a place for personal expression.

The use of props in both residential and commercial areas creates a connection between the two. Props scale down the landscape to a pedestrian level that contradicts the automobile scale of Los Angeles. Driving on the streets of East L.A. all one sees is a clutter of people, props and vendors. Walking, however, one experiences a rich, tactile landscape that enhances the enacted environment. What might seem like a visual mess from an automobile becomes a personal and vivid experience for the pedestrian.

LA YARDA: A PERSONAL EXPRESSION

Nowhere in the landscape of East L.A. is the Mexican use of space so illuminated and celebrated than in the enclosed front yard. Since many Mexican homes do not have American, suburban-style front yards, residents of East L.A. have reinterpreted them. The front yard has become, through use and design, a place for personal expression and for recreating traditional Mexican housing forms.

Houses in East L.A. are sited on their lots just like other suburban American houses, but the enclosure and personalization of front yards has greatly changed their appearance. In fact, the enclosed front yard is such a dominant element that it has altered the physical character of entire neighborhoods as well as residents' behavior patterns.

In a middle-class neighborhood, the appearance of one's front yard is a standard for being accepted into the community. In East L.A., the green, parklike setting that open front yards create in typical American suburbs has been cut up into individual slices that permit a greater range of expressiveness, create visual diversity and allow sociability to take place more readily. The appearance of one's front yard expresses one's individuality; acceptance is based on physical and social contact with neighbors.

Depending on the practical needs of the owner, the use and design of the front yard vary from junk yards to elaborate courtyard gardens reminiscent of Mexico. The maintenance of the front yard varies from house to house; one may be kept up nicely while the next is not. No one is ever penalized for not watering or taking care of his front yard.

In these enclosed front yards, the residents' private worlds unfold. All the sights and sounds from the uncontrollable street have been manipulated and tailored to the needs of the owner. The enclosed front yard acts like a room without a ceiling because of the personalization and sense of security. Things that look like clutter from outside the fences actually are as organized and purposeful as objects in a room.

Most outsiders are not prepared to read front yards and think they are unsightly. But East L.A. residents identify with these front yards because they understand and can read the personalization. Walking down a neighborhood street, one becomes aware of who might be living in each house. Residents might be outside doing something in their front yard, or the objects they leave in the yard might display traces of their lives. Toys speak of children living in a house; lots of cars and auto parts might indicate that teenagers live there. A lack of planting along the fence might indicate a dog runs around the front yard. Intricate gardens, potted plants, small statues and other elements that shelter a house from the street might indicate an elderly person resides there or that the resident is not too involved in street activity.

Social interaction takes place at the front gate.

FENCES: A SOCIAL CATALYST

One can find fences in many American front yards, of course. But for East L.A. residents, fences are a social catalyst that brings together neighbors and passersby for interaction. Fences break down social and physical barriers by creating a comfortable point between a front yard and sidewalk where people can congregate.

The use of fences in the front yard modifies the approach to the house and

Fences and threshholds help extend household space to the street.

moves the threshold from the front door to the front gate (mailboxes, for example, are hung on the fence or front gate rather than near the front door). The enclosed front yard serves as a physical barrier between the private spaces of the home and the public spaces of the street; it acts as a large foyer and becomes an active part of the household.

Stepping into the front yard from the sidewalk, one feels as if one is entering a home. The front gate or entry, sometimes made of wrought iron fencing or even masonry, can be articulated with structural elements such as arches—giving it a sense of being a building that is independent of the actual house.

The enclosed front yard becomes a large, "defendable" threshold, which, in fact, allows for more social interaction to take place. In a typical American home or apartment, which lacks a defendable threshold, there is great pressure to define social interaction because one cannot have a comfortable conversation at a front door or in a hallway. In East L.A., it is perfectly acceptable to have conversations at the front gate and not to invite people into the home.

The social interaction one experiences in the enclosed front yard is neither as demanding nor as intimate as that which takes place in a house. Since this space is public, the interaction is very casual, like being in an outdoor cafe where one could stare off for a few seconds and not offend one's companions. In the front yard, one is always aware of cars and people going by on the street. Collectively, the enclosed front yards in these neighborhoods create a very intimate atmosphere. The fences along the street break up the lawn space of each home, and the street becomes more urban than suburban in character because the fence reflects the personality of each resident. The street can now function like a plaza, and every resident can participate in the public street from the protection of his private yard.

EAST L.A. VERNACULAR

In Los Angeles, the city of suburban dream homes where architectural freedom runs rampant, the small housescapes of East L.A. seem inconsequential compared to houses designed by architects like Greene and Greene, Richard Neutra, Rudolph Schindler and Frank Gehry.

But the small, modern houses in East L.A. are distinctive because they were built by non-architects. They have evolved into what I call "East L.A. vernacular" because the combination of design and usage (people, props and physical form) is unique to this area. The houses are customized and personal; every change, no matter how small, has meaning and purpose. The colors, building materials and personal items used to embellish houses, fences and front yards offer a public face to the street.

Shy American-style homes are transformed to an extroverted form that sets the stage for the enacted environment. Each house communicates with others. People, fences and porches help extend household activities to the street. Instead of hiding behind a lawn and shrubs, suddenly each house comes forward, staking its claim to the pavement. The neighborhood feels filled in, physically and socially. The sidewalk and street feel more controlled because the household reaches right to these public areas.

The typical Mexican courtyard house and household extends itself to all four sides of the lot and is designed with a patio or courtyard in the center; this form accommodates the warm weather and reflects Spanish precedents. Because most rooms face the patio, it becomes a central point into which the flow of the household radiates. Similarly, in East L.A., the house is defined by the property line rather than the floor plan or exterior walls; the front yard and fence are integral parts of the household.

In the typical American house plan, rooms are arranged in a strong linear sequence that depends on their degree of publicness, from the front living room (public) to the back bedroom (private). But in the Mexican household, as one Mexican put it, "Most rooms are not private because many times rooms have been attached to each other as the family grows, regardless of their adjacency to other rooms. Many times one has to go through one bedroom to get to others. Many people also keep their doors open to the patio because of the hot weather."

American house plans seek to protect individual privacy through the arrangement of rooms; the typical Mexican house plan tries to keep the family separate from the general public. In East L.A., the front yard and porch can be considered semi-private rather than semi-public because the space flows out of the home to the porch, front yard and fence.

Driveways are an important feature that allows for many ephemeral uses—parking cars, children playing, barbecuing, or partying. In most cases, the driveway runs the full length of the lot on one side. The garage is placed in the back yard, rather than at the front of the house. Most houses have easy access to the driveway through a side door. The importance of the driveway increases as additional houses are built on the lot over time; the driveway serves as an outdoor hallway along which residents walk between their houses and the street.

In many American neighborhoods the use and importance of front porches has declined for various reasons, and most new homes are built without them. In East L.A., front porches have gained a new importance because many residents use them, and because they help connect the enacted front yard to the house. The porch is often decorated with personal and useful items, such as potted plants, bird cages and furniture.

LEARNING FROM THE ENACTED ENVIRONMENT

Modern structures neatly package and organize people in comprehensible arrangements of space; life is hidden behind facades. Recently, architects and urban designers have realized that the presence of people can add a rich texture to the often banal urban and suburban landscape, and they have responded by introducing street furniture, plants and vendors in the design of public spaces.

The resulting settings look like they could sustain the street life of East L.A., but there is a basic difference. In those settings, the use of props is planned and the space controls the user, rather than the user controlling the space. The enacted environment of East L.A. is not planned; the props and vendors reflect the nature of the people. The enacted environment is made up of individual actions that are ephemeral but nevertheless part of a persistent process.

People have always criticized the Mexicans of East L.A. for being nonpolitical because they do not vote. The word "politics" comes from the Greek word *polis*, or city. There are two kinds of politics in the world, theoretical and practical. Theoretical politics are the politics of politicians, who discuss how people should live their lives. Practical politics is the way we conduct our everyday lives and express our existence.

By examining the enacted environment of East L.A., one becomes aware of the politics of everyday life. The residents have created a life in their environment that says something about themselves. They may not have political control, at least in theoretical terms, but I would argue that the residents have empowered themselves through the way they use their front yards and their streets.

NOTE

1. Bruce Kelley, "El Mosco," *Los Angeles Times Magazine* (18 March 1990), 11.

27 Architect à la Mode

Deborah Singmaster

An African-American architect talks about the importance of cultural awareness.

Wilfred Achille, founding partner of multi-ethnic practice MODE 1, remains optimistic despite the problems facing black architects

Achille was born in London, but his parents come from the West Indies. It is this sort of background that he believes gives multi-ethnic practices an advantage over mainstream architects when it comes to designing certain building types. "For example, if you are designing an Afro-Caribbean elderly people's home, you know that they do not want to look out on a flower garden with grass; they want a vegetable garden that they can work and get something from." Colour is another area where the users' cultural roots must be considered: the white minimalist interior beloved of many modern architects means death to the Chinese, whereas red symbolises good luck; purple is the colour that Africans associate with royalty and luck.

At the same time, Achille stresses: "We don't want to be categorised; obviously we feel we can deal with all levels of design, like everybody else."

His time at the buyers' end of the fashion industry has given him a firm grasp of marketing skills, which he is putting to good advantage on his practice's behalf. "We don't have a direct line to work, so we have to use marketing tools. We send out letters, we advertise in specific magazines; we look in the newspapers for possible work." Competitions? "We want to do competitions but the latest Cardiff episode does not say much for the system. Zaha is a role model for us and it is very difficult for us to watch this sort of thing happening."

SOBA [Society of Black Architects] was formed in 1990 because black architects and students felt that there was nowhere they could come together to discuss the problems which they were facing in their work and training, and which are not encountered by their white counterparts. The society now has over 200 members drawn from about 30 practices and educational establishments. Achille's term of office as chairman of SOBA comes to an end this month. During the past year members have lobbied MPs about the way work is allotted to multi-ethnic practices by housing associations and local authorities. Part of the problem, says Achille, is that although black practices can get on housing association and local authority lists, this does not ensure that they are

Deborah Singmaster, "Architect à la Mode," from *Architects' Journal*. Copyright © 1995 by Emap Construct. Permission to reprint granted by the publisher.

given work. "Obviously the HAs operate equal opportunities policies: providing they have black practices on their list they meet the criteria. But there is no monitoring of the lists. It's pointless having an equal opportunities policy if it is not monitored, and it's very disheartening when you meet all the requirements but fail to get any work."

Despite his awareness of much that is wrong in the profession, Achille is not depressed or pessimistic. He senses an under-current of creativity, of things waiting to happen. "There's a buzz going on. There will be new architectural designs appearing, people will start taking more risks," he says. He maintains this faith in the face of much evidence to the contrary. A friend who attended a Millennium 2000 meeting told him that "everyone present was over 50 and there was no multicultural mix whatsoever." Asks Achille: "Who is the year 2000 for?" It's a question that a lot of people should be asking.

28 The Psychology of Sustainability: What Planners Can Learn from Attitude Research

Alice Jones

A psychologist shows how to operationalize a concept for research purposes, specifically how to ask or write questions that get realistic answers in regard to sustainability.

INTRODUCTION

The centuries old concept of finding balance between human and natural systems has emerged most recently under the rubric of sustainability or sustainable development. Although definitions of sustainability differ, at the heart of the notion is the idea that human social and economic systems should operate within the limits of the natural systems upon which they depend (see Beatley 1995a for a discussion of some of the definitions of sustainability and sustainable development). There is general consensus about the seriousness of environmental problems such as resource depletion, habitat destruction, and pollution; there is also growing—albeit reluctant—agreement that finding solutions to these problems means moving away from the mass consumerism and materialism that characterize western society and reducing our reliance on the resource-hungry growth engine to gird our local and national economies. But although we generally agree where it is we need to go, we seem a little fuzzy on just how to "get there from here." How do we overcome the inertia in our political, social, and economic systems and get down to the business of changing our consumption and lifestyle patterns?

Researchers in the field of psychology, particularly those involved in the study of attitudes and behavior, may be able to help planners find ways to "get there from here." Planners have historically borrowed and adapted theories, models and technologies from other disciplines—geographic analysis, transportation engineering, natural resources, political science, and economics, just to name a few. Planning has also borrowed from the discipline of psychology—most notably work related to the effects that physical surroundings have on humans. Examples include research on the image of the city and environmental cognition (Lynch 1960; Evans 1980), visual resource management (Zube, Pitt, and Anderson 1974), urban visual quality (Lozano 1974; Nasar 1987, 1990), the effects of urban renewal (Fried and Gleicher 1961), stress (Milgram 1970), crime

Alice Jones, "The Psychology of Sustainability: What Planners Can Learn from Attitude Research," from *Journal of Planning Education & Research*, Vol. 16, pp. 56–65. Copyright © 1996 by Sage Publications. Permission to reprint granted by the publisher.

prevention through environmental design (Newman 1972), neighborhood quality (Appleyard 1981, Rohe 1985) and considerations of culture in planning (Rapoport 1969). In addition to examining how physical surroundings affect people, psychologists also have examined the way that human behavior affects the environment. A search of the *PSYCHLit* database on the keyword term *conservation-ecological-behavior* locates nearly three hundred journal articles published between 1974 and 1986—a considerable number of which deal with aspects of energy conservation, spurred on by public attention (and abundant research funding) during the "energy crisis" of the 1970s. In addition to energy use, psychologists have explored aspects of environmentally benevolent behaviors such as recycling, water use, and littering (see Geller, Winett, and Everett 1982 for a comprehensive review of much of this literature).

Planners are professionally adept at thinking in terms of aggregations or collectives of people—neighborhoods, cities, counties, and states, for example. But this professional adeptness may actually work against us when we move into the realm of sustainability because many of the policies that we think of as being sustainable—more compact development patterns, reducing energy use and automobile dependency, limiting resource consumption and waste generation through reuse and recycling—are policies that will require *individuals* to adopt new behaviors. In the words of David Orr (1994, 62), "[sustainability] will occur when enough people choose to consume less or when scarcity is imposed by circumstances and enforced by government fiat." Only a cynical few would wish upon our children and grandchildren Orr's bleak option of scarcity and government fiat; and most would agree intellectually that "there is nothing incompatible with conservation, efficiency, environment, economic prosperity, and 'the good life'" (Geller, Winett, and Everett 1982, 5). Still, at a very basic level, there is something about the whole prospect of changing our patterns of consumption and behavior that sounds uncomfortably close to compromising our quality of life.

One psychological model that appears to have direct relevance to planning is Martin Fishbein and Icek Ajzen's (1975) theory of reasoned action, later updated by Ajzen (1985) and renamed the theory of planned behavior. Fishbein and Ajzen offer a model for how our beliefs and attitudes lead to or affect our exhibited behaviors. The aspects of the Fishbein and Ajzen model and Ajzen's modification of the model that are particularly applicable to planning will be described, and the model's specific application to certain planning activities will be discussed. Some opportunities for a broader joint research agenda between planning and psychology will then be explored.

THE THEORY OF REASONED ACTION/PLANNED BEHAVIOR

A good deal of psychologists' attention has been devoted to documenting people's expressed attitudes and how these attitudes correspond or conflict with their observed behaviors. Although some planners are familiar with certain attitude-behavior psychology research, on the whole this body of work has not crossed over into the planning literature. Cultivating an understanding of what psychologists know about how our emotions, values, beliefs, and behaviors are all tied together may help planners gain insight into the very personal nature of some of our grand visions for a sustainable future. This insight could make the sustainability discussion more productive and may help us design policy programs that will give people the appropriate motivations for adopting the behavioral changes that will make our visions reality.

Developing ways to measure attitudes was a major emphasis of social psychology research in the 1920s and 1930s (see e.g., Eagly and Chaiken 1992, Chapter 2). Underlying this research into attitude measurement was an assumption that attitudes directly shape behaviors: if someone's attitude about something could be determined, that person's behavior related to that something could be predicted. But empirical evidence challenged this assumption. LaPiere's (1934, in Petty and Cacioppo 1981, 22–23) classic study of racial prejudice demonstrated, for example, that knowing an innkeeper's negative attitudes towards a certain ethnic group did not improve the researcher's ability to predict how that innkeeper would behave in a face-to-face interaction with a member of that group.

In the realm of environmental studies, the connection between attitudes and behaviors has been similarly confusing. Why, for example, do people report overwhelming support for reducing automobile reliance and conserving energy by expanding public transportation, but far fewer people actually use it? Or why will people report concern about global water pollution, but many of those same people threaten their own local lakes and riverways through their backyard use of herbicides and fertilizers?

The most commonly held conception of the attitude-behavior relationship goes something like this: we form attitudes based on the knowledge obtained from exposure to information, and then adopt behaviors that are consistent with the attitudes we hold. Using this conception, the way to change behavior is to provide information that will lead to knowledge acquisition and then to attitude change: I am exposed to a persuasive message that smoking is bad for me; I form a negative attitude towards smoking; I quit smoking. The huge number of smokers who know a great deal about the health effects of smoking (high knowledge), and even express that they wish to or have tried to quit (negative attitude), but continue to smoke (behavior in conflict with both knowledge and attitude), demonstrates the fallacy of this model. Still, many public education campaigns designed to encourage environmentally benevolent behaviors are constructed using this information-knowledge-attitude-behavior conception, including campaigns encouraging water conservation (Mosher, Spangenberg, and Potts 1993) and participation in recycling programs (Gottman 1993).

In the mid-1970s, Martin Fishbein and Icek Ajzen (1975) proposed the theory of reasoned action to explain how attitudes and beliefs affect behavior. Briefly, the theory says that behavior is best predicted by behavioral intention, or the intention to perform the behavior. Behavioral intention is influenced primarily by two things: our attitude towards a behavior (*"I would like to plant a tree"*); and how we perceive that the people whose opinions we value will view the behavior, or our subjective norms (*"my mother would like it if I planted a tree"* or *"my friends would approve if I planted a tree"*). Figure 1 illustrates the general conceptualization of the theory of reasoned action. Note that the model includes feedbacks between the attitude toward the behavior and subjective norms. This recognizes that our personal attitudes are interlinked with those of our important social referents.

One criticism of the reasoned action model is that it does not control separately for individual characteristics such as age, gender, education, and social status because it assumes that these characteristics influence either attitude formation or the nature of the subjective norms (Davis 1985). But some have argued that this explanation does not adequately capture the influence that our social status has on behavior—particularly as it relates to access to resources or opportunities (Davis 1985; Liska 1984). Perhaps in response to these criticisms, in the early 1980s Ajzen added a third element to the model: our perceived behavioral control, or to what extent we think we are capable of performing certain behaviors (Ajzen 1985, 1991; Madden *et al.* 1992). In the tree-planting example earlier, relevant behavioral control perceptions might be: *"I can't afford what*

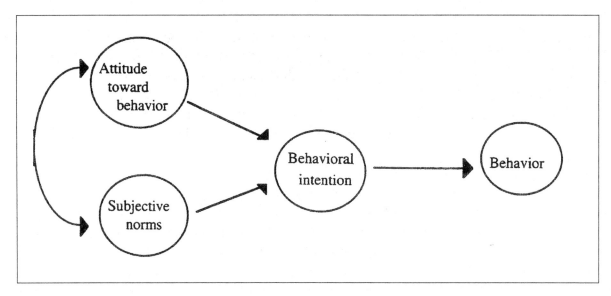

Figure 1: Theory of reasoned action.

nurseries charge for trees" or *"I don't have access to any place to plant a tree"* or, simply, *"I don't know how to plant a tree."* Ajzen named his revised model the theory of planned behavior (see Figure 2).

The factors that contribute to behavioral intention—personal attitudes, subjective norms, and perceived behavioral control—each suggest changes in the way we approach planning, particularly planning in the context of the widespread behavioral changes that will be necessary if we are to bring about a sustainable future.

Attitudes About Behaviors: The Conceptual Scale of Attitude Objects

The first component in the theory of reasoned action/planned behavior is the notion of our attitudes towards the behavior. For Fishbein and Ajzen (1975), a major issue is appropriately measuring attitudes in the first place. They argue that one reason we find conflicts between expressed attitudes and exhibited behaviors is that people are not very good at changing scales, or moving conceptually from general attitudes to specific behaviors (or from general behaviors to specific attitudes, for that matter). To predict a behavior, they said that we need to measure the appropriate attitude about that behavior. For example *"trees are good for the planet"* is a general belief, and *"I like trees"* or *"I like planting things"* are general attitudes that might—or might not—be related to a person's likelihood to actually plant a tree. Clearly not everyone who agrees with the statement *"trees are good for the planet"* is going to plant one; and *"I like planting things"* is an attitude that could be expressed by many people with no interest in planting trees—a farmer or a weekend rose gardener, for instance.

Fishbein and Ajzen identify four discrete elements of every behavior: action, target, context, and time. They argue that, if we want to predict behavior from attitudes towards attitude objects—or things about which we hold attitudes—then we must consider these four elements in specifying the attitude object. If we want to know whether people are likely to adopt a water-conserving behavior, we should not ask the question: *"Are you concerned about the world's water resources?"* or *"Do you believe that people should conserve water?"* Instead, we should ask them about the specific behavior that we are interested in: *"Would you install a low-flow shower head?"* or *"Will you replace your lawn area with low-water-using landscaping?"* It's not that people intentionally overstate their concern for world water resources, they simply do not make the necessary conceptual linkage between that general concern and their own household behavior. Fishbein and Ajzen's conception of the specificity of attitude objects dictates further that we fix these attitudes in time: *"Will you water your lawn only with a hand-held hose for the next three weeks?"*; *"Would you put a displacement device in your toilet tank today?"*

This problem of inappropriate attitude object definition, or our own ineptness at changing conceptual scales, seems particularly important to the understanding of public concerns for environmental issues because much of the information we are given about environmental problems is about phenomena that occur on fairly large geographical and temporal scales that are beyond our personal experience. Global warming is not something that we can perceive on our skin; few of us have seen a rainforest anywhere but on PBS or the *Discovery Channel*, and environmental damage often accumulates gradually over years, decades, or even centuries.

Consider the differences between Figure 3 and Figure 4. As planners, we generally conceptualize the world as a nested hierarchy like that depicted in Figure 3 in which our own planning unit (nation, state, region, city) is an element in a larger system, but is also comprised of smaller and smaller geographic units like neighborhoods, which are, in turn, collections of single households (and one colleague suggests that the figures should contain an additional unit—a single person—since households are themselves aggregations of individuals.)

But what the work of psychologists like Fishbein and Ajzen suggests is that the people for whom and with whom we plan actually conceptualize these units as depicted in Figure 4: each scale unit is thought of as a distinct entity that is separate from the other units. The *national landfill shortage* is a conceptually separate notion from *the city's solid waste*, which is, in turn, conceptually distinct from *my kitchen garbage can*. As the reordering of the units in Figure 4 suggests, the most relevant or important units are those that are closest to the individual's personal experience: his or her own household and his or her own personal referent community—a relatively tiny sphere of friends, family, neighbors, and co-workers. It is important to note that although these personal referent communities are represented in the figures with a drawing of a neighborhood—a geographically oriented "community of place" (Glynn 1986; Heller 1989)—it is more likely that the "community of interest" of most urban and suburban dwellers will be defined non-geographically through networks of family members, professional peers, and social relationships.

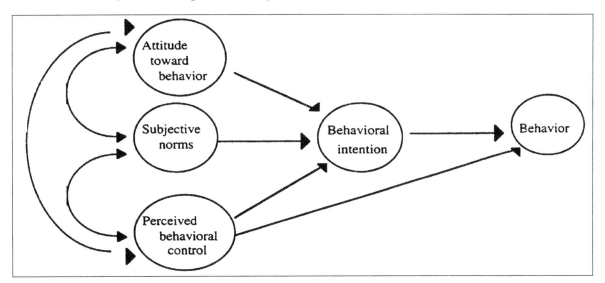

Figure 2: Theory of planned behavior.

In short, while we may be able to think about and even hold attitudes about very large units of both space and time, these attitudes may mean very little when it comes to adopting actual *behaviors*. Our behaviors come from some place much closer to home, both physically and emotionally. It may be literally impossible for us to follow the popular slogan "Think Globally, Act Locally" because what we *think* on a global scale has little to do with how we *act* on a local or personally relevant scale. Wendell Berry (1989) poetically articulated this dilemma in a commencement address to the College of the Atlantic:

> The word *planetary* ... refers to an abstract anxiety or an abstract passion that is desperate and useless exactly to the extent that it is abstract. How, after all, can anybody—any particular body—do anything to heal a planet?
>
> ... Our understandable wish to preserve the planet must somehow be reduced to the scale our competence—that is to the wish to preserve all of its humble households and neighborhoods, (pp. 16–18, emphasis original)

To deal with people's innate difficulties in making the perceptual leap from broad environmental issues to specific household or personal behaviors, perhaps the first lesson that planners can learn from Fishbein and Ajzen, is how to ask the right questions in the information gathering process. Asking people for their broad opinions or beliefs does not elicit much information about their behaviors. For example, a Canadian transportation planner recently lamented on the *alt.planning.urban* Internet newsgroup that, although surveys indicated that citizens in his city overwhelmingly supported new expansions to the public transportation system, the expansion had not attracted as many new riders as the surveys suggested.

Consider the following questions that might be asked by a transportation planner who wants to project potential ridership on a proposed light rail line by surveying people about their attitudes towards such an expansion:

Do you support public transportation?

First of all, the attitude object, "public transportation" is not the same as the target behavioral object, "a light rail line." The element of action (support) is somewhat vague, and there is no element of either time or context. Someone could answer "yes" to this question because of a positive experience in Washington, D.C. or London that would be completely unrelated to an attitude about a similar system in his or her own city.

If there were a light rail stop in your neighborhood today, would you ride the train to your place of work tomorrow morning?

This question includes all four of the important elements of attitudes towards behavior that Fishbein and Ajzen identify: a specific action (ride), target (the train), context (to your place of work), and time (tomorrow morning).

It is likely that responses to the second question could elicit more useful information for projecting potential light rail ridership than would responses to the first question. But, as one anonymous reviewer cautions, specificity may also be a serious limitation of the reasoned action/planned behavior model. People may fail to endorse a highly specific item precisely because it is specific, and planners may erroneously conclude that people are not inclined towards an environmentally responsible action simply because the attitude measurement was based on an overly specific activity. A respondent could answer "no" to the second question above because he must run errands on his lunch hour and shuttle the kids to karate class after work the next day, even if he would use a light rail system given the opportunity to adjust his schedule to it. Appropriate use of specificity in measuring attitudes requires sampling behaviors with sufficient variation in constraints.

Subjective Norms: The Influence of Others

The second major component of the reasoned action/planned behavior model deals with our perceptions of how others want us to act, or our subjective norms. It is not how the others *want* us to behave that is as important as our *perception* of how they want us to behave.

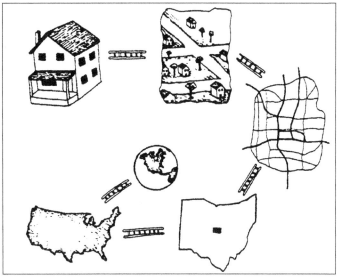

Figure 3: Planners' conception of the hierarchy of geographical scales.

To illustrate this influence of subjective norms, consider a homeowner with strong environmental values fantasizing about letting her grass grow tall enough to produce seed or replacing all of the nonindigenous species of trees and shrubs with a mix of plant materials native to the region's ecosystem. Despite these landscaping fantasies, she trims her grass because she does not want the neighbors to think she's a poor housekeeper, and her dreams of an all-indigenous yard are tempered by her awareness that, come sales time, a landscape that deviates significantly from the standard lawn-and-shrub treatment might severely limit the number of prospective buyers. According to the reasoned action/planned behavior model, this person's favorable attitudes toward the environment and towards naturalizing her yard are being influenced by perceptions about her neighbors' potential disapproval or the disapproval of potential home buyers. (Her behavior may be tempered further by local appearance regulations or health codes which are, in essence, codifications of expected norms of yard appearance.)

The work of some community psychologists illustrates that individuals are not the only sources of our subjective norms; our identity as members of groups and communities also influences our behavior. In their studies of sense of community, McMillan and Chavis (1986) identified several distinct roles group membership plays in our psychological well-being: group membership gives us a sense of emotional safety, we experience cohesiveness when we conform to a group's expected behavioral norms; we seek validation of our own values and beliefs through association with others who share those values and beliefs; and we define ourselves very often by the history of the collective culture of which we feel we are a part (for a more general discussion of the sense of community literature, see Cochrun 1994).

We are motivated to adopt behaviors that either identify us as members of groups or that enhance our status within those groups to which we belong or wish to belong. We also feel that we have the greatest influence to change the behaviors of others within the groups to which we hold the strongest ties (Cochrun 1994). For example, I feel that I am much more likely to be successful at convincing my brother or mother to purchase a few compact fluorescent light bulbs than I would be at persuading the university to replace the bank of 200-watt incandescent spotlights that burn in the hallway outside my office.

An implication of the importance of these subjective norms is that if we want to change individual behavior, one way to do so might be to make that behavior an attribute of group membership—particularly groups to which people are already emotionally tied. It appears, for example, that participation in curbside recycling increases when people see their neighbors' recycling containers set out on collection day (Gottman 1993). Planners may be able to use group membership as a way to encourage acceptance or compliance with certain policies. In addition to using existing communities or groups as mechanisms for communicating information about behaviors, we may also look to existing groups when we seek public input into the decision-making processes that help shape our visions and plans.

To truly take advantage of subjective norms, planners must first understand how our perceptions of important individuals affects our expressed behaviors and how we view ourselves as members of the referent communities and groups that are most important to us. This may mean re-thinking what is traditionally meant by "communities" or "groups" in planning. When planners solicit public involvement, they often rely on contacting organizations that portray themselves as voices of the relevant interests of the community or communities: the downtown business association is called to represent the "business community," a minority affairs agency may represent the "African-American community," the Sierra Club might stand in for the "environmental community," and a homeowners association might be contacted to represent the "neighborhood community."

But two questions arise with using these organizations as surrogates for communities of interest: the first concerns the relationship of the organization and the broader community it purports to represent—whether for internal political reasons of the organization or because of the great diversity of interests within the community. How, for example, can an organization like Stonewall Union adequately represent the "gay community" when the gay/lesbian/bisexual population includes people from all races, religions, professions, socioeconomic and education levels, and backgrounds? Planners may readily recognize that the Nation of Islam does not express views held by the entire African-American population any more than Greenpeace or the Sierra Club represent the views of all environmentalists; and planners may sometimes try to strike a balanced view of certain interests by involving more than one organization representing that interest.

Beyond this question of representation, however, is the question of member commitment. Do people value their membership in the groups with which planners interact enough to be motivated to adopt new behaviors in order to maintain their status within those groups? To the individual, choosing to attend a public meeting or become a member of a citizen task force is much like adopting a new community or group—and that new group must compete with all of the other

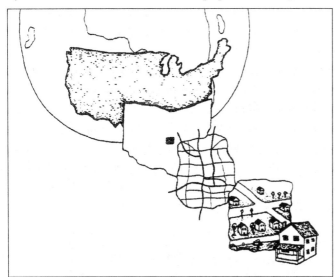

Figure 4: Individuals' conception of the distinctness of geographical scales.

referent groups and communities already of interest to that person. If the weekly meeting of the Citizen Task Force for Recreation and Park Planning conflicts with Little League night, participation in the task force simply would not be an option for many parents. But what if the park planners were to strike up a conversation with these same reluctant parents in the bleachers at the baseball game? Might planners seek public participation in comprehensive planning by going to garden club meetings, school soccer games, church socials, or perhaps by hanging out in bowling alleys on league night?

Fishbein and Ajzen's conception of the influence of subjective norms suggests that approaching people within social contexts that are personally meaningful to them could radically change the face of citizen participation in the planning process. We might gain different insights about people's wants, concerns, and needs if we were to look beyond the traditional "communities" or interest groups that typically get invited to the public table and search for the groups and communities where people already feel most committed and comfortable—the communities that have the greatest influence on their behaviors and in which they feel they have the greatest influence on the behaviors of others. And instead of asking these people to participate in public processes by inviting them into unfamiliar environments such as public hearings or open meetings, we might dispatch planners to meet them on their home turf—at their meetings and on their agendas, where we do not compromise their established loci of control.

Cultivating these groups and communities as participants in the policy formation process might have great payoffs at the implementation phase of planning. Once we have asked groups to help us formulate policy, could we then ask these same groups to help disseminate information about policies or encourage them to monitor members' compliance? If an individual received a behavioral message from a group to which he or she was already emotionally tied, the message would likely be stronger and more motivating than any billboard or public service announcement we could possibly devise.

The "What Can I Do" Factor: Perceptions of Behavioral Control

The final factor influencing behavioral intention in Ajzen's planned behavior model is the perception of behavioral control. Perceptions of minimal behavioral control could discourage people from adopting environmentally benevolent or sustainable behaviors. An apartment dweller may feel she is unable to recycle because her complex does not have on-site containers and her tiny studio apartment is too small for her to store recyclables herself. A couple may wish to add wall insulation and storm windows to their home to save energy, but do not believe they can qualify for the necessary home improvement loan; or they may want to replace their shower fixtures and toilets with water-conserving models, but simply don't have the plumbing know-how to do so.

As illustrated in Figure 2, perceived behavioral control can affect behavior directly, or it can affect behavior indirectly by influencing behavioral intentions. An example might be a tenant living in a older duplex who knows that his heating bills would be lower if the unit were better insulated. His past success in getting the owner to pay for minor repairs on the unit by offering his own labor in exchange for decreased rent may lead him to perceive that he has a pretty good chance of getting the owner to let him insulate the attic and walls. He develops a strong behavioral intention to do the work based largely, then, on his positive perception of his ability to do so. But if he calls the owner and is unable to convince him to pay for the insulation, the tenant's perception of his lack of behavioral control would directly affect his nonadoption of the behavior despite his initially strong favorable behavioral intention toward doing the work.

The interlinkages between perceived control and the two other determinants of behavioral intentions are of particular note. For example, an interested person may turn down an invitation to serve on a planning department's citizens task force studying a light rail proposal because she does not feel she has the time to commit to the meetings. This perceived lack of behavioral control may affect her behavioral intention directly (*"I'd like to participate, but I simply don't have the time"*), or it may operate by influencing her attitude towards the behavior by giving her a negative attitude towards joining the committee (*"Crimony! I don't have the time to spend in yet another useless committee meeting!"*).

Recognition of this linkage between attitudes and perceptions of behavioral control seems particularly important to environmental planning because of the broader conceptual scale at which many of our environmental attitudes are formed. People may hold positive attitudes about saving the planet, but they simply feel they have no control over the forces that create industrial pollution, rainforest destruction, or the third-world population explosion. In the face of large-scale desertification and drought-driven famine on the African continent, letting one's lawn turn brown to save a few hundred gallons of water seems like a pitifully trivial act.

To help people overcome their own perceived ineffectiveness at solving environmental problems, planners might actively try to design policy elements that help bridge the conceptual gap between broad scales such as nations and regions and those scales at which people actually feel they have some control—what Wendell Berry calls "the scale of our competence." Psychologists Geller, Winett, and Everett (1982) suggest that individual behavioral strategies will be much more successful if they are set in the supportive context of federal and state policy programs. Company sponsored car and vanpool programs have been encouraged in some areas, for example, by the creation of high-occupancy vehicle (HOV) highway lanes—that is, a system-level support for an individually initiated behavior.

These policy bridges might be represented by the ladder depicted in Figure 4 earlier. Can we develop national biodiversity plans with specific correlations or linkages to state programs, for example? We might envision a completely nested hierarchy of incremental geographical units linked by policy bridges: for a global goal such as water or energy conservation there would be specific national objectives, which would be supported by specific multi-state regional objectives, supported in turn by state objectives, supported in turn by county objectives that are connected in turn to city or town objectives, which are then connected to neighborhood or community objectives, and finally, to individual behavioral objectives. And, of course, this concept could be applied to nonpolitical geographic units a well, such as bioregions, watersheds, and landscapes (see Hersperger 1994 for an extensive review of the application of landscape ecology in planning). In building such a hierarchy, however, we must remember that, even if we as planners visualize the elements in the hierarchy as interlinked, people will likely still conceptualize these elements as distinct entities.

CONCLUSIONS: A NEW JUNCTION FOR PLANNING AND PSYCHOLOGY

Paul C. Stern and E. Scott Geller are among the psychologists who have emphasized through their laboratory and applied research the need to introduce psychological concepts and theories into the large-scale planning activities of environmental preservation and energy conservation (see, for example, Geller 1989, 1992; Geller, Winett, and Everett 1982; Needleman and Geller 1992; Stern 1978, 1992a, 1992b; Stern and Gardner 1981; Stern and Oskamp 1987).

Stern criticizes policymakers for "using concepts from information economics that lump variables such as knowledge, beliefs, comprehension of information, and trust under a single rubric of *information*, which is analyzed as an economic activity that has costs" (1992a, 1231 emphasis original). He also berates policymakers for clinging to the mythical model of information-attitude-behavior which assumes that additional information leads to attitude change and ultimately to behavioral change.

Fishbein and Ajzen's (1975) reasoned action model of behavior broadens this simplistic attitude-behavior relationship by emphasizing that, in addition to the individual's attitude towards the behavior, subjective norms also play a critical role in the behavior adoption process. Ajzen's (1985) revised version, the planned behavior model, adds perceived behavioral control as a third important element in the behavioral equation. While the reasoned action/planned behavior model is far from the only psychological model of behavior with relevance to planning, the discussion here serves to demonstrate that there are valuable tools that planners can borrow from behavioral psychology to help us achieve our environmental planning and sustainability goals (for detailed reviews of psychological contributions to environmental resource management, see Geller, Winett, and Everett 1982; Stern and Oskamp 1987).

The relationship between planning and behavioral psychology does not necessarily need to be a one-way relationship: just as there are things that planners and policymakers can learn from behavioral psychologists, there are things that these psychologists may be able to learn from planners. Stern (1992b) warns his colleagues that "it is up to psychologists to demonstrate that they can make practical contributions … [and] develop an understanding and familiarity with the languages, thought processes and institutions that dominate … policy settings" (p. 1231). As members of a discipline that is already conversant in the peculiar jargons of a broad range of government, private, and academic institutions, and with researchers and practitioners in both technical and social science realms, planners seem to be particularly well equipped for introducing psychologists to the "languages and thought processes and institutions" relevant to environmental planning and policy.

There also appears to be much fertile ground for interdisciplinary research between planning and behavioral psychology. For example, if planners are to approach people through their important referent groups, perhaps a useful area for joint research would be identifying characteristics of groups—the purpose of the group, members' motivations to comply with group norms, the organization's longevity or stability, or how the group's communication networks function, for example—that might make some groups or institutions better planning contacts than others.

Schools and churches seem like natural target institutions for building planning relationships since these institutions are often at least generally geographically oriented and might therefore serve as useful surrogates for neighborhoods. But given that many of our social referent networks are not geographical in nature, are there other communities or groups that would be equally useful? The earlier mention of garden clubs and bowling leagues may seem somewhat facetious, but are there characteristics of groups like sports teams or hobby clubs that could offer unique perspectives into the planning process? Psychologists could be well-equipped to help identify the important characteristics of groups that would make good candidates for building ongoing relationships with planners.

As planners explore the notion of sustainability as a potential guiding paradigm (see Beatley 1995b), one particularly relevant research question for collaboration between planning and behavioral psychology is: *How does adoption of one type of environmental behavior affect the likelihood that an individual will adopt another behavior?* Does participation in a curbside recycling program increase the likelihood of adopting other behaviors such as taking used motor oil to the Jiffy Lube for recycling rather than flushing it down the storm sewer?

A recent review of community recycling programs confirms that this relationship between environmentally benevolent behaviors is a common assumption among recycling program managers (Gottman 1993). Several papers presented at a national symposium of water resources educators indicate that this is also a prevalent assumption of many designers of state and municipal water conservation programs (see Lyman 1993; Koenings and Mountjoy-Venning 1993; and Jordan 1993). Fishbein and Ajzen's notion of conceptually separate attitude objects challenges this assumption, however: the behavior of rinsing vegetables in a pan instead of a stream of running water may be a reflection of beliefs or attitudes related to food preparation (*pan-rinsing vegetables helps retain vitamins*), while installing a water-conserving toilet may be related to attitudes or beliefs about home improvement (*replacing the toilet will not increase the resale value of my home as much as new wall tile will*). If this assumption is not necessarily true for seemingly related behaviors (in this case, water conservation), what about much more conceptually separate behaviors? Does participation in curbside recycling (a waste-reduction behavior) increase the probability of installing an automatic set-back thermostat (an energy-saving behavior)? The work of Weigel and his colleagues (Weigel *et al.* 1974; Weigel and Newman 1975; Weigel 1977) suggests that the adoption of certain environmentally benevolent behaviors does increase the likelihood of adoption of others at least to some extent, but the process of multiple behavior adoption is still not yet clear. Related research questions that planners and psychologists could pursue together might include, *What specific environmental attitudes are most salient in the behavior-adoption process?* and *How do people access or use general environmental attitudes in making specific day-to-day behavior decisions?*

Stern and his colleagues (Stern 1992a, 1992b; Kempton, Darley, and Stern 1992; Stern and Oskamp 1987; Stern and Gardner 1981) also suggest several avenues for joint research, including investigating attitude change among corporate executives and government policymakers who have influence over a much more significant portion of total energy use and resource consumption than do the individuals and households that have been the historic focus of conservation behavior research; understanding the decision-making process of organizations; undertaking longitudinal studies of the role of information, feedback, and persuasive communication in behavior change over years or periods of years; distinguishing the differing factors that motivate substantial one-time changes like investing in insulation from repetitive but relatively insignificant behaviors such as turning off lights in a room; and examining how citizens' groups can exert pressure on government officials to induce change through varying forms of political activism. Certainly, there should be room for planners to join behavioral psychologists in pursuit of answers to these questions.

Behavioral psychology can offer planners tremendous insight into how attitudes, values, beliefs, perceptions, and behaviors are intertwined and may perhaps even help us find ways to incorporate this knowledge into the planning and implementation of our sustainable visions for the future. Planners may be able to help reduce global, national, and regional environmental problems to the "scale of our competence" by first acknowledging the inescapable perceptual and psychological processes that separate our abilities to think and reason on broad geographical, conceptual, and temporal scales from our abilities to actually draw upon these broad conceptualizations and incorporate them into our day-to-day behaviors. The challenge to planners is to turn these fundamentally human psychological traits into assets rather than liabilities in the planning process.

Author's note: An earlier version of this paper was presented at the 1994 ACSP conference in Tempe, Arizona. I would like to thank psychologist Richard E. Petty, Jack L. Nasar, the two anonymous referees, and ACSP conference discussant Richard Bolan for their invaluable comments. I would also like to thank Sue Olcott for creating the illustrations used in Figures 3 and 4.

ALICE JONES

Alice Jones is a Ph.D. candidate in environmental planning at The Ohio State University. Her research and teaching interests involve citizen participation in community sustainability and environmental planning.

REFERENCES

Ajzen, I. 1985. From intentions to actions: A theory of planned behavior. In *Action-Control From Cognition to Behavior,* J. Kuhl & J. Beckman, eds. Heidelberg: Springer.

Ajzen, I. 1992. The theory of planned behavior. *Organizational Behavior and Human Decision Processes* 50(2): 179–211.

Appleyard, D. 1981. *Livable Streets.* Berkeley: University of California Press.

Archer, D., T. F. Pettigrew, and E. Aronson. 1992. Making research apply: High stakes public policy in a regulatory environment. *American Psychologist* 47 (10): 1233–36.

Beatley, T. 1995a. The many meanings of sustainability: Introduction to a special issue of *JPL*. *Journal of Planning Literature* 9 (4): 339–42.

Beatley, T. 1995b. Planning and sustainability: The elements of a new (improved?) paradigm. *Journal of Planning Literatures* 9 (4): 383–95.

Berry, W. 1989. The futility of global thinking. *Harper's Magazine.* September: 16–22. (Adapted from a June 1989 commencement address to the College of the Atlantic Bar Harbor, Maine.)

Cochrun, S. E. 1994. Understanding and enhancing neighborhood sense of community: A note. *Journal of Planning Literature* 9 (1): 92–99.

Davis, R. A. 1985. Social structure, belief, attitude, intention and behavior a partial test of Liska's revisions. *Social Psychology Quarterly* 48 (1): 89–93.

Eagly, A. H., and S. Chaiken. 1992. *The Psychology of Attitudes.* Fort Worth: Harcourt Brace Jovanovich College Publishers.

England, J. 1994. Public Information Officer, City of Columbus Division of water. Personal interview with the author, November 8.

Evans, G. 1980. Environmental cognition. *Psychological Bulletin* 88 (2): 259–87.

Fishbein, M., and I. Ajzen. 1975. *Belief, Attitude, Intention and Behavior. An Introduction to Theory and Research.* Reading, Ma: Addison-Wesley.

Geller, E. S. 1989. Applied behavior analysis and social marketing: An integration for environmental preservation. *Journal of Social Issues* 45 (1): 17–36.

Geller, E. S. 1992. It takes more than information to save energy: A comment. *American Psychologist* 47 (6): 814–19.

Geller, E. S., R. W. Winett, and P. B. Everett. 1982. *Preserving the Environment: New Strategies for Behavior Change.* New York: Pergamon.

Glynn, T. J. 1986. Neighborhood and sense of community. *Journal of Community Psychology* 18 (3):277–88.

Gottman, K. 1993. Planning for community recycling programs: A note. *Journal of Planning Literature* 7 (3): 291–97.

Hersperger, A.K. 1994. Landscape ecology and its potential application to planning. *Journal of Planning Literature* 9 (1): 14–29.

Heller, K. 1989. The return to community. *American Journal of Community Psychology* 17 (1):1–15.

Jordan, J. 1993. Creating public awareness: Establishing a statewide water conservation and education organization. In *Water Resources Education: A Lifetime of Learning.* See Mosher, Spangenberg and Potts 1993.

Kempton, W., J. M. Darley, and P. C. Stern. 1992. Psychological research for the new energy problems: Strategies and opportunities. *American Psychologist* 47 (10): 1213–23.

Koenings, J. and J. Mountjoy-Venning. 1993. Comprehensive water resources education techniques in Thruston County, Washington. In *Water Resources Education: A Lifetime of Learning.* See Mosher, Spangenberg and Potts 1993.

Liska, A. E. 1984. A critical examination of the causal structure of the Fishbein/Azjen attitude-behavior model. *Social Psychology Quarterly* 47:61–74.

Lozano, E. 1974. Visual needs in the environment. *Town Planning Review* 43 (4): 351–74.

Lyman, H. 1993. Water resources education: Ten ways to create public awareness of water issues. In *Water Resources Education: A Lifetime of Learning.* See Mosher, Spangenberg and Potts 1993.

Lynch, K. 1960. *The Image of the City.* Cambridge, Ma: MIT Press.

Madden, T. J., P. S. Ellen, and I. Ajzen. 1992. A comparison of the theory of planned behavior and the theory of reasoned action. *Personality and Social Psychology Bulletin* 18(1): 3–9.

McMillan, D. W., and D. M. Chavis. 1986. Sense of community: A definition and theory. *Journal of Community Psychology* 14 (1): 6–23.

Milgram, S. 1970. The experience of living in cities. *Science* 167:1461–8.

Mosher, C. D., N. E. Spangenberg, and D. F. Potts, eds. 1993. Water Resources Education: A Lifetime of Learning/ Changing Roles in Water Resources Management and Policy. Proceedings of the symposia of the American Water Resources Association, June 27–30, Bellevue, Washington. See especially papers by Hilary Lynan (pp. 249–254), Jeanne Koenings and Jane Mountjoy-Venning (pp. 183) and Jeffrey L. Jordon (pp. 293–298).

Nasar, J. L. 1987. Effects of signscape complexity and coherence on the perceived visual quality of retail scenes. *Journal of the American Planning Association* 53(4): 499–509.

Nasar, J. L. 1990. The evaluative image of the city. *Journal of the American Planning Association* 56 (1): 41–53.

Newman, O. 1973. *Defensible Space.* London: Architectural Press.

Petty, R. E., and J. T. Cacioppo. 1981. *Attitudes and Persuasion: Classic and Contemporary Approaches.* Dubuque, Ia.: William C. Brown Company. 3rd Printing 1983.

Rapoport, A. (1969). *House Form and Culture.* Englewood Cliffs, NJ: Prentice Hall.

Rohe, W. M. 1985. *Planning with Neighborhoods.* Chapel Hill: University of North Carolina Press.

Stern, P. C. 1992a. Psychological dimensions of global environmental change. *Annual Review of Psychology* 43: 269–302.

Stern, P. C. 1992b. What psychology knows about energy conservation. *American Psychologist* 47 (10): 1224–32.

Stern, P. C., and E. Aronson, eds. 1984. *Energy Use: The Human Dimension.* San Francisco: Freeman. As cited in Stern and Oskamp 1987, pp. 1070.

Stern, P. C., and G. T. Gardner. 1981. Psychological research and energy policy. *American Psychologist* 36 (4): 329–42.

Stern, P. C., and S. Oskamp. 1987. Managing scarce environmental resources. In *Handbook of Environmental Psychology.* vol. 2. Eds. Daniel Stokols and Irwin Alrman. New York: Wiley & Sons.

Stutzman, T. M., and S. B. Green. 1982. Factors affecting energy consumption: Two field tests of the Fishbein-Azjen model. *Journal of Social Psychology* 117 (Second Half): 183–201.

Weigel, R. H. 1977. Ideological and demographic correlates of proecology behavior. *Journal of Social Psychology* 103 (First half): 39–47.

Weigel, R. H. and L. S. Newman. 1975. Increasing attitude-behavior correspondence by broadening the scope of the behavioral message. *Journal of Personality and Social Psychology* 33 (6): 793–802.

Weigel, R. H., D. T. A. Vernon, and L. N. Tognacci. 1974. Specificity of the attitude as a determinant of attitude-behavior congruence. *Journal of Personality and Social Psychology* 30 (6): 724–28.

Zube, E. H., D. G. Pitt, and T. W. Anderson. 1974. *Perception and measurements of scenic resources in the southern Connecticut River Valley.* Amherst: Institute for Man and Environment, University of Massachusetts.

29 The Hidden Program of the High School (or Six Metaphors in Search of a Box)

Herb Childress

This book takes the teenager's point of view — often neglected in planning — about the experience of high school and other public places in a small town in northern California.

Very often, folk knowledge tells us things that a more rigorous study leaves behind. Regular people talking have fewer constraints upon them than experts, and tend less to cut the world into distinct subject areas. In this way, they can often speak a deeper truth. To this end, here are two brief stories.

One. A friend who owned a furniture store told me once that he'd looked at renting a storefront in the mall. He'd decided against it. "They tell you what hours you have to be open. The bell rings, and you open the store. Another bell rings, and you close the store. No, thanks. I've been to high school once already."

Two. Curtisville High English teacher George Springs returned to school from his day of jury duty, from which he'd been excused. He told his class about his discomfort and indecision, about both wanting to do his service to his community and also not wanting to be away from his classes so near the end of the semester. But he was clearly fascinated by the experience of being a potential juror. "It was a terrible way to spend a day—cooped up in a little chair, waiting around for something to happen, being told where to go and when you could leave and when you could go to the bathroom." He smiled broadly. "We were treated just like students."

It is worth trying to figure out why most of us can smile in recognition of these stories, and why, once we recognize their truth, we go ahead and replicate that meager and uncomfortable experience of high school anyway. The fact is that our physical construction of high schools reflects important but unspoken beliefs, and that both the beliefs and the construction make the ensuing experience almost inevitable.

If I were to ask you to name the physical components of a high school—not your high school, not any particular high school, but just "a high school"—what would they be? Surely there would be classrooms, and hallways. Lockers. A principal's office. A teachers' lounge. A gym. Bathrooms. Wood shop, auto shop, home-ec room. Labs for chemistry and biology, for computers nowadays. A library. Possibly an auditorium, probably a band room and a cafeteria. Storage for tables and

Herb Childress, "The Hidden Program of the High School," from *Landscapes of Betrayal, Landscapes of Joy: Curtisville in the Lives of Its Teenagers*, pp. 213–236. Copyright © 2000 by State University of New York Press. Permission to reprint granted by the publisher.

chairs. The janitor's room, maybe as part of the boiler room. A place for buses and station wagons to unload their kids, some parking for the older kids, some parking for the teachers. A football field surrounded by a track and bleachers, a baseball field, a soccer field, tennis courts.

This is all so innocent. This is the inventory of the American High School, from Riverdale High in the Archie comics to Muskegon Catholic Central, where I graduated almost twenty-five years ago. It is, however, an inventory that tells us quite a bit about what we think a high school ought to be. That we take it utterly for granted tells us quite a bit about how powerful those beliefs are.

This list, once we know how many kids are going to be at a particular school, can then have numbers applied to it: How many classrooms? How many lockers? How many toilets? How many parking stalls? Multiply those answers by their individual sizes, gotten from *Architectural Graphic Standards* or state guidelines, and you have what architects commonly call "the program" of the building, the annotated list of what ought to be included in the designed product. Sometimes the program also includes some vague introductory text about "sense of community" or "promoting interaction," but that's far less important than budget limits. The list of spaces and its associated geometric and financial arithmetic is what the design is based upon, what the school district expects and the architects provide. It can be done in its most basic form in half a day—we just did most of it already in the last three paragraphs.

When I first arrived at Curtisville High School in July of 1994, I met the principal, Jeff Dawson, for our first appointment. Mr. Dawson is a friendly sort, a former athlete and former football coach and former girls' basketball coach who moved up from history teacher to assistant principal to principal.

He asked some about my work; I'd sent him six copies of my research proposal, but they were in an untouched stack in a cabinet next to his desk, and he told me he hadn't had time to look at one. He was, justifiably, more interested in *his* major project for the year, which was to get the school shepherded through its six-year accreditation review coming up in the spring. He was honest about what he saw as the school's successes and its shortcomings—the accreditation visit wasn't likely to tell him much that he didn't already know.

After about ten minutes of small talk, he gave me a tour of the campus, completely quiet except for a handful of student workers who were painting the spruce-green trim all around. Jeff had been spending some of his summer on moving teachers into different classrooms so that all of the faculty in individual departments would be closer together—there was now an "English wing" and a "Math wing" and a "languages wing." The science and vocational wings had long been established, since the lab-based rooms were about the only ones on campus that were unique to their purposes. I saw the new computer lab full of high-performance machines, and the two-year-old "multi-purpose room" which was partly auditorium and partly big unallocated space depending on whether the telescoping bleachers were pulled out.

He spent the greatest amount of our tour on the Main Gym and South Gym, then beyond to the new infield on the Softball diamond, the just-installed bleachers on the baseball field. We finished the trip at the entry to the football field, where we stood and surveyed the newly donated scoreboard (courtesy of Rite way Trucking, who had painted their logo on it). "I used to love coming here on the night of a game," Jeff said, leaning on the rail of the track. "I really looked forward to it, it was the highlight of the week. We had some great tennis when I was coaching. I always tell people that it wasn't great coaching, we just had the horses. This year … I'll be honest with you, we'll be doing good if we win a game all season."

But the wistful former coach faded quickly and the administrator returned. "Now that I'm not coaching, I'd just as soon never come here again. I have a headache all day on the day of a home game. Last year, we had a really ugly crowd at the Port City game, some of their kids wanted to mix it up. I've started hiring security for the games now, because a few teachers just aren't enough any more. If it happens again, we're going to move the games to Saturday afternoons."

We walked back to his office and shook hands. "If you need anything at all, don't hesitate to come and see me. My door is always open." As he walked through the door of the administration building, it closed behind him.

I spent the next two days measuring hallways and classrooms, walking off the distance between the soccer field and the baseball diamond in order to draw a campus plan and a larger site plan. I didn't know it then, but between my tour and the drawing, I had seen not only the physical school but also the ideas behind it.

Curtisville High is a collection of eleven single-story buildings connected by covered walkways as shown in Figure 7. Each classroom building is between five thousand and eight thousand square feet, with the main gym and multi-purpose building much larger. In the late 1950s, when Curtisville High was planned, the California Department of education contributed a certain amount of build-

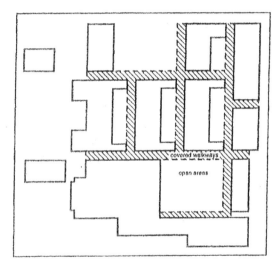

Fig.7. Curtisville High School plan

ing construction money for each student. A great number of school districts decided to maximize their classroom space and not spend any of this money on enclosed hallways, so passage from room to room was designed with less expensive courts and arcades. There is an entire generation of outdoor schools in California, an interesting idea in San Diego but not so great in Timber County where kids mill around before class in the thirty-five degree December rain.

The buildings at Curtisville are rectangular, mostly with one or two sides exposed to the weather and the others facing one of these covered arcades. The weather walls are made of concrete block; the arcade facing walls are made of plaster composition panels with batten boards at the joints, with windows that open into the classrooms at ceiling height. All of the exterior walls are painted a calm, pale green, with doors, cornice boards, and lockers in a darker woodsy green.

Within those buildings are thirty-two non-athletic classrooms, four athletic rooms, administrative offices, a library, the office for Native American education programs, a kitchen, a theater, four student bathrooms, and three teacher bathrooms. This collection of school buildings sits on about seven acres, surrounded by two acres of parking and about thirty acres of athletic fields on a quarter-mile-square plot at the outskirts of town.

In light of nationwide stories of school buildings which are literally crumbling while still occupied, Curtisville appears to be a tremendously well-maintained campus. There are few luxuries but room enough for all, weatherproof and adequately heated. The program has been fulfilled. The list of spaces has become three-dimensional and material, and everyone and everything has its place.

The program of a building succinctly expresses our beliefs about its job and about the people who inhabit it. Architects Murray Silverstein and Max Jacobson help us to read those beliefs in the building. First, they say, we have our basic definition of the building type, the image not only of the building but of the enclosed behavior that comes to mind when we say "office tower" or "shopping mall" or "high school." As their example, Silverstein and Jacobson offered an architectural definition of a supermarket: a single building of at least 70,000 square feet that offers not only food but "all needed household goods" to a population of several thousand.

Each building type has a specific arrangement of spaces that make the building type recognizable, the sort of inventory we created a few pages ago. To continue their supermarket example, Silverstein and Jacobson identified four characteristics that are always part of our understanding of a supermarket: a site which is more than half parking, located near a major traffic artery; a building which offers all merchandise in self-service displays, but which holds back-stock off the

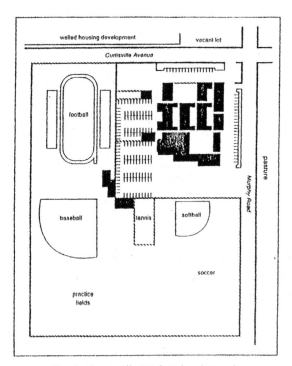

Fig. 8. Curtisville High School site plan

sales floor; a layout with the most basic food items at the perimeter and impulse items closest to the central paying area; and an environment which is controlled in every way—sound, lighting, temperature, and organization of products. These are the characteristics that give a supermarket its "supermarketness." Without any one of these internal patterns, the supermarket would cease to be a supermarket and would become something else.

These shared characteristics have larger causes, cultural patterns that mold both our spaces and our expectations. For the supermarket, Silverstein and Jacobson have identified three underlying cultural roots: the factory farm and the industrial model of food production; government policies that support agri-business over small producers; and an economic system based on large corporate ownership of supermarket chains (and their associated house-brand packagers). I think they've left some out—brand-naming that offers broad but meaningless choices, the sale of shelf space to wholesalers, the increasing gulf between farmed food and processed food—but their point remains valid: a different system of food production and distribution would result in an entirely different building type to fulfill the same functions.

Larger social patterns like these are inherently brought into the creation of any new building. The basic cultural ideas of a building type make the same basic program inevitable; beliefs and context are, as Silverstein and Jacobson put it, the hidden program. The places that result then act as metaphors for ideas that we normally don't express in words but say plainly through our actions and our creations.

The first metaphor that guides school construction and administration is the *separation of kids and adults,* removing teenagers from the community and placing them into the hands of appointed experts. The school building and grounds are both the evidence of adult desire for separation from children and teenagers and the means of separating them.

Except for the oldest schools in the most urban areas, high schools are generally constructed on huge parcels and set far away from the community they serve. Curtisville High was built on a forty-acre lot shown in Figure 8, located over a mile away from downtown. When it was opened in the early 1960s, it was extraordinarily isolated, set onto ranchland at the far north end of town. The town has grown out toward the school in the thirty-five years since its construction, but a couple of dozen placid Black Angus still graze on the lot across the street.

The school sits out at the corner of Murphy Road and Curtisville Avenue, as far away on its site as it can get from the few houses that are nearby. The school has no kitchen or lunchroom, but the "open campus" rule has been repeatedly challenged by both parents and nearby property owners who view loose kids as a breach of their security. Early in the year, the lunchtime exodus from school included fifty or so kids who walked across the soccer field to a broken piece of fence at the end of Rasnor Road. Leaving via this gap in the perimeter allowed these kids to get to the convenience store about five minutes faster, no small consideration in a forty-minute lunch period. But within the first two weeks of school, this announcement appeared in the morning bulletin: "ALL STUDENTS—WHEN LEAVING CAMPUS, please respect the rights of citizens and their property. Dispose of trash properly and stay off private property. The fence by Rasnor Road is NOT an exit—please use Murphy Road when leaving campus." That announcement (and the posting of the assistant principal next to the hole in the fence that noon) reduced the flow of kids from fifty to about five.

The request to the school had come from the manager of the apartment complex through which the students flowed on their shortcut to the Arco mini-mart. My own examination didn't turn up much trash or worn grooves in the lawns, and the kids didn't break anything or threaten anyone when I made the trek with them about twenty times over the course of the year. The perceived threat was greater than the actual events.

This supervised distance between teens and community ensures that teenagers only rarely come into contact with adults engaged in their work. Kids get to see teachers at work, and janitors; they get to watch the lady who makes their sandwiches at the Deli; they see the guy who fries potato wedges in the convenience store and the woman who runs the cash register. But they're held apart from the real economic doings of their town and the human aspects of that working life. If one of the jobs of school is to enculturate teenagers, we act counter to that if we separate them from the most basic elements of that culture: the ways in which we make our livings. (Of course, they might only learn how bored many adults are with their work, which would itself be an important—and tragic—lesson.)

Even on campus, though, kids are held separate from the adults around them. Teachers have separate bathrooms, a separate lounge and work room, a separate parking lot. Within the classrooms, there are two zones set aside for the teacher: the front wall of the classroom, an area often marked off by a desk or a lectern and an overhead projector, and behind which students are clearly out of place; and the desk in the rear corner of the room where the teacher does his or her grading and sits while supervising tests, watching the backs of heads for undue variation from stillness. Physical proximity between teacher and students is very rare at Curtisville—and it was, over the year, to become a reliable sign of a good classroom.

The administration of the school is also sharply divided from the students, both in function and in building. Students play very little role in the planning of their school or their education, planning which takes place on the site but in buildings that are never entered by students except for punishment. At Curtisville High School, like most others, being called into the principal's office isn't usually an invitation to help the school develop a more responsive curriculum.

To return to the classroom, we find much evidence of the second guiding metaphor of schools: *teaching is active, and learning is passive.* The students sit in their regularly-claimed seats (which may or may not be assigned but which must be consistent in order that the teacher might take attendance more quickly), seats which are permanently constructed as part of the desks so that kids cannot even choose a favorite distance from their writing surface. Occasionally, the desks are turned to make small groups, but the individual desk (and associated private learning) is the norm, and the kids know it; after all, that's how the payback is determined at test time.

The teacher stands, head higher than those of the students; the students sit, looking upward. The teacher moves; the students do not. The teacher is the performer, using blackboard, overhead projector, desk and podium as tools and props; the students are the audience, who (ideally) view and take notes on the performance. The audience may be set in rows and columns facing the blackboard or in three angled sets of rows and columns making a sort of level amphitheater, or in two facing sets of rows and columns like the parted Red Sea with the teacher working the resulting central aisle. Regardless, there is one person who transmits, and thirty-five who receive.

The teacher begins class and ends it. The teacher opens discussion and closes it. Educational literature is full of terms like "time on task" and "disruption" and "interruption" and "inappropriate responses," all of which are definitional ways of establishing the norm of audience silence and passive compliance. The teacher knows "where the class should be" at the end of the period, and is responsible for taking them there. This is highly unlike most adult-adult interchanges, in which even if one person is responsible for the outcome of many, the others all at least know the destination.

We have constructed a model of learning that is inherently boring and alienating exactly because it encourages this passivity, because it removes the linkage between curiosity and active, self-guided exploration. In order to see this more clearly, imagine a white-collar worker with a set of tasks to accomplish, a set of people to supervise, and a set of supervisors of her own to satisfy. More or less, she's left on her own to do her work. But once a week, there's a staff meeting in which the division manager talks for an hour. Staff participation in these meetings, while nominally requested, is neither encouraged nor necessary; the agenda comes first. Meetings like this—tedious, agonizing, eternal—are the low point in the week.

High school is nothing but staff meetings.

This passive-audience metaphor is made more literal whenever the TV and the VCR come out, which is surprisingly often. Curtisville High has spent tens of thousands of dollars in television and videotape equipment and video curricular materials over the past few years; eleven of the thirty full-time classrooms have a television and VCR as permanent equipment, with several more units available from the library on portable carts. In a minority of classrooms, television is an integral part of the course, as for example in Dan Jacobs' English classes that examine first the novel and then the film version of, for instance, *Pygmalion*. In many classrooms, though, television is a "preferred activity," a Friday treat for having been more or less orderly through the rest of the week, as when Mr. Peterson gave his Individual in Society class two periods to watch Olivia Newton-John and John Travolta in "Grease."

Video can convey information straight from some curriculum development company or the California Department of Education, which combine to put out an extraordinary number of videotapes every year. Television can be a pacifier that allows a teacher to grade papers, or helps a substitute teacher to keep from being taken for a ride by students who recognize and exploit indecision. Regardless of its use, though, the widespread classroom employment of television is a recognition and acceptance of the conception of passivity in learning, an exploitation of our shared convention that students are an audience.

This expectation of passivity extends to all school-related activities. The adult conception of "going to a football game" is to sit in one position and move only for functional purposes like bathroom and concession stand trips. When I sat in the stands and counted, I was passed by five and six times as many kids as adults in a crowd that was nearly evenly split in age. Those kids were far more likely to be in pairs and threes than the adults, who were often on solo trips to the John or the hot dog stand. The teenage conception of attending a football game is fluid: the stands and the grounds are places to meet people, have roving conversations, and only now and again to turn their attention to the remote but nominal "event." The real event is to be with friends, and that entails movement. This is a source of constant frustration to Mr. Dawson and the rest of the administration, who wish that the kids would just sit down and watch the game like their parents and the Booster Club members. Teachers and rented security guards alike are instructed before the game to keep kids in their seats and out of the aisles, a futile task diligently pursued.

Mr. Dawson passed me in the halls one afternoon at two o'clock and said, "There's nothing better than walking the halls and there's no students in it—everybody's in place." Students know that they must ask their teacher for a hall pass in order to use the bathroom during class periods; they know that they must ask the attendance office for an off-campus pass in order to see a doctor or dentist. The management of students is paramount to the success of the school in the terms that it has established, and management is always easier when those to be managed see themselves as inevitably passive.

School leaders, like those of many of our institutions, consider one of their greatest successes to be the fact that the school treats everyone the same regardless of their differences. One of the most central metaphors of education, the third in our list, is *the celebration of abstraction and the avoidance of the unique.* Students are allocated to classrooms mathematically, as are their teachers. The classrooms themselves are seen as interchangeable, one box the same as the next—in the architectural world, this is known as the "egg-crate school." And the day is divided into six egg-crate periods of equal length, with morning nominally the same as afternoon.

The human facts of these decisions are rarely discussed, although they're central to any learning that goes on. I saw students and teachers who quite simply never got along all year, to the enormous frustration of both; I saw students and teachers alike struggle to stay awake every day immediately after lunch, or consistently lose their concentration during fourth period. But counselors are charged not to let students change classes for these messy human reasons. Principal Dawson assured his teachers before the school year began that "we aren't doing drops to let kids avoid teachers or get a certain period free or get sixth-period gym."

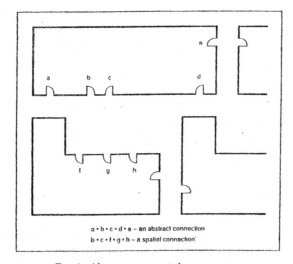

Fig. 9. Abstract vs. spatial connections

Curtisville's teachers are officially differentiated by their position on what's called the "down-and-over" chart. The District's pay scale for teachers is based both on years of employment—a scale which maxes out at twelve years, even though ten or more teachers have been at Curtisville for over twenty years—and on the number of college credits completed beyond the bachelor's degree, to a limit of sixty. Thus a teacher is monetarily rewarded by moving either down (more years) or over (through continuing education) on the chart. In the abstract terms used by the school, Dan Jacobs and Lily Chase are the same teacher, and a student assigned to either one of them for English 3 would get an equivalent experience. This is, in the experiential world, clear nonsense; it is also a belief that guides school planning.

The belief that rooms are all the same allows the administration to shunt teachers all around the school. New teachers find that they have classes in two or even three different rooms over the course of the day, and veterans can come back in the fall to a room far removed from that of the previous year. While this is recognized as unfortunate, the misfortune is expressed in terms of inefficiency and inconvenience to the teacher, and not in terms of the inability to create a stable home from which to work and to welcome.

During my initial tour of the campus, Jeff was clearly pleased that he'd been able to bring his teacher and room assignments together by departments, so that all of his English teachers were in one building, all of his language teachers in another, all of his social science teachers in a third, and so on. The facts, though, are that the teachers in these departments almost always have different prep periods and thus aren't able to collaborate during their off-times; that students can hardly "major" in a subject and thus spend most of their time in a certain region of the school, as they might on a college campus; and that the space that would have mattered for collaboration in the English department was certainly not common possession of the 500 Building (which put Mr. Springs' classroom over two hundred feet from Mr. Bauer's, and arranged them in a linear and thus not-social pattern) but common possession of the courtyard between the 500 and 600 Buildings, which could have brought all five teachers within a sixty-foot radius and in an inward-facing and thus more interactive pattern. The administrative achievement was entirely abstract and had no effect on real behavior.

The abstract, however, is easily measurable, while the actual is often impossible to enumerate clearly. Achievement is defined as a test score, for example, allowing sharp divisions to be defined (between a "B" and a "C," for instance) where none in fact exist. I picked up a scrap of paper on the hallway one afternoon; it turned out to be a computer printout of a grade report for a student in Bio 1. To that point, there had been three tests and two labs included in the grade. Her test scores were 100, 100, and 93. Her lab scores were 0 and 0. Her combined grade was printed at the bottom: 293/400 = C. Whatever this set of numbers might mean, it distinctly does not mean that she was an "average" student. It might mean that doing the labs was irrelevant to understanding the material—after all, she got three superior scores on her tests without doing the labs. Conversely, it might mean that the tests were far too simple, and that I could have walked in from the Quad and done just us well. It might mean that she had a terrible environment at home in which to do homework, and often couldn't get it done. It might mean that she was lazy, doing only what was supervised and enforced, blowing off all her other work. It might mean a lot of things, but it goes into the book as an unambiguous "293/400 = C."

The fact of Curtisville's cold, windy, and wet outdoor corridors appears nowhere on the balance sheet of maximizing educational square footage; the fact that Mara at age sixteen was accepted into Stanford's advanced program for a combined senior year of high school and freshman year of college was not taken into account by Curtisville's administration, who insisted that she take four credits of Phys Ed in her very expensive year at college in order to meet California's high school graduation requirements. Our insistence on treating everyone equally and "fairly" ensures that we treat almost no one sensibly.

The linkage of so many schools to mandated curriculum frameworks has led to a massive industry that creates and sells teaching aids in careful compliance with the California Department of Education guidelines. Teacher mailboxes overflow with catalogues from curriculum development companies offering videos, workbooks, software and CD-ROMs, and "curriculum modules" on everything from the Civil War to tobacco abuse. For the less materially-minded, there are courses, seminars, and conferences on classroom management, multi-modal learning, and integrated curriculum strategies.

Teachers are caught in the middle of this struggle, attempting to deal both with administrative abstractions and with the realities of classroom and personality and interaction. Some teachers align themselves closely to the state curriculum, using it to outline their classes over the year; they are the ones found in front of the photocopy machine, running off pages sixty-four and sixty-five of a packaged, state-approved "study unit." (The California Department of Education encourages this, of course; their standardized achievement tests are the stick that they use to punish non-compliant teachers and schools, and the phrase "teaching to the test" is heard across the land.) Others use the frameworks as a broad outline, filling in the details with personally chosen—often personally created—classroom work. Still others treat guidelines and uniformity as the enemy: Dan Jacobs, a twenty-five-year veteran, told me early in the year that "you've got to break the rules if you're going to get anything accomplished in the classroom."

Tom Fischer, an eighteen-year teacher of Auto Shop, dreaded the day that the state issued a mandated curriculum for automotive technology. "We've been lucky so far to avoid that—the other subjects got theirs a long time ago. I hate all this stuff about tests and reports and frameworks. The way I teach Auto Shop is that it's a performance-based course. Can they disassemble, rebuild, and repair an engine by the end of the school year? Can they think diagnostically and analytically? Can they go through a process and figure out what might be possible causes for a particular problem? That's what I want my students to leave with at the end of the year, a respect and an ability for analytical thinking. But the state is going to want them to pass a test on pistons and compression, and a test on lubrication, and all that junk." I asked Tom to tell me his favorite thing about teaching. He paused, then smiled. "Seeing in a students' eyes that they've already figured out something I'm explaining just before I've finished saying it."

Four months after that explanation, Tom Fischer, along with thousands of other auto shop teachers, got his three-inch-thick binder containing the Automotive Technology curriculum from the California Department of Education.

Given the model of schooling we have pursued—a standardized mass curriculum delivered to a passive audience and evaluated through measurable test outcomes reported mainly in the aggregate—it makes some sense to pursue our fourth metaphor, *economies of scale*. We strive to eliminate redundancies, to provide equivalent or greater services to greater numbers for the same expense.

When the Northern Timber Unified High School District was created in the 1950s, it was following a nationwide trend of school consolidation; in the two Wisconsin townships I'd studied earlier, the 1950s brought a state-mandated reduction from twenty-two school districts to three. The idea was to bring students into a smaller number of modern, well-equipped schools—they'd have used the term "state of the art" if it had been trendy then—in order to accomplish both an improvement in educational quality and an economic savings at the same time.

Derek Drummond, Director of the School of Architecture at McGill University in Montreal, has written recently on people he calls "institutional entrepreneurs," school administrators and hospital boards and church councils who have been driven by the same sort of "aggressive, 'bottom-line' thinking" as Wal-Mart and Microsoft. "In the belief that great efficiencies can be realized by eliminating local or community-based and supported hospitals and providing the equivalent of 'one-stop shopping' for health care in a mega- or super-hospital," he writes, "the authorities are once again disregarding the critical impact of such an initiative on the urban environment. ... hurt[ing] many citizens whose associations with these institutions are as profound as life and death."[5]

If we replace his concern over hospital mergers with a concern for high schools (a concern which Drummond has abandoned, believing probably correctly that there are few truly local high schools remaining in North America), his message is pertinent in Curtisville as well. Curtisville

High School is the home to kids who, forty years ago, would have been in different schools all around the northern third of Timber County. Curtisville draws kids from Flat Lake (five miles east); Sandy Cove (eleven miles north); Cramer Bench (twenty-seven miles north); Roosevelt (forty miles north); and all of the ranches and forest houses in between. About a quarter of Curtisville's students are from widespread communities and homes spreading over several hundred square miles.

Clearly, if the fifty or so kids who lived in Flat Lake went to an imaginary Flat Lake High School, they wouldn't have the level of material support that we take for granted in a modern high school. They wouldn't have the weight room with its full complement of Universal machines, free weights, stationary bicycles, stereo, and mirrored wall. They wouldn't have as many televisions per student, nor as many tools and specimens in the Biology, Physics, Chemistry, and Geology labs. They wouldn't have rooms full of fast new computers, and might not be linked to the Internet. They wouldn't have as much administrative support: secretaries, outreach specialists, special-needs counselors, home-study coordinators, and a continuation school.

Those are, of course, abstract ways to measure the effectiveness of high schools, measurements that obscure and preclude some others. One thing these economies of scale hide is the loss of local culture and environment. This is most clear in the communities that don't have their own high schools. Curtisville's kids and teachers alike used quick catch phrases to note the observable and acknowledged differences between kids from different communities—the Roosevelt Cowboys, for example; the Moonstone Hippies. Had the Cowboys been educated in a Roosevelt school, they might have had more contact with their at-hand environment, might have learned new ways to understand the matrix of ranching, timbering, and tourism that formed the facts of life in Roosevelt.

We might say that integration is all to the good, that we are able to bring kids out of the fairly narrow world views that characterize their small towns, that we open their vision to a new and more tolerant way of living. This is a wonderful theory, but one which is not at all put into practice because the school's official policy is that these local culture differences don't exist. Diversity is a buzzword in educational theory right now, but the diversity that's talked about at Curtisville High is packaged in the language of the mostly urban places that make up so much of the state's population. Textbooks and videos all have their obligatory white and Black and Hispanic and Asian faces, but they're all white and Black and Hispanic and Asian yuppie children. There aren't any curriculum materials that show teenagers with cowboy hats and lifted pickups and Skoal circles worn into their hip pockets; there aren't any materials that show teenagers in tie-dye and dreadlocks, carrying surfboards and playing Hacky Sack; there aren't any materials showing teenagers who shave their heads and wear white makeup and velvet cloaks and paint their fingernails black. Curtisville High School brings together as diverse a set of kids as exist anywhere in any school—though the diversity is not on the ethnic grounds that distant urban analysts believe are the important ones—and then refuses to address those contrasts as an object of study. They offer up canned "We Are the World" platitudes, delivered in shrink-wrap from Sacramento, and dismiss the differences between the Punk and the Prep, between the Cowboy and the Stoner. They might as well have left the kids at home.

But the loss of the local high school in small towns is only the most visible effect of consolidation and standardization. The larger and less often considered loss is that there is no room for the local anywhere in the state curriculum. Curtisville's campus, made for an imaginary California with no driving winter rainstorms and no cold fog, is the architectural counterpart of its curriculum, made for an imaginary student who has no environment around her, a student who is merely being prepared for entry into the national labor pool. Curtisville has a government which makes no appearance in Government class; it has an economy which isn't discussed in Economics class.[6] Curtisville has a history with no place in the History books, and a literature with no means of entry into the English curriculum. There is an amazing range of biology and geology in northern Timber County, most of which goes unmentioned in the science labs. There is a tennis team, though few kids play and no one plays well or seriously, but there are no surfing or rodeo teams because the regional school insurance pools consider those sports too dangerous. The local languages of social importance are Native American, not Spanish and French. There are Agriculture classes memorizing 1961 cotton-yield data from their thirty-five-year-old textbooks, from which most students go home and tend to their cattle and horses and sheep.

The community holds the school at a distance, both physically and socially, but the school holds the town away as well. The community-school interchange is minimal because that's the way we've designed it. The local environment is a superb resource for teaching, especially in light of the immediacy and experiential focus of teenagers, but it is entirely wasted. Curtisville didn't just appear by the hand of God; it was built by developers and speculators in response to some of the great pressures of twentieth century economics and culture. To have these teaching tools—these roads and highways, neighborhoods and small towns, the bluffs, the creeks, and the ocean—literally right outside the window and then to ignore them in favor of a curriculum designed hundreds of miles away is one incredibly telling decision.

Kristy, a girl in the junior class, was working on a college application and had her most recent report card on the desk. She seemed puzzled, and came over to ask Mara a question. "It says my GPA is 3.57, and that my class rank is 27 out of 173. But the application wants to know if I'm in the top tenth of my class, or the top fifth, or the top third. Where do I find that?"

Our fifth metaphor of *objective evaluation* has become one of the central driving beliefs of the school, and our most common form of evaluation is competition. Our schools are centered around competition, from the notion of "grading on the curve" to the constant array of state and national tests—ASVAB, PSAT, SAT, ACT, CLAS, Golden State. The results, learned weeks and months after the fact, are expressed in incomprehensible sets of incompatible abstractions. 460 verbal, 520 math, on the recentered scales. 73rd percentile. Combined score 17 out of 36. Second quartile. So many precise values linked to the inherently imprecise business of knowing.

And of course, there is the more overt competition of inter-scholastic sports. Curtisville High School fields girls' teams in volleyball, soccer, tennis, basketball, track, and softball, and boys' teams in football, soccer, tennis, wrestling, basketball, baseball, golf, cross country, and track. Three quarters of the school's site is given over to athletic fields; within the fraction that's left over, the two gymnasia take up an area equivalent to all of the classrooms in four buildings.

Curtisville fields its share of lousy teams, teams which have seasons of 0–9 or 2–14, but they have some winners as well: moving to sectional and regional competition in baseball, taking the girls' state basketball championship in the mid-'80s. Those, of course, are the teams that are remembered, with photos and trophies filling two cases along the entry to the gym. The collection tells us that school sports exist not so much to be loved and to fill our lives with intensity as to prove our worth against others.

Sport is the model that we use in other realms of education as well. An acquaintance of mine coaches junior-high kids in competitive math, calling them "mathletes" and bragging that three of them went to the state finals. Competitions abound in the arts, in music, in clubs and hobbies, as a way to make firm evaluations even in the absence of numerical criteria. It seems to be impossible to know whether or not you're good at anything unless you beat someone else doing it. Even the school's Christmas rituals of decorating classroom doors and gathering canned food for the poor are arranged as competitions.

Unfortunately, the mindset of the sports world (which is the mindset of the larger business world we expect our children to enter) bleeds into all other fields as well. Irene, who played clarinet in the school band, said, "Mr. Phelps puts all of his energy on winning superior ratings at Sectionals. It doesn't matter whether we really grow or learn anything about music, and it's not about bringing a piece of music to life that doesn't exist unless we play it. It's all about doing everything to get that unanimous superior rating. He's a really good teacher if you're a really good player, but he's not a good teacher if you're just okay."

This single-minded focus on testing brought about bizarre distortions of priorities: an English teacher who spent eight months out of the school year making sure her class could pass the State's year-end exam; a football coach who tried to recruit a star soccer player to do place-kicking on the football team instead; a band director who decided that students should play a new instrument. Amy, a senior, had played the flute since fourth grade. In her junior year, Mr. Phelps told her that the band needed a bigger sound, and switched her to the alto sax because she was a good musician and could make the change. In a convincing demonstration of the Peter Principle, Amy struggled with the new instrument for both semesters and quit the band altogether at the end of the year. She owned the flute metaphorically in knowing its feel and nuances of sound and fingering, in understanding her abilities and limitations; she owned the flute literally as well. She had no possession over the saxophone, again both metaphorically (its unfamiliarity of fingering and mouthpiece, its weight and center of gravity, the sound and shape of the notes) and literally (she was given a "disgusting school saxophone, old and beat-up, it even had mold inside it"). She now plays neither instrument, and only occasionally plays the piano.

Amy has been lost to the world of group music because of an abstract decision made in favor of a predetermined musical repertoire, a predetermined "right sound," a predetermined conception of what high school music should be about and a belief that quality can only he reliably told through ribbons won at regional competitions. The school was full of forbidden personal stereos, smuggled under sweaters and jackets at the potential cost of confiscation. They played Clint Black and Nine Inch Nails and En Vogue and Too Short, AC/DC and Nirvana and Bob Marley—music which is easy for us to dismiss but which has at least as much technical and cultural merit as "I've Got a Gal in Kalamazoo." Music was central to the experience of so many kids who could never express it through high school band, just as the desire for physical expression found outlets in non-competitive (and unauthorized) forms like surfing, skateboarding, Hacky Sack, and the mosh pit. When we look for a balance of instruments that will win us awards, the people behind those instruments have disappeared.

Perhaps most importantly, these sorts of objective evaluations are self-defeating because they serve to *limit* what we attempt to do rather than to expand it. Any time we try to offer a definitive description of what we want, we leave out essential things in our rush to be objective. Jobs with careful and precise job descriptions are deadly boring, and tend to be precarious exactly because they're so inflexibly defined; education that pursues numerical criteria of some sort or another faces irrelevance, because the criteria miss most of what makes people successful.

Teachers often noted with some frustration that they couldn't get their kids to see beyond Timber County. "There's an incredible xenophobia here," said one teacher who spent considerable time traveling through the United States and Europe. "We had scholarships all set for twenty-two students last year, to good schools like Wheaton. One applied." He shook his head. "If it's out of the county, they just won't go. These kids are as good as anywhere, but they think, 'Well, I think I'll go to CC [Coastal College, a community college just south of Port City], I'll go to Timber State.'"

We have in modern America an extraordinary assumption, one that would not have been shared by many of our grandparents. We believe in our sixth metaphor, *personal mobility*. We believe that we might live almost any place in America, and that we'll probably live in several places. The curriculum shares and encourages that expectation. Educational reforms are focused on "statewide performance standards that reflect the needs of a competitive world-class economy."

Such a seemingly common sense statement is fascinating in the assumptions it hints at. It's important to note, for example, that the conference from which that goal was drawn was sponsored by the U.S. Department of Labor, and that it took the form of a focus group for the purpose of clarifying consumer desire for a product. In this case, the consumers are nationwide "business leaders" or major employers, the producers are educators and politicians, and the products are students being prepared to compete in the future world economy.

The whole notion of statewide standards is an interesting one. Why is it particularly important that we make it clear how our students rank on some statewide or national scale? Because our large employers and major universities demand it. Uniform rankings make it easier to draw recruits from a large geographic area. Our mobility makes us easier prey for huge institutions, because people are willing to move extraordinary distances and to uproot themselves in order to pursue a career. Local people are competing against everyone in the larger region, even perhaps more than that, for the same jobs. What will happen as we continue to move into our highly touted world economy? Will we in fact require international grading of students so that we know that someone from Indonesia would be better suited to a particular San Francisco job than someone from Toledo? Who benefits from this grading and sorting technique? Clearly not the students being tested and evaluated (literally, "given a value").

It's no surprise that the curriculum, just like the campus, avoids that which is local and concrete. The local is of no worth in a national or global economy.[9] Understanding local watersheds is a negligible skill in a society that expects us to move whenever and wherever we're transferred. Local government is a futile preoccupation when zoning and building rules come from the county and state, who copy one another's rules on a national scale anyway. And the local timber and fishing economy is waning—it's far more profitable to study the stock market, that abstract and global speculative machine that drives the failure of local economies. The school district's office sign was carved out of a redwood burl, and that's as local as they felt the need to be.

These six metaphors are almost completely intertwined, all part of a single and coherent master narrative; it's hard to imagine that any of them could exist separately from the others. But take them all together and put them into a single paragraph:

> The school building and its associated program are based around placing passive kids into an isolated and homogeneous environment for mass-produced training. This training will be delivered by rule-bound experts who prepare youth at the least cost for a life of mobility and participation in the global economy. Continued participation is always contingent upon periodic competition and evaluation.

We don't say things this baldly in our mission statements, but our landscapes often let the truth slip.

Most industries have taken considerable stops toward a management strategy known as "total quality management," one of the central tenets of which is that the business exists to do exactly what the customer wants, only better. The casual observer might be surprised to see the degree to which this mindset does not exist in the high school, but that surprise is based on the illusion that the students—or perhaps the parents—are the customers.

Let us be both clear and honest about this: the student is not the customer. The student is the product. The customer is the labor market, through the proxy of the California Department of Education. If California hopes to attract new businesses and hold its existing ones, and if it hopes to decrease spending on unemployment and welfare and incarceration, then it must create an attractive business climate. In our modern economic terrain in which the desperation of labor is a resource available worldwide—whether from a manufacturing plant in Ciudad Juarez or a worldwide bookkeeping company in Seoul—an attractive business climate must include a labor force which is relatively passive, unattached to the local, willing to be continually evaluated and occasionally to lose, whether through personal fault or through accident. Those are the products that Curtisville High School is set up to manufacture.

30 Environmental Logic and Minority Communities

David R. Diaz

This reading shows how two American subcultures interact with environmentalism. Environmental racism refers to the unequal burden of pollution borne by different income groups often confounded with ethnicity and race. Assign for the issue of sustainability and subculture variation in human-environment relations.

THE IMPORTANCE OF ENVIRONMENTAL POLICY FOR MINORITY AND IMMIGRANT COMMUNITIES

The era of environmental regulations and laws has had a profound influence on the direction of environmental policies governing air, water, solid and hazardous waste, and future land use patterns. Latino immigrants/minorities located historically in declining communities need to consider assuming an active, participatory role if such regulations are to address their economic and environmental concerns. Land use and environmental laws will increasingly direct the relocation of manufacturing activity (Hayes 1987: 434–435). Market-based decisions will be restructured to a great extent by the implementation of these laws. Two issues are key. Will corporations or consumers absorb the direct costs of pollution control, and how will the political process address immigrant/minority community concerns about the effect of environmental regulations? If capital interests succeed in shifting the costs to consumers, low-income groups will be confronted with yet another historical example of regressive taxation.

Immigrant/minority organizations concerned with economic restructuring cannot afford to ignore participating in environmental debates (Anthony 1990). Inner-city neighborhoods have historically suffered from regressive land use policies (Boyer 1983: 95–97; Bullard 1994; Scott 1969: 82–83, 595–99). Ideational patterns have significantly increased exposure of area residents to severe levels of air pollution (*San Bernardino Sun Times Telegraph* 1989). During the early 1990s, basic government decisions were formulated on a diverse legislative agenda in California (Assembly Office of Research 1989).

The evolution of regional political culture has gradually acknowledged that an environmentally sound economic system is an irreversible objective. While electoral consensus does not currently

---

David R. Diaz; Marta Lopez-Garza & David Diaz, eds., "Environmental Logic and Minority Communities," from *Asian and Latino Immigrants in a Restructuring Economy: The Metamorphosis of Southern California*, pp. 425–448. Copyright © 2001 by Stanford University Press. Permission to reprint granted by the publisher.

exist (Johnson 1988), opponents to this objective have been forced to moderate their resistance (Hayes 1987: 521). Minorities will play a key role in this process regardless of their current peripheral political status. The region's new political consensus must incorporate the interests of diverse interest groups. An environmental agenda must not be formulated without strong participation by minority communities throughout the region (Russell 1989). In building political consensus, it is essential that immigrants and minorities are directly represented in policy- and decision-making government agencies and that environmental and land use-oriented literature is translated into appropriate languages. If these recommendations are not implemented, fragmentation of an environmental consensus will create serious barriers impeding regional support for a new environmental/economic mandate.

Immigrants experience many of the basic political concerns, disadvantages, and discriminatory restrictions experienced by native-born minorities. Structurally, the status of Asians and Latinos is similar to that of recent immigrants within this analysis of economic restructuring and environmental policy. This analysis does not attempt to differentiate between the structural political rights or the documented status of the two groups, and, in fact, both sectors are viewed as sharing basic, common political interests. Thus, both terms, "minority" and "immigrant," are intermingled throughout this analysis, with minimal distinction. However, in addressing the political and economic interests of immigrants who reside in predominantly ethnic neighborhoods (La Gory and Pipkin 1981: 180–81), it is important to clarify the structural limits of democracy. An important consideration is that while immigrants cannot vote, actual Latino voting patterns remain problematic, thus implying that, historically, native Latinos are not persuasively more powerful than immigrants.

Regressive land use and toxic waste issues pose serious environmental risks for minority neighborhoods (Pansing, Rederer, and Yale 1989; Russell 1989). Growth management and opposition to various development projects are mainly the focus of middle-class Euro-American-dominated organizations (Lake 1982; Popper 1981). These class fractions have developed networks on a limited set of issues. The Mothers of East Los Angeles (MELA) and the Concerned Citizens of South Central Los Angeles (CCSC) are two examples of an increasingly potent environmental politics at the local level. Both MELA and CCSC utilized regional networks to win significant political victories (Blumberg and Gottlieb 1989: 168–69; Russell 1989).

While somewhat diminished in this political era, environmental laws continue to influence economic and social restructuring, both state and market initiated. Environmental organizations must reach out, and minority groups must respond, by establishing cohesive political coalitions to advocate long-term community-oriented agendas. Affordable housing, a living wage, and a cleaner environment are essential components of a mutually inclusive political strategy if the historically regressive economic structure, the center of the urban crisis, is ever to be reoriented to effectively revitalize inner-city areas.

Impacts of Environmental Pollution on Minority Communities

While most communities suffer from dangerous levels of air pollutants due to regressive land use policies, minority areas continue to experience an inordinate burden of environmental health risks (Freeman 1973; Hall 1989). Locational analysis in Los Angeles clearly indicates that a substantial proportion of affordable housing rings the central business district (CBD) (Blue Ribbon Committee for Affordable Housing 1988, sec. 5). Their lifestyle options are between health costs and family economics (Hall 1989: 5–3, 5–6). Government agencies continually overlook the fact that a high percentage of children from minority and immigrant families reside in close proximity to areas that generate inordinate levels of industrial pollutants (Pansing et al. 1989: 30). The crisis of affordable housing has forced thousands of families into overcrowded living conditions, a situation that also severely impacts the school system. A central issue for all inner-city working class families is the health risk to children during outdoor school and recreational activities scheduled during peak (morning and afternoon) traffic periods, when air pollution levels are most severe.

The social strata at greatest risk from air pollution are school-aged children and senior citizens (Kleinman, Colome, and Foliart 1989: 4–8). Midday activity is directly impacted by the high level of stage 1 (or higher) smog alerts in the Los Angeles Basin, where high temperatures increase ozone concentrations (ibid.: 5–2). State and local air quality regulations, which constantly attempt to lower allowable air pollution thresholds, have negatively impacted the number of days children should not be allowed to engage in outdoor recreational activity. Previous State Air Resources Board action was in response to medical evidence indicating that smog is more harmful at lower levels of pollution than previously recognized (Dolan 1990).

Although playing outdoors during midday is unhealthy (*San Bernardino Sun Times Telegraph* 1989), teachers cannot be expected to keep children indoors for the entire school day. Thus, children face an increased health risk to their respiratory system and as-yet-to-be-determined long-term effects on their physical development. A significant number of schools do not have air conditioning systems to filter out some of the pollutants. In addition, where school districts have adopted a year-round school schedule to cope with overcrowding (Ong 1989: 226–27), this policy exposes more children to the worst season of pollution—the summer. The air quality problem is further exacerbated by the high levels of pollutants, which poorly maintained school buses spew into the air directly in front of schools at the beginning and end of each school day. Although children are at constant health risk, virtually no structural implementation of corrective action is evident. While recent research offers projections of the long-range health impacts from severe air pollution, the regional air quality board is mired in debates concerning pending lawsuits challenging weak implementation regulations. Only scant attention is being paid to the full extent of the crisis, much less to the future health costs that children and their families will have to endure.

In addition, minority seniors on limited incomes are placed in an intractable situation with respect to near- and long-term health care. Seniors with asthmatic conditions or respiratory problems suffer unduly from severe air pollution (Kleinman *et al.* 1989). During summer or periods of severe air pollution, seniors are often unable to perform even essential outdoor tasks (i.e., walks, trips to markets, and so on). This situation increases near- and long-term health costs for a group that can least afford another socially created burden on their living standards.

Degradation of the Environment: Life in East Los Angeles

The East Los Angeles (ELA) community is particularly vulnerable to a number of serious environmental hazards (Pansing *et al.* 1989: 6–7). ELA is a predominantly Chicano/Mexicano barrio just east of the Los Angeles Civic Center. The area is characterized by older multidensity housing in declining condition and a high concentration of public housing. Residential areas exist adjacent to heavy manufacturing districts. Many small and relatively unregulated industries, utilizing highly toxic chemicals, are located in these industrial zones (ibid.: 32–33). Entire communities were dissected and fragmented by freeway construction that occurred in the 1950s and 1960s. Many businesses continue to dispose of hazardous wastes illegally. Incidents of serious toxic contamination adjacent to elementary schools have forced emergency student evacuations.

Immigrant workers, a highly represented sector in manufacturing, confront numerous health risks at sites requiring hazardous materials in manufacturing. The Los Angeles economy is noted for the significant level of small- to medium-size industrial plants (Ong 1989: 32–33). Hazardous chemicals and chemical processes are routinely performed without adequate worker protection. A significant level of automobile- and plastics-related businesses depend on low-wage immigrant workers. Without stronger enforcement of state and federal health and safety laws, this workforce is virtually defenseless. With the demise of major manufacturing plants during the past twenty-five years, the resultant weak union structure cannot organize effectively to protect workers in small and midsize plants.

What is problematic is the absence of adequate safety equipment, the absence of training in materials handling procedures, and directed mismanagement in adhering to safety measures designed to reduce the risk of exposure to hazardous chemicals. Immigrant workers have minimal leverage because of their legal status, wage competition, and subsistence lifestyle. In a political economy increasingly polarized between upper and lower classes, health-related crises of factory workers are minimized and often ignored. While mid- and small-size manufacturers cannot afford a restive labor force, they are reluctant to reinvest capital to comply with existing state and federal regulations. The price of doing business is the health risk placed directly on immigrant laborers.

Past lobbying efforts opposing the imposition of air pollution laws provide examples of how immigrants and the working class are the sacrificial lambs in the battle of environmental legislation. Chrome plating and furniture manufacturing enterprises are at the center of this conflict. Major associations representing both industries are using economic gloom-and-doom arguments to protect their interests and generate public opposition to clean air regulations. Threats of job loss are expounded to justify limiting, circumventing, or blocking air pollution enforcement. This argument of dire economic consequence is also used to further reduce the level of worker health and safety factors in favor of long-term capital accumulation. The real health issues of the immigrants and working class are simply factored out of the public debate.

Overspray from furniture manufacturing processes, which requires massive amounts of varnish and stain spraying, escapes into the workplace and the air basin. The industry stridently avoids acknowledging the depth of the problem in terms of public or worker health. In attempting to maintain the media agenda, their only argument is job loss versus environmental protection.

The same scenario is replayed by supporters of the chrome plating industry. Chrome processing utilizes an inordinate amount of highly toxic chemicals in open vats and in dangerous workplace conditions. The industry initially fought the disposal regulations of Los Angeles that prohibit the dumping of these chemicals in the storm drain system because of serious pollution draining into the Santa Monica Bay. Their argument focused solely on job preservation, the same sloganeering used to oppose the revisions in existing clean air plans. Both industries depend on an undisciplined immigrant workforce and an absence of strong regulatory enforcement. These factors are clear examples of how immigrant communities continue to be exposed to regressive environmental dangers. Land use policies that historically ignore the basic zoning protection afforded middle- and upper-class areas substantiate activists' concerns that environmental racism, not inept planning, is the root cause of this crisis (Smith 1990).

Environmental hazards are a direct result from a system of rules that are not uniformly implemented in immigrant neighborhoods (Bullard 1994; Pansing *et al.* 1989: 92). For example, the manufacturing lobby has opposed meaningful air pollution and toxic substance control legislation for decades (Diaz 1989). The issue inherent within the crisis of the built environment is the realization that minorities experience a disproportionate burden of the health consequences from environmental degradation. Stronger laws and enforcement of environmental regulations are required for the protection of immigrant and minority communities (*Race, Poverty and the Environment* 1990). Immigrant populations, having left their economically and/or politically repressive societies, are now subsumed into another scenario where their contribution to accumulation is considered more important than their health.

Economic restructuring cannot be viewed solely in monolithic terms of increasing job volume. Job safety and workplace health considerations must prevail in the face of media sound bites from manufacturing interests threatening to abandon a given region if environmental regulations are implemented. Regulatory reforms focusing on worker health and the workplace environment should reject all attempts to force low-wage workers, especially immigrants, into the narrow choice between personal health versus a weekly wage. Immigrant communities cannot be made society's sacrificial lambs. Unfortunately, for this societal sector, continual environmental degradation at home, neighborhood, school, or workplace is the direct cost of capital's method toward evading substantial external production costs related to environmental issues.

Grassroots Activism and Environmental Strategies

By the mid-1980s, awareness of environmental issues created an opportunity for immigrant and minority communities to explore different political strategies. Political mobilization, based on protest demonstrations and petitioning of local political leaders, was supplemented by state and federal environmental regulations to protect neighborhoods from unfavorable development proposals (Russell 1989). The one environmental concern, in particular, that galvanized public sentiment was the "discovery" of illegal hazardous waste sites adjacent to residential and school areas. The emergency evacuation of children from local schools forced activists to reorient their perspective on the types of issues they should address and develop networks with groups versed in environmental law. The relationship between minority communities and environmentalists became a critical link in the eventual restoration of the built and natural environment. The importance of this relationship has been generally ignored by mainstream environmental organizations in the 1970s and 1980s (Anthony 1990).

In Los Angeles, the most significant political victory for minorities since the early 1970s was the defeat of the LANCER trash incineration project proposed for south-central Los Angeles (Blumberg and Gottlieb 1989: 1782). The success of the CCSC's strategy is attributed to the effective use of environmental analysis at a critical juncture of the controversy (ibid.).

The next major minority-based conflict occurred when MELA began a protest against the proposed location of another prison on the east side. The area, already housing the largest prison population in the free world, was targeted for a major state prison. While implementing the most innovative political and media strategy in recent memory to publicize their opposition to the proposal, the cornerstone of the opposition was an attack on the environmental impact report (EIR) prepared for the project (Pansing *et al.* 1989). As a result, the state courts mandated that a new EIR must be submitted in relation to the project (*Eastside Journal* 1990). After years of conflict over this project proposed by the governor and approved by the legislature, MELA won an important environmental victory.

Although CCSC and MELA were not the first minority organizations in the region to rely heavily on the environmental review process, their success has been publicized throughout the region. Both CCSC and MELA have effectively developed a conjuncture of environmental and grassroots politics whose political movements in minority communities have been emulated in other cities.

Environmental activism remains stifled within media confines and conventional wisdom as solely the purview of middle-class NIMBYite factions (Lake 1982). In a sense, the subtle ravages of all American racism preclude accepting the logic that low-income communities must also benefit and, more important, effectively leverage environmental regulations in localized situations. At issue is the political role that minorities are assuming in redefining how regulations designed to protect the natural environment should also benefit the urban environment. This theme has generally been overlooked by policymakers at all levels of government. Only through grassroots activism has this perception gradually eroded. Minority organizations have found environmental legislation to be among their most effective options in fighting to maintain community autonomy over land use issues.

Economic Restructuring in a Changing Regulatory Era

An orientation toward environmental logic contains inherent challenges for the future of the region and, in particular, the form and substance of industrial location policies. New regulations will significantly change transit patterns, manufacturing processes, and energy consumption levels. However, minorities cannot afford to fall into the political trap used in the past by opponents to environmental reform through the jobs/housing debate. Specifically, major economic restructuring occurring within the context of a global economy should not be confused with the impacts of environmental laws (Bluestone and Harrison 1982: 200–1). The loss of manufacturing jobs, the crisis in affordable housing, and the attack on a livable wage are all economic factors that pre-date the current environmental debate. In fact, opposition forces confuse the issue of public health and right-to-know laws by controlling the media agenda on the jobs/housing debate.

The lobby that has wrecked unions and actively shifted jobs offshore (Bluestone and Harrison 1982: chaps. 2–3), and without a credible record of advocacy for affordable housing in the last twenty years (all key minority community issues), is now attempting to assume the high moral ground of fighting against environmental regulations to protect the interests of the same class that they have reduced to subsistence living over the last fifteen years. This is the paramount ideological contradiction within the environmental debate. Essentially, capital's economic interests are being debated, not the serious consumer-oriented negative health and economic consequences that result from high levels of pollutants. Fundamentally, immigrants and minorities should question why their historic adversaries are desperately attempting, in media and public forums, to portray themselves as their main allies.

Contrary to conventional economic analysis, economic restructuring and strong environmental regulations are not destined to cause dire economic impacts on workers (Gorz 1980:130–39). Many proposals designed to restructure economic activity are labor intensive, generating a high level of skilled and semiskilled jobs (Dominiski, Clark, and Relis 1990). However, the full debate between the merits of high-tech industrialization versus small-scale environmentally sensitive production activities is only now reaching appropriate political and economic policy arenas. The issue of sustainable and long-term community growth patterns (ironically those economic prescriptions currently in vogue in the Third World) may, in fact, become the formula for First World economic survival.

Three areas of a new environmental economic system provide insight toward a formula for societal revitalization: recycling, weatherization, and solar retrofitting, all low-tech, environmentally sound production processes. Furthermore, all are extremely labor intensive. A housing industry based on energy conservation is, for example, among the most labor intensive production processes in existence (Dominiski *et al.* 1990). The economic-versus-environment debate requires a new set of social priorities centered on the linkage between employment and environmental quality. Immigrant communities would become major beneficiaries of this potential environmentally based socioeconomic restructuring.

The main question challenging the internal logic of environmentally sensitive economic development centers on its long-range prospects within a complex world economy. It is painfully obvious that a mass consumer-driven system, socialist or free market, is predicated on an extremely wasteful economic/political set of priorities (Gorz 1980). The world economy reflects the regional political economy in terms of competition for consumption classes and reduced production costs (Harvey 1985: 252–56). The political role of minorities in this scenario appears at times fruitless. Participation in societal change becomes an exercise in alienation and class exclusion. The remoteness of our political system to the average voter/nonvoter (Harper 1993: 50–51) produces a self-imposed barrier against generating public acknowledgement for necessary change (Parenti 1978).

Continued resistance to change by major industries translates into ever increasing levels of pollution. Reliance on an outdated political economy maintains a system of terminal urban poverty and deteriorating housing conditions (Gottdiener 1985: 282–83). Conversely, the service industry, the emerging employment growth sector, fails to differentiate between mass consumer goods, low-wage jobs, and high-end specialty services requiring substantial infusions of capital and/or specific marketing skills. Consequently, this drain on capital maintains immigrant workers at subsistence levels (Bluestone and Harrison 1982:220–24). The health and safety of immigrant workers are further compromised in a global economy that fails to differentiate between Third and First World when the goal is reduced production costs (Morris 1989; Robinson 1989). In effect, the status of immigrant workers has not changed from the system of exploitation that reduces them to expendable wage laborers, advanced capital's imported reserve army. The hysteria of border control politics is leveraged solely to fan racist tensions. Capital's required labor reserves for low-wage nonunion, manufacturing and service jobs is totally dependent on immigrants continually crossing the border (Muller and Espenshade 1985: 161–63, 182–83). Perpetuation of conventional economic logic provides scant hope for improved living conditions for the thousands of recent immigrants and their historic ethnic peers. The question becomes, How much longer can advanced capital systematically maintain a status quo that structurally mandates regressive environmental and class-based economic policies?

The astounding levels of pollution and its horrendous negative health impacts during the past three decades have forced opponents into a gradual retrenchment in response to the global environmental crisis. However, industrialists and their allies have responded only to the most lucrative aspects of environmental economics, addressing the consequences of industrialization (e.g., contracting for pollution cleanup processes) (Hayes 1987: 251). Capital maintains its historic resistance in addressing environmental pollution at its source, that is, industrialization itself (Daly 1977: 101,123). This traditional resistance to political interference is eroding because of a garden variety of environmental crises within the regional political economy. For example, where is society going to throw its trash in the next five years? How many more drought years can urbanization in desert areas be maintained? Finally, are we, as a society, willing to risk complete depletion of the ozone due to both an overreliance on cars and toxic-based industrial production?

At stake in the twenty-first century is political control over land use decision making, in particular the relationship among industrial, commercial, and housing location patterns. Society increasingly demands political solutions, solutions that will weaken capital's domination of a corporatist state. The response by the state is an endless debate on regulatory implementation of environmental laws (Flavin and Young 1993). Southern California is often at the center of these issues since the Los Angeles Basin is perennially the national focus for air pollution control legislation because of its nefarious pollution levels (Flink 1975: 221–23).

Public protest against traffic congestion, lack of parklands, school overcrowding, growing landfill problems, and political gridlock at the local level have also forced the issue of environmental degradation of the regional political economy on a reluctant and apathetic legislature. In response to this rising tide of protest to the excesses of urbanization, the California legislature has reviewed a series of major state land use control bills.

Ironically, regional political culture has become integrally dependent on the immigrant labor market (Ong 1989: Chap. 5). This interdependence is also reflected in urban lifestyles through daily interaction and housing patterns. As the region expands exponentially, it suffers collectively from unrestrained development activity. Immigrant families face the same urban environmental crisis impacting all classes, albeit with greater economic disadvantage. While the region benefits from cultural enrichment through ethnic diversity, popular culture also clings to racist and class-based discrimination. Immigrants are confronted with a political economy that simultaneously depends on their labor power, at subsistence-level wages, while decrying the impacts of this diversity on accumulation and reproduction. Further, reactionary political responses against immigrant populations serve to diffuse attention to the structural limits of unabated growth in geographic areas that have reached their natural environmental holding capacity.

What middle- and upper-class constituencies will not admit publicly is that their own migration and consumption patterns are far more environmentally regressive than those of the immigrant underclass (Booth 1988). The regional immigration "problem" is a cross-class phenomena. Historically, numerous "middle class" immigrants have moved into California in response to management positions and the prospects of future income growth (Starr 1985). Suburban housing (and inherently long commutes) and the high-end commodified housing market are not designed for the working class. Commodification of urban lifestyles is generally beyond the reach of subsistence-wage earners. Moreover, the environmental ravages of globalization and industrialization are not created by a class that is literally barred from the benefits of capitalism. Conversely, mass transit, higher-density housing, and reduced conspicuous consumption are structural approaches toward reducing environmental impacts of industrialization (Paehlke 1989: 247–51).

To a large extent, political opposition to implementation of a strong anti-consumerist environmental agenda is a public reaction against eventual lifestyle and consumption changes that will necessarily parallel immigrant minority community urban experiences. In a real sense, the Third World is gradually directing the First World toward environmentally sound urban lifestyles within the bastion of an advanced sector of the global economy.

Solutions to the environmental crisis require the active involvement of immigrant communities, inclusive of the region's new ethnic majority. Political change at the grassroots level is the new reality within an environmental movement attempting to reconstruct the limits of regional locational patterns (*Race, Poverty and the Environment* 1990).

Corporate- Versus Consumer-Oriented Implementation Policies

Since the 1950s, "Old Guard" opponents (transportation, manufacturing, energy, real estate, and so on) to environmental regulation have constantly forecast economic doom. This tired and redundant rhetoric remains the basis for capital's opposition despite constant growth in the national economy during this period. The Old Guard's resistance to change is a political action designed to defeat any meaningful regulatory limits on growth (Diaz 1989). As the environmental crisis worsens, public pressure for reform will result in a political solution that redirects the costs of environmental cleanup and protection on the backs of average citizens. A regressive "environmental tax" strategy defines the problem as an end-user issue while the source polluters evade their social and financial responsibility on this matter (Frantz 1990). The Southern California Association of Governments has proposed such a "solution" through a commuter fee system to reduce peak-hour trips (Southern California Association of Governments 1990; see also Knight 1990). However, it is highly questionable whether a corporatist state can resist capital's dominance over the political agenda to protect the public interest (Kann 1986: 261–63).

Immigrants at this level of the debate are subsumed within the interests of society as a whole. Their options to support resistance to the Old Guard strategy are limited. The disenfranchisement of immigrants and a discriminatory political system are the major barriers to a unified environmental and consumer opposition to a regressive environmental agenda. When important sectors of society are essentially locked out of the political process, dominant interests are free to focus on lobbying against a narrow and inept middle class (Boggs 1983). Capital's structural limitations toward corporate responsibility are also sheltered by a divided class culture that splinters consumers between the satisfied sectors and the marginal sectors. Thus, the dilemma of restructuring the global consumer society becomes mired in a theoretical debate confined to a politically fractured environmental constituency. The inherent political contradictions of the progressive reform movement (i.e., its inability to forge class linkages) at the turn of the century (Lubove 1962: 46) are being repeated by current reform movements.

Ironically, a number of political, structural, and technical factors have created conditions that limit capital's ability to effectively respond to the environmental crisis. Since capital traditionally fights environmentally related production costs, society has developed self-imposed economic barriers. An obvious one is the landfill crisis involving both solid and hazardous waste. Simply stated, the Los Angeles Basin is running out of space, and NIMBYite factions pose serious political hurdles by opposing development of new locations for commercial and industrial waste disposal sites. The past practice of leveraging regions against one another is no longer a viable option since it is political suicide to support dumping toxic poison in virtually any jurisdiction. Capital also resists absorbing the costs of state-of-the-art technologies designed to minimize the incidence of environmental catastrophe. The Superfund program, through which capitalists are paid to clean up waste sites generated by industrialization, is a classic example of politically imposed barriers created to limit capital's need to consider long-term source reduction programs (Hayes 1987: 448–49). Why should capital place major emphasis on this problem when tax resources are regressively redirected to their benefit?

Social costs in the form of tax policy and user fees have an inequitable influence on some sectors of the economy (Ingersoll and Brockbank 1986: 220). Low-income families are regressively impacted by these hidden environmental costs (Gianessi and Peskin 1980). Further complicating this fiscal issue is the implementation of new pollution reduction regulations that eventually will increase the cost of living (Mansfield 1980: 568). At the subsistence level, increased burdens translate into life choices between food, shelter, and health expenses. The imposition of recycling fees and water conservation penalties places undue burdens on families living in apartments with no direct control over collective user patterns. For example, how will families implement recycling practices in cramped living quarters where space is at a premium? On another level, can mass transit users depend on a stable fee structure, or will a rise in bus fares to cover operating losses and cost overruns on the Metro Rail project impact basic service?

Cities can develop a sliding scale of fees based on family income in relation to service charges for transit fares, water use, or solid waste recycling programs. Sanitation districts need to develop a comprehensive program for apartment dwellers and for areas of concentrated overcrowded housing. Transit rates based on income levels would ensure active ridership among low-income groups. Immigrants would be the direct beneficiaries of improved workplace conditions. Proper handling and storage of hazardous materials and recycling measures both reduce health problems and assist social requirements toward long-term waste reduction solutions. If properly designed, consumer packaging, product shelf life, and changes in the types of goods offered should not necessarily imply significant consumer price increases.

Opposition to reliance on user fees addressing environmental pollution control strategies is in the best interests of immigrant and minority families. To ensure that dramatic changes in transit patterns are achieved, mass transit fees should be subsidized for low-income groups. Local and regional government should encourage low-tech processes to achieve a broad socially generated environmental agenda, especially in the areas of recycling and the maintenance of public streetscapes. Political pressure must be maintained to force the source polluters to absorb direct and indirect costs in complying with pollution control regulations. Environmental groups have to develop networks with minority constituents to confront historical resistance to a restructured environmentally sound economic system. Without the support of the region's new majority, splintered class factions will be hard-pressed to oppose any corporate sponsored consumer fee strategies to generate necessary revenues to reverse capital's historic degradation of the environment.

Policy Challenges of the 1990s

In Washington, D.C., Congress and the Clinton administration have negotiated the final version of a revised Clean Air Act. In Sacramento, the legislature is analyzing state- and/or regional level land use measures and various avenues to control the fiscal effects of urban sprawl (California State Senate 1988). At virtually all levels of government, industrialization's environmental crisis is a major political concern. The public has forced the debate because of the evolution of the growth control movements in Northern and Southern California. For example, on the regional level, local agencies are reassessing policies related to the built environment, congestion, and housing density controls (Gottdiener 1985: 273). The social and political costs of uncontrolled urban sprawl are at the base of a renewed urgency to address growth and environmental issues.

It is essential that immigrants and minority groups enter into the political fray while the framework for an urban environmental strategy remains in a developing stage. Unfortunately, the historic impacts of a discriminatory political system impose serious problems for effective political lobbying (Parenti 1980: 302–7). The city of Los Angeles is reflective of how government bodies fail to represent the actual demographics of the region (Browning, Marshall, and Tabb 1984: 24). Furthermore, despite comprising a significant proportion of the regional populace, the vast majority of immigrants are not eligible to participate in the political process.

Economic status is another factor that inhibits minorities from addressing these issues (Browning *et al.* 1984: 81–82). When personal decisions are between urban survival or the luxury of political activism, most working-class families are preoccupied with the former.

However, the importance of the current environmental debate mandates that minorities force their entry into the political arena. The decisions made within the next five years will restructure society for the next quarter century. All facets of social and economic activity will be impacted. The availability of housing, the level and type of entry-level jobs, the type of consumer products, and household life patterns are among the major societal functions that will be radically altered from their present format. No sector can afford not to become directly involved in the process. Environmental organizations along with growth control groups alone do not have sufficient political leverage necessary to attain the environmental/economic restructuring necessary to solve the environmental crisis. A collective coalition across class and ethnic social strata would be the most potent political coalition to achieve the goals of the environmental movement.

Both MELA and CCSC are examples of the long-term political, economic, and social benefits that this type of coalition offers both constituencies (Russell 1989). These two minority organizations are examples of a broad-based political network willing to address the difficult myriad of urban issues centered on environmental questions.

The first of four necessary political steps required for forming this potential coalition is for minorities to become directly involved in legislative advocacy process at all levels of government. The second step is that a wide range of issues should be debated to generate a basic level of consensus on various urban environmental issues. Currently, minority concerns remain narrowly (and properly) focused on the defeat of regressive land use proposals. The third step entails developing a proactive urban agenda that incorporates both environmental and economic policy addressing tangible living-wage and public welfare considerations. This step requires the mainstream environmental movement to advocate aggressively for a significant increase in electoral and appointed minority representation at all levels of government and within their respective organizations. Finally, the interests of immigrants must be incorporated into all levels of the policy debate. While existing minority groups include immigrant membership, other actors need to develop a firm understanding of the problems, concerns, and impacts that a new environmental/economic/social agenda will have on capital's underclass.

Currently at the level of regional government in California, few decision-making entities reflect the ethnic composition of the region. While the Los Angeles City Council, School Board, and most recently the County Board of Supervisors have increased minority representation (only the school board has an ethnic majority), no other major county or city government in the region has significant minority representation. In addition, virtually all quasi-government entities in the region have either minimal or nonexistent minority representation. For example, the Los Angeles City Department of Water and Power Board of Commissioners has had scant minority membership. The Metropolitan Water District Board has been historically an exclusionary body. Sanitation districts have scant minority membership. While these government entities debate urban and suburban policy, allocate funds for infrastructure projects, and develop sanctions to enforce a new environmental agenda, the vast majority of users are essentially excluded from the political process. Without adequate representation at the level of the local state, implementation of these various programs will have a difficult time developing broad-based public cooperation.

The question of representation becomes paramount in this new environmental era. Immigrants have virtually no political clout other than through public protest. Minority groups in general have been successfully excluded by all-American racism, which has persisted and intensified in the 1980s (Piven and Cloward 1982). Where minority groups do have representation, their power is usually minimal (Parenti 1980: 316). At the regional level, this political influence is further diluted. In the five major counties in Southern California, only three minorities hold elected county government seats. This problem is more apparent when minority representation on special district commissions is analyzed at the regional and state levels. To spur minority community involvement in the current debate, a dramatic change in the political landscape is required. When the first member of an ethnic group is represented on a particular board or council, this step is in reality a false pretense of progress. Until governing bodies accurately reflect the region's ethnic population, societal consensus cannot be achieved on a broad-based environmentally oriented land use agenda.

A political system that engenders exclusion at virtually every level of entry (including the existing two-party structure) provides minority groups with limited options (Parenti 1980: 192–95). A major problem with achieving adequate representation is the Democratic Party's inability to maintain support for minority political agendas, especially at the state and federal levels (Browning *et al.* 1984: 254–55; Christensen and Gerston 1988: 265). In the current era, community organizations and unions are the only tangible avenues for political mobilization. Developing networks with environmental groups and sympathetic politicians provides one avenue of access. Immigrants, in particular, are pushed into a contradictory political position. While their daily labor is demanded by capital for its survival, immigrants are blamed for problems that they do not create or control. Confronted with a series of daunting political and social hurdles, immigrants and minorities cannot afford to allow a regressive political environment to limit their activism in this crucial debate over the future of regional political culture and political economy.

Life in the Clean Lane: An Environmentally Sensitive City

The environmental crisis is one of the major social challenges of this generation. In facing this crisis, American society must begin to recognize and address the fact that it is global capital's spoiled child (Monkkonen 1986: 34). The current policy debate will ultimately determine whether public health is more important than the freedom to pollute the environment as an economic expediency. A fundamental question is whether labor-intensive industries will agree to coexist in a new regulatory arena. Questions focused on economic restructuring are not simply limited to a difference of opinion over the equity of a subsistence or a livable wage. Restructuring also implies affordable housing, quality education, recreational and cultural amenities, and effective pollution control strategies.

In order to protect their economic and social interests, immigrant and minority constituencies have to develop sophisticated political strategies. In response to requests for political support for their agenda, middle-class and environmental groups, immigrants, and minorities must demand specific political concessions. These include addressing subsidies and equitable fee scales related to current and future environmental regulations and policies that are clearly directed to the needs of working-class families. For example, in return for supporting clean air plans, air quality districts should be forced to adopt a livable-wage policy. In tandem with massive transit subsidies derived from all levels of government, affordable transportation policies need to be imposed on the regional marketplace. In essence, an environmentally sound economy has to be restructured to also protect the interests of the majority of wage earners.

The convergence of a middle- and working-class collective movement in support of this political agenda is the cornerstone of the debate over economic restructuring. This difficult task necessarily demands major class concessions that may not be achievable within this economic system. In this instance, the conservative counterattack against environmental laws will have succeeded in protecting capital from the direct cost of pollution control. Capital's control of the pollution agenda would be solidified, thus allowing manipulation of the lower classes under a weak two-party system. Consequently, a corporatist state structure that recognizes the social and economic benefits of inaction would choose to remain sequestered in fraternal discussions over program implementation (Pressman and Wildavsky 1973: chap. 6).

Restructuring within the context of environmental logic would benefit society in general and immigrant groups in particular. Many of the current environmentally oriented proposals are labor intensive (Dominski *et al.* 1990). Numerous opportunities exist for generating the required level of jobs necessary to sustain a livable-wage economy. Innovative restructuring of the residential market would provide a range of skilled and semiskilled positions, including weatherization, solar energy retrofitting, water conservation, and solid waste recycling. Reducing single-occupant-vehicle trips is dependent on user acceptance of mass transit systems. Consumer trips would eventually require extended walks to retail locations that support neighborhood-oriented small businesses. This historic social pattern enhances both community culture and neighborhood-based development. Computer-directed local area networks could eventually eliminate long daily commutes, thereby creating a strong home-oriented service sector. These types of locally and globally driven employment opportunities alone would not solve the natural environmental crisis. A social justice philosophy must be implemented to recognize and celebrate human and cultural values as crucial and valid political and economic indices (Gorz 1980).

Workplace conditions are a critical factor in assessing the impact of pollution on immigrant groups. Worker health and safety are both labor-management and social environmental issues. The handling and storing of hazardous materials is a serious environmental problem. Not only are workers placed at direct health risk, but their immediate families and the surrounding community are placed at risk. New air quality regulations addressing industrial spray processes imply that workers should not be exposed to an array of toxic chemicals. Capital must be forced to control this source pollution by providing proper worker equipment and emission reduction technology. During the Reagan/Dukemajian era, workers and unions suffered from substantial reductions in the scope of enforcement agencies designed to protect workers (Mann 1986: 20). What the politicians refused to acknowledge is that society was also being placed at risk because of these cutbacks. Renewed interest in source pollution control must place the burden of direct costs on source polluters through fines, sanctions, and jail if the public interest is to be taken seriously.

By 2020, history will have rendered judgment on this nation's choice between a pollution-control-oriented economic system or environmental chaos as the legacy left for future generations. In one sense, capital cannot reverse the public momentum toward a new environmental regulatory arena. However, regardless of the type and function of environmental regulation, capital's dominance of the corporatist state ensures that political consensus alone is not sufficient to change the accumulation and reproduction process (Kann 1986: 257–63). Immigrant and minority groups have to question a system that possesses the ability to invest substantial resources in research and development for the design of new technologies while appearing disengaged in determining whether this investment benefits all social classes or solely dominant capital factions. Immigrants, structurally limited in their political and economic response to environmental degradation, must not bear the brunt of capital's minimal concern toward the environmental crisis. Trickle-down ideology translates into the worst environmental conditions for the weakest sectors of society (ibid.: 269).

If economic restructuring is to meet the needs of immigrants, an environmental component to this agenda is essential. An environmentally sound economy should incorporate new methods toward ensuring labor-intensive production capacity. Changes in workplace and household patterns, along with the reshaping of neighborhood land use policies, will generate a new level of employment opportunities. The state also has to reassert its political mandate to enforce environmental and pollution control laws. For example, placing workers at risk capriciously should not be the price for accumulation and reproduction here or anywhere else in the global economic system.

In relation to an environmental movement attempting to achieve a long-range political agenda, a coalition of minority groups is an essential facet in confronting economically driven pollution. However, immigrants and minorities must exert strong political leverage while maintaining a viable social justice agenda in exchange for their political support. Unless economic restructuring is both class and collectively based, the power of capital interests will prove to be an insurmountable barrier. In the current period, neither middle-class environmentalists, minorities, nor immigrants internally possess the political power essential to challenge capital's hegemony over the political economy. An environmentally grounded political strategy presents an optimum potential for the immigrant/minority community to achieve social justice and economic rights within the framework of protecting this generation's brief endowment: stewardship of the natural environment.

BIBLIOGRAPHY

Anthony, Carl. 1990. "Why African Americans Should Be Environmentalists." *Race, Poverty, and the Environment* 1 (1): 5–6.

Assembly Office of Research, State of California. 1989. "California 2000: Getting Ahead of the Growth Curve." Sacramento, Calif.: Joint Publications Office.

Billiter, Bill. 1981. "Chemicals Found at Site That Could Form Poison Gas." *Los Angeles Times*, October 28, B1.

Blue Ribbon Committee for Affordable Housing, City of Los Angeles. 1988. "Housing the Future: Draft Briefing Book." City of Los Angeles, Office of the Mayor.

Bluestone, Barry, and Bennett Harrison. 1982. *The Deindustrialization of America*. New York: Basic Books.

Blumberg, Louis, and Robert Gottlieb. 1989. *War on Waste: Can America Win Its Battle with Garbage*. Washington, D.C.: Island Press.

Boggs, Carl. 1983. "The New Populism and the Limits of Structural Reforms." *Theory and Society* 12 (3, May): 343–363.

Booth, Richard S. 1988. "Forging a Viable Future." In Peter Borrelli, ed., *Crossroads: Environmental Priorities for the Future*, pp. 295–308. Washington, D.C.: Island Press.

Boyer, M. Christine. 1983. *Dreaming the Rational City*. Cambridge, Mass.: MIT Press.

Browning, Rufus P., Dale R. Marshall, and David H. Tabb. 1984. *Protest Is Not Enough*. Berkeley and Los Angeles: University of California Press.

Bullard, Robert D., ed. 1994. *Unequal Protection*. San Francisco: Sierra Club Books.

California State Senate. 1988. "Growth Management: Local Decisions, Regional Needs, and Statewide Goals." Select Committee on Planning for California's Growth and Committee on Local Government, California State Legislature.

Christensen, Terry, and Larry Gerston. 1988. *Politics in the Golden State: The California Connection*. Boston: Scott, Foresman.

Daly, Herman E. 1977. *Steady-State Economics*. San Francisco: W. H. Freeman.

Diaz, David R. 1989. "The Polluters Fight Back." *LA Weekly*, December 1–7, 18. 1990. "The Battle of ELA." In Mike Davis, Steve Haitt, Marie Kennedy, Sue Ruddick, and Michael Sprinker, eds., *Fires in the Hearth: The Radical Politics of Place in America*, pp. 271–284. London: Verso Press.

Dolan, Maura. 1990. "Proposed New Smog Rule Would Trigger More Alerts." *Los Angeles Times*, August 7, A1, A18.

Dominski, Anthony, Jon Clark, and Paul Relis. 1990. *The Bottom Line: Restructuring Cities for Sustainability*. Santa Barbara, Calif.: Community Environmental Council.

Eastside Journal. 1990. "Eastside Prison Foes Strike Another Prison Win." July 4, A1.

Flavin, Christopher, and John E. Young. 1993. "Shaping the Next Industrial Revolution." In Lestor R. Brown, ed., *State of the World*. 1993, pp. 180–199. New York: W. W. Norton.

Flink, James J. 1975. *The Car Culture*. Cambridge, Mass.: MIT Press.

Frantz, Douglas. 1990. "Polluters Directing Cleanups." Los Angeles Times, June 17, A1, A30.

Freeman, A. Myrick. 1973. "Income Distribution and Environmental Quality." In Alain C. Enthoven and A. Myrick Freeman, eds., *Pollution, Resources, and the Environment*, pp. 122–137. New York: W. W. Norton.

Gianessi, Leonard P., and Henry Peskin. 1980. "The Distribution of the Costs of Federal Water Pollution Control Policy." *Land Economics* 56 (1, February): 85–102.

Gorz, Andre. 1980. *Ecology as Politics*. Boston: South End Press.

Gottdiener, M. 1985. *The Social Production of Urban Space*. Austin: University of Texas Press.

Hall, Jane V. 1989. "Economic Assessment of the Health Benefits from Improvements in Air Quality in the South Coast Air Basin." Report, South Coast Air Quality Management District, El Monte, California.

Harper, Charles, 1993. *Exploring Social Change*. Englewood Cliffs, N.J.: Prentice Hall.

Harvey, David. 1985. *Consciousness and the Urban Experience*. Baltimore: The Johns Hopkins University Press.

Hayes, Samuel P. 1987. *Beauty, Health, and Permanence: Environmental Politics in the United States, 1955–1985*. Cambridge: Cambridge University Press.

Ingersoll, Thomas G., and Bradley R. Brockbank. 1986. "The Role of Economic Incentives in Environmental Policy." In Sheldon Kamieniecki, Robert O'Brien, and Michael Clarke, eds., *Controversies in Environmental Policy*, pp. 201–222. Albany: State University of New York Press.

Johnson, Huey D. 1988. "Environmental Quality as a National Purpose." In Peter Borelli, ed, *Crossroads: Environmental Priorities for the Future*, pp. 217–224. Washington, D.C.: Island Press.

Kann, Mark E. 1986. "Environmental Democracy in the United States." In Sheldon Kamieniecki, Robert O'Brien, and Michael Clarke, eds., *Controversies in Environmental Policy*, pp. 252–274. Albany: State University of New York Press.

Kleinman, Michael, Steven Colome, and Donna Foliart. 1989. "Effects on Human Health of Pollutants in the South Coast Air Basin." Report, South Coast Air Quality Management District, El Monte, California.

Knight, Tony. 1990. "New Anti-Smog Proposals Penalize, Reward Commuters." *Daily News*, July 6, A1.

La Gory, Mark, and John Pipkin. 1981. *Urban Social Space*. Belmont, Calif: Wadsworth.

Lake, Laura. 1982. *Environmental Regulation: The Political Effects of Implementation*. New York: Praeger.

Lubove, Roy. 1962. *The Progressives and the Slums: Tenement House Reform in New York City*. Pittsburgh: University of Pittsburgh Press.

Mann, Dean E. 1986. "Democratic Politics and Environmental Policy." In Sheldon Kamieniecki, Robert O'Brien, and Michael Clarke, eds., *Controversies in Environmental Policy*, pp. 3–36. Albany: State University of New York Press.

Mansfield, Edwin. 1980. "Technology and Productivity in the United States." In Martin Feldstein, ed., *The American Economy in Transition*, pp. 563–596. Chicago: University of Chicago Press.

Monkkonen, Eric H. 1986. "The Sense of Crisis: A Historian's Point of View." In M. Gottdiener, ed., *Cities in Stress*, pp. 20–38. Beverly Hills, Calif: Sage.

Morris, Lela D. 1989. "Minorities, Jobs, and Health." *AAOHN Journal* 37 (2): 53–55.

Muller, Thomas, and Thomas J. Espenshade. 1985. *The Fourth Wave*. Washington, D.C.: Urban Land Institute.

Ong, Paul M. 1989. "The Widening Divide: Income Inequality and Poverty in Los Angeles." Graduate School of Architecture and Urban Planning, University of California, Los Angeles.

Paehlke, Robert C. 1989. *Environmentalism and the Future of Progressive Politics*. New Haven, Conn.: Yale University Press.

Pansing, Cynthia, Hali Rederer, and David Yale. 1989. "A Community at Risk: The Environmental Quality of Life in East Los Angeles." Master's thesis, University of California, Los Angeles.

Parenti, Michael. 1978. *Power and the Powerless*. New York: St. Martin's Press. 1980. *Democracy for the Few*. New York: St. Martin's Press.

Persons of Hispanic Origin in the United States, 1990. CP-3-3. Washington, D.C.: U.S. Government Printing Office.

Piven, Francis Fox, and Richard A. Cloward. 1982. *The New Class War*. New York: Pantheon.

Popper, Frank J. 1981. *The Politics of Land Use Reform*. Madison: University of Wisconsin Press.

Pressman, Jeffery L., and Aaron B. Wildavsky. 1973. *Implementation*. Berkeley and Los Angeles: University of California Press.

Race, Poverty and the Environment. 1990. "Earth Day Issue." 1 (1): 1–8.

Robinson, James C. 1989. "Trends in Racial Inequality and Exposure to Work-Related Hazards, 1968–1986." *AAOHN Journal* 37 (2): 56–63.

Russell, Dick. 1989. "Environmental Racism." *The Amicus Journal* (spring): 22–32.

San Bernardino Sun Times Telegraph. 1989. Special Report, "Smog: The Silent Killer," November 26–December 3, 1–14.

Scott, Mel. 1969. *American City Planning*. Berkeley and Los Angeles: University of California Press.

Seiler, Michael. 1981. "Brown Orders Speedy Cleanup of Toxic Dump." *Los Angeles Times*, October 29, B1.

Smith, Gar. 1990. "Freeways, Community and Environmental Racism." *Race, Poverty and the Environment* 1 (1): 7.

Southern California Association of Governments. 1990. "The Growth Management and Transportation Task Force Report." Southern California Association of Governments, Los Angeles.

Starr, Kevin. 1985. *Inventing the Dream*. New York: Oxford University Press. 1991.

The Hispanic Population by Place of Birth for the United States. Washington, D.C.: U.S. Department of Commerce. 1993.

The Foreign-Born Population in the United States. Washington, D.C.: U.S. Department of Commerce. 1993.

Wallace, Steven P. 1986. "Central American and Mexican Immigrant Characteristics and Economic Incorporation in California." *International Migration Review* 20: 657–671.

Weeks, John. 1985. *The Economics of Central America*. New York: Holmes and Meier.

Wilkinson, Tracy. 1991. "L.A.'s Turn as Urban Laboratory." *Los Angeles Times*, December 11, 1A.

World Council of Churches. 1985, 1988, 1989. *The Human Rights Situation in El Salvador*. San Salvador: "Archbishop Oscar Romero" Christian Legal Aid Service Report(s).

Zambrana, Ruth E., and Claudia Dorrington. 1998. "Economic and Social Vulnerability of Latino Children and Families by Subgroup: Implications for Child Welfare." *Child Welfare* LXXVII(1): 5–27.

Zolberg, Aristide R. 1981. "International Migration in Political Perspective." In Mary M. Kritz, ed., *Global Trends in Migration*, pp. 15–52. Staten Island, N.Y.: Center for Migration Studies.

31 Reinterpreting Sustainable Architecture: The Place of Technology

Simon Guy and Graham Farmer

This award-winning article analyzes six different worldviews embedded in architectural approaches to sustainability.

This paper examines the relationships between diverse technical design strategies and competing conceptions of ecological place making. It highlights the conceptual challenges involved in defining what we mean by calling a building "green" and outlines a social constructivist perspective on the development of sustainable architecture. The paper identifies six alternative logics of ecological design which have their roots in competing conceptions of environmentalism, and explores the ways in which each logic prefigures technological strategies and alternative visions of sustainable places. Finally, the paper discusses the implications of the contested nature of ecological design for architectural education, practice, and research.

INTRODUCTION

Susan Maxman has suggested that "sustainable architecture isn't a prescription. Its an approach, an attitude. It shouldn't really even have a label. It should just be *architecture*."[1] However, beyond this de facto professional embrace of "green" design, making sense of environmental innovation in architecture tends to be a confusing business. Glancing through the myriad of articles, reports, and books on the subject of green or sustainable buildings, we find a bewildering array of contrasting building types, employing a great variety of different technologies and design approaches, each justified by a highly diverse set of interpretations of what a sustainable place might represent. As Cook and Golton put it, "the designation 'green' is extremely wide ranging, encompassing many viewpoints and open to broad interpretation," with sustainable architecture embodying an "essentially contestable concept."[2]

Simon Guy & Graham Farmer, "Reinterpreting Sustainable: The Place of Technology," from *Journal of Architectural Education*, Vol. 54, No. 3, pp. 140–148. Published by Blackwell Publications, 2001. Copyright by John Wiley & Sons. Permission to reprint granted by the rights holder.

CONSTRUCTING CONSENSUS

While it is widely recognized that sustainability is a contested concept, much of the contemporary debate on sustainable architecture tends to sidestep the issue. Either competing environmental strategies are grouped within a single, homogenous categorization of green design with little or no reference to their distinctiveness, or the existence of a multiplicity of design approaches is identified as a significant barrier to solving what are considered to be self-evident problems such as global warming. Seen this way, sustainable buildings are assumed to merely represent differently configured technical structures, with particular pathways of technological innovation viewed as objectively preferable to others. Reflecting the "technocist supremacy" that dominates most environmental research programs, this perspective tends to ignore the essentially social questions implicated in the practice of sustainable architecture.[3] Typical are suggestions that if we are to achieve sustainable buildings then architecture should become more "objective," and that "until a consensus is attained, the ability of the architectural community to adopt a coherent environmental strategy, across all building types and styles of development, will remain elusive."[4] Such "environmental realism" is founded on the notion that "rational science can and will provide the understanding of the environment and the assessment of those measures which are necessary to rectify environmental bads."[5] Further implicit in this model of consensus is a "process of standardisation," which means that "particular local conditions" and competing "forms of local knowledge" tend to be ignored.[6]

REINTERPRETING SUSTAINABLE ARCHITECTURE

We suggest that a more appropriate way to understand this strategic diversity lies in abandoning the search for a true or incontestable definition of sustainable buildings, and instead treating the concept in a "relative rather than an absolute sense" as a "means of raising awareness of all the issues that can be considered."[7] In this we follow John Hannigan in suggesting that society's willingness to recognize and solve environmental problems depends more upon the way these claims are presented by a limited number of people than upon the severity of the threats they pose.[8] That is, the concept of a green building is a social construct. This is not to say that the range of environmental innovations are not valid—socially, commercially, or technically—in their own terms. The aim of this analysis is not to "discredit environmental claims but rather to understand how they are created, legitimated, and contested."[9] The premise is, then, that individuals, groups, and institutions embody widely differing perceptions of what environmental innovation is about.[10] Each of these actors may share a commitment to sustainable design but are likely to differ greatly in their "interpretation of the causes of, and hence the solution to, unsustainability."[11] This is a highly contested process. Design and development actors possess varying degrees of power to implement their environmental visions. By treating these competing views as environmental discourses that take material form in the shape of buildings, we can recognize the tension between alternative environmental beliefs and strategies. Thus, by adopting an interpretative framework, and by "exploring the notion of discourse, we highlight the social production of space, place, and the environment. We challenge the assumption that environment is merely a physical entity and resist the categorisation of it only in scientific terms."[12]

Table 1 The Six Competing Logics of Sustainable Architecture

Logic	Image of Space	Source of Environmental Knowledge	Building Image	Technologies	Idealized Concept of Place
Eco-technic	global context macrophysical	technorational scientific	commercial modern future oriented	integrated energy efficient high-tech intelligent	Integration of global environmental concerns into conventional building design strategies. Urban vision of the compact and dense city.
Eco-centric	fragile microbiotic	systemic ecology metaphysical holism	polluter parasitic consumer	autonomous renewable recycled intermediate	Harmony with nature through decentralized, autonomous buildings with limited ecological footprints. Ensuring the stability, integrity, and "flourishing" of local and global biodiversity.
Eco-aesthetic	alienating anthropocentric	sensual postmodern science	iconic architectural New Age	pragmatic new nonlinear organic	Universally reconstructed in the light of new ecological knowledge and transforming our consciousness of nature.
Eco-cultural	cultural context regional	phenomenology cultural ecology	authentic harmonious typological	local low-tech commonplace vernacular	Learning to "dwell" through buildings adapted to local and bioregional physical and cultural characteristics.
Eco-medical	polluted hazardous	medical clinical ecology	healthy living caring	passive nontoxic natural tactile	A natural and tactile environment which ensures the health, well-being, and quality of life for individuals.
Eco-social	social context hierarchical	sociology social ecology	democratic home individual	flexible participatory appropriate locally managed	Reconciliation of individual and community in socially cohesive manner through decentralized "organic," nonhierarchical, and participatory communities.

THE COMPETING LOGICS OF SUSTAINABLE ARCHITECTURE

Our analysis is based upon studies of completed buildings and an extensive literature review of books, articles, and reports covering issues related to sustainable, environmental, ecological, or green buildings. Careful analysis of the resulting search resulted in a typology of six environmental logics, which are illustrated in Table 1.[13] Here, we define *logic,* following Hajer, as "a specific ensemble of ideas, concepts and categorisations that are produced, reproduced and transformed in a particular set of practices through which meaning is given to social and physical realities."[14] These logics are not meant to be in any way exclusive, or frozen in time or space. As Benton and Short suggest, "Discourses are never static and rarely stable."[15] That is, through the design process of any particular development, logics may collide, merge, or coinhabit debate about form, design, and specification. The main point is that the "environmental problematique is hardly ever discussed in its full complexity." Rather, each "environmental logic tends to be dominated by specific emblems: issues that dominate the perception of the ecological dilemma."[16] Each of the logics highlight the ways in which the green building debate is framed differently depending upon competing constructions of the environmental problem and alternative concepts of what might constitute a sustainable place. These contrasting environmental discourses "mobilise biases in and out of the environmental debate," thereby shaping the subsequent design strategy.[17] In particular, each logic is underpinned by a disparate concept of the space through which environmental benefits and detriments flow and are represented; differing sources of environmental knowledge though which we come to experience and understand the environment; and distinct images of buildings in relation to the environments they inhabit. In exploring these interpretative frameworks, we illustrate how each logic prefigures technological choice within a broad design strategy premised by a specific form of environmental place making. As we highlighted above, we present these logics as separate but not autonomous. In practice, logics may merge or simply be absent as exemplified by analysis of any individual building (which we must leave for another paper). Rather than focus on the particular, our aim here is to unpack the general metalogics that frame our thinking about sustainable architecture.

The Eco-technic Logic—Buildings and the Global Place

The eco-technic logic is based on a technorational, policy-oriented discourse which represents a belief in incremental, technoeconomic change and that science and technology can provide the solutions to environmental problems. As Cook and Golton put it, "technocentrics recognize the existence of environmental problems and want to solve them through management of the environment" putting their trust in "objective analysis and a rational scientific method."[18] In the field of environmental policy, these ideas have been expressed in terms of ecological modernization, which "indicates the possibility of overcoming the environmental crisis without leaving the path of modernisation."[19] The assumption is that existing institutions can internalize and respond to ecological concerns and what is required is an integrative approach in which science, technology, and management take account of the environmental impacts of development.

A key feature of the ecological modernization paradigm is its globalizing viewpoint, which situates sustainability within a context that is distant in terms of space and time. Concerns are mainly for the universal, global environmental problems of climate change, global warming, ozone layer depletion, and transnational pollution issues such as acid rain. It is a view that the real environmental dangers are those of a "global physical crisis that threatens survival."[20] What is required is the formation of an international political consensus around the need for centralized national and global action. There is an emphasis on the concept of futurity, as suggested by the Brundtland definition of sustainability as "meeting the needs of the present without compromising the ability of future generations to meet their own needs."[21] We therefore have an ethical responsibility to distant humanity or future generations in maintaining both the stability and resource richness of the globe. The role and context of sustainable buildings becomes prioritized in terms of global action and local reaction.

In practice, these ideas are characterized by a consensual, top-down view of environmental and technological change in which a "progressive process of innovation mitigates the adverse effects of development."[22] The source of environmental problems stems from past practices not taking sufficient account of environmental concerns, and what is required is the "development, inauguration and diffusion of new technologies that are more intelligent than the older ones and that benefit the environment," and under the assumption that "the only possible way out of the ecological crisis is by going further into industrialisation."[23] This approach therefore, while borrowing much of its symbolic language from ecology, places its optimism and faith in the potential and possibilities of technological development as a panacea for our environmental ills.

In the case of building design, the emblematic issue is efficiency and, in line with global concerns, energy efficiency is prioritized. The negative environmental impacts of buildings are assumed to be the result of a variety of inefficient practices implicit within the process of building production. The resulting design strategy is adaptive but based on recognizably modern, usually high-technology buildings that attempt to maximize the efficiency of building in spatial, construction, and energy terms. This approach is perhaps best epitomized by the High-Tech school, led by British architects such as Norman Foster, Richard Rogers, Nicholas Grimshaw, and Michael Hopkins and including the work of Italian architect Renzo Piano, Thomas Herzog in Germany, and the bioclimatic skyscrapers of Ken Yeang in Malaysia.[24] Here, an emphasis on the environmental efficiency of development has stimulated a whole range of technological innovations in building fabric and servicing systems: translucent insulation, new types of glass and solar shading, intelligent facades, double-skin walls and roofs, and photovoltaics. Energy-efficient lighting, passive solar design and daylighting, the use of natural and mixed-mode ventilation, more efficient air conditioning and comfort cooling, combined with sophisticated energy management systems are all part of the High-Tech approach. The rhetoric of the ecotechnic approach tends to be overwhelmingly quantitative, success is expressed in the numerical reduction of building energy consumption, material-embodied energy, waste and resource-use reduction, and in concepts such as life-cycle flexibility and cost-benefit analysis.

The Eco-centric Logic—Buildings and the Place of Nature

In sharp contrast to the eco-technic logic with its emphasis on incremental technical change and an optimism in the adaptability of institutions to accommodate environmental demands, the eco-centric logic is founded on a need for a radical reconfiguration of values. According to Victor Papenak the "beneficial connection between economics and ecology has been systematically misrepresented by industrial and governmental apologists."[25] Here the assumption is that "the challenge of sustainable design is too big, too complex, and too uncertain to deal with as a technical problem, or even as an exercise in institutional design."[26] The eco-centric logic stems from a particular view of nature generated through the natural scientific paradigm of systemic ecology. As a framework of analysis, it emphasizes both the epistemological holism implicit in ecology and the metaphysical reality of ecological wholes. It is a discourse that stresses the dynamic interaction between the living and nonliving as a community of interdependent parts suggested by the notion of "Gaia."[27] Ecocentric discourse combines the science of ecology with an eco-centric or bio-centric ethical framework that extends moral considerations beyond anthropocentric concerns to encompass nonliving objects and ecological systems. This is expressed by Aldo Leopold's "land ethic," which portrays the earth not as a commodity to be bought and sold but rather as a community of which humans are an integral part.[28] Human responsibilities to the environment are conceived as stewardship, a kind of management ethic dictated by the biophysical constraints and limits that come not from human needs but from within nature itself. Exceeding these limits, it is argued, will have catastrophic results, with nothing less than planetary survival at stake.

This rhetoric generates a viewpoint in which nature becomes viewed as fragile and where natural equilibrium is easily disrupted. Sustainability therefore requires immediate and full precautionary protection of ecosystems and natural capital; an absolute response needing "a radical approach to rethinking building design and production."[29] The role of sustainable architecture is not simply the improvement of environmental performance, as this approach "belongs to an instrumental paradigm that is in itself complicit in our environmental problems."[30] Here, what is required is not only the development of more efficient technologies but a wider questioning of what constitutes sufficient technology; it is the latter which must define the boundaries of the former.[31] The eco-centric image of the built environment emphasizes its negative environmental impacts; in the case of buildings, the perception is that they are an unnatural form of "pure consumption" interrupting the natural cycles of nature.[32] In this sense: "Each building is an act against nature; it directly makes some proportion of the earth's surface organically sterile by covering it over, rendering that area incapable of producing those natural resources that require the interaction between soil, sun and water. As a result in ecological terms, a building is a parasite."[33] The essential mission of sustainable architecture becomes that of noninterference with nature, the ultimate measure of sustainability is the flourishing of ecosystems, and the fundamental question is whether to build at all. Where building is essential, the aim is to radically reduce the "ecological footprint" of buildings.[34] Approaches to building tend to draw directly on analogies with ecological systems as efficient, living, closed, cyclical processes, which oppose the linear, inefficient, open systems of conventional buildings. The holistic design strategies that result tend to revolve around small-scale and decentralized techniques utilizing low and intermediate technologies. There is an emphasis on reducing, or severing dependency on centralized infrastructure services of water, energy, and waste as in the autonomous house designs of architects like Brenda and Robert Vale in the UK.[35] In terms of building materials, preference is for renewable, natural materials such as earth, timber, and straw combined with a reduction of the use of virgin building materials through reuse and recycling. This approach is epitomized by Mike Reynold's work on domestic "Earthships" in New Mexico, where self-sufficient homes are made from used tires, bottles, and other waste materials, filled and plastered with earth.[36]

The Eco-aesthetic Logic—Buildings and the New Age Place

The eco-aesthetic logic shifts the debate about sustainable architecture beyond the efficient use of resources and the reduction of ecological footprints. Here the role of sustainable architecture is metaphorical and, as an iconic expression of societal values, it should act to inspire and convey an increasing identification with nature and the nonhuman world, what is required is a "new language in the building arts."[37] The eco-aesthetic logic draws on what might be termed a new concept discourse, which emphasizes spirituality in social and environmental relations and contains a strong New Age dimension. New Ageism takes an evolutionary view of world history, and "is bound together by a belief that the world is undergoing a transformation or shift in consciousness which will usher in a new mode of being."[38] As a theory of social change, it represents an idealist vision of a global universal consciousness, which begins with individual reflexivity and ecological awareness and which will eventually lead to the establishment of "whole new civilisations and cultures."[39] The starting point for change derives from a "convergence of views inherent in Eastern philosophies [and] post-modern science."[40] This new post-modern paradigm "is a new world view that is illuminated by what are called the new sciences of complexity, which includes Complexity Theory itself, Chaos Science, self-organising systems, and non-linear dynamics."[41] The eco-aesthetic logic places an emphasis on individual creativity and a liberated imagination combined with a romantic view of nature that rejects Western rationalism, modernism, and materialism; the assumption is that "the salvation of this human world lies nowhere else than in the human heart."[42] The solution to the environmental crisis requires a shift from utilitarian values to a view in which aesthetic and sensual values play a prominent role. According to John Passmore: "A more sensuous society could never have endured the desolate towns, the dreary and dirty houses, the uniquely ugly chapels, the slag heaps, the filthy rivers, the junk yards which constitute the 'scenery' of the post industrial west. Only if men can first learn to look sensuously at the world will they learn to care for it."[43]

The emblematic issue in building design is how to represent the epoch shift of the new millennium and the transition to a holistic, ecological worldview or zeitgeist. This invokes an ethical responsibility in beginning to redefine culture itself, and in creating a new universal architectural iconography that has transformative value in altering our consciousness of nature. The role of green buildings is to break free from strictly formalist interpretations of architecture, which are representative of a humanist culture with an anthropocentric attitude to nature, and "the entire direction in design suggests the development of a new paradigm in the building arts that [is] based on ecological models."[44] The rhetoric of this logic prioritizes appropriate architectural form above physical performance, expressed in Charles Jencks's assertion that "good ecological building may mean bad expressive architecture."[45] Instead it is "essential to cultivate a tradition of sensuous, creative Green Architecture," one that "delights in the ecological paradigm for its philosophy of holism, its style and the way in which it illuminates the complexity paradigm."[46] This new architectural language will be made possible by the new technologies of the information age—namely, advances in structural engineering, the ability to build curved forms through the use of computer modeling, automated production and new materials that offer the possibility to move beyond conventional notions of space and functional norms to create new forms that celebrate the environmental message. A move back towards organicism, expressionism, the chaotic, and the nonlinear is the "aesthetic … growing out of this new world view; a language of building and design close to nature, of twists and folds and undulations; of crystalline forms and fractured planes."[47] Jencks suggests that the beginning of this new movement can be witnessed in the "organi-tech" architecture of Frank Gehry, Santiago Calatrava, and Future Systems; in the "cosmic" forms of Japanese architects such as Arato Isosaki; and in the artistic fusion of landscape and architecture in the work of SITE.[48]

The Eco-cultural Logic—Buildings and the Authentic Place

The eco-cultural logic emphasizes a fundamental reorientation of values to engage with both environmental and cultural concerns. Here, it is not the development of a new universal culture which is promoted, but rather the preservation of a diversity of existing cultures. The emblematic issue is authenticity and the notion that truly sustainable buildings need to more fully relate to the concept of locality and place. The emphasis on place, or genius loci, is intended to counteract the deficiencies of abstract modernist space and is a reaction against the globalism of the International Style. Our ethical responsibilities are to resist the phenomena of universalization prevalent in modern culture, as, according to Frampton, "sustaining any kind of authentic culture in the future will depend ultimately on our capacity to generate vital forms of regional culture."[49] Arne Naess argues that we should "aim to conserve the richness and diversity of life on earth—and that includes human cultural diversity."[50] This requires a further step from ecologically sustainable development to long-range "ecosophical" development: "Any model of ecologically sustainable development must contain answers, however tentative, as to how to avoid contributing to thoughtless destruction of cultures, and to the dissemination of the belief in a glorious, meaningless life."[51]

The eco-cultural logic draws inspiration from a phenomeno-logical account of the environment and revives Heidegger's concept of dwelling with an emphasis on reinhabiting or relearning a sense of place. This unique sense of identity evolves subjectively from within nature and there is a concern for the continuity of meaning between tradition and the individual combined with the cultivation of an ecological consciousness. It implies both the development of a sense of being indigenous to a place and a responsibility for protecting landscape and ecosystems from disturbance. The approach stresses decentralization and is concerned with the characteristics of regions or bioregions, which are conceived as the basic geographical unit of a small-scale ecological society. Here a bioregion is defined by a combination of natural, biological, and ecological characteristics and by a cultural context, it is both a bounded physical terrain and a "terrain of consciousness."[52] Sustainability means living within the constraints and possibilities imposed by these characteristics, and as a design strategy, bioregionalism draws inspiration from indigenous and vernacular building approaches. These traditional building forms are seen as indicative of the way in which rooted cultures have naturally evolved appropriate lifestyles adapted to their particular physical environment.

Within this logic it is suggested that sustainable architectural approaches should move away from universal and technologically based design methodologies as these often fail to coincide with the cultural values of a particular place or people. According to Ujam and Stevenson this means "refuting the concern of certain 'Green' architects with 'Green' but culturally unsustainable technical fixes situated within existing building typologies. Adding insulation made from synthetic materials or 'Arabic-wind' towers as objects to an office block does not integrate a 'green' solution in terms of cultural considerations and sustainable design."[53] Contemporary architecture should therefore "recognize very deeply structured personal responses to particular places" if it is to be sustainable.[54] The eco-cultural logic emphasizes both the preservation and conservation of the variety of built cultural archetypes that already exist, combined with a concern for cultural continuity expressed through the transformation and reuse of traditional construction techniques, building typologies, and settlement patterns, each with a history of local evolution and use. This emphasis on the peculiarities of place, the use of local materials, and an appropriate formal response to climatic and microclimatic conditions is perhaps best expressed in the regionalist approaches of architects like Glenn Murcutt in Australia, Charles Correa in India, Geoffrey Bawa in Sri Lanka, and Hassan Fathy in Egypt.

The Eco-medical Logic—Buildings and the Healthy Place

The eco-medical logic shifts debates about sustainability from concerns about appropriate form and the wider cultural context of design towards a humanist and social concern for the sustaining of individual health. It is generated through a medical discourse that tends to relate "the health of the individual to an increasingly important condition: a healthy environment."[55] A new relationship of human beings to the environment has been legitimated through an understanding that the health of individuals is conditioned by the external environment. "By linking health to issues such as the quality of air, water and urban space, medicine has helped to make the environment an important concern."[56] This logic utilizes a medical rhetoric to focus attention on the adverse impacts of the built environment and the causes of stress that engender health problems, both physical and psychological. Medical discourse has highlighted the environmental hazards that are associated with mechanization and that accompany the "risk society."[57] Here the application of technology is not considered to be a risk-free operation, and importantly, this discourse has served to highlight that reducing the technological intensity of buildings (or society) does not necessarily "lead to a shrinking well-being: on the contrary even a growth in well-being can be imagined."[58]

In the case of buildings, the eco-medical logic tends to focus a critical attention on the interior of buildings, where the concept of sick buildings is a familiar emblematic issue applied to both working and domestic environments.[59] As David Pearson suggests, "the majority of urban built environments are poorly designed and managed, and the constant exposure to them produces stress and illness—the symptoms of 'sick building syndrome' being part of a far wider malaise."[60] Here the role of buildings as a technological barrier to a hostile natural world has been transformed; instead, we have a new image of buildings themselves as potentially dangerous environments in which individuals are put at daily risk from a variety of hazards.[61] Our health is literally threatened by the technologies that were created to protect it. In the case of the work environment, critics utilizing this logic tend to identify the technological intensity of large modern buildings, combined with a separation from nature and a lack of individual control over our immediate surroundings, as the root cause of the problem. Many people spend their lives in anonymous, universal environments which are artificially lit, mechanically ventilated, and effectively cut off from the outside world. This isolation from nature is being increasingly challenged by building occupiers, who now desire more control over their internal environments. As a result, new design principles of "environmental diversity are emerging," which envisage spaces that maintain, in the occupant, a sense of dynamics of the natural climate, of the proper condition of mankind."[62]

The promotion of naturally conditioned environments extends to the choice of materials, and the ecomedical logic draws on the disciplines of clinical ecology and environmental medicine where chemical pollution from synthetic building materials is seen as a key issue.[63] Architects such as Christopher Day have further extended these concerns to spiritual well-being, suggesting the importance of lifestyle as a complex whole.[64] What is required is "healing environments," ones in which we feel "balanced, relaxed and at one with the world," an architecture that can "honour the senses."[65] These ideals are embodied in the concept of *Baubiologie* (building biology), where the concepts of health and ecology are interwoven, and the aim is to "design buildings that meet our physical, biological, and spiritual needs. Their fabric, services, colour and scent must interact harmoniously with us and the environment ... to maintain a healthy, 'living' indoor climate."[66] This approach has inspired the buildings of Peter Schmid in the Netherlands, Floyd Stein in Denmark, the Gaia group in Norway, and the practice of Elbe and Sambeth in Germany. Baubiologie promotes the use of natural and tactile materials and traditional building methods utilizing organic treatments and finishes, natural light and ventilation, and the use of color to promote health.

The Eco-social Logic—Buildings and the Community Place

The eco-social logic extends the social agenda of sustainability beyond a concern for the individual to encompass a political discourse that suggests that the root cause of the ecological crisis stems from wider social factors. It addresses the emblematic issue of democracy as the key to an ecological society. It is only through a model of community that is created to serve common needs and goals, where humans experience true freedom and individual self-realization, that they will be able to live in harmony with the natural world. According to Murray Bookchin: "The ecological principle of unity in diversity grades into a richly mediated social principle," implicit in the term "social ecology."[67] Social ecologists believe that "human domination and degradation of nature arises out of social patterns of domination and hierarchy, patterns of social life in which some humans exercise control or domination over others."[68] Environmental and ecological destruction is therefore best understood as a form of human domination, and the more hierarchical and oppressive the nature of a society, the more likely that it will abuse and dominate the environment.

The ecological society can therefore only attain "its truth, its self actualization, in the form of richly articulated, mutualistic networks of people based on community."[69] This approach proposes the decentralization of industrial society into smaller, highly self-sufficient, and communal units, working with "intermediate technologies that are based on an understanding of the laws of ecology."[70] The aim is the creation of healthy, self-reliant societies that exercise local control, take responsibility for their environment, operate a local economy based on minimal levels of material goods and the maximum use of human resources. This logic suggests the creation of buildings that embody and express the notion of a social and ecological community in which democratic values such as full participation and freedom are the norm. It promotes the notion of building as home and seeks to challenge the feelings of alienation attached to many examples of modern architecture. It is exemplified by Dick Russell's suggestion that "we need a building metaphor that somehow encapsulates the idea of co-operative community, of a responsibility toward the earth and each other that we have abandoned."[71] Here, ethical concerns stem from the creation of buildings that have the potential to help us forge a sense of individual and collective identity. The design approach aims to express the organic formation of society with links to the natural locality within which communities are developed; and through these links, we will become more aware of our impact on the environment. The strategy deriving from this logic is as much social as technical and aesthetic, and it highlights the political issue of democratic control over technology and expertise. There is a concern for the use of "appropriate technologies," which according to Pepper, "are democratic [because] unlike high technology they can be owned, understood, maintained and used by individuals … not just a minority of 'expert' men."[72] This contrasts with the black-box anonymity of many complex building technologies, and here, the vision of building is one of an enabling, transparent, participatory process that is adapted to, and grounded within, particular local ecological conditions. Contemporary architectural approaches range from the participatory design processes utilized by Lucien Kroll in Belgium and Ralph Erskine in the U.K. to the self-build projects of Peter Hubner in Germany and a number of architects working with the Segal method in the U.K.[73] The aim throughout is to construct appropriate, flexible, and participatory buildings that serve the needs of occupiers without impacting on the environment unnecessarily by using renewable natural, recycled, and wherever possible, local materials. The vision of independent ecocommunities is more fully realized in a number of alternative communities throughout the world including the Findhorn Community in Scotland, Christiana Free City in Denmark, and Arcosanti in Arizona.

CONCLUSIONS: RECONSTRUCTING SUSTAINABLE ARCHITECTURE

In highlighting the contested nature of debates around sustainable architecture, our analysis raises significant questions about the positivistic scientific assumption underpinning the search for a consensual definition of sustainable architectural practice. We suggest that design debates and practice constitute sites of conflicting interpretations through which an often complex set of actors participate in a continuous process of defining and redefining the nature of the environmental problem itself. Debates about sustainable architecture are shaped by different social interests, based on different interpretations of the problem, and characterized by quite different pathways towards a range of sustainable futures. These competing environmental debates are not the result of uncertainty, but are due to the existence of *"contradictory certainties:* Severely divergent and mutually irreconcilable sets of convictions both about the environmental problems we face and the solutions that are available to us."⁷⁴ The analytical framework of social constructivist theory developed here and elsewhere usefully demonstrates the contingent and contextual nature of technological innovation and building design, and highlights the arguably most fundamental issue (understandably marginalized in the debate about consensus)—that the environment is a contested terrain, and that implicit within alternative technological strategies are distinct philosophies of environmental place making.⁷⁵ Environmental concerns are both time and space specific and are governed by a specific modeling of nature, this same "logic can be applied to technology and to sustainable architecture. In other words there is 'interpretative flexibility' attached to any artefact: It might be designed in another way."⁷⁶ This perspective points towards a multidirectional analytical model that recognizes how certain technological development pathways fade away, while others are "economically reinforced as members of a society come to share a set of meanings or benefits" attached to them.⁷⁷

Adopting a social constructivist perspective has critical implications for architectural practice, education, and research. Rather than searching for a singular optimal technological pathway, it is vital that we learn to recognize and listen to the number of voices striving to frame the debate and the visions they express of alternative environmental places. The search for consensus that has hitherto characterized sustainable design and policy making should be translated into the search for an enlarged context in which a more heterogeneous coalition of practices can be developed. In this sense, rather than viewing sustainable design practice as the "implementation of a plan for action, it should be viewed as an on-going transformational process in which different actor interests and struggles are located."⁷⁸

In an educational context, there is an opportunity to encourage greater reflectivity in architectural students by challenging the search for a true or incontestable, consensual definition of green buildings. If the future direction and success of sustainable architecture strategies relies on the abilities of architects to act as moral citizens by engaging in an open process of negotiation, criticism and debate, then it is vital that students are encouraged to become more sensitive to the range of possible logics of innovation that may surface in design practice. This means searching for critical methods for understanding technological innovation that transcend both instrumental and deterministic interpretations and that can begin to open "the discourse of technology to future designers in the hopes of engendering a more humane and multivocal world."⁷⁹ Multiple opinions and perspectives are not only valid but highly desirable. Further, once a diversity of possible approaches have been exposed "they might lead to a more reflective attitude towards certain environmental constructs and perhaps even the formulation of alternative scenarios."⁸⁰

Finally, we cannot ignore the ways in which particular logics of environmental innovation take root in commercial development practices. This means accepting that architecture is dependent on the contingent and dynamic strategies of those development actors with the power to implement their chosen design strategy. An important contribution of social constructivist analysis may lie in its ability to demonstrate how the power relations among competing development interests frame technological decision making and subsequent design strategies. An analysis of the changing power relationships structuring this process suggests an important future direction in research.⁸¹ Such research may help to identify those societal actors with most influence over decision making and enable practitioners and students to recognize their own position and role in the provision of more sustainable lifestyles. However, this may only be possible if, according to Hajer, "ecological politics could shed its prevailing techno-corporatist format and create open structures to determine what sort of nature and society we really want."⁸² In recognizing the socially contested nature of environmental design, we might begin to engage in a very different dialogue about sustainable architecture.

NOTES

1. Susan Maxman, "Shaking the Rafters," *Earthwatch* (July/Aug. 1993): 11.
2. Sara J. Cook and Bryn L. Golton, "Sustainable Development: Concepts and Practice in the Built Environment," *Sustainable Construction* CIB TG 16, (Nov. 1994): 677–685.
3. Graham Woodgate and Michael Redclift, "From a 'Sociology of Nature' to Environmental Sociology," *Environmental Values* 7 (1998): 2–24.
4. John Brennan, "Green Architecture: Style over Content," *Architectural Design* 67/1–2 (1997): 23–25.
5. Phil Macnaghton and John Urry, *Contested Natures* (London: Sage, 1998), p. 1.
6. Ibid., p. 9.
7. Cook and Golton, "Sustainable Development," p. 684.
8. John Hannigan, *Environmental Sociology: A Social Constructivist Perspective* (London: Routledge, 1995).
9. Hannigan, *Environmental Sociology*, p. 3.
10. See Marteen Hajer, *The Politics of Environmental Discourse* (Oxford: Oxford University Press, 1995), pp. 12–13, where the author suggests that, "the present hegemony of the idea of sustainable development in environmental discourse should not be seen as the product of a linear, progressive, and value-free process of convincing actors of the importance of the Green case. It is much more a struggle between various unconventional political coalitions, each made up of such actors as scientists, politicians, activists, or organisations representing such actors, but also having links with specific television channels, journals and newspapers, or even celebrities."
11. Steve Hatfield Dodds, "Pathways and Paradigms for Sustaining Human Communities," *Open House International* 24/1 (1999): 6–16.
12. Lisa Benton and John Short, *Environmental Discourse and Practice* (Oxford: Blackwell, 1999), p. 2. We share Benton and Short's definition of environmental discourses as "explanations of the world around us. They are deep structures which pattern thought, belief and practices, and allow us to understand why human-environmental relationships take the forms they do."
13. This analysis derives partly from an earlier analysis that interprets each logic in terms of their competing ethical perspectives. See Simon Guy and Graham Farmer, "Contested Constructions: The Competing Logics of Green Buildings and Ethics," in Warwick Fox, ed., *The Ethics of the Built Environment* (London: Routledge, 2000). We would like to acknowledge the contribution of Suzie Osborn to the literature review.
14. Hajer, *The Politics of Environmental Discourse*, p. 44.
15. Benton and Short, *Environmental Discourse and Practice*, p. 2
16. Hajer, *The Politics of Environmental Discourse*, p. 19–20.
17. Ibid., p. 20.
18. Cook and Golton, "Sustainable Development," p. 677.
19. Gert Spaargaren and Arthur P. J. Mol, "Sociology, Environment and Modernity: Ecological Modernisation as a Theory of Social Change," *Society and Natural Resources* 5 (1992): 323–344.
20. Hajer, *Environmental Discourse*, p. 14.
21. This definition of sustainability stems from the World Commission on Environment and Development (WCED). See *Our Common Future* (New York: Oxford University Press, 1987), p. 42.

22. Andrew Blowers, "Environmental Policy: Ecological Modernisation or the Risk Society?," *Urban Studies* 34/5–6 (1996): 853.
23. Spaargaren and Mol, "Sociology, Environment and Modernity," p. 335.
24. See Catherine Slessor, *Eco-Tech: Sustainable Architecture and High Technology* (London: Thames and Hudson, 1997).
25. Victor Papenak, *The Green Imperative: Ecology and Ethics in Design and Architecture* (London: Thames and Hudson, 1995), p. 46.
26. Hatfied Dodds, "Pathways and Paradigms," p. 7.
27. See James Lovelock, *The Ages of Gaia: A Biography of Our Living Earth*, (Oxford: Oxford University Press, 1989).
28. Aldo Leopold, *A Sand County Almanack* (New York: Oxford University Press, 1949), pp. 223–224.
29. John Farmer, *Green Shift: Towards a Green Sensibility in Architecture* (Oxford: WWF, 1996), pp. 172.
30. William Braham, "Correalism and Equipoise: Observations on the Sustainable," *Architectural Research Quarterly* 3/1 (1999): 57–63.
31. Wolfgang Sachs, "Sustainable Development and the Crisis of Nature: On the Political Anatomy of an Oxymoron," in Franck Fischer and Maarten Hajer, eds., *Living With Nature: Environmental Politics as Cultural Discourse* (Oxford: Oxford University Press, 1999), pp. 23–41.
32. William Rees and Mathis Wackernagel, *Our Ecological Footprint: Reducing Human Impact on the Earth* (Canada: New Society Publishers, 1996).
33. Steve Curwell and Ian Cooper, "The implications of urban sustainability," *Building Research and Information* 26/1 (1998):17–27.
34. For a full explanation of the theory of ecological footprints see Rees and Wackernagel, *Our Ecological Footprint*, pp. 7–30.
35. See Brenda Vale, *The Autonomous House: Design and Planning for Self Sufficiency* (London: Thames and Hudson, 1975).
36. See Sumita Sinha, "Down to Earth Buildings," *Architectural Design* 67 (1997): 90–93.
37. James Wines, "The architecture of ecology," *The Amicus Journal* (Summer 1993): 23.
38. See Richard Storm, *In Search of Heaven on Earth: A History of the New Age* (London: Bloomsbury Press, 1991).
39. David Pepper, *Modern Environmentalism: An Introduction* (London: Routledge, 1996), p. 27.
40. Ibid., p. 296.
41. Charles Jencks, *The Architecture of the Jumping Universe: How Complexity Science is Changing Architecture and Culture* (London: Academy Editions, 1995), p. 9.
42. Peter Russell, *The Awakening Earth: The Global Brain* (London: Arkana, 1991), p. 226.
43. John Passmore, *Man's Responsibility for Nature* (New York: Scribner's, 1974), p. 189.
44. James Wines, "Passages: The Fusion of Architecture and Landscape in the Recent Work of SITE," *Architectural Design* 67 (1997): 32–37.
45. Jencks, *The Architecture of the Jumping Universe*, p. 94.
46. Ibid., pp. 94–96.
47. Ibid., p. 9.
48. Ibid., pp. 96–136.
49. Kenneth Frampton, *Modern Architecture: A Critical History* (London: Thames and Hudson, 1985), p. 317.
50. Arne Naess, "Deep Ecology and Ultimate Premises," *The Ecologist* 18/4–5 (1988): 128–131.

51. Arne Naess, "Sustainable Development and the Deep Ecology Movement," Proceedings of the European Consortium for Political Research Conference, *The Politics of Sustainable Development in the European Union,* University of Crete (1994): 1.
52. Roger Talbot, "Alternative Future or Future Shock," *Alt'ing,* (Mar. 1996): 10–14.
53. Faozi Ujam and Fionn Stevenson, "Structuring Sustainability," *Alt'ing,* (Mar. 1996): 45–49.
54. Ibid., p. 49.
55. Isabelle Lanthier and Lawrence Olivier, "The Construction of Environmental Awareness," in Eric Darier, ed., *Discourses of the Environment* (Oxford: Blackwell, 1999), p. 65.
56. Ibid., p. 76.
57. Ulrich Beck, "From Industrial Society to the Risk Society: Questions of Survival, Social Structure and Ecological Enlightenment," *Theory, Culture and Society* 9 (1992): 97–123.
58. Sachs, "Sustainable Development and the Crisis of Nature," p. 40.
59. Sick building syndrome is a term used to describe a set of commonly occurring symptoms that affect people at their place of work, usually in office type environments. These include headaches, fatigue, irritation to the eyes, nose, and skin, a dry throat, and nausea.
60. David Pearson, "Making Sense of Architecture," *The Architectural Review* No. 1136 (Oct. 1991): 68–69.
61. See Simon Guy and Elizabeth Shove, "From Shelter to Machine: Remodeling Buildings for a Changing Environment," *Proceedings of the World Conference of Sociology,* Biederfeld, Germany (July 1994).
62. Dean Hawkes, *The Environmental Tradition: Studies in the Architecture of the Environment* (London: E&Fn Spon, 1996), p. 17.
63. See for example, Alfred Zamm and Robert Gannon, *Why Your House May Endanger Your Health* (New York: Simon and Schuster, 1980) and Debra Lynn Dadd, *The Non-Toxic Home* (Los Angeles: Jeremy P. Tarcher, 1986).
64. See Christopher Day, *Places of the Soul: Architecture and Environmental Design as a Healing Art* (London: Thorsons, 1995).
65. Pearson, "Making Sense of Architecture," p. 68–69.
66. David Pearson, *The Natural House Book* (London: Conran Octopus, 1991), p. 26.
67. Murray Bookchin, *The Modern Crisis* (Philadelphia: New Society Publishers, 1986), p. 59.
68. Joseph R. Des Jardins, *Environmental Ethics: An Introduction to Environmental Philosophy* (Belmont: Wadsworth, 1993) p. 240.
69. Bookchin, *The Modern Crisis,* p. 59.
70. Hajer, *The Politics of Environmental Discourse,* p. 85.
71. Dick Russell, "Ecologically Sound Architecture Gains Ground," *The Amicus Journal* (Summer 1993): 14–17.
72. Pepper, *Modern Enviromentalism: An Introduction,* p. 36.
73. The Segal method is a self-build timber-frame construction system developed by architect Walter Segal. For an introduction see Charlotte Ellis, "Walter's Way," *The Architectural Review* 1081 (Mar. 1987): 77–85.
74. Hannigan, *Environmental Sociology,* p. 30.
75. On the contingent and contextual nature of technological innovation and building design, see Steven A. Moore, "Technology and the Politics of Sustainability at Blueprint Demonstration Farm," *Journal of Architectural Education,* 51/1 (1997): 23–31. For arguments that the environment is a contested terrain, see, for example, Simon Guy and Simon Marvin, "Understanding Sustainable Cities: Competing Urban Futures," *European Urban and Regional Studies* 6/3 (1999): 268–275.
76. Moore, *Technology and the Politics of Sustainability,* p. 25.
77. Ibid., p. 25.

78. Norman Long and Ann Long, *Battlefields of Knowledge: The Interlocking of Theory and Practice in Social Research and Development* (London: Routledge, 1992), p. 9.
79. Barbara L. Allen, "Rethinking Architectural Technology: History, Theory, and Practice," *Journal of Architectural Education,* 51/1(1997): 2–4.
80. Maarten Hajer, "Ecological Modernisation," in Scott Lash, Bronislaw Szerszynski, and Brianne Wynne, eds., *Risk, Environment and Modernity: Towards a New Ecology* (London: Sage, 1996), p. 258.
81. Simon Guy, "Developing Alternatives: Energy, Offices and the Environment," *International Journal of Urban and Regional Research,* 22/2 (1998): 264–82.
82. Hajer, *Environmental Discourse,* p. 294.

32 Post-Occupancy Evaluation: Issues and Implementation

Craig Zimring

This article provides a historical overview of Post Occupancy Evaluations and their application in a variety of governmental and business contexts and reflects on some of the reasons of their rather limited utilization.

The United States is conducting the largest federal construction program since the Second World War, constructing some 160 new courthouses at the cost of $10 billion. After each project is completed, a post-occupancy evaluation team administers surveys, conducts interviews and observes activity in the building. These POEs are used to refine the *U.S. Courts Design Guide*, the document that has become the key document for judges, architects, project managers, and consultants in planning new courthouses (Administrative Office of the U.S. Courts, 1997).

Disney evaluates everything, all the time. The company assesses the experience of customers as they use the parks and other attractions, monitors the relationships between key design decisions and performance—such as how wide Main Street needs to be to feel comfortably busy during normal attendance levels—and records the performance of thousands of materials and products. The result is that the industrial engineering team can rapidly turn design goals into physical parameters. As a result, they have become key partners with the Imagineering group in planning and designing new properties (Weis, personal communication, March, 1999).

A group of UK architectural researchers and building scientists have teamed up with the *Building Services Journal* to conduct four evaluations annually of innovative sustainable office buildings. The buildings are published in the magazine when they are first opened and then evaluated three years later. Each evaluation involves questionnaires with users and technical assessment of energy use and building performance. The researchers have developed a growing set of benchmarks and the performances of individual buildings are reported with respect to the results for a large sample of similar buildings (Cohen, Standeven, Bordass, & Leaman, 2001a).

Postoccupancy evaluation (POE) grew out of the extraordinary confluence of interests among social scientists, designers, and planners in the 1960s and 1970s (see for example, Friedman, Zimring, & Zube, 1978; Preiser, Rabinowitz, & White, 1988; Shibley, 1982). Robert Bechtel has estimated that over 50,000 POEs have been completed; a recent Web search on *Google* turned

Craig Zimring, Robert B. Bechtel, Arza Churchman, & Arzah Ts'erts'man, eds., "Post-Occupancy Evaluation," from *Handbook of Environmental Psychology*, pp. 306–322. Copyright © 2002 by John Wiley & Sons. Permission to reprint granted by the publisher.

up over 2,700 sites that mention "postoccupancy evaluation" by name. Whereas many POEs are conducted as academic studies, numerous large public agencies have developed POE programs, such as the U.S. General Services Administration, Administrative Office of the U.S. Courts, U.S. Department of State, U.S. Department of Commerce, U.S. Postal Service, Public Works Canada, California Department of Corrections, State of Minnesota, the government of New Zealand, and many others. The California Department of General Services is starting a large POE program and the European Community is initiating an effort called IANUS, linking building evaluation to the provision of public services and focusing on the specification of indicators that show the diversity of interests and perspectives related to different actors in policy-related built-environment evaluation (Symes & Robbins, 2001). The U.S. National Research Council's Federal Facilities Council recently conducted a symposium on POE in the federal sector (Stanley & Little, 2001). And, although they do not always call them "postoccupancy evaluations," many private clients have initiated programs where they systematically assess building performance.

POEs are conducted by a wide range of practitioners for many different purposes, and there is no common definition. I propose the following definition of POE, based on Weiss' (1997) definition of *program* evaluation. However, for this chapter I will adapt for POE the definition that Weiss proposed for program evaluation more generally (Weiss, 1997):

> *Post-occupancy evaluation* is the *systematic* assessment of the process of delivering buildings or other designed settings or of the *performance* of those settings as they are actually used, or both, as compared to a set of *implicit or explicit standards,* with the intention of *improving* the process or settings.

There are five key aspects of this definition:

1. By *systematic* I mean that the POE follows an explicit, accepted methodology developed for POE or derived from social science, building science, architecture, planning, or another discipline. This can be quantitative or qualitative.
2. Although POEs have often evaluated buildings, they may also evaluate the details of the *process* of building delivery, including planning, programming, design, value engineering, construction, facilities management, and reuse.
3. POEs assess buildings while they are actually in use and, hence, evaluators can assess performance. POE complements other practices such as programming, building modeling, preoccupancy evaluation, and others.
4. Performance standards are not always explicit. They might be implicit and embedded in the methodology used in the evaluation, but they are taken to be objective, or at least *intrasubjective* in the sense that they are shared. Most evaluators view performance as multidimensional, reflecting the needs or perspectives of a range of stakeholders, such as the organization that occupies the building and the individuals who use or are affected by the building. (The relationship among different performance standards is often a key aspect of POEs, such as understanding and reconciling first cost with life cycle cost, or first cost with user satisfaction.)
5. I am reserving the term *postoccupancy evaluation* for applied studies. Although POE projects might well yield conceptual understanding and some researchers label their theoretically driven field studies "POE," this blurs the focus of POE, which is ultimately aimed at improving the built environment.

(However, I do argue that POE needs to be based on theories of building function and theories of organizational learning and change. This is explored further in the Discussion section.)

This chapter focuses on the last issue: how POE has contributed to improved buildings and building delivery processes. I focus on the distinction between two different kinds of applications of POEs: evaluations that are aimed at supporting a specific project (usually the project being evaluated, though sometimes another project) versus evaluations that are aimed at informing future projects (Zimring & Reizenstein, 1981). I emphasize this latter "feed-forward" role of POE, which has not received as much discussion as the project support role (Horgen, Joroff, Porter, & Schon, 1996; Schneekloth & Shibley, 1995).

I pay particular attention to the potential difficulties faced by large building delivery organizations when using POE for organizational learning. Because the building industry is extremely fragmented among many small clients, design firms, consultants, and contractors, the relatively few large public and private organizations can have a disproportionately significant impact on the quality of buildings.

BACKGROUND

The following section provides a brief introduction to POE. More detailed discussions can be found elsewhere, such as Friedman *et al.* (1978); Grannis (1994); Horgen *et al.* (1996); Kincaid (1994); Parshall and Peña (1983); Preiser, Rabinowitz, and White (1988); Preiser and Schramm (1997); and Shibley, (1982).

HISTORY, TERMS, GOALS, AND METHODS

POE initially developed quickly as a result of the growth of environment and behavior research—pursued by social scientists, designers, and planners who were interested in understanding the experience of building users and in representing the "non-paying" client (Zeisel, 1975). Early POEs were primarily conducted by academicians focusing on the settings that were accessible to them, such as housing, college dorms, and residential institutions (Preiser, 1994). During the 1980s, many large public agencies established more structured processes to organize information and decisions in their building delivery processes. As practices such as facilities programming became regularized and were accepted as routine, agencies such as Public Works Canada and the U.S. Postal Service added building evaluation as a further step in gathering and managing information (Kantrowitz & Farbstein, 1996).

This development of POE occurred while program evaluation was also rapidly growing. Campbell and many others had been arguing at least since the 1960s that public programs could be treated as social experiments and that rational, technical means could contribute to, or even replace, messier political decision making (Campbell, 1999). A similar argument was applied to POE, where statements of expected performance embedded in architectural programs could be viewed as hypotheses that POE could test (Preiser *et al.*, 1988).

Terminology

The term *postoccupancy evaluation* was intended to reflect that assessment takes place after the client has taken occupancy of a building. This was in direct contrast to some design competitions where completed buildings were disqualified from consideration and to other kinds of assessment such as "value engineering" that reviewed plans before construction. Over the years many theorists and practitioners have grown uncomfortable with the term *POE*. The literal meaning of the term seems to suggest that it occurs after people leave the building, and it seems to emphasize evaluation done at a single point in the process. Friedman *et al.* (1978) proposed the term *environmental design evaluation*. Other researchers and practitioners have suggested terms such as *environmental audits* or *building-in-use assessment* (Vischer, 1996). More recently, *building evaluation* and *building performance evaluation* have been proposed (Baird, Gray, Isaacs, Kernohan, & McIndoe, 1996). Despite the diversity of the practice, the term *postoccupancy evaluation* remains common for historical reasons, and I use it in this chapter for clarity.

The Scope of POE

Some researchers have argued that POE is only one component of an information- and negotiation-based approach to design decision making. For example, Bechtel has emphasized the importance of "preoccupancy evaluation" (Bechtel, personal communication, March 2000). Other authors have suggested that POE cannot be meaningfully discussed as a stand-alone practice but rather needs to be considered as one aspect of approaches that include "place-making" (Schneekloth & Shibley, 1995) and "process architecture" (Horgen, Joroff, Porter, & Schon, 1999). (These are discussed later in the chapter.)

There have been several successful examples where POE has been incorporated into a broader program of user-based programming, discussion, and design guide development (Shibley, 1982). For example, the U.S. Army Corps of Engineers initiated an ambitious program of programming and evaluation that resulted in some 19 design guides for facilities ranging from drama and music centers to barracks, and military police stations (Schneekloth & Shibley, 1995; Shibley, 1982, 1985). More recently, POE has been seen as part of a spectrum of practices aimed at understanding design criteria, predicting the effectiveness of emerging designs, reviewing completed designs, and supporting building activation and facilities management (Preiser & Schramm, 1997).

POE METHODS

As POE methods have become more sophisticated, at least two directions have emerged: (1) methods have become more diverse, and (2) standard methods packages have been developed.

Greater Diversity of Methods

With a few notable exceptions, many early POEs primarily focused on assessing user satisfaction, user assessment of building comfort and functionality, and user behavior using self-report methods such as questionnaires and interviews and direct observation of user behavior. More recent POEs now also assess the technical performance of building systems, cost, and other factors (Bordass & Leaman, 1996; Cohen, Standeven, Bordass & Leaman, 2001a, 2001b; Leaman, Cohen, & Jackman, 1995; Raw, Roys, & Leaman, 1990). Recently, Judith Heerwagen has suggested that

POEs should employ a "balanced scorecard" approach that considers issues such as financial performance, impact of the building on the business process, growth and satisfaction of employees, and impact on other stakeholders (Heerwagen, 2001). The balanced scorecard approach is discussed in more depth later in this chapter.

Developing Standardized Methods

Whereas most POEs assess the comfort and satisfaction of everyday building users, as POE methods have developed, more-standardized and specialized evaluation approaches have been developed for specific building types such as schools (Ornstein, 1997), health care facilities (Carpman & Grant, 1993), environments for young children (Moore, personal communication, July 2000), retail settings (Foxall & Hackett, 1994; Underhill, 1999), housing (Anderson & Weidemann, 1997), and jails and prisons (Wener, Farbstein, & Knapel, 1993; Zimring, Munyon, & Ard, 1988). Not surprisingly, evaluation of the white-collar work environment has been one of the most active areas for evaluation (Brill, Margulis, Konar, Buffalo Organization for Social and Technological Innovation, & Westinghouse Furniture Systems, 1984; Cooper, 1992; Duffy, 1998; Francis, 1986; Ornstein, 1999; Raw *et al.*, 1990; Spreckelmeyer, 1993; Stokols, 1988; Wineman, 1986). For example, Vischer created a standardized building-in-use survey that assesses self-reported satisfaction, comfort, and productivity (Vischer, 1996).

Some researchers have also developed standardized methods for assessing technical performance of buildings such as thermal and energy performance. The "Post-occupancy Review of Buildings and their Engineering" (PROBE) studies described above employ standard questionnaire and technical assessment techniques (Bordass, Bromley, & Leaman, 1995; Cohen *et al.*, 2001a; Leaman *et al.*, 1995). The PROBE team has conducted some 18 evaluations of buildings that were published in the *Building Services Journal* as representing technically innovative buildings. Approximately three years after commissioning, the team returns to the buildings and administers a standard building-in-use user questionnaire and monitors the performance of the heating, ventilating, and air-conditioning system, records energy use, and conducts pressure tests and other measures. The evaluation criteria are part of the standard methods package and allow the team to make links between building design and outcomes. The PROBE team has identified several variables that are good predictors of satisfaction and self-reported productivity. For instance, they have found that issues such as floor plans that offer more access to windows and higher levels of personal control over lighting, heating, and noise are strong predictors of self-reported satisfaction. Other standardized evaluation methods focus on more specific aspects of technical performance, such as the revised office environment survey (ROES) questionnaire, which assesses occupants' response to indoor air quality (Raw, 1995, 2000). The ROES survey focuses on occupants' reports of health, comfort, and productivity. The scale has been used many times and has established norms.

POE MODELS

POE methodologists have proposed several methodological and conceptual models of POE. For example, several authors have emphasized the importance of articulating different levels of POEs with different amounts of activity and resource requirements (Friedman *et al.*, 1978; Preiser *et al.*, 1988). In his influential book, Preiser advocated three levels of POEs: brief indicative studies, more-detailed investigative POEs, and diagnostic studies aimed at correlating environmental measures with subjective user responses (Preiser et al., 1988).

Although there have not been many theories of POE, many authors have used broader conceptual frameworks to organize their work. Some years ago, Friedman et al. (1978) suggested that POEs adopt an open systems framework that identifies a "focal problem" and "larger system" based on considering relationships among five elements of building delivery processes: building, users, design process, proximate-environmental context, and social-historical context. Preiser suggested that POE evaluation criteria be based on a habitability framework and has recently expanded this to include a focus on building performance evaluation and universal design (Preiser, 1994; Preiser & Schramm, 1997). As was mentioned earlier, Heerwagen has recently proposed that Kaplan and Norton's balanced scorecard approach (Kaplan & Norton, 1996) can be used in POE (Heerwagen, 2001). The balanced scorecard approach is a multistep process where organizational vision and strategy are translated into goals and objectives with quantifiable targets. The balanced scorecard is "balanced" in that it includes both financial and nonfinancial outcomes and focuses on both routine processes and "breakthrough" performance. Heerwagen has suggested that a balanced POE scorecard can focus on several outcomes: financial, business process, internal staff and professional development, and external stakeholders.

Recently, several authors have criticized approaches to building delivery and evaluation that emphasize standardization and accumulation of information. Rather, they argue that each decision-making process must be socially constructed by the participants. For example, Schneekloth and Shibley (1995) have proposed a dialogic "placemaking" process where a highly interactive process of building design and evaluation can help transform organizations and groups. They argue that programming, design, and evaluation can help organizations develop and change but only if consultants genuinely understand the values and perspectives of stakeholders rather than approaching projects with a preexisting model of correct solutions or approaches. For example, Schneekloth and Shibley have conducted many projects for the same large bank. Each of these has been different because the different participants in each project bring their own needs, values, and power relationships.

Horgen and her colleagues adopt a somewhat similar framework in their discussion of "process architecture" (Horgen et al., 1999). They criticize the prevailing "technical rational" approach to architecture and design and emphasize that the design process can be like a game where the role of consultants and evaluation is to help players clarify the impact of different moves for different players.

In sum, whereas many researchers are advancing the field by proposing specialized or standard methods that focus on a specific building type, others are suggesting that POE is most effective in a discursive framework that is different for each project.

SUMMARY

POE has become more diverse as it has developed. POEs now include a wider range of practices and have become embroiled in the larger debates about the development of knowledge and methods in the social sciences and humanities. However, as was discussed earlier, POE is by definition an applied practice, and it is not clear that it has always had the salutary impacts that were intended. Several large organizations have suspended their POE programs and many design practitioners discount their value. The following sections focus on the impacts POE has had on and particularly the roles that POE has had in individual and organizational learning.

LEARNING FROM POE

POE can both benefit a specific project and contribute to a more general knowledge base of lessons learned (Preiser *et al.*, 1988; Shibley, 1982; Zimring, 1981). The next sections discuss these potential impacts in greater detail.

Project-Based Learning

POE can help clarify important decisions about the project that is being evaluated or can contribute to the programming or design for a subsequent project. At least five kinds of project-based decisions have emerged as important in POE: (1) fine-tuning, (2) diagnosing how to aid a troubled or problematic setting, (3) deciding whether to expand the scope of an innovative design or technology, (4) deciding how to address a key "strategic" programmatic decision, (5) maintaining quality such as by incentives for performance.

Fine-Tuning

The immediate experience of a new building can have a significant impact on the subsequent satisfaction of users and their organization. Small irritants can have a large and lasting influence. POE has recently been used as a way of understanding the move-in process and helping reduce problems and misfits. For example, project managers in Santa Clara County (CA) were tired of getting a storm of requests from building users when they initially moved in. In some cases, a few weeks' use of the building clarified how people would use their spaces, and they asked for additional small items such as extra shelves or bulletin boards. In other cases, there were problems with construction or the organization changed over the course of design and construction, and the space needed to be reconfigured to fit different patterns of use.

These requests came on an ad hoc basis and were difficult to direct to contractors, suppliers, and others. Santa Clara County contracted with consultants Cheryl Fuller and Craig Zimring to create a "quick response survey" (QRS) aimed at organizing and prioritizing user needs about three months after buildings were occupied. All building users fill out a one-page questionnaire, and project managers follow up with a half-day walk-through interview of the building with the facility manager and staff representatives. The project managers would then prioritize requests and meet with the client organizations. The State of California Department of General Services is further developing the QRS and will have evaluators enter results into a lessons-learned database.

POE as Diagnosis

Occasionally a building is the subject of complaints or controversy; a POE can help to diagnose the source of problems and prioritize solutions. For example, the new San Francisco central library was an architectural landmark when it opened in 1996 but aroused controversy. The project had been controversial since its inception—books were displaced to make room for computers, a hotly debated decision in the library community—but there were complaints by the public that it was hard to find books and other services and by staff that it was difficult to manage materials. As a result, the mayor appointed an audit commission that recommended a POE, led by architect Cynthia Ripley and accompanied by a blue-ribbon evaluation team including the director of the Los Angeles library system. After conducting focus groups with staff and users, observing the use of the facility, and analyzing records, the POE team found a number of serious problems. The configuration of the spaces made operations difficult. Related books were scattered among several buildings and much staff time was spent finding and retrieving them and some were damaged in transit. Poor signage and a confusing layout made it hard for users to find their way. The report commended the architecture but recommended a targeted $30 million multiphase renovation project to reorganize the book stacks and interiors (Flagg, 1999; Ripley Architects, 2000).

In another example, the architecture firm Hugh Stubbins and Associates was receiving complaints about a recently completed office building that they had designed. The offices were stuffy and hot. They conducted a POE and discovered that the ductwork had never been connected by the heating contractors, and they were able to resolve the problems to the client's satisfaction (Zimring & Welch, 1988).

In Ottawa a group of white-collar workers walked out of a large government office building, complaining that the building was "sick." Public Works Canada commissioned a very in-depth evaluation, including detailed interviews, questionnaires, and monitoring of air quality and lighting. The study showed that the workers' complaints were justified—the air quality was poor in some locations because of interior partitions that were added after the ventilating system was designed—but that many complaints were also due to other environmental qualities such as confusing layouts as well as building management and organizational factors (Vischer, 1996).

Using POE to Test Innovation

Evaluation can help decide whether innovative buildings or building components considered for broader application. For example, the State of Minnesota Department of Natural Resources (DNR) has recently changed the way in which it manages the environment. Rather than organizing their staff by discipline, they now use a matrix management system where decisions are made by a multidisciplinary group organized by ecosystem. The DNR is creating new regional centers that include wildlife biologists, air and water specialists, and others concerned with a given area. The centers are intended to encourage multidisciplinary collaboration and to be sustainable, with low energy use and low environmental impact. The DNR contracted with a university team led by Julia Robinson to evaluate two of the initial projects. Though the centers were generally successful, the team made numerous recommendations for retrofitting and for subsequent designs. When the budget request was made for the third center, the POE report was included as an appendix, resulting in full funding of a new project for the first time in DNR's history. DNR was told that the POE was a major reason: It showed a high level of understanding of the project. Though apparently successful, this project showed some of the tensions between POEs conducted by external consultants and by internal staff. An external evaluation can bring specialized POE skills and greater objectivity, but the results can sometimes be viewed as not addressing the needs of internal staff. In this project there was some concern by the internal staff about the sustainability recommendations. An additional team was hired to create design guidelines in close consultation with staff (Wallace, 2000).

Using POE to Support Strategic Decisions

Some design decisions are strategic in the sense that they influence many later decisions within a project. These are important targets of POE. For example, the California Department of Corrections (CDC) was considering adopting the practice of having two prison housing units share a common dining room and kitchen. This concept could save many millions of dollars statewide but might lead to greater difficulty in moving and controlling inmates. The CDC and the firm that was hired to manage the prison construction program, Kitchell CEM, performed a POE of a first example of the shared dining facility, interviewing staff and observing operations. The evaluation revealed that this shared arrangement worked well, and it was repeated several times in California (Fuller, 1988).

Whereas this POE, as with most others, focuses on how well strategic decisions achieve an accepted set of goals—what Argyris and Schon (1978) have called "single-loop learning,"—POE can also be used to examine the goals themselves, what has been termed "double-loop learning" (Argyris & Schon, 1978). For example, Zimring, Munyon, and Ard (1988) evaluated an innovative jail in Martinez, California, where inmate and guards spent all of their time in small housing units that included dining and exercise areas. In this case, the "strategic decision" was to decentralize services and bring food, visitors, and education to inmates rather than moving the inmates. The study included single-loop learning—how well the facility supported existing goals of high control and low maintenance—as well as considering how a less stressful facility can help shift the goals of incarceration toward rehabilitation rather than simply supporting custody or punishment.

Maintaining Quality

POE is sometimes used to maintain quality control. For example, the drug company Ciba-Geigy contracted with the architecture-engineering firm HLW and the contractor Sordoni Skansa Construction to put their design and construction profits ($300,000 and $1.2 million) at risk for the new $39 million Martin Dexter Laboratory in Tarrytown, NY. The profits were based equally on three issues: (1) the ability of the firms to deliver the building as scheduled, (2) their ability to deliver the building within the original budget, and (3) postoccupancy evaluation. The POE was based on responses to 14 survey questions concerning the following issues: HVAC, acoustics, odor control, vibration, lighting, fume hood performance, quality of construction (finishes), building appearance, and user-friendliness. The questions were binary choice (acceptable/not acceptable), and the building had to reach 70% satisfaction to pass the test. Some aspects such as sound transmission were also assessed using physical measures; if the user satisfaction measures didn't reach criterion, physical measures could be substituted (Gregerson, 1997). The designers and contractors consulted the scientists throughout the process, showing them alternatives of the facade design and full-scale mockups of the range hoods. The building passed on all criteria except satisfaction with the range hoods, which were modified after the evaluation as a response to user input. Sordoni Skansa has since used POE in several other projects.

Decision-focused evaluation as part of a design project can be performed in an attempt to rationalize decision making by shifting the criteria for decisions from politics to data: Which decision is likely to have the best outcome? However, as the Ciba-Geigy example illustrates, an equally important role of POE can be to set up a framework for discussion and negotiation that leads to greater clarity about goals and consensual strategies for building design.

POE as Organizational Learning

POE provides the opportunity for organizational learning about buildings. By *organizational learning*, I mean that organizations are able to constantly improve routine activities, such as more efficiently providing higher-quality standard office space for a white-collar work organization, and to respond to change quickly and effectively when needed (Argyris, 1992a). Learning is organizational if it concerns the core mission of the organization and is infused through the organization rather than residing in a few individuals.

For example, since the 1970s Disney Corporation has been evaluating everything it does. Disney has at least three evaluation programs and three corresponding databases: (1) They keep track of the performance of materials and equipment and record their findings in a technical database; (2) the guest services group interviews guests about facilities and services and records predictors of Disney's "key business drivers"—the intention to return; (3) a 40-person industrial engineering team conducts continuous research that is aimed at refining guidelines and rules of thumb. The industrial engineering team explores optimal conditions: When does Main Street feel pleasantly crowded but not oppressive? When are restrooms full without undue waiting? When are gift shops most productive? This research allows Disney to make direct links between "inputs," such as the proposed number of people entering the gates, to "outputs" such as the width of Main Street.

The Disney databases are not formally linked together but are used extensively during design and renovation projects. They have been so effective that the senior industrial engineer works as an equal with the Imagineering project manager during the programming of major new projects.

Disney's evaluation process is quite rare. It uses an evaluation program to do four processes that are key to organizational learning (Huber, 1991):

1. Monitoring changes in the internal and external business environment and assessing performance
2. Interpreting and discussing the implications of results
3. Consolidating results into an organizational memory
4. Widely distributing findings and conclusions

While POE potentially provides a methodology for all four of these processes, POE practice has historically focused on case studies and supporting decision making for individual projects rather than for more general lessons learned. Even when evaluators have been able to create databases of findings, they have often been used to benchmark single cases rather than to develop more-general conclusions.

Furthermore, organizational learning is hard to do. Most organizations spend a great deal of effort taking control of their environment and maintaining stability by doing things such as setting up functional divisions, establishing reporting arrangements, and creating policies that govern behavior, most organizations are much poorer at fostering learning and at nurturing the change that often results from learning. Learning requires the will to collect data about performance and the time to interpret and draw conclusions from it. To learn we have to expose mistakes so we can improve: Most organizations don't reward the exposure of shortcomings.

In a recent survey, Thierry Rosenheck and I examined the materials from some 18 POE programs, and wherever possible interviewed participants, to see if organizational learning had occurred and, if so, to see how they were able to overcome these barriers. These findings are discussed in a somewhat different way in another paper (Zimring & Rosenheck, 2001); I summarize them here.

Is There Evidence That Organizations Actually Use POE to Learn?

In looking at organizations that have active POE programs, Rosenheck and I found that members of project teams, including project managers, consultants, and clients, tend not to be aware of POEs unless a special evaluation has been conducted to address a problem that the team is facing. Where they are aware of the POEs, team members often do not have the reports from past POEs at hand and do not use POE results in daily decision making.

Midlevel staff tend to be more aware of POE results, and particularly midlevel staff responsible for developing guidelines and standards. For example, in the U.S. Postal Service, the staff who maintain guidelines also administer POEs. The POEs conducted by the Administrative Office of the U.S. Courts are directly used by the Judicial Conference to test and update the U.S. Courts Design Guide.

We were not able to identify situations in which senior management used POEs for strategic planning. As was mentioned earlier, POEs have the potential for supporting double-loop learning (Argyris & Schon, 1978): for not only evaluating how to better achieve existing goals but also to reflect on whether the goals themselves need to be reconsidered. But we were not able to find cases in which this actually occurred.

We were not able to find many compilations of POE findings, although several organizations, including the U.S. Army Corps of Engineers, U.S. Postal Service, Administrative Office of the U.S. Courts, U.S. General Services Administration, and others, have incorporated POEs into design guides. Disney and the U.S. Department of State have incorporated POE into databases of information. These are discussed in more detail later.

It does appear that POEs are not used to their full potential for organizational learning. There are undoubtedly sometimes issues with the POEs themselves if they are not credible or well constructed, but there are also at least three organizational reasons for this:

1. Learning is fragile and difficult and many organizations have not created the appropriate conditions for it. If learning is to be genuinely "organizational," a wide variety of staff must have the opportunity to participate and to reflect on the results in a way that enables them to incorporate those results into their own practice. Potential participants must see the value for themselves; there must be incentives for being involved. Most significantly, organizations cannot punish people when POEs reveal problems with projects.
2. Many organizations simply do not make information available in a format that is clear and useful to decision makers.
3. Many organizations have not created a coherent, integrated body of knowledge that is helpful in everyday decision making. Knowledge tends to be informal and individual.

Ways to Create the Appropriate Conditions for Learning Through POE

Several organizations have overcome some of the difficulties in using POE to learn. They have used at least eight strategies: (1) Create opportunities for decision makers to participate and reflect; (2) provide access to knowledge for different audiences; (3) provide incentives; (4) reduce disincentives—create protected opportunities for innovation and evaluation; (5) reduce risk by upper management commitment; (6) focus on "learning moments;" (7) tie POE to strategic design decisions and key business drivers; (8) create organizational memory for precedents.

Create opportunities for participation and reflection by decision makers. Our research suggests that POE-based knowledge is not widely shared within most organizations. One way to achieve this sharing is through direct participation in evaluations. Seeing how a facility works and hearing directly from users make for a memorable experience. And, the process of analyzing and writing up the results of an evaluation can help decision makers reflect on the implications of the results and make links to their own practice.

A lessons-learned program initiated in 1997 for New York City to examine the success of school projects in the state was aimed at creating change by having the architects themselves involved with the POEs. The School Construction Authority (SCA), whose membership is appointed by the governor, the mayor, and the New York City Board of Education, was charged with the program. To get the program approved, SCA, under the leadership of consultant Ralph Steinglass, adopted a simple methodology: require the architect/engineer of record to conduct the POE. The rationale was that this would guarantee that designers would confront how users responded to their designs and force a lessons-learned loop in the design process. About 20 POEs have been completed. To ensure reliability, SCA reviewed the re-suits before approving the POEs. In some cases, the architects or engineers had to reschedule their interviews when they were suspected of introducing a bias or continue their investigation if they failed to include critical areas required in the study.

Provide access to knowledge for different audiences. Many organizations produce POEs as case study reports that are not widely distributed. Part of this may be due to the history of POE, which has focused on single case studies, and part may be due to the perceived disincentives to distributing information that might be seen as critical of internal efforts or individuals. Some of the problem is the simple technical difficulty of distributing printed information which has become easier with the Internet and intranet and virtual private networks. NASA makes its lessons-learned database available to all authorized staff and contractors. In the UK, the PROBE team has created an interactive Web site for the 18 buildings they have evaluated as part of the PROBE project (Bordass & Leaman, 1997).

Some organizations have overcome these impediments by creating design guides and databases of POE information. Agencies such as the Administrative Office of the U.S. Courts, the U.S. Postal Service, and the U.S. General Services Administration have created design guides that are broadly distributed.

The growth of multimedia databases has allowed organizations to distribute information more broadly. For example, the U.S. Department of State's Office of Foreign Buildings Operations (FBO) is responsible for the design and construction of U.S. posts overseas. From 1993 to 1999, FBO POE coordinator Thierry Rosenheck conducted 11 POEs of new embassies. The POEs were aimed at assessing both user response and technical performance of the buildings and building systems. Questionnaires, interviews, focus groups, site visits, and other measures were used to assess a wide range of issues, such as aesthetics, circulation, security, and maintainability. FBO contracted with Craig Zimring to develop an online database (called *LessonBase*) that consolidates all POE findings and makes them accessible for future decision making. The structure of LessonBase is aimed at confronting users with problematic situations that would cause them to reconsider their original assumptions or practices. LessonBase stories include problems, analyses of the problems, design or management solutions to the problems, and proposed guidelines or lessons for preventing the problems in the future. For example, while in many countries the ambassador's residence must be very secure, the use of institutional materials, equipment, and layouts has led to high cost and an unfriendly atmosphere. In one embassy, the ambassador initially refused to move into a multimillion-dollar facility. More careful attention to privacy and to a family setting can reduce problems and increase satisfaction.

One of the most popular features of LessonBase is the "Lessons-Learned" section where staff can add more informal lessons to the database. While LessonBase has not been fully implemented because of technical and management issues, it has been used in the planning of several new embassies and is being integrated into a comprehensive facilities management database called "Dr. Checks" developed by the U.S. Army Corps of Engineers.

Design projects represent many different professional cultures. Engineers tend to take a technical problem-solving approach. Architects are often interested in form and materials. Clients might be interested in the usability and experience of the building. Senior managers might be searching for help in setting strategic directions, whereas project managers might be interested in lessons learned about specific materials or equipment. Part of the challenge in creating any database or report is translating between these different professional cultures, and evaluators have not always been successful at doing this.

Provide incentives. The California Department of General Services is considering including the results of POEs as part of the review of qualifications when selecting consultants and contractors. Even the consideration of this idea has strongly increased architecture firms' interest in POEs. I am unaware of any POE programs that provide incentives for internal staff members to participate in evaluations, though several programs have discussed such incentives, such as providing a free vacation day as a reward for adding data to the knowledge base or providing a minisabbatical for participating in evaluations or lessons-learned programs. Disney provides a powerful, if indirect, incentive: knowledge. Only the industrial engineers have access to key POE data, and they then become valuable members of the design team.

Reduce disincentives: Create protected opportunities for innovation and evaluation. Organizational learning consultants have long pointed to an inherent contradiction in many organizations. Whereas most organizations espouse innovation and learning, they behave in ways that actively limit it. One example is a recent meeting between project managers and senior management in a large public organization. The organization had used an innovative building delivery strategy but were not familiar with it and had left out a key review step. When this became clear, a senior manager turned to the project manager and said, "We would have expected someone at your level to do better." The message to everyone in the room was clear: Avoid innovation and avoid evaluation! This syndrome—focusing on the individual rather than the performance, blaming the innovator rather than learning from the innovation—is pervasive among organizations (Argyris, 1992b; Argyris & Schon, 1978). However, some building delivery organizations have used POE to at least partially overcome it.

Some organizations have done this by explicitly sanctioning "research" with the attendant acknowledgment that innovations might not succeed. For example, the U.S. General Services Administration (GSA) Public Buildings Service has recently appointed a "Director of Research." The first director, Kevin Kampschroer, has a budget to conduct, synthesize, and distribute research, including POE. The use of the term *research* carries with it the understanding that not all efforts are successful and the budget provides some time for reflection about findings. To date, much of the research is conducted by academic consultants who bring outside learning into GSA. However, GSA is also looking at ways to broaden internal ownership of the research program.

GSA has also created an active "officing" laboratory in its own headquarters building. The lab, supervised by Kampschroer, is one floor of actual workspace that includes an innovative raised-floor heating, ventilating, and air-conditioning system and several brands of modular office furniture systems. It also explores design to support teamwork, with many small conference rooms and meeting areas. The workers are frequently surveyed and observed, and the lab also becomes a place where clients can see alternative office layouts.

The U.S. Courts and the U.S. General Services Administration Courthouse Management Group are considering developing a different kind of laboratory: a full-scale courtroom mockup facility where new courtroom layouts and technologies can be tested and refined at relatively low cost and risk. This facility, to be constructed at the Georgia Institute of Technology, would allow mock trials to be conducted and would provide training for judges, staff, and lawyers.

Another way to reduce the personal and organizational cost of experimentation is by starting small with projects that have an experimental component. The innovation can be evaluated and considered for broader adoption. For example, the U.S. Department of State Office of Foreign Buildings Operations (FBO) tries out innovations on a limited number of projects before rolling out the innovation to the larger organization. FBO has recently used building serviceability tools and methods (ST&M) (Davis & Szigeti, 1996) for programming and design review for the new embassies in Dar es Salaam and Nairobi.

In many organizations, it is risky to be the first one to try an innovation. Massachusetts Institute of Technology organizational consultant Edgar Schein has proposed that, though organizations may benefit greatly from consultants, they often find the experience of peers more helpful when they actually move to implementing an innovation. Schein has called for "learning consortia" where people can get advice from peers in other organizations and learn from their experience (Schein, 1995). He argues that, though such learning consortia may be effective at all levels of an organization, they are particularly effective among CEOs or upper-mid level managers.

Although the strategies described earlier—using prototypes, creating a laboratory, and developing a learning consortium—are quite different, all reduce the disincentives for innovation and evaluation by allowing innovation and evaluation at relatively low personal and organizational cost.

Reduce risk by securing upper management commitment. Participants in POE programs report that uncertainty about senior management's commitment to the program is a key disincentive to participation. A POE program takes 2 to 5 years to have an effect, and staff often have doubts about the depth and longevity of senior management's support. Support or lack of support can be manifest materially—through resources—as well as by more subtle means such as the use of POE in daily conversation, in performance reviews, and other ways.

Focus on "learning moments." The Administrative Office of the U.S. Courts (AO) conducts a POE program that informs design guidelines (the *U.S. Courts Design Guide*). However, the AO has achieved feed-forward by linking the design guide to a "strategic learning moment" in the development of court-houses: the negotiation between judges and the building agent (the U.S. General Services Administration) about the scope and quality level for new courthouses. In the early 1990s the U.S. government initiated the largest civilian construction program since the Second World War, projecting to spend over $10 billion on 160 new courthouses. (The creation of new judgeships in the 1980s, concerns for increased security, and new technologies necessitated new courthouses or major renovations.) However both the judiciary and GSA were being criticized by Congress for creating marble-clad "Taj Mahals." The AO initiated the POE program to identify necessary changes to the standards in the first edition of the *Design Guide,* to defend the judiciary against attack by documenting the efficacy of the design standards, and to inform the negotiation about issues such as the dimensions and materials of courtrooms and chambers. Information from

POEs was also used in training workshops for judges and staff who were becoming involved in new courthouse design and construction. This program is run by the AO, but the design guide is actually created and vetted by a committee of the Judicial Conference, the group that sets broad policy within the federal judiciary. This program is quite unusual: It is the only case that we are aware of where a POE and design guide are developed by a client organization that does not build its own buildings.

Tie POE to strategic design decisions and key business drivers. POE can be particularly successful in feedforward if it links strategic facilities decisions to the "key business drivers" of the client organization. The U.S. Army Corps of Engineers design guide and POE program was motivated by the shift to an all-volunteer army. Potential recruits said that the aging facilities were a significant impediment to recruiting and retention and the Army sought to renovate or rebuild many of its buildings (Shibley, 1985).

In the 1980s the newly privatized U.S. Postal Service (USPS) was losing customers to competitors such as FedEx and UPS (Kantrowitz & Farbstein, 1996). Focusing initially on the customer experience with lobbies, the USPS contracted with Min Kantrowitz and Jay Farbstein and Associates to conduct focus group evaluations. This has led to a large and continuing program of evaluations and design guide development. New concepts of post office design are developed, such as the retail-focused "postal store"; innovative projects are designed; the projects are evaluated; and the ideas are refined and then incorporated into design guides. This program has sustained an ongoing process of testing and refining the design guides through evaluation and experience. More recently, the USPS has de-emphasized on-site evaluations. According to POE manager Mark Nedzbala, most POEs now involve having facility managers fill out relatively brief mail-out surveys. Nedzbala has found that the open-ended responses to the questionnaire are often most valuable in refining the USPS's design guidelines because they are more specific than the scaled satisfaction responses.

Create organizational memory for precedents. A key part of organizational memory is simply knowing what the organization has done. Few building delivery organizations have good comprehensive databases that allow decision makers and clients to access past cases or to examine benchmarks. A potential use of POE is to consolidate such information and to tie it to evaluation.

CONCLUSIONS

A large number of POEs are being conducted, with a wide range of methods, goals, and heuristic frameworks. Some evaluators have created standard packages of methods, whereas others have argued that standardization can reduce the meaningfulness of evaluation and the ability of participants to take ownership of the results. Many evaluators have called for a broadening of the role of evaluation by focusing on its role in enabling a wide range of decisions about buildings and facilities management.

Despite the large number of POEs that have been conducted, POE has not had the impact that it could have on subsequent building delivery and management, partly because evaluators and their clients have not attended to the fit between POE and the organizational conditions that allow learning to go on. Though the goals of POE are inherently applied, part of this problem is actually a lack of *theory*. Somewhat adapting Weiss's model of program evaluation (Weiss, 1997), it is helpful to separate "evaluation implementation theory" from "setting operation theory." By *evaluation implementation theory* I mean a theory of action: how an organization or individual decision makers can implement the results of the POE. As was suggested earlier, this may range from creating design standards or guidelines to working intensively with a specific design team. Much of the previous section was devoted to beginning to sketch out a preliminary evaluation implementation theory and some actions based on this theory.

Much *setting operation theory*—theories about the links between design or process and other outcomes—has been only implicit in POE. However, several theories have begun to emerge. In their chapter in this volume focusing on space syntax, Peponis and Wineman present theories and evidence that the form of the environment interacts with issues such as culture, communication, movement, and wayfinding. Duffy has argued that one can link organizational characteristics, such as the number of professionals, to building characteristics, such as the length of the building perimeter that allows private cellular offices with windows (Duffy & Powell, 1997). Building serviceability tools and methods have adopted a similar approach by arguing that client requirements for office buildings can be defined in terms of some 100 scales about issues such as flexibility that are linked to specific building qualities (Davis & Szigeti, 1996).

An important role for environmental psychologists is to continue to develop both implementation and setting theories that can be incorporated into POE. Until this happens POE will continue to be a promising empirical exercise that all too often falls short of its potential.

REFERENCES

Administrative Office of the U.S. Courts. (1997). *U.S. Courts Design Guide.* Washington, DC: U.S. Government Printing Office.

Anderson, J. R., & Weidemann, S. (1997). Developing and utilizing models of residential satisfaction. In G. Moore & R. Marans (Eds.), *Advances in environment and behavior research and design* (Vol. 4, pp. 287–315). New York: Plenum Press.

Argyris, C. (1992a). *On organizational learning.* Cambridge, MA: Blackwell.

Argyris, C. (1992b). Teaching smart people how to learn. In C. Argyris (Ed.), *On organizational learning* (pp. 84–100). Cambridge, MA: Blackwell Business.

Argyris, C. & Schon, D. (1978). *Organizational learning.* Reading, MA: Addison-Wesley.

Baird, G., Gray, J., Isaacs, N., Kernohan, D., & McIndoe, G. (Eds.), (1996). *Building evaluation techniques.* New York: McGraw-Hill.

Bordass, W., Bromley, A., & Leaman, A. (1995). *Comfort, control and energy efficiency in offices.* Garston, England: Building Research Establishment.

Bordass, W., & Leaman, A. (1996). Future buildings and their services: Strategic considerations for designers and their clients. *Proceedings of the CIBSE/ASHRAE Joint National Conference, 1.*

Bordass, W., & Leaman, A. (1997). Future buildings and their services: Strategic considerations for designers and clients. *Building Research and Information,* 25(4), 190–195.

Brill, M., Margulis, S. T., Konar, E., Buffalo Organization for Social and Technological Innovation, & Westinghouse Furniture Systems. (1984). *Using office design to increase productivity.* Buffalo, NY: Workplace Design & Productivity.

Campbell, D. T. (1999). *Social experimentation.* Beverly Hills, CA: Sage.

Carpman, J. R., & Grant, M. A. (1993). *Design that cares: Planning health facilities for patients and visitors* (2nd ed.). Chicago: American Hospital.

Cohen, R., Standeven, M., Bordass, B., & Leaman, A. (2001a). Assessing building performance in use 1: *The Probe process. Building Research and Information,* 29(2), 85–102.

Cohen, R., Standeven, M., Bordass, B., & Leaman, A. (2001b). Assessing building performance in use 2: *Technical performance of the Probe buildings. Building Research and Information,* 29(2), 103–114.

Cooper, S. (1992). *We can learn from cross-cultural workplaces: A study of American executives in Japanese workplaces in the U.S.* New York: Environmental Psychology Program Graduate Center, City University of New York.

Davis, G., & Szigeti, F. (1996). Serviceability tools a methods (STM): Matching occupant requirements and facilities. In G. Baird, J. Gray, N. Isaacs, D. Kernoha & G. McIndoe (Eds.), *Building evaluation techniques* New York: McGraw-Hill.

Duffy, F. (1998). The new office. *Facilities Design and Management,* 27(8), 76–79.

Duffy, F., & Powell, K. (1997). *The new office.* London: Conran Octopus.

Flagg, G. (1999). Study finds major flaws in San Francisco main library. *American Libraries,* 30(9), 16.

Foxall, G., & Hackett, P. (1994). Consumer satisfaction with Birmingham's International Convention Center. *Service Industries Journal,* 74(3), 369.

Francis, J. (1986). *Office productivity: Contributions of the physical setting* (USA-CERL P-86/13). Washington, DC, U.S. Army Corps of Engineers.

Friedman, A., Zimring, C., & Zube, E. (1978). *Environmental design evaluation.* New York: Plenum Press.

Fuller, C. (1988). Post-occupancy evaluation: Fast feedback for planners. *Corrections Today,* 50(2), 213–214.

Grannis, P. (1994). Postoccupancy evaluation: An avenue for applied environment-behavior research in planning practice. *Journal of Planning Literature,* 9(2), 210–219.

Gregerson, J. (1997, August). Fee not-so-simple. *Building, Design and Construction,* 30–32.

Heerwagen, J. H. (2001, March 13). *A balanced scorecard approach to post-occupancy evaluation: Using the tools of business to evaluate facilities.* Paper presented at the Federal Facilities Council Symposium on Building Performance Assessments: Current and Evolving Practices for Post Occupancy Evaluation Programs, Washington, DC.

Horgen, T. H., Joroff, M. L., Porter, W. L., & Schon, D. A. (1996). Post-occupancy evaluation of facilities: A participatory approach to programming and design. *Facilities,* 14(7/8), 16–25.

Horgen, T. H., Joroff, M. L., Porter, W. L., & Schon, D. A. (1999). *Excellence by design: Transforming workplace and work practice.* New York: Wiley.

Huber, G. P. (1991). Organizational learning: The contributing processes and the literature. *Organization Science, 2,* 88–115.

Kantrowitz, M., & Farbstein, J. (1996). POE delivers for the post office. In G. Baird, J. Gray, N. Isaacs, D. Kernohan, & G. McIndoe (Eds.), *Building evaluation techniques,* New York: McGraw-Hill.

Kaplan, R. S., & Norton, D. P. (1996). *The balanced scorecard: Translating strategy into action.* Boston: Harvard I Business School Press.

Kincaid, D. (1994). Measuring performance in facility management. *Facilities,* 12(6), 17–21.

Leaman, A., Cohen, R., & Jackman, P. (1995). Ventilation of office buildings: Deciding the most appropriate system. *Heating And Air Conditioning* (7/8), 16–18, 20, 22–24, 26–28.

Ornstein, S. W. (1997). Post-occupancy evaluation performed in elementary and high schools of greater Sao Paulo, Brazil: The occupants and the quality of the school environment. *Environment and Behavior, 29(2),* 236.

Ornstein, S. W. (1999). A post-occupancy evaluation of workplaces in Sao Paulo, Brazil. *Environment and Behavior,* 31(4), 435–462.

Marshall, S. A., & Pena, W. (1983). *Evaluating facilities: A practical approach to post-occupancy evaluation.* Houston, TX: CRS Group.

Preiser, W. F. E. (1994). Built environment evaluation: Conceptual basis, benefits and uses. *Journal of Architectural and Planning Research. 11(2),* 92–107.

Preiser, W. F. E., Rabinowitz, H. Z., & White, E. T. (1988). *Post-occupancy evaluation.* New York: Van Nostrand Reinhold.

Preiser, W. F. E., & Schramm, U. (1997). Building performance evaluation. In J. DeChiara, J. Panero, & M. Zelnik (Eds.), *Time-saver standards* (7 ed., pp. 233–238). New York: McGraw-Hill.

Raw, G. J. (1995). *A questionnaire for studies of sick building syndrome* (Building Research Establishment Rep). London: Construction Research Communications.

Raw, G. J. (2000). Assessing occupant reaction to indoor air quality. In J. Spengler, J. Samet, & J. McCarthey (Eds.), *Indoor air quality handbook.* New York: McGraw-Hill.

Raw, G. J., Roys, M., & Leaman, A. (1990). Further findings from the Office Environment Survey: Productivity. *Proceedings of Indoor Air 90.* Toronto, Canada: Building Research Establishment (BRE).

Ripley Architects. (2000). *San Francisco Public Library occupancy evaluation final report.* San Francisco: Author.

Schein, E. H. (1995). *Learning consortia: How to create parallel learning systems for organization sets* [Working paper] Cambridge, MA: Society for Organizational Learning.

Schneekloth, L. H., & Shibley, R. G. (1995). *Placemaking: The art and practice of building communities.* New York: Wiley.

Shibley, R. (1982). Building evaluations services. *Progressive Architecture, 63*(12), 64–67.

Shibley, R. (1985). Building evaluation in the main stream. *Environment and Behavior,(1),* 7–24.

Spreckelmeyer, K. (1993). Office relocation and environmental change: A case study. *Environment and Behavior, 25(2),* 181.

Stanley, L., & Little, R. (2001, March 13). *Introduction: Current and evolving practices for post-occupancy evaluation programs.* Paper presented at the Federal Facilities Council Symposium on Building Performance Assessments: Current and Evolving Practices for Post Occupancy Evaluation Programs, Washington, DC.

Stokols, D. (1988). *Developing standardized tools for acing employees' ratings of facility performance.*

Symes, M., & Robbins, C. (2001). *"Literature Review" for "Indicators System for New Urban Services."* Paper presented at the European Union Framework 4 Research Programme: Key action 4 the City of Tomorrow.

Underhill, P. (1999). *Why we buy: The science of shopping.* New York: Simon & Schuster.

Vischer, J. (1996). *Workspace strategies: Environment as a tool for work.* New York: Chapman & Hall.

Weiss, C. H. (1997). *Evaluation* (2nd ed.). Upper Saddle River, NJ: Prentice-Hall.

Wener, R., Farbstein, J., & Knapel, C. (1993). Post-occupancy evaluations: Improving correctional facility design. *Corrections Journal,* 55(6), 96.

Wineman, J. (1986). Introduction. In J. Wineman (Ed.) *Behavioral issues in office design, 6–31.* New York: Van Nostrand Reinhold.

Zeisel, J. (1975). *Sociology and architectural design.* New York: Russell Sage Foundation.

Zimring, C., Munyon, W. H. & Ard, L. (1988). Reducing Stress in Jails. *Ekistics,* (332), 215–230.

Zimring, C., & Rosenheck, T. (2001, March 13). *Getting it right the second or third time rather than the sixth or seventh.* Paper presented at the Federal Facilities Council Symposium on Building Performance Assessments: Current and Evolving Practices for Post Occupancy Evaluation Programs, Washington, D.C.

Zimring, C. M., & Reizenstein, J. E. (1981). A primer on post-occupancy evaluation. *Architecture (American Institute of Architects Journal),* 70(13), 52–59.

Zimring, C. M., & Welch, P. (1988, July). Learning from 20-20 hindsight. *Progressive Architecture,* 55–62.

Author's Note: I would like to thank Bill Bordass, Arza Churchman, Joanne Green Martin Symes, and Richard Wener for their thoughtful comments. Some of this material was presented in a different form to the Federal Facilities Council *Symposium on Building Performance Assessments: Current and Evolving Practices for Post Occupancy Evaluation Programs,* Washington, DC, March 2001.

33 Environmental Correlates to Behavioral Health Outcomes in Alzheimer's Special Care Units

John Zeisel, Nina M. Silverstein, Joan Hyde, Sue Levkoff,
M. Powell Lawton, and William Holmes

Studying the impact of facilities on Alzheimer's has become a well-developed area of research. This study tested the impact of architectural features on symptoms of Alzheimer's patients and demonstrated that environmental design has bigger potential for alleviating the Alzheimer's condition than currently available medications.

Purpose: We systematically measured the associations between environmental design features of nursing home special care units and the incidence of aggression, agitation, social withdrawal, depression, and psychotic problems among persons living there who have Alzheimer's disease or a related disorder. **Design and Methods:** We developed and tested a model of critical health-related environmental design features in settings for people with Alzheimer's disease. We used hierarchical linear modeling statistical techniques to assess associations between seven environmental design features and behavioral health measures for 427 residents in 15 special care units. Behavioral health measures included the Cohen-Mansfield physical agitation, verbal agitation, and aggressive behavior scales, the Multidimensional Observation Scale for Elderly Subjects depression and social withdrawal scales, and BEHAVE-AD (psychotic symptom list) misidentification and paranoid delusions scales. Statistical controls were included for the influence of, among others, cognitive status, need for assistance with activities of daily living, prescription drug use, amount of Alzheimer's staff training, and staff-to-resident ratio. Although hierarchical linear modeling minimizes the risk of Type II—false positive—error, this exploratory study also pays special attention to avoiding Type I error—the failure to recognize possible relationships between behavioral health characteristics and independent variables. **Results:** We found associations between each behavioral health measure and particular environmental design features, as well as between behavioral health measures and both resident and nonenvironmental facility variables. **Implications:** This research demonstrates the potential that environment has for contributing to the improvement of Alzheimer's symptoms. A balanced combination of pharmacologic, behavioral, and environmental approaches is likely to be most effective in improving the health, behavior, and quality of life of people with Alzheimer's disease.

John Zeisel, Nina M. Silverstein, Joan Hyde, Sue Levkoff, M. Powell Lawton, & William Holmes, "Environmental Correlates to Behavioral Health Outcomes in Alzheimer's Special Care Units," from *The Gerontologist*, Vol. 43, No. 5, pp. 697–711. Copyright © 2003 by Oxford University Press. Permission to reprint granted by the publisher.

Key Words: Special care units, Environment, Alzheimer's disease, Non-pharmacologic treatment

This study was funded by Grant AG12343 from the National Institutes of Health, National Institute on Aging; it was carried out by a team of researchers, two of whom are designers—operators of Alzheimer's assisted living residences and four of whom are university-based researchers and statisticians. John Zeisel was the principal investigator. We gratefully acknowledge the contributions of Richard N. Jones to the clarity of the statistical explanations, and of research assistants Linda Shi to data collection and Helen Miltiades to data analysis.

This study describes associations found between seven special care unit (SCU) environmental design features and agitation, aggression, depression, social withdrawal, and psychotic symptoms of residents with Alzheimer's disease in those SCUs. The measurable effect of environment on Alzheimer's symptoms is an important topic for all concerned with the care of persons with Alzheimer's disease—including family members, service providers, care-giving staff, doctors, other health care providers, architects, and developers. Even in the *New England Journal of Medicine* the case is made for environment as an intervention (Campion, 1996). Campion argued that therapeutic physical environments can positively affect the lives of residents with dementia: "Faced with a patient with progressive Alzheimer's disease, physicians may feel they can do nothing to help. This is wrong. ... Care in a supportive environment can protect function for years" (p. 791).

This paper explores environmental treatment effects, using the conceptual model used by Beck and colleagues (1998) in their study of disruptive behavior in nursing homes. Beck's model presents disruptive behaviors as an outcome influenced both by individual factors such as gender, cognitive status, and health and by what the authors call "proximal factors," intrapersonal as well as environmental. Attributes of both the physical and the social environment are included under the title of "environmental proximal factors." Beck and colleagues identified these proximal factors but did not measure them, focusing instead on the influence of resident factors. This study measures proximal physical environment factors and statistically controls for the others.

Agitation, aggression, psychotic symptoms, depression, and social withdrawal were chosen as the dependent variables in this study because they occur frequently in Alzheimer's SCUs and often lead to other difficult to manage behaviors. These challenging behaviors are often treated with costly medications that have multiple side effects. Whereas responses to control these behaviors in the past have included the use of physical restraints (Castle & Fogel, 1998), the passage of the Omnibus Budget Reconciliation Act (OBRA) and the resulting decline in the use of physical restraints has had the unintended consequence of increasing use of pharmacological restraints (Sloane *et al.*, 1991).

For over a decade, numerous publications have discussed the treatment advantages of design features for this population (Calkins, 1988; Chafetz, & West, 1987; Coons, 1991; Hyde, 1989; Mathew, Sloane, Kirby, & Flood, 1988; Ohta & Ohta 1988; Weisman, Cohen, Ray, & Day, 1991; Zeisel, Hyde, & Levkoff, 1994). It is timely to carefully consider how environment can more humanely and cost-effectively contribute to managing and reducing these symptoms (Day, Carreon, & Stump, 2000). The literature has in fact made strong research-based arguments that proximal physical environmental characteristics of long-term care facilities significantly influence certain behaviors:

1. Camouflaged exits reduce elopement attempts (Dickinson & McLain-Kark, 1998).
2. Privacy reduces aggression and agitation and improves sleep (Morgan & Stewart, 1998).
3. Common spaces with a unique non-institutional character are associated with reduced social withdrawal (Gotestam & Melin, 1987).
4. Walking paths with multisensory activity nodes decrease exit seeking, improve mood, and engage family members (Cohen-Mansfield & Werner, 1998).
5. Residential character is associated with reduced social withdrawal, greater independence, improved sleep, and more family visits (Minde, Haynes, & Rodenburg, 1990).
6. Sensory comprehension reduces verbal agitation (Burgio, Scilley, Hardin, Hsu, & Yancey, 1996; Cohen-Mansfield & Werner, 1997).
7. Therapeutic garden access reduces elopement attempts and improves sleep (Stewart, 1995).
8. Increased safety leads to greater independence (Sloane *et al.*, 1991), which in turn is associated with fewer falls (Capezuti, Strumpf, Evans, Grisso, & Maislin, 1998).

Although compelling arguments are made for the therapeutic efficacy of an appropriate physical environment, until now little systematic research has been carried out to determine whether the special design features commonly found in SCUs are, in fact, effective in reducing symptoms and enhancing the quality of life for residents with dementia (U.S. Congress, 1992).

DESIGN AND METHODS

Overview of Methodology

Development of an Environment-Behavior Factors Model.—Before this study, an environment behavior (E–B) model was developed to identify the proximal physical environment factors hypothesized to influence behavioral and other health characteristics of residents with Alzheimer's disease in nursing home SCUs. This model and its systematic development, based on the work of established researchers and theorists (Calkins, 1988; Cohen & Weisman, 1991; Hiatt, 1991; Lawton, 1990), are explained in an earlier article (Zeisel *et al.*, 1994). A Delphi approach was used with an expert panel to test and refine the initial model and its related outcome measures. Early drafts of the model—drawn from published research findings—were distributed to panel members, each of whom was asked to rank every concept, dimension, and outcomes hypothesis on a 7-point scale indicating the degree to which particular E–B relationships represented state-of-the-art research findings. On the basis of the rankings and accompanying comments, items were deleted or combined into new concepts, and hypotheses were reformulated. Each successive draft was circulated to the group, with revised rankings returned, until there was a marked consensus improvement over earlier rankings. Those few features that continued to be ranked low by some experts and high by others in the final ranking were determined to reflect persistent state-of-research-knowledge differences in the field. These rankings were then shared with the entire expert group, and each member was asked to voice objections to the rankings, if there were any, so that these could, if possible, be resolved (Zeisel *et al.*, 1994).

The expert panel that played such a crucial role in the model's refinement included Margaret Calkins, PhD, IDEAS Inc.; Paul Chafetz, PhD, University of Texas; Uriel Cohen, AIA, University of Wisconsin; Betty Rose Connell, Atlanta VA Medical Center; Irving Faunce, Exeter Hospital; M.

Powell Lawton, PhD, Philadelphia Geriatric Center; Nancy Mace, MA, California Pacific Medical Center; Jon Sanford, Atlanta VA Medical Center; Philip Sloane, MD, MPH, University of North Carolina at Chapel Hill; and Myra Schiff, PhD, Canadian Alzheimer's Association.

An Alzheimer-specific set of testable E–B hypotheses resulted, describing potential effects of environmental conditions on health and behavior outcomes (Table 1). Each concept in the E–B Model includes two critical dimensions identified from published research literature and responses from the expert panel.

Two investigators independently used the concepts and dimensions in the E–B Model as a checklist to rate the physical environment of 30 SCUs during a 1-day site visit to each facility. During the rating procedure, both investigators separately rated every concept as "5 (high) to 1 (low)," generating an empirical indicator list of observed environmental features and conditions contributing to their ratings. Each feature and condition was photographed for later reference if independent ratings differed. The final set of indicators was organized into an environmental factors checklist to be quantitatively developed and used in future research to rank sites on these environmental characteristics (Table 2).

Investigators' ratings were compared. Where exact agreement was found, no further analysis was carried out. Where a difference was found, consensus was reached by referring to the photographs of the observed conditions, the rating scale, and the environmental factors checklist. In the few cases in which consensus could not be reached in this way, and where scores were 2 points apart on the 5-to-1 scale, a third rater was utilized and consensus reached. In the final version, the ratings were collapsed to a 3-point scale—representing "excellent," "moderate," and "poor" for each characteristic—because the direction of each assessment was considered more important than its degree.

Sample Site Selection.—Self-reported SCUs vary greatly in quality, and there is no official central or regional registration file of SCUs—a major problem that earlier SCU evaluation researchers have faced. Therefore, a nearly exhaustive list of 200 self-reported SCUs in New England and eastern New York was compiled through contact with Alzheimer's Association chapters in the study area. Calls were made to all 200 to determine which met the following definitional criteria:

- Functions as a self-contained unit,
- Is a physically distinct part of the building,
- Has dedicated staff to work on the unit,
- Restricts residents' movements to the physically distinct area unless monitored or accompanied by staff, and
- Includes on the unit only residents who have been diagnosed as having a dementing condition.

A letter requesting study participation was sent to the 52 sites that met the definitional criteria. Thirty SCUs agreed to participate, all of which were visited in the process of developing the E–B checklist (Zeisel *et al.*, 1994). A comparison of the two groups of sites—participants and nonparticipants—showed no significant differences in terms of facility size, profit and nonprofit ownership, and urban–rural location. The final 15-SCU sample was purposefully selected to maximize variability among the characteristics of the independent environmental variables as defined by the E–B checklist. By the statistical aggregation of the environmental characteristics of all sampled SCUs, clusters of independent variable conditions were created in the final hierarchical linear modeling (HLM) analysis. The purposeful sampling of the final 15 SCUs is supported by the fact that no specific SCU was treated as an independent or control case in itself.

On the basis of environmental assessments, 15 SCUs were selected that included as many of the environmental conditions as possible—high and low conditions for each of the environmental characteristics from the E–B checklist just described. For example, the few SCUs with poor exit control conditions were first expressly included in the sample to include this condition in the range of test conditions for this variable, no matter what their rating was on other conditions. The next SCU was selected to represent another uncommon environmental condition, and so on until all the conditions were filled with a balanced number of residents in each condition. Selecting facilities to ensure a full range of variation in the characteristics increases the statistical power of the analysis. A random selection approach for the final 15-SCU sample is not likely to have resulted in the extreme conditions being represented in the sample, and the analysis of significant associations would not have been possible. Obviously, the research team had no knowledge of the distribution of dependent variable conditions when the sample of residents was selected. The total number of residents in the 15-site sample was 427.

Analytic Approach.—Teresi (1994) described the problematic nature "of studies of intervention effects when institutional units (SCUs) are assigned to experimental or control conditions, but the individual is the unit of analysis ... the resulting mixed units of analysis (SCU and individual resident) can result in attenuated standard errors for the estimates of effects" (p. S252–S253). She suggested that "special modeling techniques may be needed in these situations" (Teresi, 1994, p. S253).

HLM is such a "special" technique (Bryk & Raudenbush, 1992; Bryk, Raudenbush, Seltzer, & Congdon, 1988). In their study of correlates of quality care in long-term care facilities, Bravo, De Wals, Dubois, and Charpentier pointed out that "the simultaneous study of resident- and facility-level variables calls for a statistical approach that accounts for the nested (or hierarchical) structure of the data. Hence the need for hierarchical models" (Bravo et al., 1999, p. 181). HLM was used in this study to assess the association between environmental design characteristics of SCUs (facility-level variables) and health outcomes measures of residents (individual-level variables) while taking into account quality-of-care variables (facility-level variables) and resident characteristics (individual-level variables). Nonenvironmental variables are controlled for in the analysis by averaging the effects of the environmental variables across all groups defined by characteristics of the nonenvironmental variables.

Table 1. *Alzheimer's (E–B) Factors Model*

E–B Concepts	Definition or Examples	Dimensions	
1. Exit control	Boundary conditions of each SCU: the surrounding walls, fences, doors, & how they are locked or otherwise limit & allow people to come and go.	Immediacy of control: the degree to which the exit doors are magnetically or otherwise locked vs. open but alarmed.	Unobtrusiveness: the degree to which the exit doors are camouflaged by paint or other devices, the amount of hardware, & their location along side walls as opposed to the end of hallways.
2. Walking paths	Circulation space residents use for wandering & moving around.	Continuousness w/destinations: The absence of dead-end & cul de sac corridors, & the presence of active destinations that might encourage residents there to turn around.	Wayfinding: The presence of orienting objects along the pathway, as well as wall objects that attract residents' attention & provide them a sense of being in a place.
3. Individual space	Spaces, primarily bedrooms, assigned to & mostly used by a limited number of residents.	Privacy: The number of private bedrooms in the SCU.	Personalization: The degree to which residents are allowed to & actually do place personal objects in their rooms.
4. Common space	Sizes, relationships, & qualities of spaces used by all residents in the SCU.	Quantity: The appropriate number of common rooms for the number of residents, to avoid crowding in too few rooms & to avoid "undermanning" in too many rooms.	Variability: The degree to which interior décor, furniture, & natural light provide common rooms with unique characteristics and "mood" appropriate to their use.

5. Outdoor freedom	Residents' access to common outdoor areas & the way these places support residents' needs.	Availability: The degree to which there is an adjacent outdoor space, & the degree of free access residents have to that place—doors unlocked & appropriate supervision.	Supportiveness: The degree to which the open space is a "therapeutic garden" with appropriate places to walk, sit, smell the plants, engage in safe & interesting activities, & be apart from others.
6. Residential character	The lack of institutional surroundings, including furniture & décor, wall covering, & flooring, & layout with prominent nursing station.	Size: The degree to which the size of the SCU reflects a large family space.	Familiarity: The degree to which the SCU uses residential furnishings, design features, & personal objects.
7. Autonomy support	The ways in which the facility encourages & supports residents to use their remaining faculties to carry out basic tasks & activities independently & w/ dignity, including enabling staff to avoid being overprotective.	Safety: The degree to which the unit's physical environment protects residents from injury from objects & inappropriate furniture, helps to prevent falls & injury from inevitable falls, & prevents elopements.	Prosthetic: Physical supports in the environment for residents to do things for themselves—handrails, toilet seats high enough for self-toileting, & bathtub & shower support rails.
8. Sensory comprehension	Quality of the sensory environment—acoustic, visual, thermal, odor, & kinesthetic environment in all spaces, & the degree to which these conditions may confuse residents.	Sensory management: The degree to which staff can control auditory & visual "noise" in the unit & the degree to which such sensory complexity has been controlled by design.	Meaningfulness to residents: The degree to which the ambient sensory environment is familiar to residents—smell, sights, sounds, & touch-textures.

Note: E–B = environment–behavior; SCU = special care unit.

Table 2. Environment Rating Checklist Indicators

Concept	Indicators Making Up *High* Ratings
Exit Control	
Walking paths	
Individual space	
Common space	

		Outdoor freedom
Residential character	Residential size	
	7–15 SCU residents	
	Low percieved crowding in SCU	
	Homelike character	
	Homelike noninstitutional qualities of staff dress, decor, linens, wall accessories, furniture, & lighting	
Autonomy support	Safety	
	Ease of staff surveillance in common and private spaces	
	Reduced risk of slipping & falling on flooring, furniture, carts, & hallway clutter	
	Presence of proactive measures to prevent access to sharp or otherwise dangerous objects	
	Support for independence	
	Presence of handrails in halls and bathrooms	
	Presence of devices that cue appropriate spatial behaviors	
	Prosthetic supports for independent toileting, dressing, showering, & self-mobility	
	Freedom to use outdoor space	
Sensory comprehension	Staff control	
	Staff actions that keep sensory input normal	
	Moderate level of background noise	
	Understandable sensory input	
	Meaningful sensory input—activity sounds, resident sounds, activity levels, smells, lighting, colors, heat, & touch	

Notes: Measurement problems prevented the "outdoor freedom" variable from inclusion in the analysis. Further research is recommended for this important environmental factor. SCU = special care unit.

HLM avoids inaccurate standard errors by establishing the association between an SCU characteristic and individual effects by using the sample size appropriate to their respective level of analysis. The standard errors and significance probabilities for the estimates are adjusted according to the number of data points available at each level—the different degrees of freedom associated with SCU variables versus resident variables. This avoids the attenuated standard errors that could occur if only the larger number of individuals were the unit of analysis as well as the inflated standard errors if only the smaller number of SCUs were the unit of analysis.

Using HLM analysis thus reduces the risk of making Type II—false positive—decisions about whether variables have an influence on the outcome. If only individual units of analysis were used, this would deflate the standard error of the facility-level effect, overstate its significance, and increase the risk of concluding it had a real effect when it did not (a false-positive decision). HLM was therefore used to reduce the cumulative risk of Type II errors and to more accurately estimate the actual significance of the environmental characteristics. It was judged that alternative procedures would give less valid and more uncertain results than HLM in this situation.

Dependent Variables

Behavioral Measures.—The largest in-depth national study of SCUs and dementia residents was organized and supported by the National Institute on Aging (NIA) and began in 1991. Known as the NIA Collaborative Studies on Alzheimer's SCUs, this 10-study coordinated project developed and validated a set of measures, known as the NIA Common Core "behavior, affect and activities measure and delirium assessment" Tool (NIA, 1993). To ensure validity and reliability, and to enable comparative analysis with the combined data from these studies, the present study incorporated scales from the NIA Collaborative Studies in the *resident profile* instrument, used to assess behavioral symptoms among study participants. Completed from medical records and professional judgment by a nurse-informant familiar with each resident, the *resident profile* includes scales from the Cohen-Mansfield Agitation Inventory (CMAI; Cohen-Mansfield, Marx, & Rosenthal, 1989), measuring aggressive, physically agitated, and verbally agitated behavior; the Multidimensional Observation Scale for Elderly Subjects (MOSES; Helmes, Csapo, & Short 1987), measuring depression and social withdrawal; and the BEHAVE-AD Psychotic Symptom List (Reisberg *et al.*, 1987) to measure misidentification syndrome and paranoid delusions (Table 3).

For each of the 14 CMAI items, nurse-informants indicated the frequency of the following behaviors: verbal aggression (cursing), physical aggression (hitting, kicking, biting, etc.), destroying property, self-abusive behavior, wandering, restlessness, inappropriate dress, handling items inappropriately, attention seeking, verbal repetitivism, complaining or noncompliance, making strange noises (weird laughter or crying), hiding items, and screaming. Cronbach's alpha for the three CMAI subscales was .68, .62, and .76.

Table 3. Outcome Measures

Measure	Reference	No. of Items	N	x	SD	α
CMAI (short form)	Cohen-Mansfield *et al.*, 1989					
Physical agitation		5	426	3.63	3.94	.68
Verbal agitation		5	426	2.87	3.55	.62
Aggressive behavior		4	426	3.00	3.39	.76

MOSES	Helmes et al., 1987					
Depression		7	360	5.24	5.07	.88
Social withdrawal		6	388	10.85	4.29	.79
BEHAVE-AD	Reisberg et al., 1987					
Misidentification		4	427	0.46	1.31	.64
Paranoid delusions		4[a]	427	1.23	2.15	.63

Note: CMAI—Cohen-Mansfield Agitation Inventory; MOSES—Multidimensional Observation Scale for Elderly Subjects; BEHAVE-AD—psychotic symptom list.
[a]This is a National Institute on Aging Common Core scale that uses three BEHAVE-AD items and one item from Cohen-Mansfield.

For each of the 13 items from the MOSES, nurse-informants indicated for each resident the frequency of these behaviors: depression (looked or said something depressed or sad, or made sad, depressed, gloomy, or mournful sounds, but not bored ones), being worried, tense, and anxious (looked or said something worried, and cried), being pessimistic (saying the future was hopeless or unbearable), being in good spirits (happy, smiling, cheerful), and being socially withdrawn (initiating interactions, responding to social contacts, paying attention to things around the patient, keeping self-occupied, and helping other residents). Cronbach's alpha for the two MOSES subscales was .88 and .79.

For each of eight items on two BEHAVE-AD Psychotic Symptom List subscales, nurse-informants indicated per resident the frequency of paranoid delusions (being stolen from or being harmed) and misidentification syndromes (saw someone else in the mirror, saw an imposter, or saw TV actors in the room). Cronbach's alpha for the two Psychotic Symptom subscales was .64 and .63.

Controlling for Nonenvironmental Variables.—For the physical environmental correlates of the behavioral health variables to be isolated accurately, the HLM model was used to control for potential resident-level and nonenvironmental facility-level variables—both of which were entered into the model. The first are characteristics of each resident, including cognition, activity of daily living (ADL) skills, and length of stay in the SCU. One resident-level characteristic particularly attended to in the analysis is prescription drug use. This characteristic, if overlooked, could completely distort all findings.

The nonenvironmental facility-level characteristics controlled for in the HLM analysis include staff ratio, facility size, organization, and degree of dementia friendliness. Both sets of variables, listed in Table 4, are explained in the paragraphs that follow. There were no missing data in the HLM analysis.

Resident characteristics: Individual characteristics of the residents were considered first. Demographic information included in the analysis for each resident comprised age, sex, and length of stay. Because risk of falling and associated restraining safety measures have been associated with agitation (Capezuti, Strumpf, Evans, Grisso, & Maislin, 1998; Sloane et al., 1991), a variable specifying whether or not a resident had fallen 3 months prior to the interview date was included.

Information on residents' ability to perform ADLs as well as their cognitive status was included from data in the Minimum Data Set (MDS) that the SCUs maintained for each resident. Where no MDS data were maintained, SCU nurses generated these data for each resident in the SCU. The Activities of Daily Living scale ranges between 1 and 28 and includes such items as bed mobility, walking, dressing, eating, toileting, bathing, balance, and task segmentation. Higher values indicate greater ADL impairment. Cronbach's alpha for the 28 items in the ADL scale was .78. The MDS Cognition scale from the NIA Common Core Assessment Tool was used to determine each resident's cognitive performance. The MDS Cognition scale has 13 items relating to short- and long-term memory, and to decision-making ability. Cronbach's alpha for the 13 MDS Cognition scale items was .73.

Pharmacological agents can independently affect residents' agitation, anxiety, depression, and other behaviors. These were therefore specifically controlled for statistically. Pharmacological-therapeutic drugs were classified into three categories: minor tranquilizers (benzodiazepines, anxiolytics, sedatives, or hypnotics), antidepressants, and other antipsychotic agents. Each patient's drug record was obtained and coded according to this typology, and the patient was given a score for each type of drug taken. If any drug in each of the three categories was administered, the patient received a score of 1, and if none of this type was taken, the patient's score was 0 for that drug category.

Table 4. Nonenvironmental Variables Included in the HLM Model

Resident Characteristics	Prescription Drug Controls	Facility Characteristics
Age	Minor tranquilizers	Staff/resident ratio
Gender	Antidepressants	Facility size
Length of stay in facility	Other antipsychotics	Organizational status
Fell in past 3 months		Dementia friendliness
ADL skills		
Cognition		

Note: HLM = hierarchical linear modeling; ADL = activity of daily living.

Facility characteristics: As a way to control for the possible effects of nonenvironmental characteristics of the facilities themselves, several variables were constructed to describe each facility. The number of residents per SCU was used to take into account possible effects that facility size might have on health and behaviors (Bravo *et al.*, 1999; Castle & Fogel, 1998; Leon & Ory, 1999). Because Castle and Fogel (1998) found that health and behaviors were influenced by organizational status, a dummy variable was created to indicate profit or nonprofit status.

A final scale, developed by rating each SCU's policy and procedures manual, was created to reflect the overall Alzheimer's appropriateness of the facility. Ratings were assigned to each SCU's policy and procedures manual on the basis of their Alzheimer specificity, and on the ratio of key dementia features (assessment, mission, staff empowerment, family support, community involvement, staff appropriateness, management or financial issues, and activities) to nondementia features (quality assurance, housekeeping or maintenance, nursing procedures, emergency procedures, research, clothing, incidents, record keeping, and physician services). Two researchers independently reviewed and ranked the documents on Likert scales. When 2 or fewer points apart, the two scores were averaged. When more than 2 points apart, a third rater mediated a discussion of the scores until consensus was reached.

Environmental characteristics: Each environmental factor, already explained in earlier paragraphs, was coded as two dummy variables: excellent environmental condition (yes or no) and poor environmental condition (yes or no), with the medium environmental condition as the referent category.

Descriptive Statistics

Resident Characteristics.—The sample included 308 women and 119 men, ranging in age from 53 to 102 (M = 81.14; SD = 7.8). The majority (58%) were widowed, with 29% married, 6% divorced, and the remaining single or unspecified. The largest percentage (46%) of the sample was moderately to severely dependent in ADLs, with 39% experiencing mild to moderate dependency, and 15% who required supervision only or were independent. Twenty percent had cognitive impairment rated moderate to severe, 67% rated moderate, and 13% rated mild. Prescription medication use for minor tranquilizers was 37%, for antidepressants 30%, and for other antipsychotic agents 33%, with 65% of the sample on at least one psychotherapeutic prescription drug. Twenty-seven percent had experienced a fall in the past 3 months. The average length of institutionalization was 26.63 months (SD = 20.24), with a range of less than 1 month to 151 months for a resident 95 years old.

Facility Characteristics.—The sample included 15 facilities. The size of the facilities ranged from 20 to 50 residents (M = 33.67). The clinical, 24-hour staff-to-resident ratio ranged from 0.91 to 2.50 (M = 1.54). Nine facilities were for profit and six were not for profit (one religious and two government facilities are included). On the basis of a systematic two-person analysis of their mission statement, training protocol, policies and procedures, and activities programming, the level of Alzheimer's capability of each facility was ranked. Seven facilities were characterized as highly Alzheimer's capable, three as only Alzheimer's friendly, and five as dementia unfriendly. The intraclass correlation, expressing the variability in the outcomes from residents sampled from the same facility, was 0.36. This weak commonality of characteristics by facility is possibly due to institutional policies that exclude residents inappropriate to the care available or that provide special services benefiting a particular population.

Table 5. Bivariate Correlations Among Variables

Variable	CM Total (Prorated)	MOSES (Prorated)		CM (Porated)			BEHAVE-AD (Prorated)
		Withdrawal	Depression	AB	PAB	VAB	
Privacy	**-.254**	.008	-.085	**-.204**	-.156	**-.221**	-.145
Common space	**-.222**	.079	.003	**-.173**	**-.206**	-.122	-.092
Exit control	**-.240**	**.195**	.149	-.125	**-.230**	**-.180**	-.122
Residential char.	**-.224**	.013	.025	**-.202**	-.109	**-.205**	-.085
Sensory comp.	**-.208**	.071	.067	-.136	-.144	**-.194**	-.140

Walking path	**-.212**	.044	.097	**-.191**	**-.158**	**-.135**	-.020
Mission statement	**.120**	-.071	-.010	**.101**	.073	**.102**	.019
Fell in the past 30 days	.034	-.091	**-.100**	.002	.047	.025	.012
ADL scale (28 items)	**-.185**	**.284**	**.232**	-.004	**-.323**	-.065	-.072
Length of time in institution	-.058	.065	.073	-.028	-.077	-.022	.003
No. of residents	**-.242**	.027	.066	**-.243**	-.097	**-.219**	-.042
Gender	-.009	-.091	**-.148**	-.082	-.046	**.110**	.041
Age	.001	**-.142**	**-.206**	-.040	-.063	**.109**	.046
Staff ratio	**-.194**	.016	-.049	**-.105**	**-.173**	**-.156**	**-.134**
Antipsychotic meds.	-.079	**.217**	**.459**	.039	**-.171**	-.030	.013

Notes: The figures in each cell represent the Pearson correlation between each set of variables. Boldface indicates correlations that are large enough (r > .10) and significant at p < .05. MOSES = Multidimensional Observation Scale for Elderly Subjects; AB = aggressive behavior; PAB = physically agitated behavior; VAB = verbally agitated behavior; ADL = activity of daily living; CM = Cohen-Mansfield; BEHAVE-AD = psychotic symptom list.

Facility Environmental Characteristics.—No single facility received consistent high or low scores on all its environmental characteristics. Facilities given a high rating on some characteristics received only medium scores on the remaining characteristics. Facilities scoring medium on some characteristics scored low on the remaining characteristics. Only one facility received a range of low, medium, and high scores.

Six facilities, housing 37% of the residents in the study, scored high on exit control, whereas seven scored medium (49% of the residents) and two scored low (14% of the residents). For walking paths, three facilities (18% of the residents) were high, eight facilities (50% of the residents) were medium, and four facilities, with 32% of the residents, were low. There were three facilities (16% of the residents) with excellent privacy–personalization, and six facilities each with medium and low scores with 34% and 50% of the residents, respectively. Five facilities with 27% of the residents had excellent common space, seven with 55% of the residents had medium common space, and the remaining three facilities with 18% of the residents had poor common space. Ten percent of the residents living in two facilities ranked high on residential, versus institutional, quality; the remaining eight medium-rated and five low-rated facilities each had 45% of the residents.

Five facilities with 31% of the residents scored high on autonomy support and 10 scored medium (69% of the residents). No sites scored low on autonomy support. For sensory comprehension, six facilities (36% of the residents) were high, seven facilities (46% of the residents) were medium, and two facilities with 18% of the residents scored low. There were eight facilities (54% of the residents) with excellent scores for physical access to a garden, four facilities (27% of residents) with medium access scores, and three facilities with low access scores (19% of the residents).

Although data were collected on the physical accessibility—or absence—of gardens in each of the participating facilities, data were not systematically collected on residents' actual access to these spaces. In other words, the data do not clearly indicate if doors to gardens were or were not kept unlocked during the day in good weather, whether staff only permitted residents to take walks when accompanied by staff, or whether residents had continual access. Because these attributes are so critical to the definition of "outdoor access," this variable was unfortunately omitted from the analysis. Future research must gather more extensive data on this critical environmental variable to determine the impact of therapeutic gardens on behavioral health outcomes.

Results

This section reports the results of an initial bivariate analysis as well as the final multivariate analysis used to test the model that underlies this research effort. Three types of variables—resident characteristics, nonenvironmental facility characteristics, and environmental characteristics—correlate significantly with resident behavioral health measures in the bivariate analysis. The bivariate correlations of these variables with the dependent variables were calculated by using Pearson's correlation coefficient, in order to provide a preliminary indication of which factors were likely to be related to the outcome variables. These correlations are presented in Table 5. The environmental factors tend to be correlated with the behavioral health measures in the direction predicted, except for exit control, which, without the other variables being taken into account, was associated with increased, not decreased, withdrawal and depression. This direction is reversed in the later analysis. Several of the individual and non-environmental facility-level variables are also associated with the dependent variables.

Table 6. HLM Model Elements

Characteristics	Behavioral Health Measures	HLM Equations
X_1 = Privacy	Y_1 = Anxiety/aggression (Cohen-Mansfield total)	$Y_1 = 16.4 - 2.21X_1 + 0.10X_2 + 0.50X_3$
X_2 = Falling down	Y_2 = Social withdrawal (MOSES)	$Y_2 = 0.2 - 0.82X_4 + 0.10X_5 - 0.10X_6$
X_3 = ADLs	Y_3 = Depression (MOSES)	$Y_3 = 0.6 - 0.58X_7 + 0.30X_8 + 0.70X_9$
X_4 = Common space	Y_4 = All aggression (Cohen-Mansfield subscale)	$Y_4 = 11.2 - 0.23X10 - 0.70X8$
X_5 = Length of stay	Y_5 = PA (Cohen-Mansfield)	$Y_5 = 6.6 - 0.40X3$
X_6 = No. of residents	Y_6 = VA (Cohen-Mansfield)	$Y_6 = 6.5 - 0.57X_{11} - 0.10X_{12} + 0.90X_2 + 2.10Y_1 + 2.10X_9 + 0.10X_{13}$
X_7 = Exit control	Y_7 = Psych. problems (BEHAVE-AD)	$Y_7 = 4.1 - 0.33X_1 - 0.11X_{12} + 0.38X_{14} - 0.40X_{15}$
X_8 = Gender		
X_9 = Antipsychotic meds.		
X_{10} = Res. character		
X_{11} = Sensory comp.		
X_{12} = Staff ratio		
X_{13} = Age		
X_{14} = Walking path		
X_{15} = Mission		

Notes: HLM = hierarchical linear modeling; ADLs = activities of daily living; MOSES = Multidimensional Observation Scale for Elderly Subjects; PA = physical aggression; VA = verbal aggression; BEHAVE-AD = psychotic symptom list. Characteristics are for the environment, the resident, or the facility.

The large and statistically significant correlation coefficients in the bivariate analysis do not take into account the hierarchical relationships among the variables. Therefore we consider all correlations of r < .10 to be trivial—regardless of significance, in Cohen's (1969) effect size taxonomy. Those associations that are large enough (r > .10) and significant at p < .05 are shown in boldface in Table 5.

The result of the multivariate model analysis, based on introducing potential confounders as controls, is the final test of the research model. The variables from the bivariate analysis were therefore entered in the HLM program to assess which variables remain significantly related after other factors were controlled for. The bivariate associations hold when this statistical model is used, and the exit control association is reversed once the hierarchy of variables is taken into account. A mixed HLM model was used where environmental variables were fixed, and the individual correlates were treated as random effects. The assumption of the individual variables as random effects implies that they are assumed to vary across Level 2 variables. The individual correlates were centered on the grand mean. Our research indicates that these variables, independently—and possibly interactively—are correlated with the resident behavioral health characteristics measured in this study. Seven environmental and nine resident and nonenvironmental facility factors were entered in the final model, with one environmental variable—autonomy support—dropping out in the final HLM analysis. Table 6 presents the final variables and equations used in the HLM model. This contains the variables that remained significant after the other independent variables were controlled for. For environmental factors, 49 independent significant tests were carried out. For the resident and nonenvironmental facility factors, 63 tests were carried out. Seventeen of the relationships were statistically significant, whereas only six false positives would have been expected by chance.

In Table 7 these correlates are grouped according to the dependent behavioral health variable with which they are correlated, although in this discussion of results, the findings are presented in three sections reflecting the type of variable. Variables on the left are Level 2 variables, whereas those on the right are Level 1 variables. Findings that were significant at the .05 level were reported. In addition, five associations whose significance levels do not quite attain the conventional .05 level of significance (.051 to .068) are discussed. Their trends are all in the direction suggested by the model underlying the analysis, and they are included in this discussion as exploratory findings deserving further research. For each dependent variable, the HLM analysis first controlled for all the individual and nonenvironmental facility characteristics. Then all environmental variables were entered, with nonsignificant ones being dropped sequentially until only significant ones remained. All individual and facility variables were kept in as control variables. Only significant control variables are shown in Table 7. Model assumptions were also verified. The residuals were determined to be normally distributed, indicating that this model assumption was not violated. The remaining correlates are presented in Table 7, as well as the coefficients and their standard errors for the final fixed model, and the variance components, degrees of freedom, and chi-square values for the random effects. There was no significant evidence of heterogeneity of variance, as indicated by an F test for heterogeneity of variance.

Table 7. Environmental Correlates to Alzheimer's Symptoms: HLM Analysis Results for Levels 1 and 2

Correlates		Coef.	SE	T Ratio	p Value	PF Correlates	T Ratio	p Value	Variance Com.	x^2
Behavioral Health	Design									df
Anxiety–agg. (CM total)	Privacy–personaliz. (–)	–2.21	.73	–2.87	.019	Falling down (+)	+2.443	.037	0.002	10.6 14
						ADL performance (+)	+3.799	.005	0.004	13.5 14
MOSES										
Social withdrawal	Common space variability (–)	–0.82	.40	–2.067	.068*	Length of stay (+)	+2.068	.066*	0.010	12.0 8
						No. of residents (–)	-4.009	.004	–	– –
Depression	Exit control (–)	–0.58	.26	–2.261	.050	Gender (women +)	-3.568	.007	0.380	7.6 13
						Antipsychotic meds. (+)	+2.292	.047	0.050	20.1 12
All aggressions (CM subscale)	Residential char. (–)	–0.23	.06	–3.896	.002	Gender (men +)	+2.151	.051*	0.460	12.6 12
Aggression										
Physical (CM)	—					ADL performance (–)	-3.516	.037	0.050	16.4 14
Verbal (CM)	Sensory comp. (–)	–0.57	.27	–2.156	.059*	Staff ratio (–)	-2.115	.063*	—	— —
						Falling (+),	+2.254	.050	2.070	13.0 6
						Anxiety (+),	+2.279	.048	0.890	10.1 6
						Antipsych. meds. (+)	+2.724	.024	1.060	18.4 6
						Age (+) Mission (–)	+2.323	.045	0.001	8.11 5
Psych. problems	Privacy–personaliz. (–)	-0.33	.11	-2.918	.023		-3.117	.018	—	— —
(BEHAVE-AD)	Sensory comp. (–) Walking path (+)	-0.11 0.38	.04 .15	-2.668 +2.485	.032 .042					

Notes: Findings are significant at $p < .05$. Five findings, marked by an asterisk, are in the same direction as predicted by the theoretical model but at levels that only approach conventional levels of statistical significance ($p = .051$ to $p = .068$). The varying degrees of freedom in the final column result from a different number of control variables when correlates of behavioral health are looked at. PF correlates = individual and non-environmental proximal factor correlates. MOSES = Multidimensional Observation Scale for Elderly Subjects; CM = Cohen-Mansfield; BEHAVE-AD = psychotic symptom list; ADL = activity of daily living; HLM = hierarchical linear modeling.

E–B INFLUENCES

The HLM analysis shows that physical environmental design features correlate with behavioral health, even when individual and nonenvironmental facility characteristics are taken into account. In fact, individual and nonenvironmental facility characteristics can be seen as interacting with the following attributes of the physical environment.

The degree of privacy–personalization in the SCUs studied was negatively correlated with patient scores on the Cohen-Mansfield total aggression scale. Residents in facilities with more privacy—more rooms that are individual and more opportunities for personalization—generally scored lower on this scale, representing less anxiety and aggression.

The amount of variability among common spaces in a facility was negatively correlated with patient social withdrawal scores. The degree of social withdrawal among residents decreased as the variability among the common spaces in a facility increased. Depression was negatively correlated with another environmental factor—exit design. Residents in facilities whose exits were well camouflaged and had silent electronic locks rather than alarms tended to be less depressed. A hypothesis to explain this correlation is that residents try to elope less in such settings and that caregivers—tending to consider such environments safer—afford residents greater independence of movement. Residents who experience this greater freedom, and hence have less conflict about trying to leave the SCU, feel a greater sense of control and empowerment, leading in turn to less depression. Until further research is carried out measuring personal state-of-mind variables that might be implicated in such a process, this explanation remains only a hypothesis.

Aggression and its various expressions were also correlated with characteristics of the physical environment. Persons living in SCUs with a more residential, less institutional environment expressed lower levels of overall aggression than those living in more institutional settings. Physical aggression, scored separately, did not appear to be associated with environmental design after individual and facility characteristics were controlled for, but verbal aggression appears to be correlated with environment. In facilities where sensory input is more understandable and where such input is more controlled, residents tended to be less verbally aggressive.

Finally, environmental design also was correlated with resident psychotic problems. Those living in environments scoring high on privacy–personalization tended to have lower scores on the psychotic problem scale. The same was true for those living in facilities with higher scores on sensory comprehension scores.

It should be noted that privacy–personalization and sensory comprehension were related to lower scores for more than one negative characteristic. In several of this study's HLM models where these two factors did not reach statistical significance, they were among the last variables dropped from the models. This suggests that privacy–personalization and sensory comprehension are likely to be particularly important environmental design features contributing to improved behavioral health outcomes.

Taken with other correlates of the behavioral health characteristics discussed in the paragraphs that follow, this analysis appears to provide evidence that environmental design is related to behavioral health outcomes among residents of SCUs with dementia-related health problems. Because the present research did not include measures of subjective control such as alienation and anomie, while it is clear that there are relationships between environment and behavioral health characteristics, we can only hypothesize what the specific links are which may relate them. Elaboration and exploration of the nature of these relationships must await future research.

Resident-Level Influences

Certain resident-level characteristics are shown through the HLM analysis to correlate with residents' behavioral health. The more a resident has problems performing ADLs, the more likely he or she is to have a lower total anxiety and aggression score on the Cohen-Mansfield scale. The likelihood of a resident falling, in contrast, was positively related to expressions of anxiety and aggression.

The longer a person has lived in a caregiving institution, the more highly correlated her or his social withdrawal score is likely to be. This may reflect the fact that those living longer in SCUs are also more likely to be confounded with progression of dementia or other medical conditions with a developmental process.

Gender is associated with depression. Our study shows depression to be more prevalent among Alzheimer's residents who are women than among those who are men. This is also the case for those taking antipsychotic medications—the more such medications, the greater the correlation with depression, according to our findings.

In contrast, gender is correlated with overall aggression scores in the opposite direction. Male residents are more likely to score higher than female residents on overall aggression—both physical and verbal. Ability to perform ADLs is negatively correlated with all patient scores on physical aggression, whereas a patient's likelihood of falling down, level of anxiety, age, and taking of antipsychotic medications all appear to be positively correlated with the expression of verbal aggression by residents.

Nonenvironmental Facility-Level Influences

Only three nonenvironmental facility-level characteristics appear to correlate with the behavioral health measures in this study. The larger the facility—the more residents there are in the SCU—the lower the social withdrawal scores tend to be. The higher the staff ratio, the lower are the verbal aggression scores among residents. In addition, the higher the facility scores on Alzheimer capability, the fewer reported psychotic problems residents tend to exhibit.

DISCUSSION

This research demonstrates that certain features of the physical environment in SCUs are associated with improved behavioral health among residents. The environmental features associated with both reduced aggressive and agitated behavior and fewer psychological problems include privacy and personalization in bedrooms, residential character, and an ambient environment that residents can understand. Characteristics of the environment associated with reduced depression, social withdrawal, misidentification, and hallucinations include common areas that vary in ambiance and exit doors throughout the SCU that are camouflaged.

Environments conventionally designed for the cognitively able appear to put stress on the cognitive abilities of those with Alzheimer's. One explanation for the results presented here may be that the design characteristics discussed relieve residents' cognitive stress, thus reducing their anxiety and related aggressive acts. Another is that the design features, by providing residents with greater control over their own lives, empower them and thus reduce their tendency to withdraw and even to be situationally depressed. The present research can only indicate the direction for such interpretations. More extensive research will be required to be more definitive.

The findings support and expand on the Intervention model proposed by Beck and colleagues (1998). Each of the behavioral health characteristics measured in the present study—in addition to correlating with at least one environmental factor—was also associated with resident characteristics, such as gender, cognitive status, and medications and to nonphysical facility factors such as staff ratio and Alzheimer's friendliness of the mission. This would appear to indicate a dynamic, interactive relationship between resident characteristics and environmental features on one hand and the behavioral health of residents on the other.

For design and construction, these findings have clear implications. Even though SCU design has to meet stringent fire safety requirements and construction standards that may seem rigid and imply institutional design responses, SCUs should strive to model their interior environments after homelike settings to reduce aggressive and other symptoms. Applied in design of SCUs, these findings will lead to more private and less shared rooms, variation in common room design within an SCU, common rooms for activities located at ends of hallways, and doors located along side walls whenever possible instead of at the end of hallways where they act as "attractive nuisances." Alzheimer Association chapters are already advising consumers to take environmental design issues such as these into account when determining the quality of nursing homes, SCUs, and assisted living special care programs they are considering for their loved ones (Alzheimer's Association, 2000; Raia, Zeisel, Cacciapuoti, Stout, & Rodman, 2003).

Funding for major renovation of heavily institutional nursing home SCUs must be weighed against the potential of decreased costs for medications and increases in quality of life, not merely as cosmetic alterations.

Limitations

It is possible that the significant associations found between behavioral health characteristics and environmental factors are spurious and result from their correlation with some other unspecified or poorly specified factor. If this were the case, however, it is highly unlikely that each of the environmental factors would be significant and in the direction hypothesized.

Nevertheless, the data presented here may be limited by the questions asked and the variables studied. This presents limitations that have to be considered when the results are interpreted.

There may be *unspecified factors* not included in the model that also correlate with behavioral health characteristics. Some of these may be environmental variables such as whether or not the SCUs had gardens that residents used, whether the environments reflected the cultural background of residents, or if they were maintained well or were cluttered and messy. In our analysis, we assumed random distribution of such characteristics, but these may have independent effects on the behavioral health characteristics measured.

One or more of the factors studied may have been only *partly specified*. For example, the study team identified two dimensions of exit control design: the degree to which the exit is camouflaged to reduce the likelihood of elopement, and the degree to which the doors were actually locked (magnetically or by key) versus unlocked but alarmed. Other dimensions of exit control that were overlooked may still be important for the analysis.

Limited variability may also be influencing the data. For example, although the research team attempted to have high and low independent variable scores for each factor, secure exits were a criterion for inclusion in the sample. One SCU with a large enough group of residents was found to have only a "black line on the floor" as its barrier to the rest of the facility, providing only one SCU in the cell representing poor exit control.

Nevertheless, the study analysis did attempt to rigorously control for resident characteristics and organizational factors that previous research has indicated might confound the data analysis. These included such resident characteristic variables as prescription drug usage, risk of falling, cognition, need for assistance with ADLs, length of stay in the facility, and age. Organizational factors included the ratio of staff to residents, the not-for-profit or for-profit status of the organization, and the dementia friendliness of the facility's mission.

Two major limitations can only be overcome by increased research funding in this area. Resource allocation in the research led the team to a final selection of 15 sites and 427 residents, instead of 30 sites with nearly 950 residents. There is clearly a need to replicate this research with the use of more facilities as well as to gather longitudinal data to examine in greater detail the impacts of the environment on outcomes inferred by the correlations found in this study.

FUTURE RESEARCH

This study paves the way for further exploration into environmental design as one important non-pharmacologic treatment modality for people with Alzheimer's disease (Zeisel & Raia, 2000). Future research might focus on applying a similar methodology to other environmental factors the literature has indicated might be therapeutic. These could include accessible gardens, soothing colors, non-disorienting carpeting patterns, higher lighting levels, and alternative bathing settings.

A larger sample size in future research would increase the significance of findings and would permit the inclusion and control of a greater number of variables—environmental, individual, and facility characteristics. A more diverse sample would enable researchers to test the generalizability of the study findings to a greater variety of Alzheimer care settings—assisted living residences for people with Alzheimer's, foster care settings, and at-home care in addition to nursing home SCUs.

An examination in future research of the cumulative effects of environmental features might also yield useful information. For example, is the association between reduced aggression and both privacy–personalization and unique common spaces cumulative, such that planning both together could augment the reduction of aggression more than either separately? Even more challenging and rewarding would be insight into the dynamic interactive and cumulative effects of environmental conditions with organizational factors as well as pharmacologic treatment.

A Significant Direction

This research demonstrates the great opportunity systematic attention to environmental factors opens for improving Alzheimer's symptoms. The greatest likelihood for this approach to make a significant contribution is to consider environment as one of at least three modalities—pharmacologic, behavioral, and environmental—for improving the quality of life, health, and behavior of people with Alzheimer's disease. These might well be considered three "treatments" for the disease.

As conceptual and empiric research in the area of environment and health accelerates, it is becoming increasingly clear that a combination of drug treatment, supportive environments, and focused caregiving approaches provides the highest likelihood that those with Alzheimer's disease can indeed live more satisfying lives. The stage is set for interdisciplinary intervention studies to identify the optimum balance and arrangement of these treatment modalities.

REFERENCES

Alzheimer's Association, Massachusetts Chapter. (2000). *Guidelines to assess the quality of special care units for Alzheimer's residents in nursing homes.* Cambridge, MA: Author.

Beck, C., Frank, L., Chumbler, N. R., O'Sullivan, P., Vogelpohl, T. S., Rasin, J., *et al.*, (1998). Correlates of disruptive behavior in severely cognitively impaired nursing home residents. *The Gerontologist*, 38, 189–198.

Bravo, G., De Wals, P., Dubois, M. F., & Charpentier, M. (1999). Correlates of care quality in long-term care facilities: A multilevel analysis. *Journal of Gerontology: Psychological Sciences*, 54B, P180–P188.

Burgio, L., Scilley, K., Hardin, M. J., Hsu, C., & Yancey, J. (1996). Environmental "white noise": An intervention for verbally agitated nursing home residents. *Journal of Gerontology: Psychological Sciences*, 51B, P364–P373.

Bryk, A., & Raudenbush, S. (1992). *HLM: Applications and data analysis methods.* Newbury Park, CA: Sage.

Bryk, A., Raudenbush, S., Seltzer, M., & Congdon, R. (1988). *An introduction to HLM: Computer program and user's guide.* Chicago: University of Chicago, Department of Education.

Calkins, M. P. (1988). *Design for dementia: Planning environments for the elderly and the confused.* Owings Mills, MD: National Health Publishing.

Campion, E. W. (1996). When a mind dies. *New England Journal of Medicine*, 334, 791.

Capezuti, E., Strumpf, N. E., Evans, L. K., Grisso, J. A., & Maislin, G. (1998). The relationship between physical restraint removal and falls and injuries among nursing home residents. *Journal of Gerontology: Medical Sciences*, 53A, M47–M52.

Castle, N. G., & Fogel, B. (1998). Characteristics of nursing homes that are restraint free. *The Gerontologist*, 38, 181–188.

Chafetz, P. K., & West, H. L. (1987, November). *Longitudinal control group evaluation of a special care unit for dementia patients: Initial findings.* Paper presented at the 40th Annual Meeting of the Gerontological Society of America, Washington, DC.

Cohen, J. (1969). *Statistical power analysis for the behavioral sciences.* New York: Academic Press.

Cohen, U., & Weisman, G. (1991). *Holding on to home: Designing environments for people with dementia.* Baltimore: Johns Hopkins University Press.

Cohen-Mansfield, J., Marx, M. S., & Rosenthal, A. S. (1989). A description of agitation in a nursing home. *Journal of Gerontology: Medical Sciences*, 44, M77–M84.

Cohen-Mansfield, J., & Werner, P. (1997). Management of verbally disruptive behaviors in nursing home residents. *Journal of Gerontology: Medical Sciences*, 52A, M369–M377.

Cohen-Mansfield, J., & Werner, P. (1998). The effects of an enhanced environment on nursing home residents who pace. *The Gerontologist*, 38, 199–208.

Coons, D. H. (1991). The therapeutic milieu: Concepts and criteria. In D. Coons (Ed.), *Specialized dementia care units* (p. 7–24). Baltimore: Johns Hopkins University Press.

Day, K., Carreon, D., & Stump, C. (2000). The therapeutic design of environments for people with dementia: A review of empirical research. *The Gerontologist*, 40, 397–416.

Dickinson, J. I., & McLain-Kark, J. (1998). Wandering behavior and attempted exits among residents diagnosed with dementia-related illnesses: A qualitative approach. *Journal of Women and Aging*, 10, 23–35.

Gotestam, K. G., & Melin, L. (1987). Improving well-being for patients with senile dementia by minor changes in the ward environment. In L. Levi (Ed.), *Society, stress, and disease* (p. 295–297). Oxford, England: Oxford University Press.

Helmes, E., Csapo, K. G., & Short, J. A. (1987). Standardization and validation of the Multidimensional Observation Scale for Elderly Subjects (MOSES). *Journal of Gerontology*, 42, 395–405.

Hiatt, L. (1991). *Nursing home renovation designed for reform.* Stoneham, MA: Butterworth Architecture.

Hyde, J. (1989). The physical environment and the care of Alzheimer's patients: An experimental survey of Massachusetts Alzheimer's units. *American Journal of Alzheimer's Care and Related Disorders & Research*, 4, 36–44.

Lawton, M. P. (1990). Environmental approaches to research and treatment of Alzheimer's disease. In E. Light & B. D. Lebowitz (Eds.), *Alzheimer's disease treatment and family stress: Direction for research* (p. 340–362). Rockville, MD: U.S. Department of Health and Human Services.

Leon, J., & Ory, M. G. (1999). Effectiveness of special care unit (SCU) placements in reducing physically aggressive behaviors in recently admitted dementia nursing home residents. *American Journal of Alzheimer's Disease*, 14, 270–277.

Mathew, L. J., Sloane, P. D., Kirby, M., & Flood, R. (1988). What's different about a special care unit for dementia patients? A comparative study. *American Journal of Alzheimer's Care and Related Disorders & Research*, 3, 16–23.

Minde, R., Haynes, E., & Rodenburg, M. (1990). The ward milieu and its effect on the behaviour of psychogeriatric patients. *Canadian Journal of Psychiatry*, 35, 133–138.

Morgan, D. G., & Stewart, M. J. (1998). Multiple occupancy versus private rooms on dementia care units. *Environment and Behavior*, 30, 487–504.

National Institute on Aging. (1993). *Manual of procedures: National Institute on Aging collaborative studies: Special care units for Alzheimer's disease* (Vol. 1). Bethesda, MD: Author.

Ohta, R. J., & Ohta, B. M. (1988). Special units for Alzheimer's disease patients: A critical look. *The Gerontologist*, 28, 803–808.

Raia, P., Zeisel, J., Cacciapuoti, J., Stout, M. A., & Rodman, C. (2003). *Guidelines for the care of Alzheimer's residents in assisted living residences*. Cambridge, MA: Alzheimer's Association, Massachusetts Chapter.

Reisberg, B., Borenstein, J., Salob, S. P., Ferris, S. H., Franssen, E., & Georgotas, A. (1987). Behavioral symptoms in Alzheimer's disease: Phenomenology and treatment. *Journal of Clinical Psychiatry*, 48, S9–S15.

Sloane, P. D., & Matthew, L. J. (1990). The therapeutic environment screening scale. *American Journal of Alzheimer's Care and Related Disorders & Research*, 5, 22–26.

Sloane, P. D., Mathew, L. J., Scarborough, M., Desai, J. R., Koch, G. G., & Tangen, C. (1991). Physical and pharmacologic restraint of nursing home patients with dementia: Impact of specialized units. *Journal of the American Medical Association*, 265, 1278–1283.

Sloane, P. D., Mitchell, C. M., Preisser, J. S., Phillips, C., Commander, C., & Burker, E. (1998). Environmental correlates of resident agitation in Alzheimer's disease special care units. *Journal of the American Geriatrics Society*, 46, 862–869.

Stewart, J. T. (1995). Management of behavior problems in the demented patient. *American Family Physician*, 52, 2311–2320.

Teresi, J. (1994). Overview of methodological issues in the study of chronic care populations. *Alzheimer Disease and Associated Disorders*, 8(Suppl. 1), S247–S273.

U.S. Congress, Office of Technology Assessment. (1992). *Special care units for people with Alzheimer's and other dementias: Consumer education, research, regulatory, and reimbursement issues*. Washington, DC: U.S. Government Printing Office.

Weisman, G. D., Cohen, U., Ray, K., & Day, K. (1991). Architectural planning and design for dementia care. In D. H. Coons (Ed.), *Specialized dementia care units* (p. 83–106). Baltimore: Johns Hopkins University Press.

Zeisel, J., Hyde, J., & Levkoff, S. (1994). Best practices: An environment-behavior (E–B) model for Alzheimer special care units. *American Journal of Alzheimer's Care and Related Disorders & Research*, 9, 4–21.

Zeisel, J., & Raia, P. (2000). Nonpharmacological treatment for Alzheimer's disease: A mind-brain approach. *American Journal of Alzheimer's Disease and Other Dementias, 15,* 331–340.

Received December 10, 2001
Accepted September 19, 2002
Decision Editor: Laurence G. Branch, PhD

34 A New Way of Thinking About Taste

Galen Cranz

Taste had been viewed as a way that class is expressed and reinforced, but even more generally it may be a way that people integrate different parts of the social system that they inhabit (what sociologist Bourdieu calls "habitus.") Does taste express social-economic class or personalization and identity? Can it do both? To what extent do the key concepts of pragmatics, symbolics, and aesthetics apply to architecture and urban design beyond interior design?

In the department of architecture where I teach, aesthetic issues are important criteria for judging buildings and talent. Distinguishing good design from inferior design is part of what a student learns there. This keen sense of discrimination is commonly used to privilege one thing over another and so has some distant relation to power. Because my formal education is in sociology, I think about both the powerful and the powerless, taking pains to include the point of view of the masses, the ordinary, and even the vulnerable. How can anyone with this kind of education be interested in issues of artistic distinction, so associated with taste and connoisseurship? In graduate school an art teacher once asked me how I could be a sociology major since I was good at art. Of course this was flattering at one level, but it also made me frustrated that our culture assumes an either/or choice between clarity of thought (about anything including social life) and sensory beauty. I want both.

I see art as an important part of social life—not just as a way to create distinction, but also as a way to practice personal, social and cultural integration. In our homes we have an ongoing relationship with art. Indeed, for most of us our homes are the site of more everyday art activity than any other place. Accordingly, in this essay I will focus on the ordinary practice of decorating homes to show how artistic activity is a form of personal integration as much as a form of social differentiation. I define interior decoration broadly, not as a business, but rather as a widespread general cultural practice of decorating the interior of a room or house. (Therefore, I will use the term decorator to apply to both professionals and laymen.) While the practice is general, it is more structured than we commonly assume. Almost everyone assembles two different kinds of objects—the practical and symbolic—at home—by means of aesthetics. This view of decoration makes it important by establishing its artistic and social significance.

Galen Cranz; Jean W. McLaughlin, ed., "A New Way of Thinking About Taste," from *Nature of Craft & The Penland Experience.* Published by Lark Books, 2004. Copyright by Sterling Publishing Company. Permission to reprint granted by the rights holder.

Many sociologists have recognized the importance of decoration through its connection with taste. (See bibliography.) Since the 18th century, taste has been recognized as a process of discrimination, most recently highlighted by Pierre Bourdieu's seminal study *Distinction: A Social Critique of the Judgment of Taste*. Home decor is one of the major sites for the exercise of taste. Sociologists view taste as a way that people make distinctions between themselves and others and a way that people legitimize class differences. In common speech today the word taste is used much more simply, synonymous with the preference, as in "I have a taste for natural fabrics." The artistic, the everyday, and the sociological views of taste can provisionally find common ground in a definition of taste that refers to the ability to make distinctions, evaluate, and choose aesthetic qualities in all of the arts, including those of daily living.

I am proposing a new framework for thinking about taste that offers an inclusive understanding of artistic assembly in environmental design, including home decor. Graphically and conceptually, it looks something like this:

Taste = (Pragmatics + Symbols) Integrated Aesthetically

People have two classes of objects in their homes—the practical things necessary to live in our culture and the symbolic things that express who we are, from where we have come, and perhaps where we are going. People integrate these two sets of objects into compositions by means of aesthetic principles like symmetry and color coordination. Thus, taste in decorating involves the unification of two fairly discrete categories of objects—the pragmatic and the symbolic—by means of aesthetics.

The pragmatic consists of the objects needed in a culture in order to eat, sleep, dress—toasters, beds, chairs, lamps, ironing boards. The pragmatic basis of taste is important because it differentiates taste from "pure" art, thereby placing taste squarely within the domain of utility.

Symbolic objects represent some part of a person's identity, the sum total of the groups with whom he or she affiliates.[1] They communicate about relatives, activities, achievements, travel, education, and religion. They include photographs, audio equipment, sports trophies, souvenirs, awards, diplomas, and crucifixes, all of which express different aspects of a person's identity. (A few of these objects might be handmade, but most will be industrially manufactured commodities.)

Neither category—the symbolic nor the pragmatic—is fixed. What is defined as pragmatic varies culturally. Tables and chairs are pragmatic requirements for dwelling in western cultures, but became symbols of modernization and westernization in the floor-sitting parts of the world. Moreover, the pragmatic and symbolic can overlap. For example, pragmatic things can be elaborated and overlaid with symbolic meaning. Plastic forks have different meanings than stainless steel forks, which in turn have different meanings than sterling silver forks. The pattern in which they are decorated (or not) gives us additional information about their symbolic significance. Sometimes the bare pragmatic object can be used symbolically. For example, having the "right" colander may be symbolically important to a designer.

Context is important in knowing if something is pragmatic or symbolic. For example, according to architectural historian Greg Castillo, utilitarian stoves and refrigerators installed in model homes in West Berlin became symbols of the benefits of American capitalism in the 1950s Cold War against communism. In other contexts they would be mere commodities, but here the people who displayed them and the audience who viewed them gave them symbolic meaning.[2]

Conversely, television, once a symbol of forward-looking people, is now a pragmatic necessity that only the poorest of the poor cannot afford.

These two sets of objects—the pragmatic and the symbolic—are organized in relation to one another functionally and visually, following kinesthetic and aesthetic rules that may or may not be conscious to the homemaker. Empirically, I have observed that people want to make unified tableaux out of their disparate collections of objects. It is as if pragmatic and symbolic objects are added together and then ordered (perhaps multiplied or harmonized) by aesthetic rules. These rules or conventions govern, consciously or unconsciously, the arrangement of parts, details, form, color, etc., so as to produce a complete and visually harmonious unit. These rules vary by culture. For example, rich, deeply carved texture might be more important in one culture or time period than another, depending on sources of wood, climate, shadows, myths—the list is almost endless.

Could we speak of taste in sports, finance, military action, or crime? Yes, possibly, but taste usually refers to the arts and aesthetics. The word art has a Latin root meaning to join or fit together and refers to creativeness, the human ability to make things. Our household compositions fit within this definition of art. The word aesthetics comes to us from ancient Greek, referring to our capacity to perceive, our sensitivity, hence our sensitivity to art and beauty, our taste. Domestic display also registers our sense of aesthetics. Kinesthetic has to do with our awareness of bodily movement, also implicitly involved in domestic compositions because we do not want things to be out of reach, fall on us, or be inconveniently situated. Together, objects along with the artistic and kinesthetic rules used to order them, help us communicate with one another—yes, but also with ourselves.

When we assemble our things and look at them ourselves we are psychologically integrating ourselves, not just showing off to others. I have come to see taste as much as a process about selection and assembly as it is a quality of objects, a talent in individuals, or a social status. I would like to explain how I have come to this conclusion.

First, why isn't taste in the object? Why aren't some objects more tasteful than others? In a consumer world what makes us distinctive it is not so much the specific qualities of the things we have, but their constellation. We do not make most things by hand; we can buy them fairly readily, so their material significance is not great. Instead, their relationship takes on significance. To change a collection of objects into a composition requires connecting them. Anthropologist Ellen Dissanayake, in studying the practice of craft, has noted the importance of the relationship between things: "I was intrigued with how much depended on two things and their relationship. One rock or one piece of wood is something (some thing), but once a second rock or piece of wood, or some other second thing, is placed with it, there is an immediate implicit connection between them that requires consideration." Thus, questions about objects being in good taste or bad taste lose significance. Connoisseurship, a way to distinguish one object from another or one creator from another, is often closely linked to discussions of taste but its significance fades in light of the importance of placement.

Second, is taste a quality in persons? I am not particularly interested in whether or not a person "has taste" or "has no taste." Rather, I am interested in how a person assembles the many things in his or her immediate environment. Here taste is the activity and the outcome of assembling objects artistically. It is true that some people have more skill at assembling these secular tableaux than others. This must be acknowledged, but not so much as good, bad, or poor taste. I prefer to see skill differences acknowledged as more or less developed.[3] Not all differences between people are differences in skill, but rather differences in what and how they want to communicate. People differ regarding how much interest they have in communicating in this way; some don't care about communicating about themselves through this medium.

Recently I asked graduate architecture students to make a composition of all the things that they had brought with them into the classroom. There I saw the disservice that comes from using the lens of "good" and "bad" taste. The major distinction between their compositions was in regard to how formal versus how associational they were. Admittedly, I was personally more attracted to some of the compositions than others and I would say that some were more sophisticated than others, but this exercise taught me something else. I was forced to take a more psychoanalytic point of view. The differences related more to what each student was trying to communicate—slice of student life, painterly still life, form for form's sake, mystery—than to my or anyone else's idea of "good" or "bad" taste. And some were more skilled at expressing their intentions than others.

My new framework applies to people at all levels of design skill. The differences are in the number of dimensions that people use to create aesthetic unity (color, texture, shape, size, pattern), the principles of composition (primarily symmetrical versus asymmetrical) and the scale at which they attempt to create such order.[4] In the student exercise there were marked differences in the scale of their compositions; some used a chair seat, some used the whole chair, others used a part of the wall or floor in relation to a chair.

I have learned that domestic compositions follow a developmental sequence. I first realized this after I spent a week studying how residents decorated their apartments in a housing project for the elderly in New Jersey in the 1970s. All of the units were either one-bedroom studios or one-bedroom units. Because they were identical, the only way that they could be individualized was through their decoration. The management made some suggestions as to whom I should interview in the building. The first on the list was Miss Hayworth, whom they called "the best housekeeper" in the building. To me that phrase suggested that I would see a very neat, clean place. Instead, I discovered the best "decorator," or perhaps even the best "interior designer." Today we might say that she was the Martha Stewart of Jersey Manor. Widely acknowledged as the best in the building, she had an influence on her neighbors, especially her immediate neighbor and friend Mrs. Cuff. On the basis of observing, photographing and interviewing these two and another twenty residents I developed a hypothesis which I have since confirmed in many other homes through advertisements, newspapers, movies, decorator magazines, and of course through direct observation.

Generally, we put things together that look alike. And, first, most people use color to make things match or contrast. For example, the bedroom might be all blue—the paint on the walls, the pattern of the bedspreads, the tray on the dresser, even the alarm clock. Now that even bathrooms are decorated (since about 1960) all of the items—towels, shower curtain, the cover of the tissue dispenser, even the plate for the light switch—might be the same shade of fuchsia. One resident used the orange-yellow rug that came with the unit to establish a palette of orange.

In addition to color, the more sophisticated use pattern and texture. Bas-relief metal work might be paired with a plant having a similar leaf pattern. A paper lampshade with a pattern that includes quarter inch white dots is placed near a small ivory bas-relief representation of the Last Supper because the size of the heads is the same as the dots.

The most sophisticated relate things by shape. Those with training or feeling for sculpture might collect circles, squares, or triangles together into a composition of different colors. A slightly more sophisticated move might be to assemble things of different shape and color but of comparable size and definition. A round shape might be composed with a square, triangle, or rectangle of roughly equivalent size.[5]

Regarding scale, some have the psychological or economic capacity to organize the entire wall, not just the dresser top or segment above it, and others can integrate the entire room. Beyond this scale professionals usually take over; relatively few people attempt to create visual order between rooms (the realm of architects), and fewer between inside and outside (architects and landscape architects), and yet fewer between buildings (urban designers), or cities and regions (city and regional planners). Yet the basic impulse to order practical and expressive things artistically remains in professional circles.

Reactions to those who violate the expectation that in our homes practical and symbolic things will be combined artistically help demonstrate how strong this norm is. In the New Jersey housing project of over three hundred units for the elderly, only two people were described negatively by others; one was "not a good housekeeper" and the other was "dirty." They proved to be the exception that proves the rule. In this case, the exception that exposed the workings of this way of thinking about taste. Miss Brevit was a retired nurse who decided to learn about plants and set them up all over her apartment. She went so far as to remove the doors from her clothes closet to create more shelf space for potted plants. She was unusual for several reasons: she had been a professional, she was one of only two people who took a subscription to the *New York Times*, and she had books. But her real eccentricity for the other residents was that she had very few symbolic objects and that she did not organize her things into a visual tableau. She was described as "not a good housekeeper" because her environment was primarily pragmatic.

Mr. Wheeler was not literally "dirty." Rather, he had no conventionally sentimental objects and made no artistic compositions. He was a history buff, interested in local civil engineering. He had boxes full of photographs of tunnels, bridges, and other civic works. He had files full of newspaper clippings and documents. He told me that he had much more when he lived in a house, but had to get rid of a lot of it in order to move in here. He didn't mind living amongst his own files. He violated the unwritten codes about how one should display one's stuff. He was virtually all pragmatic.

These two examples clarified for me how the pragmatic and symbolic have become discrete categories of thought in people's minds. In these two cases the neighbors were not conscious of their mental structures, and so they used other terms like "dirty" and "poor housekeeper" when the symbolic category was ignored or collapsed into one with pragmatic. Designers, too, sometimes violate this shared cultural process; for some modernist designers, having the right pragmatic objects—the right toaster, the right juicer—may be all the symbolism they allow themselves. Laymen may perceive such strict minimalist environments as "bare" or "cold," but all that has happened is that the two categories have been collapsed into one. Some people have so many sentimental objects in their place that it is hard to move around or make a meal; here the symbolic has dominated the pragmatic. These extreme cases help expose the structure of thought that we routinely bring to bear upon the process of organizing our homes.

The point of view I am developing here is that everybody decorates and so everyone composes, which is a form of psychological integration. In decorating, people create dioramas in which they actually live. The size of the composition and the way practical things are combined with symbolic ones tell us more about the person than a simple statement that they have good or bad taste. Similarly, there are no objects that are intrinsically in "good" or "bad" taste. For example, toilet lid covers, whether they are hand crocheted or industrially produced, are not "bad taste" despite what my colleagues in architecture might think. The fact that someone chooses to soften the clank of the lid on the tank and at the same time include the pragmatic toilet in an overall decorative scheme means that they are quite serious about the aesthetics of everyday living, and that their taste behavior is highly activated. For all these reason I have concluded that taste is not particularly meaningful as a property of persons or objects.

ADVANTAGES OF THIS WAY OF THINKING ABOUT TASTE

This set of ideas for thinking about interior decoration can be used to analyze how people decorate in different cultures, different classes, different genders, different age groups, and different ethnic groups and subcultures, even as it allows for and acknowledges individual variations. That is to say, we do not have to use different ideas about how people make things or decorate if we shift focus from the United States to Polynesia, from the rich to the poor, men to women, young to old, from one immigrant group to another. Because each of the elements of this framework is defined generally but analytically, we can locate each of these groups and persons at different points along the same conceptual dimensions.[6] Even though our identities are rooted in group memberships, individuals can and do express themselves visually by assembling their stuff in unique compositions. And as they change, so too do the arrangements of their stuff.

This way of thinking about taste as a special kind of composition is simple enough to apply to all scales of environmental design. It encompasses both the things inside of a room or building, the building itself, and the things outside of it. We could use the same set of ideas to talk about products, interiors, architecture, urban design, and landscape architecture. Differences between an object and a neighborhood would be recognized as different points along a continuum, rather than being used to create separate theories, disciplines, and standards of excellence for each shift in scale.

Another strength of this framework for thinking about taste is that it situates both amateurs and design professionals along a continuum. This means that we don't have to assume a sharp difference between the user and a designer or, in sociologist Herbert Gans's terms, between the audience and the creator. Bluntly, this means that the tastemaker and the most aesthetically undeveloped person share something. If everyone participates in this activity, professionals do not have to feel alienated from their audiences. They can communicate directly with nonprofessionals about this important aspect of living. Conversely, by understanding that what professionals work at for a living is an elaboration of what they themselves are doing when they do something as simple as set the table, the layperson can feel affinity with the artist, craftsperson, and designer.

Practically speaking, this means that citizens might appreciate (and hire) art, craft, and design professionals more than they do now. I do not want laypeople to be intimidated, nor to use professionals as status symbols, but rather to appreciate them for working thoughtfully and full-time to develop and refine this shared impulse to intertwine two categories of objects in a pleasing way. Laymen can learn from these professionals and benefit from their services, even as the most culturally responsive professionals are learning from popular practices. This elemental way of thinking about taste can expand the exchange of ideas about how to develop, enhance, simplify, or elaborate the artistic tableaux in which we live our lives.

Another power of this framework is that it does not require two different sets of considerations for male or female practitioners. In *As Long As It's Pink: Gender Politics of Taste,* Penny Sparke has argued that historically taste referred primarily to women's aesthetic activity within the home, and that male culture claimed the term "design" as a way to differentiate itself from the traditional female concern with "taste" in interior decoration. This perspective recognizes differences in ability and training, but makes much of the observation that the impulse to make order is shared by most people.

This simple but comprehensive (one definition of elegant) view allows us to reconsider a whole series of dichotomies as related qualities. For example, this framework allows us to consider both useful and expressive aspects, in other words both the pragmatic and the symbolic. Further, it allows us to acknowledge both the formal and the associational aspects of these works, that is to consider both form and meaning, sometimes referred to as syntax and semantics. It allows us to consider both structure and surface, both the process and its outcome, both making and display, both activity and result.[7]

This is a general set of ideas for explaining how the values implicit in the term "taste" operate in the world, potentially liberating for the insecure consumer, and especially useful for educators and professionals in planning and environmental design, architecture, art, fashion, sociology, education, and cultural studies. Most writing on taste either debunks it or celebrates it. This is a step toward learning how it works, so that as individuals or as professionals we can use its codes knowingly.

TASTE MOVES BETWEEN MATERIAL AND NONMATERIAL CULTURE

One issue remains: that of rank and class. The sociological contribution to writing about taste sees it as a form of showing off—called conspicuous consumption by Thorstein Veblen and distinction by Bourdieu—a form of rank, legitimizing class differences. In contrast, I have observed that the basic formula for artistic display is surprisingly similar for all socioeconomic classes. In the United States at least, the working class, middle class, upper middle-class, celebrities, and even artists, designers, craftspersons, and collectors follow similar rules despite differences in money, power, and education.

In discussing aesthetic cultural systems, sociologist Paul DiMaggio has made a distinction between material and nonmaterial culture, and sociologist David Gartman has observed that material culture (for example, cars and washing machines) has become a basis for equalizing social differences, while nonmaterial culture like music has become a basis for sustaining social differences. The qualifications that these sociologists have introduced in order to modify Bourdieu's strict view that all matters of taste are matters of rank can be applied to my way of thinking about taste. Pragmatic things are material and since we all need the same basic things in our Western living rooms we could say that of all the things we possess they provide the most commonality among people; despite cost differences they make us more like one another than anything else. The symbolic things introduce less equality, representing differences in education, travel, religion, etc. The aesthetic principles by which we order our pragmatic and symbolic things are nonmaterial, and they may introduce even more inequality, although design idealists, like me, see this as a way to transcend inequality.[8]

My addition to this evolving set of ideas is to suggest that taste slides back and forth between material and nonmaterial culture. Put another way, taste is a transitional category between the two.[9] Recall that taste is about placement. The mental structures used to place the objects are nonmaterial, but the objects themselves are clearly material. This makes taste, at least in the context of interior decoration, an arena in which social differences are both maintained *and* transcended. Cognitive styles of arranging objects, which the design writer Leonard Koren calls "rhetorics," are the nonmaterial part of culture, but they are inextricably fused with its material base, the objects.

Taste is a slippery concept that can be used either to transcend class differences or to confirm them. A Ming vase and a beer bottle are both material and both signify different social ranks, but in composition they could be related by form—they may have the same silhouette—which would seem to transcend class signification. However, the sculptural sophistication of looking for and seeing common shapes elevates the decorator, bringing back in the vertical element of rank.

The active, process-oriented conception of taste that I have described here suggests that we play with the relationship between our changing cognitive distinctions and the universal material plane that unites us all. Thereby, difference and similarity, distinction and wholeness are acknowledged simultaneously. The exercise of taste in the realm of interior decoration is a kind of alchemy.

Let me expand on this particular kind of transformation. The aesthetic operations that unify pragmatic and symbolic objects do not so much fuse the two as much as they temporarily relate them. These operations allow us to reconfigure objects. Very different compositions can be created with identical objects. These secular tableaux remind me of what I have heard about the late 19th century *tableau vivant*. People dressed in costumes copied from famous paintings, often of antiquity, then acted out and held poses of the figures in the paintings. They could be unfrozen, reconfigured, and frozen again. So, too, our things can be reorganized for greater convenience, greater drama, new color schemes, in response to new ideas about what is convenient, and the like. Ah, but how little we take advantage of this ability to change—except when goaded by fashion. We get lazy and let things remain as they have been, but fashion prompts us to reconfigure our stuff. Psychically, fashion helps keep us flexible. As Tom Wolfe has said, fashion allows us to conform (to group standards) and change by the same token.

Our compositions, as expressions of our wholeness, change as we pass through life. Personally we change and we express those changes through various media including the environments in which we live. The common practice of decorating, arranging our things, may help us integrate our various and multiple identities. Our identities will differ by class, but people in all classes assemble and thereby integrate their identities. Decorating may help us consolidate and integrate who we are as much as it helps us recognize and legitimate social differences.[10] This means that decorating is a cultural practice as much as a class-based practice that reflects differences in social structure. This view admits that both our previous and our current selves differ from our fellows. We express interpersonal differences and *at the same time* we express our current sense of wholeness through the choices we make in clothes, jewelry, and home decoration. A composition can be a universe unto itself. For some time during creation or deep appreciation of another person's arrangement, it is not part of a social hierarchy. In this way decoration both expresses and transcends social differences.

NOTES

1. This dimension most closely corresponds to the moral codes by which some elites identify one another according to sociologist Michelle Lamont.
2. In the late 20th century buying commercial stoves for residential kitchens became a symbolic statement more than a pragmatic accommodation to an increase in cooking skill. In fact, those who cook regularly often feel smug that those who have the commercial stoves seldom use them.
3. Accordingly, I am even willing to conceptualize taste "scores," some people scoring higher than others. But they would be scoring higher or lower at an activity rather than as human beings.
4. Theoretically, each assembly created by a person could be given a score so that levels of skill could be acknowledged, objectified, measured. Even so, the final score would not be as interesting as the scores in the different parts of the equation. Two people could end up with the same score but have very different profiles in terms of the kinds of pragmatic objects, the kinds of symbols, and how skillfully they were composed.
5. At the scale of landscape an example is architect Bernard Tschumi's design for Parc La Villette in Paris.
6. Important questions about this way of thinking about taste, decoration, and craft remain. For example, how early do children learn to manipulate these several components of taste? How are gender differences developed? Where do we get our ideas as adults?
7. For those interested in the debates about mass culture and those interested in society and economy, this perspective also allows us to consider decoration as both production and consumption, important because residents produce interior arrangements even if they buy (and in that sense consume) their component parts.
8. My grandmother, a professional interior designer, told me that it didn't matter how poor one was, if one had to sit on orange crates and shop at the five and dime and thrift stores, one could still put things together well. But her brand of democracy presumes an educated eye—not necessarily formally educated, but an eye raised to think that beauty matters. There may also be innate, not class-based, differences between people in regard to how much information they take in through the senses.
9. Curiously, while this fusion or continuum seems important, we in our culture do not want to blur the distinction between pragmatic and symbolic. That is to say, maintaining the difference between pragmatic and symbolic categories is important even as the two categories are harmonized artistically, and even as doing so creates and expresses a continuum between material and nonmaterial categories.
10. In sociological terms decoration performs an "integrative" function, not just one of "pattern maintenance."

BIBLIOGRAPHY

Bourdieu, Pierre. *Distinction: A Social Critique of the Judgment of Taste.* Cambridge MA: Harvard University Press, 1984.

Castillo, Greg. "A Home for the Cold War: Exhibiting American Domesticity in Postwar Europe." *Journal of the Society of Architectural Historians,* in press.

DiMaggio, Paul. "Classification in Art." *American Sociological Review* 52 (1987): 440–55.

Dissanayake, Ellen. *Two Orphans and a Dog: Art and Transformation.* Haystack Mountain School of Crafts, Deer Isle, Maine, 2000: 4.

Erickson, Bonnie. "Culture, Class and Connections." *American Journal of Sociology* 1021 (July, 1996): 217–251.

Gans, Herbert. *Popular Culture and High Culture.* New York: Basic Books, 1999.

Gartman, David. "Culture as Class Symbolization or Mass Reification? A Critique of Bourdieu's Distinction." *American Journal of Sociology* 972 (Sept., 1991): 421–447.

Koren, Leonard. *Arranging Things: A Rhetoric of Object Placement.* Berkeley, CA: Stone Bridge Press, 2003.

Kron, Joan. "The Semiotics of Home Decor." In *Signs of Life* in the USA, eds., Sonia Maasik and Jack Solomon. Boston: Bedford Books, 1997: 72–82.

Laumann, E. O. and J. S. House. "Living Room Styles and Social Attributes: The Patterning of Material Artifacts in a Modern Urban Community," *Sociol. Soc. Res.* 54 (1970): 321–42.

Lamont, Michele. *Money, Morals, and Manners: The Culture of the French and the American Upper-Middle Class.* Chicago: University of Chicago Press, 1992.

Levine, Lawrence. *Highbrow/Lowbrow: The Emergence of Cultural Hierarchy in America.* Cambridge, MA: Harvard University Press, 1988.

Marcus, Clare Cooper. *House As Mirror of Self.* Berkeley CA.: Conan Press, 1995.

Miller, Daniel. "Consumption and Commodities." *Annual Review of Anthropology,* 24 (1995): 141–161.

Peterson, Richard and Roger Kern. "Changing Highbrow Taste From Snob to Omnivore," *American Sociological Review,* 615. (Oct. 1996): 900–907.

Starke, Penny. *As Long As It's Pink: The Sexual Politics of Taste.* New York: Harper Collins, 1995.

Veblen, Thorstein. *The Theory of the Leisure Class.* New York: Modern Library, 1934.

Wolfe, Tom. "Introduction," in Rene König. *A La Mode: on the Social Psychology of Fashion.* New York: Seabury Press, 1973.

35 Defining the Sustainable Park: A Fifth Model for Urban Parks

Galen Cranz and Michael Boland

This article summarizes the park typology established in *The Politics of Park Design* and argues that a new, fifth model is emerging in response to the social need for ecological sustainability.

ABSTRACT

How can parks contribute to the overarching project of helping cities become more ecologically sustainable? The history of urban parks in America reveals more concern with social problems than with ecological sustainability. Four types of city parks have been identified—the Pleasure Ground, the Reform Park, the Recreation Facility, and the Open Space System—and each of them respond to social issues, not ecological ones. Yet today, ecological problems are becoming one of our biggest social concerns, so a new urban park type focused on social solutions to ecological problems would be consistent with this pattern. Using the same social and physical criteria that described the previous four models, Part I describes a fifth model, the Sustainable Park, which began to emerge in the late 1990s. Part II postulates three general attributes of this new kind of park: (1) self-sufficiency in regard to material resources and maintenance, (2) solving larger urban problems outside of park boundaries, and (3) creating new standards for aesthetics and landscape management in parks and other urban landscapes. It also explores policy implications of these attributes regarding park design and management, the practice of landscape architecture, citizen participation, and ecological education.

In the past, citizens saw parks as an antidote to cities, which they perceived as stressful, dangerous, and unhealthy places to live. Once a contradiction in terms, the sustainable city is now an intellectually and socially recognized goal. Within this framework, we now ask what contribution parks can make to the project of making cities more ecologically balanced and sustainable. Historically, urban parks responded to social problems and expressed various ideas about nature, but they showed little concern for actual ecological fitness. Today, in contrast, ecological problems may be counted among our most pressing social problems. Because ecological and social problems are now conflated, a new urban park type that focuses on solutions to ecological problems and expresses

Galen Cranz & Michael Boland, "Defining the Sustainable Park: A Fifth Model for Urban Parks," from *Landscape Journal*, Vol. 23, No. 2, pp. 102–120. Copyright © 2004 by University of Wisconsin Press. Permission to reprint granted by the publisher.

new ideas about nature can build upon the traditional social genesis of urban parks in the United States to help improve the quality of life in American cities.

PART I: A NEW TYPE OF PARK?

A Park Typology. A classic study of urban parks (Cranz 1982) described four types: the Pleasure Ground (1850–1900), the Reform Park (1900–1930), the Recreation Facility (1930–1965), and the Open Space System (1965–?). This typology includes both the shifting social purposes that parks served and the corresponding variations in designed form. Each park type evolved to address what were considered to be pressing urban social problems at that time. Table 1 summarizes the social goals, social actors, and formal characteristics for each of the four types. The *Pleasure Ground* was typically large and located on the edge of the city (Figure 1). Frederick Law Olmsted, the father of landscape architecture in America, designed many of them. He favored a pastoral style, neither wild nor urban, with curvilinear circulation and naturalistic use of trees and water. Mental appreciation of the landscape was important, but these parks were actively programmed and sports were popular, so they were not merely "passive."

Table 1. A Comparison of the Sustainable Park to Prior Park Types After Cranz (1982).

	Pleasure Ground 1850–1900	Reform Park 1900–1930	Recreation Facility 1930–1965	Open Space System 1965–?	Sustainable Park 1990–present
Social Goal	Public health & social reform	Social reform; children's play; assimilation	Recreation service	Participation; revitalize city; stop riots	Human health; ecological health
Activities	Strolling, carriage racing, bike riding, picnics, rowing, classical music, nondidactic education	Supervised play, gymnastics, crafts, Americanization classes, dancing, plays & pageants	Active recreation: basketball, tennis, team sports, spectator sports, swimming	Psychic relief, free-form play, pop music, participatory arts	Strolling, hiking, biking, passive & active recreation, bird watching, education, stewardship
Size	Very large, 1,000+ acres	Small, city blocks	Small to medium, follow formulae	Varied, often small, irregular sites	Varied, emphasis on corridors
Relation to City	Set in contrast	Accepts urban patterns	Suburban	City is a work of art; network	Art-nature continuum; part of larger urban system; model for others
Order	Curvilinear	Rectilinear	Rectilinear	Both	Evolutionary aesthetic
Elements	Woodland & meadow, curving paths, placid water bodies, rustic structures, limited floral displays	Sandlots, playgrounds, rectilinear paths, swimming pools, field houses	Asphalt or grass play area, pools, rectilinear paths, standard play equipment	Trees, grass, shrubs, curving & rectilinear paths, water features for view, free-form play equipment	Native plants, permeable surfaces, ecological restoration green infrastructure, resource self-sufficiency

Promoters	Health reformers, transcendentalism, real estate interests	Social reformers, social workers, recreation workers	Politicians, bureaucrats, planners	Politicians, environmentalists, artists, designers	Environmentalists, local communities, volunteer groups, landscape architects
Beneficiaries	All city dwellers (intended), upper middle class (reality)	Children, immigrants, working class	Suburban families	Residents, workers, poor urban youth, middle class	Residents, wildlife, cities, planet

The working class seldom used these parks because they were far from the tenements. Consequently, small park advocates wanted the city to establish parks on a few square blocks in the inner city. Eventually this movement merged with those advocating playgrounds for children, resulting in the *Reform Park* with special play equipment for children. These parks were small and symmetrical, with no illusion of countryside or nature. Their principal architectural innovation was the field house, envisioned as a clubhouse for the working class (Figure 2a).

To justify their expenditures, park commissioners during the first two eras enumerated all the social goals that parks served: to reduce class conflict, to reinforce the family unit, to socialize immigrants to the American way of life, to stop the spread of disease, and to educate citizens. In contrast, a new era was claimed in 1930 when Robert Moses was appointed commissioner of New York City's Park Department. For him, parks had become a recognized governmental service requiring no justification (Moses 1940, 3). Instead, he and park departments nationwide established uniform standards and extended service to the suburbs and urban areas that had not yet received parks or playgrounds. The major innovations were the stadium, parking lot, and asphalt ball courts—hence the term *Recreation Facility* (Figure 2b).

A generation later, a dialectic response against the perceived sterility of the Recreation Facility emerged in 1965 when Lindsay ran for mayor of New York City. He published a policy paper on parks that reclaimed parks as a mechanism of social control and reform. In defiance of previous notions of standardization, he recruited landscape architects to design site-specific recreational settings. A more artistic, participatory sensibility flourished, part of a closer tie between park programming and popular culture. Accordingly, recreation came to be seen as something that could take place anywhere—in the streets, on a rooftop, at the waterfront, along an abandoned railway line, as well as in traditional plazas and parks. Paley Park, for example, is a tiny site, violating

Figure 1. Central Park, the first Pleasure Ground in the United States. (Photograph by M. Boland)

the standards of the recreation era, and emblematic of the new ideology because it embraced the city. All parks came to be conceived as part of a network of disparate open spaces linked together, hence the term *Open Space System* (Figure 2c).

Noting that park models tend to dominate for 30 to 50 years, we conclude that these models are generational. That is, each generation has its own set of ideas about how parks can help cities, its own experience in putting these ideas into practice, and its own frustrations and victories with those models. Accordingly, we expected that our generation would formulate and realize its own model. Given the current attention to ecological fitness and sustainable development, we expected that the fifth model would focus on solving ecological problems.

Postulating a Fifth Park Model: Methods. How would we recognize the fifth model if and when we saw it? General definitions may not be of much help. Sustainability and ecological design have many different facets, so it is understandable that most definitions are very broad, but such definitions run the danger of becoming weak as guides to action. The commonly cited Brundtland definition of sustainability as meeting "the needs of the present without compromising the ability of future generations to meet their own needs" emphasizes that aspect of sustainability having to do with justice within and between generations (Thompson 2000, 12–32). However, this definition is too broad for most landscape architects, urban designers, and park planners who want to know how the general value of sustainability might be recognized and realized in the specific context of urban parks. Yet we agree with the British sociologists Simon Guy and Graham Farmer (2000) in their observations about the early stages of searching for a definition of green buildings: we might benefit by resisting the urge to find one "true or incontestable, consensual definition ... [in order to remain] sensitive to the range of ... innovations which may surface" (73–74).

As a compromise between being too broad or too specific, we started out with a loose working definition of Sustainable Parks. A working definition would allow us to identify parks that we could reexamine in order to come up with a progressively more refined understanding of what Sustainable Parks are or could be. To start, we knew that Sustainable Parks would have to have traits generally thought to increase the ecological performance of parks. To warrant being

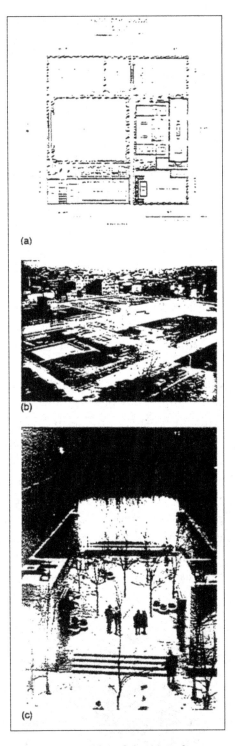

Figure 2. Examples of the (a) Reform Park (courtesy of Chicago South Park District), (b) Recreation Facility (reprinted from New York City, Department of Parks, report from 1967) and (c) Open Space System (courtesy of New York Public Library).

recognized as a distinctive model, we expected that at least some of these traits would not be found in any of the other four prior park types. These new characteristics included the use of native plants, restoration of streams or other natural systems, wildlife habitat, integration of appropriate technologies or infrastructure, recycling, and sustainable construction and maintenance practices. This working definition started out emphasizing the ecological value of parks, but we knew it would also include social values. After all, sustainability is ultimately a social concept rather than a technical or biological one because humans are responsible for the ecological crisis today.

We began the search for a new park model using a sociological technique called content analysis. We analyzed parks published in five prominent landscape journals over the previous 20 years from 1982 to 2002. We started in 1982 when *The Politics of Park Design* was published in order to pick up where it had left off. (Only *Landscape Architecture* magazine was analyzed from years 1998–2002 due to limits of the research budget and because the vast majority of the articles about parks published between 1982 and 1997 had come from *Landscape Architecture*. See Appendix A for a complete list of publications reviewed.) In the publishing world, biases are inevitable regarding editorial selection, but the bias would presumably work in favor of innovation and change—the very thing we were monitoring. Therefore, an analysis of parks featured in these publications was a useful way to detect trends or shifts in emphasis.

We found 125 parks in our analysis and have listed them in Appendix A. Each park was described based on the information contained in the published text and illustrations. We analyzed each park on identical worksheets in terms of physical form, social program, promoters, intended and actual beneficiaries, and public reaction. On the basis of this analysis, each park was coded as one or more of the park types, using a simple coding system: Pleasure Ground (I), Reform (II), Recreation Facility (III), Open Space System (IV), and Sustainable Park (V). The physical and social information gathered on each park included the following: Park Identifier (name, location, designer); Model (Pleasure Ground, Reform Park, Recreation Facility, Open Space System, Sustainable Park); Physical Form (location, size, composition); Landscape Elements (water, land, vegetation, other); Buildings; Construction Details; Program (designed purpose and unintended purposes); Promoters; Beneficiaries (intended and actual); Fate of Model in Practice (implementation, public reaction). Most parks received one number because they fell clearly into one of the park types, but some provisionally received two numbers because two types could be discerned. These cases were analyzed by a group of graduate student researchers led by the senior author to decide which type was stronger.[1]

We could not determine whether or not any of these parks actually succeeded at reducing resource use or creating self-sustaining, healthy ecological systems. Moreover, we did not distinguish between parks that merely evoked ecological symbolism and those that actually restored functioning ecological systems. This is not an evaluation of specific parks or places. At this point in history, making philosophical and ideological appeals to sustainability and ecology is enough to mark a significant change in thinking about the purpose of urban parks.

A New Park Type Is Emerging. Our analysis found that all five park types were published during this 20-year period, but Open Space Systems (46%) predominated (Table 2). The second largest category (23%) was the new fifth category, tentatively identified as *sustainable*. We conclude that a new model is emerging among landscape professionals.

Most (86%) of the parks exhibiting traits we had determined to be *sustainable* were featured in articles published after 1990. This change came 25 years after the shift to open space ideology in 1965. Since American urban park models have typically lasted 30 to 50 years, and since historically park bureaucracies have institutionalized changes in thinking about parks *after* landscape architects have begun to advocate them, we predict that the Sustainable Park will be adopted by municipal park departments between 1995 and 2015. We have already observed the number of Pleasure Grounds drop significantly from 1998 to 2002 while the number of Open Space and Sustainable Parks have increased.

Table 2. Parks described in leading landscape architecture journals analyzed by park type.

	1982–1990	1991–2002	Total
Pleasure Ground	12 (23.5%)	12 (16%)	24 (19%)
Reform Park	0 (0%)	3 (4%)	3 (2%)
Recreation Facility	12 (23.5%)	0 (0%)	12 (10%)
Open Space	23 (45%)	34 (46%)	57 (46%)
Sustainable Park	4 (8%)	25 (34%)	29 (23%)
Total	51 (100%)	74 (100%)	125 (100%)

Table 1 summarizes all five models so that the Sustainable Park can be understood within its historical context. It shows that the fifth park model is distinctive enough to merit being differentiated from the others.

The characteristics of the Sustainable Park are both induced from what we observed and deduced from theoretical writing about ecology and sustainability regarding what should be in such a park. Working inductively from our content analysis, we were able to generalize new ecological traits appearing in some urban parks. Working deductively, we reviewed intellectual work about ecological design and the sustainable design movement to widen the range of our ideas about how city parks might function ecologically. The new model is an "ideal type" in the sense of the classical sociologist Max Weber, not necessarily an ideal goal but rather a collation of all the ideas about different qualities and features of actual and future sustainable parks. No one park would have all of these features. We have tried to be comprehensive in our thinking, but we do not presume to have created an exhaustive list of characteristics. If the new type is itself developmental, so too is our collective understanding of it. We invite others to add to our list of characteristics and reorganize them as inspired and compelled. We especially hope to hear from those practitioners who will be contributing to the continued evolution of these ideas on the ground.

Figure 3. Crissy Field has many examples of resource self-sufficiency. (Photograph by M. Boland)

PART II: POLICY IMPLICATIONS

Based on both inductive and deductive approaches, we concluded that sustainable urban parks differ from traditional parks in regard to many details and at least three general principles. First, Sustainable Parks attempt to become self-sufficient with regards to material resources. Second, they can play a role in solving larger urban problems outside their boundaries when they are integrated with the surrounding urban fabric. Third, new aesthetic forms emerge for parks and other urban landscapes. As we discuss these principles, we elaborate on their many policy implications, especially those regarding the design and management of city parks, the practice of landscape architecture, citizen participation, and ecological education.

Principle I: Resource Self-sufficiency. The Sustainable Park differs from other urban park models by emphasizing internal self-sufficiency in regard to material resources. Past urban park models have not been self-sufficient, requiring instead large amounts of energy, fertilizers, plant material, labor, and water while producing noise, pesticide-laced runoff, wastewater, lawn clippings, and garbage—all of which are disposed off-site at great cost or with negative impacts. The heavy maintenance and sustained government funding required for most urban parks has endangered their long-term survival. For example, in New York's Central Park, Olmsted sought to create a naturalistic landscape that mimicked nature in aesthetic terms but not in its species composition or ecological function. In the ensuing century, Central Park slowly fell into a state of disrepair, the victim of declining budgets, increasing use, and the natural lifespan of non-native, non-regenerating landscapes. The planted woodlands were among the first landscapes abandoned in terms of maintenance and, as a result, have suffered from the spread of invasive species such as Norway maple and Japanese knotweed (Cramer 1993, 106). City parks have been subject to the vagaries of the municipal budgeting process and vacillating attitudes about the role of government. Short-term reductions in funding have often translated into deferred maintenance, prompting a vicious cycle of abandonment whereby parks fall into a state of disrepair and further abandonment by the public, both in use and funding.

Sustainable Parks employ a diverse array of strategies to reduce the need for resources and to increase self-sufficiency. These strategies are woven into every aspect of park design, construction, and management. Sustainable Parks manage to increase their ecological health in the face of funding cuts and changing recreational demands. We identified recurring strategies for increasing resource self-sufficiency, including sustainable design, construction and maintenance practices, plant choices, composting, water harvesting, public-private partnerships, and community stewardship.

Sustainable design practices that reduce resource use and maintenance are increasingly employed in Sustainable Parks. A strong example of the benefits of recycling is Crissy Field (Figure 3). The 230,000 cubic yards of soil removed during construction of a tidal marsh were used to elevate the historic airfield and new group picnic area instead of being dumped off-site or in the Bay. The plan for the restoration of Crissy Field attempted to balance natural and human history with a modern desire for active recreation and ecological restoration. The project included the restoration of unique and ecologically valuable salt marsh and dune habitats intermingled with a heavily used promenade, a board-sailing facility, beach frontage used for off-leash dog use, and a 28-acre restored historic airfield to be used for public events and active recreation. The 15,000 tons of rubble removed from the beach were ground and re-used in landscape features (Figure 4). Over 45 acres of asphalt were removed, crushed, and used beneath pathways and parking lots as road base and structural fill.

Figure 4. The West Bluff Picnic area at Crissy Field was built with earth excavated to restore wetlands. (Photograph by M. Boland)

Structures built within Sustainable Parks are sited and designed to minimize the ecological costs of their construction and ongoing use. Buildings are solar-facing, relying on natural lighting and ventilation systems. They use recycled or less energy-intensive construction materials. One implication of the concern for the ecological function of materials is that park departments work with materials experts to evaluate which materials—metals, post-consumer plastics, bamboo, wood, porous concrete vs. asphalt, flycrete—have the least long-term environmental costs under various circumstances. Swimming pools use the latest non-toxic purification systems. In practice we found examples that emphasize one feature or another. The Spring Lake Park Visitor Center in Santa Rosa, California, minimizes both construction and operating costs (Henderson 1993). The simple pyramidal structure was carefully inserted into the wooded site, so that only three trees had to be removed. The pyramid form was easy to frame and was angled to maximize the efficiency of solar panels. The structure was partially set into the earth to minimize its visual impact and increase energy efficiency. The structure is largely heated using the sun and cooled using simple, natural systems. Only on the coldest winter days is a wood-burning stove fired up to take off the chill.

Sustainable design practices have been useful in the restoration of historic Pleasure Grounds, such as New York's Central Park and Brooklyn's Prospect Park (Figure 5). The historic North Woods and Ramble in Central Park are slowly being converted to self-regenerating native woodland while preserving historic and recreational values. For example, invasive exotic Norway maples that were originally planted are being replaced by non-invasive horticultural species. To reduce maintenance and increase habitat values, park managers have adopted an attitude of letting "nature do as much of the work as possible" (Cramer 1993, 110). Historic paved edges around water features in Central Park such as the Turtle Pond have been softened and replaced with plantings of bog and marginal wetland species that are not invasive (Figure 6). Similar strategies have been employed in Prospect Park and other Olmsted parks.

Instituting these changes requires re-educating park staffs and developing new maintenance skills. Landscape architect Rolf Sauer (1998) emphasized this while he was working on Louisville's landmark park system restoration. After 20 years of training maintenance staff to "sweep concrete," they were instead trained to restore and sustain landscape as a living system. Additional management changes will be required in order to recruit scientifically trained staff, coordinate volunteers, and develop the reporting mechanisms and responsiveness expected for privately funded projects. For example, the Central Park Conservancy, working with the City of New York, has developed a zone-gardener program in which responsibility for a section of a park and coordination of volunteers

Figure 5. This sign identifies nature as a partner in the management of historic Prospect Park. (Photograph by M. Boland)

Figure 6. The softened edge of Central Park's Turtle Pond provides improved wildlife habitat. (Photograph by M. Boland)

for that section is assigned to an individual gardener. This allows for staff and volunteer training related to the specific requirements of each landscape type, whether a restored woodland, lake, meadow, or manicured historic site.

Sustainable Parks depend on native, or non-invasive, environmentally appropriate plant choices. Although many parks have been designed in the image of nature, they were rarely designed to preserve or restore ecological function. Instead, their designers often used exotic species to create the desired, naturalistic effect. Some of these exotic species, like Norway maple, Scotch broom, and water hyacinth, have invaded adjacent natural areas. Mass plantings of regularly discarded annual exotic plants were used at points of interest. Where designers did use native species, their natural succession was arrested at a particular point for aesthetic effect. By working against rather than with ecological processes, the resources (fertilizers, herbicides, pesticides, and labor) required to maintain even naturalistic landscapes are greater than if native trees and plants were used. (However, we acknowledge that some native species can take considerably more effort than a more conventional landscape to establish, particularly in formerly weedy areas or areas adjacent to degraded sites.)

Sustainable Parks not only use ecologically suitable plants (native, appropriate exotics), but plantings are done in such a way that secondary plant succession can proceed. Planting schemes use drought-resistant plants in dry climates and use water-loving plants in wet ones. Correspondingly appropriate animal life—lizards and frogs, for example, whose future might otherwise be endangered—are able to live here. The resulting regional variation in the palette of plant materials is a welcome change from the homogeneous look of most municipal parks nationwide. Planting decisions made at Crissy Field have produced a sustainable, self-regenerating landscape that requires establishment irrigation and weeding only for the first few years and does not require the application of polluting pesticides, herbicides, or fertilizers (Figure 7). With the exception of two tree species, all of the plant species are native to the Presidio and were propagated from locally collected seeds and cuttings.

Flowers still have a place in the Sustainable Park. The

Figure 7. In non-turf areas at Crissy Field, only native foredune, back dune and dune scrub species were planted. (Photograph by M. Boland)

United States could follow the example of Chinese parks where flowers are harvested as medicinal herbs. Even when strictly ornamental, flowers are also home to birds, bees, and insects. Designers can still dazzle visitors with native plants if they use them in special plant combinations and planting schemes. For example, the senior author remembers as a teenager at the Seattle World's Fair of 1962 that onions planted formally were more distinctive and special than a hothouse of exotic orchids.

New attitudes about mown turf were observed in Sustainable Parks. For recreational uses, we did not see substitutes for mown, irrigated turf, but we observed some experiments regarding grass type and maintenance. Conventional turf can be replaced with less resource-intensive native grass species. At Crissy Field, conventional turf grasses could not be used because of the danger that they might spread into the adjacent restored tidal marsh. Consequently, planners chose a mix of native grasses, the species varying depending on the conditions and expected level of use (Figure 8). Salt tolerant native rye grass and salt grass were used for turf near the shore where board sailors bring their salt-covered boards for rigging. Planners chose native red fescue and Pacific hair grass for the 28-acre historic airfield and dune-like landforms because they require little irrigation and tolerate foot traffic. Although mown like conventional turf, these native species have flourished under harsh conditions with less water and no pesticides. The tradeoff is a somewhat less uniform turf with more seasonal color variation than a conventional lawn.

In Sustainable Parks where lawns were not used recreationally, native meadows have replaced conventional turf. Rolf Sauer of Andropogon calls turf "green asphalt" because it is mowed so closely and uniformly that water runs off of it—like asphalt. As part of the restoration of the historic Louisville park system, mown meadows and savannas of heterogeneous, indigenous grasses have replaced closely mowed lawns (Figure 9). Meadows are allowed to grow 1–3 feet high, and even pathways and heavily used fields are mowed to 5–7 inches rather than 3–4 inches. Mowing was significantly reduced, thereby saving resources and protecting ecological processes. Today mowing is used in only two conditions: to maintain herbaceous meadows (to keep them from eventually reverting to woodlands), and in pathways around or through meadows. These mowed pathways play an important role. By defining the edges of meadows and making them perceivable as an *intentional* landscape, these pathways allow users to appreciate that the natural strands of grasses represent a desired effect and not a lack of maintenance or care.

Figure 8. Planners chose native red fescue and Pacific hair grass for the 28-acre historic airfield because they require little irrigation and tolerate foot traffic. (Photograph by M. Boland)

Composting is an increasingly important

practice because it recycles resources in a way that simultaneously improves the health of the landscape and lowers the cost of maintaining urban parks. For example, New York's Central Park composts its green waste and debris at a composting facility on Manhattan's Upper East Side, using its waste to improve soil quality rather than paying to have it shipped off Manhattan Island. Compost can be generated on-site from leaves, pruned branches, and from animal waste (Figure 10). San Francisco's Presidio annually composts 1,500 cubic yards of green waste and forestry debris, which is used to improve moisture retention in the Presidio's sandy soil. The compost is produced for less than it would cost to purchase it commercially. Sheep and other ruminants could be reintroduced to eliminate mechanical lawn mowing, produce natural fertilizer, and educate children. (One of the aesthetic implications is that compost could be elevated to the status of an art form, an idea developed further below.) On-site restaurants should also collect compost.

Sustainable Parks treat stormwater and greywater as aesthetic and ecological resources, as *food* rather than waste to be disposed. On-site water management includes the use of natural systems to clean stormwater and greywater, while also creating habitat for wildlife. Water runoff has been a problem in conventional parks because they have a great deal of asphalt, hard-packed soil, and mown turf. Because rainfall cannot penetrate the ground, it runs off into city sewers and causes erosion. Sustainable design practices such as on-site stormwater retention basins and permeable asphalt do double duty by accommodating visitor use and reducing runoff. At the DuPont headquarters in the Brandywine Valley, the firm Andropogon Associates installed a porous asphalt parking lot for cars that absorbs water on site. By combining these functions, woodland that was to be cut to build an on-site stormwater retention basin was preserved. With the money saved by not cutting the forest, nature trails were built and the woodland was restored (Hiss 1991).

Figure 9. Turf at Louisville's Summit Field (above) was replaced with native prairie grass to reduce runoff and increase ecological value (below). (Courtesy of Andropogon Associates)

The 20-acre tidal marsh at Crissy Field was built to restore a fragment of the large salt marsh system that originally spanned the north shore of San Francisco. In order to increase groundwater infiltration and reduce off-site storm-water flows into the bay, 70 acres of asphalt and hard-packed dirt were removed (Figure 11). Eventually, the complete restoration of the Tennessee Hollow watershed will bring three buried streams back into the open. (In regard to wildlife, the marsh fills a gap in the Pacific Flyway; prior to its construction, migrating birds had no stopping places in San Francisco. The marsh restoration was also used as an opportunity to re-establish a locally limited native plant

Figure 10. Compost is a subject "ripe" for collaboration between environmental artists and maintenance crews. (Photograph by M. Boland)

community, the back dune swale.) The Sustainable Park uses water efficiently, so sprinklers do not waste water through evaporation by shooting it into the air, but occasionally fountains might express the joyful final stages of water purification.

Sustainability refers not only to tangible resources, but also to social and cultural viability. Public-private partnerships are one kind of new social structure whereby the community may directly support urban parks. Organizations like the Central Park Conservancy, the Golden Gate National Parks Conservancy, and the Yosemite Fund were created in the last twenty years to compensate for the steady decrease in the amount of public funding allocated to parks. The non-profit Central Park Conservancy was created in 1980 to raise private funds to supplement public funding used by the New York Parks and Recreation Department to rebuild and maintain Central Park. Over the past two decades, the Conservancy has played an increasingly large role in the reconstruction of Central Park, both raising funds and implementing the restoration of the park. The Conservancy has raised nearly $300 million to fund the reconstruction of Central Park and endow ongoing maintenance and operation of the park. The San Francisco-based Golden Gate National Parks Conservancy raised over $32 million in private philanthropic dollars to fund the transformation of Crissy Field and proceeded to manage every element of its implementation, including planning, design, construction, and stewardship programs.

Community stewardship programs bring human resources to parks that governmental entities are unwilling or unable to access (Figure 12). Volunteer programs at the Golden Gate National Recreation Area in San Francisco annually provide over 100,000 hours of support to the restoration and stewardship of native plant communities and several endangered species in the park (Farrell 2001). The restoration of Central Park's North Woods started with a community advisory board

Figure 11. The Crissy Field tidal marsh filters storm water that formerly flowed untreated into San Francisco Bay. (Photograph by M. Boland)

that crafted a vision for the north woods and guided the planning process. Volunteer groups and the educational programs of nearby institutions implemented the vision. Ongoing community-based stewardship programs still guide the restoration and engage the local community in the maintenance and rejuvenation of the woodlands. While such programs clearly rely on help from outside their borders, they are self-sufficient in the sense that they rely so little on government funding. This raises a larger issue about the role of human labor, whether paid or volunteered. Strictly speaking, an ecologically self-sufficient park might not require human labor, but a Sustainable Park that is both ecologically self-sufficient and culturally satisfying still requires human care in planting and maintenance.

Principle II: An Integrated Part of the Larger Urban System. Insofar as Sustainable Parks are conceptualized as part of the larger metropolis, they can help resolve urban problems located outside park boundaries. Pleasure Grounds like New York's Central Park were conceived as an antidote to urban life, an opportunity to address the poor air quality, lack of access to sunlight, limited opportunities for exercise, and other problems associated with close urban quarters. Ensuing park models had equally well-developed social agendas and problem-solving roles for the city as a whole.

The Sustainable Park builds on this history. We identified several social and environmental urban problems that Sustainable Parks have been designed to address. These problems fall into four broad categories: infrastructure, reclamation, health, and social well-being. This list is not exhaustive, but it does summarize those strategies and tactics we encountered most frequently.

Figure 12. Presidio Stewardship Program volunteers planting a former U.S. Army landfill. (Photograph by M. Boland)

The first of these problems, the integration of urban infrastructure (waterways and roads) into parks, is in some ways a very old idea. Pleasure Grounds often played a key role in the city's transportation system by incorporating parkways that provided relatively unfettered routes for movement. Boston's Emerald Necklace is a network of roadways and parklands that shaped a significant expansion of the urban fabric. At the same time it was an elaborate stormwater retention system designed to solve a major drainage and water quality problem created by urbanization. However, the Emerald Necklace is the exception and not the rule; in many older examples, the park is only a container through which the infrastructure system passes. Rarely does the park landscape itself function as a component of the larger infrastructure system.

The Sustainable Park changes this by using parklands to treat city wastewater and stormwater. This strategy has valuable secondary benefits, including the creation of wildlife habitat as well as recreational and scenic settings. We noted different approaches to incorporating wastewater infrastructure into parks. Some utilize existing riparian systems for the treatment of urban wastewater or stormwater. Jackson Bottom Park in Hillsboro, Oregon, incorporates an existing riparian system and uses a system of ponds to retain and treat effluent, stormwater, and other types of urban runoff (ALSA Merit Award 1992, 75).

At historic Xochimilco Park outside of Mexico City, work to protect the ancient system of *chinampas* or *floating farms* not only protected an endangered historic landscape, but it also addressed water quality concerns in the area and improved wildlife habitat. (Additionally, the scheme preserved threatened farmland by increasing farm profits, making it more lucrative to farm than to sell the land for development).

In contrast, some theorists have proposed synthetic ecological systems to address water quality issues. The example we know the best is a 1991 proposal for New York City's Riverside South. Donald Trump proposed this large development for an abandoned rail yard on Manhattan's Upper West Side. The project had as its centerpiece a 23-acre park, which a consultant (the senior author) proposed should be used to address negative environmental impacts of the development (Figure 13). The proposal was to construct wetlands to treat both stormwater that might otherwise be dumped untreated into the Hudson River and sewage from 9,000 new residential units. Ornamental plantings of water hyacinths and bull rushes in the park would have created a beautiful setting while quietly removing heavy metals and other toxics from the water. Inside each apartment building, biologist John Todd's (1984) "living machines" would treat wastewater. These ideas were introduced and discussed by the public and the Trump organization in 1991–1992, but they were ultimately rejected as "untested" at such a large-scale.

A second urban problem that Sustainable Parks tackle is urban land reclamation.[2] After a century of rapid industrialization and deindustrialization, many cities contain large derelict sites within their boundaries, including former military bases, landfills, industrial yards, and obsolete transportation systems. The soil at these sites is often contaminated with heavy metals, lead paint, petroleum products, pesticides, and other toxic materials; otherwise it is unconsolidated and unstable. These conditions often make these sites unsuitable for new construction. Considering that they are often the last undeveloped sites within the urban environment, they offer an excellent opportunity for new parks. In this sense, park-making itself becomes a form of land reclamation.

Several Sustainable Parks address problems of reclamation in more specific ways. Mel Chin's bio-remediation art project outside of Denver, Colorado, made art of science. By using plants that extract heavy metals from earth, he set an example for park landscapes. The designers of both Bixby Park in Palo Alto, California, and Dyer Landfill Restoration in Palm Beach County, Florida, used a combination of ecological process and technology in an attempt to restore former landfill sites. At Bixby Park, landscape architect George Hargreaves used native grasses to clothe a series of sculptural landforms (Figure 14). Earthen dams in swales control erosion: by trapping water they also create micro-environments for native plant species. Yet fragments of industrial culture along with methane extractors and other infrastructure related to the decommissioning of the landfill remain visible, left as interpretive and mnemonic devices (Rainey 1994). The Dyer Landfill goes a step further by re-creating a wetland at a former landfill. Native cypress, live oak, Florida slash pine, and saw palmettos were planted at the same elevations one might find them in nearby natural landscapes. According to landscape architect George Gentile, native vegetation has begun to reseed itself, and many native wildlife species (the kite, ibis, raccoon, armadillo, and alligator) now use the site (Hess, 1992).

A third urban problem that Sustainable Parks address is health. The idea of using parks for teaching and maintaining public health is an old one. Medicinal gardens have been identified with ancient Egyptian, Greek, and Roman sites, and in America, the idea of the urban park as an asset to the overall health of communities is deeply embedded in our national culture. Part of the program for each of the previous four models included an effort to improve the health of urban residents.[3]

What is distinctive about the Sustainable Park is that it might be used to improve and maintain physical and psychological health even more directly than has been traditional in the United States. For example, several parks in Germany, such as the 10-hectare health park near Bottrop, have been built specifically for patients from hospitals in nearby communities. These parks facilitate inpatient and outpatient rehabilitation, support community self-help groups, and assist in the aftercare of acutely ill hospital patients. In the United States, such specialized grounds have been associated only with hospitals or other medical facilities. Physician (and architecture student) Scott Prysi proposed integrating a health clinic into a neighborhood park in South Berkeley, claiming that this would make the park more broadly ecological than it has ever been. Cranz (1982) anticipated that park programming might eventually offer holistic health classes, for example, yoga, tai chi, BodyMind Centering, Alexander Technique, Feldenkrais, etc.

A fourth problem is urban alienation, which Sustainable Parks address by seeking to increase social well-being. Many worry that urban residents feel alienated from nature and natural processes—and from each other. Contemporary park advocates believe that expanded citizen involvement

Figure 14. Bixby Park landforms are representations of, but not the product of, natural process. (Photograph by M. Boland)

Figure 15. In Berkeley, most creeks have been put under ground, veiling a critical ecological process. Strawberry Creek Park was organized around a newly revealed stretch of Strawberry Creek. (Photograph by Joe McBride)

in the stewardship of urban parks and urban farming can generate a sense of belonging and community (Franck and Schneekloth 1994, 361–362). Similarly, they claim that expanded "awareness of and contact with ecological processes in the urban environment increase one's sense of connection to the local and regional environment. Sustainable Parks encourage reconnection of citizens to each other and to the land by providing new vehicles for direct public participation in the conception, creation, and stewardship of parks. The design of Strawberry Creek Park, located in Berkeley, California, is based on this idea (Figure 15).

Advocates of the fifth model believe that this use of native plants and the re-establishment of ecological process in the urban environment can generate a sense of regional identity even in dense cities (Hough 1990). Community-based stewardship programs in urban parks, such as the Presidio Stewardship Program at GGNRA and the North Woods in New York's Central Park, provide a vehicle for urban residents to rediscover ecological processes and wild places hidden in the urban environment and to play a role in their preservation. However, we presume that users feel less connected to the region, the park, and nature when plant restoration schemes like those in Prospect Park must rely on permanent fencing to keep people off of the restored slopes (Taplin 2001).

Service learning programs, middle school and high-school stewardship programs, and in-school nursery programs affiliated with Sustainable Parks may deepen citizens' understanding of ecological processes. The Presidio Stewardship Program not only engages thousands of students in ecological restoration, but also educates them about ecological cycles and pre-Columbian landscapes in San Francisco neighborhoods (Figure 16). As part of the construction of Crissy Field, over 3,000 volunteers collected seed for, propagated, planted, and weeded over 100,000 native plants representing 73 native species (Prince 2001). The staff has reported a demand for native plantings in nearby residences and schools generated by this program (Farrell 2001). This involvement has also created more responsible park users. Clearly, engaging young people in the stewardship of native plantings in parks has the potential both to reduce intentional vandalism and to increase responsible use, thereby reducing unintentional damage as well. Reducing both types of damage is essential to protect ecological processes in urban environments.

Education plays a big role in improving the quality of life. Sustainable Parks educate by exposing the public directly to new ideas and attitudes about nature and the urban landscape. They do this in a host of ways. At Crissy Field, signage and educational waysides that explain natural processes at work, environmental education programs that interpret ecological and cultural systems, and the Crissy Center building itself have all been designed to generate a greater level of understanding, appreciation, and commitment in visitors. Even the benches, pathways, and promenade are oriented to give visitors a direct experience of the natural forces at play.

Some educational strategies are self-consciously didactic. For example, Blueprint Farm in Laredo, Texas, designed by the Center for Maximum Potential Building Systems, is conceived as an educational landscape where technology integrates human and natural systems into a "metabolic unit" (Hess 1992). The park includes organic farmland, sediment ponds to clean stormwater, cisterns to gather water for use, windmills and other appropriate technology systems to generate power, and structures built from recycled oil rigs and other salvaged materials.

Other strategies are more passive, operating as object lessons in how to manage the interface between human culture and ecological process. Temporary barrier fencing to protect "Mother Nature at work" on restoration sites offers a simple lesson. Seasonal maintenance events can also be educational. For example, prescribed burns simultaneously create more vital natural systems and educate by virtue of their drama. At the Crosby Arboretum in southern Mississippi, prescribed burns have been useful both to study the use of fire as a management tool and to educate the public using a combination of direct action followed by interpretive exhibits (Andropogon Associates 2003).

Sustainable Parks also improve quality of life by mitigating conflicts between adjacent land uses. For example, Ecton Brook Linear Park in Northampton, England, protects a stream corridor and at the same time functions as a buffer between high-density housing and adjacent agricultural land, deflecting potential conflicts regarding noise, foot traffic, pesticides, and child safety. Native plantings along the 2.5 km park have increased the density of the buffer between human uses and have increased the park's value to wildlife, serving as conduits for the movement of wildlife and the distribution of native plant species. In such instances, both homocentric and ecocentric ideas about ecological quality are fulfilled.

In the near future, community-based urban farming efforts could be instituted in parks to improve social well-being in many different ways. Right now, the San Francisco League of Urban Gardeners and the San Francisco Jail Garden Project teach job skills and fight malnutrition, thereby diminishing aspects of urban poverty. Moreover, by creating venues for collective neighborhood-based

Figure 16. Presidio volunteer monitoring a Presidio pilot project testing the survival of native species growing under non-native eucalyptus. (Photograph by M. Boland)

activity, they build community and fight crime. At the Edible School Yard at Martin Luther King Jr. High School in Berkeley, teachers use gardening as part of the school curriculum. The San Francisco League of Urban Gardeners operates the St. Mary's/Allemany youth garden in conjunction with the Allemany public housing project to provide jobs and job training for youth; they run a business that makes jelly, salsa, and vinegar, using produce grown in the urban farm. In Santa Cruz, the Homeless Garden Project employs and feeds the homeless, coordinating their efforts with social service agencies that provide support to the homeless affiliated with their farm (Lawson 2000). The idea of putting agricultural programs into parks proper may be a next step in the development of the Sustainable Park.

Principle III: New Modes of Aesthetic Expression. New types of aesthetic expression are emerging in Sustainable Parks. The form of the park itself and its relationship to the city, its style, and its management practices have moved in a more ecological direction, developing an evolutionary aesthetic, a new spatial relationship to the city, and a new role for designers. This new type may serve as a model for other urban landscapes, private gardens, and ultimately, the city itself.

Some landscape critics suggest that truly ecological parks must transcend the traditional notion of style predicated on a fixed, static image of the landscape and develop an *evolutionary* aesthetic. Louise Mozingo (1997) has argued that ecological landscapes should incorporate an aesthetic of "temporality" that moves beyond the fixed vision of the landscape and incorporates change. Similarly, Jusuck Koh (1988) has advocated an evolutionary approach to design that offers a "dynamic view of aesthetics" and a shift in focus "away from the traditional ordering of 'form' following positivistic aesthetics toward an ordering of 'process'" (185, 186). His aesthetic of "complementarity" lets the natural landscape complement, rather than hide, humans and buildings. Both landscape architect Lyle (1994) and landscape architect Thayer (1994) have emphasized that we should not camouflage technology. A number of artists and landscape architects have created landscapes that speak about ecological process (Figure 17).

Yet process-oriented things often appear messy in our current culture, so Joan Nassauer (1995) has described how designers can provide cues that an apparently untidy landscape is part of a larger plan. The importance of providing such cues became clear in a recent 2002 competition for Railyard Park in Santa Fe (where the senior author served as a juror). The program was explicit in calling for sustainable designs, requiring special attention to water and drought-resistant native species. One of the five short-listed entries followed an evolutionary aesthetic (Figure 18). It did not win in part because the jury considered it hard to sell to the public. More deliberate signs of intentional care would have tipped the balance in favor of this scheme.

Figure 17. Alan Sonfist's "Time Landscape" reconstructs a tiny fragment of Manhattan's pre-contact landscape and explores the aesthetic dimensions of secondary plant succession in the urban landscape. (Photograph by M. Boland)

An evolutionary aesthetic itself may have to become accepted in stages or steps. The first step is a simple change in materials: drought-tolerant, low-maintenance native species; recycled yard waste for soil amendment; wood

Figure 18. For Railyard Park, Ruddick Associates proposed a series of swales to slow water down, creating micro-environments in which plant succession would occur. (Courtesy of Ruddick Associates)

chips from debris for paths and mulch; recycled plastic lumber for benches; low-maintenance, local, or renewable materials. At the next stage, designers manipulate plants and topography less as static materials and more as landscapes that emerge as the byproduct of dynamic ecological systems. Taking a cue from restoration ecology, designers in a few Sustainable Parks have created diverse plant communities that emphasize both the ornamental and ecological value of plants. This is a step beyond merely replacing ornamental exotics with native species. This way of managing vegetation allows for evolutionary change in structure and species diversity over time as a result of either anthropogenic or biotic factors. Central Park's North Woods and Crissy Field are two park landscapes where this shift from a focus on species to plant assemblages has meant emphasizing the spatial qualities of different plant communities and has necessitated new approaches to planting and managing park landscapes (Figure 19). In 2002, park competitions for Santa Fe and for Fresh Kills on Staten Island have had winning and short-listed entries that emphasize evolutionary processes in their planting schemes. The recentness of such examples that demonstrate how an authentic evolutionary aesthetic might be integrated into urban parks suggests that the profession of landscape architecture has just barely begun this particular aesthetic exploration.

In contrast, some artists attempt to explore the idea of ecology in parks in primarily formalistic terms. The Village of Yorkville Park in Toronto, Canada, is a downtown plaza organized into 17 sections, each containing plants from a different local plant community. By identifying and celebrating local plant communities and local ecology, this park brings an awareness of the regional landscape into downtown Toronto. Yet these are disembodied fragments of plant communities

Figure 19. The form givers in the Crissy Field landscape are ecological variables like wind and depth to ground water. (Photograph by M. Boland)

without reference to the underlying geomorphological, climatological, and successional processes that created them in the first place. This design also gives the false impression that these plant communities can be easily replicated anywhere, can live in close proximity to each other, and are unchanging. Similarly, Hargreaves Associates landforms along the Guadeloupe River Parkway, at Bixby Park and Crissy Field—although inspired by the movement of water, wind, and soil in dynamic natural systems—are not created as the byproduct of those systems, nor are they dynamic in any ecological sense. Instead they are very precise, highly controlled representations or symbols of ecological process. Although perhaps imperfect models for how landscapes might incorporate ecological process, these evocative landscapes contain the first stirrings of an ecological (if not evolutionary) aesthetic and suggest that art can play a role in educating the public about ecological process in the urban environment. Moreover, formal designs have the potential to serve ecological purposes. Formal gardens may be better than pastoral English gardens for some animal and plant life because humans are restricted to fixed pathways (Figure 20). Birds, for example can nest and reproduce in the safety of hedges. Formally speaking, the Sustainable Park is stylistically open; it can be either naturalistic or formalistic in appearance.

Just as the Sustainable Park model suggests variety among the parks themselves, the model also suggests variety in the spatial relationship to the city between the park and the surrounding urban fabric. Instead of being conceived as an antidote set in contrast to adjacent urban life, the Sustainable Park builds on the ideology of the Open Space System by attempting to integrate open space into the city. However, it goes beyond the Open Space System by not only preserving, but also restoring open space for human viewing and activity; moreover, its ecological impulse goes *deeper* than Open Space ideology because it serves other species in the urban environment. Creating an underpass for wildlife, for example, is a recent proposal to join two tracts of land for a new park in Baldwin Hills, Los Angeles.

Eventually, this emphasis on system could have a centripetal effect on the form and distribution of parks. Indeed, the very idea of the park as a discrete locus of nature in the city may become obsolete in truly sustainable urban settlements. Instead of overall shapes predicated on aesthetic consideration or property ownership that has given rise to rectilinear or chunky parks, the configurations of Sustainable Parks will vary as an expression of the role that the land, water, air, vegetation, and animals—including humans—play in the local ecological system.

Because Sustainable Parks involve the community broadly and in myriad ways, they are no longer the specialized domain of experts and managers. Community involvement necessarily brings a different set of form-giving forces to bear on park design and management, suggesting that the idea of a developmental or evolutionary aesthetic has enormous social application (Figure 21). An evolutionary aesthetic necessarily shifts the purpose of design and the role of the designer from artist-visionary to a medium through which the forces of nature and society express themselves.

Figure 20. Birds can nest and reproduce in the safety of hedges in formal landscapes like this at Parc de Sceaux. (Photograph by M. Boland)

Figure 21. Volunteers played a central role in defining the scope and design of the National AIDS Memorial Grove. (Photograph by M. Boland)

If designers see themselves as weaving new, unexpected developments into a pattern, even shifting the pattern itself, they would embrace a role that has been likened to jazz and other improvisational performance arts. The park, gardening, and landscape professions may attract those who are gratified by working with laypeople and other experts over time to create urban harmonies on the spot.

The National AIDS Memorial Grove in San Francisco owes its existence and its form to this new role for designers and evolutionary aesthetic. A group of concerned citizens who had lost many friends to AIDS and at the same time were keenly concerned about the sorry state of parks in San Francisco conceived of the project. For them the Grove was both the restoration of a derelict portion of Golden Gate Park and a tribute to lost friends and loved ones. Members of the community, instead of municipal employees, have coordinated all aspects of the design and construction. The design was evolutionary, unfolding slowly over seven years. The overall appearance and individual elements of the Grove are not the product of a single designer's vision. Rather, the Grove has evolved from the interaction of community and site over time (Figure 22). Simultaneously, the Grove has brought AIDS education and awareness to the larger community in a non-threatening way. This project exemplifies the developmental and emergent nature of the Sustainable Park.

Where to Begin? We encourage park departments everywhere to realize these principles for Sustainable Park design. With broad policy implementation, this new standard will move from the avant-garde and cutting edge to best practice. But even as it becomes more broadly disseminated, this new model will not produce uniformity because in each bioregion, the standards will be expressed in ecologically distinctive ways. Over time, the model can be evaluated in each bioregion

Figure 22. Stones in the dry stream, "bowls" carved in boulders and inscriptions encourage direct manipulation of the National AIDS Memorial Grove landscape by visitors. (Photograph by M. Boland)

and continuously elaborated and refined through practice *on the ground*. Since ecology and sustainability are complex, people often ask where to begin and how to intervene. We recommend starting with the biggest, most expensive, most troublesome problem as the starting point. In many parks today, maintenance is the biggest problem because it is the biggest expense. Therefore, we first recommend improving maintenance practices, rethinking them radically. This means focusing on resource self-sufficiency and developing a new aesthetic from that focus. Does this priority mean that solving larger urban problems may have to wait? Not if we consider that modeling a new aesthetic that derives from self-sufficiency would also solve problems for other urban landscapes. By getting started, eventually the entire urban system will be transformed for the better.

Appendix A: Parks by Park Type (secondary rankings shown in parentheses)

Pleasure Ground (I)

Almada Park, Almada, Portugal
Andre Citroen, Paris, France (IV)
Astoria Park Extension, Queens, NY
Battersea Park, London, England
Bay Adelaide Park, Toronto, CA
Biddy Mason Park, Los Angeles, CA
Bryant Park, New York, NY (IV)
Central Park, Sha Tin, Hong Kong, China (V)
Chase Palm Park, Santa Barbara, CA
Delamont Country Park, Strangford Lough, UK (IV)
Fair Park, Dallas, TX
Forest Hill Park, Cleveland, OH (III)
Glebe Park, Canberra, Australia
Great Park, Louisville, KY (IV)
Henry Moore Sculpture Garden, Kansas City, MO
Hudson River Park, New York, NY
Lechmere Canal Park, East Cambridge, MA
Mile End Park, London, England
North Point Park, Boston, MA (IV)
Olympia Fields, Olympia Fields, IL
Patriots Square, Phoenix, AZ
Royal Botanic Garden, Kew, London, England (IV)
Socrates Sculpture Park, Queens, NY
Washington Market Park, New York, NY

Reform Park (II)

Allegheny Riverfront, Pittsburgh, PA
Landscaftslehrpark, Erfurt, Germany (IV)
Princess of Wales Memorial Park, UK

Recreation Facility (III)

Academy Courts, The Bronx, NY
Albert Park, Melbourne, Australia
Burgess Park, London, England (IV)
Gin Drinkers Bay Park, Hong Kong, China
Lake Hico Park, Jackson, MI
Lastenlehto Park, Helsinki, Finland
Merrylands Park, Sydney, Australia
Midtown Park, Duluth, MN
Paloheinan Hippu Park, Helsinki, Finland
Pearl Street Park, New York, NY
Richard Oastler Park, Leeds, England
Southwest Corridor Park, Boston, MA

Open Space System (IV)

24th Street Park, Virginia Beach, VA
All Peoples Trail, Shaker Height, OH
Bicentennial Plaza, San Jose, CA
Bouthorpe Park, Norwich, England
BUGA, Magdeburg, Germany
Cambridge Center Garage Roof Garden, Cambridge, MA
Candlestick Point Park, San Francisco, CA
Charleston Waterfront Park, Charleston, SC
Children's Park, San Diego, CA
Cleveland Meadows, Cleveland, OH
Columbia Union Marketplace, Brooklyn, NY
Courthouse Square, Toronto, Canada
Docklands, London, England
Dunbari Close Garden, Edinburgh, Scotland
Ecton Brook Linear Park, England (V)

Elcho Gardens, Calton, Scotland
First Interstate Plaza, Dallas, TX
Foothills Community Park, Boulder, CO
Freeway Park, Seattle, WA
Gene Coulon Beach Park, Renton, WA
Gore Park, San Jose, CA
Haas, Sherover, & Trotner Promenades, Jerusalem
Holyoke Heritage Park, Holyoke, MA
Imperial Beach Pier Plaza, Imperial Beach, CA
Japanese-American Plaza, Portland, OR
Jose Marti Riverfront Park, Miami, FL
Lafayette Park, Oakland, CA
Landesgartenschau, Lunen, Germany
Laumeier Sculpture Park, St. Louis, MO
Liverpool Garden, Liverpool, England
Lok Fu Park, Hong Kong, China
Los Angeles River Park, Los Angeles, CA
Louisville Waterfront Park, Louisville, KY
Martin Luther King Jr. Promenade, San Diego, CA
Memorial to the 56 Signers of the Declaration of Independence, Washington, DC
New Kirkgate, Edinburgh, Scotland
Nordsternpark, Gelsenkirchen, Germany
Post Office Square, Boston, MA
Promenade Plantee, Paris, France
Pyrmont Point Park, Sydney, Australia
Risley Moss, Warrington, England (V)
River Promenade, Indianapolis, IN
Riverfront Plaza, Hartford, CT
Royal Park, Melbourne, Australia (V)
S. Graham Brown Park, St. Mathews, KY
San Antonio River Walk, San Antonio, TX
Skyline Park, Denver, CO
South Cove, Battery Park City, New York, NY
South Waterfront Park, Hoboken, NJ
Thames Barrier Park, London, England
The Belvedere, New York, NY
Tiffany Plaza, The Bronx, NY

Tom McCall Park, Portland, OR
VOA Park, West Chester, OH
Westlake Park, Seattle, WA
Westlands Park, Greenwood Village, CO
Wolden Berg Riverfront Park, New Orleans, LA

Sustainable Park (V)

Alex Wilson Garden, Toronto, CA
Baldwin Hills Park, Los Angeles, CA
Blueprint Farm, Laredo, TX
Byxbee Park, Palo Alto, CA
Cherokee, Iroquois & Shawnee Parks, Louisville, KY
Denver Botanic Garden, Denver, CO
Dyer Landfill, Palm Beach County, FL
Fishtrap Creek Park, Abbotsford, Canada
Freedom Parkway, Atlanta, GA
Freshkills Landfill Park, Staten Island, NY
Gesundheitspark, Buttrop, Germany
Guadelupe Riverfront Park, San Jose, CA
Horseshoe Park, Aurora, CO
Jackson Bottom, Hillsboro, Oregon (IV)
Landscaftspark Duisburg-Nord, Germany
Liberty State Park, Ellis Island, NY
Long Nose Point Park, Sydney, Australia
North York Moors Park, England
Northside Park, Denver, CO
Old School Forest Preserve, Libertyville, IL
Presidio of San Francisco, San Francisco, CA
River Torrens Linear Park, Adelaide, Australia
Ross Landing Public Plaza, Chattanooga, TN (IV)
Samuel Love Greenway, Englewood, CO
St. Louis Forest Park Restoration, St. Louis, MO
Stadtpark West, Bochum, Germany
Strawberry Creek Park, Berkeley, CA
Village of Yorkville Park, Toronto, Canada
West Point Park, Seattle, WA

Acknowledgments

A major portion of this study was funded by a grant from The Graham Foundation for Advanced Study in Architecture.

Notes

1. Members of the research team were Michael Boland, Erika Conkling, Chris Heath, Rosa Lane, Lothar Maier, Jay Rambo, Nicola Probst, Scott Prysi, and Steve Middleton—students in two graduate seminars held by Dr. Galen Cranz in the Department of Architecture at the University of California at Berkeley in the fall of 1997 and spring of 1998. Additionally, graduate student Renu Desi worked with Dr. Cranz in the summer of 2002 to conduct the analysis for the years 1998–2002.
2. The most widely-known precedent for the transformation of industrial land into parkland is Rich Haag's Gasworks Park in Seattle, but it exemplifies Open Space ideology more than Sustainable ideology. This project transformed a dangerous, derelict industrial landscape into a socially useful park, emphasizing the Open Space idea that recreation could be anywhere. It did not claim ecological restoration, nor was it entirely successful as a reclamation project in that portions of the park were closed due to residual high levels of chemical contamination.
3. Pleasure Grounds were conceived as the "lungs of the city," facilitating the movement and purification of dirty urban air. The Reform Era introduced public bathing via the enticement of swimming as a public health measure. Reform parks provided opportunities for active recreation and exercise to ensure the health of urban dwellers, particularly children, while Recreation Era emphasized exercise for the entire family. Open Space Systems are reminiscent of Pleasure Grounds in their devotion to providing fresh air into the heart of cities, but their planners showed more interest in mental and social health. They emphasized re-creation, balance, and "keeping cool." The extensive open space system developed in postwar Stuttgart is a literal example of this, using convection currents to bring cool air from surrounding ridges down into the hot, dense core of central Stuttgart (Cranz 1982, Spirn 1984).

References

Andropogon Associates, Ltd. 2003. Promotional materials. Philadelphia: Andropogon Associates, Ltd.

ASLA Merit Award. 1992. *Landscape Architecture Magazine* 82(11): 75.

Cramer, Marianne. 1993. Urban renewal: Restoring the vision of Olmsted and Vaux in Central Park's woodlands. *Restoration and Management Notes* 11 (2): 106–116.

Cranz, Galen. 1982. *The Politics of Park Design: A History of Urban Parks in America.* Cambridge, MA: MIT Press.

Farrell, Sharon. 2001. Personal communication with plant ecologist at the Golden Gate National Recreation Area (GGNRA), 5 August.

Franck, Karen, and Lynda Schneekloth. 1994. *Ordering Space: Types in Architecture and Design.* New York: Van Nostrand Reinhold.

Guy, Simon, and Graham Farmer. 2000. Contested constructions: The competing logics of green buildings and ethics. In *Ethics and the Built Environment,* edited by Warwick Fox. London: Routledge.

Henderson, Justin. 1993. Pyramids of the Sun. *Architecture* (6): 82–85.

Hess, Allan. 1992. Technology exposed. *Landscape Architecture Magazine* 82(5): 38–48.

Hiss, Tony. 1991 Guardians of the green. *Countryside* (Spring): 41–43.

Hough, Michael. 1990. *Out of Place: Restoring Identity to the Regional landscape.* New Haven: Yale University Press.

Johnson, Jory. 1996. Updating Olmsted. *Landscape Architecture Magazine* 86 (3): 80–98.

Koh, Jusuck. 1988. An ecological aesthetic. *Landscape Journal (1):* 177–191.

Lawson, Laura. 2000. The community-garden movement, 1970s to present. PhD Dissertation, Department of Landscape Architecture. University of California, Berkeley.

Lyle, J. T. 1994. *Regenerative Design for Sustainable Development.* New York: Wiley.

Moses, Robert. 1940. *Six Years of Park Progress.* New York City: Department of Parks.

Mozingo, Louise. 1997. The aesthetics of ecological design: Seeing science as culture. *Landscape Journal* 16(2): 46–59.

Nassauer, Joan. 1995. Messy ecosystems, orderly frames. *Landscape Journal* 14 (2):161–170.

Prince, Carol. 2001. Personal communication at Golden Gate National Parks Conservancy, 3 March.

Raincy, Ruben. 1994. Environmental ethics and park design: A case study of Bixby Park. *Journal of Garden History* 14 (3): 171–178.

Sauer, Rolf. 1996. Master plan for renewing Louisville Kentucky's Olmsted parks and parkways: A guide to sustainable landscape management. *Forum* 13(1): 64–75.

Spirn, Ann. 1984. *The Granite Garden: Urban Nature and Human Design.* New York: Basic Books.

Taplin, Dana. 2001. Art, nature, and people: Landscape values of an urban park. Ph.D. Dissertation, Environmental Psychology, City University of New York.

Thayer, R. Gray. 1994. *World, Green Heart: Technology, Nature and the Sustainable Landscape.* New York: Wiley.

Thompson, Ian. 2000. The ethics of sustainability. In *Landscape and Sustainability,* edited by John Benson and Maggie Roc, London and New York: Spon Press.

Todd, Nancy, and John Todd. 1984. *From Eco-Cities to Living Machines: Principles of Ecological Design.* Berkeley: North Atlantic Books.

36 Cohousing: An Old Idea— A Contemporary Approach

Charles Durrett

The cohousing model, developed in the United States by Durrett and McCamant, is applied to seniors.

In villages people work together to build a schoolhouse, raise a barn, harvest the crops, celebrate the harvest and more. Similarly, residents in cohousing enjoy the benefits of cooperation, whether by organizing common dinners, social activities, or caring for an elderly resident. Both communities build social relationships by working together to address practical needs. Cohousing offers the social and practical advantages of a closely knit neighborhood consistent with the realities of twenty-first century life.

In non-industrial communities, work is integrated with the rest of life. Small towns are not divided into residential, commercial, and industrial areas; rather, residences are built on top of shops, and cottage industries flourish throughout neighborhoods. Although cohousing developments are primarily residential, daily patterns develop that begin to weave work and home life together again. Most cohousing residents go outside the community for their professional work, but there is also informal trading of skills within the community. One resident, a plumber, tends to a leaky faucet, another helps repair a neighbor's car.

Several residents make wine together. A woman who makes pottery finds her best customers are fellow residents who buy her goods for gifts. These neighbors know each other's skills and feel comfortable asking for assistance, understanding they will be able to reciprocate later.

Technological advances make it increasingly common for people to work part time or full time at home. In most living situations today, working at home can be very isolating (we know a computer programmer who could easily work from home, but chooses to drive to the office for companionship). The cohousing environment allows residents to enjoy the benefits of working at home without feeling isolated. As the trend toward working at home continues to grow, so cohousing responds: a recently-completed cohousing community in Northern California included office space adjacent to its common facilities. In addition to office spaces, this area currently includes a coffee shop, hair salon, and other commercial and retail establishments. With a tip of the hat toward traditional village life, a suite of residential cohousing units are situated above these business spaces.

Charles Durrett, "Cohousing: An Old Idea—A Contemporary Approach," from *Senior Cohousing: A Community Approach to Independent Living*, pp. 13–28. Copyright © 2005. Permission to reprint granted by the publisher.

While incorporating many of the qualities of traditional communities, cohousing is distinctively contemporary in its approach, based on the values of choice and tolerance. Residents choose when and how often to participate in community activities and seek to live with a diverse group of people. Cohousing is a "best of all worlds" solution.

What Is Cohousing?

Cohousing is a living arrangement where multiple houses (usually 20 to 30) are oriented around a common open area and a common building. These communities are custom-designed neighborhoods for residents who do not want to live in typical suburban, urban, or even rural neighborhoods where neighbors don't know each other. For seniors, it is an alternative to assisted living as well. Cohousing residents are proactive in creating viable, friendly, neighborhoods in which residents cooperate and socialize. They sometimes say they aren't doing anything new; but consciously they are creating the kind of neighborhoods that naturally existed in the past.

In addition to its social advantages, cohousing offers numerous environmental benefits. Studies show that residents of cohousing communities use about 25 percent as much energy as Americans in traditional housing, and, most significantly, use 25 percent as much household energy-overall as they did in their previous living arrangement and drive about 25 percent less. Cohousing residences are about 60 percent the size of average new American houses, and cohousing communities on average occupy less than 50 percent as much land as the average new subdivision for the same number of households. And through the power of community ownership cohousing residents actually get more and pay less.

While cohousing might be prevalent in Europe, it remains a relatively new concept in the United States. The first American cohousing projects were built in 1991. Currently, there are 100 of these communities in the country, about 20 under construction, with another 150 or so in the planning stage. The trend is catching on.

> Portions of this chapter are taken from our previous book, *Cohousing: A Contemporary Approach to Housing Ourselves,* by Kathryn McCamant and Charles Durrett. For a more detailed look at the cohousing big picture, pick up a copy of the book at any public library or quality bookseller. You can also order direct from us online at The Cohousing Company, www.cohousingco.com.

Six Components of Cohousing

Cohousing can be found in many forms—from urban factory loft conversions to suburban cities to small towns. Whatever the form, cohousing projects share six-components:

- Participatory Process: Residents organize and participate in the planning and design process for the housing development, and are responsible as a group for final decisions.
- Deliberate Neighborhood Design: The physical design encourages a strong sense of community.
- Extensive Common Facilities: An integral part of the community, common areas are designed for daily use, to supplement private living areas.

- Complete Resident Management: Residents manage the development, making decisions of common concerns at community meetings.
- Non-Hierarchal Structure: There are not really leadership roles, the responsibility for the decisions is shared by the community's adults.
- Separate Income Sources: If the community provides residents with their primary-income, this is a significant change to the dynamic between neighbors and defines another level of community beyond the scope of cohousing.

Participatory Process

One of the strengths of cohousing is the active participation of residents, from the earliest planning stages through construction. The desire to live in a cohousing community provides the driving force to get it built, and in most instances, the residents themselves initiate the project.

The number of residents who participate throughout the planning and development process varies from project to project. Often a core group of six to twelve families establishes a development program, finds the site, hires the architect, and then seeks other interested people. Sometimes a large group initiates the community, and is pared down as the project becomes more defined. Typically, all of the houses are sold or rented before the project is finished. In some cases, the resident group collaborates with nonprofit housing associations or a private developer, but even then, the residents play a key role.

The participatory process has both advantages and disadvantages, but no cohousing community has ever been built any other way. Even with the proven success of cohousing, developers hesitate to build it on their own, and couldn't if they wanted to. Experience shows that only people who seek new residential options for themselves will have the motivation to push through the planning and design process without making serious compromises.

One possible obstacle is the opposition of planning commissions and neighborhood associations, usually based on false assumptions about cohousing and clustered housing. This is a common problem for any new development, but people's unfamiliarity with cohousing can make it even more difficult. Neighbors may fear that cohousing will attract "unconventional" people, adversely affect the neighborhood, and reduce property values. Such fears are completely unfounded. Cohousing residents tend to be conscientious, taxpaying citizens, active in school and community activities. Cohousing developments have helped to stabilize neighborhoods and make them more desirable.

In spite of such difficulties, resident groups have pushed their projects through the labyrinth of barriers. When a city-council denied approval of one cohousing project, the residents built models, went to meetings, and eventually convinced the council they were respectable citizens with worthy intentions. When banks questioned the feasibility of yet another project, residents risked their own assets to convince the bank to give them the construction loan. When cuts had to be made to build within a construction budget, another group of residents insisted the architect cut the size of amenities of the individual units to preserve the common facilities. Few developers, for-profit or non-profit, would ever take such measures or risks.

Organizing and planning a cohousing community requires time for group meetings, research, and decision making. But anything worthwhile requires time and effort. People organize to build schools, town halls, fire stations and churches, so why not a viable working neighborhood? Residents volunteer their time because of their commitment to the idea and their own desire for a more satisfying residential environment. The most active members are likely to attend one to three meetings a month for one or two years.

The process can be long, but those now living in cohousing communities universally agree it was not only well worth the effort, but the best thing they ever did for themselves and their families.

A feeling of community emerges during the period when residents are working together to reach their common goal. Typically, few participants know each other before joining the group. During the planning and development phases they must agree on many issues closely tied to their personal values. Despite the inevitable frustrations and disagreements, the intensity of the planning period forms bonds between residents that greatly contribute to the community after they move in. Having fought and sacrificed together for the place where they will live builds a sense of pride and community that no outside developer can "build into a project."

Deliberate Neighborhood Design

A physical environment that encourages a strong neighborhood atmosphere is the second characteristic of cohousing. People often talk of how enjoyable it would be if they could live someplace where they knew their neighbors and felt secure. Yet, few residential developments include areas where neighbors can meet casually. Cohousing residents set out to build an environment that reflects their desire for community. Beginning with the initial development plan, residents emphasize design aspects that increase the possibilities for social contact. The neighborhood atmosphere can be enhanced by placing parking at the edge of the site, thus allowing the majority of the development to be pedestrian-oriented and safe for seniors and grandchildren alike. Informal gathering places are created with benches and tables. The location of the common house determines how it will be used. If the residents pass by the common house on their way home, they are more likely to drop in. If the common house can be seen from many of the houses, it will be used more often.

Physical design is critically important in facilitating a social atmosphere. While the participatory development process establishes the initial sense of community, it is the physical design that sustains it over time. Whether the design succeeds depends largely on the architect's and organizing group's understanding of how design factors affect community life. Without thoughtful consideration, many opportunities can be easily missed.

For senior cohousing, design must be tailored to seniors, but every possible interior safety feature does not have to be installed at the outset. It is critical that every possible measure should be taken to avoid an institutional look. A flexible building design is also important, so that the units can be modified to suit owners who are aging, and also new owners.

Common Facilities

While each private home is a complete house in and of itself, just like any traditional residential unit, cohousing communities have common areas that supplement the private houses. Private houses in cohousing can be smaller than typical houses because features such as workshops, guest rooms, and laundry are located in the common house. The common house is an extension of each private residence, based on what the group believes will make their lives easier and more economical, not to mention more fun and interesting. And since the residents won't purchase each common item more than once—one for each household—these per-household costs are dramatically reduced. One lawnmower for 30 households, for example, represents a huge savings over one lawnmower per household.

According to the Census Bureau, the average size of new homes built in the United States at the start of the 21st century was 2,324 square feet. The average private house in a cohousing community is 1,250 square feet. On the other hand, the average common house for a typical 30-unit cohousing community averages 5,000 square feet, including workshops and other buildings.

The common house, which supplements the individual dwellings and provides a place for community activities, is the heart of a cohousing community. It is a place for common dinners, afternoon tea, games on rainy days, a Friday night bar, crafts workshop, laundry facilities, and numerous other organized and informal activities. The common facilities often extend beyond the common house to include barns and animal sheds, greenhouses, a car repair garage, and in one case, a tennis court and swimming pool.

These facilities provide both practical and social benefits. For instance, the common workshop replaces the need for every family to have the space and tools to fix furniture and repair bicycles and cars. Expensive tools, such as a drill press or table saw, become much more affordable when the cost is shared by several households. Not only do residents gain access to a wider range of tools through a common workshop, but enjoy the company of others using the shop or just passing by. They may also share and learn new techniques and skills along the way.

The concept of a common space in clustered housing is not in itself unusual. Many condominium developments have a clubhouse or community room. However, a clubhouse significantly differs from a common house both in the way and to the extent the space is used. Typically, a clubhouse is rented out by individual residents for private parties, or used for owner association meetings or exercise classes. More, the clubhouse is usually small in size, which in turn provides just enough room to accommodate small-scale entertainment needs. The exception is "adult" complexes, which may incorporate a bar and a well-equipped gym into its common area. Regardless, there is no place set aside specifically for children; and most of the time the clubhouse is empty and locked—a nice touch on paper but in reality a poorly utilized afterthought. In contrast, a cohousing common house is open all day, and is considered an essential part of daily community life.

As cohousing has evolved, the common house has increased in size and importance. Today, the size of private dwellings is often reduced in order to build more extensive common facilities. These changes were dictated by experience. For instance, many residents of early cohousing developments were reluctant to commit to common dinners, thinking they would be nice once or maybe twice a week, but not on a regular basis. Yet, when the common house is designed well, common dinners have proven overwhelmingly successful, and today most new cohousing groups plan for meals in the common house several times a week, with over half of the residents participating on any given evening. Substantial space is thus allocated in the common house for pleasant dining rooms and spacious kitchens. Children's play areas are often included, so that children can be children, and adults can sit and converse in an adult-oriented environment.

The specific features of the common house depend on the interests and needs of the residents. Their use is likely to change over time in response to new community members and needs.

By allowing residents to become acquainted, discover mutual interests, and share experiences, common facilities and activities contribute greatly to the formation of a tightly knit community. These friendships then carry over into other areas. As one resident said:

> "The common house is an essential element. Through the activities there, life is added to the streets. Without it, the sense of community would be hard to maintain."

The common house is also an asset for the surrounding neighborhood. It is used for meetings, classes, union organizing, and cultural programs. A Danish cohousing group even organized a film club that attracts participants from their entire town. As the community's primary meeting place, the common house has infinite uses both for the residents and their neighbors.

Resident Management

In keeping with the spirit in which cohousing is built, residents—owners and renters alike—are responsible for the community's ongoing management. Major decisions are made at common meetings, usually held once a month. These meetings provide a forum for residents to discuss issues and solve problems.

Responsibilities are typically divided among work groups in which all adults must participate. Duties like cooking common dinners and cleaning the common house are usually rotated. As with any group of people, some residents feel they do more than their fair share while others don't do enough. This cannot be helped. In most cases, community responsibilities become less formally structured as residents become better acquainted.

Under a system of resident management, problems cannot be blamed on outsiders. Residents must assume responsibility themselves. If the buildings are not well maintained, they will have to pay for repairs. If the common activities are disorganized, everyone loses.

Learning how to make decisions as a group is not easy. Most people grow up and work in hierarchical situations. Residents must learn to work together and find the best solution. They may adopt organizational formats developed by other groups, or create new methods for themselves. It is a process of learning by doing. Residents told us that over time they become effective at working together, and effectively applied the lessons they learned at home to their work lives, or to other organizations to which they belonged.

Non-Hierarchical Social Structure

Although residents state opinions about certain issues (for example, people who frequently use the workshop might propose the merits of investing more money on tools), the community shares responsibility. The community doesn't depend on one person for direction. A "burning soul" may get the community off the ground, another may pull together the financing, and another may arrange the venue for each meeting. This division of labor is based on what each person feels he or she can fairly contribute. No one person, however, dominates the decisions or the community-building process, and no one person should become excessively taxed by the process.

Separate Income

There is no shared community economy. If the community provides residents with their primary income, this changes the dynamics among neighbors and adds another level of community beyond the scope of cohousing.

The economics of most cohousing communities are more or less like a typical condominium project. In a survey, 100 cohousing residents were asked how much money or disposable income they saved each month by living in cohousing. The standard answer was $100 to $200 per month.

A Unique Combination with Diverse Applications

These characteristics have come to define cohousing. None of these elements is unique, but the consistent combination of all six is. Each characteristic builds on the others and contributes to the success of the whole.

> "We have a lot of activities together that are not planned. Except for dinner, the unplanned activities are more fun than the planned ones." (Cohousing resident)

Although these characteristics are consistently present, their applications have been diverse. Each community is different because each was developed by the residents to address and realize their particular needs and desires.

The Architecture of Cohousing

A central path usually connects the individual homes. Often, a common terrace faces the houses and can seat everyone for dinner or other activities. There are gathering nodes along the walkway, such as a picnic table or sand box. Such nodes are associated with every five to nine houses. The houses have front porches at least seven feet deep and nine feet wide, so people will actually use the space.

The kitchen is oriented toward the common side of the house, with the sink facing the community so residents cooking or washing dishes can see people coming and going. Meanwhile, more private areas (such as living rooms and bedrooms) face the rear, or private side, of the house.

Optimally, residents can see the common house from most, if not all, of the houses and can see if others are inside. The common house generally contains a common dining room, a kitchen, a media room, a laundry room, a sitting room, and other activity rooms such as a workshop, craft room, music room, and others depending on the group's desires. In a senior cohousing community, the common house often has large guest rooms to accommodate an extended visit from family, or for professional caregivers if residents need help.

Further Considerations

Building a viable cohousing community requires that the residents remain true to more than the spirit of the ideal. As such, the following issues greatly impact how a cohousing community develops, both in the short and long term.

Community Size

While the average cohousing development accommodates 15 to 30 households, some consist of as few as nine families, or as many as 42 families. We found that housing groups with fewer than nine households who share common areas and facilities tend to function similarly to households in which a number of unrelated people share a house or apartment.

Living in such a small community is more demanding because residents depend more on each other. If one person temporarily needs extra time to concentrate on professional interests, thereby limiting community participation, the others feel the loss. Residents must be good friends and must agree on most issues in order to live interdependently. In addition, residents in small housing groups often have difficulty maintaining the energy to organize common activities over a period of many years. Larger communities can more readily absorb varying degrees of participation and differences of opinion.

The average size of a cohousing community, 40–100 people, allows residents to retain their autonomy and choose when, or when not, to participate in community activities. Many people are seeking a more supportive environment, rather than a new family type. The freedom not to participate sometimes can help to create a living environment that accommodates people's changing needs over the years.

Location

Locations of cohousing developments are limited by two factors, the availability of affordable sites and finding enough people interested in living in cohousing. The majority are situated just outside metropolitan areas where sites are affordable and yet within reasonable distance from work, schools, and other urban attractions. That said, there are no hard and fast rules about location. Some cohousing communities are located in the inner cities. By contrast, at least ten communities have been established in semi-rural settings, some of them using refurbished old farmhouses for the common house. While these developments have a "rural atmosphere," most residents will commute to nearby cities for work. Bottom line: *cohousing residents decide for themselves what location will work best for their particular desires and needs.*

Design

As already mentioned, most cohousing communities have attached dwellings clustered around pedestrian streets or courtyards, although a few communities consist of detached single-family houses. Some communities mix attached dwellings with detached single-family structures. More recent complexes have dealt with their northern climate by covering a central pedestrian street with glass, thus allowing access between residences and the common house without needing to "go outside."

Cohousing is generally a new construction enterprise because it is difficult to create the desired relationships between spaces in existing buildings. Nevertheless, several communities in Denmark adapted old factory buildings; and another adapted an old school building. In another case, residents renovated nine dilapidated row houses to create a charming community in the inner city.

While all of the newly constructed Danish developments are low-rise in scale, in both Denmark and Sweden high-rises and sections of huge housing projects have been converted to cohousing to overcome impersonal environments that encouraged vandalism and high occupant turnover.

Types of Financing and Ownership

Cohousing developments utilize a variety of financing mechanisms and ownership structures, either by choice or local ordinances: privately-owned condominiums, limited-equity cooperatives, rentals owned by nonprofit organizations, and a combination of private ownership and nonprofit-owned rental units. In each case, residents initiate, plan, and manage the community, whether or not the units are owner-occupied or rented. In Denmark, eighteen of the twenty developments built before 1982 are completely privately financed and owned, similar to American condominiums. Then, for a period, most projects took advantage of new government-sponsored, index-linked loans that structured the developments as limited-equity cooperatives. More recently, much government funding of nonprofit schemes has been withdrawn, including financial support for cohousing. Many other cohousing projects have resulted from collaborations between nonprofit organizations and resident groups to build rental units.

Other than determining who can afford to live in the development, financing makes little difference in the actual functioning of a cohousing community. Thus, cohousing differs from other housing categories, such as cooperatives and condominiums, which are defined solely by their type of ownership. Cohousing refers to an idea about how people can live together, rather than any particular financing or ownership scheme.

Priorities

The priorities of cohousing groups are as varied as the residents themselves. In addition to seeking a sense of community, some groups emphasize ecological concerns, such as solar and wind energy, recycling and organic community gardens. In other developments, residents place less priority on community projects and spend more time on individual interests such as local theatre groups, classes, or political organizations. And, of course, others are devoted to seniors.

Why Cohousing Just for Seniors?

Why would someone want to create a cohousing community dedicated to seniors? There is no simple answer, since housing is an individual choice. Mixed-generational cohousing is an option for some seniors, but regular cohousing communities typically focus their energies in places where seniors have already been—building careers, raising families, and the like. As well, concerns of younger cohousers do not usually hinge on health issues. While some seniors will find the youthful vigor of a regular cohousing community to be refreshing, others feel it's a case of "been there, done that."

So what alternatives are there? For too many Americans, who either find themselves widowed and lonely or otherwise unable to effectively care for themselves and their homes as they once did, a planned retirement "community" or assisted-care institution beckons. It's an odd predicament: most seniors have been capable, reliable people throughout their adult lives. They raised families, owned property, worked in various jobs, and/or ran their own businesses. They were active members of a larger community. But those seniors who choose the planned retirement community route too often find themselves just as alone as before, only now locked down behind the walls of a gated compound. As for the seniors in assisted-living care, they become, in effect, patients within an institution, where hired staff dictates the choice of food, the people with whom they can socialize, and the types of activities offered. At best, activities might be modified with residents input, but essentially the residents have given up control of their lives. And there's no going back.

By contrast, in senior cohousing the residents themselves make their own decisions. They are not alone, nor are they lonely. They collectively decide who will cook, what to cook, when to eat, and so on. After dinner, they go to a show or play a card game. They set up quilting racks, make music, and plan the next workday.

Since relationships are paramount in a cohousing community, residents live next door to their friends and, over time, their previous best friends (from life before senior cohousing) move in. These seniors live among people with whom they share a common bond of age, experience, and community—a community they themselves built to specifically meet their own needs. These relationships provide purpose and direction in their lives and are as meaningful as any they have ever had. This is why there is cohousing just for seniors.

37

Interview with Jaime Lerner

Architect-planner Jaime Lerner established sustainable policies city-wide in transportation, urban design, and housing.

Curitiba is considered one of the best examples of urban planning on the planet. When did you begin participating in the design of its Master Plan?

In the mid-60s, I was part of a group of architects working for the City of Curitiba, advising the mayor at the time (Ivo Arzua Pereira) in every development phase of the Curitiba Preliminary Urban Plan. We later became the Instituto de Pesquisa e Planejamento Urbano de Curitiba (IPPUC), Curitiba Research and Urban Planning Institute. Through IPPUC, I participated in the preparation of the Master Plan to guide the City's physical, economic and cultural transformation, and was elected mayor of the city in 1971. I remained mayor for three terms (1971–75, 1979–83 and 1989–92).

How can a city be an instrument for change?

A city has to have the political will to change. A city needs a strategy, which works with potentiality, not just needs. And a city needs solidarity, not as rhetoric but as a sincere understanding of the daily life of its citizens. With every problem there needs to be an equation of co-responsibility. When everyone understands what the consequences of certain attitudes are they will more readily cooperate and help bring about change. A city needs to have a daily plan and daily processes that encourage constant learning.

This is why you have designed initiatives where the citizens are involved in such things as tree planting, recycling, and keeping the gardens clean?

Yes, involvement in all aspects of city life. When we started separating garbage in Curitiba, we looked first to the children. For six months, we taught every child the importance of separating organic from inorganic garbage. The children then taught their parents. Since 1989, we've had 70% voluntary participation in this initiative. When we had a fuel crisis about 20 years ago, even

http://www.massivechange.com/media/MOV_JaimeLerner.pdf. Permission to reprint granted by the rights holder.

though we had a very good system of transport in place, everyone knew that they should rethink public transport. Curitiba has more private cars than any Brazilian city except Brasilia (500,000) yet 75% of commuters take the bus and Curitibanos spend only 10% of their income on transport. Why? Because they have a good alternative.

Jaime, tell me about the significance of the Plexiglas bus tubes you designed.

It was said for so many decades that a good system of transportation should be underground. But when you don't have the financial resources to build such infrastructure, it helps you to have more creativity. The tube, a less expensive option, gives the buses of Curitiba the same performance as a subway. We started to study this about 30 years ago and knew what was needed to create a good system of transport: it had to be fast, reliable, comfortable, and with good frequency. This meant not only putting buses in exclusive lanes like in many cities of the world, but also allowing for boarding on the same level and paying before getting on the bus. The tube supports both. In 1974, we moved 25,000 passengers per day with buses running in an exclusive lane. The system was improved regularly and now we are transporting more than two million passengers per day.

On surface, we can have better frequency and the connections are faster. Underground, you can travel faster, but it's technically impossible to have a frequency less than two minutes and the connections take longer; sometimes it takes 15 minutes or more to walk underground alone. I have nothing against subways, but the problem is that it's hard to have a complete network of underground systems. Even cities that have a few subway lines need an effective surface system. The future of mobility has to be considered in terms of integrated systems, where each piece—bikes, cars, taxis, subways, buses—never competes in the space of another.

What do the different colors of the buses signify?

The colors allow for easy reading of the system. The double-articulated buses are red. The feeder buses are yellow. The interborough buses are green. So you know by the color of the bus what kind of bus it is. If you want to build solutions for the future and have people working with you, every citizen has to understand the system very well. You have to have a commitment with simplicity. Every child should know the design of his or her own city. They should design the city even, because if you can design the city you can understand the city. If you understand the city, you will respect the city.

What is the capacity of the double-articulated bus?

300 people. I used to joke about this though: it's 300 Brazilians or 270 Swedes! As soon as the system has a very good boarding process, you can transport 300 passengers every minute very easily, which is 18,000 passengers per hour in one direction. In thirty seconds, this is 36,000 people per hour, which is a subway statistic, which is what we do in Curitiba.

Do you believe this kind of transformation can occur in any city of the world?

In my more than forty years of doing this, I'm convinced that every city in the world, no matter the scale, no matter the financial resources, can have a significant change in less than two years.

I can swear to you that this is possible and that you can make important changes. With public transportation, you can definitely make important changes. With environmental issues, you can make important changes. On the care of children, you can make important changes. It all depends on the city, but anything is possible. It's not a question of scale. Sometimes mayors use as an excuse that their cities are too big. But no, it's not a question of scale; it's a question of philosophy. Don't be afraid of the scale. Don't be afraid if you don't have enough financial resources. You can always build a good equation of co-responsibility.

Are other places in the world mimicking the Curitiba model?

It took 25 years until another city tried to do what we did in Curitiba, and that city is Bogotá, Colombia. Now, more than 83 cities in the world are doing it, including Sao Paolo. I was in Seoul, Korea, and the mayor there is removing highways in the city in an attempt to design a surface system and restore an old stream, a small river in the city that was very important to their history. Honolulu is trying to implement a surface system and I'm sure they will do it very efficiently. These are just two examples of many, many more.

This must give you a feeling of great satisfaction.

It does, for sure. I'm convinced that the most important thing to work on right now is the mobility system, which is not only a system of transport; it's the whole understanding of a city. The more we create an integration of functions the better a city will become. We don't yet have a smart car. We have a smart bus, which is a good system of transport.

Cars that are good on design are not good on the engine. Cars advanced on the engine—hybrid systems—are not good on design. Small cars are not good on the road. Cars for the road are not good for the city. Bikes are another issue. We have to redesign the bike so that it opens up like an umbrella. If bikes were more portable we could integrate them with public transport, going from door to door. I'm working on this idea with a team here in Curitiba. We're exploring how far we can go with surface transportation. Lastly, why not develop a kangaroo system for cars? Rather than having two cars—one for the road and one for the city—we could have a car that feeds energy into a very, very small car.

I like to say, cars are our mechanical mothers in law. You have to have a good relationship with your mother-in-law but you cannot allow her to conduct your life.

Jaime Lerner is the president of the International Union of Architects (IUA) and the former mayor of Curitiba, Brazil. He is the author of Urban Acupuncture.

38 Three Theoretical Assumptions Needed to Create Useful Applied Social Science Research for Architecture

Eleftherios Pavlides and Galen Cranz

Authors clarify the distinction between assessment and evaluation, between hypothesis testing and discovery science, and make a point of including architectural methods of documentation and traditional social research methods in building assessment. We conduct surveys not to evaluate buildings, but rather as part of organizational learning, to improve buildings, and expand our understanding of how people experience them. Even the very best building can be improved; even the worst has something good about it from which we can learn.

ABSTRACT

Social science research has had minimal impact on architectural practice despite efforts since the 1960's by organizations such as EDRA (Environmental Design Research Association) and IAPS (International Association of People-environment Studies) and others. This paper questions three fundamental assumptions of environmental design research that may account for the underwhelming application of this research in architecture: 1) Social science methods are suitable for evaluation of buildings. To the contrary, social science methods may not be suitable for the more global, action-oriented evaluation of buildings. More accurately and more modestly, social science methods can assess specific users' experiences of specific qualities or features of buildings. 2) Hypothesis science is the ideal for environmental design research. To the contrary, hypothesis science in environmental design research is not as productive as discovery science. 3) Architectural methods of documentation are not relevant to social science investigations of the built environment. To the contrary, accessing social information in the physical environment requires detailed documentation and evaluation of the built environment using architectural methods, similar to archeology.

Eleftherios Pavlides and Galen Cranz, "Three Theoretical Assumptions Needed to Create Useful Applied Social Science Research for Architecture," from *The International Journal of Interdisciplinary Social Sciences*, Vol. 4, No. 10, pp. 191–201. Copyright © 2009 by Common Ground Publishing. Permission to reprint granted by the publisher.

SOCIAL SCIENCES IN ARCHITECTURAL DESIGN: THREE ASSUMPTIONS RECONSIDERED

This paper explores three underlying assumptions of social science research in the area of environment and behavior and suggests an alternative approach in order to increase the utility of applied social science research for architectural design. This paper is not about what is loosely considered "research" in architectural design, namely, collecting all the information needed to program and design a building. Rather, this paper evaluates social science methods used to identify users' points of view about designed places.

Origins of Applied Social Sciences in the Area of Environment and Behavior

In the nineteen sixties several social scientists, such as Sommer[1], Winkel[2], Ittelson[3], Prohansky[4] and others, independently applied social sciences research to assess how specific buildings, ranging from psychiatric hospitals to geriatric institutions, met human needs.[5] This work cumulated with the formation of the Environmental Design Research Association (EDRA) an international, interdisciplinary organization whose annual international conference first brought together design professionals, social scientists, students, educators, and facility managers in 1969. The goal was to advance and disseminate environmental design research, in order to create environments responsive to human needs.[6]

In Europe, the International Association of People-environments (IAPS) was officially founded in 1981 to stimulate research and innovation for improving human wellbeing and the physical environment and to promote the integration of research, education, policy and architectural practice.[7] The Man Environment Research Association (MERA) was founded in Japan in 1982[8] and in Australia People And Place Environmental Research (PAPER) was founded in 1980 and its successor Environment, Behaviour & Society (EBS) (2005), also published journals and held conferences to promote social science scholarship and research on how built environments meet human needs, again with the intention of improving planning and architectural design.

However, after four decades of conferences, journals, publications, doctoral programs, and social science educational requirements by the National Architectural Accreditation Board for

---

1   Sommer applied work on sociability and layout of furniture in a geriatric facility is an early example of research that influenced design decisions. His seminal book *Personal Space* has been reissued multiple time since its 1969 publication.

2   Winkel's early work identified the design flaws of a psychiatric hospital that had catastrophic impact on the patients, and he is one of the founders of the doctoral program at CUNNY.

3   Ittelson published in 1961 a report "Some Factors Influencing the Design and Function of Psychiatric Facilities" and with Prohansky started a program of studies at CUNNY.

4   Prohansky, along with Winkel, Rivlin and Ittelson, created the first text in Environmental Psychology and the first Journal Environment and Behavior.

5   For a detailed early history of psychologists studying the designed environment and collaborations with architects who played a role in forming the Environmental Design Research Association see (Bechtel, Robert. *Environment and Behavior: An Introduction*, page 75–88).

6   http://www.edra.org/

7   http://www.iaps-association.org/what-is-iaps/some-history/ Although the official beginning is 1981, conferences have been held in various European countries since 1969.

8   http://www.mera-web.jp/english/whats.html

architectural training in the US, most practicing architects do not know that Environment and Behaviour (EB) research even exists. While various social scientists have made contributions to specific projects,[9] in general the architectural profession has not been deeply or widely affected by the environment-and-behavior literature.[10] A minor sub-literature arose attempting to explain the overwhelming absence of application of the environmental design research that with few exceptions focused on the absence of interest by architects rather than on the inherent nature of the research of this emerging field.[11] The possibility that social science research may be inherently unsuited to make direct contributions to architectural design was suggested at the EDRA 2009 40th anniversary conference in Kansas City by one of the four elders who offered reflections on past accomplishments and discussed the future of EDRA. Dr. Kaplan[12] posited that intuition plays a large role in complex decision-making, suggesting that architectural design may be more dependent on intuition than behavioral researchers have recognized.[13] Architectural design decisions and architectural evaluation can be aided by scientific inquiry but are unlikely to be based on science alone.[14]

As an architect with a PhD that combined ethnographic methods of participant observation and ethnographic interviews with architectural analysis, the first author has been teaching architecture students "Social Aspects of Architecture" for the last twenty years. Architecture students review the environment behavior literature seeking information relevant to building types. They also conduct fieldwork, informed by the synthesis of methods including photographic elicitation that the first author developed for his doctoral dissertation, in order to assess a building from the point of view of the people who use it.[15] Their research is reported to a sponsor, who is a manager

---

9   Notably Galen Cranz—a sociologist who studied the social use of parks, contributed to the winning entry by architect Bernard Tschumi for one of the most important architectural competitions of the 20th Century—and sociologist John Zeisel have proven environmental attributes affect Alzheimer's symptoms. Cranz, Galen. *The Politics of Park Design: A History of Urban Parks in America* (MIT, 1982)., and Zeisel, J., Silverstein, N., Hyde, J., Levkoff, S., Lawton, M. P. and Holmes, W. (2003) "Environmental correlates to behavioral outcomes in Alzheimer's special care units," in *The Gerontologist*, 43(5), 697–711. He has collaborated with architects who designed facilities where patients have measurably fewer symptoms.

10 While social science research has not found direct application in the architectural profession, Konstantin Kiyanenko, professor of architecture at the Vologda State Technical University in Russia, recently observed that publications emanating from EDRA have affected the discourse, the language of architectural education, and that this has had indirect influence on the architectural profession's awareness of human needs in the US in ways that do not exist in Russia.

11 Pavlides, in "The Missing Dimension in Environmental Research," in *EDRA 22*, 1991, argues that in general, environmental design research does not adequately document the physical characteristics of the environment under investigation to generate useful results.

12 Stephen Kaplan is an influential scholar in the areas of environmental design research, well known for his studies on people's relationship to nature. Kaplan, Stephen. *The Experience of Nature*. Cambridge University Press, 1989.

13 The architectural design process has been referred to by Horst Rittel and Jon Lang (among others) as a "wicked" problem or an extremely ill-defined problem that has no way of determining when the problem is solved. Lang, Jon. *Creating Architectural Theory: The Role of the Behavioral Sciences in Environmental Design*. Wiley, John & Sons, 1987.

14 *Blink* by Malcolm Gladwell summarized much of what is known in many different fields about how efficiently the unconscious mind works intuitively.

15 Parts of this dissertation have been published in a) "Vernacular Architecture as an Expression of its Social Context," with Jana Hesser, chapter in *Current Perspectives on Housing and Culture*. Edited by Setha M. Low and Erve J. Chambers. University of Penn. Press, Philadelphia, 1989, and b) "The Influence of Women's Roles on House Form and Decoration in

in an organization with responsibilities to maintain, add, or initiate new construction and who, therefore, is able to use this information. The sponsors evaluate the usefulness of the information that students obtain from interviews as well as from reviewing the environment behavior literature for the particular building type. (For this work students receive service-learning credit, a graduation requirement for Roger Williams University and some other universities.) Highlights of material from several semesters about a particular building type have been presented to experienced architects at national conferences and local professional lunch meetings. Architects who were asked to assess the usefulness of this information for architectural design indicated that this information is relevant and useful to their practice and they will use it in future designs.

The theoretical assumptions discussed below are based on the experience of teaching the "Social Aspects of Architecture" course mentioned above and "Social and Cultural Processes in Architecture and Urban Design" taught by the second author at the University of California at Berkeley. Architectural assessments combining social science methods with architectural methods are contrasted to standard Post Occupancy Evaluation or POE. This is the term extensively used for evaluating buildings from the users' point of view with methods from the social sciences.[16] POE studies use a varying constellation of techniques from the social sciences to study buildings, but they share some common assumptions, three of which are discussed below.

Questioning Three Fundamental Assumptions of Environmental Design Research that may Account for the Underwhelming Application of this Research in Architecture

Assumption 1: Social science methods are suitable for evaluation of buildings. To the contrary, social science methods may not be suitable for the more global, action-oriented evaluation of buildings. More accurately and more modestly, social science methods can assess specific experiences of specific qualities or features of buildings.

Social science methods cannot completely evaluate buildings from the users' point of view. The complexity and sheer magnitude of the number of factors affecting the architectural design process[17] make complete or full environmental evaluation unattainable if we rely only on social science methods. Building evaluation needs to address a large compilation of interrelated factors beyond human needs, including structural, economic, and code requirements, to mention a few. In educational research, *assessment* refers to individual student performance, whereas *evaluation* refers to the decision-making process that administrators and other stakeholders go through when they decide to keep an educational program or modify it. Social science methods do not address this complexity, especially the value-based component of decision-making. Lowering expectations of what applied social science research may contribute to architecture may increase the utility of applied social sciences to architecture. Technically we could say that the POE term that has come to us over 3–4 years is a misnomer. The term is well established, even used by journalists covering

---

Eressos, Greece," with Jana Hesser, chapter in *Gender and Power in Rural Greece*. Edited by Jill Dubisch. Princeton University Press, Princeton, 1986.

16   Craig Zimring, "Post Occupancy Evaluation Of Designed Environments" in *Methods in environmental and behavioral research*, edited by Robert B. Bechtel, Robert W. Marans, William Michelson, Malabar, Fla.: R. E. Krieger Pub. Co., 1990.

17   John Lang, *Creating Architectural Theory* (New York: Van Nostrand, 1987), p. 60.

architectural issues in the U.S. and the UK, and so will remain in common use, but we would like to use the term "user assessment" because it offers a more precise, modest, and realistic basis for applications to architecture.

In lieu of attempting global evaluations of buildings using social science methods, research can focus on how aspects, qualities, or features accommodate or interfere with specific activities for specific people. This kind of inquiry does not validate or question design decisions. Instead, it provides insights about issues of importance to users, especially outlier groups that are impacted by designs of the environment in ways not anticipated. Attempting to assess whether a particular articulation of architectural form meets a specific human need is useful, but it does not rise to the level of evaluation because it isolates a parameter from all the parameters that taken together shape judgment about a building. We leave evaluation to architects and decision makers working with the architects who are planning and designing buildings; they can use such applied social science assessments in their evaluation, employing a variety of rational, moral, and intuitive methods. This corrective has the advantage of changing the architects' perception of the social scientist as an uninformed, outside critic, hostile to the architect's design, to that of a modest contributor to the organization's ability to evaluate its building.

Assumption 2: Hypothesis science is the ideal for environmental design research. To the contrary, hypothesis science in environmental design research is not as productive as discovery science.

Developing a hypothesis is seldom as productive as inquiry in architectural research. Social sciences often make a claim about causal relations among variables, which can be disproven through a process that could be repeated. The roots of this scientific tradition date to the 19th century mechanistic view of the world as conceived by philosophers such as August Comte and John Stuart Mill, and is connected to a desire to bestow on the social sciences the same status as the physical sciences.[18] Social sciences were presumed to be more scientific to the degree that they resembled the physical sciences.[19] Modern theoreticians of science, such as Singer, Ackoff, and Emery, have identified limitations of the cause-effect paradigm. They proposed as an alterative that "the universe is best revealed by viewing it in terms of producer-product," which requires the recognition of the importance of a complex environment providing the context for an event to take place. They continue, "Science based on the producer-product relationship is environment-full, not environment-free. For example, moisture is a coproducer of an oak along with an acorn. There are other necessary conditions that taken collectively constitute the acorn's environment."[20]

An additional problem for architects is that hypothesis-testing research has produced findings with only limited uses for architects because it validates information already well known and understood by architects through experience. The utility of such scientific information is not to evaluate design decisions, but to educate clients about the reasons behind design decisions. For example, architects have always understood the importance of abundant daylight and value it as an essential design quality for school designs. Scientific research proving that daylight increases learning rates has helped architects defend their designs from school committees that in a misguided

---

18   Michael S. Lewis-Beck, Alan Bryman, Tim Futing Liao, *The Sage encyclopedia of social science research methods.*
19   Lee C. McIntyre, *Readings in the Philosophy of Social Science,* The MIT Press: 1994.
20   Michael Lucas, *Understanding business: environments,* Routledge: 2000 p. 30.

effort to save money attempt to eliminate skylights or reduce the percentage of windows in the envelope of a school building.[21]

Furthermore, the validation of hypotheses using social scientific methods has limited value for architectural innovation because if a question is already defined, architects are efficient at finding multiple answers to resolve it. Architectural design depends on creating forms that simultaneously address many questions and solve many problems with each articulation of form. Each individual question has multiple solutions and architects become adept at selecting the solution to each question so that solutions to all questions under consideration are co-located in one architectural form, the one finally chosen for implementation.

An alternative to testing hypotheses with observations, interviews, or experiments, is to engage in discovery science by generating databases of information, without always knowing in advance how the data will be used. This is the practice with modern biological and physical sciences where the "new approach to biological experimentation known as discovery science based on generating detailed inventories on genes, proteins, and metabolites in a particular cell type or tissue as a key information source."[22] In discovery science, observations or other methods of collecting large amounts of data are mined to see what kinds of patterns can be found.[23] If you do think you find patterns or other information, you may form a hypothesis and test it traditionally. This approach has been used in modern physical sciences most famously with the genome project and the Hadron electron accelerator. If the desire is for the social sciences to emulate the modern physical sciences, then a broader adoption of discovery science can be expected—beyond the limited application proposed here to address the practicality of making applied social sciences useful for architectural practice.

A social science technique that has proved productive in conducting discovery science in architecture is photographic elicitation interviews. In this technique, people familiar with a building through use are presented with photographs of locations in the building and are asked to discuss what activities they carry out in the places shown in the photograph, to assess in what way these places support these activities, in what ways these places interfere with them, and to explain why. This process does not impose external categories, which linguists and anthropologists call etic categories, but rather allows inhabitants to select their own criteria for evaluating an environment, what linguists and anthropologists call emic categories.

Perhaps surprisingly, responses to this kind of undirected questioning elicitations fall into patterns. In practice a lot of people use the same criteria and make similar evaluations of the places shown in the photographs, even though, theoretically, each respondent could raise a different concern. These common responses generally confirm the expectations of the architecture students and the sponsors. Even though these concerns are in some ways already known, sponsors find the overwhelming numbers of respondents who report a problem without having been prompted by a question to be an especially useful validation of its significance. Such data help sponsors make a case for funds to renovate or construct something new.

Beyond this, *unusual* responses derived from photographic elicitation interviews, frequently from small groups or outliers whose needs were previously not known, provide the most useful

---

21 Heschong Mahone Group, *Daylighting in schools: An investigation into the Relationship Between Daylighting and Human Performance*. Pacific Gas and Electric Company, 1999.

22 Sharyl J. Nass, Bruce Stillman, *Large Scale Biomedical Science*. National Cancer Policy Board (U.S.). 2003. p. 192.

23 Andrew Pollack, "Approaching Biology From a Different Angle." *New York Times*, Tuesday, April 17, 2001.

information. These atypical responses often have surprisingly general significance, which stimulates innovation. Discovery science reveals uses or experiences of the environment not anticipated by architects. For example, an unexpected response came from a high school student who came from a culture in which paper is not used for cleaning at the toilet. He reported that he could not use the school toilet because he did not have access to water. Architects experienced with school designs who were given this information found it both novel and useful, suggested multiple ways of addressing this need, and anticipated using this information in future school bathroom designs. While this kind of information does not suffice to program or design an entire school building, it helps improve programming and design by making it more inclusive to accommodate the needs of immigrant students who can not use toilets as commonly designed.

The purpose of this kind of open-ended investigation is to enrich the design process with questions that would have otherwise remained unasked and broaden the understanding of diverse uses and perceptions of the build environment. Using applied social science research to identify additional questions and problems not only allows architects to make their designs more inclusive and more sensitive to human needs, but also offers an intrinsic reward of architectural practice—creativity in problem solving. By not being proscriptive, architects' resistance to social research as a "straight jacket" can be avoided. Identifying new problems invites architects to use their creative talent, something they always value and welcome.

Assumption 3: Architectural methods of documentation are not relevant to social science investigations of the built environment. To the contrary, accessing social information in the physical environment requires detailed documentation and evaluation of the built environment using architectural methods, similar to archaeology.

A third difference between the traditional POE and the applied discovery social science advanced here is the level of documentation of the physical environment. We recommend using the standards of architecture in recording and evaluating a building before attempting to study how various users experience and use it. POEs, with some exceptions, do not create a comprehensive and extensive record of architectural form, including scale drawings in section and plan, site plans showing relationships to broader context, views, materials, qualities of light at various times, building envelope, artificial illumination, and mechanical systems. POEs typically overlook these criteria that have been taught through architectural education. In contrast, the proposed user assessment of the building combines annotated scale drawings, photographs, and diagrams to establish an objective, "etic" baseline evaluation of the building from the architect's point of view. While the architect is carrying out this objective documentation, their trained intuition is also at work, so creative insights will emerge.

The initial examination of the building using architectural methods serves three purposes. a) It generates photographic material and ideas to help design the photo-elicitation interview instrument; b) it provides visual material to help present the findings; c) it provides an etic (architect's–outsider's) evaluation against which to contrast the emic (user's–insider's) insights that result from the photo-elicitation interviews.

a) Selecting photographs and other graphic material to create a photo-elicitation interview instrument requires:

1. A thorough understanding of how to use graphic media to communicate architectural qualities;
2. Comprehending the complex simultaneity of how architectural forms address multiple functions; and
3. Performing extensive pre-testing to make sure the presentation of the visual material is both easy to comprehend by users and is productive in eliciting responses.

To design an effective interview instrument for this kind of research requires architectural graphic skills and knowledge associated with the practice of architecture.

Importantly, the use of photographs is not limited to eliciting remarks about qualities visible in photographs. Often photographs educe comments about olfactory or acoustic qualities as well as about activities in areas adjacent to those visible in the photographs. Furthermore, sometimes interviewees may point to aspects visible in the photographs that the person who took the photograph was not aware were there. For examples, a photograph of seats in a library by a staircase to the basement brought comments that it smells bad there because of the mold due to the humidity in the basement; a picture of a room in the student union brought the comment of how noisy the mechanical system is in that location.

b) The complex visual documentation with drawings and photographs is critical for presenting the findings. POE findings are sometimes presented with graphs containing summary of responses but are not supported by drawings and photographs of the architecture that the research was attempting to evaluate. However, architecture photographs and drawings are not merely illustrations of ideas but an indispensable part of the discourse, in the same way that visual information is essential to art history and archaeology.

c) The original architectural documentation and evaluation provides a basis for superimposing how some users' experiences and uses may differ from the norm and were not anticipated from the architect's original point of view. This contrast heightens awareness—for both the architecture student and the architect—of the multiplicity of experiences of buildings. The reactions of many different kinds of people can challenge one's intuition and offer good reasons for using social science research to support architectural practice.

One of the important consequences of the detail required for this initial investigation with architectural methods is that it is not accomplished in one semester by one team. The physical complexity of a single building invites study over several semesters. A building is similar in complexity to an archaeological site that typically is recorded and analyzed over many years. Work accomplished in previous years can be reviewed and expanded. Pedagogically, this has the advantage of involving students in a long term, real world project to which they can contribute in a meaningful way.

CONCLUSIONS

In this paper we argue that the limited influence of the applied social sciences on architecture might be reversed if some theoretical assumptions are challenged and reversed. We have questioned the ideal of evaluating a building, since evaluation is not even possible without a value and policy orientation. Moreover, the hypothesis-testing approach of some social science has only limited utility to architecture. Instead, discovery science raises new questions important for innovation. Further, recognition that assessments of how different groups of people, even extremely small groups of people, experience and use buildings is a lot more useful than using methods from the social sciences that require large samples, randomly selected (which raises thorny questions about how to define the population using a particular building, in order to draw a sample) for statistical significance. Finally, for applied social science to achieve its potential it needs to include in its methods those methods of recording and evaluating buildings afforded through architectural education. They provide a nuanced understanding of the built environment needed even in social inquiry.

These recommendations require that the researcher have training both in architecture and in the social sciences. In lieu of such dual training, collaboration between researchers from social sciences and architecture can work, especially if both specialists have experience in this kind of collaboration.

There are practical limitations to this kind of research, which is painstaking and labor intensive. Funds for this kind of fieldwork may be limited. One possible way to carry out this time consuming fieldwork is to have architecture students perform this work as part of their education. A course on Environmental Design Research allows students to become familiar with the Environment and Behavior literature while at the same time helping document buildings architecturally and learning to conduct photographic elicitation interviews with the inhabitants. Aggregating findings over several semesters from many universities on a database posted on the Internet could be a useful service to practicing architects.

These proposed theoretical modifications and practical recommendations to employ architecture students to perform discovery social science field research as part of their education would also provide architecture students the opportunity to review, summarize, and internalize all the work that has accumulated over several decades in the field of Environment and Behavior that currently remains underutilized. If students are educated in this way their approach to design will start with a review of what is known and they will assume that close, empirical assessment of relevant building types from users' points of view is the path to innovation and refinement of a building type. In addition to expanding the scope of applied social science research into the area of the built environment, this process would eventually also make hypothesis science research more accessible to architectural practice. As more findings accumulate, hypothesis formulation would become a more reasonable and practical aspiration. But the primary focus will always be on discovery science, since social institutions—and the buildings that support them—are always changing.

REFERENCES

Bechtel, Robert. *Environment and Behavior: An Introduction.* University of Arizona, 1997.

Cranz, Galen. *The Politics of Park Design: A History of Urban Parks in America.* MIT, 1982.

Cranz, Galen, Taylor, Amy, Broudehoux, Anne-Marie. "Community and Complexity on Campus. A Post-Occupancy Evaluation of the University of California, Berkeley, Haas School of Business," *Places, A Forum of Environmental Design, Winter,* 1997, Vol. 11, No. 1, pp. 38–51.

Cranz, G. & Young, C. The role of design in inhibiting or promoting use of common open space: The case of Redwood Gardens, Berkeley, CA. In S. Rodiek & B. Schwarz (Eds.), *The Role of the Outdoors in Residential Environments for Aging,* (New York: Haworth Press, Inc., 2006), pp. 71–94.

Cranz, Galen with Jess Wendover, Iris Tien, Mark Gillem, and Jon Norman. "College of Environmental Design, UC Berkeley Temporary Home," *Designing for Designers,* J. Nasar, W. F. E. Preiser & Tom Fisher (Eds.) (New York: Fairchild Books, 2007).

Cranz, Galen with Cha, EunAh. "Body Conscious Design in a 'Teen Space': Post Occupancy Evaluation of an Innovative Public Library," *Public Libraries,* Sept/Nov. 2006, pp. 48–56.

Heschong Mahone Group. *Daylighting in Schools: An Investigation into the Relationship Between Daylighting and Human Performance.* Pacific Gas and Electric Company, 1999.

Ittelson, W. "Some factors influencing the design and function of psychiatric facilities" *Progress Report,* New York: Brooklyn College of the City University, 1960.

Itelson, W. H., Proshansky, H., Rivlin, L., & Winkel, G. *Introduction to Environmental Psychology.* New York: Holt, Rinehart & Winston, 1974.

Kaplan, Stephen. *The Experience of Nature.* Cambridge University Press, 1989.

Lang, Jon. *Creating Architectural Theory: The Role of the Behavioral Sciences in Environmental Design.* Van Nostrand, 1987.

Lewis-Beck, Michael S., Bryman, Alan, Futing, Tim Liao. *The Sage Encyclopedia of Social Science Research Methods.* Sage, 2004.

Lucas, Michael. *Understanding Business: Environments.* Routledge, 2000.

McIntyre, Lee C. *Readings in the Philosophy of Social Science.* The MIT Press: 1994.

Nass, Sharyl J. and Stillman, Bruce. *Large Scale Biomedical Science.* National Cancer Policy Board (U.S.). 2003.

Pavlides, Eleftherios. "The Missing Dimension in Environmental Research" paper delivered at *EDRA 22,* 1991.

Pavlides, Eleftherios and Hesser, Jana. "Vernacular Architecture as an Expression of its Social Context." In *Current Perspectives on Housing and Culture.* Edited by Setha M. Low and Erve J. Chambers. University of Penn. Press, Philadelphia, 1989,

——"The Influence of Women's Roles on House Form and Decoration in Eressos, Greece" with Jana Hesser, *Gender and Power in Rural Greece.* Edited by Jill Dubisch. Princeton University Press, Princeton, 1986.

Pollack Andrew. "Approaching Biology From a Different Angle." *New York Times.* Tuesday, April 17, 2001.

Sommer, Robert. *Personal Space.* Prentice-Hall, 1969.

Zeisel, J., Silverstein, N., Hyde, J., Levkoff, S., Lawton, M. P. and Holmes, W. "Environmental correlates to behavioral outcomes in Alzheimer's special care units." *The Gerontologist,* 43(5), 697–711, 2003.

Zimring, Craig. "Post Occupancy Evaluation Of Designed Environments." *Methods in Environmental and Behavioral Research.* Edited by Robert B. Bechtel, Robert W. Marans, William Michelson, Malabar, Fla.: R. E. Krieger Pub. Co., 1990.

39 Levels of Analysis in Environmental Design

Galen Cranz

Sociologically, every scale, whether tiny or large, can be considered from a different level of analysis. Even a chair or a home has institutional, societal, and even cultural significance. Designers may consider their products from the point of view of what it says at each level.

Architecture is many things to many different people. Architectural historians often examine buildings as indicators of cultural forces; in contrast, social scientists and environmental-behavior researchers emphasize the behavior that occurs within them. I would like to introduce the sociological idea of levels of analysis to demonstrate that both levels are important and valid. In fact, not only those two levels of analysis, but also several others may help scholars, practitioners, and citizens understand the full significance of architecture. Architecture and environmental design in its broadest sense—from objects to regions—embeds values and norms and directs behavior in every society and culture.

The idea of levels of analysis came from the sociological theorizing of Parsons and Shils, who tried to create a theory of social structure abstract and general enough to apply to any social system in any cultural context.[i] It has been criticized as overly static, but in my efforts to understand architecture as a cultural practice I have found myself using this idea for many years to demonstrate to students how architecture addresses both symbolism and behavior simultaneously. It's not an either-or choice, but rather a way to judge the power of a design: the more levels it addresses and solves at the same time the more brilliant the solution.

The Levels of Analysis from Parsons and Shils are:

Cultural,
Societal,
Institutional,
Complex Organizational,
Face-to-face, primary, technical

Galen Cranz, *Levels of Analysis in Environmental Design*, pp. 1–8. Copyright © 2010 by Galen Cranz. Permission to reprint granted by the author.

In Table 1, below, I have separated technical and made explicit their assumption of:

Organism
Physical environment

The levels of analysis from Parsons and Shils are in the left hand column in Table 1. Some of the labels are self-evident, but others need clarification. **Culture** refers to **the *pattern* of values**, not just the values. For example, the values of honesty, filial piety, equality, learning, self-discipline, compassion, responsibility, friendship, work, courage, perseverance, and loyalty have different priorities in different cultures. And within one culture this pattern can change over time. For example, one Greek tragedy depicts the cultural change that was occurring when one value (obedience to father) trumped another (brotherhood) as happened when Greece was changing to a patriarchal society from a matrifocal one according to Robert Briffault in *The Mothers*.[ii]

The **societal** level of analysis corresponds to the most general, abstract, widely shared **values** that guide a people.

In modern times societies are often the same as the state, a political structure, but this level of analysis refers to the things that are shared by all the institutions in a society, including state, religion, law, economy, and education. American society and Canadian society are different even if they share many common cultural patterns like language and buildings because some of their most general values are different and, accordingly, their institutions, like health care and policing, differ from one another.[iii]

Probably the most technical term here is **institution**, because it refers to **general norms** for realizing values, rather than to an organization that one can join. The institution of higher education is different from any one of the particular universities one might be part of, like the University of California or New Jersey Institute of Technology. In everyday speech we often use the term "institutions" to refer to specific hospitals, universities, jails, schools, but here they are called **complex organizations**. These are the physical buildings and the social life that goes on in them, which translate general norms for how to do things to more local and functionally specific manifestations of those ideas. That process gets increasingly specific when we move to the **primary/technical** level of analysis where **face-to-face interaction** occurs in small groups and in relation to the tangible, physical environment. (Originally "technical" was at the same level as "primary" because technology involves direct physical interaction, but here I have represented technology separately since it is so important in architecture.) Below that, but still imbued with social meaning, is the organic world including the human organism, and below that is the physical world of air and geology, our bedrock, and also still social as the metaphor of bedrock testifies.

How values get translated into action is what sociologists call the "specification" problem. **Values and ways of thinking get manifested** far more deeply than early sociology recognized **into the physical tissue of our bodies**.[iv]

Different **disciplines** have developed to focus most of their attention on one or two of these levels, as indicated in column three. Column four indicates how scholars debate the issue of **how social change occurs**, in particular at what level social changes begins and in what direction it flows. Materialists argue that social change starts when there are changes in who owns tools; Marx in particular showed how changes in who owned the means of production created social changes, which in turn eventually created cultural changes. From this point of view culture is "superstructure" that comes after (or on top of) the more basic and fundamental power relationships are established and serves to legitimate and obscure the real power relations.

Idealists, in contrast, argue that human cultural categories, the way people think, shapes their perception of reality, including technology and the use of the material world.[v] Those are the biggest, most obvious debates in the social sciences, but others advocate the power of each of the other levels of analysis as the seat of change as well. For example, specialists in organizational behavior show how the structure of a complex organization creates a culture of its own that effects work productivity, innovation, morale, etc. Others might insist that institutional change, especially through law, is the most important agent of change. Psychotherapists and the psychologically oriented see individual well-being as the basis for social change: "be the change you want to see."

Let's consider an example of social change from recent American history. At the level of *societal* values we Americans profess belief in equality of opportunity (rather than equality per se), but at the *institutional* level that belief was translated into two separate educational systems for Euro-Americans and African-Americans. In 1954 that interpretation was changed when the Supreme Court declared that separate was not equal. Institutional segregation was no longer in place, but at the *organizational* level many states and school districts maintained the old practices, provoking the Civil Rights movement 10 years later. School districts were forced by federal troops to integrate their schools. Once equality reached the organizational level, however, it still remained—and remains today—for *individual* teachers, parents, students to adjust their attitudes and behavior. Research on self-esteem, for example, indicates that social change has to work its way into the hearts and minds of individuals. Until African-American and Euro-American children both feel that they are valued members of society equality of opportunity remains partial, because low self esteem retards performance.

Further, even our bodies are effected by social arrangements. For example, African Americans suffer disproportionately from stress and stress related disorders, and people who are financially advantaged for the last 20 years of their work lives outlive poorer people by a significant number of years. Fashionable shoes deform our feet and toes; chairs create posture problems; even ideas about being "cool" or relaxed or proper work their way into fixed muscular patterns that become relatively permanent (even thought they can be changed by means of kinesthetic reeducation).

I want to offer the possibility that **design** operates at each of these levels and has a corresponding physical, material manifestation. The fifth column indicates the correspondences between sociological thought and architectural thought. At the **cultural level** the priorities and hierarchies of values are expressed through **settlement pattern**, which refers to the way communities are laid out, which activities are housed next to which activities. For example, some re-industrial villages might use an anthropomorphic pattern with the chief at the top, religious or political functions to the right and left, residences in the torso, with agriculture and waste management at the furthest distance. Today, urban planners, who plan at the scale of the entire city, and urban designers, who plan at the scale of clusters of several buildings, also work within the framework of general cultural ideas, however contested, about appropriate relations among parts of a settlement. The American **urban grid expresses that idea** that all land is equal for the purpose of general economic expediency. Of course, that utilitarian ideal is deformed by other values, for example, the high ground with views or breeze has been sought by the wealthy for their homes. Rivers and seaside once gave priority to transit and commercial functions, but now air travel has released these locations for recreation, residence, and supporting services. Civic centers, business districts, residential, and manufacturing areas are usually separated, often by transit corridors, and this pattern expresses the idea that these functions should be keep apart; a competing idea has challenged the functional segregation of the post-war city claiming that uses should be mixed for greater convenience and round-the-clock use.

At the **societal level** architects express general values and aspirations through **symbolism** usually expressed on the exterior of buildings—architrave, bas-relief, columns, elaborate entrances, symmetrical or asymmetrical facades, choice of building materials, shapes, colors, type and placement of windows. Asymmetrical facades often connote informality in the United States, for park buildings and residences. For example, the grand Biltmore Estate in Asheville, North Carolina, the largest residence in the United States, designed to look like a European castle, has an asymmetrical facade that distinguishes it from governmental and commercial buildings that have employed the same European grandeur. When F. L. Wright wanted to express the value that buildings should relate to the surrounding land forms he massed the building horizontally and reinforced that with attention to every detail including the shape and color of brickwork and even the direction of the mortar.

Monuments epitomize societal functions because the entire structure is devoted to honoring a single event, person, or idea. The state uses history in architectural symbolism.[vi] Many towns have monuments to those fallen in WWII or to a national hero. The importance of the Statue of Liberty is at the societal level, its function to symbolize the nation.

Building type expresses the **institutional level**. This is the trickiest level to understand because sociologically the term is used differently than in ordinary usage. In ordinary usage we refer to banks and universities as institutions, but they are organizations, usually a subset of an institution like higher education or the financial system. In sociological usage an institution cannot be joined; only an organization can be joined. In architectural thinking the equivalent of the institutional level of analysis is **building type**, a *kind* of building, a set of ideas, but not yet a specific building that one can enter. Of course, an actual building can be entered and is an *example* of a type but not technically what sociologists would call an "ideal type," meaning a set of ideas about what kind of building it is. Examples of building types include the American Protestant church, the Baroque church, cathedral, mosque, temple, retail stores, shopping mall, library, courthouse, post office, ranch house, gas station, and so forth. Architecture is site specific; this is what changes it from an institution (type) to an actual building.

A **building** both expresses and influences how an **organization** sees itself. What groups and activities should be next to one another is expressed in the plan of how rooms are organized. Similarly, one can tell what groups and activities should be separated from one another (due to noise, special status, need for privacy) by analyzing the plan and the section. Some activities are front and center, others back stage, some elevated, some in the basement. Relations between rooms both horizontally (plan) and vertically (section) can be seen as an organizational chart.

Rooms are where people get together for **face-to-face** interaction, what sociologists call the "primary" level of analysis, and where they interact physically with technology. Sometimes a room can be a cell for only one student, monk, prisoner, or high status office holder, and even in these instances the room is shaping the individual's direct physical experience. Institutions, say a monastery for contemplative learning, and their organizations, say St. Albert's College in Oakland, need rooms that support their general and specific norms.[vii]

Sociologically, **objects** are part of the **technical** environment, but they are so important in the design profession that they may merit a row of their own. Clothes, tools, furniture, buildings and designed landscapes as material objects each carry or embody the intentions encoded into them by designers and other specialists from the higher (more general?) levels of analysis. The physical world is used to reinforce and even create the social world. Recall Churchill's often cited quip, "We shape our buildings and then our buildings shape us." Humans create things that in turn shape our experience—which is one of the reasons we create things they way we do. Karl Marx argued that whoever owned the means of production controlled all of society and so is often called a materialist. However, power may be the more critical issue—who owns the tools has to do with power relations, in turn, part of social relations more broadly. We can still say Marx's social theories originate at the relatively concrete level of face-to-face social relations with special emphasis on the tools of production.

The level of the physical organism—our **bodies**—is often considered below the level of social analysis because bodies are part of zoology and biology. However, the field of somatics has argued that culture and psychology both influence the shape of the human body, so it too carries culture. Chinese foot binding is a dramatic example of how culture shapes the body. Dainty feet were a cultural and erotic ideal. A man could show off his wealth by having wives with bound feet who were incapable of working; he could afford an unproductive family. In the United States and Europe today most women wear tight shoes to look elegant, not like a duck, not flat footed. Even men's shoes are slender enough to force the little toe inward so that Westerners have a deformed metatarsal joint, a mild but real version of Chinese foot binding. Chairs have produced back problems; computers have produced repetitive strain injuries. Changes in cultural ideals influence how slender or fleshy we are; the fast food industry as a whole has fattened most bodies in the industrialized world. Bodies can fight back; the goals of body conscious design are to support individual anatomy and consciousness either within the world of fashion or by changing fashion.[viii] Architecture effects bodies through haptic and tactile experiences; traditional Japanese rooms with their tatami mats and low windows invite us to sit cross legged or kneeling on the floor with the consequence of keeping hip joints open and mobile. Westerners walk on different surfaces that effect our gait; different window sizes and placements create close or far views and create more or less light for various cultural, social, institutional, and organizational reasons, and thereby effect focal length, learning, and health. (Somatic training may be more versatile in addressing various levels of analysis than behavior observation or interview data collection techniques that usually can only aggregate individual responses.)

Below all this is the level of the **physical environment**, including the **air and geology** that underlie plant and animal life. They too have been shaped by humans as anthropologists and ethno botanists have demonstrated and as we are experiencing today with species extinction, river pollution, ozone depletion, soil erosion, etc. Some have argued that man has also been shaped by the inorganic and organic environment.

Notes of the Use of Levels of Analysis

Note that "levels of analysis" is not the same as reality! This offers a way to analyze things, but in reality a building and a person perform as an embodied whole. Nor is the idea of "levels of analysis" the same as scale because a small object can be analyzed at all levels of analysis, including the most general cultural level. One might ask if science can illuminate some levels more than others? No, any level is amenable to some data collection technique. This means one has to be inventive to find indicators of the societal uses of a building as well as the behavioral uses.

Why the Idea of "Levels of Analysis" May Be Important

Introducing sociological levels of analysis into architecture is useful because this conceptual framework allows us to see and appreciate that architecture is not just a subset of material culture. Architecture works at all levels and needs to be understood at multiple levels.

In all fields this perspective keeps us from comparing this inappropriately, from comparing "apples and oranges." Saying that teaching as a graduate student is part of their education and therefore can be paid little is true at the individual level of analysis, but the organization benefits from having half the teaching force paid little so union organizers can claim it's exploitation. Having the idea of levels of analysis helps the observer understand how both claims could be true. In landscape architecture caring about whether people turn right or left at a choice point in a park pathway (behavioral level of analysis) does not explain why we have parks in the first place (the institutional level of analysis). Conversely, knowing how and why the institution of pencils, staircases, or chairs evolved does not help us design objects that do not hurt people physically. An architect will want to express the values to which an organization aspires symbolically *and* which facilitate the behaviors necessary to enact those values. Sometimes the architect will want to address the culture or change it, and of course not all buildings change or define culture equally. Art historians often identify the seminal buildings that express cultural changes and which influence many other buildings.

The concept of levels of analysis helps the academic reviewer, the scholar, the client, the user, and the architects themselves discuss several different points of view in an articulate way. This could be no more than saying that there are different points of view, but the idea of levels helps sort out the points of view according to a logic which gives structural significance to each perspective. We do not end up saying simply that people look at things differently; we can pinpoint the significance of the differences. Other scholars—I'm thinking of economists—use two general levels of analysis—micro and macro—but for analysis of the designed environment, which extends from small objects and tools to buildings, landscapes, cities, and even regions, the more differentiated concept of "levels of analysis" from sociology makes sense.

Although all scales of the built environment can be studied at all levels of analysis, it may be that they are not all equally important, or give you the same traction, differentiation. For example, a hospital building could be analyzed in regard to circulation and wayfinding at the level of individual behavior. Even when aggregated (the experiences of many are summed) in order to understand many people's experience, the level of analysis is still individual behavior. Additionally, we might also want to examine that same building for what it symbolizes about American health care and the institution of allopathic medicine. Neither approach is wrong, and neither is irrelevant to architects in practice, but they are quite different from one another, and one cannot infer that the history of the evolution of the hospital as a technical environment, separate from religion, tells us much about why the circulation is confusing or crystal clear in a particular building. (Clothes, too, can be analyzed at individual level and also at cultural level, or at the institutional level of the "rag trade," or the organizational level of Levi's.)

The concept of levels of analysis helps us identify the sources of continuity as well as change. The physical environment and the social structures at these various levels perpetuate a culture from generation to generation while at the same time the environment becomes an agent of social change both because of changes in the expression of the architecture as well as changes in the perception of the inherited architecture. Furthermore, using this concept historically to diagnose changes over time counters the criticism that the concept is static.[ix]

The field of architectural history typically (but not exclusively) uses the higher levels of analysis to focus on the cultural and national meaning of buildings); such studies usually ignore the lower levels that relate to actual behavior and experience. In contrast, the field of person-environment research also called environmental design research (typified by EDRA members) focuses on the behavioral level of analysis and neglects the higher levels of institution, society, and culture. Studio may be the place where all levels are painstakingly addressed, but studio teachers do not always get recognition from their colleagues in the social sciences for this comprehensive integration.

Table 1. Sociological Levels of Analysis, Disciplinary Correspondences, Social Change Theories, & Design Equivalent

Levels of Analysis	Sociological Anthropological Terms; the Problem of Specification	Disciplines typically concerned with this level of analysis	Direction of Social Change	Design manifestation/ equivalent; Material cultural	Examples
Cultural (e.g., Western civilization)	Pattern of Values	Anthropology, history, geography, Architectural history	Idealist (words), Formalist (all concepts without words, reptilian brain)	Settlement pattern; Urban design; site plan	Hippodamian grid reflects stratification; anthropomorphic villages (Dogan); U.S. grid; Roman; Hindu grid; feng shui; gender segregation
Societal	Values	Sociology, Architectural history	Patriot Religionist	Symbolism Style, Facade & elevation, monuments	Rustic detailing Neo-classical style Art Noveau apartment facades Statue of Liberty
Institutional	Norms, general	Sociology	Legalist Economist Educationalist	Building type; program	American Church; baroque church; cathedral; mosque; temple; retail stores, shopping malls; ranch house; cabin; library building; gas station; conservatory, etc
Complex Organizations	Norms	Sociology	Organizational consultant	Building; program.	Relations between rooms both horizontally (plan) and vertically (section)
Face-to-face Group, behavior	Norms, specific	Psychology Person-environment studies; Environmental Design Research	Psychotherapist, Social psychologist	Room	Kitchen, bathroom, bedroom, living room, den, meeting room, classroom, office, workroom, salesroom, lecture hall, auditorium
Technology	Tools, buildings as tools	Anthropology	Materialist	Objects	Clothes, tools, furniture, handrails & doorknobs, buildings and designed landscapes as material objects
Organism	Animal and plant life	Somatic Arts; Biology, both Zoology and Botany	Somatic determinist; Biological determinist	Culturally conditioned body	Feet of someone who grew up barefoot in Hawaii vs. wearing shoes
Physical Environment	Geology, air, water	Geologist Earth Scientist	Physical determinist	Physical Environment	Soil quality; air quality; water quality

NOTES

i. Talcott Parsons and Edward Shils, eds., *Toward a general theory of action*, New York: Harper & Row, 1951.

ii. Robert Briffault, *The Mothers: a study of the origins of sentiments and institutions*, Volume 3., and *The Mothers: the matriarchal theory of social origins*.

iii. See Michael Moore's film, "Sicko" that claims that Canadians are less frightened people than Americans due to societal differences.

iv. Galen Cranz, *The Chair: Rethinking Culture, Body, and Design,* W.W. Norton, 2000.

v. Historians have argued that the industrial revolution became possible only because of changes in the domestic realm where the introduction of furniture, specialization of domestic space, and the birth of privacy, and guilt as a social control mechanism (replacing shame) were cultural changes that predate all the technological changes. These cultural changes were critical prerequisites to the technological and scientific changes that followed, so culture changed technology not the other way around. Thanks to Elefterios Pavlides for this point.

vi. Larwrence J. Vale, *Architecture, Power and National Identity,* MIT Press, 1992.

vii. Bachelard, *Poetics of Space*, explores the room at the level of the collective unconscious, thereby moving it to the cultural level of analysis.

viii. www.bodyconsciousdesign.org

ix. My thanks to my friend and colleague Eleftherios Pavlides at Roger Williams University for a careful reading of this entire essay and contributing examples to Table 1. Here in particular I want to thank him for contributing these points about continuity and history.

40 How Post-Occupancy Evaluation Research Effected Design and Policy at the San Francisco Public Library

Galen Cranz

What happens to a building assessment after it has been conducted? Decision makers at the San Francisco Public Library used this information to prioritize remodeling over the 15 years after the building was first commissioned in 1995.

ABSTRACT

Architects have been exhorted to conduct more post occupancy evaluation (POE) studies of their work, but usually they do not have the money or the inclination to do so. Public buildings like libraries are more likely to receive this special attention, but still the cost of conducting such evaluations limits the number of them. For a library, Lushington and Mills (1991) maintain that a POE can help establish accountability in the complex and costly process of creating a new building, relaying in a formal report both successes and shortcomings of the library to policymakers, funding authorities, architects, builders, and library administrators. Are they right in the case of the San Francisco Public Library? The New Main Library opened April 1996 to much fanfare, followed by much journalistic criticism. Before the Library Commissioners acted to respond to these complaints, they wanted a measured, scientific assessment of how the building was actually functioning overall in regard to its many social and physical aspects. The Commissioners expected that this study would form the basis for making changes in the building itself, its operation, and management. Accordingly, they authorized a preliminary post occupancy evaluation of the library in 1997 that was expanded in 1998; the final report was made public in 2001. How have the relevant policymakers responded to this study? First, this paper summarizes the evaluations themselves, and second, it assesses their impact by analyzing newspaper coverage after the evaluations were made public and by interviewing key policymakers and stakeholders in 2006 and 2009. The occupancy research had and continues to have significant effects on policy making and managerial actions.

Keywords: post-occupancy evaluation research, public libraries, design guidelines for libraries, facilities management, policy formation

Galen Cranz, *How Post-Occupancy Evaluation Research Effected Design and Policy at the San Francisco Public Library.* Copyright © 2010 by Galen Cranz. Permission to reprint granted by the author.

INTRODUCTION

Over the last quarter-century a handful of researchers have specialized in evaluating library performance in order to improve their planning and design programming. Consequently, library planners currently have a compilation of evidence-based recommendations regarding the design of a successful library as follows. Lushington and Mills (1980) surveyed library users and made recommendations starting with the exterior of the building: visible signs should indicate opening hours and services for easy identification by passersby; ample parking close to the building, and large directional signs to lead users to a visible entrance; a building directory at the entrance. Once inside, the user should find: immediate access to materials and services; a centralized service center location visible from the entrance with professional staff present and other services radiating outward from there; well-delineated functional relationships within the building by use of carefully planned graphics, lighting, colors, and furniture arrangements.[1] Another specialist (Dewe, 1995) who focused on libraries for children and young people reports that they enjoy the choice provided by spaces with varying shapes, sizes, and lighting levels. He acknowledges that what is defined as "comfortable seating" will vary. Children, for example, "often consume books on the spot, perhaps laying on the floor and adopting poses that seem uncomfortable to the adult."[2] They prefer flexible environments with seating arrangements that they have the freedom to alter. Another study (Cranz, 2006) also found that teens would use many postures including lying down if the design of the physical environment offered choice.[3]

Schneekloth and Keable (1991) have focused on staff for whom materials processing is the central experience. Following materials through their physical acquisition and the subsequent sequence of processing that occurs through the building space leads to an understanding of "staff functions, interrelationships, adjacency requirements, and security measures."[4] Yet, Cohen & Cohen (1979) report that "too many" libraries, in the effort to create "interesting, attractive interiors to delight the eye,"[5] (with book stacks that form the shape of a pyramid or that radiate as spokes on a wheel, for example) end up with difficulties in shelving and accessing materials and accommodating growth. Instead, functionality and flexibility should be at the forefront of design, which now has to include the various machines necessary for the many different types of media that characterize today's library materials. Lushington and Mills suggest using compact storage arranged to make retrieval of materials rapid and convenient.[6] Schneekloth and Keable confirmed that flexibility

---

[1] Thanks to Iris Tien for helping review the literature of library design guidelines. Nolan Lushington and Willis N. Mills, Jr., *Libraries Designed for Users: A Planning Handbook* (Hamden, Connecticut: Library Professional Publications, 1980), 14, 16, 19.

[2] Michael Dewe, *Planning and Designing Libraries for Children and Young People* (London: Library Association Publishing, 1995), 133.

[3] Dewe, 134. See also Cranz, Galen with Cha, Eunah, "Body Conscious Design in a 'Teen Space:' Post Occupancy Evaluation of an Innovative Public Library," *Public Libraries*, Sept/Nov. 2006.

[4] Lynda H. Schneekloth and Ellen Bruce Keable, *Evaluation of Library Facilities: A Tool for Managing Change* (Champaign, Illinois: Occasional Papers, Graduate School of Library and Information Science, The University of Illinois, 1991), 5.

[5] Aaron Cohen and Elain Cohen, *Designing and Space Planning for Libraries: A Behavioral Guide* (New York: R. R. Bowker Company, 1979), 62.

[6] Lushington and Mills, 19.

of facilities and equipment allows the library to adjust to changes in function, technology, and building image.[7]

In general, we can conclude that library POEs have been useful to help planners and designers create good user experience and functional libraries. Collectively, they have highlighted wayfinding, user preference for choice in seating, staff workflow, the importance of flexibility for continuous growth and library materials and changes in technology.

Moreover, conclusions drawn from POEs can lead to organizational learning, but many organizations are reluctant to embrace the POE process. Fundamentally, POEs expose mistakes about a project that can lead to improvements, but as Zimring (2001) wryly notes, "most organizations do not reward exposing shortcomings."[8] Optimistically, Lushington and Mills maintain that for a library a POE can help establish accountability in the complex and costly process of building a new library,[9] relaying in a formal report both successes and shortcomings of the library to policymakers, funding authorities, architects, builders, and library administrators. Are they right in the case of San Francisco?

A post occupancy evaluation of the San Francisco Main Public Library was made public in 2001. How have the relevant policymakers, funding authorities architects, builders and library administrators responded to these formal written evaluations? Did the San Francisco organization learn from its mistakes or resist them? Did other libraries learn from their mistakes and successes? The goal of this research was to find out. But first, we need to summarize the major findings that emerged from these evaluations.

History and Method of the San Francisco Public Library POE

Designed by the New York architecture firm of Pei Cobb Freed and the local San Francisco firm of SMWM, the New Main San Francisco Public Library was opened April 1996 in the Civic Center to much fanfare, followed by much journalistic criticism.[10] Patronage had increased significantly compared to the Old Main, and the building was appreciated for its glamour, but published criticism highlighted numerous problems including inadequate space for book storage, difficulties in processing and retrieving books, frustration with the new automatic shading system, and dissatisfaction with computerized card cataloging. Internally, staff reported additional problems, including inadequate directional signage, noise, ergonomic difficulties, and inefficient workflow. A city audit recommended an evaluation.[11]

---

7   Schneekloth and Keable, 6.

8   Craig Zimring, "Post-Occupancy Evaluations and Organizational Learning," *Learning from Our Buildings: A State-of-the-Practice Summary of Post-Occupancy Evaluation* (Washington, D.C.: Federal Facilities Council Technical Report No. 145, National Academy Press, 2001), 43.

9   Nolan Lushington and James M. Kusack, *The Design and Evaluation of Public Library Buildings* (Hamden, Connecticut: Library Professional Publications, 1991), 119.

10   The list of 20 newspapers and journals that have covered the library's problems in the past include local as well as national papers: *SF Independent, SF Examiner, LA Times, Kansas City Star, Washington Post, Sacramento Bee, SF Bay Area, Philadelphia Inquirer, SF Frontlines, SF Chronicle, New Mission News, New York Times, Baltimore Sun, LA Downtown News, Journal Sioux City, Library Hotline, Facilities Design & Management, Library Journal, American Libraries, Architecture*.

11   Coda Partners, LLC, SFPL Strategic Audit, April 1997 (Vols. 1 + 2).

However, before the Commissioners acted to respond to these criticisms and implied demands for changes in the building and its operation, they wanted to know if the problems were significant enough to merit the expense of a systematic evaluation study. Were the problems exaggerated by newspaper sensationalism or by union faultfinding or overreaction to specific problems? After a full month in November 1997 of focus groups, one-on-one interviews, direct observations, and listening to the public at public meetings of the Library Commission, the author, who was hired to do this preliminary evaluation, confirmed that the problems were real and extensive. The author wrote a Request for Proposal (RFP) for the POE that first defined the goals and objectives of the report and then went on to define the scope of work to include specific questions under each of 5 general areas of concern—user experience, building design, maintenance and operations, potential uses for the adjacent underground Brooks Hall, and priorities for actions taking into account both cost and urgency.

Accordingly, in 1998 the San Francisco Public Library Commission with the Mayor's Office proceeded to request a post-occupancy evaluation of the New Main San Francisco Public Library. They wanted a measured, scientific assessment of how the building was actually functioning overall in regard to its many social and physical aspects. They intended this evaluation to form the basis for making any changes in building operation, management and physical remodeling. The author took the lead in writing the RFP for the POE. This document defined the goals and objectives of the POE, defined the key respondent categories, and identified key issues. The POE had to be multi-faceted, requiring assessment of the building's performance along several social and physical dimensions, and requiring recommendations for managing and prioritizing proposed changes.

The final form of the RFP issued by the Library indicated that the POE was, foremost, intended to describe and evaluate public use and reaction to the building. More specifically, public reaction was to include the opinions of specialized user groups regarding facilities designed especially for various "affinity groups," including the sight and hearing impaired, and the wheelchair bound. Additionally, the evaluation was to include staff satisfaction with all aspects of the work environments; administrative satisfaction with all departments; building performance in regard to HVAC, conveyance systems, maintenance, storage, and operable and fixed equipment, including automatic shading.

In 1998 the Commission invited professional consultants to submit their qualifications and explain their research approach, proposed schedules, proposed personnel, and work hours. Ripley Associates were selected; in 2000 they completed their evaluation, which was made public in early 2001. Ten years after the completion of the building the author of this paper conducted a further study to learn if the POE was an effective form of feedback for the Commission, the architects, the staff, and the public. First, I noted that the terms of the evaluation changed slightly from consultant to library administration to final consultant. The original intentions were modified by the Administration when they formalized the RFP for public distribution, and they were further modified in practice by the architectural office of Ripley Associates when they conducted the four month long study. The Administration, in turn, evaluated the assessments to decide which recommendations to ignore, which to pursue, and in what order.[12]

---

12   The SFPL website version of the final POE can be seen at http://sfpl4.sfpl.org/index.php?pg=2000043301.

In order to assess the effect of this research on decision making and public awareness this paper reports on the changes that have actually been made, notes newspaper coverage improvements and retrofits, and finally reports the administrators' judgment about the value of the research.

Findings from the Ripley POE and Newspaper Coverage

The Ripley assessment reported findings in the following categories:

1. functional design issues referring to the location and configuration of spaces,
2. legibility issues referring to the users' difficulties in finding materials and services,
3. capacity to house materials, services, and staff,
4. library as workplace for staff operations to serve the public,
5. facility staff operations to keep bldg well maintained and renovated as changes in public services require, and
6. audiovisual systems.

The *San Francisco Chronicle* emphasized the financial aspect of Ripley's recommended changes. Less than a year after the report's publication, in December 2000, San Francisco Public Library administrators presented a $5.3 million plan to the Library Commission for a first round of improvements for the library. A second phase was estimated to cost at least $10 million more. The reporter went on to note that the first phase contained many proposals in direct response to findings in the Ripley report.

For example, a main issue was that users could not get to the collections easily. To remedy this, a proposed $3.7 million would improve the "First Stop" on the first floor of the library, home to new additions to the library and counters for checking materials in and out, and where about 40 percent of library users visit.[13] Just before this proposal, a $106 million library bond issue had been approved by voters, $10 million of which had already been set aside for such a move of the technical services division out of the main library to make expansion of the first floor possible.[14]

The same article called attention to another major finding of the Ripley report, namely the problems with wayfinding around the library. Many people found the layout of the library confusing, and could not find the resources or materials they needed. A proposed $350,000 would be spent on improving the signs located throughout the library.[15] Ripley's report also found that users entering on the second floor had difficulty navigating to the actual entry of the library on the first floor. $800,000 of the proposal would be spent making it easier to navigate around the second floor, including building a new walkway and entrance on the second floor so patrons could directly enter the library without having to take the circuitous route down to the first floor to pass through security and then enter the library. This proposal also required the hiring of additional full-time security staff for the new entrance.[16]

---

13   Ripley report, 2000.
14   Edward Epstein, "Big Sum Needed To Fix S.F. Library: First phase going before commission," *San Francisco Chronicle* December 29, 2000, final ed.: A23.
15   Ibid.
16   Ibid.

Additionally, reporters noted that Ripley included comments from library staff that they wanted better fixtures and plumbing in the first floor restrooms to remedy regular clogging, and the desire to fix the problem of having to close the first floor restrooms during the day when the toilets were cleaned.[17]

The same article acknowledged another problem that Ripley could not solve. Less than five years after its opening, the library was already out of shelf space.[18] Little could be done to expand capacity since building height was limited by its location on Civic Center Plaza and digging down was not possible due to the base isolation necessary for earthquake safety.

How the POE Made a Difference to Policy Makers

Charles Higueras, who served as President of the Library Commission during the time that the Library was built and evaluated, said when interviewed by the author in 2006 that Ripley negotiated a somewhat narrower focus with smaller sample sizes for the public opinion surveys, having argued that the original RFP was too extensive. Even so, the report is broad in scope, and he said that the Commissioners used the study to prioritize expenditures over the years. In July 2009 Kathy Lawhun, Director, toured the building with the author and highlighted the following changes, all of which came directly from the building assessment studies.

1. Signage was changed, in two stages. The changes involved more signage, higher contrast graphics, and the circular atrium got included into the signage system as a conceptual compass or clock, one of the Ripley recommendations.
2. Automatic book sorting equipment was changed in 2003.
3. Cataloguing and technical services moved off site in 2005, so that 6000 SF of "prime real estate" on the first floor could be open to the public. All fiction was moved to the 1st floor.
4. The recommended bridge to children's section was not added, due to cost, protection of children, and the commissioners' judgment that it would "ruin" the atrium; this was the only major Ripley recommendation to be ignored.
5. Lighting was changed to more energy efficient LED lighting; new lighting in stacks; people can see better than before.
6. They replaced frosted with clear glass throughout the building, so users can see in.
7. They created a separate AV room with shelving to increase efficiency; it is the busiest place, "packed," and still needs to expand, so Lawhun wants more study about how to do that.
8. The automatic shades have not worked in years, so now permanently up or down, some replaced with manual controls. The original company went out of business. The shades are expensive to replace; management will slowly replace them throughout the entire building.
9. Compact storage for new equipment now located in the cold underground room rather than more habitable office space.
10. Most of these and other changes occurred on the first floor. For example, the loading dock, which was too high for the library delivery trucks, was fixed with the addition of a mechanical lift. Also, the first floor toilets had their plumbing replaced with devices called "Muffin Monsters" that chew up anything that is put down the toilets so that there has been no

---

17 Ripley report.
18 Epstein, Op.cit.

major clog since their installation. Additionally, another 10 big and little projects were also accomplished.

11. Management closed the first floor circulation for a year to make changes; it reopened Jan 16, 2008 with a "grand opening" with the mayor.

Did Newspapers Notice These Changes?

Newspaper coverage of the library after 2001 is scant. This suggests that newspapers like to focus on scandal (for example, books being dumped surreptitiously at night because the new library did not have room enough for them).

However, coverage picked up again. In May 2003 the *San Francisco Chronicle* reported that the library made improvements to improve the user experience. For example, *The Chronicle* reported on a noticeably slow computer catalog used to search for books in the library. The library system's computers were "reduced to a crawl" during peak hours in the afternoon.[19] By August 2003, the aging software had been replaced by a new online computer catalog system, complete with new software that could handle Asian characters, at a cost of $1.2 million. The new system improved the speed and ease of catalog searches. Said one user, "It's plenty speedy for me—it outruns my attention span."[20] In this column, "Chronicle Watch: Working for a Better Bay Area" *The Chronicle* newspaper specializes in singling out problems and then making a point to follow-up and find out what happened after their public finger-pointing.

In 2004, *The Chronicle* reported on a debate about introducing tracking devices called radio-frequency identification computer chips (RFID) into the library's materials at start-up costs of $1 million. Many had concerns about invasions of privacy associated with the chips, but its benefits, besides ease of tracking the library's collection, included remedying some of the problems outlined in Ripley's report four years before. Replacing bar codes with RFID would improve workplace conditions for library staff, a concern in the report. The library's chief workplace hazard was repetitive stress injuries caused by repeatedly sweeping bar-coded books across a scanner. In the three years prior, such injuries had cost the library $265,000 in workers' compensation claims. RFID would alleviate these injuries. It would also improve the user experience, speeding up checkout by as much as 50 percent.[21] Decreasing the time spent at checkout would better utilize library staff, a recommendation made in Ripley's report, freeing up staff to help patrons.[22]

The process required for continual improvement of the San Francisco Public Library after its construction completion has not gone unnoticed by nearby towns looking to build new libraries of their own. During the course of designing a new library facility in San Jose, CA, one recurring

---

19   Thanks to Iris Tien for summarizing newspaper coverage. Ryan Kim, "ChronicleWatch: Working for a better Bay Area," *San Francisco Chronicle* May 20, 2003, final ed.: A13.

20   Joseph De Wolk, "ChronicleWatch: Working for a better Bay Area," *San Francisco Chronicle* August 28, 2003, final ed.: A23.

21   Joe Garofoli, "San Francisco: Privacy concerns about library checkout device," *San Francisco Chronicle* March 4, 2004, final ed.: A20.

22   Joe Garofoli, "San Francisco: Privacy concerns about library checkout device," *San Francisco Chronicle* March 4, 2004, final ed.: A20.

theme for the planners was: "Don't be like San Francisco."[23] Jane Light, San Jose's library director said, "We wanted a beautiful building, but we also wanted to make sure it functioned."[24] Professional library journals and newsletters have not given the library much attention, but Light's comment reported in *The Sacramento Bee* from a professional librarian is telling.

CONCLUSION AND DISCUSSION: EVALUATING EVALUATION

In the case of the San Francisco Public Library, POE research influenced decisions about what should be remodeled.[25] Director Lawhun concluded that the Ripley recommendations were a good basis to build on; even those not used were useful to help the administration evaluate their choices and set priorities. She observed that the sequence of changes was established more by in-house considerations than by outside assessments.

This study confirms that researchers assess and decision makers evaluate, that is, establish priorities for action. The field of person-environment studies has conflated those two processes, but perhaps they need to be distinguished as they are in the field of educational assessment (of students) and evaluation (of educational programs). Accordingly, we too can assess users' experiences with a building, but let decision makers judge how to use that information to decide what changes to make in a building and in what sequence. The relationship between research and policy is real but not automatic. Finally, the need for continued study of building performance and popular demand noted by the director suggests that the assessment and evaluation are continuous processes in successful buildings and that these research processes are part of organizational learning.

---

23 Blair Anthony Robertson, "Library is one for the books: The new San Jose facility is billed as the first in the U.S. shared by a city and college," *The Sacramento Bee* July 4, 2003, metro final ed.: A3.

24 Ibid.

25 Other potent influences on decisions to remodel include lawsuits against contractors and other design professionals, but the details of those settlements are closed to the public.

41 Healthy Cities: Key Principles for Professional Practices

Roderick J. Lawrence

Lawrence, who teaches in Switzerland, summarizes the principles of the Healthy Cities movement that Len Duhl in public health at UC Berkeley initiated. Sustainability can be enacted through the lens of human health.

ABSTRACT

Building a healthy city is intentional, not haphazard. It occurs in a human context which defines and is mutually defined by a wide range of cultural and societal factors. Building and managing a healthy city involves choosing between a range of options in order to achieve numerous objectives, some of which may not give a high priority to health and quality of life. Therefore it is necessary to reconsider the construction of cities and urban development in a broad environmental, economic, social and political context that explicitly accounts for health and well-being. This paper presents the key qualities that the World Health Organization has presented as being the main constituents of healthy cities. It also discusses those prerequisites that are necessary in order to apply these principles in professional practice. The paper discusses how architecture and urban planning can promote health and sustainability. Prior to the conclusion, the author mentions some innovative achievements.

Keywords: cities, health, urban development, principles, professional practices, well-being

INTRODUCTION

Urban environments are complex with many material and non-physical constituents. Likewise, health is multidimensional. Hence both these subjects are not structured within traditional disciplines and professional sectors. Therefore, urban health ought to be considered in terms of the multiple factors that influence both living conditions and health status, as well as the interrelations between them. An ecological perspective recognises that behavioural, biological, cultural, economic, social, physical and political factors need to be considered if a comprehensive

Roderick J. Lawrence; Mostafa K. Tolba, Aleya Abdel-Hadi, & Salah Soliman, eds., "Healthy Cities: Key Principles for Professional Practices," from *Environment, Health, and Sustainable Development*. Copyright © 2010 by Hogrefe. Permission to reprint granted by the publisher.

understanding of urban health is to complement disciplinary and sector-based interpretations. In order to integrate all these dimensions, it is necessary to go beyond interpretations that rely solely on the bio-medical model of health. Multi-disciplinary and collaborative research contributions are necessary. Unfortunately, too many empirical contributions in this field use statistical methods to identify a single risk factor. In contrast, an ecological perspective adopts an holistic interpretation which rejects this kind of single causal statistical interpretation. Instead it examines the interrelations between a wide range of factors in the societal context in which they occur. This chapter argues that it is necessary to reconsider the construction of cities and urban development in a broad environmental, economic, social and political context that explicitly accounts for health and well-being. It begins with a presentation of some key concepts, definitions and interpretations of health and healthy cities. Then it presents the key principles that the World Health Organization has presented as being the main constituents of healthy cities. It also presents a few innovative approaches that have been applied successfully to integrate health into architecture and urban planning, environmental psychology and sustainability. These achievements involve a shift from traditional disciplinary and professional approaches to inter-disciplinary and trans-disciplinary research and professional practice. Hopefully, these kinds of contributions will serve as a catalyst for many more innovative projects in the near future.

What Is Urban Health?

The World Health Organization states that health is "not merely the absence of disease and infirmity but a state of optimal physical, mental and social well being" (World Health Organization, 1946). This definition is idealistic, but it has the merit of not focusing on illness and disease, which have often been considered as either temporary or permanent impairments to health, or the malfunctioning of a single or several constituents of the human body. Given that the World Health Organization's definition of health includes social well being, then the most common interpretations of health ought to be enlarged. The World Health Organization also states that the enjoyment of the highest attainable standard of health is one of the fundamental rights of every human being without distinction of race, religion, political, economic or social condition.

Health is defined in this chapter as a condition or state of human beings resulting from the interrelations between humans and their biological, chemical, physical and social environment. All these components of residential environments should be compatible with their basic needs and their full functional activity including biological reproduction over a long period (Lawrence, 2001). Health is the result of both the direct pathological effects of chemicals, some biological agents and radiation, and the influence of physical, psychological and social dimensions of daily life including housing, transport and other characteristics of metropolitan areas. For example, improved access to medical services is a common characteristic of urban neighbourhoods that is rare in rural areas. In the field of health promotion, health is not considered as an abstract condition, but as the ability of an individual to achieve her/his potential and to respond positively to the challenges of daily life. From this perspective, health is an asset or a resource for everyday life, rather than a standard or goal that ought to be achieved. This redefinition is pertinent for people-environment studies, because the environmental and social conditions in specific residential environments do impact on human relations, induce stress, and can have positive or negative impacts on the health status of groups and individuals. It also implies that the capacity of the health sector to deal with the health and well-being of populations is limited and that collaboration with other sectors would be beneficial.

A discussion of urban health should begin by clarifying what is meant by urban and what interpretation of health is applied. Although there is no consensus about the definition of "urban," which varies from country to country, the United Nations uses national definitions which are commonly based on population size. Many countries use 10,000 resident persons as a benchmark to define urban, whereas other countries including India use 5,000 persons as the referent. Other definitions of urban are based on the administrative or political authority of municipalities, especially the degree of autonomy in relation to the national or state administration. Other definitions include the socio-economic status of the resident population, especially their livelihood (e.g., the share of all employed persons having non-agricultural occupations). A combination of these characteristics could be used to interpret rural and urban areas, but this has been rare, especially in recent published research on health determinants in urban environments.

Urban health is a vast and complex subject. In order to understand the multi-dimensional nature of urban health, all the constituents of urban ecosystems and the interrelations between them should be considered over time. These constituents include four interrelated sets of hazards:

Environmental hazards including ambient air quality, ambient noise levels, soil and water contamination, and solid waste disposal.

Social hazards including criminality, violence, and community discord, as well as the lack of education and training especially for immigrants, women and children.

Economic hazards comprising the lack of affordable housing, food and water for the poorest households, permanent unemployment, and inequalities of access to diverse kinds of resources including primary health care.

Technological hazards including traffic accidents, industrial and chemical disasters on industrial sites and contamination from mass produced foods and synthetic products.

These four main sets of hazards are variable over short and relatively long periods of time. Their dispersion and effects are complex and the exposure of different groups of urban populations (e.g., children, the elderly, ethnic minorities and the unemployed) need to be understood. Biologically inherent mechanisms are mediated by the social and environmental circumstances of urban neighbourhoods. Therefore, it is necessary to interpret the health of urban populations in terms of both individual and social differences by explicitly accounting for age, gender, socio-economic class, occupational status, and the geographical distribution of the population.

Why Is Urban Health Important?

One hundred years ago, about 80% of the world's population lived in rural areas, whereas in the year 2001 about a half of the global population live in cities. The 20th century was characterised by a growth in the number, population size and total surface area of cities on a scale previously unknown, and this trend is expected to continue. Some have argued that the last century corresponded to a period of "the urban revolution" that has transformed the physical, psychological and social dimensions of daily life including housing, transport and other characteristics of metropolitan areas. Urban life has important health benefits including easy access to job markets, education, heath care, medical services as well as diverse cultural and leisure activities. However, at the beginning of the 21st century, urban health can be characterised by relatively high levels of tuberculosis, respiratory and cardiovascular diseases, cancers, adult obesity, and malnutrition, tobacco smoking, mental ill health, alcohol consumption and drug abuse, sexually transmitted diseases (including AIDS), as well as fear of crime, homicides, violence and accidental injury and deaths. It is noteworthy that in the 1990s mental ill health was integrated into the aetiology of urban health, and that the promotion of both physical and mental health were accepted as a complementary goal for national and local policy makers and professionals.

In the field of health promotion, health is not considered as an abstract condition, but as the ability of an individual to achieve her/his potential and to respond positively to the challenges of daily life. This interpretation is pertinent for urban health because the environmental, economic and social conditions in specific urban neighbourhoods may impact on human relations, induce stress, and possibly have positive or negative impacts on the health status of social groups, households and individuals. It also implies that the capacity of the health sector to deal with the health and well-being of populations is limited and that close collaboration with other sectors would be beneficial.

What Is a Healthy City?

According to Hancock and Duhl (1988), "a healthy city is one that is continually creating and improving those physical and social environments and expanding those community resources which enable people to support each other in performing all the functions of life and in developing themselves to their maximum potential." This definition of a healthy city implies that health is determined by both short-and long-term processes. A healthy city is not only a quantified outcome, such as the measurement of health status of the population. The long term goals of the WHO Healthy Cities project are to integrate health in the agenda of all policy decision-makers in cities, to create a strong partnership for health promotion between groups in the public and private sectors, and to apply a local, participatory approach when implementing projects (Werna, Harpham and Goldstein, 1998; Werner, Harpham, Blue and Goldstein, 1999; World Health Organization, 2000c).

The health status of populations in specific urban areas is not only the result of many material and non-physical constituents listed in Table 1 but also the interrelations between them. Therefore, it is inappropriate to isolate one factor from the contextual conditions in which it occurs. Instead, systemic ecological approaches ought to be applied to understand both the factors and the interrelations between them. It is recommended that although social scientists, psychologists and medical or public health researchers have not often collaborated, there are good reasons for them to share experience and apply interdisciplinary approaches.

Table 1: Qualities of a Healthy City

1. The meeting of basic needs (for food, water, shelter, income, safety and work) for all the city's people
2. A clean, safe physical environment of high quality, including housing quality
3. An ecosystem that is stable now and sustainable in the long term
4. A diverse, vital and innovative economy
5. A strong, mutually supportive and non-exploitive community
6. A high degree of participation and control by the public over the decisions affecting their lives, health and well-being

7. The encouragement of connectedness with the past, with the cultural and biological heritage of city-dwellers and with other groups and individuals
8. Access to a wide variety of experiences and resources with the chance for a wide variety of contact, interaction and communications
9. A built form that is compatible with and enhances the preceding characteristics
10. An optimum level of appropriate public health and sick care services accessible to all
11. High health status (high levels of positive health and low levels of disease).

The eleven qualities of a healthy city listed in Table 1 need to be understood and applied in specific localities using innovative empirical research and professional practice. This stems from the fact that many contributions that are meant to address health promotion and prevention have not been wholly successful, even though many urban planners, public health officers and medical practitioners are convinced they have the "right answers." There is an urgent need for innovative approaches to address the continuing failure of the wealthiest countries of the world to provide all citizens with secure employment, affordable housing and appropriate health care that meet at least minimal requirements. The failure of so-called "model" housing estates and urban planning projects constructed in the 1960s and 1970s in numerous cities around the World, clearly shows that new ideas, working methods, objectives and criteria are needed (Burridge and Ormandy, 1993; Halpern, 1995).

Our incapacity to deal with the above-mentioned problems is related to the complexity of dealing with urban health, to the compartmentalisation of scientific and professional knowledge about urban ecosystems, to the bureaucratic division of responsibilities in cities, and to the increasing diversity of living conditions between various cities and within specific cities. In addition, the lack of effective collaboration between scientists, professionals and policy decision-makers has led to the "applicability gap" in sectors that deal with urban planning, public health and many other sectors concerned with the construction and maintenance of cities. These shortcomings of mainstream scientific research and professional practice are not necessarily the result of the lack of political commitment, or financial resources, or viable propositions. They are, above all, the logical outcome of the narrow vision of so-called experts who do not address fundamental issues but only topics isolated from their urban context. In order to deal with these limitations, at least four sets of obstacles need to be overcome. First, conceptual frameworks that do not recognise the pertinence of an ecological interpretation of urban health and living conditions. Second, methodological contributions that value rational, quantified interpretations of illness and disease at the expense of qualitative interpretations of health and well-being; use and management of human and natural ecosystems. Third, the segmentation and bureaucratisation of professional knowledge and expertise often at the expense of the experience of lay-people. Finally, the philosophy and conceptual framework for the education and training of professionals and scientists is too short-sighted. Some of these shortcomings are being addressed by the World Health Organization's Healthy Cities project in order to promote health and well-being of citizens.

The World Health Organization Healthy Cities Project

The Healthy Cities project was founded in 1987 by eleven European cities and the WHO Regional Office for Europe. Today there are more than 30 national and regional networks in Europe involving about 600 municipalities, now complemented by many hundreds more in each of the regions of the world (Goldstein, 2000; Tsouros and Farrington, 2003; Werna, Harpham, and Goldstein,1998). The Health For All strategy provides the strategic framework for this project. The Healthy Cities project in the WHO European region includes four main components. First, the designated cities that are committed to a comprehensive approach to achieving the goals of the project. Second, national and sub-national networks together with EURONET that facilitate co-operation between partners. Third, multi-city action plans (MCAPs) implemented by networks of cities collaborating on specific issues of common interest. Finally, special (model) projects are being implemented in central and eastern Europe.

The Healthy Cities project involves collaboration between sectors by formulating a "City Health Plan" that identifies the interrelations between living conditions in urban areas and the health of the residents (Green, Acres and Price, 2003). It is argued that health can be improved by addressing the physical environment, and the social and economic determinants of health in all situations (such as the home, the school, the workplace). This broad interpretation has meant that equity and social inequalities are identified as key factors in cities that need to be addressed. In particular, the plight of vulnerable social groups (including the handicapped, homeless, unemployed, single mothers and street children) are ranked as a high priority for interventions. This approach is meant to focus not only on specific groups but also particular neighbourhoods where there are concentrations of vulnerable people with relatively high health risks.

Supportive Environments

The concept of supportive environment has been used in the Healthy Cities project to emphasise that policy definition and implementation should focus on all the determinants of health, not just those within the health sector (Bistrup, 1991). Therefore, it includes the role of physical environmental factors that influence health and not just the lifestyle of individuals and groups in specific localities. In addition, it is not limited to the physical characteristics of the environment because it accounts for the cultural, social, economic and political dimensions. When these dimensions are explicitly addressed then it is necessary to deal with equality and equity in societies and how these impact on health and well being in precise residential environments.

From this perspective the layout, design and maintenance of residential environments should meet the requirements of all groups of the population including the increasing number of people with special needs—in particular, the most vulnerable in society: for example, the homeless, a group that comprises an increasing number of adolescents and young adults in industrialised countries; the elderly who need domiciliary care; people with disabilities who require easy access to and within housing units; single-parent households that may need access to special child care services; refugees and immigrants that have specific cultural customs in and outside their housing unit that should be accommodated.

Links Between Health, Architecture and Urban Planning

In the 19th century, in some European countries, a sanitary engineering approach based on corrective and remedial measures was used to remove unsanitary conditions by demolishing buildings and reconstructing neighbourhoods (Rosen, 1993). Then the public concern in European countries about the health housing relationship diminished in the 20th century with the widespread provision of municipal water supply, drainage and sewage disposal, as well as public immunisation campaigns. Unfortunately, this is probably why there has been too little concern about the health impacts of housing conditions in the context of rapid urban development in European countries from the 1950s to the 1970s as well in as all other continents of the world in recent decades. According to the United Nations Commission on Human Settlements (1996), in Africa, Asia and South America more attention has been given to lack of hygiene and sanitation, access to primary health care and malnutrition in these regions than to the health impacts of housing occupancy conditions.

There has been a long debate about the reduction of mortality rates in many European countries from the late 19th century (McMichael, 1993; Rosen, 1993). It has been argued whether these reductions are more closely tied to the improvement of diet, the provision of a supply of safe water and municipal waste disposal rather than progress in medicine and health care. This article considers this debate to be misguided, because it stems from a narrow interpretation of health and health systems. When the broader definitions of health and health systems are applied, then all actions including the non personal, target area, or population interventions including the promotion of healthy lifestyles and the provision of sewage disposal are integral components of interdisciplinary strategies to promote health in residential environments. Some of these kinds of interventions were used in the late 19th century following an improved understanding of how diseases, including cholera, spread in residential areas even though the causes of such diseases remained unknown. This debate illustrates that an integrated, interdisciplinary understanding of how the health of populations in precise localities can be improved is essential if a range of interventions are to be applied effectively again at the beginning of the 21st century.

Today we know that infectious diseases stemming from unsanitary conditions are not the leading cause of morbidity and mortality in industrialised countries. Instead, non-communicable illnesses having multiple causes are the main challenge for public health. Therefore, architecture and urban planning could shift from using reactive and corrective measures to proactive approaches. The design and planning of the built environment should not only deal with removing negative health impacts but also actively promote well-being, as Barton and Tsourou (2000) have discussed. One example of an innovative approach would reconsider land use planning and transportation in and between residential neighbourhoods from a broader ecological perspective.

An interesting example of the application of this approach is public transport in the region of Zurich, the largest city in Switzerland. This region accommodates 1 million residents. The public administration has implemented government policies to promote public transport at a lower economic and ecological cost than reliance on private motor cars. Public transport is more energy efficient and less polluting than private motor cars, especially when electric motors are used for trains and trams. Public transport uses less land surface area per passenger than the roads and car parking required for private motor cars, thus conserving natural landscapes and sites for allotments and leisure activities. Since the implementation of this policy in the 1980s an electric train network has been co-ordinated with tram and trolley bus routes so that a person has access to all neighbourhoods in the region without the need to use a motor car. The implementation of this co-ordinated transport policy in the Zurich region has led to a substantial increase in the use of public transport from 363 journeys per person per year in the 1980s to 532 journeys per person per year in the 1990s.

During the same period, the city administration implemented plans for diverting road traffic from residential streets to main roads and converting some of these streets into pedestrian zones with landscaping and children's playgrounds. In addition, new residential neighbourhoods have been consciously planned with medium and high density residential buildings and other functions that are accessible for pedestrians in the region who can use public transport. The environmental, economic, health and social impacts of this vast co-ordinated policy should not be underestimated. The co-ordinated transport project in Zurich shows the wide range of benefits of collaboration spanning across several sectors and explicitly dealing with health in tandem with the qualities of the local residential environment. It stems from a critique of piecemeal approaches to road transport, car parking and traffic safety. This coordinated approach across several sectors reinterprets accessibility and mobility in and between urban areas not only in terms of public and private modes of transport but also air and noise pollution, consumption of non-renewable resources, monetary costs and public investments, active and sedentary lifestyles, as well as health and well-being. This ecological approach not only raises questions about the high priority attributed to private motor cars during the 20th century, it also shows that direct investments in efficient public transport systems and pedestrian precincts can also be considered as indirect investments to promote environmental quality, reduce energy consumption and air pollution while promoting health and well-being.

Improved Integration of Health in People-Environment Studies

A restricted disciplinary interpretation of health has hindered the development of a broad understanding of the contextual conditions of human well being in urban and suburban environments. Segmented interpretations could be replaced by studies of the mutual interrelations between humans, their residential environment and the local ecosystem as a dynamic, regulated network that can be studied as a system and in terms of its components. From this perspective, studies of people detached from their surroundings can be replaced by studies of processes and relations that occur between the non-human and human components of open, dynamic residential environments that have a precise scale and location at the microlevel of a much larger ecosystem and biosphere (Lawrence, 2001).

The Pertinence of Human Ecology

The term "ecology" derives from the ancient Greek words *"oikos"* and *"logos"* and means "science of the habitat." It is generally agreed that this term was used first by Ernst Haeckel (1834–1919), a German zoologist, in 1866. The word ecology designates a research agenda that deals with the interrelationships between organisms and their surroundings. Since the late 19th century the term "ecology" has been interpreted in numerous ways. For example, in the natural sciences, botanists and zoologists use the term "general ecology" to refer to the interrelations between animals, plants and their immediate surroundings. In contrast, human ecology is a term that has been and still is characterised by a lack of consensus about what it means (Lawrence, 2001). For example, today there is no consensus whether human ecology is a discipline, a conceptual framework, or a set of principles. Nonetheless, there is some agreement that human ecology refers to the study of the relations, especially the reciprocal relations between people, their habitat and the environment beyond their immediate surroundings. Human groups and societies establish and maintain viable relationships with their habitat through collective mechanisms that stem from their "anthropos" and generate a system of relations and networks rather than independent action. Hence, the methodological framework of human ecology studies is the analysis of people in their habitual living conditions using a systemic framework that explicitly examines the reciprocal relations between individuals, groups, the components of their habitat and larger environmental conditions.

The human ecology research agenda considers four main sets of interrelated factors: *the individual*, who has a specific genetic code with a susceptibility and immunity to illness and disease, as well as lifestyle traits; *the agent or vector* of illness and disease, including not only bio-geo-physical components of the environment but also the social and psychological dimensions of human settings; *the physical and social environment* of the individual which affects the susceptibility of the host, the virulence of bio-physical agents and the exposure, quantity and nature of the contact between host and vector; *the available resources* used by the individuals and households including housing, nutrition, money, information, and access to health and medical services which ought to be affordable for all groups of the population. This broad perspective implies that an analysis of the interrelations between multiple components of any human ecosystem is necessary. Systemic interpretations of human illness, health and local environments have a long history. They can be traced back at least as far as the Hippocratic treatise "*On Airs, Waters, and Places*" published initially about 2,600 years ago.

The distinction between biomedical models and ecological interpretations of health is fundamental. The germ theory, for example, is an incomplete explanation of human illness and disease because it ignores the contribution of numerous physical and social dimensions of the environment that can impact on health. Ecological interpretations maintain that the presence of a germ is a necessary but not a sufficient condition for an individual to become ill. They accept that some individuals become more susceptible to certain illnesses because of their differential exposure to numerous environmental, economic and social factors that can promote or be harmful to health and well-being. This interpretation does not ignore the influence of genetics, individual behaviour or primary health care. However, it maintains that, alone, these do not address possible relations between social problems and illness (e.g., inequalities) or positive social dimensions and health promotion (e.g., public education). The distinction between potential and actual health status can be the foundation for a new interpretation of health which includes the way environmental, economic, social, and technological risk factors transgress traditional disciplinary boundaries while remaining locality and temporally specific. Cues for this interpretation were provided by human ecologists in the 1920s (Lawrence, 2001).

Strengthening Links Between Health and Sustainable Development

Until recently, health and environment were generally considered by scientists, practitioners and policy makers working in different sectors. This common practice can be illustrated by major international charters and conferences beginning with the first international conference on the environment held in Stockholm in 1972, or the international conference on primary health care held in Alma-Alta in 1978. These traditional approaches to health and the environment were gradually replaced by more integrated ones during the 1990s. The World Summit on Environment and Development, held in Rio de Janeiro in 1992, endorsed a new approach to national and international development agendas and the consideration of the environment. This Earth Summit formalised a commitment to improving health and protecting the environment as two prerequisites for sustainable development which has been endorsed by the World Health Organization (1992).

During the 1990s there was a growing interest in the interrelated nature of health and the environment across a wide range of geographical scales. At the global level, attention has focussed on carbon dioxide emissions, depletion of the ozone layer, and the incidence of cancer (McMichael, 1993). At the local level, ambient air conditions in residential neighbourhoods and indoor air quality inside buildings have been considered in relation to the incidence of allergies and respiratory diseases (Schwela, 2000). This chapter is not meant to provide a comprehensive review of a number of contributions across these geographical scales, but it does show that a multidimensional research agenda can link health to sustainable development.

Prospects and Future Directions

Our capacity to deal with complex subjects including urban health, well-being and sustainability is insufficient for several reasons including the diversity and complexity of these problems; the difficulty of identifying and measuring the interrelations between them and their components; and the need to understand the relative importance of these components in precise localities, at different geographical scales and over time. Therefore, in order to deal with these complex subjects it is necessary to shift from multidisciplinary to interdisciplinary and transdisciplinary concepts and methods.

Disciplinarity, Inter-disciplinarity and Trans-disciplinarity

When dealing with complex subjects like urban health it is necessary to shift from mono-disciplinary to inter-disciplinary and trans-disciplinary concepts and methods. In order to be effective, this shift should be founded on a clarification of definitions, goals and methods (Lawrence and Despres, 2004).

Disciplinarity refers to the specialisation of academic disciplines, especially since the 19th century. Multi-disciplinary refers to an additive research agenda in which each researcher contributes but remains within his/her discipline and applies its concepts and methods without necessarily sharing the same goal. Interdisciplinary studies are those in which concerted action and co-ordination are accepted by researchers in different disciplines as a means to achieve a shared goal that usually is a common subject of study. In contrast, trans-disciplinarity refers to an approach that incorporates a combination of concepts and knowledge not only used by academics and researchers but also other actors in civic society, including representatives of the private sector, public administrators and the public. These contributions enable the cross-fertilisation of knowledge and experiences from diverse groups of people that can promote an enlarged vision of a subject, as well as new explanatory theories. Rather than being an end in itself, trans-disciplinary research is a way of achieving innovative goals, enriched understanding and a synergy of new methods.

Multi-disciplinarity, inter-disciplinarity and trans-disciplinarity are complementary rather than being mutually exclusive (Lawrence and Despres, 2004). Without specialised disciplinary studies there would be no in-depth knowledge and data. Trans-disciplinary research and practice require a common conceptual framework and analytical methods based on shared terminology, mental images and common goals. Once these have been formulated then the next requirement is to develop a research agenda.

CONCLUSION

Today, policy makers in most countries still have great difficulty in measuring, describing and explaining constancy, change and differences in health, housing, and environmental conditions in cities. Part of the difficulty has been the lack of systematic data collection. A dynamic set covering several sectors is required across a range of administrative levels and geographical scales. Alone, official statistics based on national census returns do not provide comprehensive accounts of the quantity and quality of the housing stock, urban infrastructure and services in rapidly developing urban areas, and they ignore illegal buildings in informal settlements. Today, there are several kinds of innovative techniques and tools that can be used to monitor and analyse the spatial distribution, dynamics and interrelated nature of environmental, housing, demographic and health profiles in urban areas. There have been significant developments in the collection and interpretation of data, indicators and information during the 1990s which warrant further systematic applications—for example, geographical information systems (GIS) which represent data from diverse sources (including remote sensing) in order to identify relationships between the represented components of urban areas. This relatively new approach has not been widely applied in the health sector in many countries, but its use to monitor ambient environmental conditions, the built environment and the incidence of ill health and disease warrants a commitment from public administrations at both national and local levels.

Evidence on the determinants of health of urban populations increased during the 1990s especially in relation to the socio-economic inequalities of people living in urban areas. Nonetheless, too little attention has been given to assessing the effectiveness of interventions to change these determinants in specific localities and monitor the outcomes on health. If these evaluations are not available, then policy decision making is handicapped. More research is required to evaluate different kinds of interventions that improve the built environment in urban areas in order to identify impacts on health and well-being by the collection of time series data. Environmental impact assessment (EIA), health impact assessment (HIA) and cost-benefit analysis (CBA) can be used to study interventions that are meant to promote health. Today there are too few studies which evaluate different approaches for the communication of information to inform and educate lay-people, even though studies show that the health impact of water supply and sewage disposal is influenced by the way the population uses (or misuses) new infrastructure and services. In addition, this research can identify economic, cultural and political barriers to change. An understanding of the political feasibility of policy options should include an account of these barriers as well as the legal framework and the behavioural norms and values of the population.

REFERENCES

Barton, H. & Tsourou, C. (2000). *Healthy urban planning.* London: E & FN Spon.

Bistrup, M. L. (1991). *Housing and community environments: How they support health.* Copenhagen: National Board of Health.

Burridge, R., & Ormandy, D. (Eds.), (1993). *Unhealthy housing: Research, remedy and reform.* London: E & FN Spon.

Goldstein, G. (2000). Healthy cities: Overview of a WHO international program. *Reviews on Environmental Health,* 15, (1–2), 207–214.

Green G., Acres, F. and Price, C. (2003). City health development planning. In A. Tsouros and J. Farrington (eds.) *WHO Healthy Cities in Europe: A compilation of papers on progress and achievements*, pp. 103–133. World Health Organization European Office for Europe, Copenhagen.

Hancock, T., & Duhl, L. (1988).

Hippocrates. (1849). *On air, waters, and places*. In *The genuine works of Hippocrates*. Translated with a commentary by Francis Adams. The Sydenham Society, London, 1849.

Halpern, D. (1995). *Mental health and the built environment*. London: Taylor and Francis.

Lawrence, R. J. (2000). Urban health: a new research agenda? *Reviews on Environmental Health*, 15:1–11.

Lawrence, R. J. (1993). An ecological blueprint for healthy housing. In R. Burridge and D. Ormandy (Eds.), *Unhealthy housing: Research, remedy and reform*. (pp. 338–360). London: E & F N Spon.

Lawrence, R. J. (1995). *Meeting the challenge: Barriers to integrate cross-sectoral urban policies*. In M. Rolén (Ed.), Urban policies for an environmentally sustainable world. The OECD-Sweden seminar on the ecological city, 1–3 June 1994. (pp. 9–37). Stockholm: Swedish Council for Planning and Co-ordination of Research.

Lawrence, R. J. (1996). Urban environment, health and the economy: Cues for conceptual clarification and more effective policy implementation. In C. Price & A. Tsouros (Eds.), *Our cities, our future: Policies and action plans for health and sustainable development*. (pp. 38–64). Copenhagen: World Health Organization European Office for Europe.

Lawrence, R. J. (2001). Human Ecology. In M. K. Tolba (Ed.), *Our fragile world: Challenges and opportunities for sustainable development*. Volume 1. (pp. 675–693) Oxford: Eolss Publishers.

Lawrence, R. J. & Despres, C. (Eds.), (2004). Futures of Transdisciplinarity. *Futures*, 36(4), 397–526 (special issue).

McMichael, A. (1993). *Planetary Overload: Global environmental change and the health of the human species*. Cambridge: Cambridge University Press.

McMichael, A. (2000). The urban environment and health in a world of increasing globalization: Issues for developing countries. *Bulletin of World Health Organization*, 78(9), 1117–1126.

Rosen, G. (1993). *A History of Public Health*. Baltimore MD: John Hopkins University Press.

Schwela, D. (2000). Air pollution and health in urban areas. *Reviews on Environmental Health*, 15, (1–2) 13–42.

Tsouros, A., and J. Farrington (eds.) *WHO Healthy Cities in Europe: A compilation of papers on progress and achievements*, pp. 103–133. World Health Organization European Office for Europe, Copenhagen.

United Nations. (1992). *Agenda 21: Programme of Action for Sustainable Development*. New York: United Nations Publications.

United Nations Commission on Human Settlements. (1996). *An urbanizing world: Global report on human settlements 1996*. New York: Oxford University Press.

Werna, E., Harpham, T., & Goldstein, G. (1998). *Healthy city projects in developing countries: An international approach to local problems*. London: Earthscan.

Werna, E., Harpham, T., Blue, I., & Goldstein, G. (1999). From healthy city projects to healthy cities. *Environment and Urbanization*, 11 (1), 27–39.

World Health Organization. (1946). *Constitution*. Geneva: World Health Organization.

World Health Organization. (1990). *Indoor environment: Health aspects of air quality, thermal environment, light and noise*. Geneva: World Health Organization, document WHO/EHE/RUD/90.2.

World Health Organization. (1992). *Our Planet, Our Health: Report of the WHO Commission on Health and Environment*. Geneva: World Health Organization.

World Health Organization. (1997). *Health and Environment in Sustainable Development: Five years after the Earth Summit*. Geneva: World Health Organization, document WHO/EHG/97.8.

World Health Organization. (2000). *Healthy cities in action: 5 case studies from Africa, Asia, Middle East and Latin America*. Geneva: World Health Organization, document WHO/SDE/PHE/00.02.

42 Landscape Design: Patient-Specific Healing Gardens

Clare Cooper Marcus

Professor of landscape architecture and social architecture summarizes the research literature on the healing effects of plants and discusses design strategies for gardens in hospitals.

In the last two decades, gardens with therapeutic qualities have begun to appear in U.S. and UK healthcare facilities. Now "healing gardens" are being designed to support the treatment of patients with specific conditions.

The idea that nature has a soothing, restorative effect is nothing new. From medieval monastic infirmary gardens to the landscaped grounds of nineteenth-century mental asylums, enlightened carers have recognised that access to the outdoors has a salutary effect on a person's mental and physical health. With the onset of modern medicine and its emphasis on treatment via surgery and drugs, this knowledge was lost or deemed "unscientific". High-rise construction techniques created medical settings where patients were divorced from the outdoors.

From the early 1990s a change began to happen in healthcare design—termed patient-centred care, there were marked changes in the interior design of hospitals. Then, in the late 1990s, three books appeared documenting the therapeutic value of outdoor spaces in healthcare.[1,2,3]

The era of the healing garden had arrived. Characterising the key qualities of a successful healing garden? The basics of healing garden design relate to the issue of stress, as the relief of stress helps to bolster the immune system and stimulate the body's natural healing proclivity. There is credible scientific evidence that four elements that can be supported by design help reduce stress: the distraction provided by green nature; exercise; social support; and a sense of control.[4]

The more we are engaged with the environment through all our senses, the lower are our rates of anxiety and the less we are aware of pain. Thus, a healing garden needs to provide a multi-sensory experience with colourful flowers, varying shades and textures of green, the sights and sounds of water, elements that attract birds and butterflies, fragrances, and ornamental grasses which move with the slightest breeze.

This outdoor space needs to be a garden, not a paved courtyard—a lush green setting with an optimal ratio of green to hard surfaces of 7:3. Exercise has many beneficial effects on both physical

Clare Cooper Marcus, "Landscape Design: Patient-specific Healing Gardens," from *World Health Design*, January 2009, pp. 65–71. Copyright © 2009. Permission to reprint granted by the publisher.

and mental health. Thus, depending on the size of the garden, there needs to be a variety of longer and shorter pathway loops for strolling and exercise.

These must be surfaced to reduce glare, for example, with tinted concrete, and there needs to be attention to details such as edging to prevent those using wheelchairs rolling into planting beds, and expansion joints in paving of no more than one-eighth of an inch in width to prevent the wheels of IV poles getting caught and stuck.

There is also evidence that the more social support a patient receives from family and friends, the better they are able to heal. A garden is one place where a patient and visitor can converse in private in an attractive setting. It is essential that sensitive planting design and site furnishings provide semi-private niches for one or two people or for a family group to be alone. A hospital garden, if sensitively designed, can be a place for a family to visit with an inpatient, perhaps with children and even the family dog in tow; where a person can digest the news of a troubling prognosis; where a family can wait for someone in surgery or an outpatient wait for a prescription to be filled; or where staff members can relax together on their lunch break.

GAINING CONTROL

When we enter hospital as an inpatient it is the institution that decides what we wear, when the doctor visits, with whom we share a room and perhaps even what we can eat. In short, we lose control over many issues that were ours to decide at home. The more a patient is able to exert a sense of control, the less they will be stressed. To enhance a sense of control within the garden there should be a choice of different pathways; a variety of semi-private niches to sit in; some fixed and some moveable outdoor furniture; a variety of views to enjoy when seated—some distant, some near at hand.

The material used for seating should not retain heat or cold: wood or hard plastic are preferable, while concrete, aluminium and steel should be avoided. While these form the basics of a healing garden, there are a few more requirements that are really just common sense. The garden needs to be sheltered; provide an ambience of comfort and familiarity; include plant materials appropriate to local climate and culture; have a budget for ongoing maintenance; and avoid the inclusion of ambiguous art pieces onto which sick people can project their feelings of fear and anxiety.

The garden needs to be visible from a well-used interior area (waiting room, foyer, cafeteria etc) or, if not, there needs to be adequate signage in the building to alert people to its presence. The garden needs to be accessible, not only with an automatic door and low entry lip to facilitate access by those using a wheelchair but it also needs to be unlocked.

This may seem obvious but it is sad to report that many otherwise attractive hospital gardens are kept locked at all times to prevent use. This has specifically been observed at Private Finance Initiative (PFI) hospitals in the UK. One assumes this is so because the owners do not wish to pay for upkeep. This is particularly ironic when increasing evidence points to the stress-reducing qualities of hospital outdoor space, and that this is happening in a country that has a long cultural history based around a love of gardens.

None of the above is rocket science but a healing garden needs to be a sensitive combination of restorative elements and must be designed by a landscape architect, the only professional trained to design with plant materials. (Some of the worst healing gardens I have seen were designed by artists, architects or interior designers.)

PATIENT-SPECIFIC GARDENS

In the early years of this century, specialised forms of healing gardens began to appear: gardens designed for the special needs of specific patient groups. Among these are gardens at children's hospitals, cancer clinics, rehabilitation hospitals, facilities for burn patients, for the frail elderly and for those with Alzheimer's disease and other forms of dementia. Gardens at children's hospitals, for example, need to provide for the sometimes conflicting needs of sick children, well siblings and grieving parents.

The park-like gardens at Boston and Atlanta Children's Hospitals, for example, provide well for parents but do little to distract children. A new play-garden at Seattle Children's Hospital provides plenty of interest for children but is not a place of solace for worried parents. Legacy Emanuel Hospital Children's Garden in Portland, Oregon is one of the few that does well on all counts.[5]

In the patient-specific gardens described in more detail below, the nurses, doctors, physiotherapists, psychotherapists, speech pathologists, horticultural therapists, and occupational therapists who were to guide their patients in the therapeutic use of the garden worked closely together in creating a programme which was then implemented by a professional landscape architect.

The Healing Garden at the Good Samaritan Hospital in Portland, Oregon's Good Samaritan Hospital was created by landscape architect Ron Mah, David Evans and associates working collaboratively with a team of hospital staff who now use the garden in their therapeutic work with patients recovering from strokes and brain injuries. These include physiotherapists, speech pathologists, horticultural therapists and spiritual counsellors.

The garden includes elements such as different walking surfaces for those learning to walk again after a stroke with the aid of a walker or cane; differing planter edge heights so that patients learning fine motor control can sit or lean while doing simple gardening tasks; and plant labels that speech pathologists use in their work with patients regarding speech after a stroke.[6] Similar outdoor facilities at other hospitals include slopes, steps, bridges, a range of walking surfaces and parallel bars to aid in physiotherapy. The one oversight at the Portland garden was that the team did not realise that many of their patients lived in rural Oregon and would need to learn to walk again on surfaces such as gravel or dirt, rather than the concrete of urban sidewalks.

The Play Garden at the Rusk Institute for Rehabilitative Medicine in New York City represents a similar kind of therapeutic outdoor environment, but here it is for children with brain injuries or mobility problems. While children can be led (reluctantly) through therapeutic exercises in an indoor gym, creating a play garden where they naturally engage in similar exercises has proved highly successful.

A team approach to the design ensured that the landscape architects, Johansson and Walcavage, incorporated elements recommended by the hospital staff and that these elements would be so attractive to children that they would exercise certain skills without realising they were doing so.

For example, climbing up a low grassy hill in order to slide down a slide set into the hill or climbing several steps to get into a sandbox—in both cases exercising arm and leg muscles. Turning a frog-shaped knob to start a stream flowing or undoing various bolts and latches in the door of a playhouse encourage fine motor control. In a relatively small urban site a remarkable variety of activities are encouraged while children play in the sunshine and enjoy a relaxed milieu, in contrast to the hospital interior.

THERAPEUTIC SPACES

For people with mental or psychological, rather than physical, problems, a series of remarkable therapeutic outdoor spaces are beginning to appear. Unique in this category are two gardens in Sweden for those suffering from depression or what is termed in that country as "burn-out syndrome". The Alnarp Rehabilitation Garden encompasses a two-hectare site on the campus of the Swedish University of Agricultural Sciences at Alnarp in southwest Sweden. Staff in the department of landscape architecture—namely, Patrik Grahn and Ulrika Stigsdotter—along with a horticultural therapist, physiotherapist, occupational and psychotherapists have developed a therapeutic landscape divided into a number of garden rooms.

Participants (they are not referred to as patients) who can no longer work because of depression or burn-out are recommended to the garden programme by their doctors, insurance companies or employers. They start by coming to the garden one morning a week, increasing to four mornings over a three-month period. While at the facility, patients can, if they wish, do nothing but relax in the quiet, hedge-enclosed Welcoming Garden; or they can do light gardening tasks in the greenhouse, vegetable garden or orchard; take a walk along a forest path; or relax in a large meadow. Art therapy, relaxation exercises, snacks, etc are available in a traditional house within the garden; weekly psychotherapy sessions take place in a geodesic greenhouse.

A research project is under way, comparing patient outcomes at the Alnarp garden with a control group of comparable patients who are receiving the normal treatment—resting at home, using an antidepressant such as Prozac, and having a few psychotherapy sessions. Preliminary results indicate very positive results from the non-drug, garden treatment approach.

A similar approach is being applied at Haga Hälsoträdgård (Haga Health Garden) where a green therapeutic environment has been created inside a large commercial greenhouse in a Stockholm park. The greenhouse has been skillfully redesigned by Ulf Nordfjell and Yvonne Westerberg into five rooms so that a patient can choose to lie in a hammock among olive trees, relax on a chaise-longue under a palm tree, join a group for coffee and conversation at a candle-lit table, engage in gardening tasks, or create art pieces using plant materials.

As at Alnarp, patients attend programmes for varying lengths of time and, in addition, courses on the therapeutic value of green nature are offered for human relations staff and employers to encourage them to provide green spaces at work where employees can relax at lunch or in break periods. Thus, Haga Health Garden is taking a proactive approach aimed at educating corporate, institutional and governmental employers on the value of green nature in preventative healthcare.[7]

The increasing incidence of Alzheimer's disease and other forms of dementia is a phenomenon facing the healthcare institutions of many Western nations. For example, in the United States it is estimated that 10% of those over 65 are affected by this disease, while the percentage is nearly five times that (47%) for those over 85. The U.S. Alzheimer's Association estimates that 12 to 14 million will be affected by the year 2040.

Facilities serving those with Alzheimer's disease are recognising that a garden can serve a number of beneficial purposes. Firstly, it can provide a place for exercise, especially important for the general health of older adults. It can provide a setting where people can be in sunlight, especially important for the creation of Vitamin D, the promotion of healthy bones and the establishment of regular circadian rhythms and sleep patterns.

A garden can also provide a relaxing locale for staff-led programmes in gardening, crafts, memory recall, etc. In addition, an attractive garden is a pleasant setting for family visits and may encourage such visits. The Sophia Louise Durbridge-Wege Living Garden of the Family Life Center in Grand

Rapids, Michigan (Landscape Architect: Martha Tyson) is an exemplary facility serving the needs of patients with Alzheimer's and other forms of dementia who live with their families but spend each weekday at this day centre.[8]

One entry door to the garden and a simple looped pathway encourage walking while avoiding the confusion or aggression that can occur when patients have to make a decision to turn left or right, or remember which of several doors to return to. A large gazebo, wired for sound (music is especially soothing) and for fans on hot summer days, is a popular setting for staff-led programmes. A waterfall feature provides the soothing sight and sound of water without the possibility of people getting into it (a problem with some Alzheimer's patients). A wide variety of perennial flowers popular during the youth of many of the patients provide opportunities for experiences of memory-recall led by the staff.

A small garden and orchard area is the setting for horticultural therapy activities. A recent study at another Alzheimer's facility with a garden revealed that those who spent as little as five to ten minutes of unprogrammed activity in the garden each day in the summer months showed significant improvements on a number of parameters, including aggressive behaviour, physician-ordered medication, pulse rate, blood pressure and weight gain.[9] This suggests that this kind of patient-specific garden is not only therapeutic in a general sense but also that it has measurable patient benefits that reduce the costs of drug use and staff time.

In Portland, Oregon a unique garden opened in May 2004 for the benefit of burn patients. The Oregon Burn Center Garden was designed by a team including staff treating burn patients, a horticultural therapist and landscape architect Brain Bainnson from Quatrefoil. The resulting 9,000 square foot garden serves patients in a number of ways.[10] Firstly, it provides walking paths and differing slopes for those learning to walk again (and for those rebuilding strength and endurance). It also has a number of shade structures that provide outdoor seating for patients alone or those visiting with family, as those recovering from serious burns have to stay out of the sun. The great variety of plant materials in the garden allow for sensory stimulation (fragrance, touch, vision, hearing). And because the garden is secure and private it provides a protected space for burn patients to begin taking steps toward community reintegration.

Two patient groups not appearing in the above discussion are those suffering from cancer and HIV/AIDS. What little information exists on the environmental needs of such patients suggests that a garden based on the general properties of a healing garden would serve their needs, with an emphasis on adequate shade since both populations are treated with drugs that require they stay out of the sun. In addition, plants with strong fragrances should be avoided in gardens for cancer patients since they can induce nausea for those taking chemotherapy drugs.[11]

CONCLUSIONS

Patient-specific gardens encompass a general understanding of the restorative benefits of nature,[12] together with the recognition of the needs of a particular patient population.

In each of the cases described above, the garden has become a potent treatment milieu, complementing the provisions located indoors. In this respect, such gardens represent a third stage in the recognition and acceptance of nature-based therapy in healthcare. The first stage is encompassed by examples of eighteenth and nineteenth-century hospitals where views and access to nature were intuitively considered therapeutic, but with no understanding of why. The second stage was prompted by the emergence of credible scientific evidence that views to, or even brief visits in, a green, garden setting can have measurable physiological effects such as on blood pressure and the immune system.[13]

This, together with a move to more patient-centred care in hospital design, starting in the 1990s, prompted the provision of usable outdoor spaces, sometimes termed healing gardens. We are now in what might be termed a third stage, in which the needs of very specific patient populations are being considered in the design of healthcare outdoor space. In future work, healthcare professionals, designers and researchers need to collaborate in discerning the therapeutic benefits of gardens specifically designed for those patient populations whose needs have not yet been widely discussed or explored, including children with autism, cystic fibrosis or cerebral palsy; patients with schizophrenia or Parkinson's disease; and patients recovering from heart surgery.

There are three points to add to this brief discussion. The first point is that healing gardens are on the verge of becoming a "fad". Articles on hospitals featured in glossy design magazines often tout the fact that they have a "healing garden", but when photos of such gardens are examined (or the actual garden is visited), it is sometimes anything but healing in terms of the criteria mentioned above. Perhaps we will soon need to create a certification process, not unlike the Leadership in Energy and Environmental Design (LEED) Green Building Rating System, to ensure that healing gardens meet certain basic criteria.

A second point that cannot be emphasized enough is that a healing garden must be designed by a landscape architect, and preferably one who holds a certificate in Healthcare Garden Design similar to the one offered through an intensive course at the School of the Chicago Botanic Garden (www.chicagobotanic.org/school/certificate). Such a design professional also needs to be well-versed in participatory design. All of the successful patient-specific gardens have come about as the result of a carefully orchestrated participatory process involving the designer, clinical staff, current or former patients and family members.

Only through such a process can a garden successfully meet the needs of the patients it is intended to serve.

REFERENCES

1. Cooper, Marcus C., Barnes M. A. (Eds.). *Healing Gardens: Therapeutic Benefits and Design Recommendations.* New York: John Wiley and Sons; 1999.
2. Gerlach-Spriggs, N., Kaufman, R. E., Warner, S. B. *Restorative Gardens: The Healing Landscape.* New Haven: Yale University Press; 1998.
3. Tyson, M. M. *The Healing Landscape: Therapeutic Outdoor Environments.* New York: McGraw Hill; 1998.
4. Ulrich, R. S. Effects of gardens on health outcomes: Theory and research. In Cooper, Marcus C., and Barnes, M. (Eds.): *Healing Gardens: Therapeutic Benefits and Design Recommendations.* New York: John Wiley and Sons; 1999.
5. Cooper, Marcus C. Healing Havens: Two hospital gardens in Portland win awards for therapeutic values. *Landscape Architecture Magazine* 2003; 93(8).
6. Cooper, Marcus C. Healing Havens: Two hospital gardens in Portland win awards for therapeutic values. ibid.
7. Cooper, Marcus C. Gardens as treatment milieu: Two Swedish gardens counteract the effects of stress. *Landscape Architecture Magazine* 2006; 96(5).

8. Cooper, Marcus C. No Ordinary Garden: Alzheimer's and other patients find refuge in a Michigan dementia-care facility. *Landscape Architecture Magazine* 2005; 95(3).
9. Galbraith, J. and Westphal, J. *Therapeutic garden design: Martin Luther Alzheimer Garden*. Proceedings of American Society of Landscape Architects Conference, Salt Lake City; 2004.
10. Cooper, Marcus C. For burn patients, a place to heal. *Landscape Architecture Magazine* 2008; 98(4).
11. Cooper, Marcus C. Hospital Oasis: Through a participatory design process, a failed Tommy Church garden in San Francisco is reconfigured as an exemplary therapeutic landscape. *Landscape Architecture Magazine* 2001; 91(10).
12. Ulrich, R. S. op cit.
13. Ulrich, R. S. ibid.

CPSIA information can be obtained
at www.ICGtesting.com
Printed in the USA
FSOW04n1758250816
24208FS